Keep this book. You will need it and use it throughout your career.

About the American Hotel & Lodging Association (AH&LA)

Founded in 1910, AH&LA is the trade association representing the lodging industry in the United States. AH&LA is a federation of state lodging associations throughout the United States with 11,000 lodging properties worldwide as members. The association offers its members assistance with governmental affairs representation, communications, marketing, hospitality operations, training and education, technology issues, and more. For information, call 202-289-3100.

LODGING, the management magazine of AH&LA, is a "living textbook" for hospitality students that provides timely features, industry news, and vital lodging information.

About the American Hotel & Lodging Educational Institute (EI)

An affiliate of AH&LA, the Educational Institute is the world's largest source of quality training and educational materials for the lodging industry. EI develops textbooks and courses that are used in more than 1,200 colleges and universities worldwide, and also offers courses to individuals through its Distance Learning program. Hotels worldwide rely on EI for training resources that focus on every aspect of lodging operations. Industry-tested videos, CD-ROMs, seminars, and skills guides prepare employees at every skill level. EI also offers professional certification for the industry's top performers. For information about EI's products and services, call 800-349-0299 or 407-999-8100.

About the American Hotel & Lodging Educational Foundation (AH&LEF)

An affiliate of AH&LA, the American Hotel & Lodging Educational Foundation provides financial support that enhances the stability, prosperity, and growth of the lodging industry through educational and research programs. AH&LEF has awarded millions of dollars in scholarship funds for students pursuing higher education in hospitality management. AH&LEF has also funded research projects on topics important to the industry, including occupational safety and health, turnover and diversity, and best practices in the U.S. lodging industry. For more information, go to www.ahlef.org.

HOSPITALITY SALES and MARKETING

Educational Institute Books

UNIFORM SYSTEM OF ACCOUNTS FOR THE LODGING INDUSTRY
Tenth Revised Edition

WORLD OF RESORTS: FROM DEVELOPMENT TO MANAGEMENT
Third Edition
Chuck Yim Gee

PLANNING AND CONTROL FOR FOOD AND BEVERAGE OPERATIONS
Seventh Edition
Jack D. Ninemeier

UNDERSTANDING HOSPITALITY LAW
Fifth Edition
Jack P. Jefferies/Banks Brown

SUPERVISION IN THE HOSPITALITY INDUSTRY
Fourth Edition
Raphael R. Kavanaugh/Jack D. Ninemeier

MANAGEMENT OF FOOD AND BEVERAGE OPERATIONS
Fifth Edition
Jack D. Ninemeier

MANAGING FRONT OFFICE OPERATIONS
Eighth Edition
Michael L. Kasavana/Richard M. Brooks

MANAGING SERVICE IN FOOD AND BEVERAGE OPERATIONS
Fourth Edition
Ronald F. Cichy/Philip J. Hickey, Jr.

THE LODGING AND FOOD SERVICE INDUSTRY
Seventh Edition
Gerald W. Lattin

SECURITY AND LOSS PREVENTION MANAGEMENT
Second Edition
Raymond C. Ellis, Jr./David M. Stipanuk

HOSPITALITY INDUSTRY MANAGERIAL ACCOUNTING
Seventh Edition
Raymond S. Schmidgall

PURCHASING FOR FOOD SERVICE OPERATIONS
Ronald F. Cichy/Jeffery D Elsworth

MANAGING TECHNOLOGY IN THE HOSPITALITY INDUSTRY
Sixth Edition
Michael L. Kasavana

HOTEL AND RESTAURANT ACCOUNTING
Seventh Edition
Raymond Cote

ACCOUNTING FOR HOSPITALITY MANAGERS
Fifth Edition
Raymond Cote

CONVENTION MANAGEMENT AND SERVICE
Eighth Edition
Milton T. Astroff/James R. Abbey

HOSPITALITY SALES AND MARKETING
Fifth Edition
James R. Abbey

MANAGING HOUSEKEEPING OPERATIONS
Revised Third Edition
Aleta A. Nitschke/William D. Frye

HOSPITALITY TODAY: AN INTRODUCTION
Seventh Edition
Rocco M. Angelo/Andrew N. Vladimir

HOSPITALITY FACILITIES MANAGEMENT AND DESIGN
Third Edition
David M. Stipanuk

MANAGING HOSPITALITY HUMAN RESOURCES
Fifth Edition
Robert H. Woods, Misty M. Johanson, and Michael P. Sciarini

RETAIL MANAGEMENT FOR SPAS

HOSPITALITY INDUSTRY FINANCIAL ACCOUNTING
Third Edition
Raymond S. Schmidgall/James W. Damitio

INTERNATIONAL HOTELS: DEVELOPMENT & MANAGEMENT
Second Edition
Chuck Yim Gee

QUALITY SANITATION MANAGEMENT
Ronald F. Cichy

HOTEL INVESTMENTS: ISSUES & PERSPECTIVES
Fifth Edition
Edited by Lori E. Raleigh and Rachel J. Roginsky

LEADERSHIP AND MANAGEMENT IN THE HOSPITALITY INDUSTRY
Third Edition
Robert H. Woods/Judy Z. King

MARKETING IN THE HOSPITALITY INDUSTRY
Fifth Edition
Ronald A. Nykiel

UNIFORM SYSTEM OF ACCOUNTS FOR THE HEALTH, RACQUET AND SPORTSCLUB INDUSTRY

CONTEMPORARY CLUB MANAGEMENT
Second Edition
Edited by Joe Perdue for the Club Managers Association of America

RESORT CONDOMINIUM AND VACATION OWNERSHIP MANAGEMENT: A HOSPITALITY PERSPECTIVE
Robert A. Gentry/Pedro Mandoki/Jack Rush

ACCOUNTING FOR CLUB OPERATIONS
Raymond S. Schmidgall/James W. Damitio

TRAINING AND DEVELOPMENT FOR THE HOSPITALITY INDUSTRY
Debra F. Cannon/Catherine M. Gustafson

UNIFORM SYSTEM OF FINANCIAL REPORTING FOR CLUBS
Sixth Revised Edition

HOTEL ASSET MANAGEMENT: PRINCIPLES & PRACTICES
Second Edition
Edited by Greg Denton, Lori E. Raleigh, and A. J. Singh

MANAGING BEVERAGE OPERATIONS
Second Edition
Ronald F. Cichy/Lendal H. Kotschevar

FOOD SAFETY: MANAGING WITH THE HACCP SYSTEM
Second Edition
Ronald F. Cichy

UNIFORM SYSTEM OF FINANCIAL REPORTING FOR SPAS

FUNDAMENTALS OF DESTINATION MANAGEMENT AND MARKETING
Edited by Rich Harrill

ETHICS IN THE HOSPITALITY AND TOURISM INDUSTRY
Second Edition
Karen Lieberman/Bruce Nissen

SPA: A COMPREHENSIVE INTRODUCTION
Elizabeth M. Johnson/Bridgette M. Redman

HOSPITALITY 2015: THE FUTURE OF HOSPITALITY AND TRAVEL
Marvin Cetron/Fred DeMicco/Owen Davies

REVENUE MANAGEMENT: MAXIMIZING REVENUE IN HOSPITALITY OPERATIONS
Gabor Forgacs

FINANCIAL MANAGEMENT FOR SPAS
Raymond S. Schmidgall/John R. Korpi

HOSPITALITY SALES and MARKETING

Fifth Edition

James R. Abbey, Ph.D., CHA

Disclaimer

This publication is designed to provide accurate and authoritative information in regard to the subject matter covered. It is sold with the understanding that the publisher is not engaged in rendering legal, accounting, or other professional service. If legal advice or other expert assistance is required, the services of a competent professional person should be sought.

— *From the Declaration of Principles jointly adopted by the American Bar Association and a Committee of Publishers and Associations*

The author, James R. Abbey, is solely responsible for the contents of this publication. All views expressed herein are solely those of the author and do not necessarily reflect the views of the American Hotel & Lodging Educational Institute (the Institute) or the American Hotel & Lodging Association (AH&LA).

Nothing contained in this publication shall constitute a standard, an endorsement, or a recommendation of the Institute or AH&LA. The Institute and AH&LA disclaim any liability with respect to the use of any information, procedure, or product, or reliance thereon by any member of the hospitality industry.

2113 North High Street
Lansing, Michigan 48906-4221

The American Hotel & Lodging
Educational Institute is a nonprofit
educational foundation.

Printed in the United States of America
5 6 7 8 9 10 13 12

ISBN 978-0-86612-325-9

Editor: Jim Purvis

Contents

Part III Marketing

Preface

TODAY'S HOSPITALITY INDUSTRY is an exciting—and highly competitive—career field. Hotel and restaurant careers offer tremendous potential for personal and professional growth and success, but, as with any other profession, achieving success depends on learning and applying certain principles inherent to the field. In today's hospitality industry, it is essential to have an understanding of marketing and sales.

Many textbooks, including this one, explain the theory behind successful hospitality marketing. While theory is important, it is even more important to understand how marketing theory is actually *applied* in the marketplace. Theory can explain, for example, *why* consumers purchase, but the reasons consumers spend are just facts until an industry professional *uses them* to develop an effective marketing strategy that will contribute to the bottom line. The fifth edition of *Hospitality Sales and Marketing* has been thoroughly researched and written to provide a readable and practical approach for effectively marketing hotels and restaurants. While the text explains a number of theories and concepts, it goes a step further—showing how those theories and concepts are actually applied. The illustrations and exhibits in this book include actual industry examples (forms, checklists, charts, advertising, and so on) that are used by today's industry leaders to effectively market their hospitality firms. Every hospitality marketing and sales professional, whether embarking on a new career or already a seasoned pro, plays a crucial role in promoting his or her lodging property or restaurant. The knowledge and application of the marketing, sales, and advertising fundamentals presented in this text will not only benefit the reader professionally, but, if diligently applied by hospitality marketing and sales personnel, should boost profits as well.

Hospitality Sales and Marketing, Fifth Edition, offers a number of new and expanded features. Each chapter opens with a tip or insight from a marketing and sales practitioner. Each chapter has updated illustrations and exhibits that are captioned to reinforce the chapter material. New "Marketing in Action" sidebars have been added to show how concepts presented in the text are being applied by today's industry leaders (several of whom are profiled in new "Industry Innovators" sidebars). Other new material includes Internet exercises, discussions on the use of technology for successful hospitality marketing and sales efforts, and "Going Green" sidebars that offer tips and other information on the conservation practices of hotels and restaurants that enable these companies to help the environment, save money, and attract guests who care about "green" issues. Each chapter ends with a chapter summary, key terms, review questions, and an expanded list of Internet sites for additional information. Some chapters also include appendixes and/or case studies.

The text is divided into three parts. Part I begins with an introduction to hospitality sales and marketing, then discusses marketing plans and examines the organization of a sales office in small, midsize, and large hospitality firms. Part II,

Sales Techniques, explores personal, telephone, and internal marketing and sales. A chapter on advertising, public relations, and publicity rounds out this section. Part III, Marketing, discusses some of the hospitality industry's major market segments (both individual and group) and how to reach them.

Acknowledgments

When writing a textbook, an author usually starts out with a strong idea of what the book should be like. However, before the manuscript is published, a number of suggestions are made by students, colleagues, friends, editors, and industry professionals that contribute to the author's original idea and improve the book. I particularly want to acknowledge the helpful comments and contributions of my editors and friends, Jim Purvis and Thad Balivet. Jim and Thad are part of a team of professionals at the American Hotel & Lodging Educational Institute who are dedicated to providing quality, up-to-date educational materials to students and hospitality professionals alike.

In addition to the Educational Institute, the Hospitality Sales & Marketing Association International organization is committed to setting and maintaining high standards of excellence in the hospitality industry. In 1968, HSMAI established a Hall of Fame to honor outstanding achievements in the field of hospitality sales and marketing. The pioneering activities of these industry professionals, and their active involvement in sales and marketing education and training, have helped shape today's hospitality industry, and their contributions will continue to inspire and challenge those in the industry to new levels of excellence. This book is dedicated to the men and women honored in the HSMAI Hall of Fame:

1968: Adrian Phillips, CHME
1968: DeWitt Coffman, CHME
1968: G. E. R. "Dick" Flynn
1968: Leonard Hicks
1969: E. D. "Dill" Parrish
1971: Frank W. Berkman, CHME
1971: Duane W. "Tex" Carlton, CHME
1972: Nick C. Bicking
1972: Donald B. Martin, CHME
1972: Leonard R. Oakes, CHME
1972: Robert Quain
1973: Winthrop W. "Bud" Grice, CHME
1973: Arthur F. Taylor, CHME
1974: Jim Bearce, CHME
1974: Edmund Sansovini, CHME
1975: Danny Amico
1975: John H. Sienold
1976: H. M. "Bud" Smith
1977: William Morton
1978: Sig S. Front, CHME
1978: William F. Prigge
1979: William H. Edwards
1980: E. C. "Buzz" Sherry
1982: Hugh Connor
1984: Sandy Lindy, CHME
1985: Frank Hignett, CHME
1986: Nita Lloyd-Fore, CHME
1986: George "Jack" Neumann

1987: James Knauff, CHME

1989: Neil W. Ostergren, CHME

1989: Al Bard

1991: Michael A. Leven, CHME

1992: Howard Feiertag, CHME

1993: Thomas T. McCarthy, Jr., CHME

1994: David Troy, CHME

1995: Michael Dimond, CHME

1996: John J. Russell, CHME

1996: Mervyn "Mickey" Levine, CHME

1998: David C. Dorf, CHME

1999: Irma S. Mann, CHME

2000: Robert W. Keilt, CHME

2000: Peter C. Yesawich, Ph.D.

2001: David R. Evans, CHME

2001: Bob Stein

2003: James C. Collins

2003: Richard Degnan, CHME

James R. Abbey
Las Vegas, Nevada

About the Author

James R. Abbey

James R. Abbey, Ph.D., CHA, is a professor emeritus of hotel marketing and management at the University of Nevada, Las Vegas. He also has executive experience with clubs, restaurants, and hotels. As a consultant and researcher, he has worked with many prominent companies in the areas of sales management and marketing research and strategy. The author has won awards from the Travel Research Association of America, the National Institute of Foodservice Instructors, and the Statler Foundation. He is a graduate of Michigan State University's School of Hotel, Restaurant & Institutional Management, and holds a master's degree in finance and a Ph.D. in tourism from Utah State University.

Dr. Abbey is a contributor to leading hospitality publications and is co-author of *The Art and Science of Hospitality Management* and *Convention Management and Service.*

Part I

Introduction

Chapter 1 Outline

Competencies

1. Distinguish marketing from sales and describe the marketing mix. (pp. 3–11)
2. Explain management's role in marketing and sales. (pp. 12–13)
3. Summarize the importance of marketing and sales to hospitality companies, and describe the challenge of hospitality marketing and sales. (pp. 13–15)
4. Identify trends that affect marketing and sales in the hospitality industry. (pp. 15–27)

Insider Insights

Thomas T. McCarthy, CHA, CHSE
Owner
Tom McCarthy Associates
Falls Church, Virginia

"There's no question that opportunities for hotel marketing and sales professionals are greater now than at any time in the history of our industry. I've been asked by many people entering hotel marketing and sales to comment on what makes a hotel salesperson successful. To name a few of the many ingredients, successful salespeople are true believers in their products; honest, sincere, and ethical beyond reproach; enthusiastic; optimistic; creative; motivated; and innovative."

1

Introduction to Hospitality Marketing and Sales

IN THE MID-TWENTIETH CENTURY, the typical hotel* (84.4 percent of all properties) was located in a population or trade center, had fewer than 50 rooms, and was independently owned. Only 4.7 percent of all properties belonged to a chain, and there were only two prominent chains—Sheraton and Hilton. Rooms were small, most had no telephone, and a few lacked a private bath. There was no standardization of products, amenities, or services. Rates averaged $3.75 per night. Only large properties could afford to support restaurants and bars, and hotels with swimming pools were uncommon. There were a few resorts (most were located in the mountains or near a lake or an ocean), but these properties were primarily seasonal and catered to wealthy individuals.

Beginning in the mid-1950s, however, hotels began to change, driven by changes in the society around them:

1. *Population growth.* The population began growing significantly, especially in the South, Mountain, and Pacific regions. The population also began shifting. The Sunbelt (especially Florida and Texas) and the western states (especially Colorado, Arizona, Nevada, and California) experienced a tremendous influx of people.
2. *Longer life span.* Not only did the population grow, it also began to live longer, and a significant number of new households were formed. Many of these new families relocated, moving across the country in record numbers.
3. *Improved incomes.* Family incomes improved in the postwar economy, and two-income families became more prevalent. After the belt-tightening war years, families suddenly had more money to spend on travel and leisure. It wouldn't be until the 1970s, when inflation began running rampant, that this trend would be curtailed to any great extent.
4. *Increased leisure time.* Leisure time increased when the 40-hour workweek became commonplace and additional legal holidays were given to workers. Other job market factors such as part-time work and job sharing also contributed to the increased amount of leisure time available to workers.

---

*Except where otherwise noted, the term *hotel* will be used generically to represent all types of commercial lodging properties, including motels, motor hotels, and resorts.

5. *Expanded highway system.* Construction of the 42,500-mile U.S. interstate highway system became an important factor in the number of people traveling for business and leisure. Vehicle registrations grew phenomenally and people took to the roads in great numbers.
6. *Development of suburbs.* Not only did the interstate highway system facilitate long-distance travel, it also made local travel simpler. As a result, new residential neighborhoods were established in the suburbs. These were followed by retail shopping centers, office buildings, and recreational and entertainment facilities, all of which attracted increased traffic and the need for accommodations and meeting space.
7. *Increased air travel.* Air travel also became a commonplace part of the business and leisure scene in the United States. By the early 1980s, there were over 700 airports certified for passenger service, including 23 large hub airports (in Chicago, New York City, Los Angeles, Dallas, and so on). Hub airports not only served their own cities (which were destinations in their own right), but also served as connection points for an increasing number of domestic and international flights. In addition, 35 medium-size hubs served regional areas such as the Southwest or Northeast, and 62 small hubs provided statewide connections for a growing number of business and leisure travelers.
8. *Convention center expansion.* The 1960s ushered in a booming U.S. economy. As businesses (and business and fraternal organizations) grew, businesspeople needed facilities for conventions and meetings. Some cities already had civic centers or auditoriums that could accommodate these groups; groups were generally served by a small number of downtown hotels. But as businesses expanded into the suburbs or outgrew the limited civic center facilities, there was a boom in the construction of convention hotels, both in the cities and in regional and resort destinations.

What do these factors have to do with hospitality marketing and sales? Everything! Changing times greatly affected the hospitality industry, and the industry had to evolve to meet new challenges. For example, the industry responded to the demands of road travelers with the development of chain properties such as Holiday Inn and Howard Johnson. Hotel chains introduced standardized designs, amenities, services, and referral networks and were easily recognizable to the traveling public. Later, as air travel became increasingly used by both leisure and business travelers, airport hotels became commonplace, as did hotels designed to meet the needs of business travelers, such as convention hotels, hotels with business floors and business centers, and extended-stay properties.

These developments and more recent innovations (hotel websites, for example) were driven by changing customer wants and other trends affecting the business environment and society in general. Just as changes in the past affected hospitality firms and changed the face of the industry, present and future trends will continue to influence how hotels and restaurants do business.

In this chapter we will see how management and staff develop and implement marketing and sales strategies to keep hospitality firms competitive. Since hospitality firms should be pro-active rather than reactive, we will also detail some of the trends that are affecting today's hospitality industry and see how they will influence future marketing and sales efforts.

Marketing and Sales

Because competition among hotels and hotel brands is fierce, it is no longer adequate to place a few advertisements, send a few salespeople out on personal calls, and rely on word-of-mouth referrals to fill guestrooms and property revenue centers. The need for concentrated marketing and sales strategies has never been greater in the hospitality industry. The success of today's—and tomorrow's—hospitality products will be the direct result of the combined efforts of highly trained, competent, and innovative sales and marketing professionals who are dedicated to making an impact on the ever-changing, challenging hospitality industry.

Today's hospitality firms have shifted from a strictly sales orientation to utilizing combined sales and marketing strategies. While marketing and sales are not the same, they are interrelated, and both are needed to maximize revenues. A hotel can have the greatest marketing plan in the world, but it will be wasted if the hotel does not have an effective, customer-oriented sales staff. Conversely, a hotel can employ a great salesperson, but he or she will waste time and money if target markets and goals are not clearly defined in the marketing plan.

Both marketing and sales are, first and foremost, customer oriented; every action is aimed at the ultimate goal of serving customers. But **marketing** is much broader in scope than sales. Marketing is the study and management of the exchange process. It involves those things that the property will do to select a target market and stimulate or alter that market's demand for the property's services. While marketing includes sales, it also includes a number of other elements: research, action strategies, advertising, publicity, and sales promotions, as well as a means to monitor the effectiveness of the marketing program.

Sales consists of direct efforts to sell the property by personal sales calls, telecommunication, and mailings. Although we will discuss the importance of sales later in the chapter, it is important to note that the sales process has been changed considerably by new marketing concepts that focus on what consumers want rather than on what the property has to sell.

As companies move toward a stronger market orientation, their sales forces need to become more market focused and customer oriented. The traditional view is that salespeople should worry about volume and sell, sell, sell, and that the marketing department should worry about marketing strategy and profitability. The newer view is that salespeople should know how to produce customer satisfaction, analyze sales data, measure market potential, gather market intelligence, and develop marketing strategies and plans.[1]

Marketing focuses on trend research and the development of successful sales techniques and efforts. Successful sales efforts depend on effective marketing strategies, which can be developed only by focusing on market variables—the environment in general (uncontrollable or external variables) and controllable variables inherent in the property (the marketing mix).

Exhibit 1 Marketing Mix Model

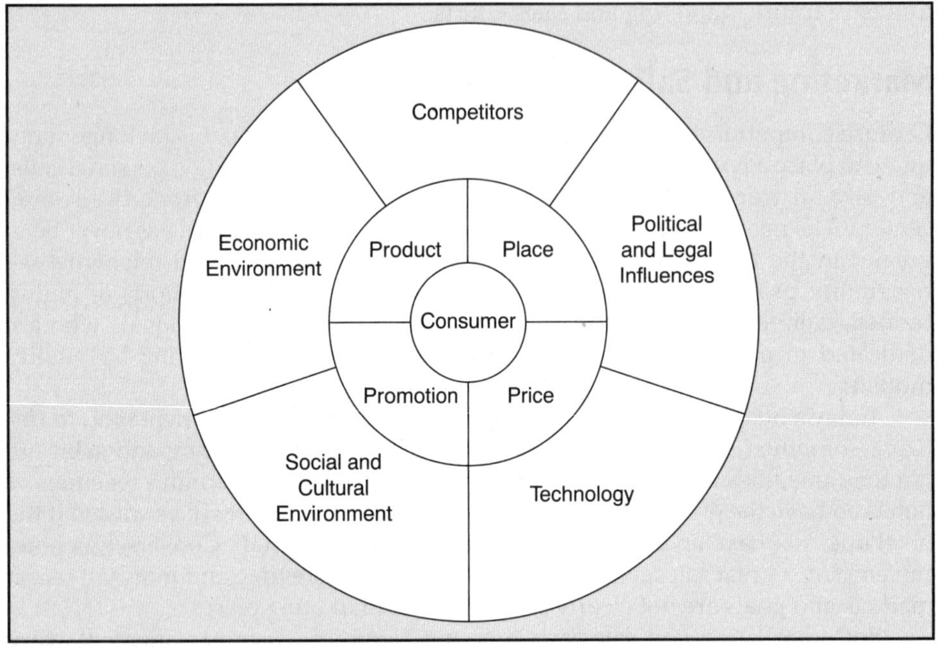

This basic marketing mix model for the hospitality industry contains the "four Ps" (product, place, promotion, and price) set forth by E. J. McCarthy in his classic book, *Basic Marketing*. Note that the consumer is the focus of the marketing mix, which is affected by the uncontrollable variables listed in the outermost circle.

The Marketing Mix

The term **marketing mix** is used to indicate the integrating of several variables to satisfy specific consumer needs. The task of the marketing manager is to form these variables into a marketing mix that meets the needs of each consumer group or market segment targeted by the property.

What makes up the marketing mix? The most widely used model of the marketing mix is the familiar "four Ps" set forth by E. J. McCarthy in his classic *Basic Marketing*. This model can be represented by three concentric circles (see Exhibit 1):

1. The innermost circle contains the focal point of the marketing effort—the *consumer.*
2. The middle circle illustrates the marketing mix of product, place, promotion, and price (the four Ps). These are termed *controllable variables.*
3. The outer circle identifies *uncontrollable variables* such as the economic environment, political and legal influences, and the social and cultural environment.

The problem with this model is that it is too restrictive for the hospitality industry, which has unique characteristics that prohibit an unadulterated application of the four Ps. This doesn't mean, however, that the hospitality industry needs

Exhibit 2 The Interaction of the Marketing Mix

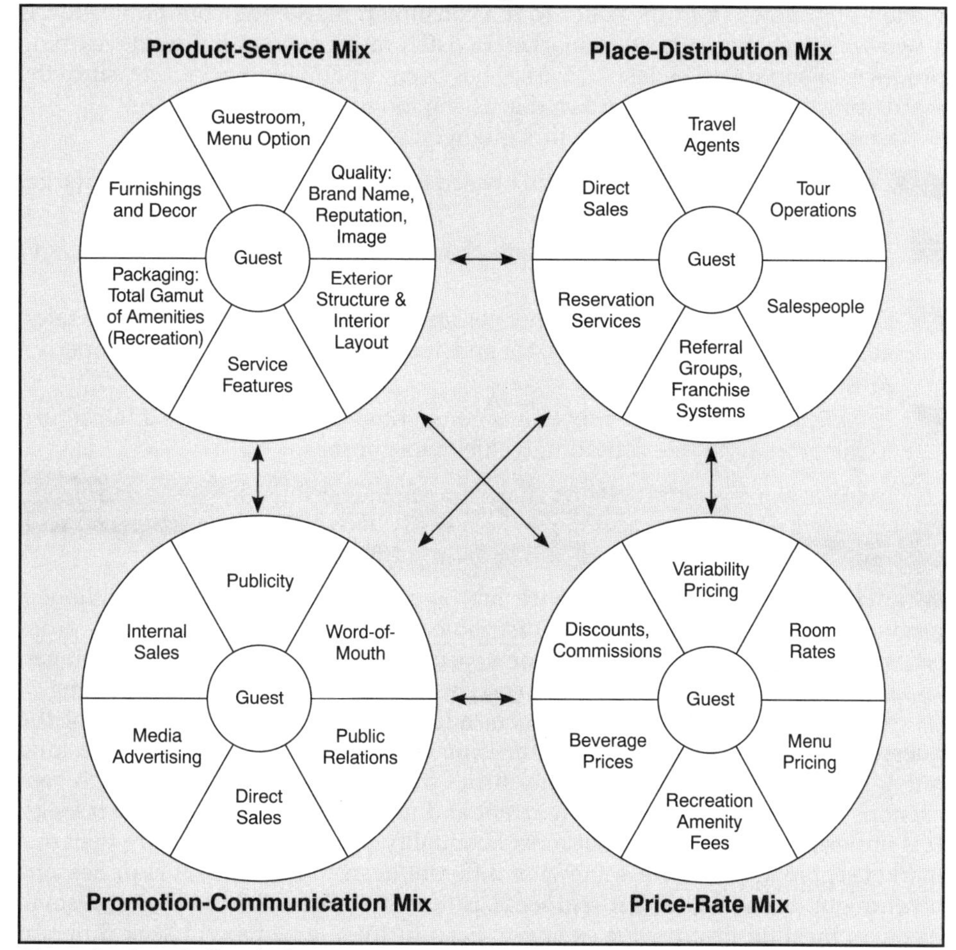

Since the hospitality industry operates in a different way from the consumer goods industry, the traditional marketing mix has been expanded in this exhibit to include those variables inherent to hospitality marketing. All of these variables must be taken into consideration when developing a marketing plan to sell hospitality products and services.

a new marketing mix. The "wheel" has already been invented; all the industry need do is add a few new wrinkles to make it work for hospitality properties.

The four Ps developed for the consumer goods industry have been broadened in this chapter to account for the unique way in which the hospitality industry operates (see Exhibit 2). *Product* has been expanded to *product-service,* because of the service orientation of hospitality properties. *Place,* the second element in the marketing mix, has been broadened to *place-distribution* to include the channels of distribution or the intermediaries who aid in the flow of hospitality products and services to guests. The *promotion* "P" is now *promotion-communication,* since marketing communication is different from promotion. With promotion, information only flows from the seller to the consumer; marketing communication is a two-way exchange. Effective marketers listen to consumers before developing products or services. The last "P," *price,* has been expanded to *price-rate,* since the word "price" is seldom used when discussing lodging accommodations.

Conceptually, the marketing mix might be seen as:

- Developing a product-service mix based on the wants and needs of the target market(s)
- Determining the most appropriate channels (place-distribution) or ways to reach the market(s)
- Determining promotion and other communication strategies, including sales, advertising, and public relations, and informing markets of the property's product-service
- Establishing a price-rate mix that is competitive and will ensure a fair return to the property while providing value to its guests

In other words, the hospitality marketing manager must have the right facilities and services (product) and make them easily accessible to guests (place) with the proper amount of promotion and at the right price.

Product-Service. The product-service mix is considered first because without a product the industry has nothing to distribute, promote, or price. Hospitality properties offer products such as guestrooms, banquet space, and food and beverages, and services such as express check-in and check-out, housekeeping, and parking.

This product-service mix must be tailored to the needs and wants of the guests sought, whether the firm is focusing on its current guest base or seeking out additional markets. A hospitality firm's offerings are based on research conclusions about its target markets (current and future) and the benefits each seeks. It is important to remember that most hospitality properties serve more than one market segment, each with somewhat different needs and wants. A Four Seasons hotel might define its market segments as families, business travelers, and small business meeting groups, for example. Each of these groups will seek different benefits from the property: the family might desire recreational amenities, the business traveler may require a secretarial service or on-site copying facilities, and the meeting group might be most interested in soundproof meeting rooms.

While the marketing and sales department cannot actually produce the physical product or render the intangible service, it is responsible for researching the guests' product-service needs and wants and then working with management to develop the property so that it meets those needs and wants. Marketing also evaluates the existing product-service mix and the property's brand name identity for possible improvements. For example, Budgetel changed its name to Baymont; the old name was believed to position the chain as an economy brand, which was inconsistent with the quality of the company's product and service levels.

The market-oriented hospitality firm attempts to match its product and service offerings to the needs and wants of its target markets, but it can face difficulty due to the fixed nature of the product. Hotel rooms and facilities are not versatile; a guestroom cannot become a suite, a convention center cannot be converted into a golf course, and a coffee shop cannot be transformed into a lounge without considerable effort and expense.

Service, the other element of the product-service mix, is considerably more flexible, but also poses problems for marketers. It is nearly impossible to standardize hotel services. The front desk agent at night cannot duplicate exactly the service provided by the front desk agent who works the morning shift. Complicated service, such as a lavish annual banquet featuring elaborate ice sculptures and exotic menu items, is impossible to re-create exactly year after year, and guests may think that such a banquet was "not as good as last year's." This is in sharp contrast to the consistency of consumer goods; the Nautilus sit-up machine used in a gym in New York will not differ from the same machine in a health club in California, and the machine will be exactly the same year after year until the model changes.

Place-Distribution. Place-distribution refers to the accessibility of the product to consumers. With consumer goods, producers use distribution channels to ship their product to consumers. In the hospitality industry, instead of the product traveling to the consumer, the consumer travels to the product.

In the marketing of consumer goods, the role of intermediaries is to ensure that the product is available to the consumer when and where it is needed, and in sufficient variety and quantity. Hospitality products—clean guestrooms, a pleasant dining experience, and so on—are neither shipped nor stored. The problems of warehousing and inventory control do not arise, making distribution much simpler for hospitality firms.

The distribution channels available to lodging establishments can be viewed as either direct or indirect. When a hospitality firm seeks to reach potential guests with its own sales force through direct mail, telephone solicitation, personal sales calls, or media advertising, the distribution channels are said to be direct. Indirect distribution channels include websites selling travel services, and intermediaries such as travel agents, tour operators, and independent hotel representatives.

Promotion-Communication. It is the task of the director of marketing to blend the most effective promotion-communication mix. Promotion is the way a hotel or restaurant communicates to target markets, and can involve advertising and direct sales techniques. Communication is different from promotion; promotion implies persuasion (something the marketer does *to* the consumer) while communication is a two-way exchange (something the marketer does *with* the consumer). Determining what the consumer wants and needs through communication is much more effective than trying to sell a product or service that is not needed.

Price-Rate. If a potential guest rejects the property and its services because of price, all of the previous efforts were wasted. Therefore, price-rate determination is one of marketing's most crucial concerns. Consumers are strongly influenced by prices, and the guests a firm is seeking to attract must be taken into consideration when establishing room rates and menu prices. Guests who stay at a budget motel have different wants, needs, and expectations from those who choose an expensive resort property.

Hotels, especially large properties, often develop variable-rate policies to meet the needs of different market groups. These policies are characterized by charging different prices to different buyers of the same product, depending on the competitive situation and the bargaining position of the buyer.

The bargaining positions of buyers (individual guests, meeting planners, and so on) will vary depending on the hotel's level of business, which can be broken down into three categories:

1. *Peak.* Also known as *in-season,* this is the period when demand for a property and its services is highest and the highest prices can be charged. **Peak periods** vary for different types of properties. A resort, for example, may experience a peak period during the middle of the summer if it is a popular seaside destination, or in the winter if it is a popular ski resort.
2. *Valley.* The **valley period,** also known as the *off-season,* is the time when demand is lowest. Reduced rates may be offered to attract business.
3. *Shoulder.* A **shoulder period** falls between a peak and a valley, and can be an excellent opportunity to build business—rooms are available and a medium or high rate can be charged. Many properties target sales and marketing efforts toward shoulder periods.

Meeting planners know they can generally negotiate better rates during valley or shoulder periods than during peak convention months, and vacationers often wait to take advantage of the off-season's reduced rates. Commercial downtown hotels, recognizing that their peak periods occur during the week, often promote special weekend package rates to encourage business during the weekend shoulder period.

A property's pricing policy can also affect its image. Upscale properties, for example, are generally cautious about offering deep discounts. In fact, if famous five-star hotels such as The Ritz-Carlton in Boston or the Regent in Hong Kong were to reduce their prices significantly, guests might become suspicious that product quality was being reduced or services curtailed. Guests at luxury properties expect to pay top rates, and marketers of such hotels feel it hurts their hotel's upscale image to discount.

Reputation can play a significant role in the pricing of hospitality products. A lodging facility may charge a higher rate for similar rooms and services because it enjoys a better reputation than its competitors. A Holiday Inn, for example, can demand a higher rate than a comparable independent property simply because of the market value travelers have placed on the chain's good reputation.

Pricing strategies may vary, depending on the goals of the property. A new property, for example, may introduce itself at low rates in order to build guest awareness and sales volume, sacrificing some immediate profits.

Marketing Mix Decisions. One element may be emphasized over another when appealing to a specific target market, but the elements of the marketing mix are interrelated, and a decision with respect to one variable usually affects other variables of the mix.

While the four Ps of the marketing mix are called controllable variables, it is important to realize that control is not absolute. For example, the lodging marketer has product limits. He or she is not free to convert conventional guestrooms to suites without substantial expense.

Insider Insights

David Fine
Director of Sales and Marketing
The Broadmoor
Colorado Springs, Colorado

"My primary function is helping to drive the group sales effort at the Broadmoor. I administer what we call our national sales team as well as our executive meeting management team. I spend time with the sales organization to grow the business for the hotel.

A lot of sales roles have changed. I'm not in a position where I have to generate a lot of reporting, because we're an independent brand. I've worked for big chains where I spent a lot of time generating information and reporting information about financials for a sales organization.

I think leadership is the key, having a pretty defined understanding of what the product is, understanding what your brand is, and then being able to clearly articulate that to your team so they can communicate that to the meeting public and to the individual leisure guest. You have to understand what your selling proposition is. And then you have to make sure your people are communicating that effectively.

I think you have to have good listening skills and the ability to absorb information and understand the scope of information and not get stuck by the minutiae.

The best people I've worked with had the ability to inject humor in the work and create a work environment that's enthusiastic, that's supportive, that's understanding of individual desires as well as collective desires.

I think a lot of our business now, a percentage of our trade, is coming through the Internet, through third-party Internet wholesalers, and a lot of high-end travelers are looking online. So clearly you have to be on top of your web product. You've got to understand the communications process and be able to speak through the Internet about what your product is and articulate what your product is online.

There's a lot of consolidation in our business today, and I think it's important that, as a sales organization, you're trying to create some level of consistency. My philosophy has been you want to build your business on very solid customer relationships and development of customers over a long period of time."

Source: Scott Etkin, "The Dealmaker," from *Lodging* magazine online, posted March 3, 2007.

Uncontrollable variables—external environmental factors—will also affect a marketing effort. A recession cannot be controlled by a marketing staff, nor can an energy crisis, natural disasters such as earthquakes and floods, or weather conditions.

Successful marketing efforts don't just happen. They must take both controllable and uncontrollable variables into consideration, and a carefully researched, planned, and managed sales effort must be developed to ensure that the property attracts guests and keeps them.

Management's Role in Marketing and Sales

On the property level, three key management positions in the marketing and sales area are the property's general manager, the director of marketing, and the director of sales.

The General Manager

The success or failure of a hotel's marketing and sales program starts with top management, and a marketing-oriented general manager is the key to a firm's sales efforts. In small to medium-size properties, the general manager may take on the responsibilities of advertising and public relations to enable the sales manager to devote his or her time to selling. The general manager may also make personal sales calls outside the office on high-priority business and spend time at the front desk during check-out, thanking guests for their business.

The Director of Marketing

Since marketing is largely a management function, it is important that the director of marketing be capable of performing a variety of management tasks, such as setting objectives and policies; making decisions; and organizing, selecting, and supervising the sales and marketing staffs.

A marketing director's supervisory tasks can be divided into five functions: planning, organizing, staffing, directing, and controlling. Planning is probably the most important. Planning is determining what needs to be done and deciding how to meet the goals and objectives set. Without proper planning, the other functions are meaningless.

Organization is also important, because a structured approach is necessary to develop strategies and utilize the marketing and sales staff to fullest advantage. Staffing—getting the right people into the right place at the right time—plays a key role in organization. Staffing also involves training employees so they can reach their highest potential, and helping them develop the ability to take on additional responsibilities.

Directing involves overseeing both programs and employees. Directing incorporates motivating and guiding the staff to do its best, and requires well-developed interpersonal skills. Controlling involves setting standards, measuring performance on a regular basis, and taking corrective action if needed.

Looking for new opportunities—and redirecting or modifying strategies that are not working well—is an ongoing process and requires the skills of a full-time marketing director. Many medium-size and large properties also use the services of a director of sales to motivate the sales staff and oversee the direct sales effort.

The Director of Sales

A director of sales differs from a director of marketing, although many properties use the terms interchangeably. The difference is that a director of marketing deals more with research and strategy and is concerned with identifying the needs and wants of consumers; a director of sales carries out marketing strategies and directs the sales staff in finding solutions to customers' problems (that is, making sales).

While marketing affects everything a hotel does, sales has a narrower focus. The most important responsibility of a salesperson is to sell the product—the property and its facilities and services—that management and the marketing and sales department have created. An effective director of sales will make sure that the sales staff is doing just that—contacting prospective or current clients and selling the benefits of the property.

The Importance of Marketing and Sales

It is important to note that both marketing and sales are vital parts of a process that fills guestrooms and restaurants and sells function and meeting room space. Both marketing and sales are necessary; neither works well without the other.

Putting business on the books is critical to every property's economic health and growth. Direct sales are as important today as they were before marketing efforts came to the forefront of hospitality promotion. Marketing activities such as publicity and advertising are one-way communications; in an industry that is consumer oriented, the value of personal contact cannot be overstated. A prospect can pick up a newspaper, read a property's ad, and remain uninvolved and uncommitted, but consider the impact of a salesperson's fifth visit to a prospect. Most prospects will be impressed by the salesperson's persistence and the fact that the salesperson really cares about determining and meeting the prospect's needs.

Marketing and Sales as a Career

The sales profession today is vastly different from what it was just a decade ago, both in attitude and method. Sales has become a scientifically designed function, from the way leads are generated, to the study of the psychology of buying, to the professional identification and handling of clients. Rather than relying on hit-or-miss efforts, sales leads are typically generated by computers relying on detailed consumer profiles or through lists scientifically developed for each property's target markets. In addition to being trained in practical sales techniques, professional salespeople are now trained in the psychology of selling and in both verbal and nonverbal communication. They are becoming experts in people-handling skills, such as the recognition of common personality types, and methods of dealing with each type of client.

Why is there so much emphasis on new techniques and sales methods? First of all, the value of a concentrated sales effort—whether a personal one-on-one sales call or an organized sales blitz—has finally been recognized. Secondly, hospitality sales has become more than just a job, more than a springboard to higher or more prestigious positions. Hotel salespeople are recognized as professionals—highly trained and service-oriented members of the marketing team.

Hospitality sales is an excellent career choice. There are many opportunities open for salespeople today. In fact, competition is so keen among hospitality firms that they are willing to pay top dollar for good salespeople.

MARKETING IN ACTION

Wyndham Hotels & Resorts: "What's Your Request?"

When Wyndham Hotels & Resorts was looking for a compelling way to differentiate its brand and build customer loyalty, it developed Wyndham ByRequest as the heart of its customer relationship marketing program. The program was designed to demonstrate how far the chain would go to personalize the stays of guests.

ByRequest membership is offered to guests with prior stays at any Wyndham property. On their third stay within 12 months, guests receive a surprise welcome in their guestroom along with a membership card and a personal profile that they can fill out at the property, on the Wyndham ByRequest website, or by calling a member phone line.

The personal profiles of some 300,000 ByRequest members are stored on a sophisticated computer information network. Once guest preferences are entered, they are communicated and tracked chain-wide.

When a Wyndham ByRequest member arrives at any Wyndham property worldwide, he or she is welcomed with a guestroom that has been tailored to his or her individual preferences. For example, the room will be located in a preferred area or level of the hotel, and the items that have been listed on the guest profile (from a specific type of pillow to a favorite magazine, beverage, or snack) will be waiting in the room.

In addition to having their profile requirements fulfilled, ByRequest members also enjoy additional benefits, including an automatic 2 P.M. checkout, free high-speed Internet access, free 800 long-distance access, airline miles, and access to an onsite ByRequest manager who will attend to any last-minute requests. Members also have a secure, personalized web page that allows them to access their profiles, communicate with the ByRequest manager at each property, and retrieve their guest folios online. Unexpected surprises, such as dining and beverage credits, complimentary in-room movies, or credits at Wyndham's resorts are added bonuses that members enjoy on a periodic basis.

The Challenge of Hospitality Marketing and Sales

Hospitality sales differs greatly from consumer goods sales in that the hospitality salesperson is selling something that has both tangible and intangible elements. The product offered (guestrooms, dining facilities, etc.) is tangible, but the services provided are intangible. Guests can't take the hotel's products or services home to use or admire; when the hotel experience is over, all they have is a memory.

Hospitality salespeople must consider the following characteristics of hospitality products and services when selling potential clients on a hotel:

1. *Intangibility.* Salespeople do not sell guestrooms or banquet rooms; they sell the use of these rooms. They must sell the benefits or the experience the property's products and services will provide to prospective clients. Since clients cannot see, touch, or use the hospitality experience before they buy, they must

rely on the hospitality salesperson's description of the property and the experiences it offers. Therefore, the salesperson's credibility plays an important role in the sale. **Service guarantees** are being increasingly used by hospitality firms to reduce the risk consumers take and build consumer confidence in a firm's promises.

2. *Perishability.* The perishability of the hospitality product presents challenges for hotel salespeople that are different from those faced by salespeople of consumer goods. An unused guestroom, an empty restaurant seat, or an unfilled tee-off time represents business lost forever. In contrast to consumer goods, the hospitality product has no shelf life; it cannot be stockpiled or inventoried to sell later. This perishability places heavy pressure on hospitality marketing and sales executives to develop innovative pricing, promotion, and planning strategies. Some hotels now charge early check-out fees, and some restaurants charge fees to customers who fail to honor their reservations.

3. *Inconsistency.* The service rendered by a housekeeper or a food server may vary greatly at different hotels or restaurants—or even at the same outlet. Maintaining a consistent level of service is essential for the success of hospitality entities, and inconsistency is a special challenge to chain properties and restaurants. Clients tend to expect the same type of experience or quality of food at each property or restaurant in a chain, but even with standardized training programs, properties and restaurants within the same chain may have very different employee skill levels and levels of service. An employee may even provide varied levels of service from day to day.

4. *Inseparability.* Production and consumption are largely simultaneous with services. The hospitality consumer comes to the property, and services are consumed at the place and time they are created. This is totally different from the sale of such consumer goods as automobiles or appliances. The purchase or consumption of consumer goods may take place several months after production has been completed. To compound the problem, guests not only come in contact with employees but with other guests as well. That makes the other guests part of the product and often affects the quality of service.

While general marketing methods used for selling tangible consumer products may be borrowed by hospitality salespeople, they must make modifications to them in order to effectively sell the often intangible products and services offered by the hospitality industry.

Trends Shaping the Future of Hospitality Marketing and Sales

Successful hospitality management requires keeping abreast of trends and acting on them before your competition does; acting rather than reacting is the key to success. The study of trends is often referred to as **environmental scanning** in marketing circles and is an integral part of hospitality sales and marketing. Trends affecting the hospitality industry include the following:

- Globalization
- Consolidation (mergers, acquisitions, and joint ventures)
- Partnership marketing
- Niche marketing and branding
- Technology
- Environmental awareness
- Guest preferences
- Relationship marketing

We will take a look at each of these trends in the following sections.

Globalization

Although countries around the world have exchanged goods and services with one another for many centuries, unprecedented opportunities for companies to expand their business globally were ushered in during the last decade. **Globalization** continues to impact the hospitality industry. U.S. hotel and restaurant chains are establishing an international presence to serve U.S. travelers and meet the demand abroad for U.S. products. Daniel Larkin, European practice leader of hospitality and leisure for PricewaterhouseCoopers, says that "it will be increasingly easier for someone who has a favorite hotel brand or brands to count on it being there whenever they travel around Europe. It'll be at least 10 years before Europe becomes like the U.S., where you can find a Marriott, Hyatt, or Sheraton wherever you go, but the trend is very clear."[2]

While the first hotels built outside the country by U.S. chains were primarily upscale properties located in capital cities, chains such as Comfort Inn, Days Inn, and Holiday Inn Express are expanding outside foreign capitals with mid-range or budget properties aimed at U.S. citizens, local business travelers, and regional tourists. Since the U.S. market is considered to have matured, it will become more important for hotel chains to look outside the country for more opportunities. Several major chains are focusing on the Asia-Pacific region.[3] Thousands of hotels are scheduled to be built in Indonesia, Thailand, China, and India over the next few years to meet the growing demand.

Leaders in globalization include major international as well as U.S. hotel chains (see Exhibit 3). Globalization is a two-way street, with several foreign chains establishing a greater presence in the United States. InterContinental Hotels Group, based in Great Britain, and the Accor chain (Europe's largest), based in France, have properties throughout the world and have built hotels in the United States.

Globalization has greatly affected the food service industry as well. McDonald's, for example, now has more than 14,000 outlets in over 70 countries, and international sales account for more than half of the company's total revenues. Other fast-food chains, including Burger King, Wendy's, Pizza Hut, Subway, KFC, and Dunkin' Donuts, are also developing franchises throughout the world, as are table-service restaurants such as T.G.I. Friday's and Sizzler.

Exhibit 3 Hotel Companies in the Most Countries

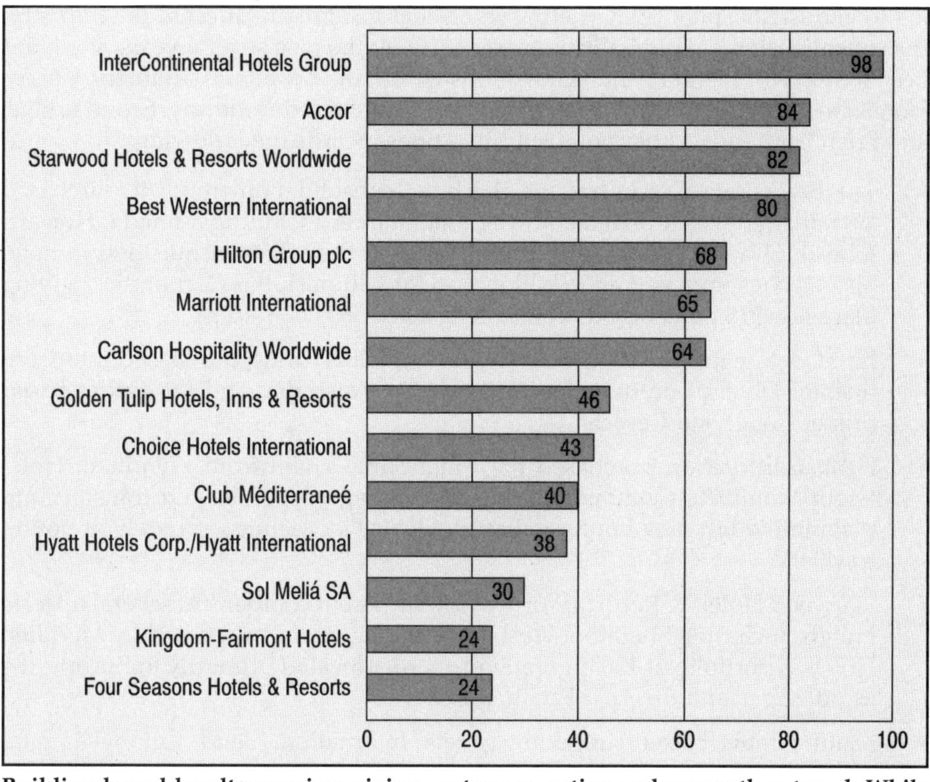

Building brand loyalty requires giving customers options wherever they travel. While U.S. chains continue to dominate the global picture, four European-owned chains are notable exceptions, with two of them—InterContinental Hotels Group and Accor—leading the way with properties in the most countries. Although Great Britain–based InterContinental Hotels Group heads the list, Starwood Hotels is expanding its portfolio in the Asia-Pacific region, with a focus on China. By the end of 2010, the company will have more than 32 new hotels in China alone under the Four Points, Sheraton, W, Westin, St. Regis, and Aloft brands. Sources: "HOTELS' Giants Survey 2001," *Hotels,* July 2002, p. 43; and Erin Sternthal, "Hotel Brand Expansion," *Travel Agent,* September 3, 2007.

The global marketplace offers both opportunities and challenges. Hospitality companies must be sensitive to cultural differences; one product or one approach does not fit all. In India, for example, where cows are sacred, McDonald's restaurants do not have hamburgers or other beef products on their menus.

Consolidation: Mergers, Acquisitions, and Joint Ventures

Globalization can be extremely costly. It requires advanced technology to process international reservations and develop marketing strategies for specific countries and regions, and there is the expense of additional promotional costs. High costs led to another hospitality marketing trend that has greatly affected the industry: the **consolidation** of hospitality companies. Over the past several years, there has been a frenzy of mergers and acquisitions within the hospitality industry. Choice Hotels International started the trend when it purchased Rodeway, Econo Lodge, and Friendship Inns. Other notable transactions include the following:

- The Blackstone Group has led the hotel consolidation trend. It purchased Wyndham International (acquiring nine brands, including Ramada, Howard Johnson, Days Inn, and Travelodge), and, in the largest acquisition in hotel history, consummated a $26 billion deal for Hilton Hotels Corporation, giving Blackstone 15 hotel brands comprising some 560,000 rooms.
- InterContinental Hotels Group, owner of Holiday Inns, purchased InterContinental Hotels, Southern Pacific Hotels of Australia, and the Dallas-based Bristol Hotels and Resorts.
- Hyatt Corporation purchased the AmeriSuites chain from Wyndham Hotel Group, completely renovating the 160 existing properties and transforming them into a hip new boutique brand, Hyatt Place, aimed squarely at young travelers.
- Starwood Hotels & Resorts Worldwide, the parent company of several upscale brands, including Sheraton, Westin, W, and St. Regis, purchased Le Meridien Hotels, a portfolio of 130 high-end properties located primarily in Europe, the Middle East, and the Asia-Pacific region.
- Saudi Arabia–based Kingdom Hotels International and Colony Capital acquired Fairmont, Raffles, Swissotel, and Delta Hotels, giving the chain a portfolio of 120 luxury hotels in 24 countries.
- In 2000, MGM Grand acquired Mirage Resorts, adding several casino hotels (including TI, the Mirage, and Bellagio) in Las Vegas and outside Nevada to its portfolio. In 2004, MGM Grand–Mirage became the Strip's largest landholder with the acquisition of Mandalay Resort Group (formerly Circus Circus Enterprises), whose properties included Circus Circus, the Excalibur, the Luxor, and Mandalay Bay. The chain now boasts properties and interest in properties on three continents.

The food service industry has also experienced its share of mergers and acquisitions. Pizza Hut, KFC, A&W, Long John Silvers, and Taco Bell, to name just one example, were all acquired by Yum! Brands Inc.

Why this frenzy of mergers? According to Bill Marriott, chairman of Marriott International, "one of the things that's driving this [consolidation] is globalization." In his view, medium-size hotel companies lack the presence and resources for the technology needed for worldwide marketing. Many industry observers predict that consolidations, mergers, and acquisitions will continue until there are four or five major hotel companies controlling the majority of hotels in the near future.[4]

Large hotel companies enjoy a number of advantages:

- More marketing clout
- More cost-effective purchasing capabilities
- More borrowing power
- More cost-saving opportunities

Consolidation has drawbacks, however. There are fears that employee layoffs will result as operations are streamlined and that the quality of hospitality products and services will suffer. Will the individual franchisees get lost at the corporate level? Will individual brands lose their distinctiveness? How will huge corporations determine which properties need the most attention, and will this attention come at the expense of other struggling properties?

Partnership Marketing

Another trend that enables hospitality companies to access new markets, expand products and services, enhance image or positioning, and better serve customers (without increasing marketing budgets) is **partnership marketing.** Partnership marketing, also known as *developing strategic alliances* and *synergism marketing,* involves two or more firms—ideally serving similar markets with noncompetitive products—joining together to benefit from each other's strengths.

There are two types of **strategic alliances:** like-kind alliances and related-business alliances. *Like-kind alliances* are those in which two or more organizations in the same business (such as several hotels) form an alliance to benefit all parties. For example, Radisson Hotels of Minneapolis, which had a large presence in North America, and SAS International Hotels of Brussels, which was prominent in northern Europe, teamed up to increase their presence in the international marketplace. SAS was given use of the Radisson name in Europe and the Middle East, where its hotels now carry the name Radisson SAS. Radisson's elaborate central reservations system is now tied to the SAS system, permitting powerful joint sales and marketing efforts around the world. Since the affiliation began, Radisson SAS expanded from 29 to 100 hotels.

Related-business alliances include hotels teaming up with such hospitality-related firms as cruise lines, food service companies, theme parks, and credit card companies to enhance their presence in the marketplace. For example, Hilton Hotels, Marriott International, and Choice Hotels have teamed up with Pizza Hut to provide pizza delivery to their guests. Other hotels are finding that having franchised restaurants or food courts on property can cut their costs while providing popular dining choices for their guests. Other related-business alliances include Marriott, Westin, Sheraton, Hilton, and Hyatt linking their frequent-traveler programs with United Airlines, which, in turn, has joined with eight other airlines around the world to better meet the needs of frequent travelers. Several restaurant chains have joint promotions with Disney and other family-oriented movie producers. McDonald's, for example, secured a ten-year exclusive partnership with Disney to promote everything from Disney movies and videos to TV shows and theme park rides in its promotional campaigns. McDonald's benefits as families flock to its outlets to collect movie-related merchandise, while Disney receives additional advertising and promotion at no cost.

Exhibit 4 Hotel Brands by Segment

Examples of Hotel Brands by Segment		
Luxury	**Upper Upscale**	**Upscale**
Fairmont	Embassy Suites	Adam's Mark
Four Seasons	Hilton	Courtyard
InterContinental	Hyatt	Crowne Plaza
Mandarin Oriental	Marriott	Doubletree
Peninsula	Renaissance	Hilton Garden Inn
St. Regis	Sheraton	Radisson
Ritz-Carlton	Westin	Wyndham
Midscale with F&B	**Midscale w/out F&B**	**Economy**
Clarion	AmeriSuites	Best Inns
Four Points	Baymont Inns & Suites	Econo Lodge
Holiday Inn	Comfort Inns & Suites	Knights Inns
Howard Johnson	Fairfield Inns & Suites	Microtel Inns
Quality Inn & Suites	Hampton Inns	Motel 6
Ramada	La Quinta Inns & Suites	Super 8
Red Lion	Wingate Inns	Travelodge

Branding (positioning properties into appropriate categories) is used by a number of hotel companies to meet the needs of various market segments—from budget to luxury travelers—to create customer loyalty. Source: Smith Travel Research. Adapted from John W. O'Neill, "Defining Segments," *Lodging Hospitality*, January 2006, p. 42.

Niche Marketing and Branding

Niche marketing—designing, building, and marketing hospitality products for specific market segments—is not entirely new. The hospitality industry has traditionally positioned itself in three broad categories or segments: luxury/upscale, midscale or mid-priced, and economy (see Exhibit 4). But now there are segments, or tiers, within these segments, and hotels are creating a number of brand names and images.

Niche marketing was established as properties became aware that there were an increasing number of market segments with varying preferences and budgets. Ramada Worldwide, for example, offers Ramada Plaza Hotels (top-of-the-line facilities designed for upscale business and leisure travelers), Ramada Inns (mid-priced properties), and Ramada Limited (limited-service properties for budget-conscious travelers). These properties are promoted differently, but each bears the familiar Ramada name. InterContinental Hotels Group, however, offers seven different brands to serve product niches from budget to full-service and extended-stay. The

INTERNET EXERCISE

Independent hotels have formed hotel associations to enable them to compete more effectively with such giant chains as Hilton, Hyatt, Marriott, and Starwood.

Log onto the Internet and research the following hotel association websites:

- Historic Hotels of America (www.historichotels.org)
- The Leading Hotels of the World (www.lhw.com)
- Preferred Hotel Group (www.preferredhotelgroup.com)
- Relais & Châteaux (www.relaischateaux.com)
- Small Luxury Hotels of the World (www.slh.com)
- WORLDHOTELS (www.worldhotels.com)

1. How does a property become a member of each of the hotel associations?
2. What inspection process is used by each association to ensure that member hotels maintain service standards?
3. Which of the associations have customer loyalty programs? Which have tiered their properties by price points?

most extensive range of brands is operated by Marriott International, which targets the price-sensitive niche with its Fairfield Inn brand; business travelers with Courtyard by Marriott; extended-stay travelers with SpringHill Suites, Residence Inns, and TownePlace Suites; and the upscale market with Ritz-Carlton, Renaissance Hotels and Resorts, and Marriott Hotels, Resorts, and Suites. In all, Marriott has 11 brands targeted to most segments of the lodging industry.

Ramada, InterContinental, and Marriott are competing for customers by offering a number of choices to fit consumers' changing needs and lifestyles. This strategy, long used by automobile companies, is known as *creating brand loyalty;* ideally, a customer who starts with the firm's basic product (a Ford Focus, for example) and is satisfied with it will stay with the firm's products, trading up as circumstances allow (purchasing a Taurus as the family grows and choosing a Lincoln when they can afford a luxury car). As with the auto industry, the hospitality industry has a strata: first-class, mid-priced, and economy properties. InterContinental, Ramada, and Marriott, among other chains, use this strategy to attract and keep their customer bases.

In order to compete with hotel chains, independent hotels and restaurants are also seeking brand recognition. Some independent properties, such as the Broadmoor in Colorado Springs, Colorado, have become a brand in themselves—the hotel has been around for close to 100 years and has developed its own identity. In other cases, independent hotels have formed associations to not only build a brand affiliation but also to take advantage of shared reservations systems and marketing efforts. These associations include The Leading Hotels of the World, which is based in New York City and represents nearly 450 luxury properties around the world (including 50 in the United States); Historic Hotels of America, which is based in Washington, D.C., and requires its members (some 211 hotels and resorts in the United States) to be at least 50 years old or eligible for the National Register of Historic Places; and Relais & Châteaux, a Paris-based firm that represents 475 independently owned hotels and restaurants in 55 countries.

Branding and positioning will continue to remain important factors in hotel and restaurant marketing. A strong brand can bring many benefits. John Russell, chief operating officer of NYLO Hotels, says of branding: "A brand is consistent, gives you confidence that it will deliver, and offers credibility and distribution.... Eighty-seven percent of purchasers prefer brands. Sixty-eight percent of all hotels in the United States today are franchised or branded."[5] Jim Carreker, president/CEO of Wyndham International, says that "clear, well-positioned brands will be the key to surviving and thriving in the new millennium. With trends toward globalization and consolidation continuing, brands will become increasingly relevant and will have the power to drive business."[6]

Technology

Technology is continually changing the way in which hospitality firms do business. Today's technology has made it easier for hotels to communicate with customers and other chain properties, is a key element in providing superior guest service, and has greatly changed the way in which hospitality firms conduct their sales and marketing efforts. While computerized reservations systems have been used for some time, the computer now offers new ways to influence purchasing decisions. Most properties have websites, and guests are also being reached through e-mails and faxes delivered via computer.

Today's guests receive more efficient service via technology with the use of automated check-in/check out kiosks, point-of-purchase sales terminals, electronic or infrared-based guestroom locks, and frequent-guest programs developed using a property's electronic data base. In addition, today's guestrooms and meeting rooms have gone high tech. It is no longer uncommon to find fax machines and connections for personal computers in guestrooms, and an increasing number of properties are offering wireless Internet connections. Properties must also offer state-of-the-art technology in their meeting facilities in order to compete for today's sophisticated business travelers and meeting planners.

Another application that is being increasingly used in hotels is the "smart card," an electronically coded all-purpose card that can serve as identification, a key to the guestroom and other property facilities, and a means of payment when shopping or dining out. At the Portofino Bay Hotel at Universal Studios in Orlando, Florida, for example, smart cards give guests special privileges at the theme park and are used as charge cards. Smart cards have become popular because of their convenience and ease of use. In addition, they can be easily invalidated if they are lost or stolen.

Last but certainly not least, technology is changing the way hotels manage their sales and marketing efforts. Yield and revenue management and other research software, computerized forms and reports, and time management systems have helped hotel sales and marketing staffs to maximize revenue. Other technological

Using Technology to Enhance Hospitality Sales and Marketing Efforts

While the hospitality industry will always be about people, today's competitive market requires that hotels and restaurants also focus as never before on the bottom line and the most effective ways to maximize their revenues. While it was sufficient to keep business financials in three-ring binders a decade ago, today's successful hospitality firms have turned to business management software applications and other technological advances for gathering, storing, comparing, analyzing, and providing access to operating and financial data in order to make better business decisions.

Even small lodging properties and restaurants can benefit from using automated "business intelligence," and there are a number of companies that provide tools for financial and customer management. Aptech Computer Systems, for example, which has provided hospitality accounting systems for 30 years, partnered with Cognos to provide even more effective tools for hospitality revenue management. Aptech later partnered with Concord Hospitality to develop specialized hotel programs to provide centralized analysis of the data required to make decisions relating to marketing strategies.

While some firms have long used computerized spreadsheets for entering and analyzing financial data, these require line-item searches for specific information. Aptech changed all that with the introduction of single-screen "dashboards" that display updated, complex information at a glance. The information is presented in visual formats that are easy to understand.

Another company that serves the hospitality industry is TravelCLICK, which provides website design and search-engine marketing strategies. The company helps hospitality firms to drive business directly to their websites and convert more online shoppers to guests. TravelCLICK's Hospitality Toolkit® web-content management system enables hospitality firms to quickly make text and image changes to their websites so they can respond to changing marketing conditions with new pricing and promotions.

In addition to using technology for enhanced revenue management, hotels and restaurants are using technology to built guest loyalty. The Marco Beach Ocean Resort on Marco Island in Florida, for example, uses a Customer Relations Management (CRM) system that stores guest information on such preferences as requested room type, food and beverage preferences, and other details. The system can be accessed by staff members throughout the hotel, which helps to ensure that the needs and expectations of guests can be anticipated and met.

advances, such as laptop computers and cellular phones, now enable salespeople to conduct business virtually anywhere while still maintaining close contact with their property or restaurant.

Environmental Awareness

Concern about the environment is no longer the province of a few fringe groups; many of today's consumers are genuinely concerned about environmental issues. Consumers are opting for more environmentally sound vacations in greater numbers, giving rise to another new industry buzz word: **ecotourism.**

GOING GREEN

Hotels and Restaurants Join the Green Revolution

For many years now, some hotels and restaurants—especially those in drought-prone areas—have employed such conservation efforts as reducing the number of times that sheets and towels are replaced for guests staying over several nights, and offering water at meals only upon request, to save both water and the energy used for laundering and dishwashing. Today, as greater emphasis is placed on the growing threat to our environment and hospitality guests actively seek out businesses that show a commitment to doing their part to protect the environment, a growing number of hotels and restaurants are stepping up their environmental efforts in such areas as:

- *Energy efficiency and conservation.* There are many methods for conserving energy, including the use of efficient technologies for heating and air conditioning units, food service appliances, lighting, and transportation; and there are alternative forms of power, including wind power, solar power, and geothermal sources.
- *Water efficiency and conservation.* Practices for conserving water include the installation of water-efficient toilets and shower heads and the use of recycled water for landscaping.
- *Sustainable food.* Using organic and locally grown food items reduces the amount of pesticides and fertilizers that harm the environment and the amount of fuel used to transport food.
- *Recycling and composting.* Items commonly recycled by "green" hotels and restaurants include such items as glass, plastic, metal, paper, ink and toner cartridges, and grease. Composting of food waste can be done either on-site or through an outside composting service.
- *Recycled, tree-free, and biodegradable products.* Recycled products are made totally or in part from processed post-consumer products. An example would be the recycled paper carry-out bags used by restaurants. Tree-free products are made from such alternative plant sources as hemp or kenaf. Biodegradable products decompose without the use of chemical agents. Biodegradable cleaners are a popular alternative to chemical products used for cleaning. Chlorine-free paper products are either unbleached or whitened with natural alternatives.
- *Green building and construction.* Green building and construction strategies include the use of environmentally friendly products such as stone and recycled materials. "Green" architecture makes use of natural sources of energy, such as skylights and solar panels.
- *Education.* Property staff should be aware of conservation procedures, follow guidelines set by the property, and be invited to share their ideas on how the property can conserve energy and resources. Guests should be advised of the hotel's conservation efforts and invited to participate in energy conservation and recycling programs. Hotels and restaurants can raise community awareness by issuing press releases about their efforts and participating in such activities as annual Earth Day events.

(continued)

GOING GREEN *(continued)*

In order to keep up-to-date on conservation technology and products, a number of hotels and restaurants are joining associations that can help them to "go green" and get the word out about their conservation efforts. The Houston, Texas–based Green Hotels Association (www.greenhotels.com), which is "committed to encouraging, promoting, and supporting ecological consciousness in the hospitality industry," was founded over ten years ago. It provides members with a comprehensive 135-page guide to assist with "going green" and offers promotional materials to raise guest awareness and explain how they can participate in a hotel's conservation efforts. The association's website also offers such information as a list of member hotels, a list of approved vendors, a catalog of environmental products, and tips on green travel.

The Hotel Association of Canada (HAC) offers a Green Key Eco-Rating Program that awards one to five green keys to hotels that meet guidelines established for such areas as environmental management, indoor air quality, solid and hazardous waste, land use, and community outreach. The program, which can be viewed on the association's website, www.hacgreenhotels.com, offers tips that can be applied by corporate environmental management, housekeeping, food and beverage operations, conference and meeting facilities, and engineering. At the time of this writing, compliance is measured by a voluntary, self-administered online audit system, but plans are in place for independently administered spot audits and inspection systems in the future.

Restaurants also have their own national environmental organization, the Green Restaurant Association (www.dinegreen.com), which has established environmental guidelines for restaurants and provides lists of endorsed products. In addition, "green restaurant" associations have been established in many cities and regions. Green My Cuisine (www.greenmycuisine.com), for example, provides environmental guidelines and certification in the San Francisco Bay area. The Green Restaurants program (www.greenrestaurants.org) serves restaurants (and environmentally conscious diners) in the Chicago area.

Ecotourism can be easily confused with adventure travel, but it is much more. Not only does ecotourism promote an enjoyment of nature (without harming the environment), but it also entails a responsibility for helping to protect the visited region.

This responsibility is shared by visitors and developers alike. Cancun, Mexico, and parts of Hawaii are examples of areas where overbuilding has destroyed precious natural resources and dimmed the beauty that originally attracted visitors. Fortunately, many developers are now preserving our fragile environment, and a number of resources have been created to help them do so. The American Hotel & Lodging Association (AH&LA) has united with His Royal Highness the Prince of Wales' International Hotel Environment Initiative (IHEI) to publish *Green Hotelier,* a magazine created to promote sound environmental practices throughout the industry. AH&LA has produced *Shaping Change and Changing Minds: Environmental*

Management for the Hospitality Industry, a video that highlights environmental case studies. As a result, an increasing number of hospitality properties have developed water conservation and recycling programs, are using recycled paper and biodegradable products, and are taking part in local conservation efforts.

In the food service industry, McDonald's Corporation switched from Styrofoam containers to paper wrappers in response to changing customer attitudes about the impact of these containers on the environment. Other innovations include reducing other packaging (by trimming the size of its napkins and straws, McDonald's decreased the amount of materials required to produce these products by two million pounds annually), using recycled materials to produce more than 200 items in its restaurants (from Happy Meal boxes to serving trays), and introducing energy-efficient restaurants.

Guest Preferences

The ability to meet the needs of hospitality customers is crucial in today's competitive environment, and hotels and restaurants must keep abreast of consumers' changing preferences and the latest demographic trends. The baby boomer market, for example, will total more than 75 million by 2010![7] These consumers have both the discretionary income and the time to enjoy travel and dining out. Knowing what baby boomers value can help firms attract them. Food service establishments that offer lighter fare, reasonable rates, and early dining hours, and hotels that emphasize safety and security, will likely capture a larger share of this market than operations that lack these features.

While today's hotel and restaurant customers fall into a number of categories, they share some of the same characteristics. Customers today:

- *Are connected.* They often use the Internet to assist in their selection of hotels and restaurants.
- *Are time-conscious.* They see time as a precious commodity, as they lead increasingly busy lives. For this reason, brands are important to them, because they represent convenience and predictable products.
- *Are demanding.* They want accurate information and are less tolerant of delays. In addition, today's travelers are sophisticated and discriminating—they expect personalized service and quality amenities.
- *Are more health-conscious.* They expect fitness facilities, no-smoking guestrooms, and healthy food options (some guests expect nutritional information on menus).

Other trends, such as the rise of the two-income family, are also making an impact on the hospitality industry. Two-income families have more disposable income, but less time. That is good news for restaurants, as these families tend to eat out more often, but the way they vacation has changed. Instead of taking extended family vacations, they are increasingly opting for multiple shorter vacations throughout the year. When they can take a longer trip, they usually choose "adventure" or "fantasy" vacations that enable them to spend quality time with their children.

Hotels are responding to today's "do-it-yourselfers" who are used to self-service (from using automatic teller machines to pumping their own gas) by offering automated check-in/check-out services and in-room self-service beverages and microwaves. Restaurants have found that buffets, soup and salad bars, and other self-service options are popular with many patrons.

Relationship Marketing

Because of the wide range of hospitality choices available, it is essential for hospitality companies to build a repeat customer base. Although the word "hospitality" suggests a warm relationship, hospitality companies as a whole have been lax when it comes to fostering bonds between themselves and guests. Today, however, hotels and restaurants are seeing their customers (and suppliers) as assets and are making **relationship marketing** an important part of their operations.

Marketing is shifting its focus away from maximizing profits on individual transactions and toward making sure that every guest is a repeat guest. This means more than providing good service—good service is *expected* by guests. It means taking the time to develop friendships with guests and making an extra effort to be sure their expectations are met and their needs anticipated for their next visit. It is no longer unusual for a repeat guest of an upscale hotel to receive cards on special occasions or to be treated to champagne or a basket of his or her favorite fruit on a birthday or anniversary.

Every hotel and restaurant should develop a relationship marketing plan to turn customers into customers for life. Good relationship marketing begins with upper managers who are committed to building customer trust and loyalty. This focus on customers needs to be emphasized and instilled by hiring and training a friendly, customer-oriented staff that is empowered to settle service discrepancies and come to the aid of guests without having to first get management approval.

Relationship marketing involves building value for the customer and giving the perception that the hotel and the customer are partners. Relationship marking creates bonds with customers by fully understanding and responding to their needs, requirements, and problems with customized personal service.

The Wyndham hotel chain is using Customer Relationship Management (CRM) to build individual guest loyalty. Dave Johnson, executive vice president of sales and marketing, says "we collect data on all customers through a central database and single out our Wyndham ByRequest members to understand them more fully. We want to know more about our guests so we can treat them better and offer them better choices. We don't say, 'Stay 10 times and you get something free.' Instead, we try to meet and exceed their needs during every stay and all the time."[8]

Relationship marketing has the potential to greatly benefit hotels and restaurants, as the best customers are those you already have (it is widely acknowledged that obtaining a new customer is five to ten times more expensive than retaining existing customers). Long-term, loyal customers also tend to spend more per visit than new customers, which can result in significant revenues. (Ritz-Carlton, for example, estimates the lifetime value of a loyal customer to average $100,000). In addition, customers who feel a relationship with a property are more prone to refer others to it.

Endnotes

1. Philip Kotler, John Brown, and James Makens, *Marketing for Hospitality and Tourism* (Englewood Cliffs, New Jersey: Prentice-Hall, Inc., 1999), p. 596.
2. Michael Shatz, "Hotel Brands Going Euro-Wide," *MeetingNews*, February 15, 1999, p. 19.
3. Erin Sternthal, "Hotel Brand Expansion," *Travel Agent*, September 3, 2007.
4. Mark Koonce, "Consolidations and Acquisitions: The Role of Sales and Marketing," *HSMAI Marketing Review*, Summer 1998, p. 20.
5. "Franchising and Branding: A Global Trend," Visiting Leaders Series, *The Hospitality Business Leader*, Fall/Winter 1998, p. 13.
6. "Execs Take a Look Into Crystal Ball," *Hotel Business*, August 1999, p. 68.
7. *Report to the Nation: Trends in Travel & Hospitality* (Washington, D.C.: Public Affairs Group, 1997), p. 19.
8. Bruce Owens, "Customer Relationship Management," *Hotel and Motel Management*, May 21, 2001, p. 36.

Key Terms

consolidation—The combination of two or more corporations to form a new corporation, by purchase, merger, or another ownership transfer. Consolidation reduces the number of companies owning brand hotels.

ecotourism—Tourism that promotes enjoyment of nature (without harming the environment); it may include efforts to protect or preserve the visited region.

environmental scanning—The analysis of trends and factors that will affect a hospitality firm's marketing efforts.

globalization—The international consolidation of big businesses and the growing trend for countries to allow the transfer of goods and services across national borders.

marketing—A system of interrelated activities formulated to plan, price, promote, and make available services or products to potential customers or guests in a particular target market.

marketing mix—The combination of the four "Ps" of marketing—product, place, promotion, and price—that is used to achieve marketing objectives for a target market.

niche marketing (branding)—Designing, building, and marketing hospitality products for specific market segments.

partnership marketing—Also known as *developing strategic alliances* and *synergism marketing,* it involves two or more firms—ideally serving similar markets with noncompetitive products—joining together to benefit from each other's strengths.

peak period—Also known as *in-season*, this is the period when demand for a property and its services is highest. Maximum rates may be charged at this time.

relationship marketing—Marketing that views customers as assets and emphasizes retaining customers by nurturing and sustaining a relationship with them.

sales—Direct efforts to sell a product or service through personal contact, telecommunication, and advertising and other promotion.

service guarantee—A promise made to customers in advance of purchasing that they can be assured of 100 percent satisfaction or they will not have to pay.

shoulder period—A period when the level of business for a property falls somewhere between its peak and valley periods.

strategic alliance—A business alliance in which the allies benefit from each other's strengths.

valley period—Also known as *off-season*, valley periods are times when demand for a property and its services is lowest. Reduced room rates are often offered during valley periods to attract business.

Review Questions

1. What changes that began in the United States in the mid-1950s had an impact on the hospitality industry?
2. What is the difference between marketing and sales?
3. What are the four controllable variables that make up the marketing mix and why must each be carefully researched and planned to ensure a successful marketing effort?
4. What are the five management functions typically inherent in the position of director of marketing?
5. How does the challenge of hospitality sales compare with that of selling consumer goods?
6. What is consolidation and how has this trend affected the hospitality industry?
7. What is niche marketing?
8. What impact has technology had on the hospitality industry in recent decades?
9. What is relationship marketing and why is it so important in today's hospitality market?

Internet Sites

For more information, visit the following Internet sites. Remember that Internet addresses can change without notice. If the site is no longer there, you can use a search engine to look for additional sites.

Accor
www.accor.com

American Hotel & Lodging Association
www.ahla.com

American Marketing Association
www.ama.org

Brinker International
www.brinker.com

Choice Hotels International
www.choicehotels.com

Destination Marketing Association International
www.iacvb.org

Historic Hotels of America
www.historichotels.org

Hospitality Sales & Marketing Association International
www.hsmai.org

Hyatt
www.hyatt.com

InterContinental Hotels Group
www.ihg.com

Interval International
www.intervalworld.com

Leading Hotels of the World
www.lhw.com

Marriott
www.marriott.com

Meeting Professionals International
www.mpiweb.org

Preferred Hotel Group
www.preferredhotelgroup.com

Ramada Inns
www.ramada.com

RCI
www.rci.com

Relais & Châteaux
www.relaischateaux.com

Restaurants & Institutions
www.rimag.com

Sales & Marketing Management
www.salesandmarketing.com

Small Luxury Hotels of the World
www.slh.com

Smith Travel Research
www.str-online.com

Travelweb
www.travelweb.com

Westin Hotels & Resorts
www.westin.com

Wingate by Wyndham
www.wingateinns.com

WORLDHOTELS
www.worldhotels.com

Case Study

Departmental Conflict at the Ultra Hotel

A quick glance out the lobby window revealed wind-blown gray clouds bunching up over the city. Storm's brewing out there, thought Rick Roland, the Ultra Hotel's marketing and sales director. In here, too, he thought as he walked past the lounges and restaurants on the ground floor of the 500-room, three-star convention property.

Unconsciously, Rick's pace slowed as he got closer to the meeting room where the end-of-the-month executive committee meeting was due to start. How ironic, he thought, to feel so apprehensive even though I'm almost ready to close on one of the biggest pieces of business I've landed in quite some time.

Taking a deep breath, Rick paused before entering the room. Images of the people waiting inside flashed through his mind: Fred Franklin, the general manager, a tough but fair boss who liked to give his staff members a chance to present their side of an argument; Norma Lopez, the no-nonsense controller with the laser-like focus on the bottom line; Claude van Fleet, the temperamental food and beverage director piloting a department through a terrible month; Camille Petrocelli, self-described "people person" and human resources director; and last, Jeanelle Causwell, rooms director, a fast-track performer, a favorite of Mr. Franklin's—and possibly my mortal enemy by the end of this meeting, Rick thought wryly.

Exhaling, Rick entered the meeting room. The meeting raced by for Rick until the moment he was waiting for. Mr. Franklin turned to him and said, "What have you got for us, Rick?"

"Well, gosh," Rick began, trying to inject some folksiness into a speech he had rehearsed a dozen times, "I'm about to land a nice piece of business for us. As all of you know, we've been after the ConveyorMatic meeting planner for months. The good news is, I think the guy's ready to commit in a big way. We're talking 250 rooms the second week of September, Sunday through Thursday, and—get this—it's a mandatory sales meeting for their big-spending sales staff, so filling up at least 240 of those 250 rooms is a cinch."

Seeing some nods and looks of interest, Rick went on. "Claude, you'll love this. We're getting three dinners, three lunches, three upgraded breakfasts, and two cocktail receptions with heavy hors d'oeuvres, which is big-time food and beverage sales—and that doesn't include spending in the outlets. It projects out to $130,000 in business for the hotel. Last year, we had only about $80,000 the same week."

"Excuse me, Rick, but isn't it hotel policy that you're only allotted 200 rooms for group sales?" Jeanelle said, launching her first salvo.

"Good point, Jeanelle, but if I book this group this year, they could be repeat customers every year. Plus, this guy is active in Meeting Professionals International, so he could give us some great referrals."

"I love it. Let's book 'em," Claude interjected, looking relieved and grateful.

"I do have to book it today, by five o'clock. That's why I want to get us all together on this," Rick explained.

"Excuse me again, Rick," Jeanelle said, "I'm sure you didn't make any promises to this group that would affect our room assignments, right?"

"Not really." Rick turned quickly to the controller. "What do you think, Norma?"

"I think we need to take a look at the numbers and make sure they're as good as you say," Norma said.

"Camille?" Rick continued eagerly.

"What?" Camille smiled, looking up from an issue of *HR Weekly*. "Oh, it sounds good; we could keep ten or fifteen people a day working for four days. Might slow down the turnover of our part-time kitchen staff."

"Rick, let's back up a minute." It was Jeanelle again, refusing to be sidetracked. "When I asked whether you'd made any promises to this group that would affect room assignments, you said 'Not really.' Could you define 'Not really' for me?"

"Well, I, uh," Rick looked down and mumbled rapidly, "I told them they could have fifty percent of their block in our new wing."

"What!" Jeanelle yelled. "You gave away my new wing! What do I tell my transient, repeat guests? My regulars stay three or four days, six times a year. You want me to tell them I'm kicking them out of the new wing? Why don't we just save time and tell them to go stay across the street from now on, because that's just what they'll do."

"But we're talking about 250 rooms!" Rick protested.

"At what rate?" Jeanelle shot back.

"Well, because of the F&B business, I gave them a discount—$79 a night."

"Wow! That's twenty percent off our regular $99 rate. Give those rooms back to me, Mr. Franklin. If we open up the corporate reservations center for discounts, I'll sell every one at $89. And I won't have to dump my best guests out of the new wing for these conveyor salesmen."

"Now, Jeanelle..." Rick pleaded.

"Now, nothing!" she snapped.

"But, Jeanelle, the F&B revenue!" Claude said, dreaming of making up last month's budget shortfall. "You know as well as I do that transient guests don't eat at the hotel. This group will mean big bucks in F&B."

"Mr. Franklin, you're the general manager; it's your call," Rick said resignedly. Jeanelle and Claude nodded in agreement. The staff leaned back, waiting for the GM's decision.

Discussion Questions

1. What reasons might the GM have for deciding to turn down the business? What conflicts on the executive committee would have to be resolved if the GM decides to turn down the business?
2. What reasons might the GM have for deciding to take the business? What conflicts on the executive committee would have to be resolved if the GM decides to take the business?

Case Number: 370CA

This case was developed in cooperation with Bill Flor and Randy Kinder, authors of *No Vacancy: A Tried & True Guide to Get More Rooms Business!*; The No Vacancy Company; Jacksonville, Florida.

This case also appears in *Contemporary Hospitality Marketing: A Service Management Approach* (Lansing, Mich.: American Hotel & Lodging Educational Institute, 1999), ISBN 978-0-86612-158-3.

Chapter 2 Outline

Competencies

1. Identify the benefits of developing long-range marketing plans and describe the makeup and function of a marketing team. (pp. 35–37)
2. Describe the first two key steps of a marketing plan: conducting a marketing audit, and selecting profitable target markets. (pp. 37–55)
3. Describe the last three key steps of a marketing plan: positioning the property, establishing objectives and action plans, and monitoring and evaluating the marketing plan. (pp. 55–64)

Insider Insights

Lynn O'Rourke
Senior Vice President of Marketing and Communications
Wyndham Worldwide Corporation

"A good marketing plan should take all of the factors affecting the success of your product into account. In putting the plan together, it's important to determine the goals and objectives of the entire organization. How the property is positioned in the marketplace is also critical. This area should not be taken lightly—positioning mistakes are costly to reverse! Once a cost-effective, action-oriented marketing plan is developed, it's important to use it. Refer to your marketing plan! Update it. Make it a working document that helps bring you well-thought-out, long-haul success."

2

The Marketing Plan: The Cornerstone of Sales

IN TODAY'S COMPETITIVE HOSPITALITY MARKET it is especially important for properties to increase their market share and profits. No business can afford to rest on its laurels, yet many hotel and restaurant owners fail to recognize the benefits of having a structured marketing plan. Having great ideas is not enough; sales, advertising, and promotional and public relations strategies must be formalized into a marketing plan that can be communicated throughout the organization. This chapter will not only explain how to develop a marketing plan, it will also provide numerous illustrations of actual forms being used in the hospitality industry today. Therefore, you are not just learning theory—you will see exactly how marketing concepts are put into practice.

The Marketing Plan

Both marketing and sales are necessary if a property hopes to effectively compete in today's marketplace. Marketing is the foundation upon which sales is built. Marketing seeks out demand, identifies the products and services that will satisfy demand, and then employs strategic sales and advertising techniques to reach customers. Without a well-defined **marketing plan** that is based on thorough research, sales efforts may be wasted.

Despite the many reasons for developing a marketing plan, some hotels and restaurants forgo using this important marketing tool, for several reasons. Some managers are so involved with day-to-day operations that all their time is devoted to short-term sales efforts rather than long-term marketing efforts. In other cases, the general manager may feel that his or her ideas are in focus and so there is no need to commit strategies to writing. Some managers find marketing planning frustrating, so they avoid it. Other properties enjoy high occupancies and their managers feel that advance planning is not needed.

Whatever the reason for the lack of a marketing plan, there are obvious benefits to long-range marketing plans. A marketing plan:

- Forces managers to think ahead and make better use of the property's resources
- Sets responsibilities and coordinates and unifies efforts to reach the property's sales goals
- Creates an awareness of problems and obstacles

- Identifies opportunities to increase market share in some market segments and open new opportunities in previously ignored areas
- Ensures that sales promotions and advertising are not wasted because of misdirected efforts

A property's marketing plan should include programs to attract business to each of the property's revenue centers, with individual programs complementing, not fighting, one another. One industry person points out that "in the minds of some hoteliers there is one hotel and one market. Brochures and sales literature usually promote the hotel as if it were one business with one market segment. In fact, it is a series of different businesses with different markets which just happen to be under one roof."[1] Market segments may vary significantly. Lunch customers are different from those who come for dinner; vacation travelers differ from business travelers; overnight convention guests have different spending patterns and needs than tour groups.

The marketing plan should be developed for at least a three-year period. The marketing strategies of many properties are planned only a year at a time, but one year is often not long enough; when sales objectives are limited to 12 months, salespeople tend to stay with the existing guest base rather than target new—and often more profitable—market segments that might take two or three years to develop. (Tour operators, associations, incentive groups, and many corporations are often committed well beyond one year.) If management is uncomfortable with a three-year plan, a compromise can be reached by setting broad goals over the three-year period and well-defined objectives and strategies for the first year of the three-year cycle. (See the chapter appendix for a sample one-year marketing plan for a single market segment—corporate/business travelers.)

The marketing plan is the property's road map. It tells you who you are, where you are going, and how you're going to get there. It spells out the steps you intend to take to gain and retain customers, increase repeat business, and encourage higher restaurant check averages and higher daily expenditures from hotel guests. It should be regularly reviewed and updated, not left sitting on a shelf to collect dust or stashed in a drawer until year's end. If you aren't reviewing and using your marketing plan on a daily basis, something is wrong with your plan.

While the marketing plan is a guide, it is not etched in stone; from time to time, certain activities will not be completed as scheduled or some action plans may be delayed or deleted due to changes in the economy, the marketplace, or personnel. Advertising and direct sales efforts may need to be increased or decreased due to these changes.

The Marketing Team

While the head of the marketing and sales department is ultimately responsible for the marketing plan, he or she should seek assistance and advice from other property staff members to ensure that all areas of the property are represented in the final marketing plan. One of the favorite sayings of Ken Blanchard, author of *The One Minute Manager,* is "None of us is as smart as all of us." A property-wide marketing team, sometimes called a *sales committee,* should be established to create and implement marketing strategies for the entire property.

The marketing team should include at least one representative from each revenue center. The team member or "team leader" from the banquet department might be the catering manager, and the head bartender could be the team leader for the lounge. Nonrevenue areas of the property should be represented as well. The director of sales may be responsible for providing input and plans relating to group business; the public relations director may be responsible for documenting successful advertising strategies used by competitors. The marketing team can also include employees who are directly involved in day-to-day operations. The principal advantage of having a marketing team is that all areas of the property are represented and no profit centers "fall through the cracks."

Once the marketing team is established, team members need to develop strategies for their revenue centers and present them to the marketing team for review and revision. The revised strategies are then incorporated into the property's overall marketing plan. Planning by the marketing team ensures that areas that might be overlooked by marketing and sales personnel are included in the marketing plan. A salesperson may know basic facts about the property's restaurant, but input from the food and beverage director—perhaps the information that the head chef has served important officials or celebrities—can result in new promotional directions that otherwise would not have been considered.

Marketing teams are excellent vehicles for unified efforts to sell the entire property. The team member responsible for a marketing strategy for his or her revenue center can often devote more time to that area than could one person from the marketing and sales department who is developing marketing plans for a number of areas. The resulting strategies, developed by team members who understand all that is involved in their areas of expertise, are often more effective than a marketing plan developed by a director of sales who has only general knowledge of the property's revenue centers.

Steps of a Marketing Plan

A good marketing plan can take a number of forms and may be developed by using any one of several techniques, but there are five key steps that must be included (see Exhibit 1):

1. Conducting a marketing audit
2. Selecting profitable target markets
3. Positioning the property
4. Establishing objectives and action plans
5. Monitoring and evaluating the marketing plan

The development of a marketing plan is a never-ending process. After one marketing plan cycle has been completed, results must be evaluated, and the process returns to the research or marketing audit portion of the cycle.

Step 1: Conducting a Marketing Audit

The foundation of any marketing plan is the marketing audit. The **marketing audit** is the research step in the planning process, and is sometimes referred to as

Exhibit 1 The Marketing Plan Cycle

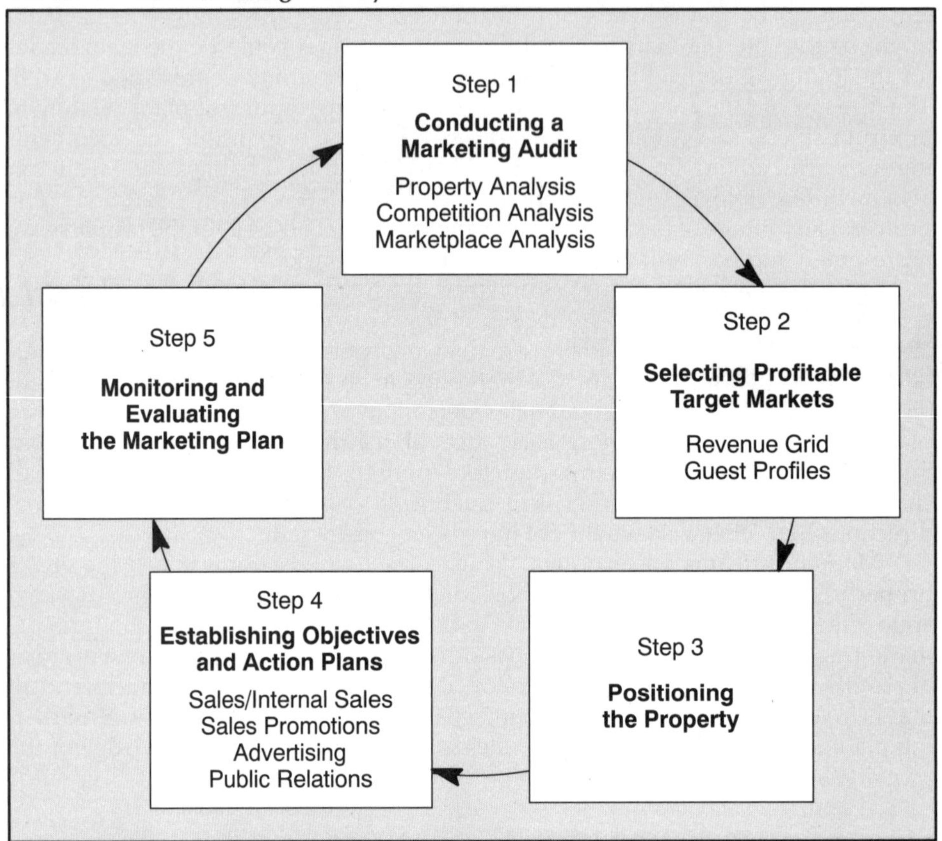

A well-constructed marketing plan is a blueprint for guiding the sales effort. These five steps provide an effective sequence that minimizes wasteful efforts and ensures a systematic approach for increasing sales.

gathering **marketing intelligence.** Systematically gathering, recording, and analyzing information about your property, your competition, and the marketplace is of great benefit in decision-making and in selecting appropriate target markets.

Hospitality firms often set up a **marketing information system** to systematically gather marketing intelligence. The marketing information system consists of the people, equipment, and procedures required to gather and analyze data to provide accurate information to marketing decision-makers. A well-designed marketing information system: (1) should be designed to provide a continuous flow of information, gathered from both inside and outside the property; and (2) should provide information that is useful. For example, statistics determining when the hotel or restaurant experiences quiet periods can be used to define marketing opportunities and establish pricing policies (see Exhibit 2).

Internal Sources of Marketing Information. The simplest marketing information system to design and implement is an internal system designed to collect data

Exhibit 2 Marketing Information System—Internal Marketing Intelligence

Marketing Information—Restaurants

1. Customer count, total sales, average check, menu sales mix by meal period
   - weekday breakfast (M-F)
   - weekday lunch (M-F)
   - weekday dinner (M-Th)
   - weekend breakfast (Sat-Sun)
   - weekend lunch (Sat-Sun)
   - weekend dinner (Fri-Sun)
2. Customer profiles—age, gender, method of payment, size of party, new or repeat customer, home and work zip codes, frequency of visits, how did they hear of you; if the restaurant is a hotel restaurant—outside or inside guest, and length of time eating
3. Seat turnover per meal period
4. Side orders, beverages, desserts, appetizers per customer, and average expenditure
5. Entrée average in dollars and popularity index of menu items
6. Sales by salesperson or server

Marketing Information—Lodging

1. Occupancy and average daily rate by
   - customer mix
   - type of room
   - day of week
2. Guest profiles
3. Occupied rooms by room type
4. Lost room revenue (average daily rate times number of rooms not rented)
5. Room sales efficiency (actual room sales divided by potential room sales; potential room sales is the revenue from a full house paying full rack rate)
6. Business turned away because property full
7. No-show and cancellation percentages

Marketing Information—Banquets and Meeting Rooms

1. Function room occupancy by meal period
2. Types of functions—profiles of group
3. Use of guestrooms by function groups
4. Popularity of individual banquet menu items
5. Sales revenue per square foot of function space
6. Average number of persons and average banquet check by type of function
7. Pattern of unused times and days

These statistics assist marketing decision-makers with establishing pricing policies, defining market opportunities, and identifying quiet and busy periods. Most hospitality chains regularly use this type of information for improving their marketing decisions. While this list may seem overwhelming at first, this data is readily available from a hotel's computer system.

from within the hotel or restaurant. This type of system can provide a wealth of valuable information while requiring less time and money than an external system. Internal information gathering methods include the use of guest histories and sales data, which can be readily obtained from guest registration information and an analysis of point-of-sale data. Information can also be obtained by using guest comment cards and in-house surveys.

In addition to guests, employees and managers are also invaluable, although sometimes overlooked, internal sources of marketing information. Front desk personnel, telephone operators, and food servers come into constant contact with guests and can provide customer feedback. Meeting with employees on a regular basis not only yields important marketing information, but also provides employees with recognition, which can increase their satisfaction and commitment to the organization.

External Sources of Marketing Information. External information is not usually collected on a daily basis due to the larger investment of time and money required. Consumer surveys usually come to mind when external marketing information is mentioned. Properties can conduct their own surveys; there are also a number of syndicated services that collect consumer information, including customer profiles, shopping behavior, customer response to advertising, and consumer attitudes and preferences. Other external sources of marketing intelligence include trade associations, trade journals and periodicals, popular periodicals, convention and visitors bureaus, travel bureaus, government sources, and the Internet. When considering which outside sources to use, it is important to ensure that the data that will be provided has been collected and measured in a valid and reliable manner and that the sampling represents your targeted customer mix.

Whether you are obtaining data from an outside source or are collecting it yourself, you will want to have specific goals and objectives in mind for the use of the data. Bill Watson, former senior vice president of marketing for Best Western, advises that "researchers must put less emphasis on data and more on the interpretation of the data. They must work toward turning data into useful information. Collecting data for its own value is like collecting stamps. It is a nice hobby but it does not deliver the mail."[2]

A complete marketing audit consists of three parts: a property analysis, competition analysis, and marketplace analysis.

Property Analysis. A **property analysis** is a written, unbiased self-appraisal used to assess the strengths and weaknesses of your property (see Exhibit 3). More than a simple checklist, a property analysis takes into account both revenue- and non-revenue-producing areas, as well as intangibles such as reputation and location.

First, a detailed room-by-room and facility-by-facility inspection should be made. Building exteriors, landscaping, and the property's sign should also be examined. The entire property should be carefully evaluated in terms of traffic flow, accessibility, eye appeal, and compatibility with local surroundings. Areas for change can be noted, but suggestions for changes must be feasible. It would not be practical, for example, for a 50-room property to spend $100,000 remodeling the outside of its building if changes in occupancy would be minimal. Only changes with a reasonable return on the investment should be considered for the final marketing plan.

Exhibit 3 Sample Property Analysis Form

PROPERTY ANALYSIS—CENTER CITY HOTEL			
AREA	**STRENGTHS**	**WEAKNESSES**	**RECOMMENDATIONS**
Exterior	Attractive and appealing, newly designed entrance Clean, good repair, freshly painted	Lack of seating/relaxing area near entrance Dumpster area visible from west wing	Veranda entrance could be more inviting with addition of comfortable chairs Construct fence to conceal trash area
Meeting rooms	Ballroom can accommodate 600 persons Ballroom overlooks river	Rooms on main level are not utilized	Convert storage rooms to meeting and function space
Parking	Convenient to rooms Lot has perimeter fence and landscaping	Driveway is in need of repair Perimeter fence is too low for security purposes Very narrow driveways at hotel entrance Difficult to enter driveway because of traffic	Repair asphalt cracks in drive Research feasibility of widening entrance
Rooms	Comfortable, modern decor Easy to keep clean Cable television Easily accessible Refrigerator in each room Effective air-conditioning	Not entirely secure Little consistency in door locking systems Small bathrooms	Install stronger window locks Install high-quality door latch mechanisms Rent out less desirable rooms last
Reputation	Friendly, clean hotel, modern, charming Courteous staff Moderate-priced rooms	Positioning is as an average facility More individual than group business Not a well-known property	Use slogan or marketing strategy Involve hotel in more community support
Location	Riverfront Accessible to expressway Popular vacation/resort area	Far from downtown and airport Two miles off main road	Develop shuttle system for groups Billboard advertising on highway

To provide the best source of information possible about a property, a property analysis should be written out, and include an objective look at the property's strengths and weaknesses. This is only one of several pages in the property analysis. Similar comparisons should be done for every area that can affect the property's profitability, including restaurants, lounges, room service, catering, convention services, and so on. This type of analysis provides a means of taking stock of what the property has to offer, what areas need to be upgraded, and what steps can be considered to improve weaknesses.

It is also important to analyze the property from a guest's perspective. In other words, management should try to see the property as guests see it. The introduction of a new menu or a heavily advertised promotion may draw large crowds, but if the staff is not ready for the increased activity or the restrooms are dirty or the parking lot full of potholes, new customers attracted by the promotion may never come back (and, worse yet, may tell friends about their unpleasant experience). Sales staff members and the property's management should stay overnight at the property to form an impression of the property as a product. An uninvolved outsider should also be invited to spend a night or weekend at the property to provide additional input.

The **occupancy and activity analysis** is an analysis of the property's past, present, and potential operating statistics, and is used to track sales history patterns over a three- to five-year period. This analysis helps determine "soft spots"—low-business periods—that most hotels and restaurants have in their sales patterns. This analysis aims to disclose sales areas that can be improved, and should be prepared for all the property's revenue centers. Most hotels keep guestroom statistics, but fewer track restaurant, lounge, and function space statistics such as total covers (meals served), seat turnover, average guest check, function room bookings, and average size of functions (see Exhibit 4). Room statistics focus on occupancy and average rate, occupancy by day of the week, geographic origin of bookings, group and individual room nights by segment and source, and the status of future group business already on the books.

One of the key summaries is the *geographic origin study.* Know who guests are, what they need and want in a hospitality product, and when and how they buy, but do not neglect to learn where they come from, as this can play a crucial part in selecting target markets and marketing effectively to market segments.

Identifying major **feeder cities** or "catchment areas" is extremely valuable; identifying which cities and zip codes most guests come from results in a more effective use of time and money. Knowing that 30 percent of a property's business traveler market comes from southern California, for example, provides more pertinent information than the general fact that 40 percent of total business comes from that state. Geographic origin information is relatively easy to obtain if the property uses computers to register guests.

While the research phase of the marketing plan is very important, the crucial exercise is not to merely collect data but to interpret property, competition, and marketplace information. The key is to "boil down" the statistical information gathered in order to select appropriate market segments and to help form strategies for reaching them.

Competition Analysis. The objectives of a **competition analysis** are to discover (1) profitable guest groups being served by competitors that are not being served at your property, (2) some competitive benefit or advantage your property enjoys that cannot be matched by major competitors, and (3) weaknesses in the marketing strategies of the competition on which your property can capitalize.

As the hospitality industry has matured, it has grown increasingly competitive. Consolidations have created bigger and more powerful brands, so, in order to achieve sales growth, hotels and restaurants are forced to capture market share

Exhibit 4 Sample Occupancy and Activity Charts

Chart 1

Monthly Room Occupancy and Average Room Rate
Three-Year Trends

	20XX/20XX		20XX/20XX		20XX/20XX	
MONTH	% OCC.	AVERAGE RM. RATE	% OCC.	AVERAGE RM. RATE	% OCC.	AVERAGE RM. RATE
OCT.	77.9%	$ 73	72.7%	$ 74	71.5 %	$ 75
NOV.	76.7	72	74.1	73	72.9	74
etc.						

Chart 2

Monthly Restaurant Food and Beverage Revenue History
Three-Year Trends (in Thousands)

	20XX/20XX		20XX/20XX		20XX/20XX	
MONTH	FOOD	BEVERAGE	FOOD	BEVERAGE	FOOD	BEVERAGE
OCT.						
NOV.						
etc.						

Chart 3

Monthly Banquet Food and Beverage Revenue History
Three-Year Trends (in Thousands)

	20XX/20XX		20XX/20XX		20XX/20XX	
MONTH	FOOD	BEVERAGE	FOOD	BEVERAGE	FOOD	BEVERAGE
OCT.						
NOV.						
etc.						

(continued)

Exhibit 4 *(continued)*

Chart 4

Monthly Function Room Revenue History
Three-Year Trends (in Thousands)

	20XX/20XX		20XX/20XX		20XX/20XX	
MONTH	FOOD	BEVERAGE	FOOD	BEVERAGE	FOOD	BEVERAGE
OCT.						
NOV.						
etc.						

Chart 5

Monthly Room Nights by Market Segment

20XX/20XX 20XX/20XX 20XX/20XX

SEGMENT/ MONTH	CORPO-RATE	ASSOCI-ATION	SMERF	TOUR AND TRAVEL	GOVERN-MENT	ETC.
OCT.						
NOV.						
etc.						

These abbreviated charts indicate the type of research that is needed in the marketplace analysis; this market research traces the property's past and present operating statistics and is basically a historical trends study. Occupancy and activity charts should be prepared and tracked for each revenue center to determine where property guests are coming from (and when) to aid in developing effective marketing strategies. In addition to the charts illustrated, Geographic Origin of Bookings and Monthly Source of Reservations charts are also used.

from their competition. Therefore, hospitality firms must not only be *customer-oriented* but also *competition-oriented.* An analysis of your property versus the competition should be made at least four times a year.

One of the principal reasons for assessing your competition is to determine how you can differentiate your property. **Differentiation** means making your hospitality firm and its profit centers different from the competition—different in a way that adds value for customers, different in a way that is meaningful. One differentiation strategy relies on differentiating your product/service by creating something that is perceived *industry-wide* as unique. For example, La Quinta Inns was the originator of the limited-service concept. The chain found a unique niche catering to cost-conscious business travelers who worked on a commission basis. La Quinta Inns was also the first chain to put the telephone on a desk rather than beside the bed, to better enable corporate guests to work and set appointments at night.

Before the competition can be evaluated, it is necessary to determine who the property's competitors are. Simply stated, competitors are generally properties in the immediate area that sell to similar market segments and offer similar products and services at similar prices. These properties are often called the **competitive set.** To get an accurate picture of your competition and help you differentiate your business, you will need to use three key forms:

1. *Competitive rate analysis.* This should compare not only competitors' rack and corporate rates, but all other rates offered (government rates, senior citizens' rates, special package plans, etc.) as well. Food service operators should evaluate competitors' menus and pricing. This analysis should be done at least four times a year. A sample competitive rate analysis is shown in Exhibit 5.
2. *Competitive fact sheets.* To gauge competitor activities in other areas, such as occupancies, group bookings, guest relations, promotional programs, and selling methods, competitive fact sheets are prepared on each competitor. Criteria may include the following:
    - *Number of rooms and their breakdown*—double/double, kings, suites, executive floor, and so on. Include the condition of the room, when it was last renovated, plans for expansion, and so on.
    - *Location*—distance from transportation hubs, key businesses, and area attractions.
    - *Overall reputation and quality*—all areas of the facility and all services offered.
    - *Meeting/banquet space and service*—number and square footage of each room; banquet menu in terms of items and pricing; physical condition.
    - *Restaurants and lounges*—outlets, hours of operation, menus and pricing, and nearby restaurants.
    - *Other amenities and services*—gift shops, indoor and outdoor pools, limousine service, valet parking, frequent traveler programs, and so on.
    - *Marketing*—size of sales staff and its responsibilities, and selling and advertising strategies (direct mail, targeting travel agents, etc.).
    - *Customer mix*—present guest mix, likely markets for the future, and so on.
    - *Positioning*—current positioning statement, chain affiliation, image, pricing policy, and points of difference in the competition.
    - *Performance record*—market share, RevPAR, sales growth, profitability.
3. *Need fulfillment by market segment.* Any competitive analysis of strengths and weaknesses should be based on market segments and the specific needs of

Exhibit 5 Competitive Rate Analysis

COMPETITIVE RATE ANALYSIS									
Hotel / Rates	Rolling Green			Arrowhead			Hilton Inn		
	Single	Double	Suite	Single	Double	Suite	Single	Double	Suite
Rack	84–92	94–102	130+	100–105	105–110	160	102–116	102–118	140+
Corporate	80	80	120	98	104	140	88	88	130
Tour	62	72	—	—	—	—	85	92	—
Convention	78–90	88–100	120+	85–100	90–105	140	88–98	94–104	130+
Club Floor	90	100	—	—	—	—	115	125	—
Government	68	78	—	85	90	—	85	90	—

This form compares the rates of your property against those of the competition. Note that all types of rates are included—rack, corporate, convention, tour, club floor, and government. In addition to benchmarking rates, hotels also gauge competitor activities in areas such as occupancies, group bookings, guest relations, promotional programs, use of advertising, selling methods, market penetration, and market segmentation mix. To monitor these areas, fact sheets are often prepared on each competitor. This comprehensive type of analysis can point out specific areas in which your property differs from the competition and can help you to determine how to set your rates in order to better compete for specific market groups.

each. Remember that your strengths and weaknesses vary from market segment to market segment based on the needs of guests within each segment, and the forms you use should evaluate how your property or restaurant stacks up against others in specific market areas. If your strengths and weaknesses are compared with those of your competition by market segment, a completely different picture can emerge depending on the segment in question. Isolating market segments and determining how your hotel or restaurant fills the needs and wants of each segment is extremely helpful in finding your competitive advantage.

Competitive measures of performance. The three most commonly used statistics for measuring your performance versus that of the competition are market share, fair share, and revenue per available room (RevPAR).

The first step in calculating market share and fair share is to set up a table of descriptive data, including each competitive property's number of rooms, available nights for sale (the total rooms multiplied by 365), occupancy percentage, and actual room nights sold over the course of the year:

	Number of Rooms	Available Rooms*	Percentage Occupancy**	Room Nights Sold
Your Property	300	109,500	76.5	83,768
Downtown Hotel	454	165,710	70.0	115,997
Airport Hotel	400	146,000	75.0	109,500
TOTAL	1,154	421,210	73.8	309,265

*Number of rooms multiplied by 365 for yearly total
**Average occupancy

The **market share** is determined by dividing the number of property room nights sold by the total market room nights sold (in this case, total room nights is 309,265). Using this formula, your property would have a market share of 27 percent based on 83,768 room nights sold, the downtown hotel would have a market share of 38 percent based on 115,997 room nights sold, and the airport hotel would have a market share of 35 percent based on sales of 109,500.

But market share alone does not provide enough information to accurately assess how well your property is doing in the marketplace. To get a more accurate analysis, you must also determine your property's **fair share**—the number of room nights your property would sell if demand were distributed based on the number of rooms in each property.

Fair share is determined by dividing the number of rooms available at each property by the number of rooms available in the market as a whole. Using the figures above, for example, your property would have a fair share of 26 percent (109,500 rooms divided by 421,210), the downtown property would have a fair share of 39 percent (165,710 rooms divided by 421,210), and the airport property would have a fair share of 35 percent (146,000 divided by 421,210):

	Market Share	Fair Share
Your Property	27%	26%
Downtown Hotel	38%	39%
Airport Hotel	35%	35%

In this example, your property's market share is one percent more than its fair share, the downtown property's market share is one percent less than its fair share, and the airport property's fair share and market share are the same. These figures show that your property is enjoying a small measure of success, while the downtown property is at a disadvantage in the market and the airport property is just holding its own. This market analysis is helpful both in terms of tracking area market trends and in measuring the impact of various marketing strategies.

Market share figures for occupancy and the number of restaurant covers are not always easy to obtain. In some cases, hospitality firms in an area agree to share average rate, occupancy, and restaurant figures. Or, a convention and visitors bureau might serve as the receiver and publisher of such data. Recently, two large private firms, PricewaterhouseCoopers and Smith Travel Research, have begun producing monthly market-specific reports to track hotel performance in major worldwide markets. Developed with the participation of major lodging chains and key independent hotels, these reports track occupancy, average daily rate, and revenue per available room by city, region, and country. The data provides market performance by current month, year-to-date for the current month, and a 12-month moving average.[3]

Comparing occupancy and average daily rate among properties can be confusing and deceptive. Another and perhaps more accurate way to determine how your property is doing against the competition is to calculate **RevPAR (revenue per available room).** This is computed by dividing room revenue by the number of available rooms for the same period. Or, RevPAR can be determined by multiplying the occupancy percentage by the average daily rate for the same period:

	Occupancy Percentage	×	Average Daily Rate	=	RevPAR
Your Property	76.5%		$ 88.00		$ 67.32
Downtown Hotel	70.0%		$ 86.00		$ 60.20
Airport Hotel	75.0%		$ 85.00		$ 63.75
	73.8%		$ 86.33		$ 63.71

RevPAR gives you the ability to compare hotels of different sizes and varying average rates, allowing you to see precisely what you are earning in relationship to your competition. Because RevPAR takes into account both occupancy and average daily rate, it is the most widely accepted comparative measure in the industry today.

A competition analysis also involves walking the properties of competitors, talking with competitors' employees, and studying the advertising of competitors. For an even clearer picture, actually staying at the properties of competitors is essential. Driving through their parking lots at night on a regular basis, paying special attention to the types of cars, the states represented by their license plates, and the number of commercial vehicles; eating in their restaurants; reading rack brochures and internal literature; and conversing with their guests are excellent ways of determining differences between your property and other properties. Check your competitors' reader boards every day (a reader board is the board on which meetings are listed in a hotel). Make notes and prepare a game plan to land these organizations next year or next quarter.

Other information needed for a competition analysis is available from a number of sources:

- Local convention and visitors bureaus
- Chambers of commerce
- Local, county, and state room tax reports[4]
- Telephone yellow pages
- Hotel chain directories
- Travel guides
- Websites of competitors

Making personal contact with other area hotel managers is also an effective information-gathering tool.

INTERNET EXERCISE

A number of firms offer information that can be useful to the hospitality industry, including the following:

- Smith Travel Research (www.smithtravelresearch.com)
  Compiles and maintains a comprehensive database of hotel performance information.
- J. D. Power and Associates (www.jdpower.com)
  Global marketing information firm that conducts independent, unbiased surveys of customer satisfaction, product quality, and buyer behavior.
- D. K. Shifflet & Associates (www.dksa.com)
  Specializes in market research and consulting services in all sectors of the travel industry. The company provides an extensive database of brands by sector and traveler type.
- Y Partnership (www.ypartnership.com)
  A marketing, advertising, and public relations agency that serves as a source of insight on consumer behavior.
- PhoCusWright Inc. (www.phocuswright.com)
  An independent travel, tourism, and hospitality research firm specializing in consumer, business, and competitive intelligence.
- PricewaterhouseCoopers (www.pwc.com)
  Offers specialized experience in the hospitality and leisure industry. Recognized for its econometric and statistical research.

Log onto the Internet and research one of these six firms, answering the following questions:

1. What services does the company offer?
2. How can the information it provides assist you in preparing a competition analysis?

Smith Travel Research (STR) prepares reports on the occupancy, average rate, and RevPAR data gathered from participating properties. Log onto the STR website and determine (by zip code) if you are located in one of the STR participation areas.

Marketplace Analysis. To plan marketing strategies, it is essential to know as much as possible about the marketplace or environment in which the property operates. A **marketplace analysis** researches the property's current position in the marketplace and reveals potential opportunities to promote the property. The marketplace analysis identifies environmental opportunities and problems that can affect business. Just a few of the marketplace factors that influence occupancy and the average daily rate are changes in demographics; positive and negative events in the community, region, state, and nation; the cost and availability of energy;

Exhibit 6 The Marketplace Analysis

MARKETPLACE ANALYSIS

Part I **OPPORTUNITIES**	**EFFECTS ON BUSINESS**
The St. Louis Airport is expanding and bringing in two new regional carriers.	Easier accessibility to the city. These airlines service several of our feeder cities.
The local college has made arrangements with several companies to hold seminars and workshops on electronics this spring and fall.	Possible room nights from students and instructors, and meeting space for meetings, classes, and seminars.
Archaeological dig in Majestic Canyon has uncovered an ancient Indian burial ground. An influx of scientists and historians have begun a major investigation of the area.	Possibility of room nights from those not wishing to sleep on site and day rooms from those who wish to shower and clean up after the dig. Also increased business in food and beverage areas.
etc.	
Part II **PROBLEMS**	**EFFECTS ON BUSINESS**
The highway from St. Louis is scheduled to be repaired in May.	Guests will experience some delays during May. However, when construction is finished, the repairs and additional lane will make access to our resort easier and faster. Also a possibility of increased restaurant business from the workers.
A new Sheraton Hotel has been proposed. Construction is to commence late next year.	This property is to be located midway between our property and St. Louis. If developed, this will be increased competition; and Sheraton is strong in the corporate market and has a good established reputation.
etc.	

This marketplace analysis looks at the environment in which your hotel operates and assesses the effects of political, economic, sociological, and technological factors (these are often termed "uncontrollable variables"). The marketplace analysis generally consists of two parts, one titled "Opportunities and Effects on Business"; the other "Problems and Effects on Business." These studies detail influences (both positive and negative) that may have an effect on your business, and provide a way to determine how these opportunities and challenges can impact your property.

government regulation; and the cost of travel. Exhibit 6, from a hotel's actual marketing plan, shows how this property's managers studied their marketplace and assessed their opportunities and the problems they faced from projected external factors. They then determined how these would affect business in order to develop marketing strategies to minimize the problems and maximize their opportunities.

Exhibit 7 Sample Marketplace Analysis Checklist

A. Local Community
1. Track trends in population and growth projections.
2. Determine demographic profiles of locals secured through census data.
3. Research local sports groups; social clubs; and trade, educational, professional, and political associations.
4. List local events and attractions—historical, scenic, cultural. List special events that attract visitors and the number of visitors who attend.

B. Local Industry
1. Assess economic and employment trends secured from Economic Industrial Commission.
2. Research proposed, new, and recently closed office and industrial complexes.
3. Document details of main employers by industry type. Information to document includes:
   a. Number of employees
   b. Names of managing director and key contacts
   c. Assessment of their lodging and function needs
   d. Expansion plans

C. Traffic Assessment
1. Assess the location of property with respect to highways, airports, and bus and train stations.
2. Determine traffic counts for highways, railroads, airports, and buses.

D. Recreational
1. List the amusement, recreational, and sports facilities that attract visitors from outside the community.
2. Obtain information on source, volume, and seasonality of use.
3. Obtain information on expansion plans, if any.

The statistics for projecting environmental effects on business can be found in census data, information from industrial commissions such as the state or city division of economic development, and industry reports such as *Sales & Marketing Management* magazine's *Survey of Buying Power*. The marketplace analysis checklist in Exhibit 7 can assist in revealing new opportunities or problems that may require attention to keep the property competitive and profitable.

Step 2: Selecting Profitable Target Markets

As mentioned earlier, many hoteliers erroneously promote a property as though it were a single business serving one market, but a hotel is actually a series of businesses that cater to a number of different markets. A hotel's guestrooms may appeal primarily to leisure travelers on the weekends and to business travelers during the week; the property's restaurant may serve a local business clientele at lunch and hotel guests at dinner; and meeting rooms may be used primarily by convention groups from out of town during the week and by local groups on weekends.

Most consumer industries are keenly aware of the importance of selling to specific market segments, and they avoid the broad market categories sometimes used in the hospitality industry. But the hospitality industry is now following suit, placing guests in narrower market segments and targeting more of those segments than ever before. This **market segmentation** consists of viewing a market as a number of smaller market segments, each segment a group of consumers with similar product and service preferences. Markets can be segmented in a number of ways: demographically (senior citizens, young marrieds); by purpose of trip (business, leisure); by benefits sought (security, business services); geographically (by zip code); by lifestyle (culture seekers, sports-minded); by usage (frequent business travelers, occasional business travelers); and by intermediary (travel agent, tour operator, meeting planner).

It is impossible, however, to be all things to all people. Properties must realistically define their product in terms of the major market segments they can best satisfy. A property should determine the market segments for which it is best suited, the areas of least competition, and modifications (if any) necessary to reach its **target markets.**

Before a property decides which market segments to target, the present **guest mix** should be determined. Determining the guest mix and the decline or growth of a market segment can be facilitated by the use of two basic forms: a *revenue grid,* which details statistics and revenue for each source of business (see Exhibit 8); and an *occupancy chart,* which provides insight into the growth patterns of each market segment (see Exhibit 9). A revenue grid is essential in determining your guest mix. The object of a revenue grid is to help you increase business from the most profitable segments and to target your resources (time, effort, and marketing dollars) to improve business from those segments that are the most profitable.

Guest Profile Information. Guest profiles also help identify the market segments to which the property is currently appealing. For best results, guest profiles should be prepared for each revenue center—guestrooms, restaurants, lounges, banquet facilities, and any other revenue-producing service (valet, laundry, health club, and so on). You can then use this information to create a clearer picture of the types of guests that patronize each revenue-producing area.

Information that should be considered in a guest profile includes the following: name of guest, address, and zip code; gender and age of guest; place or type of employment; place of residence; mode of transportation to property (car, airplane, bus, train); guest status (new, repeat, corporate); date and method of reservation; arrival and departure dates; length of stay; number in party; room rate paid; type of room chosen; type of guest (convention delegate, businessperson, leisure traveler, and so on); other purchases (minibar, room service, health club, and so on); total folio charges and method of payment (cash, credit card, company billing); and salesperson making the booking (if the guest is part of a group). This information will reveal:

Exhibit 8 Sample Revenue Grid

MARKET SEGMENTS	Room Nights	Average Guest per Room	% of Occupancy	Average Room Rate	Room Revenue	% of Room Revenue	F&B Revenue	% of F&B Revenue	Other Revenue	% of Other Revenue	% of Repeat Business	Time of Year to Promote
Individual Traveler Business Leisure												
Group Traveler Tour Convention												
Other Airline Crews Sports Teams Government												

This chart helps determine which market segments are most profitable. It not only shows occupancy and average rate, but also details all revenue from each market segment to help determine which guest mix is most profitable. Knowing the most profitable guest mix helps ensure that sales and advertising dollars are spent in the proper proportion to achieve or maintain the desired mix.

- The makeup of the present guest base
- The demographics of each guest (age, sex, marital status, family size, income, occupation, and so on)
- The point of origin, or the feeder city or area from which each guest arrives
- The average length of stay and the pattern of occupancy (revealing peak, shoulder, and valley periods)
- How guests get to the property (modes of transportation)
- Sources of reservations (toll-free number, travel agent, website, response to advertisement, etc.)
- Which segments of the market are most lucrative and which should be sought in future promotions

Compiling guest statistics by state, city, or zip code permits the ranking of geographic areas in terms of potential. Sales and advertising efforts can be concentrated on those zip codes with high potential.

When selecting markets, you should keep in mind that a balanced guest mix is ideal. A full-service hotel, for example, will want to target several markets: business

Exhibit 9 Sample Occupancy Chart

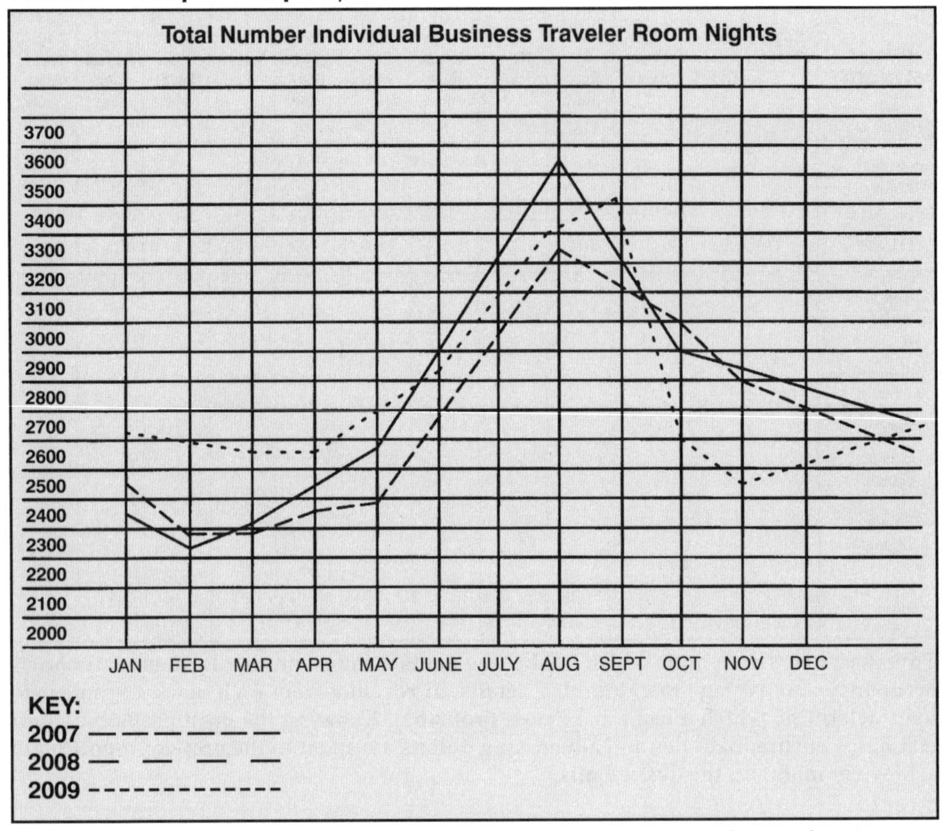

Occupancy charting details the monthly room nights for a particular market segment (in this case, the business traveler). All market segments should be charted in this way. Similar activity charting should be done for restaurants, lounges, and other revenue centers to facilitate assessment of market trends.

travelers during the week, leisure vacationers on the weekends, and local food functions, convention business, and perhaps group tours during shoulder or valley periods. This mix will ensure that the property maintains a fairly steady occupancy rate regardless of changing market trends.

The property's guest mix should be reviewed periodically. Since the objective in selecting target markets is to create the mix of business that will generate the greatest revenue and produce the most profit, changes in strategy may be necessary during the course of the year. Defining and redefining markets is a continual process, and adjustments to the marketing plan are frequently required as conditions change.

Unforeseen events, such as economic downturns, strikes, highway reroutings, and weather may alter the guest mix and result in the need for a change in the mix of business. For example, in economic recessions, corporations cut back on travel, laid-off workers drop out of the leisure market, and even senior citizens with discretionary income travel less. To fill guestrooms in such an economic climate, hotel marketers might decide to go after specialty market segments such as sports teams, family reunion and wedding business, and government travelers.

Step 3: Positioning the Property

Every property projects a certain image in the minds of the public; this perception of a property by its guests or potential guests is known as the property's *market position*. The process of designing a property's market position is known as **positioning**. It is of utmost importance for a property to communicate its distinctive position to each targeted market segment.

Positioning is not simply advertising. A property's position is composed of the hospitality it offers and the managers' and marketers' ability to create unique selling points based on the property's location, internal or external features, and personnel. Without positioning, it is impossible to determine what the property has to offer, where the property is going and how it will get there, and how the property will stand out in a highly competitive arena. Kathleen A. Girard, vice president of marketing at the Hotel Millennium in New York City, says:

> Knowing your product and how to position it is a fundamental key to success in the hotel business. You have to have a very strong identity from the moment you open your door, and you must not compromise it. Otherwise, people get confused. You have to know who your audience is, who buys. Many hotels don't know who they are. They try to be all things to all people, and certain market segments clash. Conventions clash with the individual business traveler, for example. It's better to do a few things very well than to do a lot of things in a mediocre manner.[5]

There are two basic positioning choices. First, you can directly compare yourself with the competition, competing head-on for a share of a particular market. In the fast-food business, head-on positioning is very common; Burger King, for example, promotes its burgers as flame-broiled rather than grilled. Second, you can identify a need in the marketplace and fulfill that need before the competition discovers it—that is, create a new market. Examples of this type of positioning are the extended-stay hotels of the 1990s, and today's boutique properties—small, fashionable, upscale, and highly service-oriented hotels that appeal to young, upscale consumers.

Developing a positioning strategy requires identifying the benefits that will be most important to potential guests by knowing exactly what the property has to offer:

1. Who are we? What do we stand for? What are our strengths and weaknesses? Does our property have a liability that can be turned into an asset? (The property analysis will help you answer these questions.)

2. How does our property differ from the competition? Does our property have tangible or intangible advantages over the competition? Are there areas in which we can set ourselves apart? (Your competitive fact sheets and rate analysis will provide clues.)

Re-branding and Repositioning: From "Budgetel" to "Baymont"

For most chains, staying competitive means making changes that reflect customer needs. The Budgetel chain had already been a leader in the industry—it was the first brand to mandate key card locks, offer free telephone calls, and advertise a money-back guarantee—but, although the chain offered such features as large, comfortable rooms, complimentary in-room breakfasts, and "little extras" that made the rooms feel more like home, its name conjured up images of typical budget properties with Spartan rooms and limited amenities.

After reading a *Zagat Survey on U.S. Hotels, Resorts & Spas* that called the brand "better than the name sounds," Stephen Marcus, chairman and CEO of Marcus Corp., the chain's parent company, was motivated to change the chain's name to better reflect what his properties had to offer. Marcus felt that people would feel better about staying at chain properties if the signs on the buildings reflected the brand's philosophy—while the rooms are economical, guest are not "roughing it."

The name "Baymont" was chosen because it suggests a pleasant, relaxing place and a quality image. Intended to evoke images of water and mountains, the name carried with it the notion of living the good life at an affordable price, and Marcus believed the change would associate his properties with other chains like Fairfield Inn, Holiday Inn Express, and Comfort Inn, although the rates at Baymont Inns & Suites would be lower and the chain could be promoted as a better value.

The company created a $10 million marketing campaign to introduce the new name, including developing a new logo, launching an advertising campaign, and spending some $4 million for new property signs. The name change also involved educating the chain's current customer base (business travelers, travel agents, and so on) as well as new prospects.

To better reflect the name change, Baymont Inns & Suites began offering lobby breakfasts and upgraded amenities to include hair dryers, in-room voice mail, 25-inch televisions, complimentary copies of *USA Today*, and express check-out services. Swimming pools and other amenities were also added at some locations. The name change broadened the brand's market appeal, successfully positioning the chain as a better value for the mid-market segment.

3. What areas are not producing the desired revenue or response? Are there areas that show a high potential for repeat business? (The occupancy and activity charts will help here.)
4. Which target market segments can be most beneficial to us? (Use the revenue grid to evaluate your response.)
5. What are the needs and wants of each segment? What benefits do they seek? Does the property offer any features or services that are unique?
6. Are there opportunities in the marketplace? How can we go about attracting this business?

The answers to these questions will greatly assist in the development of a position that will affect everything the property does and stands for. The property's uniqueness can then be expressed in what is known as a *positioning statement*. The positioning statement must communicate the property's advantages to its selected target markets.

The positioning statement should be targeted to market segments of sufficient size to warrant the expenditures required to attract additional business from that segment, and the property must have the ability to meet that market segment's demands. Strong positioning creates an image, outlines guest benefits, and distinguishes a property from its competition.

It is important to reassess your positioning periodically, as public perception can change. When Hilton Hotels found that its properties were perceived as middle-aged businessmen's hotels, for example, it updated its image, developing new marketing strategies for both its business traveler and leisure traveler market segments. The strategies included a "Travel should take you places" advertising campaign that consisted of catchy ads designed to illustrate how many things could happen between points on a given trip. The chain also affiliated itself with "young" brands: it sponsored the Grammy Awards show, hosted an AVP volleyball clinic at Tempe Beach Park, and offered web icons for MySpace users. Hilton's management listened to guests to ensure that Hilton properties could provide what travelers wanted most from their hotel experience—a customized, personal experience—and upgraded and renovated the chain's properties to meet traveler needs.

Step 4: Establishing Objectives and Action Plans

Once the marketing audit is completed, the target market segments identified, and the positioning established, the next step in the marketing plan is to establish specific marketing objectives. This is one of the most difficult steps in the planning process because it involves establishing goals for each market segment.

At the beginning of the year, goals such as number of room nights, average room rate, and revenue targets should be established for each month and for each market segment. Sales objectives and quotas can be developed as a result of these marketing objectives. Since marketing objectives cannot be reached without sales, it is important to answer the following questions before setting specific marketing objectives:

- Which revenue centers would benefit from additional sales activity?
- When are the peak periods? the shoulders? the valleys?
- Which marketing segments can be reached, and what priority should be given to each segment?
- What can be done to ensure increased sales in each market segment?

Marketing objectives should be simple and should be set for each market segment, revenue center, and revenue-producing service—valet, laundry, and so on. To be effective, marketing objectives must be:

1. *In writing.* Putting objectives in writing provides concise information that can be referred to as necessary by both managers and employees. Written objectives ensure that everyone has the same information.
2. *Understandable.* Performance will suffer if objectives cannot be understood by both management and staff.
3. *Realistic and challenging.* Objectives must be attainable, but they must also present some challenge to the staff. For example, an objective to maintain 100 percent occupancy year-round is unrealistic for most properties, but an objective to increase rooms business by 20 percent over the summer months is probably realistic. One way to ensure realistic goals is by *forecasting.* Occupancy and other forecasts, however, should not be based simply on prior years' performance. Factors noted in the marketing audit (changes in the economy, competitive room supply, market share, etc.) should be taken into consideration when forecasting future potential and setting goals.
4. *Specific and measurable.* Objectives must clearly define the expected results and should be as specific and measurable as possible:

   Quantity-specific. Detail expected sales in terms of number of room nights, number of covers, number of banquets, and so on. Expected dollar value (such as average daily rate or average guest check) might also be made quantity-specific, although market variables may force the reevaluation of these figures.

   Time-specific. Objectives should be broken down into annual, quarterly, monthly, weekly, or even daily objectives to make it easier to evaluate the success of marketing efforts.

   Market share–specific. Markets that offer the highest potential for the property should be targeted. This may mean going after a larger share of an existing market rather than trying to generate business from new (and possibly less profitable) market segments. For example, rather than having a general objective to "raise room occupancy," you might restate your objective as follows: "To increase room nights from the senior citizen market from 900 to 1,400 during June and July, while maintaining an average room rate of $59."

As mentioned earlier in the chapter, a marketing team is perhaps the most effective way to ensure that all revenue centers are included when setting marketing objectives. Individual revenue center objectives can be reviewed by the team to determine their feasibility, and revisions can be made as necessary before the objectives are incorporated into the property's marketing plan.

Developing and Implementing Action Plans. The heart of a marketing plan is its action plans. The statistical report generated by the marketing audit may encompass more pages, but a marketing audit alone is useless. Success comes to those hospitality marketers who make decisions and take action based on what they've learned about their property, the competition, the marketplace, and their guests. Their analysis of this data helps identify:

- What areas need sales activity (the three to six most important priorities for the coming year)
- When business is needed
- The appropriate market segments to be targeted to fulfill objectives

Once these facts are known, action plans can be created. There should be detailed action plans for *each* market segment and revenue center, and responsibility for implementing action plans should be assigned to specific individuals in each of the property's revenue centers (this accountability allows for monitoring the progress of marketing efforts).

Action plans can be as simple or as complicated as necessary. They should be very specific, incorporating the following six areas:

1. *A description of the types of business and the market segments to be solicited.* A property might wish to increase meeting room business, for example, and target local associations to help meet its goal.
2. *Target customers—a specific definition of who will be solicited.* In the case just mentioned, for example, "local associations" is not very specific. Listing the names, addresses, and contact persons for local associations will facilitate implementation of action plans.
3. *Rates/packages/promotions/special plans—a listing of the rates that will be charged for business within each segment.* To attract association business, an incentive package may be developed that includes reduced room rates or complimentary meals for association attendees.
4. *Objectives.* It is not enough to say "increase meeting rooms business." A specific goal—"increase meeting rooms business by 20 percent over weekend periods in July"—will help in establishing action steps and monitoring progress toward meeting the objective.
5. *Action steps—the specific steps that will be taken to achieve objectives.* For association business, these may include a direct mailing to all association meeting planners in the area, an "open house" to introduce meeting planners to the property, and so on.
6. *Budgeting.*

The chapter appendix provides a detailed description of how each of these areas are applied in a marketing plan.

Each action plan should include the "who," "what," "where," "when," and "why" of each step if it is to meet its objectives. If an objective is to increase covers in the restaurant next month by an average of ten per evening, for example, one action plan might be stated as follows: "Restaurant manager will contact 20 local businesses and invite owners to drop by for a complimentary dessert with dinner." This places the responsibility for implementing this part of the plan—targeting local businesses—on the restaurant manager. Another action plan to meet the same objective can be created to involve a number of employees: front desk agents can suggest to registering guests that they reserve a table in the dining room, or switchboard operators may call guests in the early evening to offer information about the restaurant's dinner special.

This scenario is an excellent example of involving a number of property employees to meet a marketing objective. The property's entire staff should always be aware of individual revenue centers and the property's overall marketing efforts. Cooperation can make it much easier to attain marketing objectives, and employee involvement may result in excellent suggestions for more effective action plans.

Budgeting. Action plan expenses must be figured into the marketing budget. Most marketing budgets include sales, advertising, online marketing/website costs, and promotional expenses; direct mail postage and handling charges; promotional premiums; and salaries of the marketing and sales staff. Individual budgets should also be established for each market segment and each action plan designed to reach that market segment. As a rule of thumb, budgeting should be broken down into quarterly segments to make effective monitoring possible. The exception is media advertising, which is often budgeted on an annual basis.

A **zero-base budget** is based on the task method; monies are budgeted at levels to get the job done, and all expenses must be justified. This is considered the best way to budget for marketing, although a number of variables—room occupancy, the business mix, gross revenues, and so on—must be taken into account when establishing a sound budget.

The principal advantage of zero-based budgeting is that it questions every expenditure. The budget is established after each detailed action plan is prepared and the amount required to complete each task estimated, rather than determining the sales budget as a fixed percentage of gross income and then deciding how to spend it. The premise underlying zero-based budgeting is that the marketing effort is budgeted at the level required to accomplish the action steps needed to capture business. While using this approach takes much more time and effort than required for percentage-of-sales, competitive-parity, or affordable-funds budgeting, this "bottom-up" budgeting ensures that the necessary funds are available to reach the marketing objectives for each target market.

In most cases, it is advantageous to develop a budget form that provides instant access to information. The budget form shown in Exhibit 10 breaks the marketing plan down into specific segments such as "Advertising," then divides these segments into expenditure categories. This type of detail is helpful for a number of reasons:

1. *It ensures that all expenses are planned for and documented.* Using a less detailed form can mean that expenses may be overlooked.
2. *It helps prevent arbitrary budget cuts.* When the budget is not broken down into specific expenditures, it is much more likely that money will be moved from one category to another without regard for the consequences.
3. *It is a step toward increased accountability for marketing plans.* Having a detailed budget provides a means of monitoring anticipated and actual expenses for each area of the marketing plan, and the budget can more easily be adjusted to meet changing trends. If a sales manager finds that direct mail campaigns

Exhibit 10 Sample Budget Form

SALES — MARKETING BUDGET — NEXT YEAR

Expenditure Item	JAN $	JAN Budget %	FEB $	FEB Budget %	MAR $	MAR Budget %	Quarter 1 $	Quarter 1 Budget %	APR $	APR Budget %	MAY $	MAY Budget %	JUN $	JUN Budget %	Quarter 2 $	Quarter 2 Budget %
Advertising																
Consumer Magazine																
Trade Magazine																
Radio AM																
Radio FM																
Television																
- Network																
- Cable																
Newspaper																
Direct Mail																
Outdoor Specialty																
Other																
1.																
2.																
Public Relations & Sales Promotion																
Trade Shows																
Sales Force Promotion																
Events																
FAM Trips																
Writers																
Tour Operators																
Travel Agents																
Others																
Receptions																
Travel Missions																
Chef Luncheon																

This is one page from a sales and marketing budget form that, when filled out, will show the budgeted funds for each expenditure item listed, broken down by month and subtotaled for each quarter. A detailed marketing budget is much better than one that simply allocates lump sums to general categories such as "Advertising," "Public Relations," "Corporate Travelers," and so on. Source: James C. Makens, *The Hotel Sales and Marketing Plan Book* (Winston-Salem, North Carolina: Marion-Clarence Publishing House, 1990), p. 227.

are more effective than billboard campaigns, for example, the next budget might see more money allocated to direct mail and less to billboards.

4. *It provides a financial road map that guides expenditures by market segment.* The allocation of marketing expenditures by target markets enables the marketing director to assess the return from specific marketing investments, such as the hire of a salesperson to develop individual corporate business, for example. This person's salary, benefits, and expenses can be directly allocated to this market segment and compared with the revenue the position generates to determine cost-effectiveness.

Perhaps the best way to establish a marketing budget is to determine a rough estimate of expenditures for each market segment, *then* develop the detailed action plans, cost each, and go back and analyze the original estimate for increases or reductions.

Step 5: Monitoring and Evaluating the Marketing Plan

The more carefully the marketing effort is measured, the easier it will be to plan future marketing activities and programs. While the cost-effectiveness of some public relations and sales promotions may be difficult to measure because of their inherent long-term effects, it is important to establish a monitoring system at the same time that action plans and specific promotions are developed.

The marketing plan should be reviewed periodically so that corrective action can be taken throughout the planning cycle. Methods of monitoring the marketing plan include the following:

1. *Record the number of room nights for each market segment.* While it may seem tedious to count and code room nights by market segment, this method results in a report that facilitates the comparison of actual results with marketing plan goals.

2. *Chart and compare the number of restaurant covers sold before and after advertising.* Evaluation should take a number of factors into consideration, including the cost of the promotion compared to the increase in profits. If profits increased by 20 percent but promotional costs exceeded the profits realized, the promotion should be reevaluated.

3. *Survey zip codes to determine which media are most effective in local advertising.* This type of analysis is especially effective for restaurant promotions and weekend hotel packages.

4. *Track prospecting results and sales production versus goals by salesperson.* If, for example, a salesperson started the year with a prospect list of 750 companies, the director of marketing might expect that one-quarter of these companies had been contacted by the end of the first quarter.

5. *Keep track of each salesperson's (1) production of room nights by market segment; (2) business booked by peak, shoulder, and valley periods; and (3) repeat business versus new business booked.*

6. *Record direct mail responses and telephone inquiries in a logbook that indicates the specific salesperson to whom each lead was assigned.* Six months later,

conversions (the actual bookings realized as a result of the inquiries) can be measured. This type of monitoring not only gives an indication of the effectiveness of the advertising piece, but may also provide insight into the strengths and weaknesses of the sales staff. If a mail campaign generated inquiries that did not convert to definite bookings, for example, the problem may lie more with the product or the sales staff than with the media.

7. *Use return mail coupons and tabulate responses to coupons distributed to guests and employees.* This can assist in determining who is using the services and products offered by the property.

8. *Use specific response techniques, such as using special telephone numbers or instructing respondents to ask for a specific individual.* These techniques can help track the effectiveness of both print and broadcast advertising.

Remember, control is an essential part of the marketing plan cycle, and periodic evaluation should be designed into the plan from the beginning. Waiting until the end of the marketing cycle can be risky. A record should be kept each time an advertising campaign is run; any strategies that do not contribute to the bottom line can be immediately reexamined.

When evaluating marketing activities, however, don't be too hasty to abandon the promotion when results aren't exactly as projected. You may be tempted to stop the present activity and replace it with something entirely new. Before doing so, take a close look at what doesn't seem to be working; sometimes, all that is needed is a little corrective action (such as moving an ad for weekend golf packages from the travel section to the sports pages).

If action plans are effective and objectives are realized within established budget limits, corrective action need not be a part of the process. But it is a painful fact that some strategies do not work. If hotel sales goals are not being met, the problem can often be traced to one or more of the following:

1. *Lack of responsibility.* The marketing team member or team leader for a revenue center has not assumed responsibility for seeing that schedules are met and evaluations of results have been made.

2. *Lack of communication.* Salespeople or other employees are not aware of their part in the marketing plan.

3. *Lack of time.* Insufficient time has been allocated for making outside sales calls or directing advertising efforts in the required markets.

4. *Lack of authority.* Salespeople have not been given the authority to commit the budget to specific marketing efforts.

5. *Lack of appeal.* Guest benefits are overrated or pricing is not competitive.

6. *Lack of control.* Outside factors (the economy, an energy crisis, inclement weather) have made it necessary to lower marketing plan goals.

7. *Lack of realistic goals.* Guests have been targeted at a time when they are not planning to buy, or sales goals are simply too high.

Whatever the reason for lagging sales, you must determine that enough time has been given for the plan to work and that corrective measures have been taken to build sales in each market segment. Objective evaluations and corrective actions may prevent costly mistakes and can lead to more effective marketing strategies in subsequent years.

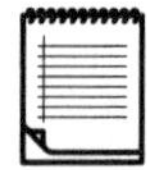

Endnotes

1. Melvyn Greene, *Marketing Hotels and Restaurants into the 90s: A Systematic Approach to Increasing Sales*, Second Edition (New York: Wiley, 1987), p. 17.
2. William S. Watson, "Letters, The New Research Responsibility," *Cornell Hotel and Restaurant Administration Quarterly*, 34, no. 5, October 1993, p. 7.
3. "PricewaterhouseCoopers, Smith Travel Research Offer Global Market Reports," *Hotel Business*, April 2000, p. 28.
4. In some areas, it is possible to get breakdowns of occupancy tax by individual property. If you know how much tax was collected each month, the monthly room revenue can be computed, and by dividing this figure by the estimated average rate, the occupancy percentage can be fairly accurately determined.
5. Kathleen A. Girard, *World Hospitality*, May 2000, p. 10.

Key Terms

competition analysis—An evaluation of a business's competition to identify opportunities and unique selling points; part of a marketing audit.

competitive set—For a hotel or restaurant, its competitive set is made up of properties in the immediate area that sell to similar market segments and offer similar products and services at similar prices.

differentiation—Distinguishing and separating your property from those of the competition.

fair share—The number of room nights a property would sell if demand were distributed based on the number of rooms in each property.

feeder city—A city other than the property's city from which guests arrive.

guest mix—Refers to the variety or mixture of guests who stay at a property or eat at a restaurant.

market segmentation—Dividing the market into groups of consumers with similar needs, wants, backgrounds, incomes, buying habits, and so on.

market share—The number of room nights a property sells compared with the total number of room nights within a market area.

marketing audit—A systematic and comprehensive evaluation of a business, its competition, and the marketplace.

marketing information system—The people, equipment, and procedures involved in gathering and analyzing data to provide accurate information to marketing decision-makers.

marketing intelligence—Information useful for marketers that has been properly analyzed, evaluated, and formatted to help marketers and managers formulate plans and make decisions.

marketing plan—A guide for marketing, sales, advertising, and promotional efforts.

marketplace analysis—An evaluation of the environmental trends and forces affecting a business, such as changes in lifestyles and societal values, economic conditions, and technology.

occupancy and activity analysis—An analysis of a property's past, present, and potential operating statistics; part of a marketplace analysis.

positioning—A marketing term used to describe the process of shaping how consumers perceive the products and services offered by a particular hotel or restaurant in relation to similar products and services offered by competitors.

property analysis—An evaluation of a business's facilities, services, and programs to determine its strengths and weaknesses; part of a marketing audit.

RevPAR (revenue per available room)—A combination of paid occupancy percentage and average daily rate; calculated by dividing room revenues by available rooms or, alternatively, by multiplying paid occupancy percentage by average daily rate; calculated to compare the revenues of properties of differing sizes and to evaluate pricing systems.

target markets—Market segments that a property identifies as having the greatest potential and toward which marketing activities are aimed.

zero-base budget—A budget that starts at zero and forces planners to justify expenditures.

Review Questions

1. What is the *shortest* time frame for which a marketing plan should be developed? What time frame is preferred? Why?
2. What are the five steps involved in developing a marketing plan?
3. What three analyses make up a marketing audit, and what are the objectives of each?
4. Why is positioning important?
5. What are four guidelines used to develop effective marketing objectives?
6. What factors should be considered when developing action plans?
7. What is a zero-base budget? Why is this considered the best way to budget for marketing?
8. How can a property's staff monitor and evaluate the implementation of a marketing plan?
9. What are seven reasons that marketing and sales staffs fail to reach their sales goals?

Internet Sites

For more information, visit the following Internet sites. Remember that Internet addresses can change without notice. If the site is no longer there, you can use a search engine to look for additional sites.

American Hotel & Lodging Association
www.ahla.com

American Marketing Association
www.ama.org

Colloquy Magazine
www.colloquy.com

Destination Marketing Association International
www.iacvb.org

First Data
www.firstdata.com

Hospitality Industry Technology Exposition and Conference
www.hitec.org

Hospitality Sales & Marketing Association International
www.hsmai.org

Informa Research Services, Inc.
www.informars.com

National Restaurant Association
www.restaurant.org

Quirk's Market Research Review
www.quirks.com

Resorts Online
www.resortsonline.com

Restaurants & Institutions
www.rimag.com

Restaurant Report On-line—Developing an Effective Marketing Plan
www.restaurantreport.com/Features/ft_marketingplan.html

Sales & Marketing Management
www.salesandmarketing.com

Small Business Administration
www.sbaonline.sba.gov/

Smith Travel Research
www.str-online.com

Statistics Canada
www.statcan.ca

Technomic Inc.
www.technomic.com

Tradeshow Week
www.tradeshowweek.com

Travel Websites
www.yahoo.com/recreation/travel

U.S. Census Bureau
www.census.gov

Westin Hotels & Resorts
www.westin.com

Case Study

Sales Underperforms Even While Meeting Budget

The Christopher Hotel is a 180-room economy/business property of a national chain located in a booming suburb of a major city. Tony, the regional director of operations, is orienting the property's new general manager, Janice.

Generally, the hotel is close to meeting most of its budgeted targets. However, when Tony compares the hotel's activity with competing hotels in the area, the picture changes dramatically. Other hotels are enjoying much higher occupancy levels than the Christopher and they are selling rooms at higher rates. The Christopher's market penetration is only 84 percent, when its baseline goal should be to achieve at least 100 percent of its fair share of the market. Tony calculates penetration rate by dividing the hotel's actual market share by its fair share (based on the proportion of rooms available in the local market).

Tony and Janice also review the Christopher's group business. Year-to-date, the hotel sold 4,796 group room nights—short of the budgeted target of 6,500 group room nights. The average room rate (ADR) for group business is down $4 from the budget.

Tony tells Janice, "While I'm here I want to investigate these problems with you and help come up with an action plan to address them. How can we increase the Christopher's penetration rate, Janice?"

"I'd start by examining what kind of new business—group and otherwise—is being generated," says Janice. "What is the mix of corporate, leisure, government, or educational groups looking for rooms? I bet that new college is putting together a sports program; visiting teams will need someplace to stay."

"You could be right," says Tony. "The school is so new that you might be too early on that idea, but it couldn't hurt to get a start with the sports program developer. Let's see what the hotel has historically done with groups." He pulls out some reports. "They've got corporate groups contributing 3,000 room nights and other groups contributing the rest of their total 4,796."

"'Other groups'? Is that how it's listed—'other groups'? Aren't there classifications within that 'other' category?" asks Janice.

Tony responds, "That's how it's listed."

Janice shakes her head and asks, "Do we have a group rooms control log to look at so we can see how individual group segments are performing? How about a pace report so we can see how group bookings kept up with budgeted amounts?"

Tony shuffles some of the papers and replies, "The previous GM did keep a GRC log and a pace report. He may not have used them to fullest advantage. He also could have kept better track of what the property's competitors were doing. That information is crucial to success, especially in this local area. In the next few months, I would like you to keep up to date on what our competitors are doing and how they're doing it."

"How good a networker was the previous director of sales?" asks Janice. "Did he have relationships with area churches, mosques, and synagogues for wedding and other special ceremony business? Was he in touch with the manager of the local convention center? How about city officials?"

"He focused more on officials of agencies serving the whole metropolitan area than on officials of this suburb," Tony replies. "Maybe he was hoping to land some of the business for conventions held downtown. He was using the right technique but on the wrong people. Our competitors here keep in touch with the city Department of Parks and Recreation. As far as wedding and ceremony groups, there's been no sales effort specifically targeting them, though some large bookings have come from that segment. I'd encourage you to pursue that option with the staff. And don't be shy about using the yellow pages of the phone book. So many salespeople use that as a last resort. Just think about all the kinds of business represented there."

"It does sound like this is a very competitive area," Janice offers. "I wonder if our sales contacts with those buyers for groups are everything they should be. How experienced are our salespeople?"

"I'm not sure, but that's another good area to look at. Now how about this problem of the group ADR?" asks Tony.

Janice picks up a management binder labeled Rate Guidelines from the GM office bookshelf. "It's great that they had some of these, though having guidelines and making sure staff know and use them are two different things. Hmm, it doesn't have a date listed; do you know when it was last updated?"

"No, I don't," replies Tony.

"That could be important; I'll check on it. Maybe we also need to change our rooms inventory management guidelines to make sure we sell out on every night when there's potential to do so," Janice responds.

Tony closes with, "I think you've got a good handle on the most pressing issues facing the Christopher Hotel, Janice. Why don't you draft an action plan in the next couple of days and we'll refine it together."

Discussion Questions

1. What factors should Janice consider when planning to increase the hotel's market penetration rate?
2. What factors should Janice consider in relation to increasing group business?
3. What initial steps should Janice take to evaluate the low average room rate for groups?
4. How can Janice find out what the competition is doing and how they're doing it?

Case Number: 370CH

This case was developed in cooperation with Lisa Richards of Hospitality Softnet, Inc., a marketing resources and support company (Sixty State Street, Suite 700, Boston, Massachusetts 02109; www.hospitalitysoftnet.com).

This case also appears in *Contemporary Hospitality Marketing: A Service Management Approach* (Lansing, Mich.: American Hotel & Lodging Educational Institute, 1999), ISBN 978-0-86612-158-3.

Chapter Appendix

Sample Marketing Plan

This is an excerpt from a hotel marketing plan. It shows one-year strategies for increasing business from one market segment—corporate business travelers.

As you read this marketing plan, note how complete and specific it is, providing a "road map" for the coming year. The strongest marketing plans result from the input of people from all areas of the property. Therefore, brainstorming sessions with key personnel are essential to developing effective marketing plans.

Corporate

1. Description

   a. Individual business travelers

   b. Relocation/Extended-Stay projects—people staying seven days or more

   c. Meetings—corporate sales, training and development, distributor and dealer, executive conferences, product presentations, stockholder, board and management meetings

   d. Catering—Christmas parties, other employee and client receptions, luncheons, dinners

2. Target Customers

a. Present local files	141 (300 by end of year)
b. Priority Accounts—largest local accounts that aren't using us at present (list to be established)	15
c. Anytown Prospects	
— Companies of over 10 employees within selected SIC numbers in following zip codes: 07314, 07315, 07318	275
— Companies of over 50 employees within selected SIC numbers in following zip codes: 07329, 07330, 07331, 07332	150
— Companies of over 100 employees within selected SIC numbers in all other zip codes within metropolitan area	100
d. All realtors within metro area	75
e. ASTD (American Society for Training and Development) members in six-state region	1,400
f. Travel agents who used us in past two years	210
Total Target Customers	2,366

3. Rates, Special Plans, Packages and Promotions

a. Regular Corporate	$ 75 sgl.	$ 80 dbl.
b. VIP Frequent Traveler Club	$ 72 sgl.	$ 72 dbl.

Membership benefits include newspaper, complimentary coffee, check cashing, points for gifts/travel, upgrade/availability.

Membership for special rate based on volume of at least one reservation per month.

c. Relocation/Extended Stay	$ 65 sgl.	$ 65 dbl.

Minimum of 7-night stay. Assign king room, refrigerator, coffee maker and supplies, no charge for spouse or children, check cashing, and newspaper.

d. Meetings — Rates depend on dates/size of meeting. Will average: $ 72 sgl. $ 77 dbl.

e. Seminar/Training/Corporate Group Package

Available on an excellent selection of specific dates

Minimum of 15 sleeping rooms includes:

	Single	Per Person Double
Room	$ 60.21	$ 30.16
Tax (6.5%)	3.91	1.96
Meeting Room	-	-
Continental Breakfast	3.50	3.50
Lunch	10.00	10.00
AM and PM Breaks	3.00	3.00
All Food Tax (4.5%)	.74	.74
All Food Service (16%)	2.64	2.64
	$ 84.00	$ 52.00

Above package including dinner:

	Single	Per Person Double
Dinner	$ 14.12	$ 14.12
Tax	.64	.64
Food Service	2.24	2.24
	$ 101.00	$ 69.00

The hotel may, at its discretion, serve group lunch and/or dinner with a preset menu in the dining room or a private room.

4. Goals/Objectives

Based on the marketing audits and a thorough review of the property, the competition, and the marketplace, we have identified midweek business as our most important priority for the coming year. We will target the corporate (individual and group) market as the primary segment to solve this need. Our objective is to increase total annual room sales revenue from $1,267,322 to $1,372,400 (an 8.3 percent increase) and to maintain an average room rate of $72 for this segment. Monthly targets are identified in the following chart:

Individual Room-Night and Revenue Goals

	J	F	M	A	M	J	J	A	S	O	N	D	Total	ADR	Room Revenue
VIP Club	100	150	200	200	200	200	150	150	175	200	150	150	2025	$72.00	$145,800
Relocation/Other Extended Stay	60	180	250	350	500	500	500	500	400	600	400	300	4540	$65.00	$295,100
Other Corporate	100	200	300	500	500	500	400	400	600	800	400	400	5100	$76.00	$387,600
Total	260	530	750	1050	1200	1200	1050	1050	1175	1600	950	850	11665	$71.02	$828,500

Group Room-Night and Revenue Goals

	J	F	M	A	M	J	J	A	S	O	N	D	Total	ADR	Room Revenue
Group Total	400	600	700	800	800	750	400	400	500	900	700	400	7350	$74.00	$543,900

Corporate Individual and Group Room-Night and Revenue Totals

	J	F	M	A	M	J	J	A	S	O	N	D	Total	ADR	Room Revenue
Combined Total	660	1130	1450	1850	2000	1950	1450	1450	1675	2500	1650	1250	19015	$72.17	$1,372,400

5. Action Steps

Sales/Direct Mail

Step No.	Method	Target Customers	No.	Details	Qtr.	Sales Days	Resp.
1	Direct Mail	a. Present local files	141–300	Send personal letters week of Jan. 5 thanking them for past business and asking them to rate satisfaction with our services by returning postage-paid return card.	1	–	M.S.

Step No.	Method	Target Customer	No.	Details	Qtr.	Sales Days	Resp.
2	Telephone	a. Present local files that don't return card	100 est.	Survey their satisfaction over the telephone. Give comp one-night stays to any who were dissatisfied.	1	4	M.S. T.M. M.C.
3	Personal Blitzes	a. Present local files	141–300	Deliver small gifts for Valentine's Day, Easter, 4th of July, Halloween, and Christmas	1 2 3 4	15	M.S. T.M. M.C.
4	Party	a. Present local files	141–300 (est. 300 pp)	Thanksgiving party to show appreciation for past business. Invite customer and guest.	4	1.5	M.S. T.M. M.C.
5	Personal calls/ Telephone calls	b. Priority Accts	15	Have contact with these accounts a minimum of once a month. Include entertainment at hotel, sporting events, or other local activities to build relationship.	1 2 3 4	1	M.S. T.M. M.C.
6	Telephone	c. Other Anytown prospects of over 10 employees in selected ZIPs	275	Call for initial qualification to determine if file should be set up (at least 50 room-nights per year). For those with potential, set up appointment with prospect at his or her office or hotel.	1	10	M.S. T.M. M.C.
7	Telephone	c. Other Anytown prospects of over 25 employees in selected ZIPs	150	Call for initial qualification (see Step 6 details)	2	6	T.M.
8	Telephone	c. Other Anytown prospects of over 100 employees All other ZIPs in metro area	100	Call for initial qualification (see Step 6 details)	2	4	M.C.
9	Personal Blitzes	d. All realtors in metro area	75	Drop off relocation brochures and do survey of needs. Set up files for those that have two or more relocations per month.	3	3	M.S. T.M. M.C.
10	Direct Mail	e. ASTD members in six-state region	200 (of 1400 total)	Do two-part mailing test of 200 throughout six-state region to determine potential for long-term training.	2	-	M.S.
				The first part of the mailing will include personal letter; meetings brochure, and postage-paid return card.		-	M.S.
				The thrust of letter will be economy, privacy, and the fact that a training meeting of 20 is a major meeting at our hotel.			
				The second part of the mailing will consist of a copy of first letter, reminder note, and another return card.		-	M.S.
11	Telephone call-backs	e. ASTD members in six states	30 est.	Respondents to mailing (Step 10) showing potential to be called within 1 day of response.	2	1	T.M.
12	Direct Mail/ call-backs	e. ASTD members in six states	1200	If response from 1st mailing is positive, additional names to be contacted as in Steps 10 and 11.	3	7	T.M. M.C.

Step No.	Method	Target Customer	No.	Details	Qtr.	Sales Days	Resp.
13	Phone Blitzes	f. Travel agents who used us in the past two years	210	Call all agents to thank for business, qualify for future. In each case talk to manager and determine whether agent should be on our mailing list.	4	5	M.S. T.M. M.C.
14	Direct Mail	f. Travel agents who used us in the past year	175 est.	Send rate letter updating them on all programs and offering complimentary rooms for their personal travel on a space available basis.	4	-	M.S.

5. Action Steps (*continued*)

Advertising

Media

Journal/South Metro (2 col. × 5″) 8 times
Journal/Central Metro (2 col. × 5″) 4 times
Connection Newspapers/Springfield (2 col × 5″) 4 times
Springfield Chamber Brochure—Annual (1 ×)
Chamber Directory—Annual (1 ×)

Merchandising

Development of the Following Brochures and Flyers

Local corporate VIP Club 4p, 2c 1,500
Relocation/Extended Stay 2p, 1c 1,500
Hotel fact sheet (group) 8″ × 10″, 2c 3,500
Meeting Packages 4p, 2c 2,500

Public Relations and Publicity

Column items dealing with prominent corporate guests or meetings will be given to major dailies as well as community media.

6. Budget

Sales

Dues/Subscriptions

Springfield and Metro Chambers, MPI $ 2,100

Entertainment (over and above normal entertainment)

Meet the Manager-Prospect
Get Togethers 12 × $75 $ 900
Thanksgiving party 300 @ $20 (cost) $ 6,000 6,900

Item	Amount	Total
Advertising		
Media		
Journal/South Metro		
2 col. × 5″ × $550 × 8	$ 4,400	
Journal/Central Metro		
2 col. × 5″ × $450 × 9	$ 4,050	
Connection Newspapers/Springfield		
2 col. × 5″ × $1005 × 4	$ 4,040	
Springfield Chamber brochure—annual $\frac{1}{2}$ pg.	450	
Chamber Directory—annual $\frac{1}{2}$ pg.	500	$13,440
Media Production		
Corporate headquarters ad	425	
Meetings ad	350	
Meetings package	450	
Chamber, individual and group × 2	800	2,025
Direct Mail		
Present local files 1,400 × $1.00	1,400	
ASTD		
#1 2-part—200 × $1.50	300	
#2 2-part—1200 × $1.50	1,800	
Travel Agent—175 × $1.00	175	3,675
Brochures/Flyers		
Local corporate VIP club 1,500	$ 1,150	
Relocation/Long Term Stay 1,500	450	
Hotel fact sheet 3,500	600	
Meeting Packages 4p, 2c 2,500	900	3,100
Other Selling Aids		
Holiday Gifts for blitzes $5 × 200		1,000
Total Corporate		$32,240

Summary

Midweek corporate business is our top priority for the coming year. The estimated 19,015 room nights is 41 percent of total rooms business. And the $32,240 is 16.6 percent of the total marketing budget.

Courtesy of Tom McCarthy, Tom McCarthy Associates, Falls Church, Virginia

Chapter 3 Outline

Competencies

1. Identify the duties and responsibilities of positions typically found in a hotel marketing and sales office. (pp. 77–85)
2. Describe how a sales office is organized, identify characteristics of successful salespeople that managers should be aware of when building an effective sales team, and describe techniques managers use to recruit, hire, train, manage, and evaluate salespeople. (pp. 85–97)
3. Explain how salespeople are compensated, and describe supplemental sales staff. (pp. 97–100)
4. List and describe typical sales meetings, and identify the types and uses of records and forms, file systems, and reports used in the marketing and sales office. (pp. 100–115)
5. Describe how automation is used in a marketing and sales office, and summarize how the efficiency of the office can be evaluated. (pp. 115–122)

Insider Insights

Danielle Babilino
Vice President Hotel Sales, Mandalay Bay Resort
Las Vegas, Nevada

"The role of the sales department is vitally important. In order to reach occupancy and revenue goals, our sales office must be organized. Standard operating procedures provide a reference for our sales and catering personnel and are a great tool for training new salespeople. When procedures and policies are clearly defined in writing, communication is improved. Successful selling and a well-organized sales office go hand in hand. It's the task of the director of sales to coordinate all sales activities so that everyone's pulling in the same direction. An organized sales office eliminates confusion, saves time, and increases guest satisfaction while maximizing profits."

3

Managing the Marketing and Sales Office

TWO TRENDS have greatly affected the way hotel marketing and sales departments do business. First, acquisitions, mergers, and consolidations have occurred in the hospitality industry at a record pace. Today, a handful of firms own nearly 100 brands; so, to increase their efficiency, these hospitality firms are consolidating their operations and relying more on regional and national sales offices.

Second, marketing functions have increasingly been incorporated into sales. More hospitality firms are focusing on the overall bottom line, not just revenue from rooms business or banquets. These firms are evaluating guest spending patterns and the potential for revenue before booking. This trend, called revenue management, has led to revenue management positions in many marketing and sales offices.

In this chapter, you will learn how today's marketing and sales departments are being structured and the methods that these departments are using to maximize efficiency. Actual industry examples and forms will be used to show exactly how well-organized marketing and sales offices are staffed and run to ensure a property's success.

The Marketing and Sales Division

Marketing and sales divisions or departments vary with the size, type, and budget of the hospitality firm. But all properties, whether large or small, should have some kind of marketing and sales department from which marketing and sales efforts are directed.

At small properties, a salesperson usually handles all types of business. He or she may call on meeting planners, travel agents, tour operators, and other sources of potential business. Still smaller hotels may have to combine sales operations under another department or even have the general manager direct marketing and sales efforts, perhaps designating one day a week for personally making sales calls.

Large properties generally have a specialized sales staff and operate out of a separate sales office. It is best, if at all possible, to have full-time sales specialists for group and individual sales. In the largest organizations, the degree of specialization is carried still further, with salespeople assigned to specific market segments: one salesperson may be assigned to association business, another to corporate meetings business, still another to tour business, and so on. Such specialization is practical only for chain operations.

Exhibit 1 Sample Organization Charts for the Marketing and Sales Personnel at Small and Midsize Properties

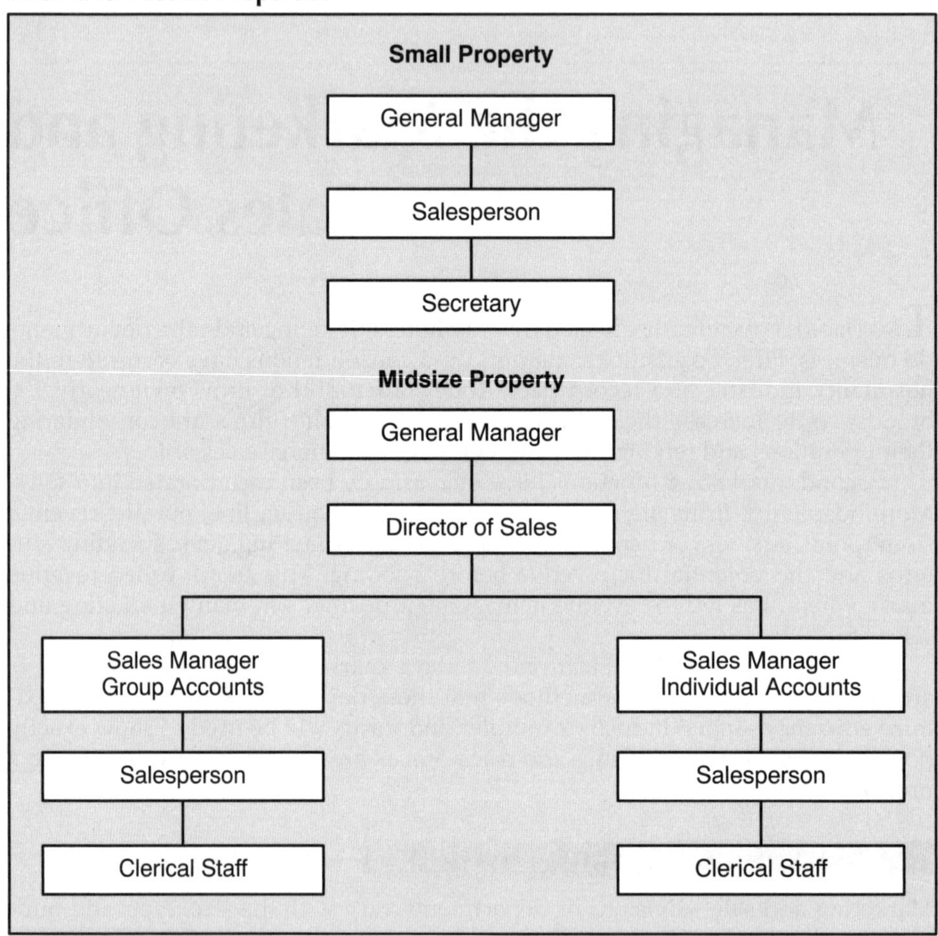

At large properties, the director of marketing handles all aspects of marketing and has a full-time director of sales reporting to him or her. However, at the great majority of small and midsize hotels, there is only a salesperson, or a director of sales and a modest staff. Since no one person can do everything it takes to market a hotel, a marketing committee should be established at these properties.

Exhibits 1 and 2 show typical organization charts for the marketing and sales divisions of small, midsize, and large properties. Although the responsibilities of the marketing and sales staff may vary among properties, a brief description of typical duties and responsibilities follows:

Director of Marketing—Considered the head of the sales effort at large properties, the director of marketing usually serves on the executive committee of the property. Some directors of marketing are actively involved in sales; others confine themselves to administering the division.

Exhibit 2 Sample Organization Chart for a Marketing and Sales Division of a Large Hotel

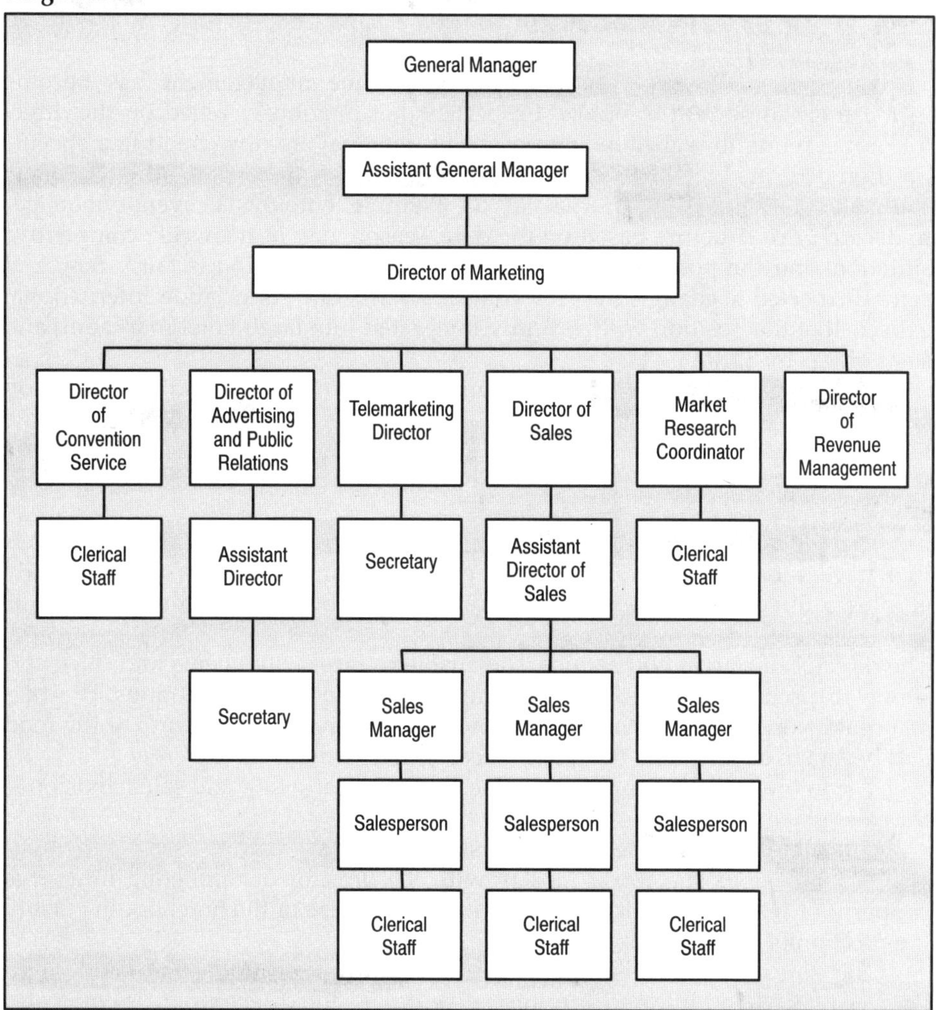

This organization chart shows the specialization that exists within the marketing and sales division of a large hotel. At large hotels and convention hotels, each salesperson may be given a specific assignment, such as individual sales, group sales, travel agent sales, international sales, and so on.

Market Research Coordinator—Many large properties employ a marketing professional who oversees the development of information regarding the history and past performance of each account being solicited. The market research coordinator may also research current market trends, the marketing and sales strategies used by competing properties, and general consumer trends. The property uses this research to develop sales strategies.

Director of Advertising and Public Relations—The job of the director of advertising and public relations is to coordinate all promotional materials, establish a good public image for the property, and help select advertising media for the property.

Director of Revenue Management—Revenue management has become increasingly important to hotels. Properties that previously relied on the director of marketing to realize maximum profit potential are now creating a specific position dedicated to forecasting supply and demand and researching the potential profitability of groups. Swissôtel, for example, employs a revenue manager to decide price structure based on the date, season, day of the week, competitive situation, and the potential of the group. While this position is fairly new and can be expected to change, the Hotel Sales & Marketing Association International expects that the position will be firmly integrated into large hotel marketing and sales offices by 2010.[1]

Telemarketing Director—This member of the marketing and sales division manages the telemarketing center and works closely with the sales staff. It is the telemarketing director's job to supervise and manage the telephone sales staff, which is responsible for developing leads, making prospecting calls, and following up on leads and previous clients.

Director of Convention Service or Convention Service Manager—Hotels that have substantial convention and group meetings business will generally employ a director of convention service or convention service manager who is responsible for overseeing the servicing of group business once it has been sold. The director of convention service is available to meet with clients and sales personnel to discuss the feasibility of bookings and the specifics of meetings. This person must work closely with all departments, coordinating the efforts of the food and beverage department, the front office, and the banquet setup crew.

The following positions form the heart of the marketing and sales division—the sales office:

Director of Sales—The director of sales is responsible for executing the marketing plan. He or she works closely with the director of marketing in a large property, or with a marketing committee when the size of the hotel doesn't justify the position of director of marketing.

The director of sales is usually in charge of the sales office and supervises the sales staff. In addition to administrative duties, the director of sales may also handle key accounts, assist salespeople when necessary, and prepare sales reports for top management (see Exhibit 3).

While the scope of this position is often argued, it is generally agreed that it is extremely difficult for one person to perform both sales and marketing functions. Since marketing includes the areas of research, public relations, packaging, direct mail, internal marketing, internal merchandising, revenue management, pricing, partnership alliances, database and Internet marketing, advertising, and external marketing, it's not likely that many individuals could accomplish these tasks and still coordinate and direct sales efforts.

Sales Manager—In small properties, this position might be synonymous with the director of sales, while, in larger properties, the sales manager would report to the director of sales. Sales managers usually assign territory or accounts to

Exhibit 3 The Role of a Director of Sales

A director of sales is responsible for several important aspects of the sales function:

1. **Coordinating with top management.** A good director of sales works closely with the general manager and other department heads, often on a weekly basis, to ensure that all the sales needs of the property are being met.
2. **Administering a sales support system.** A good sales office needs an efficient filing system, written policies and procedures, and an effective paper flow for correspondence. It is up to the director of sales to ensure that all sales systems are operating smoothly or that needed corrections are made.
3. **Training the sales staff.** The director of sales is often responsible for initial training, but must also continue to coach and counsel the sales staff. It is up to the director of sales to identify weak areas and see that the sales staff corrects them.
4. **Setting sales targets.** A good director of sales determines specific target clients in each market segment and ensures that sales calls are tailored to meet the needs of potential clients. The director of sales also evaluates business potential and steers the sales staff to lucrative areas.
5. **Evaluating sales progress.** It is up to the director of sales to have a written sales plan with definite goals in order to measure progress.
6. **Evaluating sales procedures.** The primary job of a sales office is to sell, and all non-selling functions (sales meetings, travel time, etc.) should be analyzed to be certain they are kept to a minimum. For example, the director of sales might decide to eliminate a few non-productive sales meetings to make more time for selling.

It is also up to the director of sales to determine if he or she is communicating with both sales staff and management, and if there are any problems that need to be arbitrated. If the director of sales is competent in all of these duties, he or she will ensure that the sales office runs smoothly.

salespeople, monitor the progress of salespeople, and handle their own accounts, although specific duties will vary depending on the structure of the sales office.

Assistant Director of Sales—When this position is used, the assistant director of sales serves as the chief aide to the director of sales. The assistant director of sales may manage the sales office, supervise sales staff, and handle his or her own accounts. If the sales office is headed by a sales manager, this position would be called the assistant sales manager.

Salespeople or Sales Representatives—Salespeople are the backbone of any sales organization. They are responsible for contacting, soliciting, and providing follow-up service to clients (see Exhibit 4).

Although for the sake of clarity we will refer to employees in this position as *salespeople,* in today's hospitality industry the title *salesperson* is seldom used. Salespeople are usually given titles such as *account manager* to give them increased credibility. In some operations, even members of the sales office clerical staff are

Exhibit 4 Sample Job Description—Group Salesperson

Job Title: Group Salesperson

Department: Marketing and Sales

Reports To: Director of Sales

Basic Functions: Review the marketing strategy that will obtain maximum occupancy levels and average rate with the director of sales. Responsible for all group business within the western territory.

Consult daily with the director of sales concerning the western territory and how it relates to the sales success of the hotel. Effective merchandising, prospecting, solicitation, and booking of business are among the areas that will be discussed.

Scope: The group salesperson will be the primary person responsible for booking long-term group business (long-term being more than six months out).

Work Performed: Initiate prospecting and solicitation of new accounts in the western territory; manage current accounts to maximize guestroom nights; responsible for administrative efforts necessary to perform these tasks.

Quotas for this position are:

Room nights per month:	1,200
Soft spot percentage:	20%
Phone calls per week:	
Trace/Follow-up	20
Prospecting	25
Personal calls per week:	10
New accounts per month:	10
Referrals per month:	5

The group salesperson must supply weekly, monthly, and annual reports supporting productivity standards.

Probe for client needs: rooms, suites, desired dates, day-of-week pattern, program agenda, food and beverage requirements, and degree of flexibility in each of these areas.

When available, obtain information on a group's past history; i.e., previous rooms picked up, arrival/departure pattern, and double occupancy percentage.

Review availability of clients' required dates and research any alternative dates which should be offered. The dates presented to clients should satisfy their needs while allowing the hotel to maximize occupancy and average rate.

Negotiate with clients the day or days of the week that rooms will be needed (and held), the number of rooms that will be blocked for each day of the function, and group rates (within guidelines as set by the director of sales regarding comps and function space).

Tentatively block rooms and function space in accordance with office policy.

Confirm in writing, according to office standards (via short-term contract or long-term contract and function room outline), all aspects of the meetings. Track to ensure groups receive signed contracts.

Alert all necessary departments (i.e., front office and credit) of pending tentative bookings.

Exhibit 4 *(continued)*

	Upon receiving a signed contract, process definite booking ticket, definite function room outline, and credit application.
	Oversee, manage, and track the way in which reservations are made, the pick-up of group blocks, adherence to cut-off dates, and any subsequent adjustment to room blocks (positive or negative).
	Periodically contact clients while in-house to be certain all is in order and going well; handle any last-minute needs as they arise.
	Conduct an exit interview with clients to determine level of satisfaction and ask for additional business.
	Send letter of appreciation to clients. Letter should include actual room night consumption and should be tailored to previous exit-interview discussions.
	Attend extra-curricular activities and meetings, and accept any responsibilities or projects as directed by the director of sales.
Supervision Exercised:	Supervise one secretary.
Supervision Received:	Primary supervision from the director of sales. Initial training, and retraining as needed, also received from the director of sales. Receive direction from the director of sales in regard to room merchandising.
Responsibility & Authority:	Upon satisfactory completion of rooms merchandising and operational training, the group salesperson will have the authority to confirm dates, room blocks, and rates directly with clients.
Minimum Requirements:	Bachelor's degree, preferably in business, hotel, or restaurant administration. Individual must also be professional in appearance and approach.
Experience:	Minimum of two years experience in hotel sales.
Sales Competencies:	1. Ability to negotiate. 2. Ability to prioritize and manage accounts. 3. Ability to prospect. 4. Ability to judge the profitability of new business. 5. Knowledge of product. 6. Knowledge of competition. 7. Ability to make sales presentations. 8. Ability to organize and plan. 9. Ability to utilize selling skills. 10. Ability to overcome objections. 11. Ability to solve problems and make decisions. 12. Ability to write effectively.

A job description is a detailed statement about a job, including work to be performed and organizational relationships. Job descriptions aid in the hiring process by defining the specific criteria needed to fill a position effectively; note that this sample job description lists activity goals (phone calls and personal sales calls required per week), but also lists productivity goals—performance measured by the number of room nights booked per month. Job descriptions also serve as a general guideline for training personnel. It is the responsibility of the general manager or the head of the marketing and sales department or sales office to develop job descriptions for each sales position.

The Best Hotel Sales Director I Ever Met

The best sales director I ever met:

First and foremost, has an insatiable curiosity. People blessed with curiosity will excel in their job through the process of satisfying their need to learn. Curious people crave new information. The best sales director I ever met is constantly evolving, learning, and improving.

Stays current with new technology. The best sales director has already discovered the many ways the Internet can benefit the sales effort. From researching the competition's rates and sales data to finding new prospects, the Internet has changed the way hotel rooms are sold.

Seeks to involve the hotel's general manager and others in the sales process. The process of selling is definitely not a one-person show. The best sales director invites involvement in the sales process. The best sales director I ever met shares sales successes with the entire hotel team.

Knows that hotel sales is a numbers game. Making contact with as many people as possible is an important part of being successful in hotel sales. The best sales director I ever met talks to everyone possible. This sales director makes a lot of phone calls and sends a lot of e-mails; it takes activity to produce activity.

Knows that clients, not policy, determine the hotel's services. Careful planning and execution can make almost any client request a chance for the hotel to shine. If a sales director has involved the entire hotel team in the sales process, it's amazing what can be accomplished.

Cares. The best sales director I ever met cares enough to learn from setbacks and develops tactics and strategies to offset them. The best sales director channels the pain of failure into positive action and turns great successes into examples for the future.

Source: Adapted from Neil Salerno, "The Hotel Marketing Coach," ehotelier.com, November 17, 2005.

called *account managers*. Senior salespeople are sometimes given the title of *sales executive* or *account executive*.

Clerical Staff—The clerical staff is responsible for maintaining sales paperwork, freeing salespeople to solicit clients. A good clerical staff is essential for the maintenance of sales reports, and may do research for salespeople. As mentioned above, the clerical staff is sometimes included in the *sales manager* category. In many cases, the clerical staff knows as much about the property as the salespeople, and they can often generate leads or actually sell to a client.

No matter what structure is ultimately chosen—or what positions are created within the marketing and sales structure—every effort should be made to motivate the entire staff and create a sense of teamwork. This involves instilling a sense of community, and ensuring that everyone involved—from the general manager or director of sales to the relief receptionist—shares a common direction and a willingness to play whatever part is necessary to achieve the goals set for the property.

Other Positions—Increasingly, hotels, especially large ones, are also positioning the banquet/catering department under the marketing and sales division. Although some people feel that the banquet/catering department belongs under the food and beverage division, in hotels doing extensive meetings and banquet business, control of all function space should be overseen by one person—the director of sales. This eliminates confusion and communication problems, since choices must sometimes be made regarding who will get a function room on a specific night.

In many hotels, the reservations department also falls under the marketing and sales division (rather than under the front office). Reservations is an important area in relationship to sales, since reservationists are the first to have contact with potential clients. As with banquet/catering, structuring reservations under sales can eliminate potential overbooking problems.

Organizing the Marketing and Sales Office

Whether it stands alone at a small property or is included within a marketing and sales division or department at a large property, a marketing and sales office can be organized in a variety of ways, based on a number of factors:

- The property's goals and objectives
- The budget available for marketing and sales
- Available outside assistance (travel agents, chain referrals, reservation systems, and so on)
- The total market potential and the number of people needed to take advantage of that potential

However the sales and marketing office is organized, it is crucial that all employees understand their roles in meeting the goals set forth in the marketing plan.

The Sales Area

Whether the property is large or small, the marketing and sales office may be one of the first property areas a potential client sees, and the importance of first impressions cannot be overstated.

Potential clients should be properly greeted by the sales secretary or receptionist. The sales area should be accessible but private—no "goldfish bowl" off the main lobby, but not stuck away in a basement or unused guestroom. (If the hotel has meeting and banquet rooms, the ideal location is adjacent to these facilities.) The furniture should be tasteful, the offices well lit and properly ventilated, and the design uncluttered and professional. Property information sheets and brochures, sample menus, and news clippings about your property make good pre-sale tools. The decor should include photographs of events, guestrooms, meeting rooms, and the property's staff, as well as awards received by the property. Above all, every member of the sales office—from the sales manager to the file clerks—should be knowledgeable about the property and ready to share information about the property's benefits.

Exhibit 5 Sample Interview Questions for Hiring Salespeople

1. What do you like most about selling?
2. What is the greatest lesson you have learned from your sales experience?
3. How do you organize your time to maximize your sales effectiveness?
4. What would your plan be if you were asked to sell to a market segment that was new to you?
5. How do you schedule appointments?
6. How would you rate your ability to schedule appointments? Your ability in one-to-one selling?
7. How do you service and follow up an account?
8. What information is most important to collect on competitors?
9. What do salespeople need to know about their product? What is the most important thing?
10. How did you handle a difficult client objection that you have faced?
11. Can you describe a time when you didn't quit when making a difficult sale?
12. What techniques do you use for getting by intermediaries when making telephone sales calls?
13. What has been the most difficult thing for you to learn in selling?
14. What resources do you use for prospecting new leads?
15. What is your approach to closing a sale?

Each of these open-ended questions is an opportunity for the applicant to talk about him- or herself—and for the interviewer to determine sales strengths and weaknesses.

Recruiting and Hiring Effective Salespeople

Since effective salespeople are so important to the property's sales efforts, it is essential that a good sales staff be hired (see Exhibit 5). Hiring—and retaining—good salespeople also makes good business sense, since replacement costs can be extremely high, both in terms of training a replacement and in business lost over the hiring and training period.

Consider the case of salesperson Jim Dandy, for example. Jim, an experienced sales rep, sells an average of 1,250 room nights per month at $100 each (including food and beverages)—for total revenue of $125,000 per month. Should Jim leave, the director of sales estimates it will take approximately three months to find and hire a qualified replacement—a loss of $375,000 to the property!

After the replacement is found, it may take three to six months for the new hire to work at Jim's full capacity. If the new salesperson works at one-half of Jim's capacity for the first three months and increases productivity to three-fourths of Jim's capacity in the fourth through sixth month on the job, the property has still sustained a loss of $656,250 in revenue![2] No wonder, then, hiring the right people for the job—and keeping them—is so important.

To build an effective sales team, the sales manager should be aware of a number of characteristics common to successful salespeople:

1. *Professionalism.* Successful salespeople present a professional image. They dress well, but conservatively, and are well groomed. A successful salesperson projects honesty, reliability, and enthusiasm.
2. *Ability to communicate.* Successful salespeople are excellent communicators, both when speaking and in writing. Their sales presentations are clear and interesting, they are able to build rapport with clients, and they can handle questions and objections calmly. Additionally, they are computer literate and able to use technology to communicate internally within the organization and externally with customers.
3. *Intelligence.* Successful salespeople are knowledgeable and learn very quickly.
4. *Ability to analyze.* Successful salespeople can objectively analyze their property's strengths and weaknesses and use their findings to benefit potential clients. They are also adept at analyzing clients, and are able to suggest additional products or services to meet clients' needs.
5. *Motivation.* Successful salespeople have a positive mental attitude, are confident, and are goal oriented. They understand that sales is often a "numbers game," see each rejection as a step closer to closing a sale, and refuse to let failures keep them from going after additional business.
6. *Efficiency.* Successful salespeople are experts at managing their time and sales territory. They turn waiting time into sales time, and waste little effort on unproductive activities and accounts.
7. *Persistence.* Successful salespeople use a steady and systematic selling approach, and follow up consistently on their prospects and customers. Rather than communicating through a quarterly newsletter, for example, they will make repeated contacts—a sales letter followed by a telephone or personal call, another follow-up letter or visit, and so on.
8. *Empathy.* Good salespeople are able to empathize with customers. They strive to understand the needs and wants of their prospects and clients.
9. *Curiosity.* Another quality that successful salespeople share is curiosity. They are alert to new developments that might result in business for the property, and are interested in the property's guests.

It is important to note that salespeople are not "born salespeople." Almost any enthusiastic, intelligent applicant, properly trained, can become a real asset to a property's sales staff.

Good salespeople can be found through word of mouth, advertising in newspapers or trade publications, the Internet, employment agencies, and contacts through associations or organizations that deal with the sales profession, such as the Hospitality Sales & Marketing Association International (HSMAI). They can even be found among the property's existing staff!

INTERNET EXERCISE

In order for hospitality sales professionals to work effectively, they must keep abreast of current trends and new developments in the industry. Many hospitality magazines have online sites to enable busy sales managers to readily access this type of information; some of these sites offer e-mail newsletters on a periodic basis.

Log onto the Internet and research the following hospitality magazine websites:

- www.hotelbusiness.com
- www.hmmonline.com
- www.lodgingmagazine.com

1. Do a search on three hotel marketing and sales department positions: Director of Marketing, Director of Sales, and Director of Revenue Management. What information was of the most interest to you?
2. On which site(s) did you find information useful for managing a sales office?
3. What types of articles provided valuable success strategies and tips for hospitality sales?

Training Salespeople

Once selected, salespeople (even experienced new hires) must be trained.[3] Salespeople must be given the training they need before they are sent to the front lines. Effective initial training can mean the difference between bookings and lost business, but far too often sales training consists of a tour of the property and a slap on the back, and then the new hire is urged to hit the bricks and get some business. Far more extensive sales training, however, is crucial for salespeople to sell productively. The most effective training is tailored to each individual and is not a one-time effort; there should be opportunities for continuing education after initial training, such as seminars or sales skills workshops. Job coaching and testing are also important tools for success.

Each salesperson should have a firm foundation in the following key areas:

- Property knowledge
- Office procedures
- Performance standards
- Salesmanship

Property Knowledge. Thoroughly knowing the property gives salespeople confidence when making sales calls. Each new salesperson should have a complete tour of the property to become familiar with the property's staff; the facilities, services, and products offered; and the strengths and weaknesses of the property. To assist salespeople (old and new) in gaining and retaining product knowledge, most hotels develop a **property fact book,** which typically includes a general description of the property; the number and types of guestrooms; room rates and booking policies; food service available, including the hours of operation, seating capacities, and menus; the layouts, capacities, and descriptions of meeting and banquet facilities; audiovisual equipment available; recreational facilities; and information about transportation and area attractions (see Exhibit 6).

Salespeople should also be presented with an overview of the entire operation and shown the role they play in reaching the hotel's financial objectives. It is important that new salespeople learn about the financial status of the property. Salespeople need to understand the economics of the hotel, and should be coached regarding:

1. The property's rate structure.
2. The profit contribution of each of the hotel's revenue centers. While margins may vary from one property to another, departmental profit margins run about 75 percent for guestroom sales, 15 percent for restaurant food sales, 40 percent for beverage sales, and 35 percent for banquet revenue. Because of its high profit margin, the major source of profits lies in guestroom sales rather than the food and beverage area.
3. The present percentage of business from each market segment, and the targeted optimum business mix.
4. The property's slow business periods, so that sales efforts can be directed to times when business is most needed. The negative effects of booking low-rated business during peak periods, or reserving banquet or function space for local groups when that space could have been reserved for groups needing guestrooms, should be explained.
5. The targeted average rates for each market segment, and authoritative guidelines for quoting rates.

Office Procedures. Each salesperson should know the sales office routine. A supervisor should explain sales office hours; the office computer system; booking policies; the function and guestroom control books; sales forms and reports; paper flow; and past, present, and future promotional material.

To avoid confusion and poor communication, each salesperson should have just one boss. Each salesperson should know the chain of command in the sales office, and how he or she fits into the general sales picture. Salespeople should also know how much of their work can be delegated to the sales clerical staff.

Equally important is knowledge of the office's **standard operating procedures (SOPs).** SOPs are written instructions explaining how recurring business activities should *always* be handled. Each property has different policies regarding expense reports, VIP and complimentary room policies, and booking procedures, so it is essential that salespeople know the guidelines and limits set by the property. SOPs should be in writing, and salespeople must study and learn them.

Performance Standards. Every salesperson should know exactly what is expected of him or her in terms of deadlines, sales quotas, numbers and types of sales calls (personal, telephone, and so on), correspondence, and inter-property communications. New salespeople should be given a detailed, written job description, specific long-term and short-term goals, and a territory or number of accounts. A

Exhibit 6 Outline for a Property Fact Book

OUTLINE FOR PROPERTY FACT BOOK		
GUESTROOM INFORMATION	**RESTAURANTS & LOUNGES**	**MEETING & BANQUET FACILITIES**
Priority I	**Priority I**	**Priority I**
Number of rooms	Seating capacity	Location of meeting rooms
Number of singles/ doubles/suites	Number of tables and types	Square footage/seating capacity
Size of rooms—square footage	Atmosphere/interior design	Utilities available
Number of floors	No-smoking sections	Exhibit space
Phones in rooms	Dress requirements	Meeting room rental rates
Fire alarms/detectors in rooms	Pricing by restaurant	
Rooms for the disabled	Restaurant positioning	
No-smoking rooms		
Amenities in rooms		
Priority II	**Priority II**	**Priority II**
Room rates	Menu style/theme	Function room furniture
Check-in/check-out times	Types of food by restaurant	Audiovisual capabilities
Priority III	**Priority III**	**Priority III**
Customer mix	Entertainment	Banquet seating capacities
Average occupancy by day of week	Reservation policy	Banquet menu
Average length of stay by segment	Cocktails available	Theme parties
Sales budget	Wine cellar/list	Outside services
Profitability by segment	Food served in lounge	Types of banquet specialties
Group check-in/check-out procedures	Special promotions	Beverage service
Front desk staffing	Opening/closing times	Banquet staffing levels

New salespeople cannot learn everything about a property in their first week. To help them gain knowledge in a logical order, questions about each area (guestrooms, restaurants and lounges, meeting and banquet facilities, etc.) should be arranged by priorities. At the end of week one, a salesperson should master all Priority I questions; and each week, master another priority level. The director of sales should assign the responsibility of updating and maintaining the property fact book to one specific person in the sales department.

good sales manager will give a new salesperson at least one or two high-potential accounts. It is discouraging to new salespeople to only get accounts that no one else wants. Success builds enthusiasm, so some "live" accounts should be given to new hires.

It is important that salespeople understand the market segments they are expected to target. A salesperson working with corporate group accounts, for example, will have to learn the common procedures used by corporations for booking guestrooms and meeting facilities.

It is vital that new salespeople learn how to recognize profitable and unprofitable accounts. Some accounts produce more business than others, and it is usually up to the individual salesperson to determine which accounts are producing—and, consequently, which accounts should receive more of the salesperson's time.

Salesmanship. It is important to note that instruction in the psychology of selling is part of successful sales training. More and more properties are realizing the value of training salespeople to recognize motivations for buying decisions and the types of buyers salespeople will typically encounter. The information presented in the following section is just a sample of the many different theories, systems, principles, and hypotheses available to salespeople seeking to learn more about sales psychology.

The personality types of buyers. Learning to recognize a client's basic personality type can greatly increase a salesperson's chances of selling to him or her. Personalities can be divided into four basic types: the director, the socializer, the relater, and the thinker (see Exhibit 7).[4] Remember that these types are generalizations, and an individual may have traits of more than one of these personality types. What follow are guidelines, not hard-and-fast rules.

The **director** is interested in getting results quickly, and is assertive and often blunt. He or she is interested in facts and the bottom line. To successfully sell to a director, salespeople must be prepared, organized, fast-paced, and to the point. A director must be made to feel that the decision to buy is his or her own; it is best for the salesperson to present two or three options and let the director select the one most suitable.

The **socializer,** on the other hand, is playful and talkative. Socializers enjoy the opportunity to talk about personal ideas and opinions, and are usually in no hurry to end a discussion. To successfully sell to socializers, salespeople must be stimulating and interesting but give socializers the chance to speak. Socializers usually respond to stories or illustrations that relate to them and their goals.

Like the socializer, the **relater** is a people person. Relaters tend to view things in terms of how they affect people and relationships. Relaters also need a lot of reassurance once the sale has been completed. To successfully sell to a relater, salespeople must be supportive and somewhat personal. They must never seem to be in a hurry to get the sale and terminate the contact. It is important that salespeople study the relater's feelings and emotional needs as well as his or her business needs.

The **thinker** is an idea person who is precise, efficient, and well-organized. Thinkers are not interested in just words; they must be won through actions, and it is important that they be given solid, factual evidence to digest. To successfully

Exhibit 7 Four Personality Types

Source: Adapted from information developed by Jim Cathcart of Cathcart, Alessandra & Associates, Inc.

sell to a thinker, salespeople must be well-prepared and have all the answers to any questions the thinker might ask. Since thinkers are task-oriented, they will get right to the point and will want the facts presented in a logical manner. In fact, logic is the key word when dealing with thinkers; they want logical solutions to problems. Documentation is essential when dealing with this personality type.

Training Techniques. Although methods of training vary from property to property, there are several common techniques that many properties use:

1. *Simulated sales calls.* These are sales calls acted out by the sales staff. A new salesperson can make a sales presentation and be critiqued by other staff

members. When videotaping is used, the new salesperson can view his or her performance and make corrections as necessary.

2. *Double calling.* There are three types of **double calling**—calls on which a new salesperson is accompanied by the director of sales or a senior salesperson. On *joint calls,* supervisors are there as equal team members to help sell. On *coaching calls,* supervisors observe but do not take part. On *model calls,* supervisors conduct the sales call to demonstrate selling skills. There are drawbacks to double calling, however: it takes two people to make the call, and the new salesperson may feel nervous, resulting in a poor presentation.

3. *Market segmentation drills.* Since all selling is based on customer needs satisfaction, it is important that salespeople understand the needs, characteristics, and requirements of each market segment. New and experienced salespeople can meet to discuss market segment characteristics and the sales tactics that work best with each segment.

4. *Case study exercises.* In this training exercise, a hotel's sales staff is challenged to formulate a sales action plan for a property other than its own. It may be a competitor's property or an imaginary property. This exercise hones sales strategies that may then be applied to the staff's own property.

5. *In-basket drills.* The trainee is given a stack of written communications (letters, messages, memos, and directives) to act on within a limited period of time. This exercise provides insights into how well the salesperson judges priorities and uses time.

The success of sales training can be measured by the performance of the sales staff. At the end of training, each salesperson should be able to:

- Explain the property's marketing plan.
- Prepare a property fact book.
- Conduct sales tours of the property.
- Understand how accounts are established and approved, the property's policy on advance deposits for groups, and credit policies of the hotel as they apply to functions.
- Research information on current and potential accounts.
- Prepare sales correspondence.
- Prepare for and complete sales calls.
- Prepare sales call and booking reports and interpret monthly sales progress reports.
- Use the sales office's computer system.
- Use the sales office's filing system.
- Analyze the financial performance of the sales office by interpreting the income and expense items on the hotel's profit and loss statement that are directly affected by the sales office.

Time spent giving the sales staff a firm training foundation is time well invested. The value of continuing education for the sales staff is also important. In-house seminars and industry courses such as those offered by the American Hotel & Lodging Educational Institute will help ensure that a sales staff develops to its full potential.

Managing Salespeople

Managing hospitality salespeople is a specialized type of personnel management for several reasons.[5] First, in today's highly competitive market, it is often necessary for salespeople to be away from home and family for extended periods of time. Salespeople are also away from the sales office, making it difficult for them to form close ties with the rest of the property's sales team. Additionally, the business of selling can have certain psychological effects. For example, it is normal for a salesperson to get depressed or feel discouraged if he or she has put on a dynamic presentation and the client doesn't buy.

A sales manager must become involved in a number of areas to ensure that sales volume goals are met or exceeded and costly personnel turnover is kept to a minimum. Sales management involves training and motivating salespeople, scheduling them and assigning accounts, and supervising them.

Scheduling salespeople involves analyzing both the needs of the property and the strengths and weaknesses of individual salespeople. If a property targets business travelers, for example, it is important to select a salesperson who can relate well to and is well-received by this market segment. In addition, other factors must be considered when assigning salespeople to accounts. Does the account require extensive travel? If so, is the salesperson free to travel, or does his or her family situation prohibit extensive travel? Is the salesperson people oriented or detail oriented? Would he or she work better with decision-makers who are "directors" or "relater" types? Does the salesperson have good time management skills, or instead require close supervision?

Even if the sales manager places salespeople in accounts suitable for their talents and strengths, salespeople still need motivation on a periodic basis. In most cases, money is a less effective motivator than personal recognition. It is important that salespeople be given incentives, of course, but it is often more effective to provide personal encouragement, especially if the salesperson is having an "off" period.

Supervising the efforts of the sales staff is an ongoing process, but it is often difficult to gauge effort in selling situations. Many sales managers feel that monitoring sales quotas is enough, and a periodic review of a salesperson's weekly activity report (see Exhibit 8) is all the supervision given. Other sales managers more closely supervise their personnel by periodically testing them on their knowledge, including asking them to give sample presentations to ensure that their performances are up to property standards. Their personal quotas are also reviewed on a regular basis to ensure that they are performing to the best of their ability.[6]

Assigning Account Responsibility. One of the key elements of sales management is the assigning of accounts. Unfortunately, this is often done in a haphazard manner. A director of sales may have three salespeople, for example, and decide to

Exhibit 8 Sample Weekly Activity Report

Weekly Booking Activity Report

Page ___ of ___

Hotel ____________________ Reporting Period ________ Year ________

Name of Group	*DCT	Dates	Room Nts	Room Rates	Room Revenue	Food Covers	Bev. Covers	F&B Revenue	MTG RM Revenue	**DES.

*D - Definite
C - Cancellation
T - Tentative
**Designation
N - New Business
R - Repeat Business
U - Unsolicited Business
CW - City Wide
SO - Regional Sales Office

	Room Nights	Covers	$
Group Rm Sales			
Group Rm Cxl.			
Net Sales			
Total Food			
Total Beverage			
Total Mtg. Rm.			
F&B Cxl.			
Mtg. Rm. Cxl.			
Net Sales			
TOTAL NET SALES			

	Per Calls			Telephone Calls			Correspondence		
	WK	MTH	YTD	WK	MTH	YTD	WK	MTH	YTD
GM									
DDS									
DOS									
SR									
SR									
SS									
TOT									

Manager ________ Sales Director ________ Date ________

A weekly activity report is used to monitor the performance of the sales staff. This form not only tracks the number of sales calls made and other activity goals, but also details room nights booked and the dollar value of group business. (Courtesy of Quality Inns)

assign one to each targeted market segment: one to corporate business, one to the leisure market, and one to tour and wholesale business. While this may seem adequate on the surface, how equitable—and effective—are these assignments if 65 percent of the property's business comes from the corporate market, 30 percent is from leisure travelers, and only 5 percent comes from tours?

The director of sales may realize this, and decide instead to put two of the salespeople on corporate accounts; one will handle corporate group business while the other will handle individual transient business. But this arrangement leaves other business, such as catering, relegated to yet other contacts at the property—a situation that can pose problems, since most businesses prefer to work with one individual, and the property is wasting valuable time and labor by having two or more people servicing the same account.

One answer to this dilemma is to assign salespeople to particular accounts rather than to market segments. That is, give one salesperson responsibility for all business generated by an organization. Rather than having three or four salespeople calling about different segments of a company's business—corporate, individual, relocation, catering, and so on—managers may assign one salesperson to an account as the property's contact for all types of business. This type of account assignment is helpful both to the client, who can now contact one person for all company needs, and to the salesperson, who can learn the client's preferences and build the rapport necessary to solicit additional business.

When assigning account responsibility, several factors must be considered. These include the number of accounts, the geographic area (territory), and the market segments that will be covered by each salesperson. In terms of the number of accounts, the general manager or director of sales must determine how many can be adequately handled. It is usually best to assign the same number of accounts to each salesperson rather than having one responsible for 500, another for 250, and so on.

The location of accounts must also be considered when determining the number of accounts a salesperson can adequately handle. A salesperson assigned to a local area, for example, would have far easier access to his or her accounts than a salesperson who must spend a great deal of time traveling to service accounts. The market segment(s) assigned to salespeople can also be a determining factor in the number of accounts to be assigned. A salesperson handling the account of a large corporation, for example, may have to spend more time on this account, which could involve monthly meetings, quarterly sales rallies, and a large yearly convention, than a salesperson who is handling the account of a nonprofit organization that stages one benefit a year.

Since there are so many variables in assigning account responsibility, account assignments should be evaluated periodically. This allows the sales manager to make adjustments when necessary, such as assigning additional salespeople to a particularly productive market segment or repositioning a salesperson who shows particular strengths in a marketing area.

Evaluating Salespeople

Evaluating the hotel's salespeople plays an important part in evaluating the success of the property's sales efforts—and can be a key in motivating salespeople to do a better job. When evaluations are seen as a tool to make them more successful, salespeople are more likely to be receptive to the idea of periodic evaluations. Sales managers can create this atmosphere by stressing that this is the primary purpose for evaluations and establishing two-way communication that allows salespeople to respond to management perceptions and make suggestions on how to improve the sales process.

Evaluations often involve looking at how well the salesperson met personal quotas. While it is important to reach activity quotas such as number of phone calls and personal sales calls made, performance goals such as room nights booked and revenue generated are better indicators of effectiveness. Quality of calls is more important than quantity. A salesperson can make more than the assigned number of calls, but still bring in less business than expected.

Performance appraisals can also cover a number of other areas:

- Number of new prospects developed. A ratio of two to three new leads per ten cold calls is acceptable.

- Amount of time spent selling. Appointment calls take more time than cold calls. Thirty minutes to one hour is appropriate for appointment calls, while salespeople can generally make three to four cold calls on new prospects in one hour.
- Number of proposals sent out.
- Number of follow-ups on trace files.
- Number of site inspections conducted and business generated.
- Percentage of room nights booked during high-need times for the property.

Salespeople can be rated as "strong," "proficient," or "improvement needed" in each of these areas. General comments on overall progress are also often included at the conclusion of the evaluation. Evaluations should be used to determine what steps need to be taken to improve performance in weak areas. Specific goals, action steps to achieve these goals, and a timeline for each step should be outlined for the salesperson.

To improve sales performance, evaluations should be made on at least a quarterly basis and on preset dates, allowing ample time for management to prepare for the evaluation and conduct the evaluation itself. Waiting for a yearly review leaves too much time for minor areas of difficulty to develop into major problems. Frequent evaluations allow for timely feedback that can enhance the salesperson's performance. Frequent feedback also allows management to determine if suggested changes are actually being put into action.

With new salespeople, frequent evaluations are especially crucial. Managers must take the time to work with these salespeople on at least a weekly, or, better still, a daily basis to ensure that they understand what is expected of them.

To assist with evaluations, each salesperson should be required to maintain a **reader file.** A reader file is a file folder that contains copies of all internal and external memos and correspondence. This file can be reviewed on a weekly basis by the director of sales or general manager to make certain that each salesperson's appraisal is based not only on the volume of correspondence, but on its quality as well.

Compensating Salespeople

Most properties pay a new salesperson a straight salary for the first six to twelve months on the job. This policy enables new salespeople to establish a client base, since most commissions are paid only after business is realized. After the prescribed salary-only period, salespeople are usually compensated on a salary plus commission basis.

There are many variables for determining the salary structure for salespeople: the geographic area, the level of experience, salaries offered by competitors, and sales quotas are a few examples.

Sales Incentive Programs. Sales incentive programs offer rewards separate from a salesperson's regular pay and commissions, and are provided to build team spirit, give extra recognition to good performers, and reduce sales staff turnover. Incentive programs can also be used to spark competition between departments. Incentives may include cash bonuses (on top of commissions), merchandise (cars, furs, and so on), vacation trips (in the case of chain properties, sometimes to another property in the chain), or a combination of rewards. No matter what type of incentive program is developed, it must be designed to give individuals or departments a specific reward for meeting a specific objective. Such programs should also be designed to benefit the property by encouraging salespeople to bring in extra revenue when the property most needs it.

Supplemental Sales Staff

It is often impractical or uneconomical for individual hotels to be represented nationwide by their in-house sales staff. Therefore, many properties have looked for ways to supplement their staff's sales efforts.

Regional and National Sales Offices. A regional sales office usually consists of a regional director of sales, area directors of sales, senior account executives, account executives, a research director, an office manager, and a clerical staff. Regional sales personnel often work in individual hotels within the region before advancing to the regional level.

A hotel chain's regional sales office may present workshops, seminars, and receptions to attract local executives desiring to learn more about the chain, and may provide news releases and feature columns for use in local newspapers. While the responsibilities of regional sales offices are typically directed toward promotions and public relations, the offices can also scout potential business and develop sales leads in a particular geographic area. For example, a regional sales office for Hilton in Chicago not only sells Hilton's Chicago hotels to people in other cities; it also sells Hilton hotels from all over the country to people within a prescribed radius of Chicago.

Regional sales offices maintain extensive records regarding business prospects in the region. The regional office's computer data banks can offer concise listings of group business and provide information on a client's needs and past meeting history. These systems give instant electronic access to group booking data, including availability and rates. With such information at their fingertips, many regional sales representatives are now empowered to block space, print out proposals for any hotel on the system, and book business on the spot. The hotel's director of sales is then notified by electronic mail for approval of the agreement.

Today, most U.S. hotel chains have regional offices in major cities such as New York, Los Angeles, and Washington, D.C., particularly if the chain serves groups. Washington, D.C., for example, has over 25 regional offices to serve the potential business of that city. A number of hotel chains also maintain a regional sales office at their corporate headquarters. This allows the close monitoring of the chain's operations, and is especially effective if corporate headquarters happens to be located in an industrial or population center or in a popular travel destination.

Hotel Representation Companies. Many properties are turning to outside hotel representatives for sales assistance. These **independent hotel representatives** or "reps" serve as out-of-town or market-source business representatives for noncompeting properties. Hiring independent hotel representatives is often more economical than setting up a sales office.

Since hotels have different needs, the services provided by reps can vary widely. In some cases, the rep may be hired as a field salesperson, soliciting clients who are impractical for the hotel's in-house staff to reach. A property in Florida, for example, may find it more economical to hire a rep in Boston than to send its own salespeople to that city. Other hotels use large representation companies, such as the Krisam Group and Washington, D.C.–based Associated Luxury Hotels. Services provided by these firms include consulting, market analysis, advertising, and public relations in addition to field sales.

Technological advances have allowed large hotel representation firms to go global, and many have either developed their own global reservations systems or have partnered with large reservations companies. The advantage of a worldwide reservation network for independent hotels is that it gives them the same ability to distribute their guestrooms as chains such as Hilton, Marriott, and Hyatt. The principal global representation firms include London-based Supranational Hotels, Frankfurt-based SRS-World Hotels, Calgary-based VIP International Corporation, and Dallas-based Pegasus Solutions.

Since a property's rep is an extension of the property's own sales and reservations offices, it is important that the property choose a rep who understands the property's marketing needs. There are several questions that should be answered before selecting a rep:

1. Does this rep represent any major competitors?
2. Does this rep specialize in our property's target markets?
3. Can this rep provide individual attention to our property or does his or her workload preclude working closely with our sales staff?
4. Can this rep's marketing contacts and sales techniques benefit our property?
5. What is this rep's record of client satisfaction?
6. Does this rep operate adequate facilities—telephone services, field sales staff, reservation capabilities, and so on?
7. Can this rep deliver the supporting services (advertising, computerized booking, and so on) our property needs?
8. How does this rep compare in cost with other reps who represent properties similar to ours?
9. Does the rep have offices or contacts in the cities that are likely to be our major market areas?
10. Is this rep truly interested in representing our property?

You may wish to consult similar-size properties who are using a representative that you are considering. Ask them about the effectiveness of the representative, especially in regard to areas in which you feel you may have difficulties.

It is also important to determine how the independent hotel rep will fit into the property's sales organization and how the rep will be paid. Will the rep be a salaried agent of the property, or will he or she become an extra salesperson who works on a commission basis only? A rep is often hired on a contract basis—paid a set fee plus a predetermined commission percentage on the volume of business that he or she directly books for the hotel. It is important with commission arrangements to set clear booking and pricing guidelines; reps should be given acceptable rate structures to ensure that they don't "give away the house" just to receive their commissions!

Once a rep has been selected, the property's sales staff should establish a defined line of communication between the property and the rep. The rep's productivity and level of service will largely depend on input from the property.

Developing the Marketing and Sales Office Communication System

For a marketing and sales office to operate at maximum efficiency, clear lines of communication must be established both within the sales office and with other areas of the property. Good communication ensures that all members of the property's sales team have the same information and that potential problems are kept to a minimum. A sales and marketing office relies on various methods to communicate ideas and information, including holding meetings, keeping sales records, and establishing filing systems.

Sales and Marketing Meetings

Regularly scheduled meetings are an essential part of a successful marketing effort. To ensure maximum production and communication, the head of the sales office may want to hold brief daily meetings with salespeople to discuss daily sales calls and the next day's schedule. He or she may also schedule various other meetings, including:

- Weekly staff meetings
- Weekly function meetings
- Monthly sales meetings
- Marketing committee team meetings
- Annual or semiannual sales meetings for all employees

No matter what type of meeting is held, it should be meaningful. A meeting should not be held just for the purpose of getting together. For maximum effectiveness, a meeting should always have an agenda, be held at a time that does not conflict with selling time (perhaps at 7:30 A.M. or 4:30 P.M.), last less than an hour, and, last but not least, be productive. For maximum effectiveness, minutes of the meeting should be distributed to attendees, and the hospitality firm should create a method to measure the results of strategies and tactics discussed during the meeting.

Weekly Staff Meetings. Weekly meetings of the sales staff should be conducted by the head of the sales effort—the director of marketing and sales, the director of sales, or the sales manager (the person heading up the meeting will vary depending on the size of the property and the structure of the marketing and sales department or sales office). These meetings should include the general manager and any department heads whose departments will be discussed. Topics that may be covered in a typical weekly staff meeting are new business prospects, tentative and new bookings, conventions, client service procedures, promotions, publicity, and lost business. An open discussion and brainstorming period should be a part of weekly sales meetings to encourage a mutual exchange of ideas and information.

Weekly Function Meetings. These meetings are held with department heads to review upcoming group events. At these meetings, departments involved in serving groups review each group's meeting agenda (commonly called the specification sheet or meeting résumé) item by item to ensure that everyone understands what is going to take place and to nail down any last-minute details. The property's convention service manager will generally chair these meetings.

Monthly Sales Meetings. These meetings are held to discuss tentative and definite bookings for the next month or quarter, review progress made in achieving sales goals, and discuss new property promotions. Monthly sales meetings are usually attended by all sales personnel.

Marketing Committee Team Meetings. These meetings involve department heads and knowledgeable representatives from each area of the hotel. They are essentially "meetings of the minds" to ensure that every area of the property is adequately covered in the property's marketing plan. The frequency and types of meetings held by marketing teams are usually determined by the head of the marketing and sales department or the general manager.

Annual or Semiannual Sales Meetings for All Employees. These meetings are held to discuss the marketing plan with the property's entire staff. Such meetings provide an opportunity to obtain ideas and suggestions from all employees. The marketing plan presented to the staff can be fairly simple and abbreviated, but it should give all employees an overview of the function of the marketing and sales department and outline each employee's role in the plan. Sales and advertising programs should also be discussed.

Sales Records and Forms

Sales records are a vital part of a sales office's communication system. They are important in servicing accounts and generating repeat business. It is essential that salespeople familiarize themselves with sales forms, learn to complete them properly, and file them in accordance with sales office procedures. In sales offices with computers, the data from the forms is input by the clerical staff, and the information is used to produce a variety of computer-generated reports and analyses.

In most cases, the salesperson's involvement with sales records will begin with a **call report,** a form generated during a sales call on a prospective client (see Exhibit 9). The call report is then placed in the organization's or individual's account file, and a notation for follow-up is placed in the trace file. (Account and trace files will be discussed later in the chapter.)

When a sales presentation is made, a tentative booking is usually offered if no definite booking is sold (see Exhibit 10). Once a definite booking has been made,

Exhibit 9 Sample Sales Call Report

054492

EMBASSY SUITES

Sales Call Report

Trace Date ____________________
(Month) (Year)

Type of Call: ______Personal
______Telephone
______Walk-in/Call-in

GENERAL INFORMATION

Account Name ____________________
Division/Department ____________________
Address ____________________
City ____________ State _____ Zip _____
Telephone ( ) ____________________

Individual Called ____________________
Title ____________________
Other Contact(s) ____________________

REMARKS

SAMPLE

ACTION STEP

Potential for other Cities ____________________

Sales Representative ____________________
Date of Call ____________________

File Copy

Welcome to the Suite Life®

This form is used by salespeople to document information gathered from personal, telephone, or walk-in sales calls. The form provides for general information about the account, remarks on the needs of the group, and action steps that can be taken to sell business to the account. A notation to call the account on the date indicated on this form will be placed in the trace file for the salesperson's future reference. Note the line at the top of the form for a trace date for follow-up. (Courtesy of Embassy Suites, Inc.)

Exhibit 10 Sample Booking Form

METROPOLITAN BUSINESS FORMS - DALLAS, TX

ANATOLE DALLAS CONVENTION BOOKING FORM

DATE: ______

Booked By: ______

Assisted By: ______

______Definite ______Tentative ______Option

Decision Date: ______

Group

Contact

Phone

Address

City State Zip

Assigned To:
Convention Services: ______ Catering ______

Reservations:
____Direct
____Res. Card
____Rooming List
____Housing Bureau
____Cut Off Date

Comp Policy
____1 per 50
____Spec. Staff Rate
No. ______ Rate ______
Extra Comps ______

Scope
____Nat'l
____State
____Corp.
____Tour/Travel
____Market

Attendance:

Overflow:

Billing:
____I.P.O.
____Rm/Tx To Master
____All to Master
____Catering to Master
____Advance Deposit

Rates: Singles	Doubles	Suites	Concierge

Guest Room Block:

Day/Date	Room/Suites
TOTAL ROOM NIGHTS	

Special Instructions:

Credit References:

Meeting Space ______Yes ______No

Meeting & Catering Requirements: EXHIBITS ______Yes ______Number ______ Set Up ______ Tear Down

DAY	DATE	TIME	FUNCTION	SETUP	ATTENDANCE	ROOM	RENTAL

Book Administrator ______ Date Posted ______

FILE

This sample booking form, for booking firm convention dates, is one form that may be used to process sold business. In some sales offices, there may be separate forms for tentative and firm bookings as well as change forms that reflect changes to an initial booking. (Courtesy of Anatole Hotel, Dallas, Texas)

the salesperson may be required to write and/or sign a contract with the client. If the original booking information changes, a change sheet is required. If the meeting or convention is cancelled, a lost business report must be filled out and filed with the sales manager (see Exhibit 11).

While most hotels today use computerized systems for recordkeeping and managing marketing and sales efforts, some smaller properties still use manual systems. If a computer system is used, it is still customary to maintain "hard copy" files and maintain a paper trail of customer business. Even when correspondence, contracts, and other documents inherent to sales efforts are sent electronically (via e-mail or fax), they are usually printed out and placed in a customer file.

In this section, we will discuss the basic forms that are used for the sales function. We will first show the manual versions of each before illustrating its computerized counterpart. Later in the chapter, we will show how computers are used to manage the service function and how technology can enhance sales efforts.

The Function Book—Manual Version. The key to successful function and banquet space control is the hotel's **function book**. This record shows the occupancies and vacancies of function and banquet rooms and aids in the effective planning of functions.

Function books are normally divided into pages for each day of the year, with sections set aside for each meeting or function room. Information recorded in the function book includes the organization or group scheduling the space; the name, address, and telephone number of the group's contact person; the type of function; the time required for the function; the total time required for preparation, breakdown, and cleanup; the number of people expected; the type of setup(s) required; the rates quoted; the nature of the contract; and any other pertinent remarks to assist property personnel in staging a successful function. Function book entries are always made in pencil because changes can occur even when a commitment seems firm.

To prevent mismatching of entries or double-bookings, a property should have just one function book maintained by only one person. In many cases, the person having control of the function book is the senior sales executive, but because sales personnel often travel frequently, the senior sales executive may designate one clerk to coordinate all entries.

When a property has a catering department, it is wise to locate it close to the marketing and sales office so that the function book can be easily shared. (Like the sales office, the catering department does its own selling, usually soliciting local banquets and functions.)

Having a single person control the function book is essential. It is not uncommon for the sales office and the catering department to compete for the same function space. At some properties, sales office and catering department managers who want to reserve function space must submit a function book reservation sheet (see Exhibit 12) to the person in charge of the function book. This ensures that difficulties do not arise from a decentralized, undefined procedure of recording function arrangements.

There may be instances in which the same space is desired by two groups. In this case, sales managers will try to determine the best "fit" for both the hotel and

Exhibit 11 Sample Lost Business Report

OPRYLAND HOTEL

Group Booking Status Change or Lost Business Report

Today's Date ____________ Salesperson ________ FILE # ________

Month Day Year

Current Meeting Dates ____________

New Meeting Dates ____________

Organization ____________

Contact ____________

Address ____________

____________ / Phone # ________

- ☐ Group Name Change
- ☐ Contact Name Change
- ☐ Change in # of Rooms
- ☐ Change in dates
- ☐ Tentative Cancellation
- ☐ Def. Cancellation

STATUS CHANGE

YEAR	DAY													
	Date													
	Rms													

Reason for Cancelling (Tentative or Definite) ____________

Where is Business going? ____________

Comments ____________

This form is used to document any business either cancelled or changed. In some sales offices, change forms are separate from a lost business report, and serve to note changes in the name of the group, the name of the contact person, the number of rooms reserved, and/or booking dates. A lost business report, which can also be a separate form, documents bookings which have been either tentatively or definitely cancelled. This form is used to follow up on the reason(s) for the cancellation, and is forwarded to the head of the sales office for review. (Courtesy of Opryland Hotel, Nashville, Tennessee)

Exhibit 12 Sample Function Book Reservation Sheet

US Grant HOTEL

FUNCTION BOOK RESERVATION SHEET

Group Name ______________________ Comments ______________________

Contact ______________________

Address ______________________

Phone ______________________

Dates In House ______________________

AGENDA

DAY/DATE	TIME	FUNCTION	SET-UP	# OF PEOPLE	ROOM NAME

Meeting Space Charges:

Sales Rep ______________________

Date ______________________

Option Date ______________________

Date Entered ______________________

Entered By ______________________

At many properties, sales office and catering department managers fill out reservation request forms and submit them to the one person responsible for monitoring the hotel's function space. Use of forms such as this one helps prevent double-bookings. (Courtesy of US Grant Hotel, San Diego, California)

the group. Factors to be considered are the likelihood that the space will actually be filled, the estimated profitability of each group, the status of the group (regular client or new business), the likelihood of repeat business, the long-term profitability of each group, the possibility that one group would consider an alternate date, and the group's convention history.

The Guestroom Control Book—Manual Version. Every hotel soliciting group business should have **a guestroom control book**. A guestroom control book is used to monitor the number of guestrooms committed to groups. The guestroom control book should list the number of guestrooms allotted to each group and indicate whether the allotment is firm or tentative. To make changes easier, entries are penciled in.

Most properties want a mix of group, individual, and tour business, so they establish a maximum allotment of guestrooms available to groups. This quota is usually set by the general manager and the head of the marketing and sales department, and special care must be taken to ensure that the sales staff does not exceed the prescribed allotment.

Because front desk, reservations, and sales office employees all book guestroom business, it is important that they all be aware of group allotments. The guestroom control book provides the marketing and sales office with the maximum number of guestrooms it may sell to groups on a given day. The remaining guestrooms (and any rooms allotted to groups that are not sold) are available for individual guests—these are the rooms that can be sold by front desk and reservations staff. Therefore, there should be constant communication among these personnel to avoid any overlapping room sales.

The guestroom control book is kept in the marketing and sales office and is usually administered and controlled by the director of sales. In large hotels with a sizable volume of group sales, however, entries are often coordinated by a diary control clerk, who is so called because the guestroom control book is called the hotel diary at some properties.

The guestroom control book is used to record all pertinent details regarding group room sales, including confirmations, options, and holds on rooms. A *confirmation* is definite group business that has been confirmed in writing and gives the specific dates on which the group will be staying at the hotel. An *option* is given when a group is unable to make a firm confirmation of room dates—perhaps an approval by a superior is required. A tentative *hold* is then placed on the rooms requested and an *option date* (or *release date* or *cutoff*) is set. The group must then confirm the requested rooms by the option date or release the rooms to enable the property to sell them to other clients. Reputable hoteliers will not confirm other orders for the requested rooms during the hold period. If a second group is interested in the same dates, this group may be given an option after being told about the first group's option. This puts the second group in a position to book if the first group releases the rooms on its option date.

The Function Book and Guestroom Control Book—Automated Versions. Most hotels have computerized their function book and guestroom control book. This method still provides control, since only authorized personnel can add or change information (while information is being changed, the system goes into a "read

Exhibit 13 Sample Function Book Report

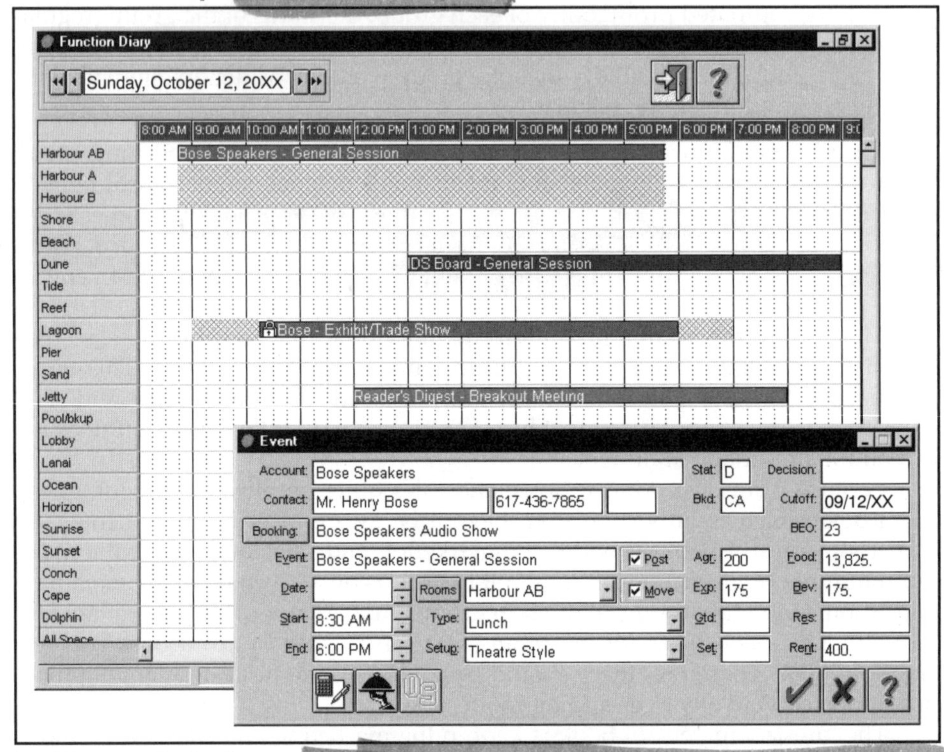

In this computerized report, function rooms are listed down the left side of the screen, and hours of the chosen day are displayed across the top. Functions are blocked by room and time of day, and pop-up windows give easy access to details about functions, including booking status, cutoff date, revenue forecasts, account contacts, and so on. Source: Delphi 7/Newmarket Software Systems, Inc., Durham, New Hampshire.

only" mode until the information is updated). The information, however, is readily available to salespeople, either in-house or from a remote location.

Sample function book reports can be displayed on a salesperson's terminal or printed as a report to banquet and convention service departments (see Exhibit 13). These reports list each function room and give an overall picture of the property's monthly activities to prevent double-booking and ensure that any space available is readily apparent to salespeople.

Before Hyatt Hotels updated their function books, says Gordon Kerr, Hyatt's senior vice president of management information systems, "each hotel kept this giant diary with function room bookings written in it. If a customer called Hyatt headquarters in Chicago to book a function room in San Francisco, for example, the manager of the San Francisco hotel had to be called to check availability. Customers eager to book space would wait hours, or even days, to receive a reply. By that time, many would-be customers had found space elsewhere. With the computerized system, Hyatt users can check availability and book function rooms at any connected hotel from any hotel in the network."[7]

Wendy Bonvechio, director of sales and marketing, Sheraton Seattle Hotel & Towers, says that "automation is very important to our business. Customers have seen a drastic change in how quickly their requests are processed since we automated several years ago. A problem that has been completely eliminated is the inevitable double-booking that occurred with the manual systems. With automation, the computer won't allow you to double-book. Our customers demand automation because it's quicker, makes us more efficient, and virtually eliminates mistakes. It's no longer an option, but a necessity in order to compete in today's market."[8]

Also available are sales and catering software packages that supplement information on the function sheet. An automated sales system can produce kitchen reports (menu items needed, listed by preparation area), room setup reports (resources requested for events on function sheets), and revenue forecast reports (anticipated revenue based on function sheets).

The guestroom control book can also be computerized. A major challenge for non-automated sales offices is maintaining an up-to-date and accurate guestroom control book that indicates the status of guestroom sales to groups. For example: a meeting planner calls and requests the best rate the hotel can offer for 50 rooms for three nights in April. The planner also requires a general session meeting room and three breakout rooms. To respond to this request, the salesperson would first have to match availability dates in April in the guestroom control book with open dates for four meeting rooms in the function book. The salesperson would also want to double-check the accuracy of the information in each book with several members of the sales staff—and check with the department manager—before quoting a rate.

In an automated sales office, however, the salesperson would be able to respond much more quickly. Both the guestroom control book and the function book could be displayed simultaneously on the salesperson's computer terminal and the salesperson could use a search function to match the meeting planner's needs with the property's guestroom and meeting room availability. This would enable the salesperson to check the status of the meeting planner's preferred dates and suggest alternate dates if the requested dates are booked. In many cases, rates are also programmed into the system, eliminating the need for the salesperson to check with the department manager for rate quotes.

In addition to being displayed on a computer terminal, information in the guestroom control book can easily be printed in concise, accurate computer reports (see Exhibit 14). These reports, too, offer instant access to the same information to authorized staff members. "Definites" and "tentatives" are clearly defined to prevent booking errors.

Filing Systems

There are several types of filing methods that may be used for storing client data and other sales information. These methods fall into three general categories:

1. *Alphabetical filing.* Records are filed in alphabetical order by the title of the organization, firm, or association with whom the property is doing business.

Exhibit 14 Sample Guestroom Control Report

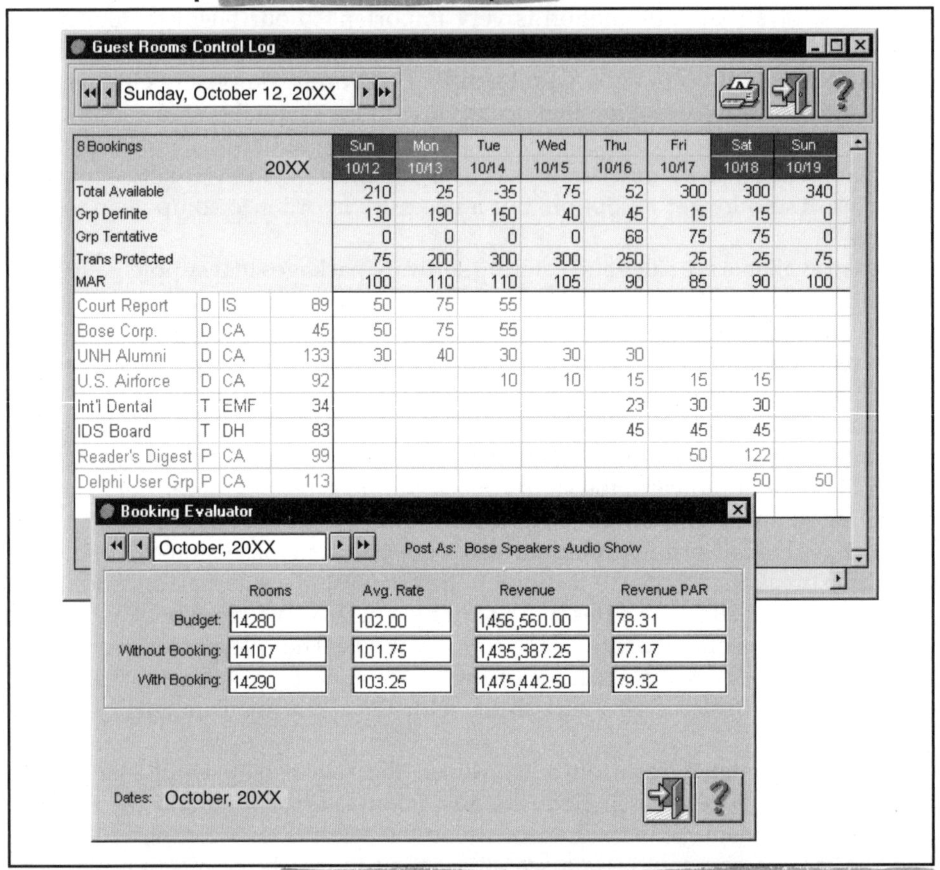

8 Bookings			20XX	Sun 10/12	Mon 10/13	Tue 10/14	Wed 10/15	Thu 10/16	Fri 10/17	Sat 10/18	Sun 10/19
Total Available				210	25	-35	75	52	300	300	340
Grp Definite				130	190	150	40	45	15	15	0
Grp Tentative				0	0	0	0	68	75	75	0
Trans Protected				75	200	300	300	250	25	25	75
MAR				100	110	110	105	90	85	90	100
Court Report	D	IS	89	50	75	55					
Bose Corp.	D	CA	45	50	75	55					
UNH Alumni	D	CA	133	30	40	30	30	30			
U.S. Airforce	D	CA	92			10	10	15	15	15	
Int'l Dental	T	EMF	34					23	30	30	
IDS Board	T	DH	83					45	45	45	
Reader's Digest	P	CA	99						50	122	
Delphi User Grp	P	CA	113							50	50

	Rooms	Avg. Rate	Revenue	Revenue PAR
Budget:	14280	102.00	1,456,560.00	78.31
Without Booking:	14107	101.75	1,435,387.25	77.17
With Booking:	14290	103.25	1,475,442.50	79.32

This computerized report allows users to assess the impact of the bookings of individual groups on budgeted targets for rooms sales, average rate, and revenue per available room (RevPAR). A summary according to booking status is displayed in the shaded portion of the upper window, and individual groups are listed below the summary according to date and room status ("D" stands for "definite," "T" stands for "tentative," and so on).

Source: Delphi 7/Newmarket Software Systems, Inc., Durham, New Hampshire.

Many properties also file the names of contact people in alphabetical order. This system seems to be the easiest to implement and use.

2. *Keyword alphabetical filing.* Client information is filed alphabetically by a general category keyword that appears in the name of the client's organization; the Association of Petroleum and Oil Products would be filed under "Petroleum," for example. While this system has its advantages when a firm or organization's exact name is not known, the system may also make multiple entries under several keywords necessary for some accounts. For example, perhaps the hotel serves a police fraternal organization. The account could be filed under "Police," "Fraternal," and "Law Enforcement."

3. *Numerical.* Sales files are assigned a number and a corresponding set of file cards is kept by account number, with the name of the account listed after the number. This system is often used with computers—the salesperson or sales clerk can either key in the account number or, if the account number is not known, type in the name of the account.

Once the filing method has been established, the next step is to determine the elements of the filing system. Most hotels use three separate files to record client information: the master card file, the account file, and the trace file.

The Master Card File. Master cards are instrumental in establishing data banks of information on the needs of clients. Each master card (in a manual system, usually a standard index card) contains a summary of everything needed for an effective sales effort: the organization's name, the names and titles of key executives, addresses, phone numbers, month or months in which the group meets, the size of the group, where the group has met in the past, the group's decision-maker, and other pertinent data that can help to obtain or keep that account's business. In many cases, a trailer card—an additional card that lists divisions or departments within the account's organization—may be filed behind the master card to serve as a source of additional business.

The master card file is also a cross-reference. It can be used to see if an account file exists for a particular group without having to go to the file cabinet to look. Master card files are also used to create mailing lists and quickly obtain addresses or phone numbers for additional sales efforts or follow-ups.

Master cards are often color-coded to draw attention to specific areas of consideration: geographic location, months of meetings, follow-ups required, and size of group. Some properties also arrange master cards alphabetically by market segment. For example, IBM and Xerox would be sorted alphabetically under "Corporate Business." Other properties may not separate master cards by market segment, but may use a color code system to easily identify specific market segments within the file—an association account may be flagged in blue, a government account in yellow, and so on.

Some properties keep a geographic file of master cards. These cards are organized according to the geographic location of the decision-maker. This type of file enables sales personnel to quickly identify accounts in cities to which they are traveling. Salespeople can simply pull the names of the decision-makers located in the area they are visiting and call on them during the sales trip.

The computerized version of the master card file enables the salesperson to instantly access the account and add an unlimited amount of material to each account file. The file can be broken down into several screens (or windows) that provide a variety of additional information: account history, name of contact person, specifics on follow-up calls, or remarks that can assist other members of the marketing team in the absence of the salesperson who made the call (see Exhibit 15).

The Account File. An **account file** is a standard-size file folder holding information needed for serving a client's basic business needs (see Exhibit 16). An account file is started at the time of initial contact with a prospective client and may include

Exhibit 15 Sample Computerized Master Card

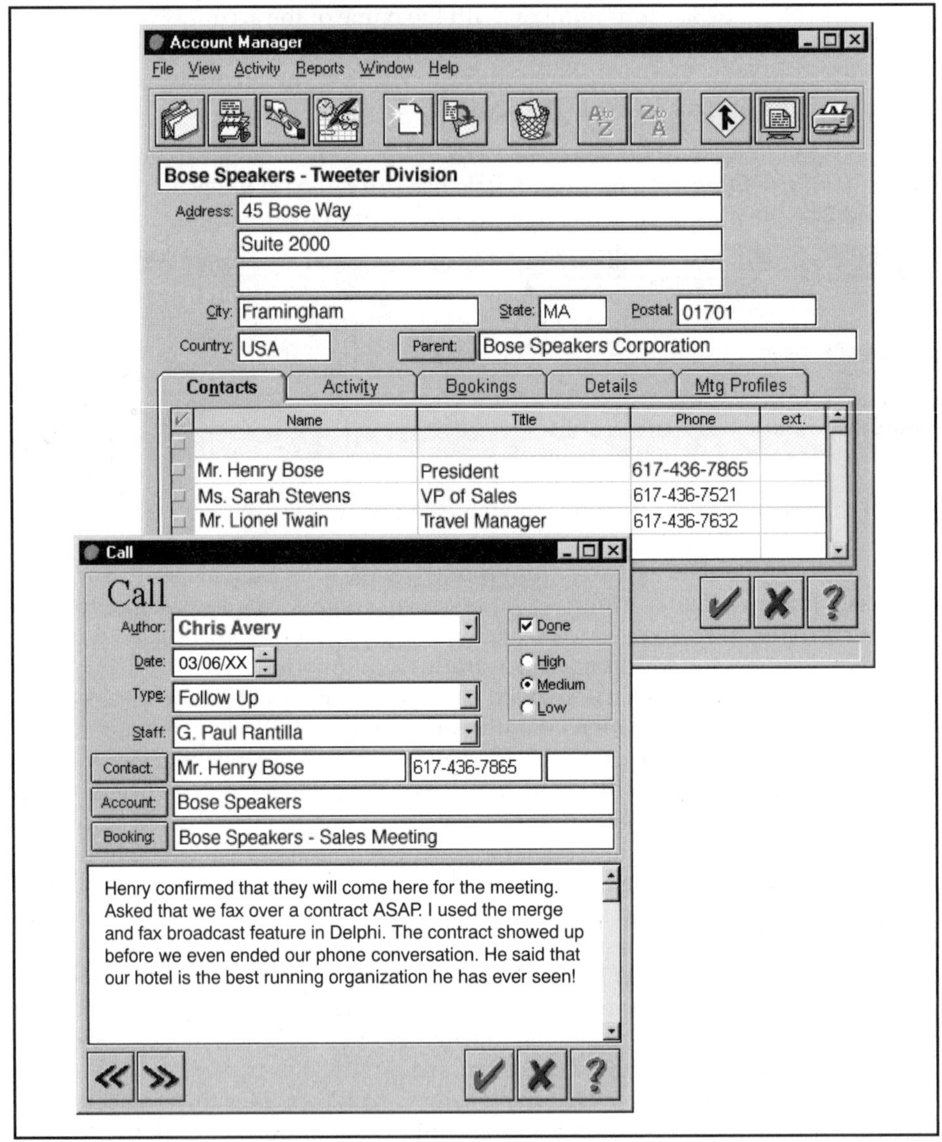

This computer program allows a salesperson to get detailed information on an account instantly. There are separate windows for the account's contacts, sales call activity on the account, a history of the account's bookings, and so on. Source: Delphi 7/Newmarket Software Systems, Inc., Durham, New Hampshire.

programs from previous conventions or meetings the organization has held, convention bureau bulletins, and information relating to the organization that has appeared in newspapers or trade journals. Sales reports and all correspondence

Exhibit 16 Sample Account File

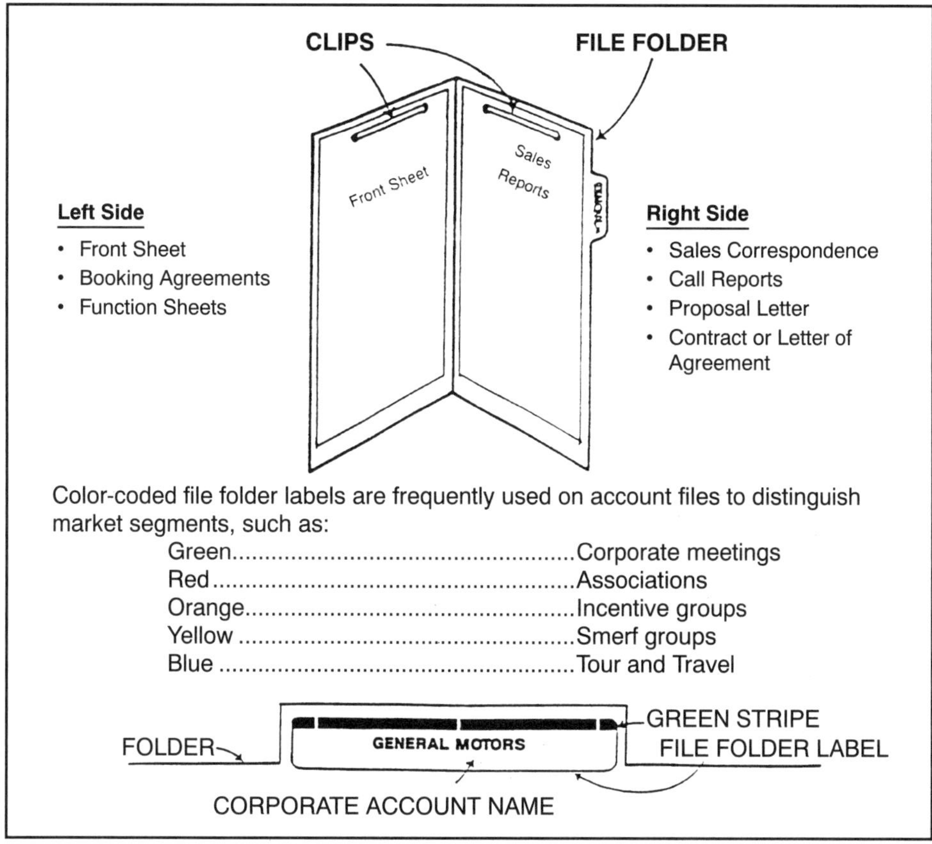

The account file is usually kept in a standard file folder and contains all of the group's information, including sales call reports, tentative and definite booking information, function sheets from past business, and correspondence generated relating to the booking. Information is placed in the file in chronological order (with the newest on top) and secured with clips to prevent loss. Like the master file, account file folders may be color-coded to call attention to specific characteristics of the group.

relating to previous efforts to secure business should also be in the file. All information in the account file should be in reverse chronological order—that is, the newest paperwork first. Account files are usually filed alphabetically.

The account file includes files on potential business as well as files on groups currently booked at the property and groups that have booked with the property in the past. Like master cards, account files are often color-coded by geographic location or, more commonly, by market segment. When a color-coding system is used, the colors used for the account files should correspond to the colors used for the master cards.

When an account file is removed, a guide card noting the name of the group, its file number, the date of removal, and the initials of the person removing the file

Exhibit 17 Sample Manual Trace File

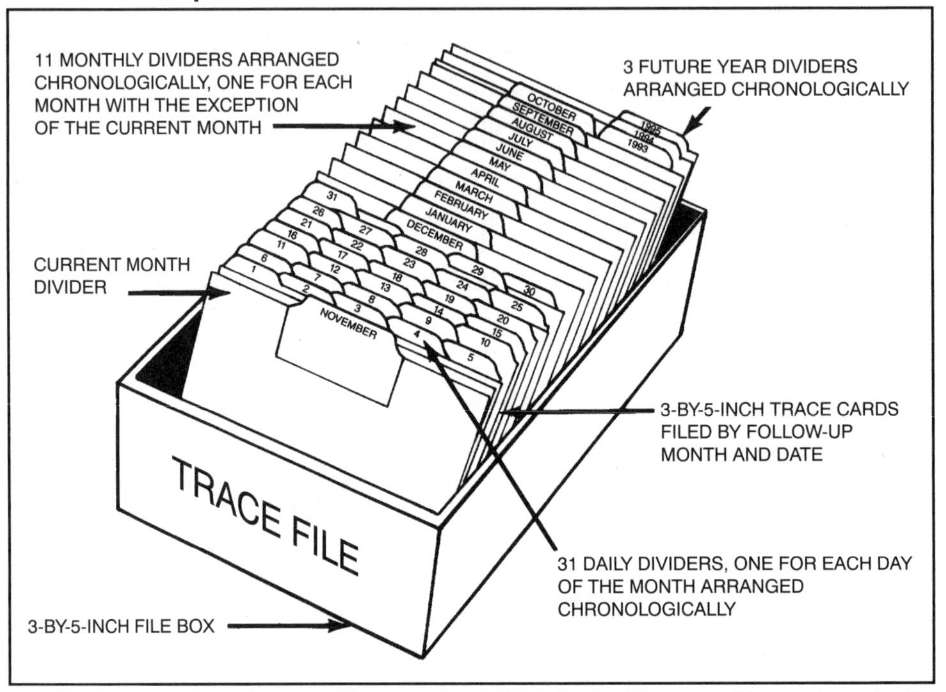

A salesperson can use the trace file as a sales call reminder. The trace file consists of a file box, 12 monthly divider cards, 31 numbered divider cards, 3-year future cards, and 3-by-5-inch index cards sometimes referred to as *trace cards*.

should be left in the file drawer in place of the file. This ensures that the sales staff will always know the whereabouts of the file.

The Trace File. The trace file, also known as a tickler file, bring-up file, or follow-up file, is an effective aid for following up an account. A reminder note or card is filed in the trace file by month and date; as seen in Exhibit 17, daily dividers are arranged chronologically for the current month. The system is used as a reminder of correspondence, telephone calls, or contacts that must be handled on a particular date.

How the trace file works. Suppose a client has reserved space for a training meeting at the property in April. The salesperson will want to contact the client no later than February 15 to finalize meeting plans, so the salesperson would slip a note or an index card (often called **a trace card**) dated February 15th into the February trace divider. On February 1, the notes and trace cards for February would be arranged according to date, and the reminder to contact the meeting planner would be placed into the 15th slot. This system, as long as it is updated and checked daily, works well, costs very little, and takes very little time to implement. An added bonus is that if a salesperson is transferred or leaves the property, there is a record of future contacts to be made that can be followed up by other members of the sales team. A trace system is absolutely essential, since most salespeople are responsible for 300 to 400 accounts. This type of system eliminates reliance on memory and ensures good follow-up.

In a computerized sales office, the trace file is automated. A trace report is printed for each salesperson every morning, and the salesperson can look at each entry and decide whether to move it to another day or act on it. Traces that have been acted upon will no longer appear on the trace report; traces awaiting action will continue to appear on future trace reports until action is taken.

Several computerized versions of the trace file are available. Specialized hotel software, such as Delphi, not only reminds salespeople of important dates, but also offers additional sales tools. The computerized trace report shown in Exhibit 18, for example, breaks down the day's business into several categories. The salesperson can take advantage of this to prioritize his or her work and schedule each day to make the most of sales opportunities. But even salespeople who do not have access to hotel-specific software can use other computer programs, such as Microsoft Outlook, to help organize their work. The Outlook program features a daily calendar and task list.

The Automated Marketing and Sales Office

A typical marketing and sales office generates an incredible amount of paperwork, and a great part of each day is spent in managing the information collected through prospecting, selling, booking, and reporting. At many properties today, much of this time-consuming and costly effort is handled with one of sales' most effective tools: a computer system.

In this section, we will take a closer look at how today's computer technology is drastically changing the face of the sales and marketing office. We will see how the computer is not only helping to eliminate time-consuming paperwork, but also how it is being used to personalize presentations, create lists of potential contacts, and forecast future demand for guest and meeting rooms.

Benefits of Automation

Hospitality industry professionals agree that, before computers, perhaps as much as 70 percent of a salesperson's time was spent on non-sales activities, such as call tracing, checking the availability of rooms, blocking rooms and space, and simply running back and forth to filing cabinets to retrieve information. The computer has changed all that. No longer is it necessary to search for lost files or prepare reports by hand; this data is readily available on individual computer terminals.

The benefits of an automated sales office are many. Computers:

- Allow tedious tasks to be accomplished quickly and efficiently.
- Allow immediate access to sales information.
- Facilitate personalized mailings based on the data in their memory banks.
- Reduce the risk of human error. When specific procedures are implemented, there is less chance of information being lost or misplaced.

Exhibit 18 Sample Computerized Trace Report

The Durham Resort

Morning Report for Ralph Johnson
September 21, 20XX

Rooming List Due

Group Name	Date	Day	Room Type	Agree	Block	Pickup	New Block
Mt. Hope Radiology Dept.	2/ 2/ 02	Wed	Run of House	25	25	_____	_______
	2/ 3/ 02	Thu	Run of House	25	25	_____	_______
	2/ 4/ 02	Fri	Run of House	300	300	_____	_______
	2/18/02	Fri	Run of House	25	25	_____	_______

Deposits Due

Group Name	Arrival Date	Trace Date	New Status/ New Trace Date
Acorn Dry Cleaning	3/20/02	1/10/02	_______ ___/___/___

Verbal Definites - Contract Due

Group Name	Arrival Date	Trace Date	New Status/ New Trace Date
Jacobs Wedding	9/1/02	1/15/02	_______ ___/___/___

Tentatives - Decision Due

Group Name	Arrival Date	Trace Date	New Status/ New Trace Date
Automobile Travelers Assn	3/24/02	11/20/01	_______/ ___/___/___
Arizona Building Company	4/30/02	12/20/01	_______/ ___/___/___

Leads - Decision Due

Group Name	Arrival Date	Trace Date	New Status/ New Trace Date
Balloon Industries	2/1/02	11/1/01	_______/ ___/___/___

Source: Delphi Newmarket Software Systems, Inc., Durham, New Hampshire

This report not only replaces the cumbersome manual trace file, but also offers additional sales tools to the salesperson. The trace report, for example, breaks down the day's business into several categories. The salesperson can take advantage of this feature to prioritize work and schedule each day to make the most of sales opportunities.

- Store information that can help the sales office direct specific sales promotions or programs to prospective clients or individual guests based on zip code, desired time periods, areas of interest, and so on.
- Simplify mass mailings, generating mailing lists (often by zip code or group type) in a fraction of the time it would take a secretary to sort through records and type letters to specified target groups.
- Enhance communication among properties, greatly facilitating the sales effort in large hotel chains.

The proliferation of personal computers and the variety of software available from a multitude of vendors have made data processing an increasingly effective and accessible tool in hotel marketing and sales offices. Tim Grover, regional director of sales and marketing for Starwood Hotels & Resorts Worldwide, states:

> For any hotel sales force, automation is critical. Delphi (computer software for hotel sales and catering) has more than 80 percent of the market; it is considered the "Microsoft" of hotel sales and catering systems. They have a Windows-based version for managing sales contracts, group room blocks, and catering space. It is also user-friendly and can generate a variety of reports. Delphi software also functions as an excellent contact manager. Every conversation with a client about an event is documented and accessible to our entire sales team. And, finally, it helps us manage our revenue more efficiently. Knowing what's on the books at any given time for both room sales and catering is a valuable asset that benefits both the customer and the hotel.[9]

Among its many applications, the Delphi system provides an "Available Dates Search" that attempts to match the needs of a prospective group with those of the hotel by providing a list of best available dates to accommodate the group (based on projected occupancy). This allows a hotel salesperson to quickly tell if a specific date is available. If an association executive calls to arrange a meeting for April 7–10, for example, a salesperson or any authorized person in the marketing and sales office can use a computer to immediately check the status of these dates, and suggest other days that the computer indicates are open if the requested days are already booked.

Additional Applications of Automation

Besides eliminating much of the drudgery of keeping records and accessing the information necessary to sell to and service customers, computers are playing an increasing role in improving sales and marketing efforts and the efficiency of property salespeople.

In this section, we will take a look at database marketing; home-based and virtual offices; lists, reports, and analysis applications; and yield and revenue management applications.

Database Marketing. One of the most important ways in which computer technology is being used is assisting the marketing and sales department in organizing and analyzing information about individual guests and groups. **Database marketing** involves using information from routine sources—guest folios, registration cards, customer surveys, the group histories of meetings, and so on—to build relationships and market the property's services most effectively.

Database management programs enable properties to store and sort such information as client bookings (including the expected and actual number of attendees), types of functions booked, average room rates for groups or individuals, average checks in restaurants, and even guests' personal preferences (nosmoking rooms, items used in a minibar, and so on). Armed with this information, a salesperson can target groups that meet at times at which the property most needs business, or the property can anticipate the needs of an individual guest or group, building rapport and customer loyalty.

As competition has increased in the past decade, hotel operators are scrutinizing marketing expenditures more carefully than ever. Since it is five to seven times more expensive to acquire new guests than to retain existing ones, database marketing has become an essential tool for establishing relationships and retaining guests.

Home-Based and Virtual Offices. Many of today's properties and their salespeople are using technology to create "virtual offices." Laptop computers enable salespeople to tap into the property's or chain's computer system from remote locations to check for room availability, rates, and other information needed by clients. Most laptops are equipped with fax modems, enabling salespersons to generate proposals for customers and immediately fax them to them. Salespeople are also using e-mail to send correspondence and documents to clients.

Swissôtel, a chain with properties in the United States, Europe, Asia, and the Middle East, was one of the first hospitality firms to "go virtual." Their national account team in the United States is equipped with laptop computers and cellular phones that enable salespeople to get immediate availability and rate information. The laptops are also used to send and receive faxes and, since property photos and detailed information about guestrooms and meeting space is stored in them, the computers can be used to customize presentations for meeting planners. Swissôtel president and CEO Andreas Meinhold says that "in a sense, Swissôtel has packed its bag and taken itself on the road using specially adapted laptops and connectivity links. Because our salespeople are tapped into the property-management system, they're able to operate out of their virtual office as if they were behind the front desk of any Swissôtel. Our account managers will be able to spend their time selling, not focusing on administrative tasks. They can work when they want and where they want, and really spend their time focusing on our customers' needs."[10]

Since salespeople armed with a laptop computer, a cellular phone, and an e-mail address can maintain close contact with both their home property and their customers, a number of hotel salespeople are now home-based. Sheraton, for example, estimates that about half of its Starwood salespeople are home-based, and chains such as Marriott and Radisson have discovered that home-based salespeople save on the expense of establishing regional sales offices. Mike Beardsley, vice president of sales and marketing for Marriott's western region in Santa Ana,

Exhibit 19 Sample Sales Performance by Market Segment Report

Sales Source Activity Report by Market Segment
Sales Performance Market Segment
Sales Activity between 12/6 and 12/21
Arrivals beginning 1/1

Booking Source: Ralph Johnson

Market Segment	Room Nights		Average Rate		Room Revenue		Food Revenue		Beverage Revenue	
	Current	(+/−)	Current	(+/−)	Current	(+/−)	Current	(+/−)	Current	(+/−)
Corporate										
TENTATIVE:	0	0	0.00	0.00	0	0	0	0	0	0
DEFINITE:	130	130	125.00	125.00	16,250	16,250	1,150	1,150	0	0
National Association										
TENTATIVE:	435	−262	170.00	35.00	73,950	−20,145	250,000	221,851	6,100	1,420
DEFINITE:	1,267	1,267	128.80	128.80	163,195	163,195	73,149	73,149	12,680	12,680
Regional Association										
TENTATIVE:	0	0	0.00	0.00	0	0	0	0	0	0
DEFINITE:	2,225	85	134.24	2.58	298,704	16,949	41,190	0	13,845	0
SHERF										
TENTATIVE:	0	−360	0.00	−135.00	0	−48,600	0	−10,657	0	0
DEFINITE:	360	360	135.00	135.00	48,600	48,600	10,657	10,657	0	0
Social										
TENTATIVE:	0	0	0.00	0.00	0	0	0	0	0	0
DEFINITE:	0	−25	0.00	−94.00	0	−2,350	0	0	0	0
State Association										
TENTATIVE:	0	0	0.00	0.00	0	0	0	0	0	0
DEFINITE:	550	450	115.45	20.45	63,500	54,000	153,991	150,000	5,000	5,000
Tour & Travel										
TENTATIVE:	0	0	0.00	0.00	0	0	0	0	0	0
DEFINITE:	50	50	120.00	120.00	6,000	6,000	4,320	0	1,170	0
TOTAL										
TENTATIVE:	435	−622	170.00	35.00	73,950	−68,745	250,000	211,194	6,100	1,420
DEFINITE:	4,582	2,317	130.12	0.50	596,249	302,644	284,457	234,956	32,695	17,680

Source: Delphi/Newmarket Software Systems, Inc., Durham, New Hampshire.

California, supervises 50 field salespeople, 30 of whom work from home. Beardsley says that when salespeople evolved from being property-centered to account-centered, the location of their offices became almost irrelevant.

Lists, Reports, and Analysis Applications. An automated sales office can quickly generate lists and reports that would take hours to produce manually. Computers can store mailing lists of prospective clients, previous guests, and organizations and associations. These lists can be printed out in a variety of applications—by zip code, by type of guest or prospect, and so on—and can be merged into word-processing functions to provide personalized sales letters. Computerized systems make short work of large mailings, providing cost-effective, targeted advertising and promotion for the property.

Data entered into computer systems is often used to generate reports, such as a sales performance by market segment report (see Exhibit 19) that analyzes a salesperson's booking activity by market segment during a specified time period.

This report is valuable to both the salesperson and the director of sales for evaluating performance, and is just one example of the various types of reports that marketing and sales offices can generate.

Market analysis begins with master cards or other basic information on present and potential business. The computer sorts the information into several categories, generating reports that give the sales staff access to a number of statistics at a glance. Reports may include arrivals and booking dates, length of stay, rates, room type chosen, or other information, such as the zip code areas that produce the most business or the types of rooms that are most popular during a particular season of the year. These statistics are a vital tool to help management plan sales strategies.

Yield and Revenue Management. The computer also plays an important role in market analysis. Computer technology has made it easier to maximize a property's earning potential with two important tools: yield and revenue management. **Yield management** is a technique that is used to maximize room revenues. A hospitality firm's "yield" is based on a simple percentage that compares its revenue potential versus the revenue realized:

$$\frac{\text{Revenue Realized (actual sales receipts)}}{\text{Revenue Potential (potential revenue if all the property's rooms were sold at full rack rates)}} = \text{Yield}$$

Until computer technology was available, the most crucial part of yield management—predicting or forecasting demand—was tedious and haphazard at best. Collecting both historical and current information allows hotels to control their inventory and pricing by forecasting demand on any given day and then adjusting prices to maximize revenue.

To better use yield management, many properties have formed forecast committees or yield management teams that meet regularly to evaluate demand trends. These teams usually consist of executives from reservations, sales, and the rooms division, and may also include marketing and front office personnel. These executives meet regularly to forecast demand and establish systems and strategies for dealing with changing demand patterns.

Revenue management takes yield management a step further. This technique, which is being increasingly used in the hospitality industry, not only assesses a group's potential for room revenues but also looks at the group's projected impact on the property's overall bottom line. Revenue management takes into consideration the size of the group, its spending history (not just in terms of rooms, but overall spending at the property's other revenue centers—restaurants, recreational facilities, etc.), and its potential future revenues (additional bookings by the group and individuals, referrals, and so on).

Because revenue management has become such an important part of hotel operations today, there are revenue management consulting companies, as well as computer programs such as Maxim Revenue Management Solutions' e.FLEX, which help managers forecast and maximize net profit contributions from every piece of hospitality business. Hospitality properties that do not want to invest in

MARKETING IN ACTION

The Mandarin Oriental San Francisco Relies on Technology for Success in its Sales and Marketing Efforts

The Mandarin Oriental San Francisco, a luxury hotel with 158 rooms, faced the challenges of anticipating and predicting competitive set information and processing this information quickly and accurately in order to offer the most optimal daily rates. In order to do so, the hotel's director of revenue management, who is responsible for providing up-to-date information to hotel management, upgraded from the hotel's IDeaS platform to IDeaS V5i™ because of the newer version's enhanced reporting.

Melanie Cooke-Kridech, the director of revenue management for the hotel, says that "as market demand continued to change, I needed to be able to communicate the necessary information to the organization in the most concise, effective way. We chose to upgrade to the newest IDeaS version because it provided smart, simple technology that allowed me to generate reports and process information quickly and accurately."

The IDeaS V5i™ offers a Decisions Module, a Group Pricing Module and a Best Available Rate (BAR) Module that provide a spectrum of valuable data, easy-to-read graphics, and information on key hotel performance indicators. Routine reports generated by the system include graphical depictions of monthly Estimated Room Revenue, Occupancy Average Daily Rate (ADR), and Revenue Per Available Rate (RevPAR). The system is highly user-friendly, online, accessible, and highly viewable.

"Research that once took me a full day now takes about 30 minutes," according to Cooke-Kridech. "I use the forecasting tools and export it directly into Excel, simply cutting and pasting data into presentations I'm already working on. This allows me to rapidly provide my colleagues with the information they need.

"Since deploying the IDeaS system, I've saved a significant amount of time, and my colleagues have increased confidence in my reporting due to the heightened accuracy of my work. Because of the increased accuracy, we are maximizing our revenue to the best of our ability."

Source: A case study adapted from the Integrated Decisions and Systems, Inc. website, ideas.com, March 2008.

their own software can take advantage of subscription services that allow them to use revenue management software on a monthly basis.

Evaluating the Marketing and Sales Office

Even established marketing and sales offices should not be regarded as permanent or unchangeable. If sales responsibilities are not being handled in the most efficient way possible, the head of the marketing and sales office should seek ways to improve procedures. Periodic reviews can help ensure that sales duties are handled properly.

This involves taking a look at a number of factors. Are lines of communication open with both the sales staff and the property's other departments? Has authority been clearly delegated—and is the scope of that authority understood? Are duties and responsibilities being carried out? Is there an adequate support staff to help sales personnel spend as much time as possible selling?

The following six additional questions should also be considered when evaluating the sales and marketing staff:

1. Does everyone understand that the customers' needs come first and that the role of the marketing and sales organization is to fill those needs?
2. Does everyone on the marketing and sales staff have a thorough understanding of the marketing plan?
3. Does everyone on the marketing and sales staff know the property, the competition, and the marketplace from top to bottom?
4. Do salespeople have a clear understanding of their goals and do they submit a weekly call plan that includes a list of assigned accounts to be traced and followed up?
5. Is there a system in place for the proper maintenance and security of account files, including trace and follow-up reports?
6. Are all necessary elements for operating a successful marketing and sales office in place—that is, a written marketing plan, employee job descriptions, standard operating procedures, an efficient filing system, a system for monitoring sales performance, a training program for new employees, and a continuing education program for veteran salespeople?

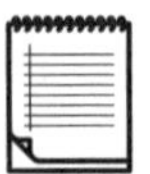

Endnotes

1. Lalia Rach, Ed.D., "The Current and Future Marketing Professional," *HSMAI Marketing Review*, Fall 1998, p. 22.
2. One half of Jim's monthly capacity of $125,000 is $62,500; three-fourths of Jim's capacity is $93,750. Three months at half capacity ($62,500) equals $187,500; three months at three-fourths capacity ($93,750) equals $281,250. Therefore, the new salesperson brings in $468,750 in revenue in the first six months ($187,500 + $281,250 = $468,750). However, Jim Dandy would have brought in $750,000 during those six months ($125,000 × 6 = $750,000). Subtracting the new salesperson's revenue ($468,750) from the revenue Jim Dandy would have brought in had he remained at the property ($750,000) shows that the new salesperson's revenues are $281,250 less than Jim Dandy's would have been ($750,000 – $468,750 = $281,250). Adding this revenue shortfall to the revenue lost during the three months it took to find and hire the new salesperson ($125,000 × 3 = $375,000) reveals that the property lost $656,250 during this nine-month period ($375,000 + $281,250 = $656,250).
3. For more information on training, see Debra F. Cannon and Catherine M. Gustafson, *Training and Development for the Hospitality Industry* (Lansing, Mich.: American Hotel & Lodging Educational Institute, 2002).
4. The information in the following section was developed by Jim Cathcart of Cathcart, Alessandra & Associates, Inc., and is used with permission.
5. Some of the material in this section was adapted from Richard R. Still, Edward W. Cundiff, and Norman A. P. Govoni, *Sales Management: Decisions, Strategies, and Cases* (Englewood Cliffs, N.J.: Prentice-Hall, 1988).

6. For more information on hospitality management, see Jerome J. Vallen and James R. Abbey, *The Art and Science of Hospitality Management* (Lansing, Mich.: American Hotel & Lodging Educational Institute, 1987); Raphael R. Kavanaugh and Jack D. Ninemeier, *Supervision in the Hospitality Industry,* 4th ed. (Lansing, Mich.: American Hotel & Lodging Educational Institute, 2007); and Robert H. Woods, *Managing Hospitality Human Resources,* 4th ed. (Lansing, Mich.: American Hotel & Lodging Educational Institute, 2006).
7. Courtesy of Hyatt Hotels Corporation Sales Automation System, *Datamation.*
8. William Duncan, "Booking Streamlined by Next Generation of Hospitality Software," *Convene,* November 1994, p. 40.
9. "How Technology Is Refining Hotel Operations," *Convene,* December 1999, p. 124.
10. Laura Ross-Fedder, "Computers Empower Swissôtel Sales Staff," *Hotel & Motel Management,* May 8, 1995, p. 4.

Key Terms

account file—A standard-size file folder holding information needed for serving a client's basic business needs. Account files may also be computerized.

call report—A document that provides general information about an account (address, contact person, etc.) as well as remarks on the needs of the group and action steps that can be taken to sell the hotel's products and services to the group.

database marketing—Attracting and retaining customers by using information in the computer databases that a firm maintains on past, current, and potential customers.

director—An assertive person interested in getting results quickly. One of four personality types of buyers.

double calling—Making sales calls with two salespeople—usually a new salesperson accompanied by a more experienced salesperson.

function book—The master control of all banquet space, broken down on each page according to banquet room or restart, with a page for each day of the year. Function books may also be computerized.

guestroom control book—A book used to monitor the number of guestrooms committed to groups. Guestroom control books may be paper-based or computerized.

independent hotel representative—An individual who offers hotel reservations to wholesalers, travel agents, and the public. An independent hotel representative or "rep" may be paid by the hotels he or she represents on a fee basis or by commission. Many of them also offer marketing and other services.

master card—An index card that contains a summary of everything needed for a sales effort, including the organization's name, the decision-maker(s), key contacts, addresses, telephone numbers, and so on. Master cards may also be computerized.

property fact book—A collection of information about a property, its products and services, and its management's policies that is designed to help prospects, travel intermediaries, journalists, and new staff members become familiar with the property. May be paper-based or computerized.

reader file—A file containing copies of all internal and external memos and correspondence generated by a salesperson, useful for reviewing that salesperson's performance.

relater—A person who tends to view things in terms of how they affect people and relationships. One of four personality types of buyers.

revenue management—The practice of assessing a group's overall profitability. Not only is the group's impact on guestrooms and meeting rooms revenues assessed, but also its spending in other areas (restaurants, retail, and so on) and its potential for future business.

socializer—A playful and talkative person. One of four personality types of buyers.

standard operating procedures (SOPs)—Written instructions explaining how recurring business activities should be handled in the sales office.

thinker—An idea person who is precise, efficient, and well-organized. One of four personality types of buyers.

trace card—A 3-by-5-inch index card used as a reminder to call a client or check a cut-off date, filed by callback date. The trace card function may also be computerized.

yield management—A hotel room pricing system that uses a hotel's computer reservations system to track advance bookings and then lower or raise prices accordingly—on a day-to-day basis—to yield the maximum average daily rate. Before selling a room in advance, the hotel staff forecasts the probability of being able to sell the room to other market segments that are willing to pay higher rates.

Review Questions

1. What factors influence the organization of a marketing and sales office?
2. What positions are typically found in the marketing and sales offices of small, midsize, and large properties?
3. What are nine characteristics common to successful salespeople, and what training tools are used to develop salespeople to their full potential?
4. What is the role of a regional or national sales office?
5. What are the functions of independent hotel sales representatives?
6. What are some typical sales records and forms, and what are their purposes?
7. What are the three basic files used in a marketing and sales office? How are they used?
8. How have computers benefited marketing and sales offices?
9. What are some of the things that should be considered when evaluating a marketing and sales office?

Internet Sites

For more information, visit the following Internet sites. Remember that Internet addresses can change without notice. If the site is no longer there, you can use a search engine to look for additional sites.

Advertising Research Foundation
www.thearf.org

American Advertising Federation
www.aaf.org

American Marketing Association
www.ama.org

Destination Marketing Association International
www.iacvb.org

First Resort Software
www.firstres.com

Group 1 Software
www.g1.com

Hospitality Industry Technology Exposition and Conference
www.hitec.org

Hospitality Jobs Online
www.hospitalityonline.com

Hospitality Sales & Marketing Association International
www.hsmai.org

Hospitality Valuation Services International
www.hvs.com

Hotel Training.com
www.hoteltraining.com

Meeting Professionals International
www.mpiweb.org

MICROS Systems, Inc.
www.micros.com

Newmarket International
www.newmarketinc.com

Resort Data Processing, Inc.
www.resortdata.com

Sales & Marketing Management
www.salesandmarketing.com

Signature Worldwide
www.signatureworldwide.com

Sorry! No Vacancy
www.no-vacancy.com

Case Study

Selecting a Salesperson

Sales consultants Claude Wise and Cyril Smarts had a rough time convincing owner/operator Jean Pennypincher that hiring a sales staff for her 12 limited-service properties would revive lagging profits. However, they finally convinced her to hire one part-time salesperson, with no benefits, to work at the Springtime Inn—the hotel with the greatest potential. Jean agreed that if this person was successful at the property, she would hire additional salespeople for the other 11 properties.

Claude and Cyril advertised the position and narrowed down the applicants to four finalists. From a previous interview with each of them, the following information was gathered (note: some of the information would be illegal to request during a job interview; such information was volunteered by the candidates):

Harriet Fisher

Harriet was looking to re-enter the hospitality industry after a five-year hiatus. She mentioned that both her children will be in school, and she would like to work from 9:00 A.M. to 2:30 P.M. each day. She does not need benefits. She previously worked three years as an account executive for a midsize hotel. She has one year of junior college.

Juan Carlise

Juan is a senior in a university hospitality program and has completed three-fourths of the curriculum. He also has served an internship as a guest-service representative at a luxury hotel and worked at the front desk of a local midsize hotel for the past four years. He speaks English and Spanish fluently. He's looking to work 20 hours a week.

Amy Adler

Amy has worked at a retail clothing store for the past eight years. She has a junior college degree. She's interested in a job with better weekday and fewer weekend hours. She's hoping to make enough money to return to school for a four-year degree.

Warren Jordan

Warren recently retired from the navy after a 20-year career. One of his last assignments was Bachelor Quarters Officer, for which he helped implement the BQ Quality of Life standards on his base. He receives military retirement pay and benefits. He's looking for a job with flexible hours that will provide a challenge and some extra money.

Claude and Cyril developed the following ten questions to ask these four applicants during their final interviews:

1. If you were independently wealthy, what would you be doing right now?
2. What was your worst encounter with a salesperson, and how would you have improved that sales experience?
3. I'm sure you've been rejected before in a business situation. What were the circumstances, and how did you handle it?
4. Would you give us an example of a time when you had to be persistent, and would you describe the result?
5. Would you rather sell something or help someone buy?
6. This position is part of a pilot test. If it is successful, we will be hiring a salesperson for each of the other 11 properties. What would you bring to the table that would help us make this pilot program a success?

7. If the pilot test is successful and we hire additional salespeople, do you see yourself managing this sales force?
8. If you could be anything other than a human, what would you be?
9. What do you like to do when you're not at work?
10. You will be given a set of weekly goals, such as 10 personal calls and 20 telephone calls a week. How would you manage your time to achieve these goals?

They carefully designed the questions so that some of them focused on sales and managerial skills while others presented open-ended opportunities for applicants to talk about their personal values, habits, lifestyles, and more. After interviewing each candidate, they reviewed the audiotapes they made of each session. The answers they received to each of their ten questions follow.

HARRIET FISHER

1. **If you were independently wealthy, what would you be doing right now?**

   "I'd hire a private tutor and take that person and my entire family and travel. I'd make sure the girls got to see all the wonders of the world they only read about now. It'd be a fantastic education for them to meet people from different cultures and see historic buildings and places."

2. **What was your worst encounter with a salesperson, and how would you have improved that sales experience?**

   "The worst salesperson I met was actually at a hotel. This salesperson had described a three-day vacation package to a family that wanted two rooms. What she *didn't* say was that the price was per person, not per room. The father, surprised at what a great price they were getting, asked if she was certain that the quoted price was for all four of them. It was a low-occupancy week, and I'm sure the salesperson was anxious to book the family. Once they arrived at the hotel, the front desk agent told them the price was twice what they expected. Despite the fact that they had traveled twelve hours by car to get to the hotel, the father was ready to walk out and take his family back home, canceling their vacation. The salesperson should have been clear about the package or offered them a less expensive package at rates they were willing to pay."

3. **I'm sure you've been rejected before in a business situation. What were the circumstances, and how did you handle it?**

   "Well, yes, I've been rejected—though I generally try to avoid it! One of the reasons I'm applying for this job came out of a recent rejection. I applied for a personal loan to buy a recreational vehicle. I was turned down because I wasn't employed. They wouldn't let me use my husband's income or my home as collateral. My first instinct was to switch banks. I did apply for a loan for the same amount at a credit union. I haven't heard back from them yet. If I'm turned down there, too, I'll bide my time and apply for the loan again after I've worked for several months."

4. **Would you give us an example of a time when you had to be persistent, and would you describe the result?**

   "Potty training. I can't think of anything that requires more persistence than that. The result is that my youngest child is going to nursery school in 'big girl' panties instead of diapers—and I assure you, that wasn't a foregone conclusion!"

5. **Would you rather sell something or help someone buy?**

   "I'd much rather help someone buy what they want. I really hesitated before taking my first sales job at the Hot Springs Hotel. I never saw myself as a salesperson. But I loved the job because I was able to help people have a successful experience, whether they were on a business or pleasure trip, and really help meet their needs. I always tried to create a win-win situation."

6. **This position is part of a pilot test. If it is successful, we will be hiring a salesperson for each of the other 11 properties. What would you bring to the table that would help us make this pilot program a success?**

   "I know the needs of transient and group guests. I can really help them see the benefits of staying at the Springtime Inn. I have experience in hotel sales, and I'm confident I can surpass the goals you outlined."

7. **If the pilot test is successful and we hire additional salespeople, do you see yourself managing this sales force?**

   "I can see myself managing the process—at least initially. I have strong organizational skills and could help set up processes to be copied by other people. As much as I enjoy working with people, though, I'd prefer not to be a manager. My last job was very high-stress and, while I enjoyed the challenges, I'm at a different stage in life now. When I go home, I don't want to take my job with me or worry about the performance of my employees. I'm no longer on the high-powered, career-at-all-costs track."

8. **If you could be anything other than a human, what would you be?**

   "I'd want to be a cat. They're loving, yet independent. They communicate blissful happiness, but aren't afraid to hiss and stick up for themselves when threatened."

9. **What do you like to do when you're not at work?**

   "What *don't* I like to do would be an easier question to answer! My oldest daughter is active in competitive ice skating, and I take her to a lot of practices. I also make her outfits and help sew outfits for several other girls. I like to ski, go sledding, hiking, rappelling, fishing, and canoeing. I used to be involved in Habitat for Humanity when the girls were younger, but I no longer have the time."

10. **You will be given a set of weekly activities and goals. How would you manage your time to achieve these goals?**

    "I would start out by breaking the weekly goals into daily goals. I would then sort my calls geographically. I really believe that for every five minutes spent planning your work, you save ten. I would want to arrange my calls and visits so that I have a half-hour free at the end of each day. That way, if something runs longer, I wouldn't have to push whatever I was working on at the end of the day to the next day. And if that half hour ends up empty, I could spend it preparing for the next day."

JUAN CARLISE

1. **If you were independently wealthy, what would you be doing right now?**

   "I'd set up a fellowship in my name at the university to pay the tuition of hospitality students who show a lot of promise. Then I'd buy a hotel that could double as a training school for the university."

2. **What was your worst encounter with a salesperson, and how would you have improved that sales experience?**

   "It was a car salesman—surprise! I was all ready to buy a car. All I wanted to do was take the paperwork home and fill it out. I had a date that night and I really wanted time to go home and get ready—I didn't want to hang around the dealership after I'd made up my mind. But the salesperson kept hounding me, telling me that if I didn't sign right now, the model I wanted might be sold out by the next afternoon. I said if he could sell all those cars, then bully for him—he didn't need me to buy. Then he said I might not get the color I wanted. I think I told him three times I was willing to chance it. Finally, I got so disgusted I gave him back his paperwork and left. He could have sold me a car if he hadn't kept up the high pressure, 'gotta-have-it-now' sales pitch. Now he'll never have me for a customer. He'd have been much better off to let me leave with the paperwork and then follow up with a phone call the next afternoon."

3. **I'm sure you've been rejected before in a business situation. What were the circumstances, and how did you handle it?**

   "Hey, you've got to be cool about rejections. I was rejected for two internships before I got a really great one last summer at a luxury hotel. I handle rejection by learning why I was rejected, how to prevent it the next time, and by trying again somewhere else."

4. **Would you give us an example of a time when you had to be persistent, and would you describe the result?**

   "Persistence is my middle name. I had to be persistent to get into college and to get an internship. I have to be persistent every day at work to get the room attendants to report room status in a timely manner."

5. **Would you rather sell something or help someone buy?**

   "I like to sell. I enjoy being a salesperson and bringing in high occupancy rates. Certainly, you want to help the customer buy your services. And I definitely don't believe in badgering customers beyond their tolerance. However, it's important to ask for a sale. A good salesperson can find at least one property service to sell to just about anyone."

6. **This position is part of a pilot test. If it is successful, we will be hiring a salesperson for each of the other 11 properties. What would you bring to the table that would help us make this pilot program a success?**

   "I bring a good education, motivation, and excitement. The first thing I'll do to help you meet your goals is meet my goals. Then I can provide an analysis of how my sales techniques can help your other properties excel. I'll also make sure I generate more business than I could possibly support alone—especially part-time."

7. **If the pilot test is successful and we hire additional salespeople, do you see yourself managing this sales force?**

   "I've spent several years preparing myself for a managerial position in hospitality. I believe that once I graduate, I'll be ready to manage the other people you hire and lead them through the same growth process that I'll be leading this first hotel through."

8. **If you could be anything other than a human, what would you be?**

   "I'd want to be a book. That way I'd be immortal and constantly contributing to other people's knowledge and enjoyment."

9. **What do you like to do when you're not at work?**

   "I enjoy fixing up old houses. I've got some buddies who have carpentry and electrical skills, and we contract out our services to fix up old homes. We're currently restoring a house built in 1885. It's got some great woodwork and an unusual root cellar. By the time we're done with it, it'll look like new—at least, what new was a century ago."

10. **You will be given a set of weekly activities and goals. How would you manage your time to achieve these goals?**

    "I'd make a to-do list with each of the goals and the tasks needed to complete those goals. Then I'd prioritize them and start working on them according to priority. I'd start with the 'A' task and work at it until it was done, then go to the 'B' task, and so on until I was through my list."

AMY ADLER

1. **If you were independently wealthy, what would you be doing right now?**

   "I'd buy an island up north where it snows a lot and live in a huge log cabin with a large fireplace. I'd have food flown in every week, and just curl up and read, watch television, and knit."

2. **What was your worst encounter with a salesperson, and how would you have improved that sales experience?**

   "It was a telephone solicitor. He called at eight o'clock in the morning. I'd been doing inventory at the store the night before and hadn't gotten home until 2 A.M. The last thing I wanted was for the phone to ring at eight o'clock. I was half asleep when I answered the phone and didn't fully wake up until the solicitor asked for my credit card number. I told the caller I didn't want to buy anything. He said I'd already agreed and the conversation was taped. I told him again I didn't want anything and hung up. A week later I received a cellular phone and a bill. I sent it back, but it took months to get them to stop sending me threatening letters. How would I make it better? Well, I'd certainly be sure that the customer I was talking to was fully awake and understood the purchase conditions—I wouldn't just read a script. Neither would I be rude to customers and tell them that they *have* to buy whatever I'm selling."

3. **I'm sure you've been rejected before in a business situation. What were the circumstances, and how did you handle it?**

   "When we were opening the outlet store, I had a great idea for setting up a perpetual inventory. It was rejected because of silly politics. Once I realized the new manager liked doing things her own way, I just put my idea in a memo and did what I was told."

4. **Would you give us an example of a time when you had to be persistent, and would you describe the result?**

   "We were opening a store at the mall down the road from here. I was temporarily relocated to help the store set up. The person I was working with had never opened a clothing store before and had a lot of strange ideas about how clothes should be displayed. I had to be very persistent and diplomatic to make sure everything was set up in a way that would be conducive to sales."

5. **Would you rather sell something or help someone buy?**

   "I prefer to sell; I'd much rather have an item and try to sell it than waste a lot of time with customers who are uncertain of what they want. You can make a lot more sales when you work at selling something specific."

6. **This position is part of a pilot test. If it is successful, we will be hiring a salesperson for each of the other 11 properties. What would you bring to the table that would help us make this pilot program a success?**

   "I've been a salesperson for a number of years. I've helped open new stores and helped turn around low-performing stores. I'll be able to do the same with your hotels. I'll bring my experience with start-ups to help your hotels find new markets and meet the needs of those markets."

7. **If the pilot test is successful and we hire additional salespeople, do you see yourself managing this sales force?**

   "I think I could. I'm very good at working with people. In retail, you get all types. I've always enjoyed solving problems for employees and customers."

8. **If you could be anything other than a human, what would you be?**

   "I'd want to be a cruise ship. Except for a few days in ports, I'd be spending most of my time out on the seas—and that seems like a wonderfully peaceful and relaxing existence."

9. **What do you like to do when you're not at work?**

   "I like to make crafts. I have several nieces and nephews I enjoy making things for. I also enjoy renting videos. I especially like British comedy."

10. **You will be given a set of weekly activities and goals. How would you manage your time to achieve these goals?**

    "Those sound like very reasonable goals. I'd plan to do two personal calls a day and four telephone calls."

WARREN JORDAN

1. **If you were independently wealthy, what would you be doing right now?**

   "Probably not much different than what I'm doing now. I'd probably get a bigger house, a new car, all that sort of stuff. I'd still be looking for a challenge, though. Granted, I wouldn't be applying for this job; instead, I'd probably open my own business."

2. **What was your worst encounter with a salesperson, and how would you have improved that sales experience?**

   "My worst experience by far was trying to buy an engagement ring for my wife. The jewelry store salesperson at the first place I went to refused to show me a moderately priced ring. I was on a military salary and didn't want to go into debt for the ring. The salesperson kept telling me that it was an investment, and that I'd be showing how much I loved my fiancée by the size of the diamond I picked. When I asked to see a smaller ring, she said, 'Why are you marrying her if you don't love her enough to get her a decent ring? You want her to be embarrassed?' I walked out at that point. Fortunately, I found another salesperson at another store who was helpful. It's this person who epitomized how I would handle the situation. She asked me what my budget was and then showed me a number of different rings with different settings. She asked about my fiancée's style and taste. Then she offered to engrave the ring with our wedding date, once we set the date. She did such a nice job that I went back to that store the next year when I got a bonus and bought my wife a pair of diamond earrings."

3. **I'm sure you've been rejected before in a business situation. What were the circumstances, and how did you handle it?**

   "The situation that is most memorable was the first time I was turned down for a promotion to lieutenant in the navy. I smarted for about a day, but then I met with my commanding officer and asked him why I had been turned down. He helped me outline the steps I could take to make sure I qualified next time. Then I followed those steps."

4. **Would you give us an example of a time when you had to be persistent, and would you describe the result?**

   "When I was manager of bachelor housing, I had a building manager who acted as though his budget was just a guideline, not a requirement. As a consequence of his poor budgeting, several of his building's requirements went unfunded. At first, I thought he just didn't understand the importance of the budgetary process, or that perhaps he didn't know how to fill out the budget forms. As it turned out, he was just biding his time until he was rotated to another position. That may have been fine for him, but I found it unacceptable. I had to hound him continually to fill out every form and make sure he could justify his numbers. I had to take measures with him that none of my other building managers required, but the end result was that I got an accurate budget out of him to submit to navy command."

5. **Would you rather sell something or help someone buy?**

   "I'd rather help someone buy. It's of no value to sell people something they don't need. There are many more long-term benefits to finding out what customers want and meeting those needs than to selling them something they don't need or want. The latter philosophy leads to too many one-time customers."

6. **This position is part of a pilot test. If it is successful, we will be hiring a salesperson for each of the other 11 properties. What would you bring to the table that would help us make this pilot program a success?**

   "I bring to you strong organizational skills and the expertise of someone accustomed to managing people and resources. I'll help you reach your goal by being so successful that it won't be necessary to justify hiring other salespeople to the hotel owner. Instead, she'll wonder how she lasted so long without them."

7. **If the pilot test is successful and we hire additional salespeople, do you see yourself managing this sales force?**

   "I think I would be the ideal person to help you select and supervise your new hires. As I mentioned before, I have extensive experience managing people, and I'm very good at establishing and implementing processes."

8. **If you could be anything other than a human, what would you be?**

   "Hmmm, that's a hard one. I guess I'd want to be a mountain. That way I can be kind and gentle, yet strong and powerful."

9. **What do you like to do when you're not at work?**

   "I'm the vice president of a local hospital board. We have several projects I'm currently working on. I chair the publicity committee, and we are promoting a fundraising campaign that starts next month. I also like to take the kids fishing and go golfing."

10. **You will be given a set of weekly activities and goals. How would you manage your time to achieve these goals?**

    "First I'd determine when the best time is to reach each client I wanted to contact. Then I'd schedule my calls according to premium success times. I'd also analyze how I spent my time so that I could eventually look for ways to increase my output by a given percentage each month."

Discussion Questions

1. What are the strengths and weaknesses of each applicant?
2. Which applicant would you hire? Why?
3. Which applicant do you think Claude and Cyril hired? Why?

Case Number: 370CD
This case was developed in cooperation with Bill Flor and Randy Kinder, authors of *No Vacancy: A Tried & True Guide to Get More Rooms Business!*; The No Vacancy Company; Jacksonville, Florida.

This case also appears in *Contemporary Hospitality Marketing: A Service Management Approach* (Lansing, Mich.: American Hotel & Lodging Educational Institute, 1999), ISBN 978-0-86612-158-3.

Part II

Sales Techniques

Chapter 4 Outline

Competencies

1. Describe the objectives of various types of personal sales calls. (p. 137)
2. Identify sources for prospecting individual and group business and explain how salespeople qualify prospects as potential clients. (pp. 138–146)
3. Describe how salespeople can prepare for presentation sales calls and project a professional image when making presentations. (pp. 146–156)
4. Summarize the five steps of a presentation sales call. (pp. 156–169)
5. Explain how salespeople can improve their productivity through efficient time management and key account management. (pp. 169–176)

Insider Insights

Greg Hendel
Co-Owner, Best Western Host Hotel
Palm Springs, CA

"Some people refer to marketing and sales as prospecting, but I like to think of it as detective work. A good salesperson is constantly asking questions. "Who's coming into town?" "Who uses rooms of this type?" "How can we determine additional sources for our business?" Marketing and sales are limited only by a salesperson's imagination!"

4

Personal Sales

THE PERSONAL SALES CALL is often the most effective means of customer contact, especially when directed at volume movers of the leisure, business, and meetings market. A personal sales call is used to build rapport with clients or potential clients and sell them the property's products and services.

There are several types of personal sales calls:

1. **Cold calls** or *prospect calls,* which can either be made in person or by telephone, are usually made within a small geographic area with a minimum amount of time spent on each call. Generally, little is known about the person or organization being called on; this is strictly a fact-finding or exploratory call. The objective is not to make a sale, but to gather information so that a selling strategy can be developed and a follow-up visit made. Of course, if you run into someone really interested in doing business, you can present the property's benefits and try to make a sale.
2. **Public relations calls** or *service calls* are made on companies and individuals who are already clients. These calls serve to promote goodwill and indicate your willingness to meet the future needs of the client.
3. **Presentation calls** (also called *appointment calls,* since appointments must often be made with busy prospects) are made to individuals, committees, or groups to explain how your property can meet their needs and to ask for their business. Therefore, you should obtain as much information as possible about prospects before making presentations. It's important to target the organizations' decision-makers and use effective visual aids and other support materials. You must be organized and confident—ready to make a strong presentation, overcome objections, and ask for the sale.
4. **Inside calls** are made to walk-ins inquiring about the property or to group buyers, such as tour operators, travel agents, and meeting planners, who have been invited to tour the property.

This chapter looks at the components of successful face-to-face salesmanship, beginning with a discussion of the importance of prospecting and the need for thorough preparation before making a sales call. Next, the chapter focuses on the presentation sales call, and describes how pre-presentation planning and the five basic steps of a presentation sales call can lead to bookings for the property. The final sections of the chapter discuss time and key account management.

Prospecting

In today's competitive environment, few hotels can be certain that their current client base will be adequate for the future. Prospecting for new business is essential and should be a continual part of hotel sales. Relationships with individuals and groups must constantly be cultivated to ensure that the hotel keeps pace with market trends and the competition. But properties should not just send salespeople out to find new business by going up and down the street and knocking on doors. According to Tom McCarthy, who has over 35 years in hotel marketing, properties need a planned approach to prospecting:

> For example, a salesperson might have a territory that includes 35,000 companies. If a salesperson can qualify 20 new prospects a week, it doesn't take much figuring to determine that the salesperson can qualify about 1,000 accounts a year.
>
> Wouldn't it make more sense to work with a list broker and pick the 1,000 companies in advance that will be assigned the salesperson (based on proximity, size, and type of business), rather than just telling the person to "hit the bricks"? Do we think the person will call on the best 1,000 out of the 35,000 by chance?
>
> Here we are, working with computers and sophisticated software and still living in the 19th century when it comes to the most basic principles of prospecting.[1]

Many salespeople see prospecting as a difficult, frustrating, and thankless job. Prospecting, however, is the lifeblood of sales because prospecting identifies the individuals or groups that may become the property's client base of the future. At a minimum, each salesperson should be making 10 to 15 calls per week on *new* prospects.

To whom should you prospect? David Jones, once a senior-level sales manager with Marriott and now a professor at San Francisco State University, says that "the prospecting process begins by understanding who your best customers are and what makes them such good customers. It is far more effective to find customers like the ones you do business with today than to try and start from scratch with potential customers who may not even want what you have to offer."[2]

Therefore, look at your present customer mix and go out and get more of the same. Prospect research information is as close as the sales office files. The function books and other records from previous years are excellent sources of prospects. These records provide information on groups that have booked and not returned, the names of key contact persons, and the names of satisfied past clients. Don't waste valuable time on "dead" files, however. If these accounts had any merit, they would not have been relegated to the dead file. Unless something has changed—a merger, perhaps—that would warrant additional attention to an inactive account, it is better to pursue accounts with more promise or prospect for new business.

Other sources for prospect research include:

1. *Referrals from past and present clients.* In addition to being excellent prospects for future bookings, satisfied clients can also be excellent sources for leads. Not only might your clients personally recommend the property to friends

MARKETING IN ACTION

When Signature Inns, an emerging lodging chain, wanted to build name recognition, it developed a number of strategies, including an aggressive personal selling effort concentrated in each hotel's home community and the surrounding area.

In addition to making monthly service calls to the ten organizations that generated the highest revenue the previous month, staff members at each property in the chain also depend on prospecting to find new business. For example, each property's assistant general manager, who is expected to make at least 15 outside calls weekly, contacts local businesses of all sizes, using various sources of information to identify the businesses, including the chamber of commerce, telephone yellow pages, local newspapers, and industrial lists. Reader boards of local competitors are also studied to determine which organizations are having meetings and other functions in the area.

Local prospects are contacted either in person or by telephone, while promotional materials are mailed to businesses in the surrounding communities. Businesses that respond are contacted in person, and the people there are asked during the visit if they might know of other firms that might be interested in using Signature properties.

The "personal touch" of each property's sales team is credited for making the difference when it comes to name recognition and the generation of additional room nights and revenue.

or business acquaintances, they may also have an extensive sphere of influence within other areas of their own organizations—or with peers from other firms. Asking current clients to identify others who might be interested in your property's facilities and services is an excellent business practice called **referral prospecting.** Some salespeople even use their network of satisfied customers to help them with booking new business. They have found that an enthusiastic call from a good customer to a new prospect is a great door opener and a positive influence on the booking decision.

2. *Other departments within large corporations or groups that the property is currently serving.* If the property is dealing with one department within a large corporation or association, there may be a number of other departments within the organization that need hotel accommodations or services. Don't be content with a single piece of business from a company. Account penetration—that is, seeking business from all divisions within a company—is the sign of a successful hotel salesperson.

3. *Local organizations and companies.* You should not neglect local firms when prospecting. Business directories, chamber of commerce publications, and industry reports will often yield important information. A local firm, for example, may be a branch of a national organization and the potential source of a large amount of business. The local library, convention and visitors bureau, and state industrial commission are also excellent sources for local

leads. Most offer publications that list businesses according to the Standard Industrial Classification (SIC), developed by the federal government. In many cases, your property may already have a breakdown, by SIC code, of business booked; this makes it particularly easy to target other businesses from the same category. In addition to the SIC code, which categorizes virtually every type of business, many publications also list businesses in terms of geographic area, volume of business, number of employees, and names of officers. This information is particularly useful in determining the prospects that would most likely be interested in your property's facilities. *Size, proximity,* and *type of business* are key criteria when developing your prospect list. It is normally best to first identify those companies that are the largest, closest to your property, and in the same or similar businesses as those that you already successfully serve.

4. *Community contacts.* Don't discount the potential of casual contacts. Delivery and repair personnel; department store managers, who entertain suppliers and often come in contact with residents new to the area; real estate salespeople, who deal with new residents and help to relocate corporate executives; funeral directors, who are often asked to recommend lodging facilities for friends of the family who arrive from out of town; and even service station attendants, who are often asked for directions and information on places to eat or stay, are all excellent sources for a number of types of business.

5. *Front desk personnel.* Many individual guests have the potential to bring group business to the property. The front desk staff can provide referrals that may result in additional individual or group business.

6. *Other property employees.* Many property employees belong to groups or organizations such as bowling leagues and church groups that can become potential clients. You should ask staff members for leads.

7. *The property's competitors.* You can even get prospect leads from the competition, so knowing what competitors are doing and whom they are serving is important. Consider these questions when researching competitors:

   - Who are our top three direct competitors?
   - What are the five major accounts for each competitor?
   - How many room nights is each account booking and at what rates?
   - What will it take (lower rates, better product-service, more promotion, etc.) to get our competitors' major accounts to use our facilities?

8. *Other sources.* You can find both individual and group business through a number of other sources. Exhibit 1 lists several sources for prospecting for new business, the key contacts you should be talking with, and the potential business you can expect from them. The local newspaper is an excellent starting point; a careful review of the business, local news, and sports sections—as well as local advertisements—can prove productive (a single newspaper could result in 15 to 25 promising leads). Leads may include names of people and businesses that have recently located to the area; presidents, officers,

Exhibit 1 Sources for Individual and Group Business

Companies

Potential business: Guestrooms, meeting rooms, office and holiday parties, retirement and award banquets, training schools and employee indoctrination sessions, recruiting programs, sales incentives (vacations for top-producing salespeople, etc.).

Sources: Chamber of commerce listings, Polk's city directory (available in libraries), telephone directory yellow pages, business sections of newspapers, Association of Corporate Travel Executives directory, leads from clients and acquaintances, competitors' function boards (the listing of daily functions that is usually posted in the lobby or meeting area).

Contact persons: Sales managers, personnel and training directors, department or division officers or heads, traffic managers, key secretaries.

Local Clubs and Professional and Fraternal Organizations

Potential business: Guestrooms for guest speakers, regularly scheduled chapter meetings, installation of new officers (banquets), holiday parties, special project events, state and regional conventions.

Sources: Chamber of commerce listings, telephone directory yellow pages, newspaper stories, leads from clients and acquaintances, competitors' function boards.

Contact persons: Local community professionals, fraternal organization administrators, club officers and members, key secretaries.

Hospitals, Schools, and Government Agencies

Potential business: Guestrooms, meetings and seminars, recruiting programs, parties, award banquets, training schools, conventions.

Sources: Chamber of commerce listings; telephone directory yellow pages; government, school, and hospital directories; leads from clients and acquaintances; competitors' function boards.

Contact persons: Directors and administrators, athletic directors or team managers, department heads, military recruiting officers, key secretaries (court bailiffs and judicial secretaries, secretaries to principals, etc.), personnel and public relations managers.

Family Social Functions

Potential business: Guestrooms for out-of-town family members (for family reunions or funerals), guestrooms for out-of-town wedding guests, a honeymoon guestroom or suite, receptions, rehearsal dinners, showers.

Sources: Retail store managers, church officials, newspaper stories, leads from clients and acquaintances.

Contact persons: Family reunion organizers, retail store managers, church officials, the bride or her parents, the groom or his parents, friends or relatives of the wedding party or family.

Travel Industry Accounts

Potential business: Guestrooms (individual and corporate), guestrooms for bus tours, tour bus meal stops, familiarization seminars.

(continued)

Exhibit 1 *(continued)*

Sources: American Society of Travel Agents membership directory, National Tour Association membership directory, telephone directory yellow pages, mailing houses, newspaper stories, leads from clients and acquaintances, competitors' function boards.

Contact persons: Company presidents; national sales managers; local airline, bus, and train station managers.

Professional and Trade Associations

Potential business: Guestrooms for guest speakers or members, regularly scheduled chapter meetings, installation of new officers (banquets), holiday parties, state and regional conventions, meetings and seminars, special project events, auxiliary activities.

Sources: Chamber of commerce listings, telephone directory yellow pages, newspaper stories, leads from clients and acquaintances, competitors' function boards.

Contact persons: Executive directors, association officers, local association members, committee chairpersons.

and committee persons of local civic and social clubs; sponsors of sporting or entertainment events; newly engaged couples; couples celebrating anniversaries; sponsors of class or family reunions; or businesses sponsoring special events.

9. *The national level.* Although it is always best to begin with "backyard" prospecting, it is also important to target travel intermediaries such as meeting planners, corporate travel managers, incentive travel buyers, travel agents, tour operators, and tour wholesalers. Lists of these travel intermediaries can be found in directories issued by national organizations (these directories can be found in large libraries). Many travel intermediaries belong to professional associations that offer allied memberships to hotel salespeople. By joining these associations and attending their meetings or conventions, you can network with travel intermediaries and develop relationships that may lead to increased sales.

10. *Networking.* Networking within professional associations and your community is the most important thing you can do to further your career and reach your property's sales goals. Networking involves building and nurturing relationships with as many business associates as possible to help you generate new leads. Get involved in civic and service organizations or in groups designed specifically for the purpose of networking. Membership in hospitality industry organizations can help you make invaluable contacts who can assist you with learning the "hot buttons" of prospects. Since the purpose of networking is to meet new people who may be helpful in generating business, it is important to attend as many meetings and gatherings as possible. While you will certainly want to tell people that you are in hospitality sales, this is not the time for a sales pitch. By listening rather than talking, you can garner information that will help you determine whether new contacts are future

prospects. Hand out your business card and collect the business cards of new acquaintances, making pertinent notes on the backs of the cards to assist you with follow up.

11. *The Internet.* The Internet has become a prominent source for lead generation and solicitation. You can search for companies by name, access financial data, and find key executives through financially oriented sites without leaving the comfort of your office. Since the computer is playing an increasingly important role in sales and marketing, you must become comfortable with today's technology to be successful in the hospitality field.

Once prospect research has been done, goals can be set. If, for example, the sales department's goal for each salesperson is to develop three new accounts a week, it may be necessary to set a prospecting goal of 15 contacts per week to realize three new prospects. Many hotel sales offices assign such specific goals, while others allow individual salespeople to set their own goals within property guidelines. In either case, you should keep accurate records of prospecting efforts for evaluating your progress in meeting goals (see Exhibit 2).

To free up salespeople for selling, many properties are using other employees for the prospecting and qualifying functions. Front desk personnel, reservationists, and sales secretaries can be trained to develop leads, or properties may employ a staff of telephone prospectors strictly for that purpose.

Qualifying Prospects

Qualify and *quantify* are two of the most important steps in the solicitation of any account. Unfortunately, not every prospect qualifies as a potential client; in many hotels, 80 percent of business is generated by 20 percent of their accounts. It is important, then, to determine which leads offer the most potential for business; in other words, you must qualify your prospects.

Full qualification involves gathering all the information necessary to place a dollar value on the potential business from the account. For example, a company executive may indicate that she has 40 executives visiting from out of town two days each month of the year, a three-day sales training seminar for 25 persons twice a year, and the need for 10 room nights per month for visiting clients. This makes it possible to estimate the potential yearly dollar volume from this account for your property—$98,100:

40 persons	×	2 days	×	12 months	=	960 room nights	×	$80	=	$76,800
25 persons	×	3 days	×	2 months	=	150 room nights	×	$70	=	$10,500
10 persons	×	1 day	×	12 months	=	120 room nights	×	$90	=	$10,800
										$98,100

By estimating potential value, you can focus on "big dollar" accounts, the key prospects that could really make a difference in occupancy and revenue should they become steady clients. Simply estimating potential revenue is not enough, however. The potential may indeed be there, but are there other factors that may affect the account's profitability? To fully determine if the prospect is indeed qualified involves three basic criteria: financial status, the need for the product or service, and the ability to purchase.

Exhibit 2 Sample Sales Prospect Card

Prospect's Name ______________________________

Company Name ______________________________

Address of Prospect ____________________ Telephone ______________

Type of Business ______________________________

Pertinent background information on the company and/or contact person:

____

____

____

Prospect's estimated sales potential in:

Room Nights ______________

Meetings/Banquets ______________

Dollars ______________

Facilities and/or services needed by prospect:

____

____

Has the prospect been qualified? ☐ Yes ☐ No

Action required to:

a. Qualify the prospect ______________________________

b. Follow-up ______________________________

Salesperson's Name ______________________________

Date of Contact ______________ Follow-Up Date ______________

To make the most of a sales call, it is helpful to have some basic information about the needs of a prospect. A sales prospect card can help a salesperson determine how to best structure his or her presentation to appeal to the needs of the client.

Financial status information may be obtained from national or local credit rating organizations as well as from annual reports. This information will provide an overview of the prospect's financial standing and enables a salesperson to weed out certain prospects. An organization that does a low volume of business, for example, probably cannot afford an upscale property for a business meeting or convention. Spending time on such an account would likely be a waste of time for

Reaching the Decision-Maker

No sales effort succeeds unless it is directed at the person or persons with the authority to make the decision to buy. Reaching the decision-maker is crucial, but often difficult—decision-makers may vary from company to company and even from year to year. To reach decision-makers, you must:

- *Ask the right questions.* To find the decision-maker, you have to ask the right questions: "Who coordinates your meetings?" is not a good question; the person who coordinates the details of a meeting may not be the actual decision-maker. It is far better to ask, "Who is responsible for deciding which hotels your company uses for meetings?" With this approach, you will be able to make immediate contact with the decision-maker rather than having to deal with one or more "go-betweens," saving valuable time and effort.
- *Start at the top.* Another approach, which may require slightly more time and effort (but which may also prove profitable), is to start at the top of the company and work downward. While speaking with the company president may not result in an immediate booking if he or she isn't personally involved, a president is seldom hesitant about referring you to the right person, and the recommendation of the president is a great door opener when dealing with his or her subordinates.
- *Look for the leaders.* Yet another effective strategy is to get to know the "star performers" in a company or organization. By identifying and cultivating relationships with them, you can reap dividends in the future—when they succeed today's key decision-makers.

When it comes to approaching decision-makers, it is natural for young salespeople just starting out to be a little shy about calling on prospects who are much older and in high positions. In most cases, however, these prospects will understand that you are just starting out; in fact, a young person sometimes brings out the paternal or maternal instincts in some prospects and they will do all they can to help you. So don't follow the natural tendency to call on people who are of the same age and career level as you are. The important thing to remember is that you need to call on those people who can give you business and further your career.

a salesperson from an upscale property. Conversely, a large, multimillion dollar corporation might be interested only in upscale accommodations for its executives and meeting attendees; a salesperson for a budget property would probably be unable to solicit business from a corporation of that size.

Need for the product or services offered by the property can be determined by researching the prospect's previous buying record. This information can be obtained through telephone surveys, by contacting the prospect directly, or through information supplied by clients or other business contacts. Has the prospect used other facilities similar to those offered by the property? Is the prospect's company part of a chain or conglomerate that may be affiliated with other hospitality properties? Does the prospect have a need for the special services offered by the property?

The prospect's ability to purchase is based on a number of factors. Even if a prospect's company is financially secure, there may be budget limitations for travel and business expenses, or restrictions on which hospitality properties may be chosen (the company may have a preferred list of acceptable accommodations). Other companies, although prosperous, may still be risky from a salesperson's point of view: payment may have to be routed through corporate offices, the company may be in the midst of a reorganization or takeover by another company, or the prospect's authority for buying may be limited. When qualifying a prospect, therefore, it is important to do your homework in these areas.

Preparing for the Presentation Sales Call

Once a qualified prospect has been called on and has expressed an interest in the property, a presentation sales call can be made.

Although you should approach each presentation sales call with confidence, you should realize that not all presentations lead to a sale. There are three reasons within a salesperson's control why a presentation sales call fails:

1. Planning for the call was inadequate.
2. The salesperson was anxious or nervous.
3. The salesperson failed to reach the decision-maker.

All of these problems can be overcome if you thoroughly prepare for your presentation.[3] Why should you do your homework? Because thorough preparation results in:

1. *Increased credibility.* A prepared salesperson knows what the property has to offer, has translated property products and services into benefits, and has determined the needs of the client before attempting to make a presentation. A client will have much more confidence in you if you know the property and how it can benefit the client.
2. *Increased confidence.* Salespeople must sell themselves as well as the property; a nervous or anxious salesperson can lose an important sale. Knowing the product, the competition, and the client increases your self-confidence and ability to influence clients.
3. *Increased probability of reaching the decision-maker.* Research gives you a better chance of talking to the right person, which means a better chance of making a sale.

Pre-Presentation Planning

To be effective, pre-presentation planning should include property research, competition research, and client research.

Property Research. You must have a thorough knowledge of your property. There are two basic methods of improving property knowledge: studying a property fact book, and developing a working knowledge of all the property's departments. The facts obtained through either method should be studied, memorized, and updated when necessary.

The property fact book. Your property fact book should include pertinent information on the following:

- General property description—location, age, layout, and so on
- Guestrooms—number, types, rates, special rooms, amenities, security
- Restaurants and lounges—number, hours, menus (including room service menus), seating capacities, types of seating, entertainment, special promotions
- Meeting and banquet facilities—number of rooms, seating capacities, services offered, banquet menus, rates
- Audiovisual equipment—types of equipment offered, availability, and prices
- VIP packages—amenities and prices
- Transportation—availability and rates, with special attention to airport transportation
- Recreational facilities—types, rates, hours, lessons available, rental equipment, supervision
- Outside services—secretarial services, shopping services, and so on
- Vendors—florists, photographers, musicians, and their rates
- The community and surrounding areas—area attractions (locations, fees, hours, group rates, etc.) and community atmosphere (rustic, metropolitan, suburban, and so on)
- Guests and finances—guest profiles; present guest mix; optimum guest mix; peak, valley, and shoulder periods; average daily rate from each market segment

During a presentation sales call, products and services listed in the property fact book should be presented as benefits to the client (see Exhibit 3). A property's total number of guestrooms, for example, may not be important to a client, but he or she may be influenced by amenities, room dimensions, the number of no-smoking rooms, check-in/check-out times, deposit policies, or other property fact book information presented as benefits to meet specific needs.

A good exercise for new salespeople touring their property is to list every feature of the property they think a guest might desire—wireless Internet, flat-screen televisions, a private floor for corporate executives, full-length mirrors, a desk with a telephone, well-lit bathrooms, and so on—and write down how these features will benefit guests.

As a salesperson, not only do you need to know your property, but you also must be sold on your property to sell it to others. Always try to view your product from the customer's point of view. If you were a prospect, why should you choose your hotel over another?

Exhibit 3 Turning Features/Services into Benefits

Feature/Service		Benefit
"We have electronic door locks	SO THAT	you will enjoy a feeling of security."
"We offer 24-hour room service	SO THAT	you may enjoy a meal in the comfort of your own room."
"Every room has a desk with a telephone	SO THAT	you can work in your guestroom efficiently."
"Every room features a complete package of name-brand amenities	SO THAT	you can travel light."
"We have express check-out	SO THAT	you can enjoy the convenience of a timely departure."
"As for our beds, the mattresses are firm	SO THAT	you're sure to enjoy a comfortable night's sleep."

The selling sentence can also be reversed—starting with the benefit and backing it up with the feature. The word "because" would link the benefit to the feature:

Benefit		Feature/Service
"You will enjoy a feeling of security	BECAUSE	we have electronic door locks."
"You can enjoy a meal in the comfort of your room	BECAUSE	we offer 24-hour room service."

Salespeople who present only features or services rely on their prospects to interpret how those features or services can benefit them. Instead, salespeople should try to influence the client's interpretation by always linking features or services with benefits—and explaining to prospects how the features or services will benefit them and enhance their meetings. To assist you in thinking "benefits," the words "so that" can be used to link the two. The selling sentence can also be reversed, using the word "because" to link the benefit to the feature or service.

Competition Research. You must know as much about competitors' properties as your property to sell successfully against the competition. It is almost impossible to sell your property if you are unable to show clients how your property can serve their needs better than the competition can. By taking a hard, objective look at competitors' properties, you can note strengths and weaknesses and emphasize your property's strengths in areas that relate to client needs. One salesperson was able to book a weekend convention after visiting a competitor's property and noting that his own property's ballroom—although approximately the same size as his competitor's—seated 40 additional guests. Research allows you to downplay those features and services in which a competitor has an advantage, and play up those areas in which your property can best serve the client. Exhibit 4 is an excellent tool for determining your strengths and weaknesses in relationship to your competition.

Exhibit 4 Sample Competition Analysis—Need Fulfillment by Market Segment

COMPETITIVE ANALYSIS
NEED FULFILLMENT BY MARKET SEGMENT

Needs and Wants of Target Markets	Competitors			
	Rolling Green Resort	Hilton Inn	Arrowhead Conference Center	Comments
Corporate Meetings Market				
AV equipment	1	3	3	Our access to outside AV firms is limited
Security	3	2	2	
Training atmosphere	2	2	2	
Space on short lead time	3	2	3	Our secluded location is a benefit to corp planners
Soundproof meeting rooms	2	2	1	
Master account billing	3	2	3	
Efficient check-in, check-out	2	2	2	
Wake-up, message service	2	2	2	
Quality food service	2	2	3	
Association Meetings Market				
Comp. room policy	3	2	2	We offer 1 comp for 40, rather than 1 comp for 50 rooms booked
Exhibit space	1	3	1	
Accessible location	1	3	2	
Overflow arrangements	1	3	2	
Assistance with housing	2	2	2	
Spouse programs	2	3	2	
Reasonable room rates	3	2	2	Key: 3= superior 2 = average 1 = poor
Recreational amenities	3	1	1	
Convention coordinator	3	2	2	

A competition analysis can take many forms, including just a simple feature-by-feature comparison of the competitors' facilities with your own. The most pertinent information can be gained by evaluating how your property "stacks up" in specific market areas. This is one type of form used to compare the services offered to each market segment. Isolating target markets and determining how well your property fills the needs and wants of each segment is extremely helpful in finding your competitive advantages. This form illustrates just two market segments. You should assess the needs and wants of all market segments you are targeting. The key is to find a difference that makes a difference to each targeted market.

When analyzing your competition, you must remember that your strengths and weaknesses differ from market segment to market segment, based on the needs of prospects within each segment. For example, while your secluded location may be an advantage to corporate meeting planners, it may be a weakness to association meeting planners who are looking for downtown sites offering a wide selection of activities for their attendees.

INTERNET EXERCISE

Log onto the Internet and find Lodging Hospitality's website at www.lhonline.com. In the "Search" box, type in "Tom McCarthy," then click on "Go." (Tom McCarthy, a leading hospitality sales trainer, was quoted in the "Prospecting" section of this chapter.) Review three articles by McCarthy that relate to personal sales. What additional information did you learn?

Information required for competition research may be obtained through visits to the competition, inquiries to competitors' properties, and studies of the competition's marketing plans and annual reports. In researching the competition, don't overlook the competition's sales methods, pricing strategies, promotional methods, and sales staff size and ability. In addition to comparing features and services, you must consider such intangibles as the reputation, friendliness, and service standards of other properties.

Client Research. Before calling on clients, learn as much as possible about them and their organization. Information is available from a number of sources: other clients who know the client, annual reports, Internet sites, business directories, articles, trade journals, and membership directories and lists.

The information obtained during pre-presentation research allows you to tailor a presentation for each client. Needs, characteristics, and requirements vary from one market segment to another, and you must gain an understanding of these differences before making sales calls.

Good salespeople are empathetic; they can put themselves in the other person's shoes. They understand their clients' viewpoints and concerns, and they consciously question, "If I were this prospect, why would I choose my hotel?" Never sell what you wouldn't buy yourself. Selling a meeting room that won't meet the customer's needs is short-sighted. It is better to refer customers to a competitor rather than sell them something that would displease them and ruin your credibility.

To become knowledgeable about market segments, their needs, and requirements, you should:

- *Study research done on market segments.* Periodicals such as *Lodging Hospitality* and *Nation's Restaurant News* regularly report on the needs of market segments.
- *Study what is happening in the industries of your key customers.* For example, if a good percentage of your business comes from insurance meetings, subscribe to publications such as *Insurance Conference Planner* and *The Meeting Professional,* which detail what is happening in the insurance field.
- *Brainstorm with hotel staff to complete a customer needs analysis for each market segment* (see Exhibit 5).

Thorough knowledge of the property, the competition, and the client can lead to booked business.

Exhibit 5 Examples of Market Segment Needs

Relocation/Extended-Stay Executive

- Large guestroom, work area, closet
- Refrigerator
- Health/fitness center
- Variety of food
- Safety deposit boxes

Retail Travel Agent

- Competitive commission rates
- Commissions paid promptly
- Toll-free reservation service
- Assurance the hotel will service their clients
- Good stock of current hotel brochures

Sports Teams

- Assignment to one area of the hotel
- Split folios when team members pay their own expenses
- Free meeting space for pre- and postgame meetings
- Extra security
- Excellent meals
- One contact in the hotel

Different market segments have different requirements. To more effectively sell to each segment, hotel salespeople must take the needs of each segment into consideration, and prepare presentations that address these needs.

The Sales Kit

Before making a sales call, you should prepare a well-organized and professional sales kit. Only the information pertinent to the client's particular needs should be included; too much information results in clutter and appears unprofessional.

Information basic to nearly every sales call includes a general **property information sheet**—a summary of what the property has to offer. A property information sheet should include the location of the property, the number and types of guestrooms, a description of the atmosphere of the hotel, parking information, number and types of restaurants, meeting room capabilities, and special amenities and features.

A meeting and banquet room information sheet may also be part of the sales kit. It should cover each meeting room's seating capacity (figured for various setups) and breakfast, lunch, dinner, and break menus. Floor plans for each meeting area are also important.

Testimonials or endorsement letters are often included in the sales kit. When using endorsement letters, however, the market segment targeted is a prime consideration; a training director is more likely to identify with an endorsement letter from another training director, for example, than with a letter written by a motorcoach tour organizer.

While they are not usually considered part of the sales kit, business cards also play an important role in a sales appointment. You should have at least three business cards readily available for each sales call—one for the receptionist, one for the secretary, and one for the prospect. Business cards should not be carried in the sales kit, but in a convenient pocket.

Information in the sales kit is more meaningful if it is accompanied by visual aids such as 8 × 10 color photographs of rooms, restaurants, banquet facilities, and the exterior of the property. A map of the hotel's general vicinity indicating transportation terminals and nearby attractions can also prove beneficial. For best results, list major attractions below the map, along with the mileage from the property to the attractions.

Today, many salespeople carry laptop computers on sales calls, allowing prospects to take virtual tours of the property, view past functions, and read recommendations from satisfied customers.

Projecting a Professional Image

Once the precall research is complete, it is time to attend to personal factors that can affect the success of the sales call. You are an official representative of the property, and your appearance, attitude, and approach to clients can mean the difference between new business and a negative response. Remember, you never get a second chance to make a good first impression.

First and foremost, never smoke, chew gum, or drink during a sales call. These activities detract from the presentation and may create a communications barrier. Other distractions or unnecessary materials (coats, umbrellas, newspapers, literature for other sales calls, and so on) should be kept to a minimum. Leave any unnecessary items outside the office and avoid distracting motions such as shuffling papers and fumbling with visual aids.

Never neglect the importance of punctuality; salespeople who are habitually late for appointments are wasting their time and their clients' time. They also send the message that the client is not important to them.

Other factors in projecting a professional image include nonverbal communication, voice quality, listening skills, and negotiating skills.

Nonverbal Communication. Nonverbal communication plays an important part in how your presentation will be accepted by the client and can be divided into four general categories: appearance, the handshake, territorial space, and body language.

Appearance. Your appearance (especially your hairstyle) is the first thing a client notices. For this reason, you should have a well-groomed and inoffensive hairstyle.

Your wardrobe is another important success factor. You should wear conservative clothing that suggests success and authority. Dark suits for men and conservative, tailored suits for women project an image of stability and credibility, setting the stage for a businesslike presentation. Clothes should be clean, well-pressed, and appropriate for the region's business community.

Even the most expensive wardrobe won't erase negative impressions caused by bad grooming. Hair should be clean; makeup moderate and well-applied; fingernails neatly manicured; and perfume, cologne, or after-shave kept to an acceptable level for business.

The handshake. The handshake, when done correctly, helps establish an atmosphere of mutual respect and leads into a positive presentation. As a general rule, you should extend your hand first and maintain eye contact with the client while gripping the client's hand firmly. The handshake should be fairly brief. A long handshake may cause discomfort for a new client because it implies intimacy, but a limp "cold-fish" handshake should also be avoided—it implies unfriendliness.

Territorial space. Cultural differences affect how physical distances between people are perceived. For simplicity, we will discuss four categories of physical distances between people: public space, social space, personal space, and intimate space.[4] Since any unwelcome invasion of these spaces can make the client defensive, an understanding of territorial space is essential to successful selling.

Public space is a nonthreatening area over 12 feet (3.7 meters) away from potential clients. This type of space is the best type to use when selling to a group, because a group usually feels more at ease and more willing to communicate at this distance. This much distance is not particularly helpful when making a presentation to an individual, however, as it limits his or her involvement.

Social space is an area four to 12 feet (1.2 to 3.7 meters) from the client, and may be an ideal beginning area for a presentation to an individual, especially if you are not acquainted with him or her. Clients often use a desk to maintain this distance.

Personal space is an area two to four feet (.6 to 1.2 meters) from the client, and is often the closest you may get to a client. Depending on a person's background, even this distance may be too close, and barriers (desks, tables, and so on) may be used by some clients to protect their personal space.

When clients are comfortable with you, they may invite you into their personal space zone; this gesture shows friendliness and greatly enhances your chances of giving a successful presentation. If you are given a choice of a seat in the social space (in front of the desk) or in the personal space (beside the client on the side of the desk), you should indicate friendliness and interest by accepting the chair in the personal space. However, chairs should not be moved closer unless the client is a friend. To do so might be an unwelcome intrusion into the client's personal space, which could lessen the chance for a sale.

Intimate space is an area within arm's length of the client and is usually reserved for close friends and loved ones. A salesperson's invasion of this space may be offensive or cause the client to feel dominated or overpowered.

Body language. One of the most interesting parts of nonverbal communication is **body language**—signals sent from a person's face, arms, hands, legs, and posture. Your body language is very important to your presentation. Your body should be erect to project confidence, you should smile to show warmth and interest in the client, and your gestures should complement, not detract from, the sales presentation.

Understanding body language can increase your chances of making a sale. Since nonverbal communication tends to be spontaneous and unconscious, people tend to believe the nonverbal message even if it contradicts what is being said. Therefore, it is important to make a conscious effort to display positive body language:

- Face—Maintain a pleasant expression, make appropriate eye contact with the client, and smile frequently.
- Arms—Keep them relaxed and uncrossed.
- Hands—Offer a firm handshake; make arm gestures with extended hands, palms open.
- Legs—Cross them in the direction of the client or leave them uncrossed.
- Posture—Lean forward to express interest or sit upright to project confidence and credibility.

You should also be alert to any negative body language sent by the client. *Caution signals* include the client leaning away from you, very little eye contact, puzzled facial expressions, a neutral or questioning tone of voice, crossed or tense arms, clasped hands, fidgeting, or legs crossed and turned away from you. *Disagreement signals* include the client leaning away from you, retracted shoulders, a tense face, a wrinkled brow, very little or no eye contact, arms crossed over the chest, hand motions expressing rejection or disapproval, tense or clenched hands, or legs crossed and turned away from you.

It is important to deal with negative body language as soon as you note it. In the case of caution signals, you can depart from the planned presentation and ask questions to encourage the client to express attitudes and opinions. By listening carefully, you can address the client's concerns, modify your presentation, and possibly reestablish rapport.

When disagreement signals are evident, it is important to *immediately* stop and adjust to the situation. Again, you may use questions to determine what is wrong, and it is acceptable to let the client know you are aware that something upsetting has occurred. Direct questions, such as "Have I said something that you do not agree with?" can be used to reestablish communication and lead the client back into the areas in the presentation that caused concern.

Voice Quality. Every sales presentation must be clear and understandable to be effective. The human voice is a persuasive instrument when used properly, and it is vitally important that you learn to use your voice as a selling tool.

You should be aware of the importance of voice tone, inflection, and enunciation during a sales call. Avoid slang and technical jargon. Use words that your customers understand. Speak slowly. If you speak too quickly and do not allow the client to speak, the client may feel overwhelmed by a verbal barrage.

A salesperson's accent may also be a factor in giving a presentation. A New Englander may need to adapt to the slow drawl of westerners, for example. If you are uncertain of how you sound to others, you may wish to tape-record your voice to analyze strengths and weaknesses.

Listening Skills. At the other end of the spectrum, you must know when to stop talking. You need to show a genuine interest in your clients' needs, and listening is an important part of building rapport.

There are a number of ways to increase your listening efficiency. First, when the client is speaking, face him or her and eliminate as many distractions as possible. Show the client that you are really listening by maintaining eye contact (without staring) and nodding in agreement. Appropriate facial expressions are another nonverbal way to assure the client that you are listening.

Pay careful attention to what is being said; this is not the time to be thinking about what to say when the client stops talking. It is often effective to repeat, in your own words, what has just been said, as you understand it. Avoid adding content when rephrasing and refrain from agreeing or disagreeing with the client; the important thing is to communicate to the client your understanding of what was said.

Being attentive to the client, taking notes, and not interrupting while the client is speaking can build listening skills and sales success.

Negotiating Skills. Listening plays a key role in yet another important sales skill: negotiating. Negotiating involves two or more parties coming together to reach an agreement for their mutual benefit. This process should be viewed as a friendly, problem-solving partnership, but many salespeople are fearful and uncomfortable in a negotiating situation. This shouldn't be the case; negotiating can result in a win-win situation for both the property and the prospect if handled properly.

The first step involves preparation by gathering information. Knowledge is power, and a successful salesperson will thoroughly research four key areas: his or her product, the competition, the prospect's position, and the property's position. We have already discussed the importance of property and competition research.

There are several key factors to consider when evaluating the prospect's position:

1. *Deadline.* How soon will the function be held?
2. *Competitors.* Is the prospect negotiating with other properties as well? If so, how well can your property compete in terms of product, services, and prices?
3. *Past problems.* Has the prospect experienced problems with another property? Knowing what went wrong enables you to point out features and benefits that will ensure that disasters will not be repeated.
4. *Budget.* Knowledge of the prospect's past and present event budgets is essential. How much has the prospect been willing to spend on similar events in the past? Is price a major concern?
5. *Other key issues.* What are the prospect's other concerns? The availability of special services, such as transportation, VIP check-in/check-out, or special meals? Payment arrangements? By knowing what is important to the prospect in advance, you can be ready with a solution that is equitable to both parties.

6. *Decision-maker.* Is the prospect the decision-maker or will he or she have to "sell" the property to another party? If another decision-maker is involved, you must provide the prospect with enough information and supporting material for an effective presentation.

The property's position is usually based on profitability requirements—how badly the property needs the prospect's business. Will this business fill a particular need—generate revenue during a "soft" period, for example? (Steering groups to dates when the hotel or restaurant needs business is an important part of negotiating.) Will it be necessary to forgo this piece of business because more lucrative accounts take precedence during a particular time period? Or does this prospect have unreasonable demands that are not cost-effective?

When evaluating these points, it is essential to consider opportunities for future business. Would servicing a minor function for the client today result in additional, possibly more lucrative business tomorrow? Are there other departments within the company that might use the property's facilities in the future?

Trade-offs or concessions are often part of negotiating, and the property must set its limits. Many salespeople think they must give something away to close a sale, but successful salespeople do not enter into discussions with that attitude. They sell value, and offer concessions only when absolutely necessary. Concessions should not cut too deeply into the property's profitability. Free meeting space may be offered if the prospect agrees to pay standard room rates, for example, or rooms may be upgraded if the prospect agrees to pay standard banquet costs. Successful negotiating is a give-and-take process, but the goal is that both parties are satisfied.

The Presentation Sales Call

Regardless of the type of sales call, you must have a planned objective for the call, whether it is to establish a personal relationship with the client, invite the client to visit the property, qualify the client for potential business, or obtain a provisional or definite booking. It often takes five to seven contacts with a potential customer before you actually book any business. If every call you make has a specific objective, one call tends to set up the next: your initial contact objective may be to qualify the account; the second, to get the prospect to the property; and so on. (Incidentally, if you are inviting a prospect to your hotel or restaurant, always do so during a busy time; a busy hotel or restaurant tends to increase believability of your claims.) In general, some type of commitment from the client is the main objective of any sales call. Having an objective in mind helps keep you on track.[5]

Most presentation calls are set up by appointment. Making an appointment shows respect for the client and saves time for both you and your prospect. With an unannounced call, it is likely that you may only get three to five minutes of your prospect's time; by making an appointment, you can usually arrange a meeting of 15 to 30 minutes, adequate time for you to give an effective presentation. Once you have made an appointment with the client and have prepared yourself for a presentation sales call, there are five steps that should be followed for maximum success:

1. Opening the sales call
2. Getting client involvement
3. Presenting your property
4. Overcoming objections
5. Closing and following up

These five steps follow the same order in every presentation sales call, and most can be prepared in advance. If steps are skipped, the sale is unlikely to be made.

Step 1: Opening the Sales Call

All sales calls begin with an opening. The opening should put the customer at ease, establish rapport, and build the prospect's confidence and trust in you. The opening includes an introduction and a purpose statement, benefit statement, and bridge statement.

Introduction. The first step is to introduce yourself and your property: "Good morning, Mr. Smith. I'm Terry Jones from the Red Rock Resort in Boulder, Colorado." If you have already spoken with the client, either in person or over the telephone, it is appropriate to say something like, "Good afternoon, Mr. Baker. It's nice to see you again" or "Hi, Jean. It's a pleasure to finally meet you after talking with you on the telephone."

During the introduction, offer a brief but firm handshake, maintain eye contact, and present a business card. Then, you should immediately begin to build rapport through a brief conversation (mutually interesting "small talk") or, better yet, by expressing interest in the prospect.

Communicating your knowledge of your prospect's organization or needs is particularly effective (this information can usually be obtained through client research). A comment such as, "I've heard so much about what your firm has been doing in the field of laser technology, and I've been looking forward to meeting you and finding out more about laser surgery" can go a long way in building rapport.

Purpose Statement. Soon after the introduction, state the purpose of the visit. Are you calling to present a new idea, service, or product? To renew a business relationship? Avoid at all times such statements as, "I just wanted to touch base with you" or "My boss wanted me to call on you." During a presentation sales call, the purpose of your visit is to make a sale, so you should say something like, "I'd like to discuss your need for meeting facilities."

Benefit Statement. The next step in the opening is to present a benefit (or benefits). The benefit statement is the most important part of the opening, because it gives the client a reason to listen to you. Most clients become interested in a hotel's facilities and services only if the facilities and services can benefit them directly. Therefore, it is important to not sell the product; you must sell what the product can do for the client. In other words, you must be a problem-solver, rather than a product-seller.

Bridge Statement. Once you have stated property benefits, you are ready to lead into the body of the sales presentation. Bridge statements are a way of asking for permission to continue the sales call, and are usually made in the form of a question: "Would you be interested in learning how other companies such as yours have benefited from our frequent guest programs?" or "Ms. Townes, is it all right if I take a few moments to ask some questions and jot down some notes about your business to give me a better idea of how we can serve you?"

These questions ask for a response from the client. If the client is not interested in answering these questions, permission to continue has not been granted, and you can thank the client for his or her time and ask for an appointment in the future. If these questions elicit positive responses, however, you have received permission to continue, and can proceed to the next phase of the sales call: getting client involvement.

Step 2: Getting Client Involvement

Step two in the sales call focuses on determining the client's specific needs and involving the client by asking questions. *Questioning always precedes any sales presentation;* this is a fundamental rule. Questioning and presenting are separate steps. *Always* complete the questioning before presenting—don't question and present, question and present, and so on. This type of approach results in a "stop-start" sales call that tends to confuse prospects and can cause them to lose interest.

Getting client involvement serves several purposes. Involvement helps build the client's interest and helps you determine the client's needs and the areas of greatest importance to the client. You should take notes during this step; these notes should later become a part of the client's account file. Questioning helps you custom-tailor the sales call. With the knowledge gained during this questioning step, you can anticipate objections and adjust your presentation accordingly.

Questioning. The use of questions such as, "Don't you agree?" "Does that sound fair?" "What do you think?" help you identify areas of concern to the client. Such questions can also be used throughout the presentation itself, either at the beginning or end of a sentence. For example, if a meeting planner is visiting the property, you could show him or her the ballroom and ask, "Would this room be suitable for your closing banquet?" Or, in showing the property's executive suite, you might say, "Your president would like this suite, wouldn't he?" Asking these types of questions involves the prospect in the presentation and enables the salesperson to check for understanding. Does the prospect see the benefit in what the property has to offer?

You need to ask two types of questions: **closed-ended questions** and **open-ended questions.** Closed-ended questions generally require a specific reply and can often be answered in one or two words. "How many training meetings did you stage last year?" is a closed-ended question. Open-ended questions give clients the opportunity to express their feelings and knowledge. For example, you might say, "In researching your association, I noticed that last year's attendance at your annual convention was at an all-time high. Why do you think last year's meeting was so successful?" The client's answer may give clues about what is important to the client.

Questions can also be divided into three broad categories: *fact-finding* questions determine specifics and facts; *feeling-finding* questions reveal the feelings, attitudes, and opinions of the client; *problem-solving* questions uncover the problems faced by the client and pave the way for the presentation.

Fact-finding questions can be closed-ended questions such as, "How long have you been with the Builder's Association?" or "How often do you hold these meetings?" Open-ended fact-finding questions can prove more effective; by asking open-ended questions ("Could you tell me about your needs for hotels in our area?"), you can determine some of the client concerns you need to address during your presentation.

To effectively sell to a client, you must accurately determine a client's feelings. This is done by asking such feeling-finding questions as, "What factors are most important to you personally in deciding on a lodging site?" Other examples of feeling-finding questions are: "What did you like about last year's convention?" and "What do you think would make this year's meeting an even greater success?"

Problem-solving questions focus on the considerations that weigh most heavily on the client's mind. By beginning problem-solving questions with a statement that demonstrates the concerns of others in a specific area, you may get a more honest response: "Ms. Jones, many of our clients tell us they're concerned about delays during check-in and check-out. Do you have any concerns in that area?" The client is encouraged to reply since he or she knows others have the same concern, and you can then respond.

Your goal with these types of questions is to discover the prospect's "hot buttons." Tom McCarthy says that

> hot buttons are a customer's most important needs, the things that will play an important role in the decision for the business. If, for example, you know the four factors most important to a particular prospect, you're in the driver's seat if you give extra emphasis to each of these hot buttons in your presentation and show why your hotel can provide what the prospect is looking for better than the competition can. To give a truly tailored presentation, it's important to determine each prospect's hot buttons and their degree of importance before giving your presentation.[6]

The most important skill in gaining client involvement is *listening* to the client's responses. The successful salesperson is an active listener who can identify and relate to the prospect's needs and desires. Careful listening can help you anticipate and overcome objections in order to close the sale.

As alluded to earlier, a salesperson can be a better listener by truly listening instead of trying to think of his or her next question while the prospect is speaking. Salespeople may find it helpful to have an informal script of standard fact-finding, feeling-finding, and problem-solving questions for each market segment. Having these questions pre-scripted and memorized can increase a salesperson's comfort level, as he or she will have a checklist to help get needed information. The salesperson is then free to focus on what the prospect is saying, knowing that he or she will not forget pertinent questions that should be asked.

Successful salespeople not only listen closely, but, whenever possible, they reinforce and confirm by agreeing with the prospect. **Rewarding remarks** such as "Right," "I understand," "That's great," and "I agree" encourage the prospect to continue—especially when they are reinforced by positive body language such as smiling, leaning forward, maintaining good eye contact, and nodding in agreement.

After you have established rapport during this questioning phase, you may use a transition statement ("Now that I understand your needs, I can show you how our property can—") to lead into step three of the presentation sales call—the presentation.

Step 3: Presenting Your Property

You should have a prepared, rehearsed sales presentation that addresses the needs of each of the major market segments the property has targeted; for example, a general sales presentation for meeting planners that relates specifically to the needs of that segment. But successful salespeople do not stop there; they custom-tailor this basic presentation to the needs of the particular meeting planner they are calling on, based on their research and questioning of the client.

Every hotel and restaurant has lots of features. However, in your presentation, you should only mention those features and services that are relevant to your prospect's needs. If the prospect only needs a meeting room for 50 persons, presenting the virtues of your ballroom, its stage, and your sophisticated audiovisual equipment is likely to turn off the prospect. Furthermore, your property's features must be turned into benefits—what the prospect will get from the feature. For example, if the prospect mentions that location is very important when choosing a restaurant for entertaining clients, you might say, "You mentioned that proximity to your office is a key factor in your decision. Our restaurant is just around the corner from your office" [feature] "so that you can walk to our restaurant and avoid the long delays of midday traffic" [benefit]. Every time you describe a feature of your property, you should explain how this feature will benefit the prospect (refer back to Exhibit 3).

There are three skills required for a successful presentation: organization, effective speaking, and intelligent use of visual aids.

Organization. Writing a presentation in advance is a good way to ensure that all important points are covered in logical order. You can then give the client an overview of the presentation ("I want to explain how our hotel will eliminate the concerns we've discussed") and present each point individually. At the end of the presentation, you can summarize the points covered. A presentation checklist containing the key elements of the opening and presentation can be a useful planning aid (see Exhibit 6).

Effective Speaking. The most important ingredient in effective speaking is enthusiasm. No salesperson wants to sound "canned." If you have memorized your presentation, make a special effort to put feeling and energy into your voice. Every salesperson's voice and manner should express a sincere desire to assist the client. Avoid using hospitality jargon.

Exhibit 6 Sample Presentation Planning Checklist

Presentation Planning Checklist

1. Who is the client? ______________________
   Company Name ______________________
   Type of Business ______________________
   Contact Person ______________________
   Address ______________________
   Phone ______________________
   Receptionist's Name ______________________
2. Date and time of appointment ______________________
3. Statements of client problem and/or opportunity as related to my offering:
   ____
   ____
4. Major buying motives of the client (if known):
5. Objectives of the presentation:

Major	Minor
____________	____________
____________	____________
____________	____________

6. Important guest benefits to be stressed:
   ____
   ____
7. Evidence needed to support my claims (competitive comparisons, public relations pieces, testimonials, etc.):
   ____
   ____
8. Other information needed (color photographs of the property, list of guest references by market segment w/phone numbers, etc.):
   ____
   ____
9. Sales tools required (brochures, audiovisual equipment, samples, etc.):
   ____
   ____

(continued)

Exhibit 6 *(continued)*

10. To start the presentation, I will:
    a. Build rapport in this way: ____________________

    ____

    b. Capture attention and interest and move on to the presentation in this way:

    ____

    ____

11. I anticipate these objections during my sales presentation:

Objection	Response
____________	____________
____________	____________
____________	____________

12. To close the sale, I will ask for the business in this way:

    ____

    ____

The use of this type of form enables a salesperson to plan each phase of a sales presentation. The form provides space to list objectives, benefits to be stressed, sales aids needed, ways to overcome objections, and techniques to close the sale. Source: Adapted from Danny N. Bellenger and Thomas N. Ingram, *Professional Selling Test and Cases* (New York: Macmillan, 1984), pp. 167–168.

Besides monitoring yourself for proper voice tone, inflection, and enunciation, make sure you are not using gestures or facial expressions that could distract the client.

Visual Aids. Visual aids are an important part of your sales presentation, as people retain more of what they can both hear *and* see. Visual aids such as pictures, charts, and graphs also build credibility. It is seldom enough to simply state the benefits of property products or services; visual aids provide proof and increase believability. Ideally, you should carry visual aids that have been specifically selected for each target market.

Many salespeople use a stand-up presentation book of 8 × 10 color photos of the property when calling on a prospect away from the hotel. The book provides prospects with a visual tour of the property, and should be organized as if the salesperson were doing an on-site tour. Photos should start with the entry and the lobby before focusing on guestrooms, restaurants, meeting room setups, buffets, and so on. If the prospect indicates that his or her need is for a meeting with no distractions, the salesperson can skip over the photos of the property's recreational facilities and focus on meeting rooms. A presentation "book" can also be created electronically and presented to clients via the salesperson's laptop computer.

In addition to brochures, color photographs of the property, reports of favorable publicity, testimonial letters, and third-party endorsements, there are a number of more sophisticated visual aids available. Some recent innovations include portable videotape and film equipment, multimedia presentations, and laptop-generated visuals. You should not make indiscriminate use of these high-tech visual aids, however. When using visual aids, the guideline should be: use the simplest and most effective method to increase believability. A well-planned presentation supplemented with endorsement letters and a presentation book containing pictures of past successful functions may be just as effective as a multimedia show. The important thing is that your visual aids relate to the needs of the client.

If a presentation book, brochure, or endorsement letter is used to increase believability, however, don't give up control of the item during the presentation itself. Rather than handing the item to the prospect, continue to hold onto it and explain features and benefits relevant to particular photos. If you give the brochure or presentation book to the prospect before or during the presentation, the prospect may become distracted and thumb through it while you are talking.

Closing the Presentation. When you have concluded the presentation, a transition phrase, which may be as simple as, "Do you have any questions?" can lead to the next step of the sales call—overcoming any objections expressed by the client.

Step 4: Overcoming Objections

Step four of the sales call deals with those times when the client has objections to your sales presentation.[7] Objections can occur at any time (one salesperson had his business card torn up by a client before he even got started), and there is no reason to panic when an objection is raised. Some objections are a client's way of asking for more information—and some may offer an opportunity to close the sale!

Objections can be verbal or nonverbal. If a client asks a number of pointed questions about food and beverage service, for example, it is possible that he or she has heard negative reports about the property's food and beverage operation. On a nonverbal level, clients may move back, clench their fists, become restless, glance sideways, or cross their arms when there is an objection to a suggested benefit.

Since objections can arise at any time, you must always be prepared to address them. Most objections should be handled immediately. The exception is an objection concerning price: if you talk about price too early, the client may think about rates throughout the presentation instead of paying attention. Deal with all other objections as soon as they come up. If you don't, the client may think you are trying to avoid them and you lose credibility.

Address objections with empathy and without arguing. You may need to ask questions to clarify the objection. If you feel that questions are necessary, do not interrupt the client. Wait until the client has finished voicing the objection, give a sympathetic response, and *restate the objection* in your own words before asking questions.

The majority of sales objections are predictable. You can minimize objections in a number of ways (see Exhibit 7) and prepare answers to common objections well in advance of the presentation. This is one area in which pre-presentation

Exhibit 7 Handling Objections During a Sales Call

Objections will be raised in most sales calls. But salespeople can take several steps to avoid objections, and have several options for taking positive action when an objection is raised.

WAYS TO MINIMIZE OBJECTIONS

- *Listen* to your prospect. Don't interrupt; let the prospect finish talking about concerns before responding. Be alert for body language that may signal unspoken objections.
- *Empathize* with your prospect. Try to see the prospect's needs and concerns from his or her point of view. Show respect for prospects, and reassure them that you understand their needs.
- *Convince* your prospect. If a dialogue seems to be headed for trouble, restate benefits or offer additional benefits. Show proof of these benefits, such as a testimonial letter from another client.

WAYS TO HANDLE OBJECTIONS THAT ARE RAISED

- *Direct response.* Clarify the objection (by asking a question or restating it in your own words) and respond directly with a solution.
- *Compensating benefit.* When the objection is valid—a meeting room will not be available until 8:00 A.M., and a group of members will be arriving at 7:00 A.M., for example—offer a compensating benefit, such as complimentary coffee and donuts while the members wait.
- *Indirect denial.* When an objection is raised, acknowledge it (don't directly agree with the prospect, but simply say, "I see," or "I understand"), but then show how your property is still able to meet the prospect's needs.

RESPONSES THAT SHOULD ALWAYS BE AVOIDED

- *Never* assume that you understand the objection from the prospect's point of view. Always clarify the objection by asking questions or restating the objection in your own words. You should not attempt to address an objection until you thoroughly understand why your prospect has the objection.
- *Never* argue with or respond negatively to the prospect. This includes criticizing the competition or trying to intimidate your prospect or make him or her look foolish.
- *Never* take the objection personally—or give up. In many cases, an objection is just the prospect's way of getting assurance that the property is indeed interested and can meet his or her needs. Don't make the mistake of getting up to leave too early—always try a close ("Mrs. Jones, if our property can provide the equipment you need, shall we confirm for June 13th?").

Objections are simply a way of asking for more information. When prospects object to a point in your presentation or ask questions, they're actually indicating interest in your property. Start a three-ring binder with three dividers for each of the three types of objections. Every time you find a response to be effective, write it down and place it in the appropriate section of the notebook. This takes a little work, but will help you to sell more effectively—soon you will have a complete book of "scripts" for each category of objection.

planning really pays off: you have a better chance of dealing successfully with objections you anticipate. Brainstorming with other salespeople about the client is an extremely effective technique for preparing answers to objections. When a number of people are involved in the creative process, more ways to handle an objection can be developed. These answers can be written down and memorized by the entire sales force.

Types of Objections. Objections fall into three basic categories:

1. Price or rate
2. Product or service
3. Lack of interest

Price or rate objections ("Your competition offers a better rate" or "My wife and I can't afford to spend that much for a wedding reception") can often be deferred to the end of the presentation, after you have had the opportunity to further detail the benefits offered for the price quoted. "Putting price aside for a moment, what else, if anything, is of concern to you?"

Product or service objections ("Our previous experience at your property was not very good" or "Your guestrooms just don't compare with those offered at newer properties") can be handled in a number of ways. One way is to restate the objection and offer a positive response to the objection:

Salesperson: "Mr. Stubbs, from your comments I gather that you don't feel our location is suitable for your training meetings."

Client: "That's right."

Salesperson: "What is it about our location that concerns you?" (Because of thorough pre-presentation research, the salesperson has a good idea of what the client's objection will be.)

Client: "I guess the biggest problem is arranging transportation for our delegates."

In this scenario, the salesperson has identified the client's concern and can then present a benefit offered by the property that will answer that concern: complimentary bus transportation to and from the airport, bus station, and train terminal.

A salesperson can also agree with an objection but point out a compensating benefit:

Client: "Your room rates are $10 to $15 higher than your competitor's."

Salesperson: "Yes, our room rates are higher, but our hotel offers 24-hour transportation to the airport, a complimentary breakfast in our deluxe coffee shop, and the finest room service in the area."

Lack of interest objections can be handled by questioning the client about his or her feelings about present arrangements:

Client:	"We're happy with our present hotel."
Salesperson:	"Is it the facilities or the service you are most pleased with?" (The salesperson is already aware that the client has complained about the poor service she received at a recent award banquet.)
Client:	"Their meeting rooms and audiovisual equipment are excellent. But sometimes we have had problems with the food service."
Salesperson:	"So you need a hotel that can equal your existing hotel in meeting rooms and audiovisual assistance, but provide better food service. Ms. Stern, our property has an excellent reputation for food service, and we can meet or exceed the meeting room and audiovisual services offered by your present hotel."

When answering objections, never knock the competition or downgrade their product or services. This tactic insults the client's judgment if he or she uses the services of the competitor, and may provoke the client's natural reaction to speak up and defend his or her previous decision. It can also destroy your credibility as an advisor.

There may be times when you are unable to overcome an objection (a meeting planner or training director may say "no" to a sale and mean it), but, in many cases, objections can be answered to the satisfaction of the client.

Step 5: Closing and Following Up

Many salespeople enjoy presenting their product, but hesitate when it comes to closing. Closing is not difficult, however, when you understand some fundamental principles involved.[8]

There are two basic types of closes: test closes and major closes. **Test closes** try to draw a reaction from the client. For example, when a salesperson shows a client a meeting room and asks, "How do you like our meeting facilities?" the salesperson is hoping to get a favorable response from the client.

Test closes can be used throughout a presentation to build an "agreement staircase" that will make the major close easier. You should use test closes at least once during each phase of your presentation. Asking questions that invite a positive response helps to get the client to say "yes" and be more receptive to the presentation. Using test closes also helps solidify key points and lets you know where you stand with the client before attempting a major close.

Using test closes throughout your presentation also helps to eliminate an onslaught of objections at the end of it. Asking such questions as, "Would this guestroom be acceptable for your attendees?" or "Would your attendees enjoy the breakfast buffet?" not only identifies your key points but also provides the opportunity for you to address objections immediately, rather than having to deal with a number of objections at the conclusion of your presentation.

A **major close** is a question or statement that asks for the sale. The major close should elicit a commitment on the part of the client and should be attempted as soon as the client has reached a peak of excitement.

Before attempting a major close, you should keep in mind that some closing situations are better than others. For example, trying to get an affirmative answer from a client who has been sitting in a cramped sales office for 20 minutes is more difficult than getting a positive response from a client who is basking in the luxury of a suite or lush atrium lobby.

There are a number of major closing techniques that can be used (see Exhibit 8). You can determine if a client is ready for a major close by observing these clues:

- Continual agreement throughout the presentation.
- The client's agreement to your response to an objection.
- Repetition of a benefit by the client.
- Positive nonverbal signs—the client smiles frequently or reexamines property brochures, for example.
- The client requests further details or asks questions throughout the presentation.

After using a major close, stop talking and give the client the chance to think things over and respond. Far too many salespeople get nervous after a major close and blurt out information or otherwise distract the client from making a decision.

It is also important to refrain from talking too much after the sale has been made. Too much talking can actually result in the loss of the sale if you say something that brings up doubts or objections that the client had not previously considered! After the sale has been made, thank the client and leave as soon as politely possible. The one exception to this rule is when you are attempting to get the names of other potential clients.

Closing is a skill that can be learned and improved like any other. Salespeople who are uncomfortable with closing should remember that clients *expect* salespeople to ask for the sale.

Following Up. You should follow up all presentation sales calls. If a sale was not made, follow-up can consist of a brief thank-you letter. The letter should be accompanied by additional material not given to the client at the time of the presentation and any materials specifically requested by the client, such as a copy of the property's contract, rate sheets, maps of the area, and so on.

If a sale was made, following up is even more important. Following up after a sale consists of providing excellent post-sale service. Certainly, follow-up service takes time, but it is usually easier and more cost-effective to keep a client satisfied than to replace a dissatisfied client.

Follow-up confirmation of a sale is extremely important, especially with group business. While a firm handshake may have closed the sale with the client,

Exhibit 8 Examples of Major Closing Techniques

Technique	Characteristic	Example
Direct Close	The salesperson asks for the business directly.	"May I reserve the space on a definite basis?"
Summing-Up Close	The salesperson summarizes the benefits and then asks for the business.	"Our meeting rooms are more than adequate to accommodate your group, the rates I've quoted are within your budget, and the dates you desire are available. May I reserve the space for you?"
BIQ Close	The salesperson uses the following format: "***B**ased on ______, **I**'d like to suggest ________." **Q**uestion: "__________________?"	"Based on the success that other companies in your field have had in using our meeting facilities, I'd like to suggest that we book your training seminar in our Gold Room. Does that sound good to you?"
Assumptive Close	The salesperson assumes that the sale is a sure thing.	"Shall I block 45 rooms for you?"
Alternative Choices	The salesperson suggests a choice between two positive alternatives.	"Would you prefer that your trainees be housed in our standard rooms or in the Tower section?"
Contingency or Closing on an Objection	The salesperson makes an agreement based on a concession from the property (overcoming a final objection).	"If we can revise the awards banquet prices to fit within your budget, then could I have your definite commitment?"
Trial Order	The salesperson suggests that the client try the facilities for an evaluation period.	"Why don't you book just one of your training seminars with us?"
Special Offer	The salesperson provides an added inducement.	"If you confirm next year's convention before the end of this month, we can offer this year's rates."

Clients *expect* salespeople to ask for the sale, and salespeople can do so in two ways: test closes (which are designed to draw a reaction from the client); and major closes, a question or statement that asks for the business. The approaches listed above are examples of major closes. Source: Adapted from Tom Hopkins, *Mastering the Art of Selling* (New York: Warner Books, 1995).

INTERNET EXERCISE

Log onto the Internet and, using a search engine such as Yahoo! or Google, type in "steps in the sales process." Review three sites from the list of matches. How are the sales steps mentioned in each site similar to those detailed in the chapter? How are they different? What additional information did you learn about the sales process?

most meeting or other group business also requires a signed proposal, contract, or confirmation agreement. Prompt attention to paperwork and other post-sale details reinforces the client's belief that he or she chose the right property.

Keeping the client informed between the time of the sale and the time of the meeting, convention, or other function is one of a salesperson's post-sale responsibilities. Meeting planners in particular want to be kept posted on the number (and often the types) of guestrooms actually reserved by members of their group(s), changes in hotel personnel, potential hotel labor problems, and any other changes that might affect their function.

It is also important to check with the client during the function. This might be done during a coffee break or meal function when the client is free. If the client says the audiovisual equipment for a meeting is not working well, for example, you can immediately see that the problem is corrected. This personalized attention shows the client and the meeting attendees that the property is genuinely interested in the needs of the group.

Follow up is required to build long-term relationships. Remember: customers don't care how much you know until they know how much you care. Be sure that your customers know that you care about them and the success of their functions.

After the function, a phone call or letter to determine client satisfaction is advised. Never assume that a lack of complaints means the client was satisfied; you must make sure that the client was pleased with the hotel and its service. If the response is positive, you can seek rebookings at a later date and ask the client for the names of others who would benefit from the services provided by the property. Exhibit 9 summarizes the five steps of the selling process.

Improving Sales Productivity

Sales is a highly competitive field, and you should constantly monitor your performance in a number of areas. In sales, good presentations are not enough. Results are what counts, and good salespeople must look at their actual productivity and search for ways to improve it.

In order to measure your productivity, you must first have a written list of goals; goals keep you on track and allow you to gauge your success. The basis for goals should always be the hotel's marketing plan, and success should be evaluated in terms of achieving the optimum customer mix set by the property. An evaluation may show, for example, that although you are seemingly productive, you are not generating the type of business desired by the property.

Exhibit 9 Steps in the Selling Process

Step 1: Opening the Sales Call
The opening consists of an introduction, a purpose statement, a benefit Wopening must interest the client enough that he or she wants to hear more.

Step 2: Getting Client Involvement
The object of this step is to build rapport and get the client to talk about problems and needs. Most sales are made or lost during this step.

Step 3: Presenting Your Property
This is the heart of the selling process. During this step, the salesperson explains the hotel's products and services to the client. It is impossible to overemphasize that the salesperson must sell *benefits,* not features, and that the salesperson must serve as a problem-solver.

Step 4: Overcoming Objections
Resistance is a normal and expected part of the sales process. When clients raise objections, they are not necessarily reacting negatively to the salesperson's proposal, but may only be seeking clarification of it. A solid objection gives direction to the sales effort—it tells the salesperson what he or she needs to do to make the sale!

Step 5: Closing and Following Up
A successful close is the ultimate objective of the sales call. Closing is asking for the sale, and a good close is a logical finish to a good sales presentation. Following up is the crucial work to ensure client satisfaction after the sale.

The sales process is a systematic series of actions that directs the prospect toward a buying commitment. Just as with learning how to play golf, tennis, or any other activity, there is a specific sequence to follow for optimum success. If you learn these sales steps in this specific order (not taking them out of sequence or skipping any steps), problems can be eliminated and your potential for success increased.

Once corporate and personal goals are clearly defined, you can use two invaluable tools to attain these goals: time management and key account management.

Time Management

Good time management is crucial to a successful sales career. Time management starts by knowing where time goes. You should keep a daily log for a minimum of two weeks to determine how much time you spend on sales activities; paperwork; meetings; telephone calls; unproductive activities such as travel time, interruptions, waiting on the telephone, and waiting at appointments; and other activities. Once you see where your time is going, you can establish priorities—urgent, important but not urgent, and tasks to be delegated—to ensure greater production.

Your workday should be planned. Non-selling tasks should be eliminated during prime selling times, and emphasis given to work items with deadlines. Hotel salespeople should be using 60 to 75 percent of their time selling aggressively.

Daily planning involves reviewing information to ensure that available time is used for maximum effectiveness. Getting an overview of daily responsibilities and activities as early as possible promotes more efficient handling of appointments and prioritizing of "to-do" lists. Perhaps the last 30 minutes of each day should be set aside to prepare for the next day's activities.

Weekly planning does not focus on the minute details inherent in daily planning, but is used to define objectives and set goals for the coming week. In many cases, for example, Mondays may be used for scheduling appointments and supplemental sales activities, Tuesdays through Thursdays set aside for extensive selling efforts, and Fridays spent finishing uncompleted tasks and planning next week's activities.

Monthly planning focuses on major events, such as conventions, community events, and so on, and sets general sales goals and strategies based on those activities. A large convention, for example, can provide the opportunity to secure future business—and may prove to be more profitable to the sales effort than prospecting during that week.

In order to use time most effectively, time spent on routine work should be minimized. Delegate routine tasks if possible. A sales secretary can handle a simple inquiry letter, for example. Other routine paperwork, which can take up much valuable sales time, should also be delegated to the clerical staff.

If delegation is not possible, group similar tasks to save time. Since clutter breeds confusion, you should try to generate as little paperwork as possible. It is important for you to learn to file, not pile. Each piece of paper should be handled just once—by personal action, delegation, filing, or discarding.

The saying "Time is money" is especially true for salespeople. There are a number of ways for you to save time and money during everyday activities.

When on the road making personal calls, you can prospect for new business by making short cold calls between scheduled presentations.

When making telephone calls, it is important that you know exactly what you want to talk about and that you have all the information needed to answer any questions that might arise. If the office is automated, a personal computer greatly facilitates obtaining information. In nonautomated offices, you should have immediate access to clients' files, property information, function book information, and so on. When you are prepared, the business portion of the call should go quickly, allowing time for rapport-building small talk with the client.

Personal telephone calls may be handled by a secretary or through an answering machine. You may set aside a small block of time each day for personal calls, but family and friends should be asked not to call at the office except in an emergency.

Drop-in visitors can mean potential business, and time should be allocated for them in daily scheduling. You can discourage lengthy stays by a visitor who is "just looking" by offering property brochures or pamphlets and encouraging the visitor to look them over and call back with any comments or questions, or suggesting a convenient time for an appointment. In many cases, the clerical staff can answer questions for drop-in visitors, freeing the sales staff for more productive work.

Habits of Highly Successful Hotel Salespeople

Daily Disciplines (or "Eating the Elephant One Bite at a Time")
Successful salespeople take their goals for achieving revenue, prospecting, making sales calls, etc., and break them down into monthly, weekly, and daily activities. For example, they know how many prospects they need to locate per day and per week in order to meet their prospecting goals.

Prioritize Activities
Salespeople who know how to prioritize their activities call on those prospects most likely to produce revenue before they do the trace calls to say "hello" to existing accounts. They make time to prospect for and qualify prospects using the Internet and other resources, but they do it in non-prime sales time.

Think Revenue, Not Just Rooms
The successful salesperson pays attention to the property's revenue management strategy and understands that the name of the game is revenue, not rooms. The revenue management strategy informs their prospecting activities.

Whales and Tunas
Successful salespeople know that they need a mix of both large and small groups and accounts to meet their revenue goals and balance out the group calendar. Some salespeople only want to pursue the big or "glamour" accounts (the whales). A problem with that strategy is that it takes much longer to land whales than the smaller, less flashy accounts (tunas).

"Intrapreneurs"
Successful salespeople treat their market or their territory like a business—their business. They function as "intraprenuers" within the organization.

Personal (Brutally Honest) Analysis
Successful salespeople evaluate their strengths in order to leverage them into landing more business ... and maybe even a better position for themselves. They are also honest about the areas where they could use some training and/or support and actively ask for it or seek out opportunities to get the training they need.

Sense of Urgency
Successful salespeople have a sense of urgency about working their plan, because they know that if they fall too far behind, it will be very difficult to catch up. They stay late when they have to and ask to leave early when they are caught up.

Source: Adapted from Carol Verret, "Habits of Highly Successful Hotel Salespeople," posted on Hotel-Marketing.com, September 29, 2005.

Travel time can be turned into productive time by using it to catch up on reading (if driving, you can listen to motivational tapes or mentally plan the workday) or correspondence (every salesperson should have access to a hand-held cassette recorder). On the road, you can save time by planning ahead, keeping a realistic schedule, and combining meetings with meals. Luncheon appointments or dinner meetings should be scheduled with high-priority clients; this is prime selling time that shouldn't be spent alone or with low-potential prospects.

THE HOTEL DIRECTOR

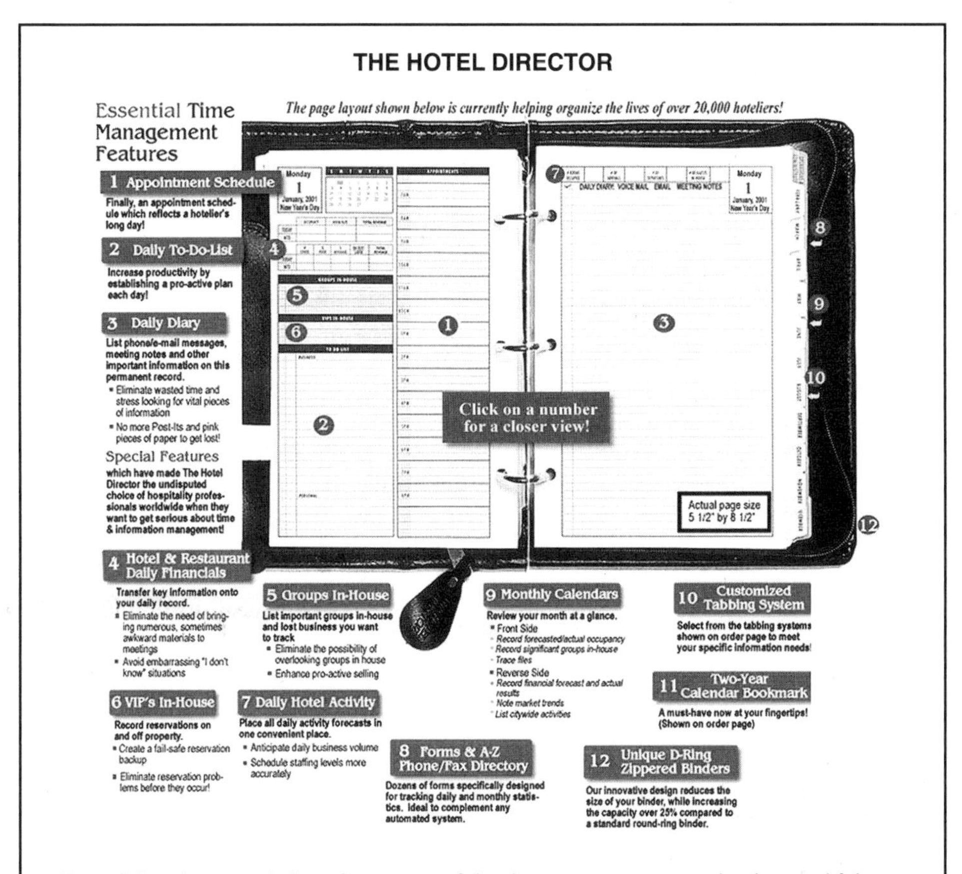

Two of the characteristics of a successful salesperson are organization and follow-up, two activities made easier through the use of a good time management system. "The Hotel Director" was designed by hotel sales professionals to meet the unique needs of hotel salespeople.

Today's salespeople are also using more high-tech devices, such as laptops and personal digital assistants (PDAs), to manage their sales efforts. Laptops are a must for today's sales staff on the road. They are used by busy salespeople to update information, make contacts with customers and prospects by e-mail, and keep in touch with the sales department back home to check on updated sales information. Software programs on the laptop can help them manage their time as well.

PDAs such as the BlackBerry and Treo provide wireless access to e-mail, phone service, and the Internet, and provide features such as a calendar, address book, task list, memo pad, and calculator to help keep salespeople organized and productive. The BlackBerry, which also features maps, offers a Corporate Data Access feature that provides access to a property's Customer Relationship Management (CRM) database and other pertinent corporate information.

Today's hospitality salespeople can best manage their valuable selling time through the use of organizers and computerized tools that are designed to provide essential information in one convenient place.

Efficient time management can mean increased sales for the property. Each salesperson should be able to account for productive sales time and efforts. While on the subject of time management, sales managers should remember that it's a good idea for salespeople to be empowered to quote rates and make decisions without having to check with their supervisor. If salespeople cannot negotiate space, dates, and rates, clients will view them as "second stringers." It is a time-saver to have salespeople who are trained and empowered to make decisions.

Time management plays a major part in the second aspect of personal planning, key account management.

Key Account Management

A typical salesperson at properties of all sizes handles 300 to 400 accounts. Landing new accounts does not mean that you must manage an ever-increasing number of clients. New accounts with high potential will replace those with the lowest potential for business, so that the total number of accounts you service will remain relatively stable, as you continually increase the quality of the accounts being followed.

With so many accounts to manage, how much time should you spend on an account? One way to establish a strategy is to practice **key account management,** which involves ranking accounts according to their profitability. This is important, because in most cases 20 percent of a salesperson's accounts generates 80 percent of the business. Prioritizing helps you allocate time to the most promising accounts.

A salesperson's accounts fall into three general priority categories—high, medium, and low—whether they are established accounts or potential sources of business. Accounts can also be assigned levels that reflect the account's impact, present or potential, on the property's sales:

- *Level 1.* These are new accounts with high potential, or present accounts with high potential but lower than expected profitability. These accounts should be your top priority. As a general rule, you will make a minimum of five personal calls and five telephone calls to each of these accounts annually.
- *Level 2.* High potential accounts that are already providing an acceptable share of business. While these accounts deserve a high investment of time, they don't require the amount of personal attention needed for Level 1 accounts. (These accounts will typically be serviced with four personal calls and four telephone calls annually.)
- *Level 3.* New accounts with medium potential, or present accounts that have medium potential but aren't providing an acceptable level of business. (These accounts are generally serviced with three personal calls and three telephone calls each year.)
- *Level 4.* Accounts that have medium potential and are providing an acceptable level of business. (These accounts may require two personal calls and two telephone calls annually.)
- *Level 5.* New or present accounts that have low potential and do not warrant a great deal of your time. These accounts may be given token attention over

Exhibit 10 Key Account Management Spreadsheet

KEY ACCOUNT MANAGEMENT SPREAD SHEET			
Name of account and key contact	# of times account was called on last year	# of times we expect to call on account this year	Estimate of room night potential from account
Stubbs Insurance Mark Steward	4 Personal calls 4 Telephone calls	5 Personal 5 Telephone	25 r.n. x 12 mo. @ $75 = $22,500 20 r.n. x 12 mo. @ $80= $19,200 30r.n. x 2 days x 4 @ $72=$17,280 125r.n. x3 days @ $75 = $28,125 Total $87,105

KEY ACCOUNT MANAGEMENT SPREAD SHEET			
Estimate of food and beverage potential	Estimate of meeting room revenue potential	Total potential dollar value of account	Level of account priority (Level 1 through Level 5)
40% of Room Revenue = $34,842	4 Workshops - Complimentary function space Product Showcase - 1.00 per square foot for exhibit hall = $10,000	Rooms $86,105 Food & Beverage $34,842 Meeting Space $10,000	Level 1 — High Potential Account

Prioritizing accounts can be accomplished easily if a salesperson takes a look at all of his or her accounts and judges them by the same criteria. A spreadsheet such as this one provides a place for data and enables the salesperson to see the profit potential of each account at a glance. The director of sales can review these spreadsheets with salespeople on a periodic basis (usually the end or beginning of a year) to reassess priorities.

the course of the year. (You may visit once annually while on a sales trip or prospecting, or may make a telephone call to the account after all other business has been taken care of.)

How do you determine an account's level of potential? Most information on present accounts comes from internal invoices (past performance records, advance registrations, survey sheets indicating potential booking dates, and so on), while other information on present and new accounts, such as credit information and references, can come from outside sources.

To help rate accounts, you should list every account on a time management spreadsheet (see Exhibit 10). A spreadsheet includes such important information as the name of the account, the name of the contact person, how often each account was called in a certain time period, how often each account is expected to be called in the future, an estimate of the account's guestroom revenue, revisions of this estimate after review, and the account's priority level. It is important that this spreadsheet be kept up-to-date, because factors such as personnel changes, mergers, and the economy may affect an account's potential profitability.

It is fairly easy to determine the amount of time that should be spent on each account in light of the spreadsheet information. The number of calls must be proportionate and manageable, and will vary with the number of clients each salesperson serves, the property's geographic location, and other commitments the salesperson may have.

It is becoming increasingly common for salespeople to be given full account responsibility. This means that one salesperson (rather than three or four) is responsible for soliciting all types of business—individual business travelers, group meeting business, banquets, social events, and so on—from a company. Having one salesperson per account saves time for customers (they are not dealing with several salespeople) as well as the salesperson (one salesperson can more effectively service an account in less time than three or four salespeople working independently). If full account responsibility is the policy at your property, this needs to be considered when ranking your accounts.

Once your accounts have been rated, you can discuss the ratings with your supervisor, develop a strategy for each established and potential account, and begin the exciting job of selling your property.

Endnotes

1. Tom McCarthy, "Get Your Sales Management Ready for the 21st Century," *Hotel and Resort Industry*, December 1990, pp. 30–31.
2. David Jones, "Prospecting in a Down Economy," *HSMAI Marketing Review*, Fall/Winter 2001, p. 46.
3. See also the videotape *Hospitality Sales: Preparing for the Sale* (Lansing, Mich.: American Hotel & Lodging Educational Institute).
4. Charles M. Futrell, *ABC's of Selling* (Homewood, Ill.: Irwin, 1985), p. 77.
5. See also the videotape *Hospitality Sales: Making the Sales Call* (Lansing, Mich.: American Hotel & Lodging Educational Institute).
6. Tom McCarthy, "Hot Buttons Put You in the Driver's Seat," *Lodging Hospitality*, May 15, 1999, p. 14.
7. See also the videotape *Hospitality Sales: Overcoming Objections* (Lansing, Mich.: American Hotel & Lodging Educational Institute).
8. The art of closing is also explored in Tom Hopkins, *Mastering the Art of Selling* (New York: Warner Books, 1995) and the videotape *Hospitality Sales: Closing the Sale and Following Up* (Lansing, Mich.: American Hotel & Lodging Educational Institute).

Key Terms

body language—Signals sent from a person's face, arms, hands, legs, and posture that indicate his or her thoughts or mood.

closed-ended question—A question requiring a specific answer, an answer that often can be given in just a few words.

cold call—A fact-finding or exploratory call on a prospect with whom there has been little or no previous contact.

inside call—A sales presentation made to walk-ins who inquire about the property.

intimate space—An area within arm's length of an individual.

key account management—A system that ranks sales accounts according to their profitability. Key account management helps organize a salesperson's time and ensures that a property's most profitable customers are given top priority.

major close—A question or statement at the end of a sales presentation that asks for the sale.

open-ended question—A question that gives individuals an opportunity to express their feelings and knowledge.

personal space—An area two to four feet (.6 to 1.2 meters) from an individual.

presentation call—A type of sales call during which the salesperson presents the features and services offered by the property and attempts to close the sale.

property information sheet—A summary of what a lodging property has to offer, including the number and types of guestrooms, a description of the atmosphere of the property, the number and types of restaurants and meeting rooms, and so on.

public relations call—A call to maintain the relationship and goodwill enjoyed with a client.

public space—An area over 12 feet (3.7 meters) away from an individual.

referral prospecting—Asking current clients to identify other individuals or businesses that may be interested in doing business with your property.

rewarding remark—A remark such as "Right," "That's great," or "I agree" that reinforces or confirms what an individual is saying and encourages him or her to continue talking.

social space—An area four to 12 feet (1.2 to 3.7 meters) from an individual.

test close—A statement or question posed by a salesperson during a sales presentation that seeks to evoke a positive response from the client.

Review Questions

1. What are the four types of sales calls?
2. What are some sources for prospect research and what are three basic criteria for qualifying prospects?
3. What three areas should be researched for effective pre-presentation planning?
4. What are the five basic steps of a presentation sales call?
5. What are the elements of a sales call opening?
6. Why should product features be converted to benefits?
7. What are three basic types of objections and what are some of the techniques used to overcome objections?
8. When should a sale be closed?

9. How can salespeople improve their productivity?
10. What is key account management?

Internet Sites

For more information, visit the following Internet sites. Remember that Internet addresses can change without notice. If the site is no longer there, you can use a search engine to look for additional sites.

American Marketing Association
www.ama.org

Destination Marketing Association International
www.iacvb.org

Hospitality Sales & Marketing Association International
www.hsmai.org

International Advertising Association
www.iaaglobal.org

Meeting Professionals International
www.mpiweb.org

Sales & Marketing Management
www.salesandmarketing.com

Sales and Performance Group
www.redhotsales.com

Chapter 5 Outline

Competencies

1. Describe the basics of effective telephone communication in relation to hospitality marketing and sales. (pp. 181–185)
2. Identify various types of outgoing telephone calls related to the marketing and sales function. (pp. 185–188)
3. Describe the steps involved in making a telephone appointment call, and describe sales calls, promotional calls, service calls, and public relations calls. (pp. 188–196)
4. Identify various types of incoming telephone calls related to the marketing and sales function, and describe how hotels handle them. (pp. 196–203)
5. Describe telephone sales blitzes and telemarketing operations. (pp. 203–209)

Insider Insights

Thomas A. Elbe
Vice President of Sales, Concorde Hotels

"The telephone is valuable not only as a selling tool, but also for prospecting and qualifying potential business. While there are many sources for client lists, the information on these lists is limited, and it would be impossible to qualify each listing face-to-face with an expensive face-to-face sales call. By using the telephone, you can inexpensively and efficiently determine if a client has the potential for your product."

5

Telephone Sales

THIS CHAPTER WILL OUTLINE the basics of telephone communication, describe how to handle outgoing and incoming calls in a professional manner, and provide an in-depth look at telephone sales operations. The telephone is an important business tool, but "good or even acceptable telephone manners have never been taught in our schools, despite the reality that proper handling of a phone call is one of the most important skills one needs in the business world. It is often the first point of contact a customer has with a company, and it can build or destroy good relations and trust—in seconds."[1] While face-to-face selling is the most effective way to sell, the telephone, if used properly, can be one of the most economical ways to find—and sell to—prospective guests and clients. Salespeople and other employees can use this sales instrument to do the following:

- Search for sales leads
- Qualify accounts (identify prospects who are most likely to buy)
- Make sales appointments
- Blitz a market to reach prospects and clients
- Service both local and geographically isolated accounts in an economical and timely manner
- Assist guests in making reservations and arranging for return visits to the property
- Sell additional services to registered guests (these may include restaurants, recreational amenities, room service, and so on)
- Receive direct mail response inquiries
- Convert inquiries generated by ads (especially ads with toll-free numbers) into sales
- Secure market research data quickly
- Reactivate former accounts
- Announce promotional news to clients and generate business for special promotions
- Follow up bids, proposals, direct mail campaigns, and leads developed at trade shows

Since the telephone is used in these and many other different ways, telephone sales may be delegated to several groups of employees within a property.

Incoming calls for individual guest reservations may go through a front desk or reservations staff; calls promoting room service or the property's restaurant may be made by switchboard operators; sales calls may be handled by salespeople or top management. No matter how calls are delegated, both incoming and outgoing calls play an important role in a property's overall sales and marketing effort.

Large independent hotels and hotel chains may employ a telemarketing staff to research data, sell, and/or set appointments for the sales staff. Telemarketing—used solely or in combination with media advertising, direct mail, and face-to-face selling—is being increasingly used to build business, offer better service, and generate market data. In this chapter, we will discuss this trend in marketing as well as detail the telephone's value as both a sales and public relations tool.

Basics of Telephone Communication

Many telephone calls are potential sales calls, so it is important that property employees have good communication skills. Telephone selling is more difficult than face-to-face sales because you can't read the prospect's body language during a telephone call or see the prospect's office decor, which often provides insights into the prospect through family photographs, trophies, and recognition plaques.

Since a friendly smile and a firm handshake can't be conveyed over the telephone, the words you use and your pronunciation, tone of voice, and delivery take on greater importance. Methods most commonly used to make a good impression over the telephone include telephone etiquette, telephone communication skills, and listening skills.

Telephone Etiquette

The lodging industry offers more than just rooms and guest services. It offers hospitality, and friendliness and courtesy are an important part of any interaction between a property employee and a potential guest. When using the telephone, property employees must communicate warmth and a willingness to be of service.

Unfortunately, sensitivity, empathy, and politeness are often lacking in telephone calls selling hospitality products. The salesperson who employs these courtesies, then, can stand out from the crowd and make a positive impression. You can get this "edge" from the very beginning, by simply asking the prospect if it is a convenient time to talk!

If it is a bad time for the prospect, sales efforts are hampered before they even begin. By respecting the prospect's time, you greatly increase the chances of a successful future contact. If the prospect suggests calling at another time, it is important to follow through. Many salespeople fail to follow up, perhaps losing the opportunity to make a sale.

Telephone etiquette begins by letting the potential guest know that he or she is important to the property. One way to do this is to use phrases that will put the potential guest at ease and show the property's concern for him or her (see Exhibit 1). It is important that the property's representative be polite and understanding and that the unseen guest feels that someone is concerned about what he or she has to say.

Exhibit 1 Sample Telephone Etiquette Guidelines

THIS IS BETTER	THAN THIS
Answering the Call	
"Days Inn Reservations, Mr. Eaton speaking. How may I help you?"	"Days Inn Reservations."
"Days Inn Reservations, Ms. Wood speaking. How may I help you?"	"Days Inn, can I help you?"
Making Sure	
"Would you repeat your name for me please?"	"What name did you say? I can't hear you."
"Would you spell that for me, please?"	"What did you say? Talk a little louder."
"I'm sorry. I didn't get the name of the person."	"I can't understand what you're trying to say."
Acknowledging	
"Yes, Mr. Martinez. I'll be happy to request that for you."	"OK, I'll do what I can."
"Yes, Ms. Jones, I'd be glad to check that for you."	"All right. Let me see."
Leaving the Line	
"Would you mind waiting while I check, please?"	"Just a minute."
	"I'll try to find out."
Returning to the Line	
"Mr. Glazer, thank you for waiting. I have that information."	"The date on that reservation was June 18."
"Ms. Muzzall, I'm sorry to have kept you waiting."	"Are you still waiting?"
Completing the Call	
"Thank you for calling Days Inn, Ms.Yang."	"Bye-bye." "OK." "So long." "That's OK." "All right, bye."

Courtesy of Days Inns of America, Inc.

There are a number of other ways salespeople can make a good impression:

1. *Adequate preparation.* Always have pertinent information at hand before calling a client. By being prepared, you can organize your thoughts, be ready to answer questions, and avoid wasting the client's time.
2. *Adequate time.* Take steps to make sure you will not be interrupted while calling a client. An interruption can irritate a client and may result in the loss of a sale. Clients deserve your undivided attention.
3. *Direct contact.* Always dial the call personally. It can irritate a client if a secretary or receptionist places the call and the client is put on hold or asked to wait for you to come to the phone.
4. *Courtesy and respect.* Intermediaries (secretaries, receptionists, clerks, assistants, etc.) should be treated courteously. Being arrogant or disrespectful greatly decreases chances of getting through to a prospect.
5. *Brevity.* Calls should be kept short and to the point unless the client wants to chat. When the call has been completed, let the client hang up first. Avoid giving the impression of being in a hurry, and never slam the receiver down while the client is still on the line.
6. *Timing.* It is important to respect the hours kept by clients. As a general rule, avoid calling during the late-afternoon or early-morning hours. Of course, the client's time zone should also be considered.

These simple guidelines will go a long way toward building courteous telephone habits among the sales staff. But sales and goodwill can be increased even more by understanding how to speak effectively over the telephone.

Telephone Communication Skills

You should check yourself often on these important communication skills:

1. *Tone of voice.* Your voice should reflect sincerity, pleasantness, confidence, and interest. It is especially important to have a "verbal smile"—something you can achieve by smiling as you speak. Also, too many salespeople make the mistake of shouting into the receiver, especially on long-distance calls. Speak into the receiver as if the client were sitting across the desk.
2. *Pitch.* A low-pitched voice is desirable. Low voices carry better and are more pleasant to the listener.[2]
3. *Inflection.* Avoid talking in a monotone. Enunciate clearly and emphasize key words; you can generate interest by the way you raise or lower your voice.
4. *Understandability.* Avoid talking with anything (gum, a cigarette, pen or pencil, etc.) in your mouth, and be careful not to talk too fast.
5. *Enthusiasm.* Add spirit to your words. Enthusiasm is contagious and infuses your call with energy.

It is a good practice for employees who use the telephone a lot, whether they be salespeople, switchboard operators, front desk agents, or top management, to check their voices on a tape recorder. Every employee should work to develop a pleasant telephone voice free of slang, jargon, and irritating habits. An enthusiastic, well-modulated voice is half of a successful telephone call.

Listening Skills

The other half of a successful telephone call is listening to what the prospective client or guest has to say. A salesperson in particular should be aware of several keys to good listening:

1. *Limit talking.* No one can talk and listen at the same time. The prospect should get a chance to air his or her views, and these views should be given careful attention—no interrupting or jumping to conclusions before the prospect has finished speaking. As a general rule, if the prospect does most of the talking during a telephone sales call, it is much easier to make a sale because you will know the prospect's needs and concerns.
2. *Get involved.* It is usually much easier to be enthusiastic and alert when sitting erect; leaning back and relaxing often interferes with listening. You should also try to put yourself in the prospect's place, listening for clues to what is important to the prospect. You can learn a great deal about the prospect's needs by the way things are said. Successful salespeople also get involved by empathizing with the caller. Phrases such as "I know how you feel" are excellent ways to show the prospect that what he or she is saying is important to you.
3. *Ask questions.* Asking questions generates prospect involvement and shows that you are interested. Questions are an effective way to keep the prospect talking and gather additional information. Ask, "Why is that important to you?" or "What else can you tell me about that?" and take notes as the prospect shares views and needs. These responses can be used later in a presentation to build support for the sales message.

Outgoing Calls

Outgoing telephone calls can be divided into a number of categories: prospect calls, qualifying calls, appointment calls, sales calls, promotional calls, service calls, and public relations calls. Since most salespeople use the telephone to set appointments rather than make a sale, this section will focus mainly on appointment telephone calls.

Prospect and Qualifying Calls

The objective of **prospect calls** is to gather information and learn the names of decision-makers. Many calls that start out as prospect calls end up as qualifying calls. **Qualifying calls** determine if prospects need or can afford the products and services offered by the property (see Exhibit 2). Qualifying calls are not sales calls, but are used to find out if an individual or company warrants an in-person sales call. This can be determined by asking several questions:

Exhibit 2 Sample Prospect Qualification Form

Prospect Qualification Form

COMPANY NAME: ______________________________

ADDRESS: ______________________________

CITY/STATE/ZIP: ______________________________

PHONE: ______________ CONTACT: ______________

1. *Introduction*: "My name is ________, and I'm calling you on behalf of L'Ermitage Hotels located in West Hollywood/Beverly Hills. Can you tell me who handles the travel and meeting arrangements for your company?"

   ____

   ____

2. After locating the right contact, state the purpose of your call and ask if any of the company's business travelers stay overnight in the Los Angeles area. If so, ask "Are you familiar with our hotels?"

   ____

   ____

3. "Do you use an outside travel agency?"

   ____

4. If so, "What is the name of the agency involved?"

   ____

   OR

   "Do you use an outside travel agency? If so, may I ask which one you work with?"

   ____

5. "Can you estimate how many room nights annually you reserve in the Los Angeles area?"

   ____

6. "Aside from individual travel, do you hold meetings in the Los Angeles area?"

   ____

   "How often?" ______________________________

7. "Would you be interested in speaking with one of our sales managers regarding our corporate rate program for your upcoming meetings?" ______________

8. Thank the individual for his or her time, and state that you will follow up in an appropriate manner (via telephone or by sending brochures and a general information letter).

Forms such as this one are used to determine if corporations or firms have a need for the hospitality firm's products or services. Qualifying saves time and money by ensuring that salespeople call on promising accounts. (Courtesy of L'Ermitage Hotels, Beverly Hills, California)

- Does your company have a need for hotel accommodations, meeting rooms, or banquet facilities?
- How many people travel for your company? What is the destination of most company travel?
- Who decides where your traveling staff stays? What hotels are you currently using?
- Who usually makes the reservations for your traveling staff?

If a prospect seems a likely candidate for an in-person sales call, further information may be gathered by asking these questions:

- How many meetings does your company hold throughout the year? What times of the year are meetings normally held? How long do they last?
- What types of meetings do you typically hold? What types of facilities do you need?
- How do you decide where to hold a meeting? What criteria do you use to decide on a location?
- When are location decisions made, and who makes them?

When researching information on national corporations, it is necessary to probe deeper and get the answers to these questions:

- Does the corporation have a travel department or a corporate travel directory that advises the corporation's business travelers of properties in which they are authorized to stay? Who heads the department for corporate travel?
- Who decides which properties are used? Who makes guestroom and meeting room reservations? Why are certain locations chosen?
- Is there a written contract or any kind of obligation to the property currently being used? If so, when does this obligation expire?
- How many people travel for the corporation? How many guestroom nights are reserved? What department has the most travelers?
- Do business travelers pay their own bills or are accommodations billed to the corporation? Do travelers pay on a per diem (by the day) basis?
- From which company properties do most business travelers originate? What is the destination of the majority of the corporation's business travelers?

A good approach to take when making telephone prospect calls is to follow a simple who, what, when, and where format:

Fact-Finding Question	Follow-Up Information Generated
Who?	Future account data—name, address, etc.—as well as description of prospect's business.
What?	Prospect's needs for guestrooms, meeting space, catered events, and other facilities/services.
When?	Months, weeks, or specific dates for which hotel facilities or services are needed.

Where?	Properties with whom the prospect is currently dealing.

The answers to these questions will give the information necessary to prepare a sales presentation. You are now in a position to answer exactly how your property can meet the prospect's needs, and, when appropriate, you can end the prospecting call with a request for an appointment.

Appointment Calls

Telephone **appointment calls** are used to briefly introduce a prospective client to the features and services offered by the property and ask for an appointment to meet face-to-face (see Exhibit 3). The object of an appointment call is to get the prospect to agree to an appointment, not to make a sale. Appointment calls save time for the salesperson and the prospect because they allow time for both to prepare for a future face-to-face sales presentation. Having an appointment also reduces the likelihood that the sales presentation will be interrupted. Pam Lontos, a sales trainer, says that "with proper telephone techniques, appointments are easy to make and will increase sales dramatically. An appointment made ahead of time improves one's chances of getting in to get the sale. That's because the client or prospect has allotted time to listen to you. They also are more receptive to being sold because you have shown respect for their time by phoning ahead to make at appointment at their convenience."[3]

Before making an appointment call, you should have all necessary information available—prospect sheets, account records (if any), prices, firm and tentative booking dates (if applicable), and general property information. (You gather this information not because you expect to make a sale, but to have it available in case the prospect asks questions.) Plan and write down what you will say. Developing an outlined presentation will help you organize your message.

Like face-to-face selling, the telephone appointment call is made up of several steps:

1. Reaching the decision-maker
2. Opening the call
3. The presentation
4. Overcoming objections
5. Setting the appointment

Reaching the Decision-Maker. If a prospect call has not been made, you can learn the name of the decision-maker through an intermediary at the firm or corporation. While intermediaries can be helpful in providing the name of the decision-maker, they can also prove to be obstacles when it comes to reaching him or her (see Exhibit 4). Appealing to the intermediary's sense of responsibility—presenting ideas that might help the decision-maker, for example—often helps you avoid the objections and barriers that intermediaries can present.

Prepare an opening statement. You must initiate the conversation when the telephone is picked up, so you should prepare an opening statement. Since the

Exhibit 3 Sample Appointment Telephone Call Dialogue

Reaching the Decision-Maker

"Hello, my name is Dan Stern. Could you help me by giving me the name of the person who makes the convention planning decisions for your firm?"

Opening the Call

"Good morning, Ms. Merrill. My name is Dan Stern. I'm with Complete Resorts International. I'm calling to explain one of the most innovative programs in convention planning available today!"

The Presentation

"Our unique services will help you save time and money on all of your convention meeting room and banquet needs. We have recently developed a program that includes three exciting features to help you stage successful meetings: your own private operations-headquarters room adjacent to the meeting area; the use of our hotel's limousine to pick up your VIPs; and your own personal meeting aide—a fully qualified staff assistant, supplied by our hotel—to handle any last-minute problems for you!"

Setting the Appointment

"I know you will be as excited as we are about our new services that will help you stage successful meetings. When can we meet for just 30 minutes to discuss your upcoming convention for your independent distributors?"

"Which day would be best for you, Tuesday or Wednesday?"

"What time is most convenient for you on that day, 10:00 A.M. or 2:00 P.M.?"

"Great! I'll see you on Tuesday at 2:00 P.M. in your office at 1234 Goodsale Road just west of the Interstate. Thank you for your time, Ms. Merrill. I'm looking forward to meeting you in person. Have a good day!"

Note that in setting the appointment, the salesperson did not set up the possibility of a "no" answer, but asked a forced-choice question that gave the prospect a choice of two alternatives: Tuesday or Wednesday. Other typical forced-choice questions include: "Would you prefer to meet in the morning or afternoon?" and "Is the beginning or the latter part of the week best for you?"

Once you have reached the decision-maker, there are three parts to a telephone appointment call: opening the call, the presentation, and setting the appointment. Note that the salesperson identified himself and his property, stated the purpose of his call, and explained how the prospect would benefit from an appointment by appealing to her need for saving time and money on banquets and conventions.

intermediary is paid to protect the time of the decision-maker, an introductory statement such as "This is Donna Scott from the Concorde Hotel. May I speak with Bob Cross?" is not likely to get you through the ring of protection surrounding most decision-makers.

Instead, you should appeal to a need—of either the decision-maker or the company—and to the intermediary's sense of responsibility: "The reason I'm calling

Exhibit 4 Reaching the Decision-Maker

Intermediary:	"Why do you want to know [the name of the decision-maker]?"
Salesperson:	"I'm putting together a list of people who would like to be kept abreast of some of the ways other local businesses are reducing their costs through the use of training meetings. I'm sure your manager would be interested in receiving this information."
Intermediary:	"What is the purpose of this call?"
Salesperson:	"I'm sorry, but I can only discuss that with your manager. Can you put me through to her, please?"
Intermediary:	"Is this a sales call?"
Salesperson:	"No, I'm not trying to sell anything on the phone. I'm just doing research on how area businesses are meeting their training needs. I was hoping that your manager could give me some ideas."

Handling the objections of a secretary, receptionist, or other intermediary is often necessary to determine the name of or reach the decision-maker. These questions are typical of those used to screen calls; the responses given are guides to handling these objections.

today is because our hotel has recently developed an incentive tour package that other top incentive companies have said is the best hotel value in years. I'd like to ask Mr. Cross a few questions to determine if this would be of any value to him." This type of opening, spoken in a confident, expectant tone of voice, will appeal to the intermediary's need to keep the decision-maker abreast of ways to save time and money for the firm.

Develop respect and rapport. Since many decision-makers rely on their secretaries or associates to screen calls and advise them of calls worthy of reply, it is important to show respect to intermediaries. Learn the names of secretaries and receptionists and list these names in your diary of clients' telephone numbers. Calling the intermediary by name is highly effective, as is timing the call so it will not interrupt a busy schedule. (You should especially avoid making calls on Monday mornings and Friday afternoons.) Timing the call shows that you respect the time of both the intermediary and the decision-maker.

Don't leave a message. There may be times when a decision-maker cannot be reached. In most cases, when you are told that the decision-maker is out of town, out on a business call, or on the telephone, the intermediary is telling the truth, but you should be concerned if you are repeatedly told, "He isn't available," "She's in a meeting," or "He's in conference." In these cases, *never* leave a message asking the decision-maker to call back. If the intermediary says, "He's on the phone, may I take a message?" a proper response is, "May I hold?" Or, you may ask the intermediary to suggest a time when it is more convenient to call. This technique is both polite and effective because it puts the intermediary's credibility on the line. You can call back and begin with this type of statement: "Good afternoon, Ms. Smith, this is Ms. Jones calling from Best Resort. When I called before, you suggested that this would be a good time to reach Mr. Sullivan. Is he in?"

Getting Past the Gatekeeper

"Gatekeepers" are intermediaries—secretaries, receptionists, and others—who act as filters for all telephone messages. For maximum success, it is important to build a good relationship with intermediaries, because they are the people who decide whether to put your calls through. Always show respect to gatekeepers and demonstrate that your purpose is the same as theirs—to provide assistance and solutions to their bosses.

Engaging the gatekeeper's interest with a good opening statement is an effective way to ensure that you will get through to a decision-maker. In the following example, we will take a look at how Bonnie Jackson, a salesperson for the City Inn, convinces the gatekeeper, Ms. Wright, that her call will benefit the decision-maker, Ms. Fraser.

Appeal to a Need

"Good morning, Ms. Wright." (The intermediary's name has been obtained from the switchboard operator.) "This is Bonnie Jackson from the City Inn. The reason for my call is that most companies want their visitors to receive personalized, VIP treatment at affordable prices. I'd like to talk with Ms. Fraser about some unique new programs we've designed to give your visitors the best possible hotel experience here in our area, at a price that other top companies tell us is the best value in town. Is Ms. Fraser available?"

At this point, Ms. Wright could either put Bonnie through to Ms. Fraser or give Bonnie some reason why she is unavailable, such as "She's in a meeting" or "She's out of town."

Rather than simply asking when Ms. Fraser can be reached, further questioning is often appropriate.

Verify the Validity of the Need

"Ms. Wright, I mentioned personalized VIP treatment for your visitors at an affordable price. Is this important to your company when selecting a hotel for your visitors?"

If Ms. Wright indicates that this need isn't very important, Bonnie can probe further to discover "hot buttons."

Determine the Most Important Need

"What single factor is most important for your company when selecting hotels for your visitors?"

If Ms. Wright indicates that convenience to the office is the most important factor, for example, Bonnie can reopen her approach, using the uncovered need to spark interest.

Reopen

"I'm glad to hear that convenience is important, Ms. Wright, because we're just five minutes away, which means that your visitors won't waste valuable time going back and forth to your office. Do you think Ms. Fraser would like to hear about our hotel and the many other benefits we can offer your visitors?"

This process demonstrates that if you fail to interest the intermediary with your opening statement, you can find out what other factors are of interest and reopen with a new statement. The gatekeeper will see that what you have to offer will benefit the decision-maker, and it's amazing how often the prospect magically reappears at his or her office or gets out of conference once you have sparked the intermediary's interest. Therefore, it's important to test your opening statements. Keep track of those that work best, and revise and strengthen the wording of those that don't, in order to reach more decision-makers than you thought possible.

Source: Adapted from a series of articles by Tom McCarthy in *Hotel and Resort Industry.* Used with permission.

Opening the Call. Once you have reached the prospect, a good opening is essential to hold the prospect's interest. As with a face-to-face sales call, you should introduce yourself, give the name of the property you represent, and immediately state the purpose of the call. A statement such as, "The reason for my call is that most companies want to house their relocating executives in hotels convenient to company headquarters. Our hotel is located just three blocks from your offices, and we are now offering a special corporate program" is far more effective than opening with "I just called to say hello" or "I'm calling because my general manager suggested you might be a good account, and you're on my list of prospects to call today."

Presenting a benefit—and showing sincere interest in meeting a prospect's needs—is a vital step in opening a call. Developing rapport is important at this early stage, and there are several techniques that can be used to make the prospect more receptive to the presentation to follow.

First, use the prospect's name often. In most cases, the more you use it (without becoming overly familiar or offensive), the better the prospect will feel toward you.

Another good way to build rapport is to use a third-party endorsement. You might say: "Mr. Pritchard, a friend of yours—Jane Steward of Woodcraft, Incorporated—suggested that I call because she felt you would be interested in our banquet facilities." The use of third-party endorsements gives credibility to the sales message and provides a common meeting ground between you and the prospect.

An appointment call should be kept short, unless the prospect wants to chat or ask questions. If it is obvious that the prospect is busy or in a totally unreceptive mood, try to get a brief message across and offer to call back at a more convenient time. If the prospect seems interested or at least willing to listen, you can move on to the presentation.

The Presentation. For an appointment call, the purpose of the presentation is to get the prospect interested enough in your property to agree to a face-to-face meeting. During the presentation, refer to your notes, if necessary, to make sure you stay on track. Remember to sell the benefits of the property to the prospect, rather than just list property features. In telephone selling, you must paint "word pictures." Benefit statements must be specific. When talking to a meeting planner, for example, it is far better to give a descriptive benefit ("When you book your meeting with us, your group is assigned to one person who has the authority to ensure that everything is handled to your satisfaction; this person will have all the answers for you at every stage to make sure your meeting is successful") than a vague benefit ("We have a great convention service department").

The use of power words such as "excellent," "guaranteed," "quality," and "successful" greatly enhances a presentation and can generate prospect interest. Power words are words that have more "sales power" than others. Power words are dynamic, expressive, and highly descriptive, helping clients to "see" the hotel's services over the phone. Power words are an important part of a sales vocabulary, along with personal words like "you," "me," "we," "us," and "our."[4]

The importance of power words is well-known in the industry. Jeff Erickson, a hospitality sales and marketing trainer, says that when his salespeople call a

Exhibit 5 Overcoming Common Prospect Objections

Prospect:	"I'm not interested."
Salesperson:	"I can understand that you might not realize the values offered by our resort from just a brief explanation over the phone, Ms. Kingsbury. But didn't you tell me that you were considering an incentive package for your top salespeople? I'd like to show you in person how our resort can give you just the package you need—at a good value."
Prospect:	"I don't have time to see you now."
Salesperson:	"Mr. Portigo, I realize you have a busy schedule. That's why I want to invite you to visit our hotel for a complimentary lunch or dinner. We can discuss your convention needs over a delicious meal, without taking a lot of time from your business day."
Prospect:	"Just send me a brochure."
Salesperson:	"I'd be happy to send our brochure, but I'd prefer to deliver it personally so I can answer any questions you might have and explain how groups similar to yours have benefited from our facilities and services. Would 1:30 on Wednesday or Thursday be a good time to visit with you?"
Prospect:	"We can't afford to hold outside training seminars."
Salesperson:	"I know you are aware that sales is a highly competitive area, and that training has proven to be an effective sales tool. Our low rates make it possible for firms like yours to hold sales training seminars at a price you can afford."

Common objections should be anticipated, and responses readied, before a salesperson makes a sales call. These are typical objections that might be voiced by a prospect.

prospect or client, "they use the pronoun 'we' instead of 'I.' Using 'we' communicates they have the power of the company behind them. We have three words we stress, 'please,' 'thank you,' and 'you.'"[5]

Overcoming Objections. Be prepared to overcome objections to specific points of the presentation. It is much easier to handle objections if you have planned some answers to common objections and have backup material available that will support your claims (see Exhibit 5). Positive public relations pieces and complimentary letters from satisfied customers are important aids. Such material also can be read before a call to give you the enthusiasm you need to sell the benefits of the property.

As with in-person selling, it is very important during an appointment telephone call to listen carefully to objections and avoid arguing with the prospect. The prospect's objections will often provide clues that will enable you to revise the presentation to address the prospect's needs or concerns.

Setting the Appointment. Since most appointments are made or lost during the first few minutes of the telephone call, you will want to ask for the appointment early. By offering choices of a day—"Would Wednesday or Thursday be more convenient?"—you can lead the prospect into a commitment to a face-to-face sales call.

Sometimes the prospect may be unwilling to set an appointment or may request that you send additional information or a brochure for review. If you are unable to get an appointment during the conversation, make arrangements to call back on another day:

Salesperson: "I'd be happy to send a brochure on our sports program. If you receive it by Tuesday, would you have a chance to review it before the end of the week?"

Prospect: "Oh, certainly."

Salesperson: "Good! I'll give you a call next Friday morning to see if you have any questions."

This type of approach opens the door for the salesperson's next call:

Intermediary: "What is this regarding?"

Salesperson: "Mr. Prospect is expecting my call to discuss the literature I sent regarding saving money on your school's team travel expenses."

If an appointment is made, end the call by confirming the date, time, and location of the appointment, express thanks, and promise to follow up the conversation with additional details (property brochures, menus, etc.) and a letter confirming the date of the face-to-face meeting. Ideally, this meeting should be held at your property so you can show the prospect the property's features and facilities.

Sales Calls

Telephone **sales calls** may be made by a salesperson or by a telemarketer working with a sales script. Hotel chains and many large independent hotels work with specially trained telephone sales teams that call on prospects and concentrate on getting bookings or commitments by phone. Unlike an appointment call, the objective of a telephone sales call is to make an immediate sale, and the caller must either close during the conversation or make arrangements to call back on another day.

Just as in a face-to-face sales presentation, it is important that you sell benefits rather than features when you sell over the phone. If you tell a prospect, "We have electronic door locks," you've only done half the job; you can't assume that the prospect will understand the benefits of this feature (added security, for example). People buy benefits, not features, and benefits must be clearly spelled out to avoid misinterpretation by the potential guest or client.

Closing Techniques. There are several techniques that can be used to close a telephone sale.

Asking for a sale can be as simple as saying, "Shall I reserve a meeting room for your district managers on Monday, July 12th?" However, this technique limits the prospect to a yes or no response, and limits you to one specific area.

A more effective technique is to *assume a sale*. Assuming a sale assumes a "yes" answer on the part of the prospect: "All right, Mrs. Grauberger, I'll confirm your group at our Lakeview Downtown Inn on the 30th of November. As I said, the rates are $42. Now let me read back the booking requirements."

Forced-choice questions encourage the prospect to choose from the alternatives presented by the salesperson. Examples of forced-choice questions include: "Shall I book your tour group for Friday night or Saturday morning?" and "Would your distributors like to try our buffet when they arrive or will they be dining in our Red Lion restaurant?" Forced-choice questions make an effective close because they create a choice between positive alternatives; the salesperson is asking not *whether*, but *which*.

The *pause close* is uniquely effective in telephone selling because silence in a strictly audio medium is difficult for most people to tolerate. A typical pause close may be set up as follows: "Okay, Mr. Fritz. Can I go ahead and book you at the Bayside Inn in Bayport at $65?" (Pause.)

The first person to speak following the pause loses. If the salesperson speaks, the prospect is taken off the decision "hook"; if the prospect speaks, he or she must make a decision.

Closing on an objection acknowledges the prospect's objection, but counters the objection with a benefit (or benefits) and asks for the sale: "That may be true, Mr. Butler. However, the guestrooms will have tables, making your employees' stay more conducive to post meeting work sessions. Shall I reserve the large meeting room or the two small ones?" or "I agree, Mr. Morton, that our property is away from the big city and its entertainment, but imagine how distraction-free this sales meeting will be! How many rooms will you be needing?"

A *series-of-minor-agreements close* summarizes the positive statements made by the prospect: "You agreed that our location was suitable. And didn't you say that our 'Budget Meeting Plan' is just what you're looking for? Then may I set up your annual sales meeting for the 20th to the 25th?"

As you can see, there are a number of effective telephone techniques that may be used in obtaining a commitment from a prospect. Even though many telemarketing operations use a standardized telephone sales script, telemarketers as well as salespeople should become familiar with these closes.

Promotional Calls

Promotional calls can be made by salespeople, the telemarketing staff, or top management to introduce special promotions. For example, one hotel advertised in community newspapers to promote its wedding reception package. The ad requested that recently engaged couples contact the catering sales manager by dialing the "hot line" telephone number listed in the ad. The catering sales manager added to the business generated from these incoming calls by calling couples who had recently announced their engagements in the local newspaper and explaining the wedding reception package. The property was able to secure 15 new accounts in one week!

INTERNET EXERCISE

Log onto the Internet and research the following websites:

- www.signatureworldwide.com
- www.telephonedoctor.com
- www.hospitalitysoftnet.com

1. What telephone sales training does each provide?
2. What new ideas were offered on each site?

Service Calls

Client satisfaction and loyalty can be developed through **service calls,** whether the calls are made just to keep in touch or are follow-up calls to clients after a sale has been made. Clients need to know they are important, and service calls are essential to maintaining and building business for the property. If changes are anticipated before a function, or if problems occur during a function, a service call does far more to show concern and smooth over the situation than a letter.

Public Relations Calls

Public relations calls are made to generate goodwill. In one case, a restaurant manager made low-key telephone calls to past regulars who had not been to the restaurant for some time. The impact was immediate—the restaurant had 25 additional covers per day! Such person-to-person contact can generate additional rooms business as well. If a general manager picks up the telephone to respond to a guest's complimentary letter, it can have a great impact on the guest—he or she is more likely to feel that the property values his or her business and will want to return.

Incoming Calls

No matter what type of call is received by a hotel, it is essential that the caller receive a positive first impression. When a call is answered at the hotel, the spotlight is on the person representing the property, and any unprofessional behavior, such as carrying on a conversation with a co-worker while the caller is on the line, may result in thousands of dollars in lost business.

It is both a courtesy and good business to answer the telephone *promptly.* When a call is not answered right away, the caller may become impatient and hang up; waiting time always seems longer than it is, and time is especially valuable to busy executives. Nancy Austin, co-author of *A Passion for Excellence,* explains how many callers may feel:

> During the first ring, we can hardly wait to speak to someone on the other end! But by the third ring your patient customer has already decided, "This is it, if they don't answer the phone I'm calling the next hotel." And by six rings, forget it! They are so thoroughly disgusted that if they

> are asked for a recommendation, the research shows they will *go out of their way* to "disrecommend" that place that didn't bother to pick up the phone. And you know why? They say, "They didn't care."[6]

To make matters worse, many properties and their salespeople have made increasing use of voice mail. According to industry professionals—and hospitality customers—voice mail is a mixed blessing. While voice mail can be used to ensure that calls are not missed when a salesperson is on another call, most customers want to talk to a live person—immediately. Customers who have to go through a voice mail menu only to find that the salesperson (or the entire sales department) is on voice mail are understandably frustrated—and may take their business elsewhere. Therefore, there should *always* be someone in the sales department available to speak directly to a prospect.

If a salesperson must be on voice mail (he or she is on vacation, for example), it is important to keep the customer in mind. Be specific on when you will return (in a day? a week? two weeks?) and provide an alternative way to reach you, or direct callers to someone else who can assist them immediately. Keep in mind that your voice mail message may need to be changed to reflect changes in your schedule. Any calls received should be returned as soon as possible—within 24 hours, if possible. In other words, use voice mail properly to make it easy—not frustrating—for clients to do business with your hotel or restaurant.

Once the telephone receiver is picked up, the hotel's representative must be ready to talk. Whether the call is to the switchboard, the reservations department, or a sales office extension, the property's representative should begin the call with a greeting, the name of the property, his or her name, and a courteous phrase: "Good morning! This is the New York Hilton; Tom Baker speaking. How may I help you?" Once the caller responds, it is important to learn his or her name and use it early in the telephone conversation.

At times it is necessary to put a caller on hold. "Hold" is not synonymous with "ignore." If a call cannot be routed or a question answered without leaving the line, the caller should be given an explanation of the delay. Instead of just saying, "Please hold," the employee should ask for permission to put the caller on hold (for example, "May I put you on hold for just a minute while I find that information for you?") and wait for a response, rather than assume that the answer is always yes. If the caller is kept on hold for more than a minute, he or she should be given progress reports. The person waiting may be told, "Mr. McClendon, I'm still checking on your reservation. Do you mind waiting a little longer?" These progress reports assure the caller that he or she has not been forgotten, and may prevent the caller from getting irritated. When the employee returns to the line, it helps get the caller's attention to begin with his or her name: "Mr. Sullivan, I have those figures for you now" or "Ms. Mercer, thanks so much for holding." This shows courtesy to the caller and may prevent having to repeat all or part of the information.

Sometimes the caller must be transferred. Far too often, the caller is transferred throughout the hotel before reaching the proper party. To avoid this situation, every attempt should be made to determine the purpose of the call and identify the correct person who can help. Then the call can be transferred to the

INTERNET EXERCISE

Log onto the Internet to do some research on *Hotel & Motel Management* magazine's website: www.hotelmotel.com. Type in "Doug Kennedy articles" or "reservation sales" in the search box and review three articles by Kennedy relating to reservation sales techniques. What new information did you learn?

right party with a statement such as, "The catering manager, Mr. Philip Rodriguez, would be glad to take care of that for you. Shall I transfer you to Philip, or would you prefer to leave your name and number so he can call you?"

Incoming telephone calls that can lead to sales fall into three basic categories: reservations, responses to advertising, and inquiries.

Reservations

For many years the telephone has played an important role in making reservations. Today, coupled with sophisticated computer systems, it is an even more effective sales tool. At small properties, reservations duties may be handled by a small reservations staff or the front desk agents, while at larger properties reservations may be handled by an extensive in-house reservations staff.

Since the reservationist (or front desk agent) is often the public's first contact with the property, more and more emphasis is being put on the training of reservations personnel. Because of the sales-oriented nature of the position, reservationists must be trained in the importance of professionalism, product knowledge, and basic selling techniques. A number of hotel properties and chains, such as Amelia Island Plantation in Florida and the Grand America Hotels and Resorts chain, have instituted extensive training programs to maximize sales while cutting down on the time reservationists spend on the telephone, tying up phone lines. At the Amelia Island Plantation, reservationists use an 11-point script that covers all of the information and selling points needed to secure business. Grand America's program focuses on sales (converting inquiry calls to reservations) and personal knowledge of the guest to enable reservations staff to tailor benefits to guest needs.

Reservations agents should be trained to recognize the difference between a simple inquiry ("Does your hotel have a sauna?") and someone interested in buying. A growing number of today's consumers do research on the web prior to calling a hotel, so chances are that many of them already know details about the property, such as whether the hotel has a sauna. It's more important that reservationists be well-versed in the steps of the selling process in order to obtain the maximum benefit for the hotel.

Central Reservations Systems. In addition to their own reservations personnel, many properties use a **central reservations system (CRS)**, accessed through a toll-free telephone number, to facilitate bookings. This approach has proven so successful that many properties now operate two or more toll-free systems: one to serve the public and another for the exclusive use of travel agents or corporate meeting planners.

Maximizing Telephone Reservations Calls

Knowing the type of traveler (business or leisure) who is inquiring about hotel reservations is important when quoting rates and upselling business. The following two scenarios show how this knowledge can enable hotel reservationists to meet the needs of the potential guest:

Business Traveler

Customer: "I'd like to make a reservation."
Agent: "Certainly. Can you tell me what date you will be arriving?" (The customer explains which dates she wants to reserve.)
Agent: "Let me check those dates for you. Will you be traveling on business or for pleasure?" (The customer replies that she is traveling on business.)
Agent: "We do have availability for your dates. The room we have has a large work desk with a separate phone and modem hook-up. It's ideal if you need to work in the room or check e-mail. We also have an exercise room and a restaurant and lounge, so you don't have to leave the hotel to get a bite to eat or if you want to entertain. The rate is $119. Shall I reserve that for you?"

Leisure Traveler

Customer: "I need to check on a rate for next weekend."
Agent: "Great. Can you tell me what date you will be arriving?" (The customer replies.)
Agent: "Let me check those dates for you. Will you be traveling on business or for pleasure?" (The customer replies that he will be vacationing with his family.)
Agent: "We do have availability for your dates. The room we have will be perfect for your family. It has two double beds, plus there is a sitting area with a couch near the TV. The couch pulls out into an additional bed, so there will be plenty of space for your family. We also have a great restaurant on-site and a pool and game room, so there will be things for the children to do. The rate is $129. Shall I reserve that for you?"

Note that the agent in both of these cases mentioned amenities that were of benefit to each specific customer. Additionally, agents should try to upsell rooms when appropriate, perhaps offering a room with an ocean-front view to leisure travelers, for example.

Source: Adapted from Lisa Richards, "Quoting the Rate to Capture the Sale," *The Rooms Chronicle,* Vol. 11, No. 3, p. 6.

A CRS, whether designed for a single property or a chain, includes a database that features such basic information as property facts (number of rooms, room rates, booking policy, etc.); information about area attractions and events; and travel information (nearby airports, transportation available, etc.). In the case of chain systems, the CRS database will also have information on other properties in the chain.

In addition to highly trained personnel, computer technology, and toll-free numbers, there are other advantages to a CRS:

1. A CRS can help with yield management. Most of today's central reservations systems can be updated online to reflect changing market conditions and rooms inventory (as rooms are filled, rates can be changed on the screen).

And the CRS can assist in filling rooms with the market segments most desirable to the property. If a property wishes to fill 85 percent of its rooms with group business travelers and allocate only 15 percent to transient business, it can reflect this inventory on the computer screen.

2. A CRS is an effective tool for measuring sales and marketing efforts. Most systems provide detailed reports that show exactly where business is coming from—what types of rooms are being sold at what rates, how many rooms are being sold through travel agents, how many group bookings are realized, and so on. These reports can be used to evaluate promotional efforts and discover weaknesses in the property's marketing strategy. An absence of travel agent bookings, for example, may mean that there is a problem with paying commissions promptly.
3. A CRS can evaluate its own effectiveness—statistics generated can be used to calculate the "conversion factor"—the percentage of toll-free calls converted to sales.
4. CRS computer technology has not only made it easier to make reservations and track sales efforts, but, ironically, has increased personalization. Details of a past stay can be stored on the computer and called up to enable reservations personnel to "remember" the guest and facilitate the reservations transaction. This application alone makes a CRS a valuable sales tool (provided its database is current).

To ensure that a CRS is providing good representation for your property, you should check the system periodically (at least quarterly) by calling the CRS and making a reservation at your property to check: (1) whether information given out by reservations agents about your property is up-to-date, (2) the selling techniques of reservations agents, and (3) how fast a reservations request is processed. In hotel-chain jargon, this is called "shopping your franchise." Shopping your franchise should not be a haphazard effort. "Mystery shoppers" should use realistic scenarios and ask a reasonable number of questions to test reservationists for product knowledge and their willingness to accommodate the needs of potential guests (see Exhibit 6). If areas for improvement are detected, managers should always try to say something positive about a reservationist's performance before discussing what could have been done more effectively.

Responses to Advertising

One of the most effective advertising methods used by hoteliers today is the listing of a toll-free telephone number in print ads. Since people are more likely to respond if the call is free, this method of advertising is an excellent source of immediate reservations and business leads and can generate a large number of calls.

Toll-free calls are often handled by a telemarketing staff that tries to get either a firm commitment for a reservation or information to pass along to a hotel salesperson. With today's technology, a salesperson can quickly e-mail a proposal to a prospect and refer him or her to the property's website for more information. These immediate responses can give you an important edge over your competition.

Exhibit 6 Sample Mystery Shopper Form

PROPERTY RESERVATIONS
Test Calls

Property____________________ Site #_________ Phone #_____________

Date________ Day of the Week________ Time________ Res Date_______

Answer within 3 rings	Y	N	# of rings________________
Warm greetings	Y	N	Comments________________
Agent gave name	Y	N	Name____________________
Match day w/date	Y	N	Comments________________
Qualify Caller (Repeat Guest)	Y	N	Comments________________
Qualify Caller (Corp, Senior, Leis.)	Y	N	Comments________________
Quote 3 benefits	Y	N	1. ____________________
			2. ____________________
			3. ____________________
Do benefits match qualification	Y	N	Comments________________
Used guest's name	Y	N	Comments________________
Attempt to upsell	Y	N	Comments________________
Asked for the sale	Y	N	Comments________________
Quote guarantee policy	Y	N	Comments________________
Thank you for calling/reserving	Y	N	Comments________________

Tone of agent Excellent Good Fair Poor

Notes:____

Many properties employ "mystery shoppers" to evaluate how well reservation calls are handled. These shoppers may use a form such as this one to help them evaluate reservations personnel. Reservationists should be trained in the areas that will be evaluated, and notified in advance that mystery shoppers may be used from time to time to evaluate their performance.

Inquiries

Excellent leads for prospective business come in the form of inquiries from people who call the property on the recommendation of friends, acquaintances, or business associates who are familiar with the property; or from people responding to advertisements, mailings, brochures, fliers, or other promotions (which were designed—often at a cost of hundreds or thousands of dollars—to generate this interest). Inquiries can generate a significant amount of business, but many hotels fail to capitalize on these leads by either ignoring or mishandling them. Properly handling inquiries can result in a steadily increasing contribution to the property's guest base.

Since inquiry calls often come directly to the switchboard, switchboard operators should know where to place these calls. Individuals may be routed directly to a reservations agent; group accounts may be referred to the hotel's sales staff or the general manager. At small properties, telephone inquiries are often handled directly at the front desk. These calls may come in while front desk personnel are especially busy registering guests. Too often, there is a tendency to treat inquiry calls lightly. However, callers with inquiries usually want a room or seek information about accommodations, and they should be given prompt attention. If front desk personnel are too busy to handle the call, the caller should be transferred to another hotel employee (a salesperson, the sales director, etc.) who can give immediate attention to the call.

Once an inquiry call is received by the sales department, it should be handled in the same manner as other sales calls. The salesperson should be courteous and interested. Since no precall research has been done on the prospect, it is especially important to listen and ask open-ended questions to determine the caller's needs. Prices or rates should not be given until the exact nature of the business is determined, and the salesperson should discuss benefits rather than features. Handling an inquiry call also includes trying to close business at that time, but even if the call does not result in immediate business, it is important to follow up. Sending additional information by fax, mail, or e-mail—and keeping a trace card (computerized or paper) on the prospective account—may lead to business in the future.

Because many people perceive hotels as "24/7/365" businesses, it is especially important to establish a plan for handling calls that come in after the marketing and sales office is closed. Author Doug Kennedy gave this report on how after-hours inquiries were handled when "mystery shoppers" called the front desk of randomly selected full-service hotels after 7:00 P.M.:

- 47 percent simply asked the caller to call back the next day.
- 24 percent transferred the call to the marketing and sales department's voice mailbox without notifying the caller.
- 22 percent also transferred the call to the marketing and sales department's voice mailbox, but they did at least notify the caller that they were doing so, and that someone from sales would return their call the following day.
- 7 percent provided a detailed explanation that salespeople usually handled such requests, that the marketing and sales department was closed for the day, and then offered to take a message and/or transfer the call to voice mail.[7]

Since inquiries may lead to business for the hotel, it is important to make a good first impression on the caller. At the very least, it should be explained to callers that a salesperson can best handle their inquiries, and they should be given options for leaving messages or asked if they would like to have a salesperson follow up. It also makes a good first impression to offer basic information, such as, "While I have you on the line, are there any basic questions you may have about our property?" or "If you want to take a virtual tour of our property right away, you can visit our website at www...."

Telephone Sales Operations

The telephone can be used in creative ways to boost sales. Two of the most common ways are telephone sales blitzes, which can be extremely effective for small to mid-size properties, and telemarketing, which is used primarily by large properties.

Telephone Sales Blitzes

Telephone sales blitzes are usually used to gather information, but they can also result in immediate sales. A telephone sales blitz is especially effective for properties that cannot afford expensive computers and other telemarketing technology; these properties are finding that they can still use the telephone "the old-fashioned way" to generate business.

A successful telephone sales blitz begins with organization. The property's general manager or sales team usually targets a particular geographic area or market segment and develops a plan for contacting as many people as possible within a short period of time.

One advantage of a telephone sales blitz is that virtually any staff member can participate, since usually the prime objective is to gather information, not sell. Reservations agents, night auditors, secretaries, and other staff members can easily be trained to use a script to ask specific questions and record the answers on a form for follow-up (see Exhibit 7).

Telemarketing Operations

In today's world of skyrocketing personal sales call costs, **telemarketing** is an effective sales tool that provides person-to-person contact, immediate feedback, and the flexibility of a variety of approaches without the costs of a personal sales call. While telemarketing is often confused with general telephone sales, the two are worlds apart. Telemarketing is characterized by systematic use of the telephone, often by a special staff of highly trained telemarketers, along with computers and other technology that provide instant access to information.

A good telemarketer can speak with up to 50 decision-makers a day.[8] Using a carefully scripted message, telemarketers can simply gather information or present a sales message and close the sale.

Telemarketing should not be taken lightly. Hotels should refrain from pulling secretaries or clerks from other departments to attempt telemarketing duties. A highly trained staff, dedicated to the telemarketing function only, is the most cost-effective way for a property to use this form of selling.

Exhibit 7 Sample Sales Blitz Form

THE SALES BLITZ: DECISION-MAKER IDENTIFICATION						
	BUSINESS			CLUBS, CHURCHES AND OTHER NON-PROFIT ORGANIZATIONS		
Person Contacted	Makes Reservations for Visitors	Makes Reservations for Company Banquets and Meetings	Uses Local Restaurants for Business Lunches	Makes Reservations for Visitors	Makes Reservations for Company Banquets and Meetings	Uses Local Restaurants for Personal Enjoyment
1. Name Title Phone						
2. Name Title Phone						
3. Name Title Phone						
4. Name Title Phone						

This sales blitz form helps a salesperson or other hotel employee record the names of decision-makers and indicate what types of business they might book at the property.
Source: James C. Makens, *The Hotel Sales and Marketing Plan Book* (Winston-Salem, N.C.: Marion-Clarence Publishing House, 1990), p. 217.

All telemarketers should have good communication skills; persistence; the capability to bounce back from rejection; good organizational skills; the ability to adapt to new situations and different types of clients; and, most important, the enthusiasm, friendliness, and flexibility that can result in increased sales.

Telemarketing Scripts. Telemarketers use telemarketing scripts designed to communicate effectively with prospects and either make a sale or gather information so that salespeople can follow up on the call. A telemarketing call report can be completed and given to the property's sales representatives for evaluation and possible follow-up (see Exhibit 8).

Most telemarketing scripts begin with an introduction that breaks the ice and explains the purpose of the call: "Good morning, I'm Mary Kelly, representing Best Rest Inns. I'm calling to ask you a few brief questions regarding your company's use of meeting rooms and accommodations for your traveling salespeople. Any

Exhibit 8 Sample Telemarketing Call Report

TELEPROSPECT CALL REPORT

DATE ____________________

ORGANIZATION ____________________

ADDRESS ____________________

____________________ TELEPHONE ____________________

KEY CONTACT ____________________ TITLE ____________________

ADDITIONAL CONTACTS ____________________ TITLE ____________________

____________________ TITLE ____________________

POTENTIAL	YES	NO	FREQUENCY
GROUP			
INDIVIDUAL			
MEETING			
OTHER			

HOTEL(S) CURRENTLY PATRONIZED ____________________

ACTION ____________________

TRACE ____________________

REMARKS ____________________

____

SIGNATURE

Many telemarketers who prospect for leads use a form similar to this one to build an information base of organizations that may constitute potential business for the property. (Courtesy of L'Ermitage Hotels, Beverly Hills, California)

information you can provide will be extremely helpful. My first question concerns the number of meetings you hold each year." This type of introduction immediately involves the respondent.

The content of a telemarketing script will, of course, depend on the property's telemarketing objectives (see Exhibit 9). Is the script designed to gather information only? Is it designed to generate leads for follow-up by salespeople? Does it offer a benefit or special premium in return for a booking? No matter what the objective, a telemarketing script is usually:

Exhibit 9 Sample Telemarketing Script: Follow-Up Survey

TELEMARKETING SURVEY

Hello____.

This is ______________________ from the Sheraton Naperville Hotel. I'm calling to thank you for staying at the Sheraton Naperville. I was hoping you would assist me by answering a few questions about our hotel so we can serve you better.

1. Which of the following describes your reasons for visiting Naperville?

   Corporate Business   Training   Convention   Sales Call   Other

   If other, explain: ____

2. Did you select our hotel personally, or was the reservation made by another individual? If by another person, then who (i.e.: secretary, travel agent, other)?
3. Was this your first stay with us?   Yes   No
4. Using the following scale, how would you rate your general impression of our hotel?

   Excellent   Above Average   Average   Fair   Poor

   Comments:

5. How would you rate our registration services?

   Excellent   Above Average   Average   Fair   Poor

   Comments:

6. What was the quality of our housekeeping services?

   Excellent   Above Average   Average   Fair   Poor

   Comments:

7. Did you dine in any of our restaurants during your stay?   Yes   No

   How would you rate them?

	Excellent	Above Average	Average	Fair	Poor	Did Not Use
Atrium Restaurant						
Banquet Service						
Beaubien Dining Room						
Cafe al Fresco						
LaSalle Drinkery						
Room Service						
Comments:						

8. Are you aware of any of the following special services we provide for our guests?

			Send Information
The Concierge Floor	Yes	No	___
Our Video Check-Out	Yes	No	___
The Guestroom Refreshment Bars	Yes	No	___

Exhibit 9 *(continued)*

			Send Information
The Pool and Sauna	Yes	No	___
Our Sheraton International Club	Yes	No	___
The Meeting and Ballroom Facilities	Yes	No	___
Our Special Meeting Packages	Yes	No	___

Would you like to receive information on any of these services?

9. Did you need or use information on the surrounding area? Yes No

   Comments:

10. Would you like the Sheraton Naperville to have any of the following services?

    A Hotel Library Yes No

    A Jogging Trail Yes No

    Cable Television Yes No

    Health Club Facilities Yes No

11. How often do you get to Naperville?

    More than once per month

    4 to 12 times per year

    1 to 3 times per year

    First visit

    What is your average length of stay?

    1, 2, 3, 4, 5, or more days

12. Would you choose the Sheraton Naperville for your next visit? Yes No

13. Can I make a future reservation for you at this time? Yes No

In appreciation for your taking the time to assist us in serving you better, we would like to send you a complimentary room upgrade or a certificate for a complimentary breakfast in our Cafe al Fresco. Which would you prefer? (Room Upgrade Breakfast)

Our records show your address as ______________________

Is this correct? Yes No

(If incorrect, fill in correct address) ______________________

____

What are the correct spelling of your name and your correct title?

____

Thank you again for your help. We look forward to seeing you at the Sheraton Naperville again soon (or appropriate date if a reservation was made).

Many properties use telemarketing surveys such as this one to follow up on their guests. Information generated by the survey can be entered into a computer to determine areas of guest interest. The information can also be used to tailor a letter or follow-up telephone call to the needs of the guest. Respondents to this survey receive a complimentary room upgrade or breakfast. (Courtesy of Sheraton Naperville Hotel, Naperville, Illinois)

MARKETING IN ACTION

The Kingsmill Resort & Spa in Williamsburg, Virginia, sought to determine its best course of action to achieve a specific goal: *Complete client satisfaction to ensure rebooking without sales costs.* To do so, the resort's managers asked a number of questions: "How are our salespeople best employed?" "How can we keep our salespeople happy?" "How do we reduce sales costs?"

The Kingsmill decided to hire telemarketers to determine a meeting prospect's profile. After being given cold leads by a sales manager, the telemarketing staff obtained the following information for each potential prospect:

- Meeting frequency
- Time(s) of the year
- Types of meetings
- Length of meeting (arrival and departure dates)
- Number of attendees
- Type of property preferred and why
- Purchase center and responsible individual
- Any other pertinent information that would help an account executive prepare a presentation

Once a potential prospect was qualified in this way, the information was turned over in a written report to the area account executive, who then telephoned those prospects likely to do business with the property for an appointment—or, if feasible, arranged for the prospect to visit the property. (Sales literature normally was not given out until a face-to-face meeting with the prospect.) After the sale was made, the client was turned over to the property's conference planner, who was responsible for preparing the sales contract or letter of agreement and following through every step of the way until the end of the meeting.

This strategy eliminated the need for salespeople to prospect. They no longer wasted valuable time contacting prospects unsuitable for the property, and they were able to devote 100 percent of their time and energy to selling. That made the salespeople happier, and also meant that fewer salespeople were needed, which reduced costs for the resort.

1. *Short.* Long surveys or presentations may irritate prospects or cause them to lose interest. It is important not to take too much of the prospect's time.
2. *Specific.* The script should be to the point. Benefits should be spelled out early.
3. *Simple.* Long words and hotel jargon should be avoided to ensure that the presentation is readily understandable. It is better to ask, "Would you prefer a room with two double beds?" rather than "Would you prefer a double-double?"
4. *Structured.* The script should flow from general questions to more specific or sensitive areas. For example, it is far easier to build rapport with a prospect if the telemarketer begins by asking general questions about the prospect and his or her type of business, instead of immediately starting off

with questions about how much the prospect has paid for meeting space or accommodations.

A telemarketing script must keep the prospect on the line long enough to gather information, get a message across, or close a sale. To do this, the script must get the prospect involved and present a benefit of interest to the prospect. Eliciting reaction to one program versus another builds interest, as does asking for the prospect's opinions, or including interesting stories and analogies that relate to the prospect's background.

Telemarketing Programs. Since telemarketing is so important, it is essential that a telemarketing program—whether established in a large regional or district office for an entire hotel chain, or headquartered at an individual property—be as disciplined as any other form of direct selling. There should be carefully developed production forms, professional training of telemarketers, continuing supervision, and tracking of results. If in-house staff is used to fill telemarketing positions, a training program should be implemented and an experienced telemarketing professional hired as either the program director or a consultant. An example of a successful telemarketing program is the Days Inns' Automatic Telemarketing System (ATMS).

Days Inns' telemarketing operation focuses on three primary markets—the motorcoach business, group business, and the corporate market; and three secondary markets—travel agents, travel agent consortiums, and tour operators. The telemarketing program combines experienced telemarketing operators with a computer software package that includes prospect and guest tracking, an inventory of available literature and mailing materials, telemarketing representative productivity tracking, automatic telephone dialing, a program for rapid retrieval of booking information, guest booking histories, a room inventory, a directory of properties, complaint and complaint follow-up records, a program for developing effective telemarketing scripts, and marketing research functions.

In evaluating its program, Days Inns management found that 5 percent of telemarketing calls resulted in immediate bookings and 20 percent generated appointments with salespeople; 60 percent of the prospects contacted wanted to have further information sent in the mail; only 15 percent had no interest. The program was extremely cost-effective. In the first year of the program's operation, six telemarketing representatives were responsible for over $3 million in bookings.[9]

Telemarketing can be an efficient tool to pinpoint prospects, sell to serious buyers, and keep in touch with regular clients and guests. For optimum success, telemarketing programs should be developed based on a detailed marketing plan and executed with a great degree of professionalism.

Endnotes

1. Ruth Hill, "Harnessing the Power of the Telephone," *HSMAI Marketing Review*, Spring 2001, p. 62.
2. From a speech by Bruce J. Orr, AT&T National Market Manager for the lodging industry, at an AH&LA convention in Las Vegas, Nevada.
3. Hill, p. 63.

4. A helpful resource for building a "power word" sales vocabulary is Richard Bayan, *Words That Sell*. The book is available from Caddylak Systems, 500 Fillmore Ave., Tonawanda, NY 14150, and at Amazon.com.
5. Jeff Erickson, "Telephone Techniques," *HSMAI Student Bulletin*, September/October 1990.
6. From a speech given at an AH&LA convention in San Francisco, California.
7. Doug Kennedy, "The Proper Handling of After-Hours Leads Can Set You Apart from the Competition," *Hotel & Motel Management* website, May 28, 2002.
8. Robert A. Meyer, "Understanding Telemarketing for Hotels," *The Cornell Hotel and Restaurant Administration Quarterly*, August 1987, p. 26.
9. From a speech given by John Russell at a Hospitality Sales & Marketing Association International midyear workshop in Nashville, Tennessee.

Key Terms

appointment call—A telephone call made by a salesperson or other representative of a business to briefly introduce a prospect to features and services offered by the business and ask for an appointment to meet face-to-face.

central reservations system (CRS)—Part of an affiliate reservation network. A central reservations system typically deals directly with the public, advertises a central (usually toll-free) telephone number, provides participating properties with necessary communications equipment, and bills properties for handling reservations.

forced-choice question—A question that seeks to limit an individual to choosing from the alternatives presented by the questioner.

promotional call—A telephone call made by a salesperson or other representative of a business to introduce special promotions.

prospect call—A telephone call made by a salesperson or other representative of a business to gather information and learn the names of decision-makers.

public relations call—A telephone call made by a salesperson or other representative of a business to generate goodwill.

qualifying call—A telephone call made by a salesperson or other representative of a business to determine if a prospect has a need for or can afford the products and services offered by the business.

sales call—A telephone call made by a salesperson or other representative of a business to make a sale.

service call—A telephone call made by a salesperson or other representative of a business to follow up after a sale has been made or merely to keep in touch with a client.

telemarketing—The systematic use, often by a specially trained staff of telemarketers with access to computers, of the telephone for marketing or sales purposes.

telephone sales blitz—The systematic use of the telephone, usually for a short period of time, to gather information, qualify prospects, or in some other way further the marketing and sales success of a business.

Review Questions

1. Why is telephone etiquette important? How can using proper telephone etiquette lead to additional sales?
2. What three techniques can enhance your listening skills?
3. What are types of outgoing calls?
4. What are the five steps of a telephone appointment call?
5. What are techniques that can be used to get past intermediaries?
6. What closing techniques can be used to get a commitment when making a telephone sales call?
7. What types of incoming calls can lead to sales?
8. What is a central reservations system and how does having such a system add to sales?
9. What is a telephone sales blitz? What role does a telephone sales blitz play in sales?
10. Why are properties turning to telemarketing as a sales tool?

Internet Sites

For more information, visit the following Internet sites. Remember that Internet addresses can change without notice. If the site is no longer there, you can use a search engine to look for additional sites.

Advanced Business Teleservices, Inc.
www.abtc.com

American Marketing Association
www.ama.org

Business By Phone, Inc.
www.businessbyphone.com

Destination Marketing Association International
www.iacvb.org

Full Circle International
www.full-circle.co.uk/overview

Hospitality Sales & Marketing Association International
www.hsmai.org

MarkeTel
www.predictivedialers.com

Meeting Professionals International
www.mpiweb.org

Phone for Success
www.consultants-mall.com/phone.htm

Quirk's Marketing Research Review
www.quirks.com

Sales & Marketing Management
www.salesandmarketing.com

TeleSales, Inc.
www.telesales.com

Case Study

Overcoming Rate Resistance—Among the Sales Staff

Conversations stopped as Fran walked into the meeting room where the sales staff of the 263-room Park View Hotel had gathered. The director of sales surveyed the anxious faces that turned toward her as she approached.

"Lighten up, folks," Fran said reassuringly. "This is a strategy session, not a wake. I know you're all aware I had a meeting with the general manager last week, and he'd like us to make a few changes to our marketing plan. I'd like us to sit down together and brainstorm ways to solve some problems we identified in our meeting."

Fran passed around a handout as the salespeople took their seats. The objections started as soon as they began reading the agenda.

"Get rid of 5,000 room nights of our corporate contract business? That's crazy!" said Angela. "Most of my best accounts are corporate preferred. I worked hard to get those accounts and I'm not dropping them now."

"Where are we going to find the customers to replace these 5,000 room nights?" Michael asked. "You can't just expect that kind of new business to come strolling through the door right away."

Murmurs of agreement filled the room. "And how am I supposed to break it to my accounts that they're not going to get their preferred rate anymore?" asked Tanisha. "I wouldn't know what to say, and I don't think I could sound real convincing."

Fran raised her hands. "Let's take this one step at a time. Here's the situation. The hotel has too much contracted business at a low rate. Some of these accounts have had the same rate for the past two years. We need to replace about a third of this business—about 5,000 room nights—with higher-rated transient and group business. I'm not saying we're going to get rid of all our contract business. I just want to evaluate which accounts we should keep, which ones might accept a higher—but still discounted—rate, and which ones don't make good business sense to keep."

Fran stood up next to a flip chart and uncapped a marker. "Let's set up some criteria for reviewing our contract accounts. What kinds of things should we look at? I'll start." She wrote, "Keep accounts with attractive arrival/departure patterns."

She continued to write as the staff began calling out ideas.

After a coffee break, Fran called the group together again. "Great work, folks. Now let's think about how we're going to replace that contract business with some new business that will bring in more revenue. I'd like to make a list of market segments and sources we could solicit more strongly. Then we can evaluate which areas we should concentrate our sales efforts on. Any ideas?" Fran worked the flip chart again.

That job done, Fran turned to the issue Tanisha brought up earlier: how to tell clients about the change in the hotel's corporate preferred rate policy. Together, the staff decided they would be more comfortable and effective if they had scripts to work from.

Fran assigned two of the sales staff to write some scripts that everyone could use when talking with their accounts, whether they were increasing their rate or eliminating their preferred rate. As the meeting adjourned, Fran still heard grumbles from some of the salespeople. "My work's not done yet," she thought, and began planning her next steps for helping her staff accept these new rate changes.

Discussion Questions

1. What are some of the criteria the sales staff could use to evaluate whether a corporate contract account should be retained or dropped?
2. What factors should the staff consider when determining new sources of business to replace the displaced contract business?
3. What would the scripts look like that the sales staff could use when talking to clients about the rate change?
4. How can Fran help her staff become comfortable with the changes in the hotel's rate structure?

Case Number: 370CJ
This case was developed in cooperation with Lisa Richards of Hospitality Softnet, Inc., a marketing resources and support company (Sixty State Street, Suite 700, Boston, Massachusetts 02109; www.hospitalitysoftnet.com).

This case also appears in *Contemporary Hospitality Marketing: A Service Management Approach* (Lansing, Mich.: American Hotel & Lodging Educational Institute, 1999), ISBN 978-0-86612-158-3.

Chapter 6 Outline

Competencies

1. Describe internal marketing and employee empowerment. (pp. 215–221)
2. Define "internal sales" and describe the general manager's role in internal sales. (pp. 222–223)
3. Summarize the role of employees in internal sales and discuss relationship selling, employee training, how employees can apply sales skills, and employee sales incentive programs. (pp. 223–237)
4. Explain how internal merchandising works in guest-contact and back-of-the-house areas. (pp. 237–241)
5. Describe how special services and in-house promotions can be used for internal marketing and sales efforts. (pp. 241–244)

Insider Insights

Judi Del Ponte
Marketing Manager, Marriott's Brighton Gardens
Sun City, Arizona

"At the Sheraton Gateway Inn where I worked as a sales manager, we operated with a small sales and marketing staff. But the people behind the front desk played an extremely critical sales role. Front desk agents knew important information about nearly every guest who stayed at our property. They knew what type of room the guest preferred, and whether the guest wanted a special service or convenience such as extra towels or a wake-up call. That gave front desk personnel a tremendous opportunity to make positive impressions that kept guests coming back. I can't emphasize enough how important it was for our sales staff and the front desk to work as a team."

6

Internal Marketing and Sales

MARKETING THE PROPERTY is everyone's business. Every employee, from the general manager to the bellperson, makes an impression on the property's guests—an impression that can leave guests looking forward to their next visit or send them packing in a hurry, never to return. Industry leader Howard Feiertag states:

> There's been tremendous growth in conducting business in our industry with technological innovations. We see it online with interactive websites, e-mail, and other Internet and intranet methods. However, technology will never replace the need for hospitality salespeople. Getting individual room reservations through the Internet will continue, but the bulk of the buying of rooms, meals, and services will always be through our people—reservationists, front office employees, catering/banquet staff, and sales staff. Every employee, regardless of type of job or function, is involved in selling.[1]

In this chapter, we will discuss the vital areas of internal marketing and internal sales, and focus on how employees in every department can generate additional sales—and repeat business for the property—through suggestive selling, cross-selling, upgrading, merchandising, and promotional techniques.

What Is Internal Marketing?

Internal marketing and internal sales, while interrelated, are not the same. The major difference between the two is the target audience. Internal marketing seeks to sell *employees* on the property and their importance to its success. Internal sales is directed toward *guests already at the property*, and is a systematic plan to meet guest needs and increase revenues. While marketing externally to key market segments is obviously important, marketing efforts should first be directed internally to employees.

Why is internal marketing needed? When selling any product, complete product knowledge—and personal belief in the product—is crucial. But what about hospitality products? The hospitality product is an intangible, an experience—and the primary factor in guest satisfaction is the quality of service rendered. Since service is so important, every employee should understand the product and his or her role in the success of the operation. Management must sell employees on the hospitality product and the importance of each employee's role in generating guest satisfaction. According to the internal marketing concept, employees are just as important to please as guests if employees are to provide the levels of service needed to compete in today's marketplace. Therefore, employee satisfaction and guest satisfaction are interrelated; there is an absolute correlation between the two.

Employee satisfaction results in less employee turnover. If employees are sold on the value of their jobs and their role in achieving customer satisfaction, and are well trained and supported by management, they will likely stay with their employer longer than employees who are frustrated and insecure in their positions. Veteran employees usually provide better service to guests. The Rosen Centre Hotel in Orlando, for example, has been able to maintain a consistent quality product over the years due in part to the hotel's ability to retain employees who were on hand to open the hotel. That impressive record is partly the result of involving the employees in defining and creating guest services and figuring out the best way to deliver those services. By having employees directly involved in the decision-making process, guest services are enhanced and employees tend to stay, because they have a stake in the property's success.

Many other hotel chains and independent properties have developed structured internal marketing programs. The Ritz-Carlton, for example, has implemented self-directed work teams in an effort to improve guest satisfaction. This policy gives workers "shared leadership" at their property, giving them more control in day-to-day activities and motivating them to provide even better customer service. Many management tasks at the Ritz-Carlton have been transferred to the hourly staff. These include scheduling, interviewing, selecting team members, and forecasting budgets. Payroll costs were significantly reduced as managerial staff went from a ratio of one for every 15 employees to one for every 50. John Russell, general manager of the chain's 399-room hotel in Tysons Corner, Virginia, says that "the self-directed team approach has resulted in happier employees, lower turnover, fewer mishaps, and improved problem-solving, all of which contribute to a high level of customer service."[2]

Establishing an Internal Marketing Plan

Like marketing externally to customers, internal marketing to employees requires a systematic approach:

1. Encouraging managers to treat employees with the same care and consideration that they extend to guests.
2. Creating employment opportunities that allow employees to grow through involvement and training.
3. Empowering employees to deliver quality service.

A one-day seminar on providing quality service by an outside trainer will not work. Management must develop a strong service culture and demonstrate this attitude daily. A Four Seasons hotel manager said that the moral cornerstone and business philosophy of the company is the "Golden Rule"—that is, treating others as you wish to be treated. Isadore Sharp, the founder and CEO of Four Seasons Hotels and Resorts, says that "once we determined to make service what we're known for—once we redefined luxury to mean not decor but service—our employees became our most important asset, because they deliver that service. We work hard to create a work environment that allows them to be their best, to feel a part of what's happening, to feel respected."[3] Another Four Seasons general manager put it this way: "A lot of companies talk about the importance of their people. But at Four Seasons we try to show it in every way that we can. Companies that keep their eye on profit, and not on the people who make the profit, are like soccer players who keep their eye on the scoreboard and not on the ball."[4]

Since employees are the key to good service, having the right employees is critical. Having the right employees begins with the hiring process. A firm's competitive strength is predicated on its ability to recruit and develop a quality workforce. Most successful hospitality firms today don't hire employees based on previous experience, but on attitude. You can train someone for a job; you can't easily train them to have the right attitude. Therefore, attracting and retaining friendly, service-oriented employees is paramount. One Marriott manager asks prospective employees, "Are you prepared to serve?" He wants to know if making customers happy makes them happy. If somewhere deep down they don't have the desire to help people, they're not right for the job. It's easier to hire friendly people than to train people to be friendly.

Once the right employees are hired, they should be empowered to provide quality service to guests. Ellen Sinclair, Vice President of Human Resources for Benchmark Hospitality, says that "our way of doing that is through communication—talking about what's going on, sharing the numbers, how we're trying to build revenues and involve our people in the process. If you communicate what the challenges and strategies are, employees are more willing, because they understand that they are part of the solution."[5]

Commonwealth Hotels, a management company that owns Hilton, Embassy Suites, and Hampton properties, also promotes employee empowerment. Commonwealth sponsors daily meetings with individual departments at their hotels. At these meetings, employees are briefed on upcoming events and given the opportunity to provide their insights, air their grievances, and request specific action. This type of dialog helps to keep employee satisfaction high. Employees are also granted a certain degree of decision-making to solve guest problems, helping them develop pride in, and ownership of, their work.

Authors William H. Davidow and Bro Uttal talk about Embassy Suites in their book, *Total Customer Service: The Ultimate Weapon,* emphasizing that Embassy Suites uses an upside-down organization chart to dramatize the idea that the front-line employees, the ones who deal with guests, are the most important people in the organization. Embassy Suites also gives employees a stake in the company's success by linking everyone's salary to hotel performance. Employees are shown the results of daily guest interviews along with the hotel's occupancy rate and cleanliness scores, and when a hotel meets or exceeds its quarterly targets, employees get a bonus based on their hourly rate and the number of hours they worked, rather than based on their position.

Training and Supporting Employees. Hospitality firms that practice internal marketing spend a lot of time training and supporting their employees. They treat their employees the way they want their employees to treat their guests.

MARKETING IN ACTION

Four Seasons Hotels and Resorts: Cultivating Satisfied Guests

At Four Seasons Hotels and Resorts, the company's top priority is a satisfied guest. Concern for the customer starts with top management and flows through the operation. The company philosophy is based on three basic principles:

1. *A shared spirit.* Hire motivated people, train them to be the best they can be, and offer them an environment in which to flourish.
2. *An enduring culture.* Adhere to an ethical code of behavior: the Golden Rule. Quite simply, this means treating others—guests, business partners, suppliers, and employees—as one would wish to be treated.
3. *Carried globally.* Four Seasons aspires to treat its staff members as they in turn treat guests. This has been the essence of the chain's success in exporting the Four Seasons brand to new markets.

Isadore Sharp, the company's founder, says, "The foundation of our success is the many people of Four Seasons who have maintained their commitment to excellence over the years. By taking pride in what they do and in being the best, they have created a company that is now acclaimed the world's best hotel company."

Four Seasons' corporate culture encourages employees to go the extra mile and respond with concern and dedication to customer needs. Employees are never penalized for trying to serve a customer. For example, Rod Dyment, a doorman at Toronto's Four Seasons, once got on a plane to Washington, D.C., to deliver the briefcase of a guest who needed key documents for a meeting the next day. Dyment's first concern was taking care of the guest. He didn't worry about getting his boss's approval. Upon his return, Dyment was not reprimanded or terminated—he was made Employee of the Year. At another Four Seasons hotel, a front desk agent gave the proverbial shirt off her back to a guest. Upon hearing that the airline had lost the guest's luggage and she had an early morning business meeting, the agent loaned the guest a suit of clothes to enable her to attend her meeting suitably attired. "We can build beautiful buildings—everybody else can, too," Sharp says. "How our employees serve their guests is the thing that can't be copied."

Four Seasons has shown that putting the guest first leads to profits; the company enjoys above-average financial performance and profit percentages that many hotel chains only dream about.

Sources: Adapted from *Four Seasons—Four Decades* (Four Seasons' website, 2002) and Jeff Higley, "The Man Behind the Brand," *Luxury Hotelier,* September 2007.

The Cincinnati Marriott Northwest has created a guest service and training program designed to encourage the staff to "treat each guest as if they were part of the family." Continuous guest service training is conducted, and the 170 staff members are encouraged to "go the extra mile" to ensure that guests will repeatedly return to the hotel. Some of the key elements of this guest service training include:

INTERNET EXERCISE

Log onto the Internet and go to *Hotel and Motel Management* magazine's website at www.hotelmotel.com. In the search box, type in "Howard Feiertag articles." Howard Feiertag, a noted hospitality sales trainer and a member of the faculty at the Department of Hospitality Management at Virginia Polytechnic Institute, was quoted in the opening paragraph of this chapter. Review two of his articles that relate to internal marketing and sales. What additional things have you learned about internal marketing and sales from these articles?

- Address each guest by name, if possible.
- Establish eye contact within 20 feet of the guest.
- Smile at the guest when you get within 10 feet of him or her.
- Answer a guest with, "It's my pleasure" rather than "You're welcome."
- Escort a guest to his or her destination each time, rather than just pointing the way.
- When a guest asks something of the employee, the employee should realize that he or she owns the request, rather than giving the request to some other employee.

This training program was developed to differentiate the hotel from its competitors. To create and reinforce an obsession with service, in every meeting the general manager discusses the importance of satisfying guests and reiterates that the hotel is committed to achieving 100-percent guest satisfaction. On Friday afternoons, the general manager invites the entire staff to gather for a pep rally during which guest letters and cards are read. This meeting helps heighten the loyalty of the staff and creates a family feeling.

The success of this training program is remarkable. The hotel has:

- Received number-one ratings for guest satisfaction in the Marriott system four times.
- Received the number-one rating for "top Marriott suburban property" four times.
- Earned a 96 percent approval rating on Marriott's opinion survey.

Kent Bruggeman, the general manager, states:

> Our staff takes pride in saying they work at one of the top 15 Marriotts in the world. And I recognize them every day for the contribution they make to the success of the organization. They know they are valuable because we take every opportunity to show them how important they are. Providing the guest with a superior experience is the only sustainable advantage that anybody has in our industry, and our employees are the ones who make the experience happen.[6]

Getting an overview of the operation—and each employee's importance in each area—during training sessions promotes a sense of pride in employees, which can shine through in guest contacts. All employees, guest-contact and back-of-the-house employees alike, must see their jobs as opportunities to promote guest satisfaction. A maintenance worker, for example, is not only fixing a television set—he or she is helping to ensure guest satisfaction. The dishwasher is not just preventing the return of a chipped glass to the dining room—he or she is making sure the property doesn't give a bad impression to a guest.

Empowering Employees to Deliver Quality Service

As alluded to earlier, **employee empowerment** is crucial to quality service and is a very important step in an internal marketing program. Employee empowerment gives employees the authority to make on-the-spot decisions to respond to guest needs—decisions that were previously relegated to those higher in authority.

In addition to building employee morale, employee empowerment also benefits guests (see Exhibit 1). At Guest Quarters Suite Hotels, for example, employees are now authorized to handle special requests or guest concerns related to quality issues immediately. Long waits while an employee checks with a supervisor are eliminated, and problems can be solved on the spot, greatly reducing guest frustration.

Employee empowerment is crucial in the food service industry as well. Tim Firnstahl, the founder of SGE, Inc., a restaurant management company in Seattle, set an objective of making sure that guest satisfaction in all of his restaurants was guaranteed. He developed a plan that included the company slogan, "Your Enjoyment Guaranteed. Always" (YEGA), and all 600 of his employees signed a contract that they would follow through on the YEGA promise. Firnstahl empowered employees to make the YEGA objective workable: "In the event of an error or delay, any employee right down to the busboy could provide complimentary wine or dessert, or pick up an entire tab if necessary."[7]

For empowerment to work for the good of all concerned, however, there must be clearly understood guidelines. In some hotels, for example, a front desk agent may be given parameters for changing guest bills. In most empowerment situations, decisions made are relative to the employee's responsibilities. A housekeeper, for example, could offer a reduced rate or other benefit in response to a guest's complaint about a room not cleaned satisfactorily, but would have no authority to respond to a guest complaint about dining room service.

To promote effective employee empowerment policies, many properties develop "empowerment surveys" that seek employee input on such areas as frequent guest complaints, obstacles hindering employees from responding to complaints, and what authority employees need to better serve guests. Two major hotel chains, Marriott and Omni Hotels, offer seminars and employee training to ensure that employee empowerment policies are effective. Marriott's Total Quality Management (TQM) seminars help managers understand employee empowerment policies. Omni offers extensive employee training, including its "Power of One" program, which teaches employees how to manage service situations.

Exhibit 1 Empowering Employees to Provide Guest Satisfaction

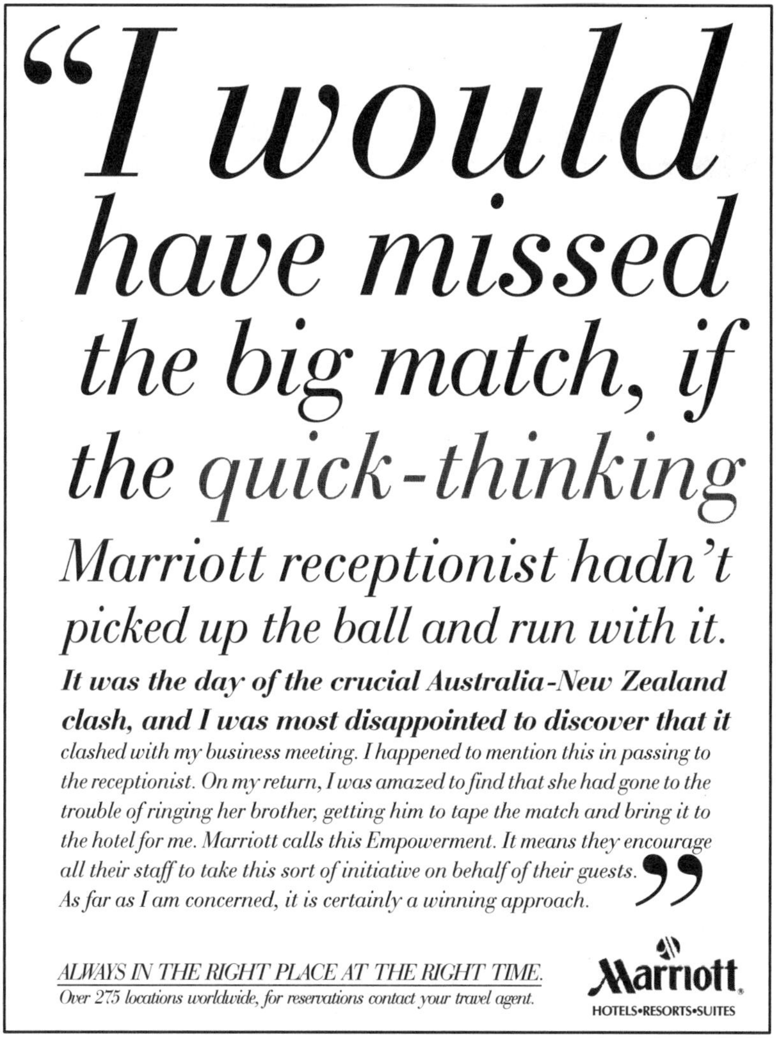

"I would have missed the big match, if the quick-thinking Marriott receptionist hadn't picked up the ball and run with it.

It was the day of the crucial Australia-New Zealand clash, and I was most disappointed to discover that it *clashed with my business meeting. I happened to mention this in passing to the receptionist. On my return, I was amazed to find that she had gone to the trouble of ringing her brother, getting him to tape the match and bring it to the hotel for me. Marriott calls this Empowerment. It means they encourage all their staff to take this sort of initiative on behalf of their guests. As far as I am concerned, it is certainly a winning approach."*

ALWAYS IN THE RIGHT PLACE AT THE RIGHT TIME.
Over 275 locations worldwide, for reservations contact your travel agent.

This ad details an instance in which a Marriott employee "went the extra mile" to ensure guest satisfaction. The ad promotes the policy of Marriott's managers to "encourage all their staff to take this sort of initiative on behalf of their guests," and shows just one example of how employee empowerment benefits the chain's customers. (Courtesy of Marriott)

Employee empowerment is expected to play a major role in selling hospitality products in our service-oriented economy. As more properties discover that empowerment increases guest satisfaction, gives employees a sense of worth, and saves the property time and money, empowerment programs will become an essential component of good property management.[8]

What Is Internal Sales?

Internal sales can be defined as specific sales activities engaged in by various employees of a property, in combination with a program of internal merchandising, to promote additional sales and guest satisfaction. The main objective of internal sales is to increase sales by promoting effective guest-employee relationships. Management can encourage these vital relationships in three ways:

1. Provide an environment conducive to good guest-employee relations
2. Instill pride (both in the property and in the value of their respective positions) in employees
3. Provide training that encourages employees to become more helpful to guests

The sales impetus must start with top management and filter down to employees. It is up to management to support and encourage employees in internal sales efforts, and to provide internal sales training, product training, and motivational programs. An enthusiastic management team can produce an entire staff that sells with enthusiasm.

There is a tremendous profit potential for internal sales, because in-house sales efforts are directed toward a captive audience. When selling to in-house guests, sales costs are minimal. Each additional dollar spent results in nearly pure bottom-line income. If every hotel guest could be induced to spend just $2 more per day, the additional sales for a 200-room property running at 80 percent occupancy (and an average per-room occupancy of 1.5 persons) would be $175,200 per year![9]

In order to be effective, in-house sales efforts must be continual. A one-month program is usually effective for only one month. An internal sales program should be a tied to the property's marketing plan, designed for the entire hotel (not just one department), and developed as a systematic yearly plan rather than a one-shot blitz. Internal sales, like external sales, should be planned for and directed to high-priority market segments and given special emphasis during periods when business is most needed.

The Role of the General Manager in Internal Sales

The attitude of the hotel's general manager will greatly influence the success of an internal sales program. If the general manager is not customer- and sales-oriented, it is unlikely that the staff will be highly motivated. A good general manager recognizes the value of guest satisfaction and sets goals to attain guest goodwill—and repeat business—by using effective internal merchandising (discussed later in the chapter) and developing sales-oriented employees. A general manager can develop a sales-oriented staff by:

- Hiring sales-oriented employees
- Training employees in sales techniques
- Motivating employees to sell

Hiring Sales-Oriented Employees. Sales-oriented employees can greatly increase in-house sales. The human resources department at large properties, or the general manager at smaller properties, should develop sales-oriented job descriptions and be able to recognize sales-oriented applicants. When new employees realize that selling is part of their job and sales is the lifeblood of the property, they will be more willing to learn sales techniques.

But while sales skills can be taught, personality can't, making it especially important to hire a staff that possesses attributes essential to selling a hospitality product. Many hotel managers "hire the smile and train the skill." Employees—especially those who will have direct contact with guests—should be "sparklers," people who are sincere in their warmth, enthusiasm, and concern for guests.

The late Michael Hurst, a successful restaurant owner, used an interviewing strategy to judge his applicants' enthusiasm and ability to interact with guests. His interviews always included the question, "What's the funniest thing that's ever happened to you?" If the applicant became animated and told a story with enthusiasm, Hurst knew he had a winner.[10]

Training Employees in Sales Techniques. Once an employee has gained a thorough knowledge of the property and the benefits the property offers to guests, sales training can help the employee learn the types of selling required for the position (upgrading, suggestive selling, cross-selling, etc.) and learn to recognize verbal and nonverbal clues from guests. These clues include tone of voice and body language; employees as well as salespeople should be well versed in how to "read" others. This knowledge will enable employees to better sell to a receptive guest, and help them know when not to approach a guest (perhaps the guest is angry, wants privacy, and so on).

Motivating Employees to Sell. One of the ways the general manager can motivate employees to sell is by convincing them that they can, indeed, become effective salespeople. Armed with this confidence—and management encouragement—employees can put their skills to work to earn more money for the property. Many properties also offer incentive programs to encourage employees to sell.

The Role of Employees in Internal Sales

Many employees make hundreds, even thousands, of guest contacts weekly, so involving employees in internal sales (and using their ideas and suggestions) is essential if a property wants to keep guests coming back. Twenty years ago, most guests didn't have much of a choice; perhaps there were only one or two hotels at their destination. Today, however, hospitality choices abound, and it is especially important to build guest loyalty to avoid losing even a small part of your current guest base to competitors.

Relationship Selling. Most hospitality managers have concluded that it is less expensive to retain existing guests than to acquire new ones, and are focusing on building relationships with their current guests. Relationship selling (also called *relationship marketing*) can be defined as building guest loyalty by creating, enhancing, and maintaining a relationship with guests.

Industry Innovators

Isadore Sharp, Founder
Four Seasons Hotels and Resorts

Isadore Sharp, who earned a degree in architecture from Tyerson University in Toronto, opened his first hotel on Toronto's Jarvis Street in 1961. By 2008, his Four Seasons Hotels and Resorts chain encompassed 75 properties worldwide, a success story that would not have been possible without the "four pillars" that Sharp established over the chain's history:

- **Quality:** "We will only operate medium-sized hotels of exceptional quality with an objective to be the best." — 1972
- **Service:** "True luxury will be defined not by architecture or decor, but by service. So we must make the quality of our service our distinguishing feature and a competitive advantage." — 1976
- **Culture:** "We will create a work ethic based on the Golden Rule to give our people a framework to pursue a superior service culture." — 1980
- **Brand:** "We will grow as a management company and build a brand name synonymous with quality." — 1986

Sharp ensured that his goals would be met by beginning with his employees and creating a company that radiated warmth from the head office down through the ranks. He hired only the best, most motivated people he could find. When the Four Seasons was preparing to open a hotel in New York, for example, it received 43,000 applications; only 17,000 were selected for an interview, and just 500 were ultimately hired. Already feeling like an elite group, these 500 employees were encouraged, just as all Four Seasons employees are, to take pride in their jobs. The company's policy of loyalty to its employees encourages them to show loyalty to the chain's guests.

Sharp's philosophy of warmth, coupled with the empowerment of his employees to go above-and-beyond to ensure guest satisfaction, has resulted in a staff that delivers the quality service that has become a trademark of the chain.

Sources: Erin F. Sternthal, "Going for the Gold," *Travel Agent*, December 9, 2002; and Jeff Higley, "The Man Behind the Brand," *Luxury Hotelier*, September 2007.

There are several ways for properties to learn more about their guests so they can build relationships with them. One commonly used method is the use of guest profiles. Guest profiles can be developed in a number of ways, from obtaining information from registration forms to conducting guest surveys. In order to be effective, however, guest profiles must contain information that will enable property personnel to determine individual guest needs.

Another, more personal, way to gain guest knowledge is via the input of property employees. Almost every employee, no matter how limited his or her actual guest contact, can assist in contributing guest information. Room attendants, for example, have access to "clues" such as special requests from guests (for extra towels, early turndown service, or the local morning newspaper, for example). Food servers can glean invaluable information—food and beverage preferences, dietary restrictions, and so on—in casual, friendly conversations. This type of input makes it easy to provide favorite items for the guest's next stay—a thoughtful gesture that can build priceless goodwill.

Relationships can be enhanced and maintained through follow-up. Follow-up can be a telephone call from the general manager or a guest service representative, a thank-you letter, or a quarterly newsletter.

Employee Training. Employee training should include a number of areas that will enable employees to assist guests and build rapport. These areas include:

- Knowing the property
- Knowing the community
- Interacting with guests
- Learning sales skills

Knowing the property. If employees do not know what the property has to offer, they cannot promote it. As part of the orientation process, every new employee should be given a complete tour of the property. All employees should learn an abbreviated form of the property fact book. They should also be informed of special promotional packages, special events, and other property happenings.

To sell effectively, hotel employees must sample the product. Food servers should taste every item on the menu so they can make a specific, personal recommendation if asked by a guest. Front desk agents will do a much better job of upselling if they have actually slept in the property's suites. It costs little to have employees stay at the hotel (employees can become "guests" on a slow Sunday night, for example), but the benefits of such stays can be great.

Knowing the community. Employee knowledge of the area surrounding the property can be helpful in two ways: employees can encourage guests to extend their stays by suggesting attractions to visit, and offering suggestions gives employees an opportunity to build good relationships with guests.

Employees should be able to do more than just provide a brochure on an area attraction or quote from a fact sheet. Properties can ensure that their staff is well informed and helpful by (1) encouraging employees to keep abreast of area events and attractions (including hours, prices, and services); (2) holding training sessions that provide local area information and fact sheets that stress guest benefits; and (3) encouraging the staff to personally experience local attractions (most guests will ask the employee if he or she has been there).

Because of the high potential for word-of-mouth referrals, many attractions offer complimentary tickets to hotel staff. Even if complimentary tickets are not available, management should still encourage employees—especially those in the sales and marketing departments and in guest-contact positions—to visit nearby places of interest so they can tell guests or potential clients about them. Royce Kardial, general manager of the Best Western Rancho Grande in Wickenburg, Arizona, takes her employees on field trips to museums and other local attractions.

Interacting with guests. Positive interaction with guests is crucial to making a good impression and generating repeat business.[11] One of the key departments for doing so at any property is the front desk. Front desk employees are not clerks; they are sales representatives. They are very often the first contact that a person has with a property, and a guest's entire perception of a property may be shaped by the way he or she is treated by front desk personnel.

Most properties recognize the value of retaining a friendly and competent front desk staff. Not only are operations smoother, but it is far easier to build a relationship with guests when the front desk staff is familiar to them. Many properties offer incentives to encourage employees to make a career of front desk operations, and front desk employees are often given the opportunity to add their input to improve operations. Through empowerment programs, front desk agents are given increased authority to make service decisions and otherwise resolve guest problems.

But front desk personnel are not the property's only representatives; every employee makes an impression, and should be trained in the areas of proper appearance, courtesy, and personal habits (food servers should be taught that it is not acceptable to touch their hair or mouths while serving guests, for example). Every employee should be reminded that each guest is valuable, and a friendly smile and a willingness to assist are vital in building rapport. It is especially important to make guests feel welcome. Employees should anticipate the needs of guests, learn details of previous visits if applicable, and call guests by name whenever possible.

Using names. Calling guests by name is one key to repeat business. Remembering guests' names shows a special caring—a respect for guests as individuals. In today's automated world, people appreciate recognition more than ever before, and there are a number of ways employees can learn and use names:

1. Before a guest registers with the hotel, the bellperson or porter can look for names on luggage tags.
2. The front desk agent gets guests' names upon receiving the completed registration forms. He or she can begin calling guests by name, and may ask the bellperson to "show Mr. and Mrs. Lewis to their room, please." The bellperson can then begin calling guests by name also.
3. New computerized telephone systems automatically display the room number and the guest's name on a monitor whenever a guest calls the switchboard from his or her guestroom. The operator can greet the guest by name: "Good afternoon, Mr. Herndon. What can I do for you?"
4. Switchboard operators can use names when making wake-up calls. A cheery, "Good morning, Ms. Ricker. It's seven o'clock. Would you like room service to bring you a fresh pot of coffee and a Danish?" is much more hospitable than, "Hello, it's seven o'clock."

5. In restaurants, the host can greet the guest by name if the guest has a reservation, and pass the guest's name along to the food server.
6. Any time guests use credit cards, there is an opportunity to learn and use names. Local patrons of the restaurant or lounge can be recognized in this way, or by simply asking them their names and welcoming them back to the property.

Name recognition works both ways. Not only do most guests appreciate the recognition accorded them by the property's staff, they also like to see familiar faces and greet staff members by name. Many properties use nametags that display the employee's name and home state. These can be excellent conversation starters: "You're from Michigan? I went to school there—at MSU!"

Handling complaints (service recovery). There are times when it is impossible to please a guest. In some cases, a guest's unhappiness is justified—service may be slow, there may be an error in reservations or payment arrangements, or a guestroom may not be ready on time. Sometimes guests may simply be taking out their frustrations with other circumstances on the nearest available person. In either case, however, employees must respond to complaints in such a way that goodwill is restored.

An angry guest can be transformed into a loyal one if his or her complaint is handled efficiently and patiently. To do so, you must remain calm and determine the exact nature of the complaint. While it is natural to want to tell a guest to calm down, this approach should be avoided, because it may make the guest feel that you think the complaint is unimportant—which can make the guest even angrier. Instead, you should ask questions to determine the exact reason for the dissatisfaction.

Once you have identified the guest's complaint, take immediate action. If you cannot handle the situation personally, immediately contact a supervisor or other person in authority. In some cases, however, complaints cannot be handled on the spot—perhaps authorization has to come from the home office, or from a person who is not available. In this instance, you should make a definite commitment to the guest to follow up.

If a guest points out a problem with the property's products or services that the property resolves after the guest has gone home, the guest should be contacted by mail or telephone, thanked for bringing the problem to the staff's attention, and told how the property dealt with the problem. In many cases, guest complaints have led to the improvement of problem areas at a property—resulting in better service and increased guest satisfaction.

Since complaints can serve a useful purpose, guests should be given an opportunity to voice them. Some unhappy guests want to be heard, and have no qualms about writing a complaint letter, making a telephone call, or demanding to speak to the manager. Resolving problems for these "squeaky wheels" is far easier than dealing with the typical unhappy guest who never expresses his or her dissatisfaction; he or she just leaves the property to tell hotel or restaurant "horror stories" to friends and business associates.

Property personnel can avoid this by trying to gauge guest reactions, or simply asking, "How was everything?" when guests check out. In many cases, guests

Strategies for Handling Complaints

To ensure guest satisfaction and repeat business, it is essential to handle guest complaints promptly and efficiently. The points below offer a brief overview of the steps that should be taken to resolve guest complaints:

- Make it easy for guests to give feedback. Show a willingness to hear their complaints. Get employees in the habit of asking about complaints and writing them down on a standard form.
- Provide help to guests quickly. Studies have shown that 95 percent of guests with small problems and 82 percent of guests with big problems stay with the company that upset them if the complaint is fixed quickly. People who have to ask more than once for a resolution are less satisfied. Inform guests of the approximate length of time it will take to resolve the complaint.
- Give authority to line staff to settle complaints; this builds the guests' feelings of trust. Having to get permission only delays the resolution of the complaint and creates further dissatisfaction.
- Make sure you do not further inconvenience the guest. Doing so will only make him or her angrier.
- Provide an alternative if an immediate solution cannot be found.
- Tell the guest what will be done so the problem won't happen again.

Source: Adapted from John T. Bowen and Stowe Shoemaker, "Loyalty: A Strategic Commitment," *Cornell Hotel and Restaurant Administration Quarterly*, February 1998, pp. 14–17.

will volunteer information when asked directly. Or, to make it easy to complain without having a face-to-face confrontation, properties can offer a complaint hot line or toll-free number.

Learning sales skills. Sales skills help employees make the most of sales opportunities in their particular areas of guest contact. Most properties have features in common—swimming pools, in-room cable television, 24-hour room service, and so on—so what makes your property different? A guest usually needs help to recognize a benefit, and that's where the guest-contact employee comes in. A benefits-oriented employee will not simply mention the property's lounge; he or she will offer a benefit: "You'll really enjoy the relaxing atmosphere after a long day of business meetings."

Once employees understand the benefits-oriented sales approach, there are several sales techniques they can use. Three of the most effective are upgrading or upselling, suggestive selling, and cross-selling.

Upgrading reservations is an effective way to increase revenues, but very few front desk or reservations staffs are trained to use upgrading techniques.[12] Although most hotels have several room types and prices, there is often no prescribed formula for selling rooms; employees simply quote a price and make no attempt to sell additional services or amenities.

One reason for management's reluctance to tell employees to try to sell rooms with higher rates is that they fear guests may be offended or feel pressured. However, a caller may be unaware of varying rates and amenities, and may appreciate the property's efforts to place him or her in a room that meets specific needs. Meeting specific needs is an important part of upgrading, and employees must be trained to listen to guests and make suggestions for an appropriate accommodation.

Front desk and reservations agents should be trained to recognize when and how to upgrade a guest's request. Upgrading can be accomplished without pressuring a guest by using one of three methods:

- Top-down
- Rate-category-alternatives
- Bottom-up

The **top-down method** is used to encourage guests to reserve middle- or high-rate rooms. It begins with the front desk or reservations agent enthusiastically recommending the guestroom sold at the highest rate. The guest may either accept or reject the recommendation. In the latter case, the agent moves down to the next price level and enthusiastically discusses the merits of this accommodation. The guest may perceive the lower rate as a compromise on the part of the agent and be more open to accepting this recommendation. If the rate quoted is still unacceptable, the agent drops to the next-highest rate, continuing this process until the guest is satisfied with the price quoted.

The **rate-category-alternatives method** is an easy and effective way to sell middle-rate rooms to guests who might otherwise choose a lower rate. The front desk or reservations agent provides the guest with a choice of three or more rate-category alternatives, and puts no pressure on the guest. In most cases, people will attempt to avoid extremes: choosing the lowest rate could cause the guest to feel cheap, while choosing the highest rate might make the guest feel unnecessarily extravagant. Under these circumstances the logical decision would be to choose the middle rate.

The **bottom-up method** is used when a guest has made a reservation but has requested a low-priced room. Initially, reconfirm the reserved room ("Mr. Harper, we have you confirmed in a very nice room"), but question the guest to see if he or she is aware of upgraded rooms or perhaps a suite. If the guest is interested, present the upgraded rooms as a unique opportunity ("We're offering a special rate this week for our deluxe rooms. For only $10 more you can enjoy a room with a view of the ocean, or, for an extra $25, you can have a deluxe room with two continental breakfasts. These rooms usually run higher, but during this promotion, we're offering them at these special rates.") By mentioning the normally higher rates, you are positioning the rooms as a good value and enhancing the guest's stay at only a small increase over charges anticipated by the guest.

It is much easier to show—and sell—the differences in rooms by using photographs. An effective sales tool for front desk personnel is a loose-leaf notebook of large color photos of the different types of guestrooms offered by the hotel. Simply telling a guest about an ocean-view room is not as effective as showing the room—and the view—in a photo.

No matter what method is used to upgrade a reservation, guests should *never* feel they are being pressured; sales pressure has no place in the hospitality industry. Rather, internal sales should be aimed at giving guests the opportunity to purchase additional products and services or to "trade up" from those already purchased. To do this, it is important to convey that guests are not just buying a room, but a home away from home, and that their needs are important to the property. By combining upselling techniques with a knowledge of guest needs, front desk employees can sell a pleasurable experience to guests while increasing revenues.

Suggestive selling is the practice of influencing a guest's purchase decision through the use of sales phrases[13] (see Exhibit 2). Almost any employee can use this sales technique in most areas of the property. Suggestive selling may be used in all of a property's food and beverage outlets, for example. A host may inform guests of the special of the day after greeting them; a food server may suggest a cocktail before dinner, an appetizer, the special of the day, or a dessert; a bartender may suggest a specialty drink. The power of suggestion is also a good way to introduce new menu items, promote low-overhead food items, and increase the server's tip base.

Food servers can follow these guidelines for suggestive selling:

- *Avoid asking questions that require a yes or no answer.* It is far more effective to give the guest a choice. For example, ask: "Which dessert would you like from our dessert cart?" rather than "Would you like dessert?" If the guest orders a steak, ask: "Would you like a red or a rosé wine with your steak?" rather than "Would you like a glass of wine with dinner?"
- *Suggest in specific terms.* Don't just suggest an appetizer, suggest a specific item such as fried zucchini, shrimp cocktail, or escargot. For even more effectiveness, paint a word picture for guests. It is far more effective to say: "Our catch of the day is rainbow trout stuffed with a delightful mixture of shrimp and fresh crabmeat, lightly floured and sautéed in butter, and garnished with fresh lemon," than to say, "Our catch of the day is stuffed trout."

Suggestive selling can also be used in other revenue centers at the property. The health club attendant may suggest a relaxing massage after a workout; the golf pro can suggest a new set of clubs from the pro shop after a private lesson; the front desk agent can suggest a return visit during a special promotional period.

Of course, suggestive selling is used in the sales department also. Rather than simply taking room night orders during busy seasons, salespeople should suggest dates that best meet the property's needs. If Tuesday is a typical sellout or high occupancy night, for example, a salesperson might suggest another night of the week to clients. Monitoring competitors' bookings may also point to suggestive selling strategies. If the property is likely to sell out during a particular week due to overflow from a competitor's booking of a large convention, salespeople can suggest dates in the weeks before or after to maximize revenue potential.

Cross-selling in advertising is simply using media in one area of the property to promote a different area of the property: a tent card in a restaurant may advertise another specialty restaurant or a sale in the pro shop, a poster at the front desk can promote the health facilities and spa, the matchbooks in the restaurant may advertise the property's lounge. Employees can also cross-sell; employees working at one facility may suggest that a guest take advantage of other facilities and services offered at the property. Employee cross-selling can begin at the front desk when the front desk agent recommends the property's restaurant. To assist front desk

Exhibit 2 Sample Sales Phrases

Situation	Suggested Sales Phrases
Front Desk	
Early morning check-ins	"Our valet service can have your suit pressed and returned to your room within an hour while you freshen up."
Early evening check-ins	"Do you enjoy Spanish music? We are featuring Carlos, one of the finest Spanish pianists in the country, in our La Mancha lounge."
	"Have you seen the exciting Hawaiian revue in our main showroom? It's almost like being on the Islands!"
	"If you'd like to have a refreshing drink to help you unwind, our Baron's Pub is located in the east wing near the coffee shop. Besides offering the best drinks in town, the Pub features continuous entertainment from 7:00 P.M. to midnight."
Late evening check-ins	"Our excellent room service is still available. Here's the phone number, sir."
Checking out	"Would you like me to make your return reservation for you now?"
	"Your next stop is Orlando, and our chain has another hotel there. Would you like me to con firm a reservation for you?"
Restaurants	
After taking the order for an entrée	"Would you care for a manhattan or a martini while you wait for your order?"
	"We've just received a new shipment of 1952 French champagne. Shall I bring you a bottle, or would you prefer to see our regular wine list?"
After the main course	"Would you like a B&B or a Drambuie to finish your meal?"
	"Would you care to try our new after-dinner coffee? We add a dash of brandy and top it off with whipped cream. We also offer Irish coffee."
Lounges	
While handing guests a drink list	"Exotic drinks are a house specialty. Perhaps you'd like to try a Scorpion, one of our most popular drinks."

(continued)

Exhibit 2 *(continued)*

In hot weather	"Would you like a nice, cool Tom Collins or would you prefer one of our refreshing fruit drinks?"
In cold weather	"Our bartender makes the best hot Tom and Jerry available anywhere. Would you care for one to warm yourself up?"
Room Service	
After delivering a meal	"Have you tried our Captain's Table restaurant yet? Tomorrow night they'll be featuring a special seafood buffet that I'm sure you'd enjoy."
When coming to clear	"Don't forget that we're available 24 hours a day. If there's anything else you'll need, you can reach us at extension 123."
Valet Parking	
Before parking the car	"Welcome to Complete Resorts. If you like Hawaiian cuisine, you'll love our Lanai Buffet. It's on the second floor above the pool area."
When delivering the car	"I hope you enjoyed your stay. Don't forget that we'll be having a special Western Barbecue next week. I'm looking forward to seeing you then."

Every guest contact presents an opportunity to sell additional features and services. Sales-oriented employees can greatly increase a property's profitability and build guest goodwill.

employees in promoting the restaurant, a special display might be posted within sight of the front desk, and copies of the restaurant's menu could be available for guests to examine. A sincere invitation to visit the property's facilities—along with display advertising or other aids to enhance the employees' presentations—can greatly increase revenues and make guests feel welcome.

Every employee must be thoroughly knowledgeable about all aspects of the property's operations before cross-selling can be fully effective. All employees, not just the food servers, should know the hours, specialties, dress requirements, and atmosphere of each of the property's restaurants. If a bellperson recommends the property's seafood restaurant, for example, it is not enough to mention the restaurant's name. What feature of the restaurant would make it worth the guest's visit? The food? A special buffet? The atmosphere? The low prices?

Employees should also be aware of special promotions (two-for-one coupons, discounts, weekend packages), pool and health club hours and services, live entertainment offered (if the property offers live entertainment, employees can be invited to hear the entertainment so they can give personal endorsements), and special services (valet, laundry, child-care or baby-sitting services, secretarial assistance, complimentary transportation, and so on).

Applying Sales Skills. Most guest-employee contacts are potential sales situations. To ensure that employees learn about all the property's revenue centers and develop effective sales approaches, managers might have employees participate in role-playing and periodic testing. Employee sales skills can be evaluated and changed as necessary during these training sessions to ensure that each guest-employee encounter will be productive.

What follows is a list of property areas and personnel that are particularly important to internal sales.

Switchboard. The switchboard operator is often the first contact that a prospective guest has with a property, so switchboard operators should answer calls in a pleasant manner that conveys a sense of welcome. Since the switchboard serves as an indicator of the property's efficiency as well as hospitality, calls should be answered promptly and transferred to the proper department without delay.

The switchboard operator can also direct guests to the property's revenue centers. A call from the operator in the late afternoon can recommend the hotel's dining room or room service. Since guests have to eat somewhere, this is often all it takes to keep them at the property. Operators can also make suggestions for restaurants or room service when they make wake-up calls.

Reservations. The industry has recently taken notice of the influence of the reservations department and its impact on revenues. Therefore, reservation sales agents are increasingly reporting directly to the marketing and sales department instead of the rooms division.

Since the basic function of the reservations department is to turn a prospect into a guest, the reservations staff should be trained to be "order-makers" instead of "order-takers"; that is, they should be well-trained in sales and public relations, as they can help a property generate additional revenue through securing and upgrading bookings and handling after-hours sales leads. A pleasant and informed reservations agent who is aware of upgrading and suggestive selling techniques can increase the number of room nights sold at higher-than-standard rates.

While it is important that the reservations staff have a guest-oriented approach, equally important is a knowledge of room types, prices, special rates, and hotel packages. Staff members should have a complete knowledge of the property and an understanding of what determines the differences in price among the hotel's guestrooms. An ocean-view room, for example, may cost more than a comparable room on the other side of the hotel; the same guestroom may double in price during periods of peak demand.

When potential guests telephone for a room after the house is full, reservations agents should offer alternatives in an attempt to keep business. For example, the reservations department might adopt a waiting list system. The reservations agent can tell the caller: "I'm sorry, Mr. Jackson, we currently have no rooms available, but we often have last-minute cancellations. If you will give me your phone number, I'll call you immediately when a room opens up." If the reservations department is too busy to make callbacks, the agent might assign the guest a reference number and suggest that he or she call again after the 6:00 P.M. cutoff for holding reservations.

Suggesting that the caller change his or her arrival date is a selling technique that is seldom used, but could prove of immense value. While this certainly won't work with all guests, many business and leisure travelers will change their plans to stay in their "first choice" hotel. The reservations agent can make this option attractive with a statement such as: "Ms. Steward, we are presently booked to capacity and have several names on a waiting list for Wednesday, November 30. But if you could change your travel plans, we have several attractive suites available on Thursday, December 1."

Front desk. As mentioned previously, front desk personnel play a pivotal role in hotel sales. They can generate additional revenue for a property by capturing walk-in business, upgrading reservations during check-in, marketing in-house facilities through suggestive selling, and securing return reservations during check-out. Therefore, they should be thoroughly trained in sales techniques. (At many properties, front desk personnel report to the sales department instead of to the rooms division.)

Interacting with front desk employees is often the guest's first *personal* impression of the property, and it is here that hospitality begins.[14] Each guest should be greeted with a warm smile and a sincere, friendly welcome, *not* a curt, "Do you have a reservation?" A repeat guest should be greeted by name and with a warm "Welcome back." From this point on, guests have *names,* not just room numbers.

The check-in function should be handled with a minimum of delay. To encourage guest loyalty, guests should be made to feel far more important than a computer screen or a few sheets of paper. Paperwork unrelated to registering the guest should be put aside until registration is completed. Additional help should be called if a long line forms.

As mentioned earlier, front desk personnel often have the opportunity to upgrade existing reservations. A low-key approach is best: "Since you made your reservation, two better rooms have opened up: one with a mountain view for $58, the other with a Jacuzzi for $62. Would you be interested in moving to one of these rooms?" Such an approach may increase room revenues and guest goodwill. The guest is being sold a better experience, not just a more expensive room.

Check-in is also a good time to mention special coupons or discount offers and suggest hotel facilities and services. The front desk agent can ask if the guest would like a wake-up call, and use this opportunity to make sales suggestions: "Fine, Ms. Zimmerman. We'll call you at 7:00 A.M. Would you like room service to deliver our breakfast special of hot coffee, a cheese omelet, and freshly squeezed orange juice at 7:30?"

Too often, hotel guests are unaware of what the property has to offer. Suggesting valet service, a light snack in the coffee shop, a relaxing swim or whirlpool in the health club, or room service—even if the guest declines—increases guest awareness, which may generate additional sales at a later time.

Another key sales opportunity is securing return reservations at check-out. Many business travelers return to town on a monthly, or even weekly, basis, and guests might decide to try another hotel or be forced to stay elsewhere if your property is sold out on a return visit. Front desk personnel should always determine the guest's plans for returning ("Are you planning to be back in the area anytime soon?") and invite departing guests to stay at the hotel again. Booking a return reservation should be made as simple as possible for the guest ("Since I have your information right here, I can go ahead and confirm that for you right now" or "I'll put your next reservation in the system and send you a confirmation later today"). If the departing guest is planning to visit another city, offer to make a reservation in your chain's property there.

Food and beverage. Good service, which includes a friendly attitude and a timely delivery of the food or drink ordered, is the key to guest satisfaction and sales success in the food and beverage department.[15] In addition to increasing sales, good service ensures that the guest has a favorable experience and will want to return.

Food servers who share with guests their knowledge of the food, its ingredients, methods of preparation, and preparation times add to guest involvement in the property, which can increase profits. A good sales approach by the server also results in spending less time answering questions, thus avoiding guest irritation.

Food and beverage service offers practically unlimited opportunities to make use of suggestive selling techniques. It is imperative that food servers offer enticing suggestions that describe a delicious item: "Have you tried our award-winning cheesecake, topped with fresh strawberries and a dollop of whipped cream?" is much more effective than "Would you care for anything else?" A food server can give the guest a choice of two or more items and state why the guest should choose one of them. For example, "Would you like a shrimp cocktail to start or would you prefer our freshly made onion soup? The shrimp arrived just this morning and are absolutely fresh, and the onion soup is excellent—the chef prides himself on making the best onion soup in the city." Suggestive selling benefits guests, food servers, and the property alike, as it can lead to increased guest satisfaction, increased tips for servers, and increased revenues.

Cross-selling can also be used by food servers. Room service personnel can suggest the dinner special in the main dining room or a special breakfast buffet for busy business travelers. A food server in the gourmet restaurant can ask guests if they have tried the "traveler's lunch" in the coffee shop. These soft-sell techniques are excellent methods of raising revenues and exposing guests to facilities they might not have tried (and might later recommend to friends).

Service personnel. Service personnel fall into two basic categories: employees who frequently have contact with guests, and employees who work in back-of-the-house areas who seldom see guests. A great deal of guest interaction is usual for the valet parking staff, door attendants, bell staff, and housekeepers, while guest contact is not as pronounced with maintenance crews and back office personnel.

Service employees with a great deal of guest contact have excellent opportunities for suggestive selling. If the hotel is near an airport, the hotel's limo drivers can sell the hotel's facilities and the local area as they drive guests from the airport to the property. A valet parker can welcome guests and ask if they have tried a particular property restaurant. A bellperson can promote the property's restaurants, lounges, laundry and valet services, and other amenities as guests are shown to their rooms. As guests leave, the door attendant or valet parker can suggest they return for a promotional event or special hotel package. In all of these guest contacts, it is important that the service staff be sincerely friendly without being pushy.

While employees who have less guest contact may be limited in their selling capacities, they "sell" the hotel by their appearance, attitude, and attention to

Exhibit 3 Sample Reservations Incentive Program

Schedule of Bonuses

Upgrade Bonuses

$10 Upgrade to Poolside	$1.00 per night
Upgrade to Bi-level or Fallback Rate	$3.00 per night
Upgrade to Bi-level or Rack Rate Suite	$5.00 per night

Booking Bonuses

Reservation booked under Rack Rate	$ .50 per night
Reservation booked at Rack Rate	$1.00 per night
Reservation booked at Poolside Rate	$1.50 per night
Reservation booked at Suite Fallback Rate	$3.00 per night
Reservation booked at Suite Rack Rate	$5.00 per night

This is a very liberal bonus program with lots of opportunities to increase your monthly take home pay by $50, $100, or even $200. Every time you upgrade or book a guest, just make a copy of the reservation with the appropriate information, and put the copy in your folder, located in the count room.

The person who converts the most room nights during the quarter will be eligible for a grand prize (to be determined) at the end of the year.

This is an excerpt from an incentive program developed by a Best Western property. Reservations agents are given bonuses for room conversions and upgrades monthly, and a grand prize is awarded at the end of the year. Source: From a speech by Robert A. Rauch, CHA, at Best Western's annual convention in Las Vegas.

small details. A friendly greeting from a pool attendant and the cheerful attitude of the maintenance crew can help make a guest's stay memorable.

Employee Incentive Programs. Employee incentive programs can be an effective means of motivating employees to sell and of tracking sales results. In the hospitality industry, most reward programs have traditionally been based on achieving certain labor or food costs or meeting sales objectives. Management may establish an incentive program for front desk or reservations agents who upgrade reservations (see Exhibit 3), or may provide a bonus to split among the front desk staff for every night on which occupancy reaches a predetermined target. In the property's restaurants, management may promote contests to reward suggestive selling and give bonuses to the servers who sell the most desserts. Other incentive programs may include a cross-selling contest with prizes to employees or departments sending the most guests to a specific restaurant. The bellperson who sells more laundry or dry cleaning services than average and the telephone operator who makes breakfast sales with morning wake-up calls can also be rewarded.

To ensure maximum results, staff recognition and/or incentive programs should:

- Be tied to results that translate directly to bottom-line dollars. This is especially true of incentive programs that offer cash rewards.

- Be tied to results that are due to employee performance.
- Reward both individual and team performance. While it is important to recognize individual performance, the best programs allow everyone to win.
- Be tied to goals that are challenging yet attainable.
- Start and end on a relatively short-term basis. Weekly is ideal; monthly is acceptable. Employees may lose interest or not give their best performance if a program drags out too long.
- Be easy to understand by employees and easy to monitor by managers.

Incentive programs must include methods of tracking results. A discount coupon that bears the name of the food server who has recommended the lounge, a business card or coupon from the bartender that the guest can give to the host of the specialty dining room, a special two-for-one invitation to the lounge show from the bellperson—all three examples provide a means of tracking the effectiveness of both the promotion and the employee.

When developing any incentive program, management should realize that while incentives in the form of cash, merchandise, or trips are often used to motivate employees, recognition is as important as the reward for many workers. Honoring top-producing employees with photographs and plaques that are prominently displayed, writing up success stories for the property's newsletter, and even recognizing outstanding employees at a special ceremony or awards dinner can mean more to some employees than monetary rewards.

Internal Merchandising

Internal merchandising is the use of guestroom guest service directories, restaurant tent cards, lobby display cards, elevator cards or posters, bulletin boards, and other promotional items to promote the property's facilities and services (see Exhibit 4).

Technology also plays a part in internal merchandising. The Hilton chain is one of several hospitality organizations that utilize a "video magazine." Video magazines may be shown in either the hotel's lobby (guests can watch the presentation on special monitors set up near comfortable chairs) or in guestrooms through the use of an in-house channel. The Hilton's one-hour video showcases the facilities and services of the host hotel as well as detailing the history and sights of the host city. The Hilton's video magazine changes monthly and is slightly different for each property, but each video provides traveling tips; features geared toward the business traveler; and information on other hotels in the chain, with a suggestive-selling message to book into one of these properties.

Internal merchandising should be carefully planned and controlled. All internal merchandising posters and print materials should be *professionally* done, and should be changed regularly. (There are few things less appealing than stained or torn tent cards or guestroom directories.) As a general rule, there should be attractive, persuasive internal merchandising media in each area of guest contact.

Exhibit 4 Sample Lobby Display Cards

Targeting in-house guests, these display cards promise a lively setting for singles to meet on Friday nights, a romantic and elegant atmosphere on Saturdays, and an elegant Sunday brunch with live entertainment.

Guest-Contact Areas

The Lobby. Posters displayed in the lobby should promote all of the property's food service outlets and other property features. Lobby posters should be placed in high-traffic locations. Posters on walls and columns where they can be illuminated are eye-catching. Many properties find that the use of transparencies—slide-like posters illuminated from behind—is especially effective.

Guestrooms. Essential information should be located in one attractive guest service directory whenever possible; the usual practice of cluttering a room with tent cards, folders, notices, and fliers does little to promote readership. Guest service directories should be attractive and small enough to be carried (they make excellent promotional pieces). Most important, they should not only list services offered, but also include *complete* information, including telephone extensions. (Many hotels are now giving out mini-directories upon check-in. These pocket-size directories not only promote property facilities and services, but also serve as room key or room card holders. This increases the likelihood of guests carrying the promotional literature with them.)

In addition to the guest service directory, the property may opt for a simple message placed on the television set or on the nightstand. One effective technique is the use of a message like the following, signed by the chef:

> My specialty tonight is beef Wellington. Please call 9049 to reserve a table.
>
> Chef Lambert

A guestroom sales technique used by the Grand Hyatt in New York is extremely effective. The hotel's managers designed a unique room service menu that is, for all intents and purposes, a picture book. The menu, which is left open on the guestroom desk, features a photograph of the finished dish on one side of the page and a description of the dish and its ingredients on the other. Door hanger menus (completed by the guest and picked up at 2:00 A.M.) also serve to merchandise room service.

Elevator Floor Landings. Many guests walk out of a hotel to breakfast in an outside restaurant simply because they do not know their hotel serves breakfast. Attractive signs in a glass-framed cabinet located next to the elevator call button can feature the property's restaurants, bars, and lounges, and the services and hours of each. The elevator area can also be used to promote valet or laundry services, entertainment offerings, and special upcoming packages such as a family discount package, a ski weekend package, and so on.

One of the most effective restaurant display posters used near elevators is found in the Marriott Southeast in Denver. When the guest pushes the call button on the elevator, a display case on the wall next to the call button lights up. Almost without exception, guests immediately read the restaurant poster in the display case as they wait for the elevator to arrive.

Elevators. Many properties hang framed posters within elevators to advertise their restaurants. It is curious that some posters are placed in the rear of the elevator,

Annual Internal Merchandising Plan				
	Placement	Merchandising Piece	Message	Cost
Jan.	Lobby Display Front Desk/Counter	Poster/4-color Counter Display/4-color	Weekend Escape	$150.00
	Coffee Shop	Table Tent	Sunday Brunch	$ 75.00
	Elevator Entrance Elevator Walls	Display cards	Sunday Brunch Valentine's Day Special	$300.00
	Lounge	Wine Bottles Hanger Piece	Valentine's Day Special—Champagne Split with Dinner	$ 75.00
Feb.	Lobby Display Front Desk Counter	Poster/4-color Counter Display with Flyers	Murder Mystery Weekend	$200.00
	Coffee Shop	Table Tent	Conference Package	$ 95.00

Planning an Internal Merchandising Strategy

A marketing committee is important to ensure that all areas of the property are represented in the marketing plan. While internal marketing can play an important role in generating revenue, it is an area easy to neglect. Too often, internal marketing takes a back seat to more aggressive forms of marketing, and efforts are piecemeal, resulting in outdated, worn, or poorly designed posters, tent cards, and guestroom directories.

In order to ensure that the property derives the greatest benefit from internal merchandising efforts, several steps should be implemented:

Step 1: Plan

An internal merchandising program should be planned on an annual basis and tied to the marketing plan and marketing priorities. A review of occupancy and activity reports will indicate which areas need merchandising, when merchandising is most needed, and what type of promotional material will be most effective for reaching targeted guests.

Step 2: Coordinate

One person from the marketing committee should be responsible for coordinating and managing the internal merchandising plan. A planning chart, such as the one illustrated above, will (1) help to ensure that major traffic areas and revenue centers are covered, and (2) detail the costs of promotional pieces.

Step 3: Evaluate

Results should be evaluated throughout each promotion by charting and comparing sales before and after placement of merchandising materials. Each evaluation should include an assessment of the promotional costs in comparison to the profits realized. If problem areas are found, materials may need to be placed in alternate locations or redesigned for better results.

since most guests face forward or look upward when riding. A sign in the rear gets a momentary glance—if the car is empty! Attractive posters positioned on the elevator's side walls may be printed on both sides and should be rotated to reflect the meal(s) being served during a particular time period. To make the cards more appealing and persuasive, they should feature a mouth-watering photograph rather than just copy.

Restaurants and Lounges. Restaurant promotion can begin at the restaurant's entrance with an attractive poster announcing the day's specials. Inside the restaurant, well-designed menus can serve as promotional pieces, and tent cards (one per table is ideal) can promote specialty dishes or other restaurants on the property. Lounges can be promoted through matchbooks, tent cards, attractive drink or snack menus, and souvenir items. For lounges featuring entertainment, a souvenir program or an autographed photograph of the performer mounted in a folder embossed with the property's logo makes an effective promotional piece.

Barber and Beauty Shops. Hotels with barber and/or beauty shops can sell the captive audience in these shops on the property's restaurants, bars, lounges, special facilities, and reservations services through the use of posters mounted in strategic locations.

Reservations or Convention Desk. Properties with a reservations or convention desk can have fliers, brochures, and other promotional material readily available in attractive displays. Local attractions might also be promoted to encourage longer stays by guests.

Cashier's Desk. Many properties provide interhotel reservations information and souvenir items (key chains, postcards, etc.) at the cashier's desk to encourage repeat or new business. Many properties offer such souvenir items as shoehorns, key chains, and garment bags, but neglect to imprint the property's telephone number on them. All giveaway items should have the hotel's name, address, and telephone number printed on them to make it easy for former guests to call the property to make return reservations. It is surprising how many people can picture a great hotel or a pleasant restaurant experience in their minds, but can't remember the name of the property after a short period of time.

Back-of-the-House Areas

Posters and bulletin boards in back-of-the-house areas that detail current sales promotions, selling suggestions, and incentive programs can stimulate employee selling and remind employees that they can powerfully influence a guest's decision to return to the property.

Special Services and In-House Promotions

Special Services

Another effective way to sell the hotel to guests is to offer special services that will make their stays enjoyable and productive. Because of the large size of the

INTERNET EXERCISE

Log onto the Internet and visit *Hospitality Upgrade* magazine's site at www.hospitalityupgrade.com. This magazine, which is the leading publication for providing technology information on the hotel and restaurant industry, is published three times annually. Subscription to the magazine is free to qualified readers. (You may want to subscribe to keep abreast of the latest in hospitality technology trends—just click on "Contact Us" on the homepage, then the "Click Here to Subscribe to Our Magazine" link, and choose "Student" when filling out the "Subscribe" information.)

1. Click on the "News" link and then the "News Archive" link. Identify four hotels with which you are familiar and read about how they have employed technology to benefit their properties.
2. Be prepared to report on how two hotels have used technology to improve their sales and marketing efforts.

business traveler market, some hotels offer business centers—24-hour offices with personal computers, photocopiers, fax services, electronic mail capabilities, and secretarial services. Other properties may promote food and beverage service targeted at business travelers: continental or buffet breakfasts, designated business lunch hours to quickly and efficiently serve busy executives, and combination meeting/dining rooms.

To attract families, properties may offer supervised play activities, package tours to local attractions, in-house baby-sitting services, children's menus, and amenities such as cribs, high chairs, and play equipment.

Limousine service or other transportation to and from airports, shopping centers, and area attractions are also special services properties can use to promote themselves. Other special touches—free coffee, free newspapers, in-room closed-circuit television, complimentary samples of local produce (apples, raisins, nuts, etc.) or products (wines, chocolates, and so on), and fresh flowers also play an important part in creating an atmosphere that will make a guest feel welcome and generate repeat business and referrals.

In-House Promotions

Many properties sponsor **in-house promotions**—special events, contests, drawings, two-for-one coupons, and so on—that can make a stay more enjoyable and generate additional revenue.

One example of an internal promotion is a secretaries' club—a program that involves the secretaries of corporate guests in a number of planned activities. By guaranteeing corporate room rates, providing an exclusive telephone number or a direct contact person at the hotel, and ensuring VIP treatment for guests referred by these secretaries, a solid corporate business base can be built and maintained. To keep secretaries motivated, properties may offer health club privileges (or discounts), complimentary or discounted meals and drinks at food

The Omni Shoreham in Washington, D.C., developed a month-long food festival with a Parisian theme to attract guests and locals to its charming Monique Café et Brasserie. The festival was publicized in-house with posters throughout the hotel and at the café's entrance.

and beverage outlets, annual lunches or receptions, annual gifts (roses, chocolates, a free weekend getaway, etc.), and other amenities to secretaries participating in the program.

Other promotions designed to encourage repeat business may include frequent traveler programs; promotional giveaways—all guests in the hotel are given a gift, but must fill out a redemption coupon to receive it (these coupons provide information that can help generate repeat business); and special packages for frequent guests or a specific target market.

The property's food and beverage outlets can benefit from in-house promotions such as two-for-one specials, discount coupons, special activities and contests, and "get acquainted" teas or cocktail hours.

The number of ways to promote to guests who are already at the property are practically unlimited. By developing creative approaches and fun-filled activities, and awarding appropriate gifts or prizes, the property can greatly increase its base of business and leave its guests eagerly looking forward to the property's next special promotion.

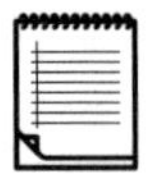

Endnotes

1. Howard Feiertag, "High-Touch Still Beats High-Tech," *Hotel and Motel Management*, March 1, 1999, p. 34.
2. Roland Leiser, "Ritz Reduces Turnover With Self-Directed Work Teams," *Hotel & Motel Management*, 4 March 1996.
3. Jamie Malanowski, "A Man for All Seasons," *Four Seasons—Four Decades*, 2002, p. 14.
4. Frank Davies, "The Prague Experience," *Four Seasons—Four Decades*, 2002, p. 9.
5. Taryn Schneider, "The Human Factor in Achieving Success in Troubled Times," *HSMAI Marketing Review*, Winter 2002, p. 23.
6. Elizabeth Johnson, "More Than Service With a Smile," *Lodging*, August 1999, p. 31.
7. Timothy W. Firnstahl, "My Employees Are My Service Guarantee," *Harvard Business Review*, July–August 1989, p. 29.
8. Empowerment is discussed further in the videotape *Managing Quality Guest Service* (Lansing, Mich.: American Hotel & Lodging Educational Institute).
9. 200 guestrooms × 80% = 160 rooms rented × 1.5 persons per room = 240 guests per day × 365 days per year = 87,600 guests × $2 additional expenditures each = $175,200 per year.
10. From a lecture given by Michael Hurst at the University of Nevada, Las Vegas.
11. Rebecca Olwa, "Technology Trends," *Hotels*, June 2002, p. 79.
12. Information on upgrading reservations is provided in the videotape *Sales: A Winning Formula* (Lansing, Mich.: American Hotel & Lodging Educational Institute).
13. Suggestive selling techniques are discussed in the videotape *Front Office: Guest Relations* (Lansing, Mich.: American Hotel & Lodging Educational Institute).
14. For a more detailed discussion of front desk procedures, see Michael L. Kasavana and Richard Brooks, *Managing Front Office Operations*, 7th ed. (Lansing, Mich.: American Hotel & Lodging Educational Institute, 2005).

15. Information on providing good food and beverage service is provided in the videotape *Smart Service for Great Banquets* (Lansing, Mich.: American Hotel & Lodging Educational Institute) and in the videotape *Food & Beverage: Suggestive Selling* (Lansing, Mich.: American Hotel & Lodging Educational Institute).

Key Terms

bottom-up method—An upgrading technique used when a guest has already made a reservation or has requested a low-priced guestroom. The front desk or reservations agent simply suggests extra amenities or the merits of a more expensive room, without pressuring the guest.

cross-selling—In internal merchandising, cross-selling is using media in one area of the property to promote a different area. Employees can also cross-sell: employees working at one facility can suggest that guests take advantage of other facilities and services offered at the property.

employee empowerment—A program or philosophy that gives employees the authority to make on-the-spot decisions to respond to guest needs—decisions that were previously relegated to those higher in authority. Employee empowerment is part of the process of developing an internal marketing program.

in-house promotion—The use of contests, special events, giveaways, and creative activities to stimulate sales and encourage guest satisfaction and repeat or referral business.

internal marketing—A concept that sees employees as "customers" who must be sold on the property they work for and convinced of their importance to its success.

internal merchandising—The use of such promotional items as tent cards, posters, and directories to promote a property's facilities and services on-site.

internal sales—Specific sales activities engaged in by various employees of a property, in conjunction with a program of internal merchandising, to promote additional sales and guest satisfaction.

rate-category-alternatives method—An upgrading technique that encourages guests to reserve middle-rate guestrooms. The front desk or reservations agent provides a guest with a choice of three or more rate-category alternatives; in most cases, the guest will seek to avoid extremes and choose a middle-rate room.

suggestive selling—The practice of influencing a guest's purchase decision through the use of sales phrases.

top-down method—An upgrading technique that encourages guests to reserve middle- or high-rate guestrooms. A front desk or reservations agent recommends the guestroom sold at the highest rate first and moves down to the next highest price level if this rate is too high. The process continues until the guest is satisfied with the price quoted.

upgrading—A sales technique that seeks to move a guest to a better accommodation or class of service.

Review Questions

1. What is the difference between internal marketing and internal sales? Why is each important?
2. What is "employee empowerment," and how can hospitality firms use it to meet guest needs?
3. What is the role of the general manager in internal sales? In what three ways can he or she develop a sales-oriented staff?
4. What is relationship selling? Why is it so important to a hospitality firm?
5. What are the four areas that should be covered in employee training to better equip employees to assist guests and build rapport?
6. What are three methods front desk agents and reservationists can use to upgrade a guest's request for a guestroom? How are they used?
7. What are some of the ways hotel employees can apply sales skills?
8. What are employee incentive programs? How are they used to motivate employees to sell?
9. What is "internal merchandising"? How and where can internal merchandising be used to build sales?
10. What are some examples of special services and in-house promotions hotels can use to build business?

Internet Sites

For more information, visit the following Internet sites. Remember that Internet addresses can change without notice. If the site is no longer there, you can use a search engine to look for additional sites.

American Marketing Association
www.ama.org

Adweek Online
www.adweek.com

The CEO Home Page
www.ceohomepage.com

Creative, the Magazine of Promotion and Marketing
www.creativemag.com

Destination Marketing Association International
www.iacvb.org

Hospitality Sales & Marketing Association International
www.hsmai.org

Meeting Professionals International
www.mpiweb.org

Sales & Marketing Management
www.salesandmarketing.com

T.G.I. Friday's Worldwide
www.tgifridays.com

urhospitality.com
www.urhospitality.com

Chapter 7 Outline

Competencies

1. Outline the reasons that hospitality firms advertise, and describe types of advertising. (pp. 249–268)
2. Describe how hospitality firms develop and execute advertising plans, and summarize how hospitality firms use advertising agencies. (pp. 269–279)
3. Describe the role of public relations and publicity in reaching prospective guests. (pp. 279–287)

Insider Insights

G. Douglas Hall
Consultant, Four Seasons Hotels and Resorts
Toronto, Ontario, Canada

"I believe in advertising. But the key is to use it properly. I'm a firm believer in research. It doesn't have to involve a large, expensive consumer study; research is often just listening. Listen to your hotel guests, listen to your competitors, listen to the people who report to you. Be consumer-directed; that's the basis of all advertising. Tell your customers about the benefits they'll enjoy, not just the features you offer. And don't let the fact that thousands of people will see your advertising deter you from speaking directly to the customer as if you were selling face-to-face. Good advertising copy talks to one person: your ideal prospect."

7

Advertising, Public Relations, and Publicity

WHILE DIRECT SELLING is the backbone of hospitality sales, advertising, public relations, and publicity are important supplements to the sales effort. Advertising makes a prospect aware of your property or restaurant before you make a sales call, while publicity and public relations can help keep your establishment's name before the public and lend credibility to your sales and advertising messages.

Because advertising is widely used in the hospitality industry, and because public relations and publicity can play an important part in the success of sales presentations, it is important that you know what types of advertising are available and that you learn how public relations and publicity are used to supplement direct selling and advertising efforts.

Why Advertise?

Hospitality firms advertise for a number of reasons:

- *Advertising reaches a vast audience.* Advertising has the potential to be seen or heard by thousands of people who are sources of sales or leads.
- *Advertising is relatively inexpensive.* The cost per reader or listener can be quite low compared to that of direct sales efforts.
- *Advertising prompts audience response.* Coupons, reply cards, telephone numbers, website addresses, and e-mail addresses included in advertisements can open doors to future sales.
- *Advertising demonstrates competitiveness.* Since most hospitality firms advertise, you must give readers or listeners an opportunity to compare benefits and features—especially when you can present superior benefits or answers to consumer needs.

Advertising is an invaluable tool that can target the market segments you have not yet reached and offer additional information to those prospects who already have a favorable impression of your hotel or restaurant.

Types of Advertising

The types of advertising that hospitality firms use include print, broadcast, electronic, direct mail, outdoor, collateral, and alternative-media. Each type has inherent strengths, but each also has limitations that must be considered before you develop an advertising strategy.

Print Advertising

Print advertising media include newspapers, magazines, and directories.

Newspapers. Newspapers are used by the hospitality industry more than other advertising mediums for a number of reasons:

- *High readership.* Most newspapers reach a large number of readers; newspaper ads can be an effective way to reach your audiences. In some cities, one newspaper dominates; an ad in such a paper gives firms easy access to their local community and to markets in specific geographic areas. You can also use ethnic and special-interest newspapers to reach targeted market segments.
- *Flexibility.* Newspapers offer a choice of ad sizes and, unlike other media (such as magazines and radio), are not limited in the number of ads that can be placed; as advertising increases, more pages are added to the newspaper to accommodate the ads. In addition, with newspapers you can place last-minute ads or easily change existing copy, which makes newspapers an ideal medium in which to place ads for newly created packages or special offers.
- *Low advertising rates.* Newspapers offer the potential of reaching thousands of potential guests at a relatively low cost, and newspaper ads can be an even bigger bargain if the newspaper offers low local-advertiser rates or bulk rates.

With all these advantages, it might seem that newspapers would be the perfect advertising medium. But there are drawbacks. Newspapers may be cluttered with ads, and your ad may be surrounded by the ads of competitors or placed next to an undesirable advertisement. Newspaper production quality is poorer than that of most magazines; the paper is coarse and color does not reproduce well on it. Newspapers are less visually exciting than magazines.

For maximum effectiveness, newspaper ads must stand out from the news stories and other ads surrounding them. This means using an eye-catching line drawing or photograph or an attention-grabbing headline (see Exhibit 1). The copy must promote a benefit of interest to your desired audience and must always include a way for the reader to respond (a telephone number, e-mail address, etc.).

Few people actually read the entire newspaper, so ads must be placed where they have the most potential to be seen by targeted audiences. Sunday travel magazines or sections can be used to sell leisure travel, while business sections, society pages, sports pages, and food and entertainment sections can be used to promote hotel packages and restaurant specials.

To introduce a new feature or to attract the attention of readers looking for information, an **advertorial** may also be used. This type of advertising may look like a regular article, but always bears a notation that identifies it as a paid advertisement (see Exhibit 2).

Magazines. Magazines are an excellent advertising option, since many **consumer** and **trade magazines** target a specific readership. Other advantages include:

Exhibit 1 Effective Newspaper Design Elements

This ad for the Ocala Hilton is an excellent example of a newspaper ad that successfully uses the basic principles of newspaper ad design. A good newspaper ad has an eye-catching headline or illustration (this ad has both); the graphics used here increase the property's image of sophistication. The ad's type is large enough to read and the copy is reduced to essentials.

- *Production quality.* Most magazines offer slick, high-tech production capabilities, with such advertising options as full-color ads, multipage spreads, and special effects (pop-up pages, fold-out sections, etc.).
- *Wider scope.* Most magazines are national in scope, which allows your ad to be seen by more people.
- *Longer life.* Unlike newspapers, magazines are saved, generally read more than once, and often shared with others.

Exhibit 2 Sample Advertorial

(ADVERTISEMENT)

Las Vegas casino tests a radical slot machine; If it doesn't pay off, it gives back your money

LAS VEGAS—Lady Luck Casino Hotel has installed a bank of slot machines that can't win a penny for the house. They actually lose money.

The machines either give players a payoff up to $1,000.00, or give back the money the customer put in.

In the first few months of testing, 59 players hit $1,000.00 jackpots on the radical "Can't Lose" machines. The casino says "thousands" have hit smaller payoffs of $2.00, $5.00, $10.00, $20.00, $50.00, $100.00 and $500.00.

"Most dollar slot machines are set to hold 3% to 10% for the house," said Alain Uboldi, Lady Luck General Manager. "These new machines do the opposite. They're set to pay back 20% to 30% to the customer—or give back his money."

Each out-of-state customer with Lady Luck's "Best Casino Fun Book in Las Vegas" gets a pull on one of the special machines. And four times a day the casino holds drawings and lets the winners play for three minutes each.

"People were skeptical at first," said Uboldi. "They didn't believe we would give back their money on a losing pull. It was tough to convince some people they were risking nothing."

The machines are located in the casino's "Welcome Center." Besides the free pull, the casino presents players with their photos, free drinks, a free long distance call and a shrimp cocktail for 25 cents.

Lady Luck's unusual offers are part of a strategy to introduce a new 16-story highrise called the "Luxury Tower," and two new restaurants.

"We took a look at Las Vegas fun books and found they all had one thing in common—they weren't fun," said Uboldi. The casino then produced its new "Best Fun Book in Las Vegas" as a satire, but Uboldi says the response has been "positively overwhelming."

The book is written in campy prose that brags about the hotel's "ferociously delicious" $2.49 buffet, offers a tongue-in-cheek "$8.00 for $10.00" slot tokens sale and admits the casino "must be crazy" for guaranteeing that a player's first card in blackjack will be an ace.

As a zany final touch, the casino rigged its parking payment machine to pay a $25.00 jackpot to every 2,000th user.

The "Best Fun Book in Las Vegas" is free to out-of-state residents, 21 years or older. Uboldi advises readers of in-flight magazines to "just tear out this page and bring it to our Welcome Center to get the book." Lady Luck is at 3rd & Ogden, downtown Las Vegas.

For a complimentary copy of the book by mail, send this story to "Best Casino Fun Book in Las Vegas", Lady Luck Casino/Hotel, P.O. Box 1060, Las Vegas, NV. 89125.

Or call free, 800-634-6580. ■

AMWE

Advertorials differ from typical print ads in that they appear to be feature stories or editorials. This advertorial reads like a feature story, but note the word "Advertisement" at the top that identifies it as paid advertising. (Courtesy of the Lady Luck Casino/Hotel, Las Vegas, NV)

Disadvantages of magazine advertising include the long lead time (this precludes promoting last-minute specials or short-term packages), higher production costs, and the possibility of your ad being placed next to that of a competitor.

Effective magazine advertising is visually appealing and targets a specific audience. Ads in consumer magazines should promote the special features or atmosphere of your establishment (see Exhibit 3). Ads in trade magazines, on the other hand, must supply all the information needed for the buyer to make a decision (see Exhibit 4).

Directories. Directories fall into three categories: general, hotel, and trade. General directories include dining guides, the telephone book's yellow pages, and so on. Hotel directories list hospitality products and services and are published for both individual travelers and travel intermediaries. Directories published by the American Association of Retired Persons (AARP) and by auto clubs are examples of those published for individual travelers. Publications such as the *Hotel & Travel Index, OAG Travel Planner/Hotel & Motel Redbook,* and *Official Meeting Facilities Guide* are used extensively by travel intermediaries such as travel agents and meeting planners to compare hotel facilities. Trade directories are published

Exhibit 3 Sample Consumer Ad

Consumer ads often promote the atmosphere of a hotel or restaurant, and usually feature the firm's positioning statement or photographs that project what a guest can expect to experience. This award-winning ad for the Hay-Adams Hotel in Washington, D.C., expresses elegance and personal service.

for members of specific industries or professions, such as the American Society of Travel Agents (ASTA).

There are two ways to advertise in directories: listings and display ads. In some cases, a listing is just that—a line that gives the name, address, and phone number of your hotel or restaurant. In other cases, a listing may consist of a paragraph or two of information that may include your location, the services you offer, rates, and so on.

Exhibit 4 Sample Trade Ad

When it came right down to it, Bob Talley didn't care about our space.

Bob Talley, Manager, Association Services Division

"I could have gotten that anywhere. What I needed was experience."

Everyone who knows the business knows that the Sheraton Washington is one of the largest meeting and convention hotels on the east coast. 1,500 guest rooms and suites. 60,000 square feet of meeting and banquet space, including 34,000 square feet of ballroom area and 26,000 square feet of breakout meeting space. 95,000 square feet of permanent exhibit space. But that's *not* the main reason why Bob Talley's clients like the American Federation for Clinical Research meet here. No. They come to the Sheraton Washington because they're guaranteed something they can't find just anywhere. Experience.

"The people are what sold me. And the people are what keep me coming back."

You can tell the world that you've hosted every major group imaginable. *But*, if they don't come back, you've got nothing but an empty claim.

At the Sheraton Washington, they come back alright. Major associations. Fortune 500 companies. But not because of our 72-foot permanent registration desk. Or the ten separate loading docks we offer for easy access to our exhibit hall. No, they're coming back for one simple reason. Our people.

That's the way it should be. And that's why the first thing we do is assign every group their own personal meeting coordinator. One person who oversees everything. One person to call if you have a question. A request. Or even a problem.

"A convention is a big investment. I wanted mine well-protected."

A comfort level. That's exactly what we offer at the Sheraton Washington. A convention services staff whose experience combined, totals over 100 years. A staff of 1,000 who cater to large groups, day in, day out, year after year. And a hotel that's dedicated to only one thing. Successful meetings.

So, let's face it. You probably already know we've got the space. The amenities. Like seven different restaurants and lounges. Two huge outdoor pools. Even a Metro subway stop right on our grounds. But when all is said and done, the reason you should hold your meeting or convention at the Sheraton Washington should be what Bob Talley's was. Simply put, because we do what we do *so well*.

For more information, call John Hyland, Director of Marketing at (202)328-2000.

Sheraton Washington Hotel

SHERATON HOTELS, INNS & RESORTS WORLDWIDE

Circle # 110 on Reader Service Card

Unlike consumer ads, trade ads are information-oriented; they usually promote such benefits as price, efficiency, or services offered to meeting planners and other travel intermediaries. The credibility of this ad is enhanced by the photograph of an actual meeting planner and the use of his quotes throughout the ad.

Many directories, however, offer the opportunity to purchase display advertisements. You should vary the advertising copy in your display ads according to the type of directory in which it will appear. An ad in a general directory, such as a yellow-pages ad, requires only an eye-catching headline or graphic and basic information (your name, location, special features, and so on). When advertising in hotel or trade directories, however, your ad will need to appeal to either consumers or travel intermediaries. As with targeted magazine advertising, consumer ads should feature your amenities and atmosphere, while ads directed toward travel intermediaries should be information-oriented and include rates, booking information, meeting room capacities, travel agent commissions, etc.

Broadcast and Electronic Advertising

Both broadcast and high-tech electronic advertising media have the potential of reaching large numbers of consumers at one time. While broadcast media (especially radio) have been around for some time, there are a number of new options for television advertising, and hospitality firms are using videos to both sell to and inform guests. In addition, electronic media, including the Internet, CD-ROMs, and fax machines, make it possible to reach prospects faster than ever before—and enable prospects to interact with hospitality firms in exciting new ways.

Radio. Radio is the oldest broadcasting medium and is often used by hospitality firms. Its greatest advertising strength is that 83 percent of the U.S. population tunes in to radio daily. Other advantages include:

- *Low costs.* It costs less to reach consumers on a cost-per-person basis through radio advertising than it does through newspaper advertising. This fact allows a firm to advertise frequently and to build its image in the community. Advertising rates often include the cost of producing the ad (charges for the announcer, for background music, etc.).
- *Flexibility.* You can reach a variety of target audiences through radio by advertising during those time periods when targeted audiences are listening.
- *Effectiveness.* Radio is one of the most effective media in building consumers' recognition of advertisers and retention of slogans or messages.

However, radio does not transmit visual images that could back up an advertising message, and ads cannot be saved for future referral (in many cases, people are listening when they are engaged in something else—driving, working, etc.—and they may not be able to jot down details of your message). Listeners may confuse your ad with other ads if they listen to many different radio stations and messages. And because of the widespread listening audience, ads must be broadcast over several different stations at frequent intervals for maximum effect.

The most successful radio ads grab the listener's attention and focus on only one idea to keep his or her interest. In some cases, a catchy slogan or jingle can be used to build name recognition for your firm. You may want to use a celebrity to lend credibility to your ad (see Exhibit 5).

Television. While television is an excellent saturation medium and can enhance your message with visuals, hospitality firms do not use television advertising extensively for a number of reasons. First, there is the high cost of airtime and

Exhibit 5 Sample Personality Radio Ad

ANNOUNCER: Hi, Tom Bodett for Motel 6 with some relief for the business traveler or anyone on the road trying like the dickens to make a buck. Well, money doesn't grow on trees and I'm probably not the first person who's told you that, but maybe I can help anyway.

Why not stay at Motel 6 and save some of that money? 'Cause for around 22 bucks, the lowest price of any national chain, you'll get a clean, comfortable room, free TV, movies, local calls, and long distance ones without a motel service charge.

No, we don't have a swinging disco or a mood lounge with maroon leather chairs and an aquarium where you can entertain your clients, but that's O.K. I got a better idea. Take the money you save and meet that client in town. Besides, they probably know all the best places to go anyway. Let them tell you what they know best and you do what's best for business.

Call __________ for reservations at Motel 6. I'm Tom Bodett for Motel 6 ... and we'll leave the light on for you.

Many properties use celebrities to promote their hospitality products. Motel 6 employed Tom Bodett (and the chain's slogan, "We'll leave the light on for you") to pull the chain out of a five-year slump—and catapult its radio spokesperson to national prominence. Tom Bodett ad courtesy of Motel 6 and the Richards Group (an advertising agency).

production. Television advertising rates are for airtime only; the production of television commercials can add thousands of dollars to the price quoted for the advertising time. It is also impossible to accurately target your audience. While commercials can be aired in specific time slots, there is no guarantee that the message will reach your desired audience (during commercials, viewers often change channels, leave the room for a snack, etc.).

You have many television advertising choices today—local stations, networks, "superstations," cable, and so on—so it is important to determine audience demographics and develop ads that will be watched. A successful television ad grabs the viewer's attention, is visual, and has an identity all its own. Its tone should give viewers an idea of what to expect when they visit your hotel or restaurant, and all your future advertising should build on the image that your ad projects, so that consumers will recognize your firm's name.

Video. Video provides a way for prospects to see what a property or restaurant has to offer before they visit, so many hospitality firms use **video brochures** or **video magazines** to showcase their products and services. Video has the advantage of being able to showcase:

- *Facilities at their best.* Videos can show each dining facility, banquet room, and meeting room in its most attractive condition.
- *A variety of setups.* Prospects can see exactly what different setups look like in a hotel's banquet and meeting rooms, and hotels and restaurants alike can exhibit theme decorations or special amenities.

- *Seasonal attractions.* Videos give travel agents, meeting planners, and individual travelers the opportunity to see a property year-round. If a site visit for a spring meeting takes place in the fall, for example, a video can show the property's garden in bloom; summer visitors could be made aware of nearby winter sports opportunities, which might encourage them to return for a winter stay.

Most videos run for four to six minutes, which should be enough time to present your benefits without losing the prospect's interest. For best results, videos should be professionally prepared and should reflect your positioning.

The Internet. The Internet can be a powerful tool when marketing to meeting planners, travel agents, and other sources of group business; it is also being used increasingly by individual consumers as a way to research vacation and other travel options and book travel.

There are a number of ways in which hospitality businesses can use the Internet for advertising. One option is to list your property or restaurant in online directories, such as HotelsOnline. Online directories range from local to international in scope. Online directories for restaurants may focus on specific types of cuisine. Another option is to sell rooms or travel packages through such travel service providers as Expedia, Orbitz, or Travelocity. In addition to listings, these sites offer hospitality businesses the opportunity to buy advertising or become a sponsor of a feature on the site. You can also be listed or advertise on other travel-related sites, such as a site serving your city or local area. Yet another option is to purchase "banner" advertising (ads that will take readers to your site when clicked) on sites frequently visited by consumers within your target markets.

In today's high-tech world, it has become necessary for hospitality properties to have a web presence of their own. The Internet allows hotels and restaurants to create their own websites and provide an overview of their products and services. Information about expansion plans, rate changes, changes in personnel, and so on can be made available to consumers very quickly. This is especially important as more and more travel professionals and consumers turn to the Internet to compare rates and services.

Most hotel chains have websites that provide links to individual properties within the chain, but it is advisable for both chain and independent properties to create a web presence of their own that provides all the information necessary for potential customers to make a buying decision. A website should be as attractive and interactive as possible, with features designed to appeal to the property's targeted markets. "Virtual tours" are a popular feature, and some properties, such as the Mandalay Bay Hotel and Casino in Las Vegas, even design their virtual tours to appeal to specific types of customers.

A trend that is changing the face of Internet advertising is the explosive growth of **social media**. It has become increasingly common for people to join online networking communities such as MySpace, Facebook, and YouTube, where they share information, photographs, videos, and music. Travel-related social sites, such as TripAdvisor, offer travel tips from consumers, and these sites can be excellent advertising vehicles for hospitality firms. Visitors to online discussion

INTERNET EXERCISE

Log onto the Internet and visit Mandalay Bay Resort and Casino's website at www.mandalaybay.com. Click on each of the "motion tours" offered to five different types of potential guests—"the Connoisseur," "the Escapist," "the Player," "the Party Goer," and "the Professional."

1. How do the tours differ for each type of guest?
2. Click on the "Conventions" tab at the top of the home page and then click on the link to the 3-D tour of the hotel's convention space.
3. Visit the websites of two other hotels. How do these sites compare with Mandalay Bay's site? What features impressed you most about each site?

boards—especially those for travel-related topics—can also prove to be invaluable by spreading the word about your product and services. In order to help hospitality firms reach out to the tech-savvy consumers who frequent social media and social networking sites, the Hospitality Sales & Marketing Association International and the Travel Industry Association have partnered to produce an educational report, *The Travel Marketer's Guide to Social Media and Social Networking*.

One of the tools that hospitality firms can use to establish a presence in the world of social media is the **blog**—an online journal of frequently updated articles or comments ("posts") that is easy to create and can be imbedded with images, hyperlinks, and video and audio features. In February 2006, Starwood Hotels launched its public blog (www.thelobby.com), which can be accessed through the Preferred Guest Program pages on the company's hotel brand websites. The blog features a number of travel-related posts that contain links to relevant hotel information. J. W. "Bill" Marriott, Jr., the Chairman and CEO of Marriott International, launched his own blog (www.blogs.marriott.com) in January 2007. One of the few industry leaders to have a personal blog, Marriott's focus is on keeping in touch with his guests through his monthly commentary and photographs.

Another way to reach out through the Internet is the **podcast**, a downloadable audio recording that is simple and inexpensive to create. When Motel 6 wanted to bring their slogan, "We'll leave the light on for you," to as many guests and potential guests as possible before the Christmas holiday, they created their first podcast, which featured Tom Bodett, the voice in the chain's "light on" commercials. Although the podcast was seasonal—Tom presented the "Top 6 Reasons to Stay at a Motel 6 During the Holidays"—the podcast continued to generate interest long after the holiday. That led to the development of other podcasts that can be downloaded from the media portion of the chain's site, including podcasts featuring American zoologist and TV personality Jack Hanna, who offers helpful hints for traveling with pets.

CD-ROMs. While many potential guests do not have Internet access, personal computers can be found in most U.S. businesses and in many homes. Therefore,

CD-ROMs—computer discs that can store a great amount of data (including text, visuals, sound clips, and programs)—can serve as an effective substitute for an Internet presence.

CD-ROMs have a number of advantages over video brochures. First, they have higher storage capacities than videos. Second, CD-ROMs are more durable than videos; the shelf life of a CD-ROM is approximately 100 years and the discs cannot be erased by magnetic fields. Finally, they can be easily and inexpensively reproduced (many are duplicates of Internet sites) and mailed.

You can create your own CD-ROM presentation or advertise on "destination" CD-ROMs, such as those developed by convention and visitors bureaus, or on your chain's CD-ROM. As with other advertising, your presentation should reflect your positioning and offer benefits pertinent to your targeted audience.

Fax. Fax (facsimile) transmissions are another electronic option that can help you get the word out quickly about your hotel or restaurant. Fax messages can be easily and inexpensively prepared and can be used to reach prospects in two ways: broadcast fax and fax-on-demand.

Broadcast faxing is used to get a message to a number of prospects at the same time. This method is often used by hotels that target meeting planners, travel agents, and other travel intermediaries, and by restaurants that service nearby office complexes. You can use your existing leads to identify prospects or you can contract with an outside firm that sells databases of the fax numbers of the prospects you are trying to reach.

Fax-on-demand is a system in which the hospitality firm gives selected travel intermediaries or other target markets a special fax number they may call to receive its latest information at any time—even when the sales office is closed. When they dial, your machine faxes them the information you specified most recently. This option can be extremely cost-effective for hotels or restaurants that already enjoy a guest base of repeat customers; these customers have already experienced the firm's offerings and simply need current information.

Direct Mail Advertising

Direct mail is one of the most popular forms of hospitality advertising because it is:

- *Targetable.* Direct mail pieces are sent directly to the prospects with the most potential to become customers.
- *Personal.* Automated word-processing equipment that can rapidly produce thousands of letters (each addressed to a different person or firm) gives a "first copy" appearance, which makes recipients more apt to feel that they are important to the hotel or restaurant.
- *Conspicuous.* A direct mail piece does not become lost in media clutter.
- *Flexible.* Direct mail offers flexibility in the types of pieces available and the timing of mailings. Direct mail pieces can be any size or shape, as long as they meet postal codes; can be printed on various types of paper; and can include such attention-getting features as pop-ups, scratch-off pieces, and even specialty items.

- *Designed for prospect involvement and action.* All the information the prospect needs is in a single form that is convenient to use; reply cards or toll-free numbers make it easy to respond.
- *Easily cost-controlled.* Pieces can be as simple or elaborate as your budget will allow, and costs can be further controlled by limiting the size and number of mailings.
- *Easily tested and measured.* The effectiveness of direct mail pieces can be gauged in several ways, such as tallying the return of reply cards, monitoring the response on toll-free numbers, and coding pieces that are sent to various areas or markets.

There are some disadvantages to using direct mail, however. First, even when it is professionally produced, direct mail may be considered junk mail by consumers (some people develop a negative image of a firm that sends direct mail). Second, mailing lists may be expensive or become ineffective quickly. Finally, direct mail is becoming more costly; postage costs have been rising steadily, as have costs for the production of direct mail pieces and for the preparation of mailings.

Successful direct mail pieces, whether they be letters, special fold-out pieces, or packets with a number of components (see Exhibit 6), should always be eye-catching and should promote benefits important to the targeted customer. If direct mail pieces are part of a series of mailings, they should reflect a common theme as well as complement your firm's image.

The most carefully designed direct mail pieces will be a waste of money, however, if they are sent to the wrong audience; a good **mailing list** means the difference between the mailing's success or failure. Mailing lists fall into three categories: commercial lists, general lists, and house lists.

Commercial lists can be compiled from several different sources and are sorted according to geographic areas and other demographics such as median income, home value, head of household, and so on. Commercial lists can be obtained from list brokers, association boards, and magazines. Most of these sources sell or rent their lists. Before purchasing a complete list, most hospitality firms do a **test mailing.** This means purchasing part of the list to gauge consumer response; additional names may be purchased if the test mailing's results warrant it.

General lists are usually obtained through business directories or the membership rosters of associations. Business directories can provide good lists of key decision-makers, as can publications such as the *Encyclopedia of Associations.*

House lists are prepared by your hotel's or restaurant's staff. Names and pertinent information can be obtained from guest registration cards, customer surveys, and even contest entries. House lists can be the most effective of all list types, even though they require preparation time. House lists provide information that can help in direct mail decisions (customer preferences, income, geographic locations, etc.). Customers on house lists have already experienced your firm and are usually open to receiving additional information about your products and services.

Outdoor Advertising

Outdoor advertising includes a firm's signs, off-property billboards, and displays that can be used both on and off the firm's premises.

Exhibit 6 Sample Direct Mail Package

AS WINTER GROWS NEAR, AND YOUR THOUGHTS TURN TO GOING SOMEPLACE WARM, MAY I SUGGEST PERHAPS THE WARMEST PLACE IN NEW ENGLAND.

THE RITZ-CARLTON.

As General Manager of The Hotel, I would like to invite you to share in some very special weekends we have planned for our guests. Romantic weekends by the fire. Weekends of fantasy and enchantment. Even a weekend of social savvy for children.

Where could you find a more personal holiday gift, or a more well-deserved reward for yourself than overlooking The Public Garden? The Ritz-Carlton.

Please call soon for reservations or return the enclosed reservations card. The Hotel Staff looks forward to your visit. And we all wish you a most joyous holiday season.

Sincerely,

Sigi Bräuer
General Manager

P.S. If you wish to present a Weekend to someone as a gift, please reserve as soon as possible so we may send a
alized Gift Certificate in time for the holidays

This direct mail package, which included a cover letter, direct mail piece, reservations/order form, and reply envelope, was used in conjunction with The Ritz-Carlton's newspaper advertising to promote winter weekend packages to upscale prospects throughout New England and New York. (Courtesy of The Ritz-Carlton, Boston, Massachusetts)

Signs. In addition to identifying and calling attention to your property or restaurant, a sign can be used to promote unique features or specials or to advertise special events. A sign can serve as a public relations tool to welcome groups as well.

While a well-designed sign can enhance name recognition, on-property signs may have the disadvantage of low viewership and may become lost in the clutter of nearby signs, especially those that are larger or more spectacular than your own.

Signs can be as simple as a painted board or as complex as a three-dimensional, free-standing sign, complete with an electronic reader board. Signs must reflect the atmosphere of the hotel or restaurant to be effective. While a steak house in the style of a ranch house can attract business with fairly inexpensive rustic signs that conjure up images of the Old West, a hotel-casino on the Las Vegas Strip would require an elaborate sign of neon or bright lights to rival the glittering signs of its competition.

Billboards. Signs appear on the grounds of a hotel or restaurant, but billboard advertisements are placed away from the property at strategic locations on well-traveled streets and highways.

Billboards offer a large display area. Their main disadvantage is that you cannot use extensive copy for your message. In-town billboards can be read more completely, as traffic is slower and readers may be stopped at traffic signals, but billboards facing busy highways do not share this advantage.

To get the attention of passersby, both the design and the copy of your billboards must be eye-catching. Even a simple painted or papered billboard can be illuminated for effect. If your budget allows, you can make use of cutouts, inflatables, or other design elements. **Cutouts** are illustrations that extend beyond the billboard itself; they both add interest and make the billboard seem larger (see Exhibit 7). Methods of adding depth include using **inflatables,** which are similar to cutouts but are made of heavyweight nylon, and using computer-generated graphics with changing designs and messages.

Whatever type of billboard you use, make it readable with simple, bold lettering and contrasting colors. Billboards should be designed to be read quickly from left to right, and copy should be kept to a minimum; let your illustration tell your story and use your copy only to indicate your name and location.

Displays. Displays can be used both in-house and off-property to promote products and services. Posters, transit cards, and scale models are types of displays.

In-house displays typically include posters in lobbies, elevators, parking garages, and other high-traffic areas. These materials are designed to promote or cross-sell and are seen by a fairly limited audience.

Off-property displays include transit cards, which can be placed inside vehicles used in public transportation (buses, subways, etc.) and on the outside of taxis, buses, and other vehicles. In addition, displays can be placed at transportation terminals; many deplaning passengers make last-minute lodging and dining decisions.

Other potentially successful venues for off-property display advertising include stadiums, arenas, bus shelters, park benches, and trade shows (trade show attendees are already in the market for hospitality products and services).

Collateral Materials

Virtually all hospitality firms use **collateral materials** in one form or another. Collateral materials include printed materials, such as brochures, posters, fliers, and tent cards, and specialty items designed to promote your products and services.

Exhibit 7 Three-Dimensional Billboards

The prestigious image of the Hilton chain is preserved in creative billboards which feature motion and three-dimensional images. This "Pot o' Gold" billboard is enhanced through the use of "gold coins" that rotate on the display area. (Courtesy of Donrey Outdoor Advertising, Las Vegas, Nevada)

Collateral materials can be very versatile and are often designed for specific groups, such as current guests or travel agents. While some collateral materials are designed to be used in-house, the majority (especially brochures and specialty items) are used as a supplement to regular advertising.

Fliers, for example, are often used to promote new items or specials or to introduce a firm to prospects in its neighborhood (this is often done by restaurants), as they are simple and inexpensive to prepare. More elaborate fliers can be used as inserts in direct mail pieces or included in materials sent out by convention and visitors bureaus or chambers of commerce in response to inquiries.

Property **brochures** can be separated into two categories: rack brochures and convention brochures. *Rack brochures* are consumer-oriented and are designed to showcase a hotel's facilities and amenities. They should be designed to reflect the property's image. A brochure for a dude ranch can use paper and artwork with a western look. A family-oriented resort's brochure should feature photographs of families enjoying leisure activities; a luxury property's brochure should be elegant and reflect the status sought by upscale guests.

Brochures usually consist of four, six, or eight panels, depending on the amount of information and the number of photographs or other artwork it will contain. Effective rack brochures have the following elements:

- *A cover that reflects your positioning.* A brochure's cover must be designed to induce readers to read the rest of the firm's message. The cover should reflect the firm's positioning, promise a consumer benefit, and include the firm's name and location. In most cases, a single, large cover illustration is more effective than several smaller photos.
- *Photographs that heighten your establishment's image and "sell" your establishment.* Photographs of special architectural features, guestrooms, and recreational amenities can help increase a prospect's desire to visit your hotel or restaurant, and your biggest attraction should be featured in the largest photograph (if all photos are the same size, nothing stands out as being particularly significant). Photographs work best when they include people enjoying your amenities, but it is important to show people that reflect the type of guests for whom the brochure is intended—photographs of families for a family-oriented brochure, and so on.
- *Effective copy.* Brochure copy should include your positioning statement, highlight your most popular features and benefits, and urge the reader to take action (reply cards or toll-free numbers are usually included). Some properties and chains that target a number of market segments develop individual brochures for each one; each brochure is designed to promote the benefits most important to its market segment (see Exhibit 8).
- *Headings that highlight key facts.* Even if a reader skims over the material, the headings will highlight the brochure's main points. In addition, special copy or graphics can be used to promote your main features.

Unlike rack brochures, which are designed to promote your establishment's atmosphere, *convention brochures* are information-oriented, designed to provide meeting planners with the facts they need to select sites. Convention brochures typically feature scale drawings of meeting rooms and list their dimensions and capacities, provide information on banquet and beverage service, and detail special services and facilities that are available to groups (see Exhibit 9).

Whatever type of brochure you use, never skimp on quality. Your brochure should always be professionally printed on paper that best complements the image you are trying to project for your firm.

Tent cards may be simple three-fold cards or elaborate fold-together pieces that can be used for both suggestive selling and cross-selling. You can place tent cards that feature dessert specials or exotic drinks on restaurant or lounge tables, while tent cards that advertise a property restaurant or lounge may be placed in guestrooms.

Many hotel and restaurant chains offer tent cards or a combination package of tent cards and posters through corporate advertising departments. If you wish to design your own tent cards, keep copy brief; using a tempting photograph will sell more effectively than words. You can have your tent cards printed in one or two colors, as is usually done, or create a full-color piece if your budget permits.

Specialty items are items that are imprinted with the name of your hotel or restaurant; they may include key chains, ballpoint pens, coffee mugs, and other merchandise. They are economical sales tools that can be remarkably effective.

Exhibit 8 Sample Targeted Brochures

For best results, brochures should target individual market segments. Each of these Days Inns brochures was developed for a specific market: businesspeople, sports teams, government workers, educators, and senior citizens. (Courtesy of Days Inns of America, Inc.)

Their primary advantage is that they can keep your name in front of prospects at a very low cost. Each time a meeting planner uses your complimentary coffee mug, for example, he or she is reminded of your establishment, as is a former customer who uses the logo glassware of a local restaurant.

There are disadvantages to specialty-item advertising, however. In some cases, the small size of items makes printing a long message impossible; you may only have room to print your firm's name and telephone number. Also, specialty items are sometimes thrown in a drawer and forgotten.

To make the most of specialty-item advertising, set a specific objective, such as getting your name before the public or attracting more business from travel agents. If your objective is simply to get recognition, all that is necessary is to select a premium that will reflect your image; if your objective is to reach travel agents, you may want to develop a strategy that involves providing a number of specialty items. Those who use this strategy should focus on a specific theme; if you want to build summer business, for example, offer beach-related items such as logo sunglasses and beach balls.

The most important factor in specialty advertising is selecting premiums that reflect your positioning. A luxury hotel, for example, should offer high-quality

Exhibit 9 Sample Convention Brochure

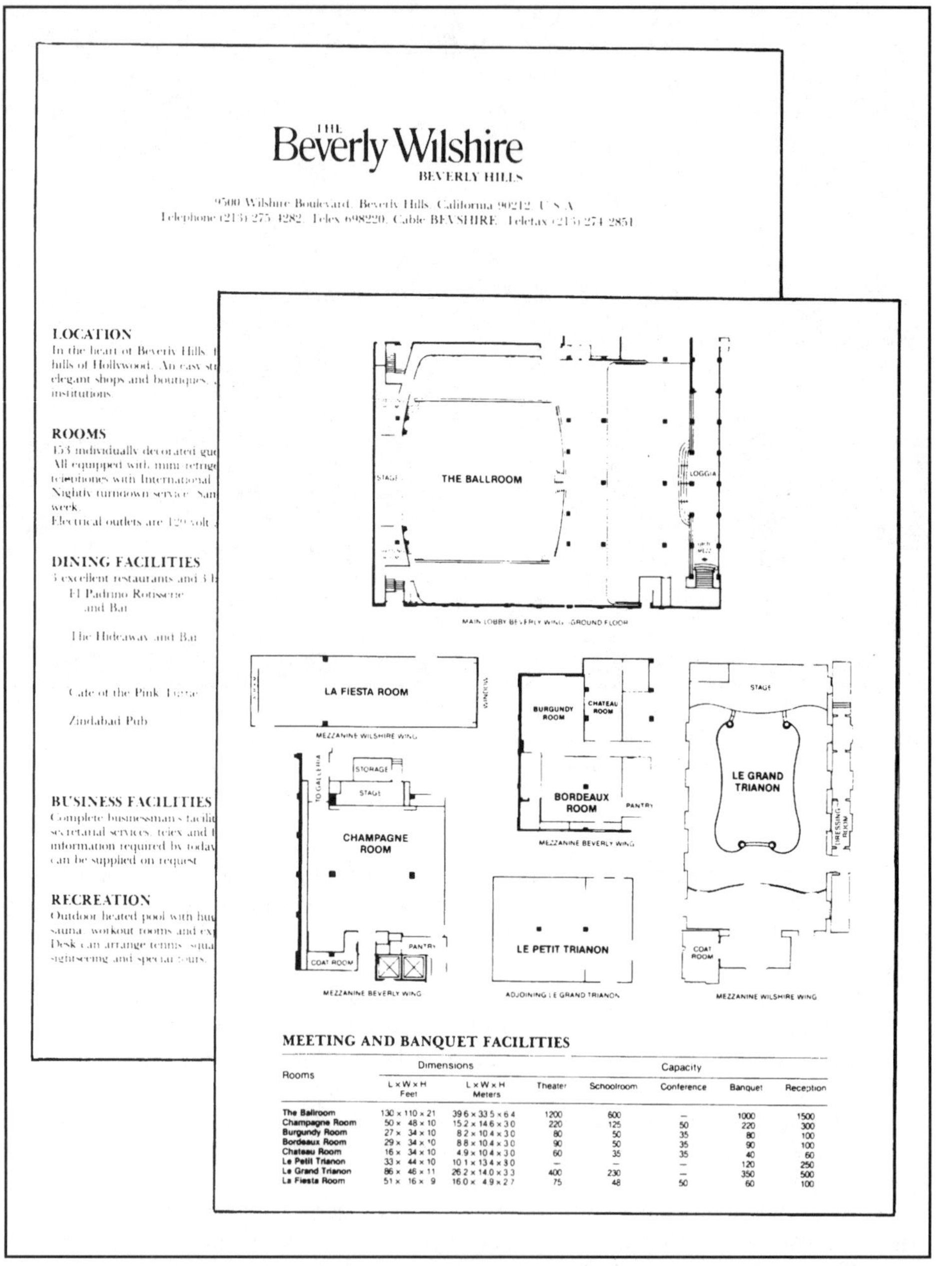

MEETING AND BANQUET FACILITIES

Rooms	Dimensions		Capacity				
	L × W × H Feet	L × W × H Meters	Theater	Schoolroom	Conference	Banquet	Reception
The Ballroom	130 × 110 × 21	39.6 × 33.5 × 6.4	1200	600	—	1000	1500
Champagne Room	50 × 48 × 10	15.2 × 14.6 × 3.0	220	125	50	220	300
Burgundy Room	27 × 34 × 10	8.2 × 10.4 × 3.0	80	50	35	80	100
Bordeaux Room	29 × 34 × 10	8.8 × 10.4 × 3.0	90	50	35	90	100
Chateau Room	16 × 34 × 10	4.9 × 10.4 × 3.0	60	35	35	40	60
Le Petit Trianon	33 × 44 × 10	10.1 × 13.4 × 3.0	—	—	—	120	250
Le Grand Trianon	86 × 46 × 11	26.2 × 14.0 × 3.3	400	230	—	350	500
La Fiesta Room	51 × 16 × 9	16.0 × 4.9 × 2.7	75	48	50	60	100

Unlike rack brochures, convention brochures must provide detailed function room and banquet information for meeting planners. This sample convention brochure lists the property's location and general amenities on the second page and room layouts and capacities on the third. Other convention brochures may rely more heavily on photographs of function facilities. (Courtesy of The Beverly Wilshire, Beverly Hills, California)

items, while a family-oriented motor inn can effectively choose cheaper items that appeal to children.

Specialty items may be ordered in a number of ways. Some hotels and restaurants order items through advertising specialty companies, and many chains publish specialty-item catalogs that feature everything from playing cards to clocks (see Exhibit 10). Items ordered from chains will be of most benefit to hoteliers if they are imprinted with the chain's toll-free reservations number.

Alternative-Media Advertising

In addition to these common advertising options, there are several **alternative-media advertising** options. These include:

- *Movie theater advertising.* Many movie theaters offer "commercial" time either before or between features. Using this medium can be especially effective prior to holidays (especially Christmas) and days on which it is traditional to eat out, such as Valentine's Day or Mother's Day.
- *Sponsorship advertising.* Hotels and restaurants can often participate in "special nights" at sports arenas or other entertainment facilities. On such nights your name can appear on such items as seat cushions, sports bottles, and other premiums given to fans, which generates community goodwill at a relatively low cost.
- *In-flight advertising.* Your advertising message can be printed on boarding passes or displayed on the screen before the start of an in-flight movie. The Meridien Hotel used another creative approach; it printed ads inside the wrappings of sandwiches served on shuttle flights from Boston to New York City.
- *Inserts in billings.* Advertising messages can be included on the billings you send to your current customers, or you can prepare a special piece that can be included in the billings of hospitality-related firms, such as rental car agencies, travel agencies, and credit card companies.
- *High-flying advertising.* This type of advertising includes ads on hot air balloons or on banners towed by airplanes.
- *Retailer tie-ins.* Another popular option is advertising on the back (or sometimes the front) of a cash register tape. In addition, you can team up with a retailer to have advertisements printed on the store's packaging, or leave fliers or coupons to be given away with purchases.

Alternative-media advertising options are limited only by your imagination, but your choices should be carefully evaluated to make sure they fit the positioning and objectives of your property or restaurant. Advertisements that are perceived as being too cute or in bad taste may do more harm than good in the long run, as can teaming up with a firm that does not complement the image of your hotel or restaurant.

Exhibit 10 Sample Chain Specialty Items

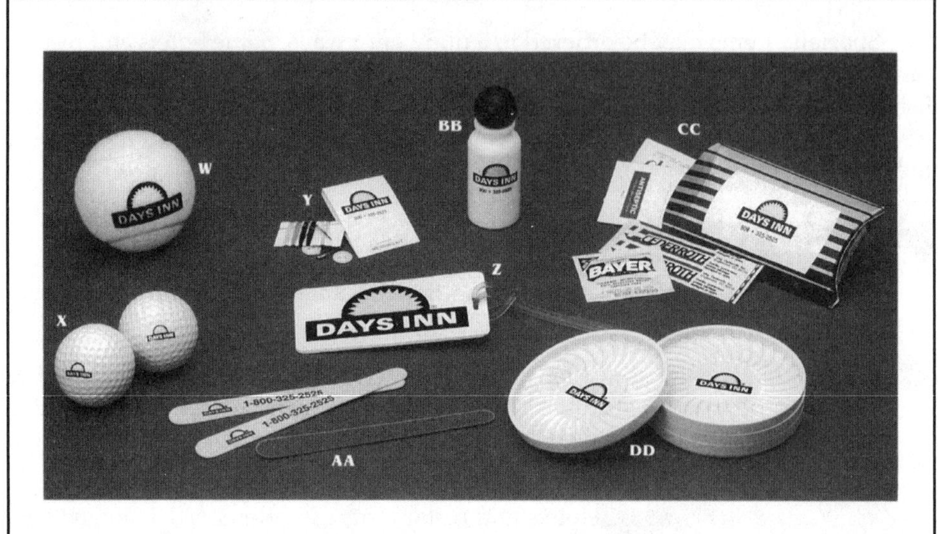

W. Tennis Balls The same **Dunlop** ®Championship tennis balls that are used in most major pro and amateur tournaments. Suitable for all types of courts. 3 Balls Per Can. **Minimum Order: 4 Cans**

X. Golf Balls Blue Maxfli ®golf balls have been a favorite of country club business and professional golfers for over a generation. Super high energy cores give extra distance to every stroke and the exterior is covered by a tough-to-cut cover. 3 Balls Per Sleeve. **Minimum Order: 4 Sleeves**

Y. Days Inn Sewing Kit 6 colors of thread, a needle, buttons, and a safety pin to handle most mending emergencies. This is one room give-away your customers will surely use! **Minimum Order: 50**

Z. Luggage Tag Executive tag with plastic strap holds a business or identification card (included). Makes a wonderful complimentary convention or conference gift. **Minimum Order: 50 Tags**

AA. Days Inn Emery Boards An inexpensive way to welcome your guests. Each board has a fine and a coarse side for neat manicuring. **Minimum Order: 100**

BB. Hand Lotion What a soft sell — Soothing Balm Argenta lotion in a **Days Inn** Logo bottle. Each once bottle holds 85 applications. **Minimum Order: 50**

CC. Survival Kit All life's little necessities in one neat kit! Includes: moist towelette, antiseptic, aspirin, antacid, adhesive bandage, and a HELP decal. **Minimum Order: 50**

DD. Plastic Coasters They hold any size glass, bottle, mug or cup — while protecting room furnishings! America's top-selling line of coasters. White Only. **Minimum Order: 50**

EE. Stadium Cup Employees and guests will enjoy this sturdy plastic cup for all their cold beverages. Holds a full 12 oz. Yellow or White. **Minimum Order: 50**

FF. Days Inn Coffee Mug Toast **Days Inn** round the clock with this mug that looks like ceramic but is ultra chip proof, break resistant plastic for both hot and cold beverages. Microwave and top rack dishwasher safe. Black Only. **Minimum Order: 12**

Chain hotels often have the option of ordering specialty items from a catalog prepared especially for the chain. This page from a Days Inns catalog shows a variety of items—from emery boards to tennis balls—that can be used as inexpensive promotional giveaways. (Courtesy of Days Inns of America, Inc.)

Developing an Advertising Plan

Advertising in all forms is used to accomplish the following goals:

- Attract potential guests' *attention* and create product awareness.
- Create an *interest* in potential guests' minds. This is not the same as creating product awareness; potential guests must become interested enough to want additional information.
- Turn prospects' interest into a *desire* to experience the property or restaurant for themselves.
- Generate *action* on the part of prospects.

Since there are so many advertising options, it is necessary to develop a plan that will enable you to meet these goals through the most effective advertising. Your advertising plan should always be considered a part or an extension of your overall marketing plan. Your positioning statement should help determine the content of your advertising, and the overall marketing budget plays a key role in how much advertising is scheduled and where.

Once you have determined how you will be positioning your firm in your advertising, you can decide which strategy will work best for your advertising message. The three advertising strategies most commonly used are differentiation, segmentation, and a combination of these two.

Differentiation emphasizes how your property or restaurant is different from its competitors. To be effective, you must have meaningful differences that are readily identifiable to potential guests. When using differentiation, however, do not use ads that boost your image by making claims that either directly or indirectly derogate other hotels or destinations—a technique that may discredit the industry as a whole.

A *segmentation* strategy can also be used to advertise your property or restaurant. The basic premise of this advertising approach is that a target market can be carved into smaller segments. The business traveler market, for example, can be segmented into women business travelers, incentive business travelers, meeting planners who book business for large groups, and so on.

A *combination* strategy involves selecting specific market segments and then differentiating your hotel or restaurant from the competition by offering unique benefits that will be of interest to that audience. This strategy is often used by small hospitality firms that can focus on one asset and then advertise to the market segment that would be attracted to that asset.

No matter what strategy is used, your advertising must cut through the media clutter and promote your firm in a memorable and cost-effective way. Four characteristics—reach, frequency, consistency, and timing—play important roles in all successful advertising strategies.

Reach refers to the number of different individuals or homes exposed to an advertising message at least once during a specified time period (a two-month promotion, for example). Generally, advertising costs will be higher as reach goals increase. Added reach will require more advertisements or the use of additional **media outlets.**

Frequency is a measure of how many times the average person in the target market is exposed to the advertising message over a specified time period. It generally takes a number of exposures to a print ad or radio or television commercial to familiarize prospects with the name or image of your firm and to prompt them to respond. Set the frequency of your advertising according to the urgency of your message. A specific event or promotion, for example, will require a large number of ads placed within a relatively short amount of time to attract the attention of the public.

Many hospitality marketing experts feel that frequency is more important than reach, due to the spur-of-the-moment nature of many decisions about where to lodge or dine. They feel that advertising is more likely to be remembered if it was seen within a week of the decision rather than a month or two previously. Peter Yesawich, president of Ypartnership (a marketing, public relations, and advertising firm), supports this philosophy:

> In media terms, the way to maximize the impact of your current [advertising] program is to trade reach (the total number of prospects exposed to your message) for frequency (the number of different times exposed). For example, rather than run an advertisement six times in six different publications, you should run 12 times in the three publications that deliver the most qualified (responsive) audience. The increased frequency will bring the audience to a "critical mass" of exposure faster, thereby producing quicker and better results.[1]

Consistency plays an important part in consumer recognition of your hotel or restaurant. Your advertising will be far more effective if it has a consistent look and, in the case of broadcast media, a consistent sound. A property or restaurant that positions its print ad elements (headline, illustration, body copy, pricing, logo, etc.) in the same order and uses ads of the same size will be recognized more often than one that tries a different look with each of its print ads. When broadcast media are used, time frames, jingles or other sound effects, the announcer, and the message should be similar for easier recognition.

Timing involves scheduling advertising for those times when it will be most effective. The Newspaper Advertising Bureau recommends timing advertisements to coincide with seasonal sales patterns—promoting summer vacation packages just before the season, promoting your holiday dinners shortly before the holidays, and so on.

There are three common advertising-timing patterns: continuity, pulsing, and flighting. Suppose the Quality Hotel wants to place 90 radio ads over a period of 30 days. If it follows a pattern of **continuity**, it will schedule the ads evenly over the 30 days (it might schedule three radio spots per day for 30 days, for example). A **pulsing** pattern is an uneven distribution of ads over a given time period (one radio spot every day over the 30-day period, with additional spots on Thursdays, Fridays, and Saturdays to generate additional weekend business, for example). **Flighting** means advertising only as needed over a given time period (distributing all 90 ads on the Sundays and Mondays within the 30-day period to promote a Monday-night dinner special, for example).

Exhibit 11 Selecting Target Market Segments

When determining the most effective use of advertising, it is important to target key market segments. Hilton Hotels and Resorts selected five key market segments and identified the media choices that would best reach each segment:

Target Market Segment	Media Choice
Frequent Business Traveler	In-flight publications such as United's *Hemispheres,* USAir's *USAirways Magazine,* American's *American Way,* Delta's *Sky,* and Air Canada's *En Route* Daily newspapers such as the *Wall Street Journal* and *USA Today;* weekly news magazines such as *Time* and *Newsweek;* and business publications such as *Forbes, Fortune,* and *Business Week*
Leisure/Vacation Traveler	National and regional full-page consumer ads in *Condé Nast Traveler, National Geographic Traveler, Southern Living, Sunset,* and *Travel & Leisure;* trade ads in *Travel Weekly*
Corporate Meeting Planner	National trade publications such as *Meeting News, Meetings and Conventions, Successful Meetings, Gavel, Business Travel News,* and *Medical Meetings*
Large Convention/Trade Show Customer	National and regional ads in targeted publications such as *Customer Convene, Best's Review, Association Meetings,* and *Association Management*
Bounce Back Weekend/Summer Vacation Market	Local and regional newspaper and magazine ads; ads in national publications such as *USA Today*

Placing Advertisements

Decisions regarding the placement of your advertisements should be based on where and when they will be most effective. In particular, you should select the media outlets in which to place ads based on the ability of each to:

- Reach the largest number of potential guests at the lowest cost per guest
- Deliver an adequate selling message
- Sell the property or restaurant rather than merely identify or announce it
- Repeat your message on a frequent basis
- Be flexible enough for special promotions
- Cover your firm's targeted marketing areas or audiences (see Exhibit 11)
- Offer the least "waste" coverage

- Best benefit your property or restaurant in terms of image and prestige
- Fall within your advertising budget
- Be affordable without sacrificing other important media coverage

To determine where to advertise, you must also know how guests choose your property or restaurant. If, for example, the majority of your hotel guests make reservations through travel agents, you should advertise in travel agent directories. On the other hand, a downtown restaurant that attracts mostly walk-in guests will benefit most from billboard advertising or ads on local radio stations.

Knowing which media reach your potential guests, however, doesn't provide all the answers you need to decide where to advertise. If your guests say they listen extensively to radio, for example, you will still need to determine exactly which stations they listen to in order to best communicate your message.

You can get information on the circulation or audience of print and broadcast media outlets from a number of sources. Newspapers and magazines issue **publisher's statements** that list their circulation, subscription rates, distribution, and other pertinent information, such as the type of readership they serve (see Exhibit 12). Additional information can be found in *Newspaper Rates and Data* and magazine directories published by the Standard Rates and Data Service.

Statistics on radio audiences can be obtained from two major sources. Arbitron monitors radio stations and develops various reports, such as local market reports and reports on listenership for various times of day. Birch Radio is a monthly service that issues reports based on telephone recall interviews, which measure audience response to messages previously heard. These reports, coupled with a comparison of radio advertising rates (see Exhibit 13), will help you determine which stations are the most cost-effective outlets for reaching your targeted audiences.

Television stations are monitored by Arbitron and the ACNielsen's Nielsen Station Index (NSI). They compile statistics such as the total audience reached by a program, the ratings for specific programs, and the demographics of the viewing audience. These figures should help determine the cost of airtime as well as your choice of a station that will reach your targeted audience.

Billboard advertising is monitored by the Traffic Audit Bureau (TAB), an independent organization supported by advertising agencies and billboard companies. TAB verifies the number of billboards and their effect on a given market.

In addition to gathering market statistics, you should take a firsthand look at media options. Study media outlets to determine if their content and image would enhance your message (and to see who is already advertising in them). In the case of a consumer magazine, for example, would your advertising benefit from the publication's image, or is the publication a poorly produced, controversial vehicle, so that advertising in it would reflect negatively on your hotel or restaurant?

Once you have selected the advertising media that seem right for you, your next step is to place your advertisements within each medium to ensure maximum exposure to your message.

Newspaper ads should be placed in the section in which they will most likely be read by your target audience—the Sunday travel section to reach leisure travelers,

Exhibit 12 Sample Publisher's Statement

VERIFIED AUDIT CIRCULATION
13366 BEACH AVENUE, MARINA DEL REY, CALIFORNIA 90291-9990 • 213 306-1577

20__

MAGAZINE
PUBLISHER'S STATEMENT

6 MONTH PERIOD
ENDING 6/30/

1. HOTEL & TRAVEL INDEX
NAME OF PUBLICATION

2. One Park Avenue — ADDRESS; New York — CITY; New York 10016 — STATE

3. Ziff-Davis Publishing Co. Inc. — PUBLISHING COMPANY; ADDRESS; CITY; STATE

4. 1937 — ESTABLISHED 5. Quarterly — FREQUENCY 6. (212) 555-5625 — TELEPHONE

7. **FIELD SERVED:**

HOTEL & TRAVEL INDEX serves owners, presidents, partners, managers, sales and other executives of retail travel agencies and wholesale tour companies, corporate travel managers and other corporate executives and departments requiring travel information; airlines, railroads, steamships, and other transportation companies; hotel reservations departments; hotel and motel representatives and other travel related services.

8. **AUDIT OF CIRCULATION**

	PAID	CONTROLLED	TOTALS
Individual (subscriptions or controlled)	45,617		45,617
Group (paid only)		XXXX	
Association (paid only)		XXXX	
Single copy sales (paid only)		XXXX	
Bulk (paid or controlled)			
TOTAL AVERAGE (QUALIFIED) CIRCULATION PER ISSUE	45,617		45,617
TOTAL AVERAGE (NON-QUALIFIED) CIRCULATION PER ISSUE (advertisers, agencies, file, samples, etc.)			5,048
TOTAL AVERAGE COPIES PRINTED PER ISSUE			50,665

9. Verification of Accuracy of Circulation List and Receivership will be determined in the Annual Field Verification and Market Research being conducted presently on the SPRING 20__ issue and which will be made a part of the Annual Audit Report.

Publishers' statements provide a circulation breakdown to help a marketing and sales staff determine if the publication will reach targeted market segments. This publisher's statement also provides a circulation audit. Circulation audits, usually performed by a third party, are much more reliable than individual publication research and break down circulation by qualified (paid) circulation and nonqualified circulation (free issues that are sent to advertisers, used as sample copies, and so on). Only the first page of the statement is shown here; other pages provide invaluable information about the publication's distribution.

If a publication is unfamiliar, it is a good idea to ask for a sample copy or a list of current advertisers. The fact that the numbers look good in a publisher's statement doesn't necessarily mean that the publication will meet the needs of the property. Its pages, for example, might be cluttered with the ads of competitors, or the editorial content may not match your positioning and image. Source: *Hotel & Travel Index.*

Exhibit 13 Sample Radio Rate Cards

KNEWS 970 RATE CARD NO. 9

30 Second Announcements
MORNING DRIVE
5 AM - 10 AM

FREQ.	1 WK	4 WKS	13 WKS	26 WKS
1 - 14X	$37.00	$35.00	$33.00	$28.00
15 - 19X	36.00	32.00	30.00	27.00
20+	33.00	28.00	27.00	24.00

MIDDAY
10 AM - 3PM

FREQ.	1 WK	4 WKS	13 WKS	26 WKS
1 - 14X	$22.00	$21.00	$19.00	$17.00
15 - 19X	21.00	20.00	18.00	16.00
20+	19.00	18.00	16.00	15.00

AFTERNOON DRIVE
3 PM - 7PM

FREQ.	1 WK	4 WKS	13 WKS	26 WKS
1 - 14X	$27.00	$25.00	$23.00	$21.00
15 - 19X	26.00	24.00	22.00	20.00
20+	23.00	21.00	20.00	16.00

KNEWS 970 RATE CARD NO. 9

30 Second Announcements
1/3 TOTAL AUDIENCE PLAN (TAP)
5 AM - 7 PM

FREQ.	1 WK	4 WKS	13 WKS
1 - 14X	$26.00	$24.00	$22.00
15+	22.00	20.00	18.00

1/4 TOTAL AUDIENCE PLAN (TAP)
5 AM - 10 PM

FREQ.	1 WK	4 WKS	13 WKS
1 - 14X	$24.00	$22.00	$18.00
15+	20.00	18.00	16.00

7 PM - 10 PM
$13.00

LATE NIGHT
MIDNIGHT - 5AM
$8.00

For 60 second rates, add 30% (multiply by 1.3).

10 second rates on request

PROGRAM RATES ON REQUEST

All schedules paid in advance receive 10% in bonus commercials.

Contracts earning consecutive week discounts or weekly frequency discounts cancelled or reduced prior to end date are subject to short rate.

Radio stations receive their revenue from the sale of airtime, and rates vary widely—even in the same market. Most radio stations issue rate cards that provide advertising information and the station's rates for advertising spots at various times of the day. (Courtesy of KNEWS, Las Vegas, Nevada)

the sports section to promote golf packages, a restaurant guide or entertainment section to advertise food specials, and so on. There is often an additional charge for a **premium position buy**—the purchase of an ad position on the top of the page beside reading matter. This position is sometimes called *full position* and is usually worth the extra money, as your ad is not placed where it is less likely to be read (the bottom of the page, in a clutter of other advertisements, etc.).

Magazines also charge extra for some ad positions, including the back cover, the insides of the front and back covers, and the center spread (a double-page spread in the center of the magazine). Some hospitality firms cannot afford the additional expense of these advertising options, but there are other choices that can enhance ad readership:

1. Three single-page ads that appear on consecutive right-hand pages
2. Two single-page ads that appear on right-hand pages in different sections of the same issue
3. A two-page spread
4. A full-page ad on a right-hand page
5. A full-page ad on a right-hand page with a strip (one-column) ad on a left-hand page[2]

Other magazine advertising options that heighten readership include the use of **gatefolds** (oversized pages or portions of pages added to a regular page) and *inserts*, which can range from a simple business reply card to a full-page color section bound into the magazine.

Radio ads should be placed by market and time. To reach people in the 18-to-30 age bracket, for example, progressive rock, soft rock, adult contemporary, and golden-oldie stations are effective. Since most people in this age-group either work or go to school, the best times to reach them are **drive times** (6:00 to 10:00 A.M. and 3:00 to 7:00 P.M.), in the evening after 7:30 P.M., and on weekends after 10:00 P.M.

Radio airtime is sold in several ways, from *fixed-position spots*, which ensure that your message is run in a specific time slot, to **weekly plans** that may run your ad at different times each day.

Television ad effectiveness—and costs—depend on the station, time slot, and time of year. Generally, ads in **prime time** (8:00 P.M. to 11:00 P.M.) cost most, since that is when a majority of viewers are watching, although costs may rise during special programming (the Olympics and other sports events, for example).

To be effective, your television ad should be aired on a station that is most likely to reach your targeted audience and whose airtime is not cluttered with other ads. It doesn't matter if these are not hospitality ads; many viewers simply change channels or walk away when constantly barraged with advertising. Have your ad positioned in a program that will enhance your image, even if doing so means higher costs. You may also consider a **sponsorship**—either presenting a program as the sole advertiser or doing so in cooperation with other advertisers.

With billboard advertising, location should be a primary consideration. Before purchasing billboard space, drive by the potential location and determine its visibility (the closest distance at which the billboard becomes visible and then readable while traffic is moving at the maximum legal speed) and the number of other billboards in the immediate vicinity. Also consider other factors, such as highway construction scheduled for the near future near the location (a detour can mean drastically reduced readership).

Billboard space is usually purchased for one to three years, and space contracts are available in two forms: rotating or fixed. **Rotating plans** ensure that your message is seen in a number of areas; the display location is changed on a periodic basis (usually every 30 to 60 days) and gives the impression that you are advertising all over town.

Fixed plans or *permanent plans* provide billboard advertising at one location only. This type of plan is usually purchased when the location provides heavy coverage—on a freeway, for example. For maximum effectiveness, billboards limited to one location must be creative—even spectacular—and must directly reach the target audience.

Budgeting for Advertising

Perhaps the most crucial part of an advertising plan is its budget. Before establishing an advertising budget, you should consider a number of variables that will affect the kind of advertising budget you will use:

- *The size and type of hospitality firm.* The size of your hotel or restaurant and the types of services and facilities it offers will greatly influence the amount of money necessary to effectively advertise it. Typically, it costs far less to advertise a standard highway property than a luxury resort.
- *The competition.* Although an advertising budget should not be established simply to match funds being spent by competitors, the level of your competition's advertising activity should help determine how much you will have to advertise to receive a fair market share.
- *Marketing objectives.* The advertising budget should be tied directly to your overall marketing plan. If you want to expand your facilities or target new markets, you may decide to invest more in advertising. If you enjoy a comfortable guest base and are experiencing a steadily increasing flow of new guests, you may want to concentrate advertising efforts on direct mail or in-house promotions, which are usually far less expensive than broadcast or national print advertising.
- *Target markets.* The number and sizes of your target markets will affect the amount of advertising needed to reach potential guests. A hotelier targeting a regional market will spend less than one who is attempting to attract guests from across the country.

After you have established your budget, review it periodically. Analyze advertising results on an ad-by-ad or campaign-by-campaign basis, and make adjustments if goals are not being met. An ad campaign's contribution to the bottom line will help determine whether it's necessary to change strategies or media outlets.

To stretch an advertising budget, you may use cooperative advertising or reciprocal advertising. **Cooperative (co-op) advertising** involves advertising in conjunction with another advertiser. There are two types of cooperative advertising: horizontal and vertical. *Horizontal co-op advertising* involves similar businesses, such as several hotels that pool resources to promote their destination city. *Vertical co-op advertising,* on the other hand, involves several different types of businesses, such as a hotel and an airline that co-sponsor an advertisement that will benefit both parties. Vertical co-op advertising is more common than horizontal co-op advertising.

Cooperative advertising offers the advantages of shared advertising costs, identification with another prestigious product or firm, and a number of media options. On the downside, parties may equally share advertising costs but may not receive equal benefits, and some advertising agreements may have conditions that are less than ideal for one or more of the participating advertisers.

Reciprocal advertising, also called *due bill advertising* or *trade-out advertising,* is the exchange of hospitality products or services (rooms, food and beverages, etc.) for advertising space or airtime. This type of advertising can be especially effective for firms with limited advertising budgets, but any firm can benefit if it carefully controls when its rooms and meals can be used. Rooms can be made available only during slack periods, and meals can be limited to breakfasts, or dinners on slow nights. A property may receive an additional return on its trade-out if a radio station manager, for example, who is given free use of the property's health club stays and buys lunch. Publishers, advertising executives, and broadcasters are usually influential, and word-of-mouth endorsements of your property or restaurant to their business associates and friends can further add value to a reciprocal-advertising agreement.

In addition to these advertising options, hotels or restaurants that belong to chains can realize great savings by participating in their chain's advertising programs. Chains conduct national advertising programs and develop **shell ads** for their individual outlets. Shell ads contain basic advertising elements, such as graphics and chain information, but leave room for franchisees to add their own specific information. Some chains also offer *donut ads*—radio messages complete with sound effects and a few seconds of time for franchisees' individual messages.

Monitoring Advertising

There are three ways to monitor the cost-effectiveness of your advertising:

1. Cost per thousand (CPM)
2. Cost per inquiry (CPI)
3. Cost per conversion

Cost per thousand refers to the cost for reaching one thousand potential buyers, and is calculated as follows:

$$\text{CPM} = \frac{\text{Cost of advertisement}}{\text{Vehicle circulation}} \times 1{,}000$$

Cost per inquiry can be used to evaluate both the response to a specific advertisement and the cost of soliciting each potential customer. CPI can be determined as follows:

$$\text{CPI} = \frac{\text{Cost of advertisement}}{\text{Total inquiries generated}}$$

Inquiries don't always result in sales, so to determine the actual value received for the cost of advertising, actual sales (conversions) must be measured:

$$\text{Cost per conversion} = \frac{\text{Cost of advertisement}}{\text{Total conversions}}$$

These formulas may be used to determine the effectiveness (or lack of it) of a particular advertisement or advertising campaign. If results do not prove cost-effective, you should analyze both the advertising and the media outlets used. Perhaps the advertising itself is not effective, or the ad is fine but the selected media outlets are not reaching the intended target audience. Once you determine the problem, you can make the necessary adjustments and reevaluate the ad or campaign in its revised form.

Advertising Agencies

Since developing an overall advertising plan or creating a single ad campaign within a workable budget can be a complicated process, many hospitality firms, especially small properties and restaurants, seek assistance from **advertising agencies.** Advertising agencies can be extremely helpful in making media decisions that will cut through media clutter and make the best use of your advertising dollars.

There are several types of advertising agencies: full-service agencies, à la carte agencies, creative shops or boutiques, and media-buying services.

Full-service ad agencies mainly use full-time staff and are usually structured into four departments: the creative department handles the development and production of ads; the media department selects specific media and places the ads; the research department serves as the firm's marketing arm; and the business department handles the agency's business affairs. These agencies may be independent operations or may have branches or affiliates that can provide coverage wherever their clients' products are sold.

À la carte ad agencies, also known as *modular services,* are usually full-service agencies that offer selected services on a negotiated-fee basis. A property or restaurant may use this type of agency for one-time productions of ads or their placements.

Creative shops or *boutiques* offer creative services on a free-lance, per-job basis. These agencies are usually staffed by free-lance artists and writers and may develop into full-service agencies as their client bases grow.

Media-buying services do not offer creative services, but specialize in buying print space and airtime. This type of agency can prove useful to hospitality firms with in-house advertising departments.

When selecting an advertising agency, it is important to consider these factors:

- *The agency's longevity, reputation, and experience with hospitality firms.*
- *Who will handle your account?* What is his or her experience level? Who would handle your account if he or she were not available in an emergency?
- *The number of accounts the agency handles, including the number and types of hospitality firms.* Might the fact that it services any of these other accounts present a conflict of interest?
- *The services the agency provides and how it would work with your firm.* Will it help with research, direct mail advertising, in-house promotions, and so on?
- *The number and types of media with which the agency is experienced.* Can the agency provide a list of the media outlets it has used, the contact persons at

each outlet, and statistics related to each outlet's effectiveness? Can it provide samples of materials it has used or developed successfully for hospitality industry campaigns?

- *How the agency would be compensated.* Would it work for a fee, a commission, or a combination of both?

After a preliminary investigation, a selection committee composed of key employees (the general manager, the director of marketing and sales, the sales director, the rooms manager, and so on) should visit each of the agencies being considered. This serves two purposes: it involves employees in the choice of an agency, and it gives your staff the opportunity to observe how the agency conducts business.

Once the field has been narrowed to two or three agencies, schedule a formal meeting with each of the top choices at your place of business. At these meetings, each agency should present its final advertising proposal and outline what it would do for your property or restaurant. You should not expect this presentation to include actual ads or ad ideas for your firm; instead, the sample presentation should detail the types of advertising that the agency thinks will work best for you. The presentation should also include suggestions for the types of materials that the agency thinks would best promote your firm. In many cases, this presentation is supplemented by examples of ads the agency has developed for related services or products.

In an ideal situation, the advertising agency you choose to work with becomes part of your sales team—familiar with your marketing plan, aware of your positioning statement, and willing to work with you to ensure that your image is presented as effectively and economically as possible.[3]

Public Relations and Publicity

While advertising is a powerful sales tool, especially since the content and timing of the message can be controlled, there are other ways to keep your name in front of the public and generate a positive image for your hotel or restaurant. Coupling your advertising with public relations and publicity can enhance your reputation and lend credibility to your sales efforts.

Public Relations

Public relations can be defined as the process of communicating favorable information about a hospitality firm to the public. Public relations includes positive guest relations, publicity (which will be discussed later in this section), and other interactions with the public and the media (see Exhibit 14).

Public relations efforts start at the hospitality firm itself with making each guest's experience memorable. But it is "outside" public relations efforts that will build name recognition and attract new customers. Ideally, these future guests will be in the target markets you specified in your marketing and advertising plans.

Developing a Public Relations Plan. For any public relations effort to be successful, it must start with objectives and action plans that are integrated into your overall

Exhibit 14 Award-Winning Public Relations Efforts

The following are examples of public relations efforts that were given awards by the American Hotel & Lodging Association at its "AH&LA Stars of the Industry" national awards program.

Omni Shoreham Hotel, Washington, D.C.

In recent years, Rock Creek Park, a scenic section adjacent to the hotel, had fallen into disrepair because the National Park Service did not have the budget or the employees to maintain it. Omni Shoreham employees took it upon themselves to contract with the Park Service for a long-term, grassroots clean-up campaign of a portion of the park. More than 150 hotel employees committed to 8,000 labor-hours over a 12-month period. The hotel contributed food and beverages for a picnic for workers the day the cleanup began.

Omni Shoreham employees were among the first groups to join in preserving and enhancing the national parks under the "Save Our Parks" program. Besides providing a community service, the project also promoted a spirit of cooperation among the hotel staff.

Treasure Island Inn, Daytona Beach Shores, Florida

Treasure Island Inn's "First Mates" organization consists of volunteers representing every department of the hotel. First Mates involve themselves—and the hotel—year-round in community and philanthropic activities. First Mates help with such charitable endeavors as United Way fund-raisers and membership drives, American Cancer Society walk-a-thons, American Red Cross blood drives, and the March of Dimes. First Mates are also active in a "Christmas for the Needy" project. First Mates and other hotel employees promote the arts in the local community by hosting a number of fund-raising events and dinner theater performances at the hotel. Through the efforts of First Mates, Treasure Island Inn has become a model for other businesses in the community of how to become involved in public health, arts, and environmental awareness programs.

Sheraton New Orleans Hotel, New Orleans, Louisiana

For the opening of its new Waterbury Conference Center, the Sheraton New Orleans sought to emphasize the center's historic site. The state-of-the-art conference center is located on the former site of the Waterbury Drug Store, a long-time New Orleans landmark. To promote the grand opening of the center, the hotel mailed press kits and invitations to key media people. A week before the event, "medicine bottles" were hand-delivered to media representatives as a reminder of the event, calling further attention to the historic significance of the new center's location. The grand opening was well attended by local media as well as many local corporations. The event resulted in numerous stories in local and national publications.

marketing plan, targeted toward your important market segments, and timed to reduce soft spots in covers or occupancy. Your plan should include what you hope to accomplish, when you can best reach target markets, and, perhaps most important, who will be involved in these efforts and what these people will do.

Selecting a Public Relations Staff. While every employee plays a role in developing and maintaining a positive public image of your hotel or restaurant, outside public relations efforts require specialized strategies. Whatever the size of the property or restaurant, it is best that a *professional* public relations person or staff be employed or contracted. Small firms may rely on one person or an outside agency; larger properties may engage a staff with diverse capabilities or work with an outside agency. Chain hotels and restaurants can take advantage of chain public relations staffs and programs.

An in-house public relations person or staff may have many responsibilities: developing local promotions, contacting the media with news releases, writing promotional literature, and perhaps writing a column for a local publication. At properties with large public relations staffs, a director of public relations is responsible for developing, implementing, promoting, and publicizing programs or special events that are designed to get the attention of the media—and of desired market segments.

Public Relations Agencies. If you decide to contract with an outside public relations agency, the guidelines for agency selection are very similar to those for ad agency selection, including the agency's location, longevity, reputation, experience, and fees. To weed out agencies with unsatisfactory plans or exorbitant rates, you should request proposals that outline how each agency would support your marketing objectives. Once you have selected an agency, you should work closely with it. An employee can be appointed to keep your agency representative aware of happenings at your establishment. For closer contact and better results, the representative should be invited to sit in on important staff meetings, treated as a member of the marketing and sales team, and expected to provide monthly or quarterly reports on the results of the agency's efforts.

Publicity

Publicity, the media's gratuitous mention of your firm, is one of the most effective promotional tools available to the hospitality industry, yet few properties include publicity in their marketing plans. Publicity supports advertising, lending credibility with unbiased third-party mentions and endorsements.

While publicity can be unplanned, such as when a celebrity visits your establishment and talks to media representatives about his or her stay, planned publicity, such as getting the word out about expansions and special programs, is more likely to promote your firm in positive ways.

A relatively new—and sometimes controversial—form of publicity is **buzz marketing**. While hospitality firms have long recognized the importance of word-of-mouth referrals from satisfied guests, some businesses are taking word of mouth a step further by employing "agents" to try out new products and services and spread the word about them. Companies such as Hershey's, Procter & Gamble, and Ralph Lauren hire agencies that recruit "real people" who fit the companies' targeted demographic to try their new products and spread the word about them (this can be done in a number of ways—from just talking to friends, to posting comments on the Internet). The concept is getting increased media attention, and this trend may impact the hospitality industry in the future—hotels may "test market" everything from guestrooms to new menus in this way, while restaurants can use the concept to evaluate new food items or packaging.

Publicity Planning. A well-developed plan can lead to favorable publicity, which can attract new business, remind previous guests about your establishment, and build community goodwill. Such a plan begins with knowing what your firm has to offer, including its history, facilities, services, staff, and marketing and sales goals. An exciting marketing concept, employees who have excelled in special fields, and upcoming events you are sponsoring are all interesting to the media.

Once you know what you have to offer, you will want to develop interesting promotional materials and get to know the media that can help you build your image in print and over the airwaves.

Developing Promotional Materials. Several types of promotional materials are typically used in conjunction with public relations and publicity campaigns. **Press kits** typically include:

- *A letter of introduction.* Typed on your firm's letterhead, this letter explains the nature of the materials enclosed, gives permission to use them, and gives the name and telephone number of a contact person who can provide additional information and assistance.
- *A summary sheet.* This lists what is in the press kit.
- *Fact sheets.* Written in a non-narrative style, fact sheets include information about the general design and appearance of the establishment, guest services, food and beverage outlets, parking facilities, safety features, and names of key personnel.
- *A basic news release.* This is a short, general article (usually no more than 500 words) in narrative form about your property. Written on a news release form or your property's letterhead, this two-page (maximum) article highlights the range of special facilities and services available at the property, your unique features (unusual architecture, murals, fountains, and so on), and other basic information that may be of interest (see Exhibit 15).
- *Photographs.* These may be interior and exterior shots of the property or photos of business and recreational amenities, menu items, unusual table settings, or other items that may be of interest to the public. Photos should always be in black and white and no smaller than five by seven inches (13 by 18 centimeters).
- *Biographies and photographs of key personnel.* Biographies of key personnel may lead to feature stories. Profiles should be short, factual, and interesting, and should be accompanied by a sharp black-and-white photo of the subject.
- *News clippings.* Previous press coverage shows that the property or restaurant was considered newsworthy in the past and may give a journalist an idea for a new slant on a subject that was covered earlier.
- *Advertising materials.* Brochures, pamphlets, fliers, videos, and other materials provide additional information and appeal.

Since media personnel may receive hundreds of press kits each year, it is important that your press kit make a positive first impression. All materials should be attractively presented in a sturdy folder that features your logo and the

Exhibit 15 Sample News Release

FOR MORE INFORMATION:
Peggy A. Gredington or
Todd E. Vasel
AMESBURY LTD.
(555) 123-4567

Background Information:

MAYFAIR SUITES: A HISTORIC LANDMARK

The doors of Mayfair Suites reopened in downtown St. Louis following a $20 million renovation that restored the historic hotel's original charm and elegance.

The 320-room Mayfair Hotel--as it was originally named--opened in 1925 under the ownership of Charles Heiss, a former busboy from Heidelberg, Germany. Today, the European charm Heiss brought to the hotel remains evident in the hotel's service, accommodations, and restaurants.

Added to the National Register of Historic Places in 1979, Mayfair Suites now has 184 guest units, a result of room enlargements and renovations over the years. Most are one-bedroom suites complete with parlors, dressing areas, and baths. Four 18th-floor penthouse suites offer living and dining areas; baths with Jacuzzis, showers, and dressing rooms; fireplaces; and magnificent cityscape views.

- more -

806 St. Charles Street / St. Louis, Missouri 63101-1507 / 314-421-2500 / 1-800-444-3313
Member Preferred Hotels Worldwide

This first page of a news release features the elements most desired by journalists. It is typed (double-spaced) on property stationery, starts roughly a third of the way down the page to leave room for an editor's headline, and includes the name of the property's contact person. (Courtesy of Mayfair Suites, St. Louis, Missouri)

name, address, and telephone number of both your firm and your media contact person.

A **news release** is a news story about a special event, a celebrity guest, a new promotional program, or another interesting topic that is sent to the news media in hopes that it will generate an article, an interview, or other media attention. Before writing a news release, it is important to know the media and their needs and to send the story to the most appropriate media outlet. If a particular story seems most appropriate for a particular department in a newspaper, for example, you can send it to that department's editor along with ideas, statistics, and photographs that would enhance the story.

While it is best to send a specific story to only one media outlet, general news can be written up in a news release and sent to many media outlets. This enables each outlet to determine the release's value—and allows each to develop its own individual story.

Periodic newsletters sent to media representatives may also generate story ideas. Newsletters keep your name in front of the media at a relatively low cost.

Travel Writers. Another way to encourage publicity is to invite travel writers to your establishment. Travel writers write about modes of transportation, hotel accommodations, and business and vacation destinations.

Travel writers may be either staff writers or free-lance writers. Staff writers work for specific publications, and their assignments are often arranged through an editorial staff. Free-lance writers work as independent agents and may either sell their ideas for stories to a publication or write stories and then try to market them.

Because travel writers vary in their styles, abilities, and markets, it is wise to develop guidelines to ensure that travel writers have the expertise to make the most of their visit. While few writers take vacations at a property's expense, you should qualify all travel writers who will be receiving discounted rates. With staff writers, a call to the publication is usually all that is necessary; free-lance writers, on the other hand, are harder to qualify. While many belong to professional organizations such as the Society of American Travel Writers, you must often rely on the writer's reputation alone.

To maximize a travel writer's visit, make clear exactly what your property will provide (in many cases, food, beverages, and incidental costs are covered by the travel writer) and what you expect in return for the writer's stay. Although travel writers are guests of your property, they are also critics obligated to present an honest view of their stay.

To create a favorable impression, you should be prepared. What is the writer's itinerary? Specially scheduled events and appointments should not cut excessively into the writer's time; neither should overtaxing activities. Schedule travel writer visits when the property's schedule is relatively free so that he or she isn't ignored. When conducting tours of guestrooms or facilities, show only one in each category.

After the visit, send the writer any informational materials that were not sent in advance of the trip. Follow up with a short note expressing the hope that the writer enjoyed his or her stay. A few weeks after the visit, you may call the writer's editor to get an idea of the coverage your property will receive. After reviewing the finished article, you should send a letter of thanks to the writer, even if the story contains negative elements (public relations includes enhancing relationships with everyone, even an unhappy travel writer).

In addition to travel writers, both staff and free-lance restaurant reviewers may generate publicity for your restaurant. Unlike travel writers, restaurant reviewers often visit unannounced to get an unbiased view of your food and service, but you can also contact a reviewer at your local newspaper when you make major changes, such as remodeling or hiring a new head chef.

Press Relations

It is easier to establish or maintain an effective public relations program if your property or restaurant enjoys a good relationship with the press. To develop good media relations and get the most from media coverage, you should consider several factors. First and foremost, your public relations person or staff must understand media interests. Media outlets must appeal to audiences and generate interest to keep readers and viewers. Publishing or airing interesting features or news stories is one way the news media seek to appeal to audiences.

Good public relations staffs are aware of the elements required for a good news story—and of the problems faced by the media. Therefore, they maintain good press relations by following these guidelines:

1. *Prepare news releases properly.* Always double-space to allow for editorial revisions, and include a "who, what, when, where, why, and how" paragraph.
2. *Avoid duplication.* Except for general news releases, do not submit the same story to a number of media outlets; write the story from a number of angles to offer outlets a measure of exclusivity.
3. *Be honest.* If questions arise, deal with them candidly, straightforwardly, and quickly.
4. *Respect deadlines.* Deadline pressure is a fact of life for most news media representatives, and news releases and conferences should be timed with deadlines in mind.

It is also important to get to know the local media, from reporters to editors and station managers. If you develop good relations with news media personnel, unfavorable publicity about your firm might be played down at a future time. Knowing the local media representatives helps when you are asked for a personal interview (either in print or on the air) or when there is a need for a news conference. Personal interviews can generate good exposure for your property and serve as a powerful public relations tool. Being familiar and comfortable with the interviewer can help greatly in reducing stress and in coming across as open and natural.

There may be times when a news release or an interview with one member of the media is not adequate. Perhaps your hotel or restaurant has experienced a labor dispute or a disaster, and it is important that the facts be presented to all of the media at once to avoid speculation or misrepresentation.

If there is sufficient cause for you to schedule a news conference, follow these guidelines:

1. *Schedule appropriately.* Except when the time of a news conference is dictated by a disaster or emergency, try to select a day and time convenient to the schedules of the news media.
2. *Be prepared.* Have special press kits available that relate to the presentation, and be sure that the speakers are adequately prepared with background information or fact sheets and answers to possible questions.
3. *Keep the conference brief and to the point.* Limit the presentation to around 15 minutes and follow it with a question-and-answer session.
4. *Be aware of media requirements.* Have adequate space for the reporters and their equipment, and provide sufficient electrical wiring and outlets. Avoid using white backdrops or table covers, and display your logo on the lectern or conference table.
5. *Maintain good press relations.* Provide adequate parking and a representative to greet press members. If time permits, provide coffee or refreshments. Provide press kits to media members who were unable to attend; this should be done the same day, if possible, and immediately after the conference in emergency situations.

It is important that you develop a public relations strategy to handle emergencies or other situations that can generate bad news. Proper planning can limit potentially negative publicity and reinforce a positive public image. One of the most important elements in handling sensitive subjects is the designation of one spokesperson. This helps minimize conflicting reports and misrepresentations of facts. Your entire staff should be aware of this policy and should refer all media representatives' questions to the spokesperson.

In most sensitive situations, the media receive information at a news conference so that each media outlet receives the same information at the same time. The spokesperson can then answer questions and describe positive actions being taken. If the press raises difficult questions, the spokesperson should never reply with "No comment," but should provide the reasons that he or she cannot answer. It is illegal to answer certain questions (perhaps the next of kin have not yet been notified, for example), and further investigation may be required to answer some questions.

There may be times—no matter how good press relations have been—when a media report is slanted or contains misleading or incorrect information. In some cases, your image may be such that a negative story will not affect business and it is best to let the story die. In other cases, however, the negative publicity may be damaging and you should deal with the error.

The first step is to contact the writer or broadcaster who made the error and discuss it. Present your case and back it up with facts in a friendly, professional manner. If you cannot reach a satisfactory solution, contact the editor or station manager and ask for a correction, retraction, or apology. Most media representatives are as eager as hotel managers to maintain good public relations and will cooperate by offering rebuttal time or an additional story to correct errors.

Conclusion

As you can see from this chapter's overview of the advertising, public relations, and publicity arenas, there are hundreds of options you can choose from to get and keep your name before the buying public. Determining which ones will be most effective requires a substantial amount of time and decision-making. To make the most of advertising, public relations, and publicity, you must keep abreast of the latest developments in these fields, study the advertising and public relations strategies of your competitors, read books on the technical aspects of each area you wish to pursue, and request information from organizations that serve the hospitality industry, such as the American Hotel & Lodging Association and the Hospitality Sales & Marketing Association International.

Endnotes

1. Peter Yesawich, "Planting Seeds for Growth," *Hotel & Resort Industry,* January 1992.
2. Top five points from Starch Tested Copy, Starch INRA Hooper, Inc., as reprinted in "Advertising Positioning"; Magazine Publishers Association; CARR Reports.
3. Material in this section was adapted from information provided by Tom McCarthy, owner, Tom McCarthy Associates, a hotel marketing consulting firm.

Key Terms

advertising agency—A company that furnishes advertising and marketing services to clients. Ad agencies may be paid by receiving a commission from the media or a predetermined fee from the client. Types of advertising agencies include à la carte agencies, creative shops or boutiques, full-service ad agencies, and media-buying services.

advertorial—A combination of an advertisement and an editorial statement, written by the advertiser, that looks more like a news story than an advertisement.

alternative-media advertising—This involves placing advertising in non-traditional places such as movie theaters, ballparks, and hot air balloons.

blog—Personal or corporate online journals that offer reporting and/or opinions about people, things, and events. Blogs are designed to allow readers to post responses or comments, so the most successful blogs generate a high degree of interactive dialogue.

brochure—A printed folder containing descriptive or advertising material; rack brochures target individuals, while convention brochures target meeting planners.

buzz marketing—The use of high-profile entertainment or news to get key influencers (celebrities, sports figures, bloggers, etc.) and others to talk about a brand or pass along a marketing message online or in personal conversations. Closely related to viral marketing, in which marketers use preexisting social networks to produce increases in brand awareness or to achieve other marketing objectives by using video clips, interactive Flash games, advergames, chat rooms, text messages, and other techniques to encourage people to pass along a marketing message voluntarily. Buzz marketing is said to have more credibility with consumers, since the message is received from a friend or colleague rather than through a more formal promotional method such as a television commercial or print ad.

collateral materials—Specialty items (such as key chains) and printed material (including brochures, folders, posters, fliers, and tent cards) used to advertise products and services.

consistency—In advertising, refers to the design of advertising messages so that they have a similar look or sound for easier audience recognition and greater cumulative impact.

consumer magazine—A publication designed to appeal to the general consumer market, in contrast to a trade magazine.

continuity—An advertising pattern in which ads are distributed evenly over a given time period.

cooperative (co-op) advertising—A pooling of marketing dollars by several businesses for promotional purposes in order to increase market impact or reduce marketing costs. Types include horizontal and vertical co-op advertising.

cost per inquiry (CPI)—The cost of advertising based on the number of inquiries the advertising generates.

cost per thousand (CPM)—The cost of reaching 1,000 households or individuals.

cutout—A type of billboard advertising in which part of the illustration extends beyond the display board itself.

drive time—The commuting hours during which radio listenership is highest and the most money can be charged for airtime: 6:00 to 10:00 A.M. and 3:00 to 7:00 P.M.

flier—A printed advertisement intended for distribution to potential clients or guests.

flighting—An advertising pattern in which ads are distributed on an as-needed basis over a given time period.

frequency—A measure of how many times the average person in a target market is exposed to an advertising message over a specified time period.

gatefold—Oversized page or portion of a page added to a regular magazine page.

inflatable—A design element made of heavyweight nylon that adds a three-dimensional effect to billboard advertising.

mailing list—A list of the names, addresses, and, in some cases, titles of persons to be reached by direct mail. It can be a commercial, general, or house list.

media-buying service—A type of advertising agency that specializes in buying print space and radio and television time. A media-buying service does not offer creative services.

media outlet—An individual newspaper, radio station, television station, magazine, directory, and so on, where advertising can be placed.

news release—A news story about a special event or other interesting item that a business sends to the news media in hopes that it will generate favorable coverage of the business.

podcast—Multimedia files (audio or video) that are distributed over the Internet for playback on personal computers or mobile devices such as MP3 players. Many podcasts are available free of charge, while others must be purchased.

premium position buy—The purchase of a specific position for your newspaper or magazine ad. A premium is paid for this preferred position; otherwise, the ad appears in a *run-of-paper position*—that is, wherever the publisher decides to place it.

press kit—A collection of news releases, fact sheets, photographs, news clippings, and other material, often attractively packaged, that is designed to give journalists background information about an organization.

prime time—The times when broadcast media viewership or listenership is highest and when the most money can be charged for advertising on these media; for television, prime time is 8:00 to 11:00 P.M.; for radio, 6:00 to 10:00 A.M. and 3:00 to 7:00 P.M.

public relations—A systematic effort by a business to communicate favorable information about itself to the public in order to create a positive impression.

publicity—The gratuitous mention in the media of an organization's people, products, or services.

publisher's statement—A statement by a publisher that includes information about circulation (broken down by paid subscriptions, number of copies available at newsstands, circulation of regional editions, and so on), subscription rates, advertising rates, mechanical requirements for ads, and deadlines for submitting ads.

pulsing—An advertising pattern in which ads are distributed unevenly over a given time period. "Pulses" or high concentrations of ads may be placed at the same time each day, week, month, or year, however.

reach—In print, the number of individuals or households estimated to be in the readership of a given publication or group of publications. In broadcast, the number or percent of an audience exposed to one or more announcements or programs.

reciprocal advertising—The exchange of an advertiser's products or services to pay for all or part of the medium's time or space. Also called *due bill advertising.*

rotating plan—A method of buying billboard advertising space in which the advertiser's message is moved from one billboard location to another at stated intervals to achieve more balanced coverage of a market.

shell ad—A predesigned ad developed by a hotel or restaurant chain's corporate headquarters that individual franchisees may use with minor modifications, such as inserting the address and phone number of the outlet.

social media—The term used to describe the tools and platforms that people employ to converse with each other and publish/share content online. These tools include blogs and podcasts as well as sites designed to share photos, videos, graphics, bookmarks, and other content.

specialty items—Sales tools such as candles, coffee cups, T-shirts, or beach towels that bear the business's name and other advertising information. Also called a *premium.*

sponsorship—A method of advertising in which an advertiser presents a radio or television program as the sole sponsor or in cooperation with other advertisers.

tent card—Suggestive-selling print advertising typically placed on restaurant tables or in guestrooms.

test mailing—Sending out an inexpensive direct mail piece to some of the names on a mailing list to measure the response rate before sending a more expensive piece to all of the names on the list.

trade magazine—A specialized publication designed to appeal to people in specific industries or professions.

video brochure—A short video (typically four to six minutes) that presents a property's products and services and is designed to be viewed off-site.

video magazine—A video designed primarily for on-site viewing that promotes a property's products and services and may provide information on reservations services, upcoming promotional packages, and local attractions.

weekly plan—A method of buying radio airtime in which your ad is aired from ten to 40 times per week. The times the ad is aired depends on whether a total audience plan, a morning-afternoon-night plan, a run-of-station plan, or a best-time-available plan is purchased.

Review Questions

1. Why do hospitality firms need to advertise? What factors should be considered when planning an advertising strategy?
2. What types of media are available for print advertising, and what are the advantages and disadvantages of each?
3. What types of broadcast media are used by hotels and restaurants, and what are the advantages and disadvantages of each type?
4. What high-tech advertising options can be used with traditional methods, and what target markets can be most effectively reached with each?
5. Why is direct mail considered an effective way to reach prospects? What factors should be considered to make the most of a direct mail campaign?
6. What are the types of outdoor advertising and what role does each play in promoting awareness of hospitality firms?
7. What are the types of collateral material hospitality firms use, and what are the advantages and disadvantages of each?
8. What methods do hospitality firms use to monitor the effectiveness of advertising?
9. What is the difference between advertising, public relations, and publicity? Why is it necessary to have separate strategies for each?
10. How can a lodging property or restaurant maintain good press relations, and how can hospitality firms counteract negative publicity?

Internet Sites

For more information, visit the following Internet sites. Remember that Internet addresses can change without notice. If the site is no longer there, you can use a search engine to look for additional sites.

ACNielsen
www.acnielsen.com

Ad Council
www.adcouncil.org

Advertising Educational Foundation
www.aded.org

Advertising Research Foundation
www.thearf.org

American Advertising Federation
www.aaf.org

American Association of Advertising Agencies
www.aaaa.org

American Society of Travel Agents
www.astanet.com

Arbitron
www.arbitron.com

Destination Marketing Association International
www.iacvb.org

Hospitality Sales & Marketing Association International
www.hsmai.org

International Association of Business Communicators
www.iabc.com

Mailing Fulfillment Service Association
www.masa.org

Media Central
www.mediacentral.com

Meeting Professionals International
www.mpiweb.org

National Association of Broadcasters
www.nab.org

Newspaper Association of America
www.naa.org

Official Airline Guide
www.oag.com

Outdoor Advertising Association of America
www.oaaa.org

Public Relations Society of America
www.prsa.org

Radio Advertising Bureau
www.rab.com

Sales & Marketing Executives International
www.smei.org

Sales & Marketing Management
www.salesandmarketing.com

Standard Rate and Data Service
www.srds.com

United States Postal Service
www.usps.gov

urhospitality.com
www.urhospitality.com

Web Digest for Marketers
www.wdfm.com

Part III

Marketing

Chapter 8 Outline

Competencies

1. Summarize the criteria business travelers use to make lodging decisions, identify types of frequent business travelers, and describe the women business traveler segment. (pp. 295–303)
2. Explain how hospitality properties are meeting the special needs of business travelers. (pp. 303–311)
3. Describe how hospitality properties are reaching business travelers. (pp. 311–319)

Insider Insights

Raymond E. Schultz
Past President & CEO, Homewood Suites, Inc.
Memphis, Tennessee

"Extended-stay hotels balance the convenience and service of a traditional hotel with the comfort and atmosphere of a home or apartment. The feeling of being 'right at home' is what extended-stay hotels such as Homewood Suites are all about. Each of our hotels features a 'community' concept, with residential-style units built around a central hospitality center and swimming pool/recreation area. We've empowered every employee to make guests feel at home. Whether it's baking a cake for a guest celebrating a birthday away from home, or working with the local school district to schedule a temporary bus stop at the hotel for a relocating guest's child, it's this attention to service that has helped achieve occupancy levels that currently lead the segment."

8

Marketing to Business Travelers

THE BUSINESS TRAVELER MARKET accounts for about half of all room revenue, so it is a very important market for most hotels. While business travel is expected to grow at a slower pace than in the past, and the percentage of Americans who take business trips is declining, the number of trips business travelers make is increasing. Business travelers can be a lucrative market for properties of all sizes and price ranges. Upscale properties realize about 60 percent of their business from this market segment; mid-level properties, about 45 percent; and economy properties, about 35 percent.

Over the past few years, new products and services for the business traveler have emerged, such as business floors, in-house business services, in-room workstations, and even entire hotels designed specifically for the business traveler. For example, Wingate, a product developed by Wyndham, is a totally new type of hotel that's designed to meet the needs of business travelers. Many established chains have also created new business-traveler-oriented products; InterContinental Hotels Group targets this market with Holiday Inn Select hotels, while Sheraton offers Sheraton's Four Points. New brands making headway in this segment are Aloft by Starwood Hotels, Hotels Indigo by InterContinental, Hilton Garden Inns, and Hyatt Place.

Another important trend in this market segment has been the introduction and growth of extended-stay properties. The first extended-stay properties included Marriott's Residence Inns and Hilton's Homewood Suites. Today's "hot niche" is extended-stay properties targeting the middle-income business traveler market; properties appealing to this market include Choice's Mainstay and Marriott's TownePlace Suites.

Many business travelers, especially GenXers, want their business trips to include social interaction as well as work. To appeal to this group, many hotel brands are revamping their public spaces—especially their lobbies—to be hip, appealing places to mix both business and pleasure. Hyatt Place, for example, has reconfigured the traditional lobby into "the gallery," which consists of three activity areas: a "cozy corner," where guests can sit and relax or work on their laptops; a "grab and go" area that offers salads and sandwiches for take-out; and a "guest kitchen" area where guests can select made-to-order food via a touch-screen menu. Marriott International offers a "great room" approach, providing "zones" where guests can work, meet, and dine. Starwood tags its hotel lobbies as "living rooms" and invites guests to linger and socialize in them, while the Embassy Suites brand, which is already known for its open-air atriums, has introduced European-style cafés at its properties.

Another trend in business travel is appealing to socially conscious business travelers and their companies by offering "green" properties and "green" meeting space. A growing number of companies book individual business traveler and group meetings business based on the commitment of a hotel to environmentally sound practices.

Because of the diversity of this market segment, properties of all sizes and price ranges can capture some of its business. In this chapter, we will discuss different types of business travelers and see how properties are meeting their needs.

Business Travelers

While statistics on this market vary from year to year (and from source to source), one survey of U.S. business travelers reported that:

- 92 percent of all business travelers spent at least one night away from home on their most recent trip;
- 73 percent stayed in hotels or motels;
- 78 percent are members of a hotel points reward program;
- 66 percent "always" or "often" stay at the same hotel chain;
- the average length of stay was 4.3 nights; and
- more than half paid $50 or more per night for their accommodations; 11 percent paid $100 or more per night.[1]

These statistics explain why properties are developing special amenities and services to attract business travelers.

Of all the different types of travelers, business travelers are perhaps the most knowledgeable and sophisticated, and they have definite preferences regarding the selection of a hotel:

1. *Convenient location.* Approximately 78 percent of all business travelers rated this factor as the prime reason for choosing a hotel.
2. *Room rates and amenities.* Over 55 percent of all business travelers cited room rates as a factor in hotel selection. In addition, business travelers look for value in terms of amenities. Free Internet and long-distance access, complimentary shuttles to and from airports, and complimentary breakfasts can help draw business travelers.
3. *Recommendations of friends and colleagues.* Over 87 percent of business travelers make their own decisions regarding accommodations, and many (35 percent) base their decisions on the recommendations of colleagues or friends rather than on the recommendations of travel agents (11 percent); 22 percent make a choice based on corporate or company policy.
4. *Previous experience with the property.* Previous experience with a property or a chain figured as a selection factor with 33 percent of the business travelers surveyed. The respondents favored chain properties for their consistency and

predictability; 41 percent said chains offered better service and 16 percent preferred chains for ease in making reservations.

5. *Facilities.* Meeting facilities influenced 33 percent of the respondents, while restaurants and food service were important to 22 percent. Restaurants and food service tend to be more important to business travelers who travel frequently, especially to women business travelers. Most women business travelers prefer to dine in their hotel rooms and were more likely to select hotels on the basis of extended-hour or 24-hour room service.
6. *Frequent traveler programs.* Hospitality firms have patterned their frequent traveler programs after the airlines' programs, which seek to develop loyalty by rewarding repeat customers. Hospitality firms' programs have doubled in the last ten years. One of the oldest, Marriott's Honored Guest Awards, has been replaced with Marriott's Rewards, a program offering points for every dollar spent in the hotel (and bonus points for car rentals and travel on participating airlines). Points can be redeemed for room nights or upgrades, air miles, destination bonuses (theater tickets and spa packages), and specially selected merchandise. It is expected that the use of frequent traveler programs, which generate more than $35 billion annually in revenue from all guests, will continue to rise as the trend toward brand loyalty continues.[2]

Business travelers can be divided into two general categories: frequent and occasional. Frequent business travelers are responsible for approximately 50 percent of all business generated by this market segment and are more easily targeted; therefore, in the following section we will focus on them. Occasional business travelers are typically "traveling salespeople" traveling on their own. To reach them, hotel salespeople should ask local corporate clients for referrals, since occasional business travelers are probably calling on many of the same corporations. Most of the programs and services developed for frequent business travelers are attractive to occasional business travelers as well.

Frequent Business Travelers

Frequent business travelers spend an average of 21 nights a year away from home on business, largely on sales trips, and use hotels or motels 76 percent of the time. They are typically employed in managerial, sales, or professional positions and are well-educated (67 percent hold four-year college degrees) and affluent (67 percent earn over $35,000 per year, while 44 percent earn more than $50,000 annually).[3] While this group is largely male, an increasing number of frequent business travelers are women. This statistic should lead to increased hotel revenues because women tend to use in-house food and beverage services more than men do.

Several independent surveys have helped hotels design services for frequent business travelers. A MasterCard survey,[4] for example, asked the question, "Assuming that the primary considerations of location, room price, and cleanliness were comparable, what other factors are most important in making a lodging selection?" The following factors are accompanied by the percentages of frequent business travelers who found them important:

Selling Economy Lodging to the Business Traveler

After the Marriott hotel chain took a look at the no-frills business traveler segment, it decided to provide a product that would meet the needs of business travelers who typically take six or more business trips per year, expect to pay $45 to $65 per night, and pay for their own lodging (no expense accounts).

The chain's economy product, Fairfield Inn, is the result of extensive independent research undertaken to determine the needs of economy-minded business travelers. As a result of the research, Fairfield Inn was developed to include a number of amenities requested by frugal business travelers while keeping its rates in the $45 to $65 range:

1. *King-size beds.* Room options include one king-size bed (preferred over queen-size beds) or two double beds.
2. *Free cable television.* Top-line cable programming was a preference; a satellite dish at each property brings in three premier cable channels (HBO, ESPN, and CNN) as well as local programming.
3. *Television remote controls.*
4. *Thick towels.* These were a top guest preference over the standard "postage-stamp-sized" towels found at other economy properties. Fairfield Inn's towels are the same as those found at more expensive Marriott properties.
5. *Free local phone calls.*
6. *A comfortable chair.* Recliners have complicated parts and are difficult to maintain, so upholstered chairs and ottomans are provided for relaxation.

- Restaurant on premises (32 percent)
- Quality service (22 percent)
- Room appointments (14 percent)
- Sports and recreational facilities (14 percent)
- Ambiance (11 percent)
- Entertainment on premises (10 percent)
- Prior knowledge (10 percent)
- Safety and security (3 percent)

The survey further revealed that there are three distinct groups of frequent business travelers: no-frills travelers, cost-plus travelers, and extroverted-affluent travelers. By studying the requirements of each group, you can create or revise amenities and services to attract one or all of them.

No-Frills Travelers. The largest group in the MasterCard survey (36 percent), **no-frills travelers,** is made up largely of middle- to upper-management men and

7. *Large desk.* Business travelers' rooms must also serve as work spaces, so Fairfield Inn provides large desks. Guests can spread out papers and still have plenty of room to work.
8. *Alarm clock.* Since many business travelers worry about missing a wake-up call, alarm clocks are provided along with the wake-up service option.
9. *Coffee and tea in the lobby.* Rather than providing the more expensive individual hot water dispenser, Fairfield Inn brews coffee and tea every morning and serves it in the lobby. This option gives guests a chance to circulate.
10. *Swimming pool.* Although swimming pools were included mainly for weekend leisure guests, business travelers may take advantage of this recreational option.
11. *Inside or outside room entry.* While some business travelers prefer the convenience of parking their cars next to their guestroom doors, others prefer the security of an inside entry. Fairfield Inn provides both types of guestrooms at all of their properties.
12. *Smoking or no-smoking rooms.* Again, guests requested a choice, so 25 percent of Fairfield Inn rooms are no-smoking.
13. *Long-cord telephones.* Long cords allow business travelers to make calls while working or moving around the guestroom.
14. *Separate vanity.* This amenity helps speed up morning activities if there are two or more people in a room.
15. *Meeting room.* A meeting room off the lobby is available on a first-come, first-served basis.
16. *Vending machines.* Vending machines provide snacks, juices, and soft drinks. Other machines dispense valet items that guests may have forgotten to bring.

In addition to marketing the physical amenities, stressing the quality of service is an important part of marketing Fairfield Inn properties to business and leisure travelers.

women primarily interested in a clean, comfortable, and quiet room at a fair price. No-frills travelers show little interest in hotel-sponsored social events. In fact, the businesspeople in this group are almost hermitlike in their business travels. They are not as interested as the other two groups in meeting people, staying where they are known, staying at fashionable hotels, or socializing.

To attract this segment, limited-service hotels, including La Quinta, Red Roof Inns, Hampton Inns, and Holiday Inn Express, are being built around the country. At these properties, which do offer some amenities (such as free breakfasts, free local telephone calls, and dataports in rooms), guests are not paying for large lobbies, room service, and other services and amenities they do not use. Another primary draw is consistency; guests know that they will get the same services and amenities at every property in the chain—at a savings of up to 20 percent over full-service hotels.[5]

Although they have higher budgets than cost-plus travelers, no-frills travelers are also likely to stay at budget properties. Properties that do not have facilities such as swimming pools, saunas, tennis courts, and putting greens, and properties that do not feature large bars or organized social activities have an excellent opportunity to attract this group. No-frills travelers were the only group to express a definite preference for a particular property atmosphere: quiet. Properties wishing to meet the needs of this group must convey a sense of peace and quiet.

Cost-Plus Travelers. This is the next-largest group of frequent business travelers (34 percent). Like no-frills travelers, these travelers are extremely cost conscious, often to the point of forgoing convenience in favor of a lower room rate. Although **cost-plus travelers**—typically salespeople and middle-management executives—are often on strict expense accounts, many pride themselves on their ability to find bargains, and they look for amenities at no-frills prices.

Cost-plus travelers are more interested in being sociable than no-frills travelers. A restaurant's operating hours, the availability of hospitality suites or lounges at which to meet peers, and no-cost amenities are important to cost-plus travelers. Doubletree seeks to appeal to these travelers by offering Doubletree Club Hotels. These hotels feature a Club Room that includes a café; a mini-office, called a Personal Harbor, for travelers who must get work done on the road; an Activity Table, for those who want to work on the Internet while having a drink and watching television; and a small meeting room that seats up to six people. These facilities are available at no charge to guests. Other hotel chains that target this segment are Marriott, Hilton, Holiday Inn, and Ramada.

Cost-plus travelers are generally more loyal or brand-oriented than the other two groups. Cost-plus travelers are more apt to belong to frequent traveler programs—both because of the value offered and because of their loyalty to a property. Although cost-plus travelers are more likely to stay in a mid-priced property on an interstate highway than in a first-class downtown hotel, they can be attracted to other properties if the price is right.

Extroverted-Affluent Travelers. This group, which made up 30 percent of the frequent business travelers in the MasterCard survey, holds the promise of generating higher sales per room than either of the other two groups. **Extroverted-affluent travelers** are typically young and affluent, and are either professionals, top-level executives, or self-employed. They are more likely to have travel agents or corporate travel managers book their reservations, and they demand the best in amenities and service.

Extroverted-affluent travelers are not concerned with saving money (either on business or pleasure trips) and demand fashionable properties. More than the other two groups, extroverted-affluent travelers put a high priority on amenities. Recreation facilities, live entertainment, and restaurants offering the finest decor and cuisine are important to them, and having a good time is more important than the expense. This group is also more likely to add vacation time to a business stay.

While these travelers make their own decisions when selecting a property, they are more likely to be influenced by the suggestions of friends and colleagues than any other group. They generally prefer such chains as Four Seasons, Ritz-Carlton, and Hyatt, or boutique hotels such as Starwood's W Hotels; these hotels offer the extra services and amenities they want.

Women Business Travelers

Women are an important segment of the business traveler market. This segment has grown at a phenomenal rate: while women made up only one percent of the business traveler segment in 1970, today they account for 45 percent of business travelers. Women already constitute 50 percent of business meeting attendees and 51 percent of all meeting planners; therefore, hotels and restaurants should take a close look at the wants and needs of these travelers.

Although businesswomen express many of the same preferences (location, rates, etc.) when making a hotel selection as their male counterparts, they appreciate different things when they travel. A survey conducted by Pennsylvania State University for Baymont Hotels found that security is the top consideration for 86 percent of all women travelers, and the cleanliness and attractiveness of properties are other important factors in booking. In contrast, these factors were important to only half of male business travelers.[6]

Since women tend to be more loyal repeat guests than men, it is especially important that a property provide the features most important to women travelers:

1. *Security.* Security-conscious women tend to comparison-shop hotels for security features, and most women consider door chains, dead bolt locks, and door "viewports" or "peepholes" essential guestroom features. Many women prefer hotels with both a single entrance close to the front desk and an atrium, where all rooms open into a central, well-lit area. Women also prefer hotels that feature an inside restaurant, room service, and a well-lit lobby. Valet parking or a brightly lit parking garage are other security essentials.

   A property can add to a woman's feeling of security by following the security procedures that are in place for all guests, such as making sure front desk agents, restaurant staff, and valet parkers do not call out room numbers; refusing to give out room numbers to callers or visitors; and instructing bell staff to leave the guestroom door open and check the room before leaving the guest. Of course, proper guestroom key control is a must.

2. *Comfort and service.* Women, like men, appreciate clean, attractive, well-lit rooms and friendly, courteous service. Amenities such as full-length mirrors and skirt hangers are popular with women. Exhibit 1 lists the amenities most popular with women business travelers.

   Women are more influenced by good service than men; an unsatisfactory experience in this area will irritate women business travelers and make them less likely to return. Hotel staff should be trained to treat women in a courteous and businesslike manner. Many women will react negatively to overly familiar terms such as *honey* and *dear.*

3. *Convenience.* Most businesswomen prefer to have a space set aside in their guestrooms for work or meetings (at the very least, they should have a desk with a telephone and good lighting). This is one reason suites are finding increased popularity with women—the bed is in a separate room, away from the business area. When suites are not available, foldaway beds are sometimes used, although these meet with mixed reactions.

Exhibit 1 Amenities for Women Business Travelers

1. Twenty-four-hour room service
2. Laundry service and one-hour emergency pressing
3. Well-lit desk space
4. A morning newspaper and the opportunity to order breakfast via room service the previous night
5. Shampoo, detergent, and sewing kits
6. Upgraded lighting in bathrooms
7. Lighted makeup mirrors, hair dryers, and irons and ironing boards
8. Additional electrical outlets for grooming appliances
9. Adequate closet space, and closet bars hung high enough to accommodate formal gowns
10. Skirt hangers and full-length mirrors
11. Sufficient towels and washcloths
12. Twenty-four-hour fitness and sauna services
13. Concierge floor lounges
14. Spa services

While women business travelers cite the same general preferences for selecting a hotel (location, cleanliness, etc.) as their male counterparts, they have different requirements when it comes to amenities.

4. *Facilities.* Because women tend to stay on the property more than men do, facilities such as swimming pools and fitness equipment are attractive to them. Sixty percent of women consider hotel exercise facilities desirable, compared with 34 percent of men.[7] And since more women business travelers are traveling with children, they give properties that can provide facilities and programs for accompanying family members prime consideration. Women business travelers also prefer hotels that provide a café or bistro atmosphere rather than a sports bar or lounge environment—and they look for healthy food choices. Spa-type menus that include organically grown fruits and vegetables, meats from organically fed animals, free-range poultry, and whole-grain breads are becoming increasingly popular.

Not only will women soon account for half of frequent business trips (worth an estimated $160 billion) in the near future, but they can also be expected to generate more than $20 billion in leisure travel in the coming years. And since businesswomen take more mini-vacations than businessmen, typically spend 25 percent more in restaurants than male business travelers, and often meet with associates while at the property, it is important that properties provide the security, comfort, and service that will appeal to this growing market segment.

MARKETING IN ACTION

"Women on Their Way" by Wyndham

When Wyndham International recognized that more women were traveling on business, it began a program to target women business travelers by meeting their special needs. As with any successful marketing effort, Wyndham's "Women on Their Way" program began with research; the chain held a contest devised by Wyndham's public relations firm. The question, "What's your most important travel tip?" generated an overwhelming response and led to the formation of a special website (www.womenontheirway.com) and an advisory board that determined and addressed the needs of women business travelers.

Cary Jehl Broussard is vice president of marketing for the "Women on Their Way" program. Under her direction, the program partnered with other organizations for women, including the Susan G. Komen Breast Cancer Foundation, the National Association of Women Business Owners, the National Association of Female Business Executives, and ivillage.com to provide additional input for the program and more networking opportunities for women.

Thanks to the insights gathered through its "Women on Their Way" program, Wyndham has made giant strides in its services and amenities for women. For example, based on input from its advisory board, Wyndham now offers a pre-call from room service five minutes before food is delivered to guestrooms, to ensure that the guest is prepared. Other services include lighter fare on room service menus, improved bath and in-room amenities, and libraries where women can go to relax instead of having to sit in a bar. Services planned for the future include special TV exercise programs in guestrooms and assistance with personal business while on the road.

The "Women on Their Way" program enabled Wyndham to increase its share of this lucrative market segment. The chain is now the leader among the women business traveler segment, serving 59 percent more women business travelers than its competitors. Its response to meeting the needs of women business travelers is being increasingly emulated by other properties, which are now offering such amenities and services as personal escorts to guestrooms, women's magazines in guestrooms, and special programs for working mothers.

Sources: Robyn Taylor Parets, "Industry Leaders Who's Who," *Lodging,* May 2000, p. 45; "The Road Warriors," *ICP,* January/February 2000, p. 23; "Sol Melia Enhances Women Business Traveler Services," *World Hospitality,* June 2000, p. 10; "Women Equal Windfall for Wyndham; Program Garners $300M Plus in Revenues," *HotelBusiness,* September 21–October 6, 2002, p. 58.

Meeting the Needs of Business Travelers

Properties are meeting the needs of business travelers in a number of unique ways. Some hotels have introduced women-only floors, but these have met with mixed reviews; many women prefer not to be segregated. Other amenities and services developed to appeal to business travelers include executive or business floors, business centers, health and fitness centers, high-tech and other special amenities, in-room refreshment centers, frequent traveler programs, and all-suite/extended-stay properties. Most of these amenities and services have met with wide approval, especially the concept of executive or business floors, and we will take a closer look at each of them in the following sections.

Executive or Club Floors. Properties that cater to a number of markets often find themselves in a quandary when it comes to providing the services needed by different types of travelers. There are two possible solutions to this dilemma: build new properties designed specifically for a targeted group (as was done by Wingate) or modify existing properties to accommodate the needs of particular segments. In many cases, the latter was found to be the more cost-efficient solution, leading firms to create "a hotel within a hotel." Peter Banks, the general manager of New York's highly successful Rihga Royal Hotel, explains his effective hotel-within-a-hotel segmentation strategy this way:

> We had to segment the market. If we tried to make the hotel upscale-upscale, there was not enough business at those high rates to fill us up. If we wanted to take it down low, then we could fill it up but we wouldn't generate enough revenue to pay the mortgage. What we had to do was segment the market and come up with different products for those segments. The 50 Pinnacle Suites on the top floors of the hotel, targeted to the upper market tier, have more amenities, such as chauffeur-driven limousines, cellular phones, private phone lines, suite faxes, etc. The mid-tier Imperial Suites, from the middle of the hotel to the 43rd floor, appeal to an upscale business market; while they have fewer amenities than the Pinnacle Suites, they have pagers, faxes, and CD and stereo tape players, among other amenities. Royal Suites are the standard accommodation marketed to the corporate market on a contract basis at a fixed rate.[8]

The major chains are staunch promoters of the concept of "a hotel within a hotel"; the Sheraton and Hilton chains offer Tower Sections, Hyatt developed a Regency Club, and Marriott created a Concierge Level. These facilities have proven extremely popular, especially with upscale guests, who appreciate having a club or floor reserved exclusively for their use, and with business travelers, who appreciate having the services they need conveniently available.

Executive floors or club floors are designed to provide a secure, comfortable environment in which to meet peers, conduct business, or relax after a busy day. These floors, which require a key to gain access, offer areas in which business travelers can work as well as special lounge areas where cocktails and continental breakfasts are served. Although guests on club floors pay a premium rate, services and amenities vary, which has led to the introduction of new club floor formats that enable properties to promote these floors as a "hotel-within-a-hotel" and worth the price.

Club floors are being increasingly marketed to three major niche markets: women, GenXers, and families. Women business travelers see club floors as secure and private places to meet with clients or just relax with a drink. GenXers prefer to work and socialize in public spaces rather than stay in their rooms. Business travelers who are accompanied by their families realize the increased value of the free breakfasts and other amenities offered on club floors. (It is important to note that some business travelers prefer club floors because there are fewer children, but many families make use of club floor lounge facilities on weekends, when there are fewer individual business travelers.)

INTERNET EXERCISE

Log onto the Internet and visit the following websites:

- Fairmont Royal York (www.fairmont.com/royalyork)
- Peabody Orlando (www.peabodyorlando.com)
- Sheraton Hotel and Towers Chicago (www.sheratonchicago.com)

Compare the club floors of each hotel and answer the following questions:

1. What specialized services and amenities are offered by each property?
2. Approximately how much are customers charged to stay on the club floors of these hotels?

The Hilton Towers Concierge Class offers express registration, complimentary breakfasts and refreshments, evening turndown service, a daily newspaper, and an exclusive lounge for executive travelers. Other products catering to this market include the Holiday Inn Crown Plaza's Club Executive Floor and the Ritz-Carlton's Club Level. The Club Floor at the Biltmore Hotel in Los Angeles offers a library, television center, game room, billiard room, and bar.

New amenities that are being introduced for executive or club floors include the allergen-free environment at Wyndham hotels (Wyndham charges 5 to 25 percent extra for these club rooms); free wireless Internet and a Microsoft Surface tabletop computer that allows guests to order songs or download photos on Sheraton club floors; and numerous new food options—Hilton has launched late-night food and drink offerings for its club floors, while the Ritz-Carlton is offering free lunch foods. The new club lounge at the San Francisco Ritz-Carlton has a fireplace and an automated cappuccino machine, and its amenities range from the free use of iPods to pet-walking services.

Executive floors or clubs require special promotion. Hotels use direct mail, press releases and other forms of publicity, and advertisements in magazines and newspapers such as the *Wall Street Journal* to reach upscale business travelers. Exhibit 2 shows an example of an ad promoting executive floors. Word-of-mouth referrals and personal calls on corporations have also generated business for these special floors. Properties hope these floors will help change the image of businesspeople from harried travelers to pampered executives relaxing in facilities as comfortable and secure as their own homes.

Business Centers. Most major hotels find that having an on-site business center is a competitive must; while many business travelers like to work in their rooms, others prefer not to work and sleep in the same room. Business centers vary in terms of services, but most offer secretarial services, fax machines, modems, and photocopying equipment; others provide computer rentals, administrative services, and even private offices that can be rented on a daily or hourly basis. Some are staffed 24 hours a day, while others are accessible for self-service after hours.

It is interesting to note that while business travelers expect properties to have business centers, they do not always use them when they are available. Since the

Exhibit 2 Executive Floors and Clubs for Business Travelers

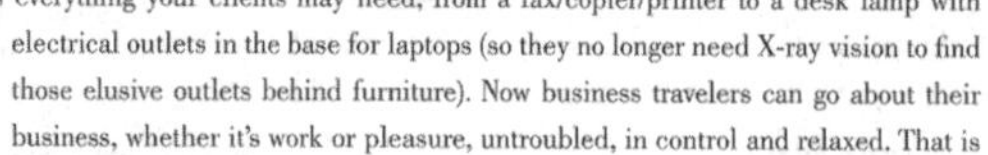

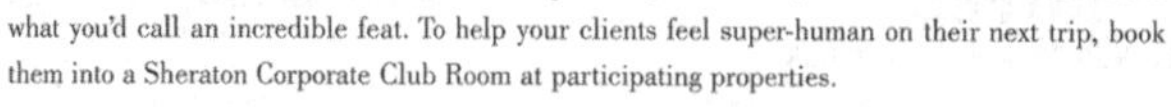

Monday, April 14, 1997 **7**

Many chains, such as ITT Sheraton, have introduced special executive floors or clubs for business travelers. This ad promotes the chain's Corporate Club Room, which offers business amenities that include a fax/copier/printer and a desk lamp with electrical outlets in the base to enable the businessperson to plug in his or her laptop computer. Other amenities commonly offered include large work desks, business supplies and services, and personal amenities such as terry robes, turndown services, and free newspapers and coffee. (Courtesy of Sheraton)

cost of equipping and staffing business centers may outweigh the need for them, an increasing number of hotels are outsourcing these services. Chains such as Hilton and Marriott have contracted with business service firms including Kinko's, Office Depot, Pitney Bowes, and Executive Express to offer business services on-site or close to their properties. In many cases, these firms can offer services at a price far lower than what hotels otherwise would have charged.

Health and Fitness Centers. An increased awareness of stress—and its impact on productivity—has led many business travelers to pursue more healthy lifestyles, including dietary changes and a commitment to regular exercise. While properties have offered the standard swimming pool for years, it is not unusual today for properties catering to business travelers to offer a complete array of exercise options. These may include tennis courts, jogging trails, or complete health clubs featuring state-of-the-art exercise equipment, whirlpools and saunas, and even exercise instruction or personal training.

Hyatt Hotels has launched its StayFit@Hyatt program, which offers the latest in cardio and strength equipment, exercise programs, a comprehensive yoga program, and knowledgeable support staff at its properties across North America and in the Caribbean. The workout programs, which are consistent throughout the chain, enable business travelers to adhere to the workout routines they have been accustomed to at home so they can stay in shape while on the road. Westin Hotels took the exercise concept a step further with its Westin WORKOUT Room—guestrooms that are equipped with either a Reebok Tomahawk XL Indoor Cycle or a Life Fitness Treadmill as well as other equipment, including adjustable dumbbells, a stability ball, yoga mats, and other Reebok workout equipment. WORKOUT Rooms, which start at an additional $20 above standard rooms, also feature in-room health and fitness reading material as well as guides to nearby running and jogging routes.

High-Tech Amenities. When business travelers come to town, they don't come to relax; they come to do business. Therefore, properties that cater to this market should provide an environment conducive to conducting business. Not only do many business travelers spend one to two hours a day working in their hotel rooms, they increasingly travel with laptop computers, cellular phones, pagers, and other high-tech devices. Therefore, hotels that wish to attract business travelers must offer the right mix of amenities to help these guests conduct business more efficiently. A study featured in the *HSMAI Marketing Review* identified the technology amenities and other business services most desired by business travelers (see Exhibit 3).

While some guestroom business amenities, such as work areas and data ports, have been offered for some time, properties are continually developing new amenities to meet the needs of today's business guests. At the 190-room Nine Zero in Boston, for example, the property was determined to put an end to a "pet peeve" of guests—having to crawl under tables to unplug telephones to access lines for their laptop computers and fax machines. The property responded with in-room work spaces with oversized desks, ergonomic chairs, and flip-top access to high-speed Internet and dataport connections—all within reach of an easy-to-use printer/fax machine, CD player, and large TV.[9]

Exhibit 3 Technology Amenities and Business Services Desired by Business Travelers

In order of importance: 1 = Not important at all, 2 = A little important, 3 = Somewhat important, 4 = Important, 5 = Very important

Amenity/Service	Rating
In-room temperature controls	4.51
Easily accessible electrical outlets	4.32
Alarm clock	4.25
Remote control TV	4.19
Phone on desk	4.16
Additional data line accessible to desk	4.01
Electronic key cards	3.56
High-speed Internet access	3.55
Express check-in/check-out	3.53
Voice-mail	3.50
Business center	3.46
In-room coffee maker	3.38
Central 800 reservation number	3.31
Online reservation capability	3.27
Automatic teller machine at hotel	3.08
Extended information about hotel online	3.07
Portable/speaker phone in room	2.91
Smart card read capability	2.76
Wireless Internet access in hotel	2.68
Pay per view	2.44
Video conferencing capabilities	2.41
In-room personal computer	2.27
In-room printer	2.27
In-room fax machine	2.15
Wireless access to hotel website	2.10
Web TV	2.00

Source: F. J. Demicco, C. Cobanoglu, and M. Cetron, "Balancing High-Tech and High-Touch Hospitality," *HSMAI Marketing Review,* Spring 2003.

Another popular service offered to business travelers is technical assistance. Tim Aubrey, vice president of technology at Fairmont Hotels & Resorts, says that "Fairmont takes direct responsibility for offering, delivering, and supporting guests' technological needs. Most of our guests use the network for real business purposes and tend to be online for hours, not just minutes. They are working as effectively in our hotel rooms as they would be in their own offices."[10] To minimize technical problems that can interfere with efficiency, the chain offers a complimentary 24-hour "Fairmont Virtual Assistant," a technical-support hotline manned by each property's IT staff. Problems that cannot be handled at the property level are referred to system managers at other properties. Technical support services are also offered by other hotel chains, such as InterContinental, which developed

CyberAssist to provide guests with technical expertise in a wide range of areas—from problems with e-mail systems to eliminating computer viruses.

Marriott Hotels & Resorts, which offers 32-inch LCD high-definition televisions and the only digital plug-in panel in the hospitality industry, took a different approach to assisting guests with their high-tech amenities. The chain developed an advertising campaign that combined live-action and computer-generated images to demonstrate how to use their new guestroom technology. The campaign featured three 15-second television spots that demonstrated how guests could use the combination TV and plug-in panel to connect their laptops to the monitor, split the screen to watch TV and work simultaneously, play their own music through the system's 25-watt speakers, view their digital pictures, and play videos from camcorders.

Guestroom amenities most requested by business travelers include multiple phone lines and enhanced work areas with oversized desks, comfortable chairs, and adequate lighting. Properties wishing to attract business travelers have responded with some or all of these amenities, and most major hotel chains now promote guestrooms designed specifically for business travelers.

Other Special Amenities. Premium-quality mattresses, upgraded linens and bedding, and high-definition flat-screen televisions in guestrooms are among business travelers' most wanted amenities. Other special amenities appreciated by business travelers include complimentary copies of newspapers (including the local daily paper and the *Wall Street Journal*), free coffee and tea, express check-in and check-out (some properties now offer automated check-in and the ability to check out via in-room TV), and free cellular phones or beepers. Luxury properties are offering such amenities as poolside computer rentals, in-room exercise equipment, and direct baggage check-in from the airport to accommodate their business travelers.

Complimentary Breakfasts and In-Room Refreshment Centers. Today's business travelers rate complimentary breakfasts among their top "perks." A full American breakfast included in the room rate is preferred, although continental breakfasts are also perceived as an added value.

While **in-room refreshment centers** (also called *minibars*) have been standard amenities in European hotels for many years, only relatively recently have U.S. properties offered this convenient—and highly profitable—service to guests. Minibars, which a hotel can purchase or lease, provide a convenient way for guests to refresh themselves or entertain in the comfort of their rooms. Favorite minibar items include light beer, spring water, soft drinks, peanuts, and Scotch. Other items, such as juices, snack foods, and other mixers and liquors are usually stocked as well. Minibars are often linked to the hotel's computerized billing system for immediate posting of charges.

Frequent Traveler Programs. The growing number of business travelers has also prompted the development of frequent traveler programs. InterContinental Hotels Group offers Priority Club, Hyatt Hotels has Gold Passport, Starwood offers Preferred Guest, and there are also Marriott's Rewards, Ramada's Business Card, and Hilton's HHonors, to name just a few. These loyalty programs offer a wide variety of

INTERNET EXERCISE

Log onto the Internet and visit the following hotel web pages that feature frequent traveler reward programs:

- Marriott Rewards (www.marriottrewards.com)
- Hilton HHonors (www.hiltonhhonors.com)
- Starwood's Preferred Guest (www.spg.com)

1. Which program is the newest of the three?
2. Which of these hotel companies has the fewest number of hotels worldwide? Which represents the most brands?
3. How many different levels of membership are offered by each program?
4. What is the policy of each in regard to point expiration?
5. Most hotel loyalty programs partner with such other service providers as airlines, cruise lines, and car rental firms. Which of these three programs participates with the fewest number of service partners?

benefits to their members, such as discounts, premiums, and special hotel services. Business traveler membership in frequent traveler programs totals in the millions.

While many frequent traveler programs are available at no cost to guests, some chains charge a nominal membership fee to cover start-up costs. Chains and properties often offer elite levels in their frequent traveler programs to pamper their upscale customers; those on elite levels (usually 5 percent or less of frequent travelers) enjoy such amenities as complimentary upgrades to suites, private club rooms, and complimentary transportation to the airport.

All-Suite/Extended-Stay Properties. When they were first introduced, all-suite properties were designed to provide an alternative to hotels with traditional guestrooms. The two-room suites, featuring a living room and a separate sleeping room, were typically larger than guestrooms and provided an environment (a room other than a bedroom) that lent itself to doing business. In addition, the suite was perceived as a better value than a traditional guestroom and was favored by women business travelers and travelers who were staying for several nights.

Over time, these properties proved ideal for extended-stay travelers (those staying five nights or more) and relocating employees and executives. Extended-stay travelers appreciated the extra room and the convenience of a full kitchen, and were further courted with special weekly and monthly rates. The relocation market was a natural for this type of room arrangement, and the demand for "all the comforts of home with the convenience of a hotel" led to the development of properties designed specifically for extended-stay guests.

The relocation market differs from the extended-stay market in that relocating guests intend to stay in the area permanently. Studies have shown that uprooted employees can lose productivity and suffer from emotional stress, so those who design extended-stay properties must take steps to soothe guests' fears and to make their transition into their new environment less stressful. Residence Inn, an upscale property that caters to the relocation market, has identified four areas of importance to today's transferees and their families:[11]

1. *A homelike atmosphere.* A homelike atmosphere is important to 58 percent of this market segment. These travelers want a peaceful introduction to their new city and want to be able to come "home" to relax. Most suites, therefore, are equipped with full kitchens and the amenities typically found in a home.
2. *Residential-style housing.* Buildings that look residential are important to 36 percent of this segment. Residence Inn meets this need by offering both single-story studios and two-story townhouses, designed together as a neighborhood surrounded by landscaping and recreational facilities.
3. *Price.* Of those surveyed, 32 percent listed price as an important consideration. Residence Inn's suites are priced competitively with hotels and offer a sliding-rate scale based on the length of stay. In response to increasing demand for mid-priced properties, Choice Hotels now offers MainStay and Marriott offers TownePlace Suites, a mid-priced alternative to its upscale Residence Inns.
4. *Reduced relocation stress.* Residence Inn helps lessen relocation stress by offering grocery-shopping services, arranging for baby-sitters, and providing orientation activities; Hawthorn Suites offers free breakfast buffets and hospitality hours and free daily newspapers in addition to grocery-shopping services; and Homewood Suites offers continental breakfasts and evening social hours. In addition, properties can help by providing "libraries" of local information (brochures, fact sheets, etc.) and knowledgeable staffs that can answer guests' questions.

When striving to meet the needs of relocation guests and other business travelers, it is important to remember that this busy guest is not simply interested in amenities; he or she is primarily concerned with avoiding hassles. Business travelers want to get their jobs done without having annoyances and frustrations get in the way. Business travelers are not just paying for a room; they are paying for a hassle-free working environment.

Reaching Business Travelers

Business travelers are relatively easy to locate. Some, in fact, might be vacationers staying at the property who will be traveling on business sometime during the year. But in today's competitive market, you cannot rely on repeat guests or word-of-mouth referrals to reach business travelers. You must actively solicit specific business-traveler market segments. Properties must first find out who makes business reservations, and then target those sources.

Surprisingly, over 60 percent of business travelers make their own reservations—and a growing number of these reservations are being made via the Internet. Peter Yesawich, in a speech to the Best Value Inns lodging chain, stated that almost six out of ten business travelers say they use the Internet to plan some aspect of their business trips. Therefore, developing a website, dedicating a portion of your website to business travelers, and advertising on websites frequented by business travelers can be effective ways to reach potential business guests.

Frequent Traveler Programs: Do They Really Build Loyalty?

Guest loyalty is very important to hotels, especially in today's highly competitive market. It takes fewer marketing dollars to maintain customers than to cultivate new ones, but loyalty is difficult to achieve. Many business travelers don't travel enough to form brand preferences; others have lodging decisions made by corporate travel departments. Still others are limited in their lodging choices by budget constraints.

Hotel chains have increasingly wooed desirable guests—business travelers who travel extensively, have expense accounts, and aren't terribly price-sensitive—with frequent traveler programs. Nearly all of the major hotel chains have some form of frequent traveler reward program, but are these costly programs more cost-efficient or more likely to build loyalty than guest recognition programs?

Rewards programs have become routinely expected by business travelers. Peter Blyth, president of Radisson Development Worldwide, says, "We are in a situation now where if you do not have a reward program you are at risk. The question is how effective it is. We believe that the offering we have is unique. Yet uniqueness is a claim made for their programs by all major players. An objective must be to capture guests into collection programs early in their traveling careers so that they are loath to abandon uncollected points by switching to another hotel group."

Blyth points out one of the problems of rewards programs—they are no longer points of differentiation for hotels. While rewards programs may generate some loyalty, research has shown that most business travelers have multiple frequent-guest memberships. Therefore, many industry professionals question the long-term value of rewards programs, which are designed to buy customer loyalty rather than earn it.

Earning loyalty means building meaningful personal relationships with guests. "Customer relationship management" through data-mining travelers' preferences can be expensive and time-consuming, but it has proved to be more effective for building guest loyalty. Many business travelers find recognition more important than getting awards, and they will remain loyal to hotels and restaurants that recognize them as individuals.

Sources: Jonathan Hart, "Global Hotel Strategies," *Financial Times,* 1999, p. 100; Ken W. McCleary and Pamela A. Weaver, "Are Frequent-Guest Programs Effective?" *Cornell Hotel and Restaurant Administration Quarterly,* Vol. 32, No. 2 (August 1991): p. 45; and Ed Watkins, "Service, Not Points, Builds Guest Loyalty," *Lodging Hospitality,* September 18, 2004.

Business-traveler business can also be obtained from corporations in the immediate vicinity of your property. Local corporations are often the sources of national business from traveling salespeople or state, regional, and national meetings. These corporations can be identified through a number of sources:

- Office building locator boards
- Chamber of commerce listings

The Extended-Stay Market at a Glance

Extended-stay properties are attractive to two market segments: business travelers who want "more than a room," and the relocation market. Extended-stay hotels, with their separate living rooms, complimentary "perks" such as breakfasts and cocktail hours, and homey atmospheres serve as "temporary residences" and are especially attractive because their features are available at rates comparable with standard hotel rooms.

Accommodations: Extended-stay accommodations are typically larger than most conventional guestrooms. Extended-stay units generally offer combined living/working areas, separate bedrooms, and kitchenettes. Work areas are equipped with desks, ergonomic chairs, and telephone lines (some offer a personalized direct telephone number). Accommodation options can range from a deluxe studio to a two-bedroom/two-bath unit.

Amenities: Typical amenities include an on-site business center, daily complimentary breakfast, complimentary evening manager's reception, on-site laundry facilities, and recreational amenities. Some properties offer full kitchens fully stocked with essentials such as dishes, cutlery, and linens. On-site 24-hour convenience stores can be found at some extended-stay hotels. Other services, such as grocery shopping services and child care, are also available, usually at upscale extended-stay properties.

Pricing: There are three pricing tiers for extended-stay properties:

Upscale ($500+ per week)—Hawthorn Suites, Homewood Suites by Hilton, Residence Inn by Marriott, Staybridge Suites by Holiday Inn.

Mid-price ($250–$500 weekly)—Candlewood Suites, Extended StayAmerica, Homestead StudioSuites Hotels, MainStay, Summerfield Suites by Hyatt, TownePlace Suites by Marriott.

(continued)

(continued)

Economy (less than $250 weekly)—Budget Suites, Crossland Economy Studios, Hearthside by Villager, Studio 6, Villager Premier.

Average Length of Stay: Five to 14 nights, 75 percent; 15 to 28 nights, 16 percent; over 28 nights, 9 percent.

Demographics: Male, 64 percent; Female, 36 percent; average age, 46; average household income, $67,200.

Market Growth: Extended-stay occupancy was 72.4 percent in 2007, a rate about nine percent higher than the occupancy rate of the hotel industry overall. It is projected that some 295,500 extended-stay guestrooms will be available in the near future.

Marketing: With the varying concepts and services offered by extended-stay properties, it is important to position your property to appeal to particular target markets. A complex designed as a residential community, for example, would be more attractive to the relocation market than to a business traveler looking for a comfortable working environment. Business travelers would probably find a property that offers meeting rooms and a business center more appealing.

- Competitors' function boards
- Local newspaper articles
- State and regional publicity materials

Business travelers throughout the nation can be targeted by obtaining the names of corporations and decision-makers through:

- Business publications and directories
- Travel publications
- State industrial commissions
- Mailing list brokers
- National trade conventions

Potential business leads obtained through these sources should first be screened to determine market potential before any costly sales efforts are initiated. This screening may be done in the form of a direct mail questionnaire or a telemarketing survey, and a computer can be used to categorize responses.

As in all sales efforts, a direct approach will probably be the most effective for reaching potential business guests. You may employ sales letters, telephone calls, and even personal sales calls. Some properties locate a potentially profitable area and use a sales blitz to saturate the market and obtain business. A sales blitz can be effective if it is properly planned and monitored and if collateral materials, follow-up information, and personal contact supplement the blitz. Microtel Inns & Suites, for example, developed a program called "Everybody Sells," in which teams from Microtel's corporate office visited each property for a few days to develop business through a sales blitz. Using contact lists developed from a variety of sources, the teams, sometimes accompanied by hotel managers and front desk agents, made cold calls on corporate entities and coached hotel personnel on selling and follow up. While not all the calls resulted in business, the blitz increased revenues and name recognition for the individual properties, and the information gathered was entered into the company's database to be used for future direct mail and telemarketing campaigns.

In addition to contacting business travelers directly, properties can reach business travelers through these sources:

- Corporate travel managers
- Secretaries' clubs
- Travel agents
- Tour operators
- Real estate agents and relocation services
- Independent hotel representatives in key feeder cities

Corporate travel managers often plan travel for company executives and are excellent sources of referral business. The job of a corporate travel manager is to research the market, plan travel for employees, and book travel arrangements. According to a study for the *Hotel & Travel Index,* more than half of hotel bookings made for company employees are made directly by corporate travel managers.[12]

The corporate travel manager is also often responsible for negotiating rates with hotels. While most hotels offer a corporate rate of 10 to 15 percent off their rack rates, large corporations can negotiate their own volume rates with hotels. Large firms that will provide a large number of room nights may receive a "corporate contract" rate that can average 15 to 35 percent off rack rates.

It is especially important to build relationships with corporate travel managers. One study found that 65 percent of corporate travel managers say their relationship with a salesperson is "very important" when selecting hospitality properties. In fact, the survey showed that if their hotel contact moved to a new property, 13 percent of corporate travel managers would "definitely" be more likely to steer their business to the new property, and another 60 percent would consider doing so if the new property met their needs.[13] Hotel salespeople, therefore, should maintain direct contact with their property's current base of corporate travel managers, and seek out potential new business by making personal contact with other corporate travel managers or by attending conferences and trade shows for this lucrative source of group business.

Many corporate travel managers are members of such professional organizations as the National Business Travel Association (NBTA) and the Association of Corporate Travel Executives (ACTE). Both NBTA and ACTE have memberships of more than 2,000 corporate travel managers representing over 400 corporations and business organizations and may prove to be excellent sources of business leads. Hotel and restaurant marketers wishing to reach these corporate travel managers may join both associations as allied members.

Secretaries' clubs are another effective way to reach business travelers. Secretaries often serve as travel intermediaries and decision-makers, and creating a club to let them know that they are appreciated can build repeat business. These clubs are primarily social organizations and offer such perks as quarterly appreciation luncheons, flowers on the members' birthdays, and other incentives to secretaries who refer guests to the property. Many properties offer discounts on amenities at the property, free room nights, and other property-related rewards for members who book certain volumes of room nights. The Sheraton Meridian's Inn-Siders Club, for example, offers discounted food and drink tickets, the use of recreational facilities, and quarterly prizes to secretaries who provide the most bookings.

Travel agents and tour operators influence the lodging choices of many business and leisure travelers. Real estate agents and relocation services may be sources for leads regarding people in the local community who will be moving or people new to the community who need a place to stay temporarily. Independent hotel representatives may serve to build both new and repeat business.

Properties can also target business travelers through advertising, promotion at trade shows, and public relations and publicity. In some cases, chains promote their properties nationally. In others, chains provide resources for promotion and advertising on a property-by-property basis. Homewood Suites by Hilton, for example, has developed an on-line Marketing Tool Kit that provides media strategies, internal brand marketing programs, and custom print advertisements that maintain the chain's standards and create a consistent look for promotions by individual properties.

Advertising can take a number of forms, depending on the business traveler segment you are targeting. Print advertising can be especially effective (see Exhibit 4), as long as ads are designed to show benefits and amenities that will attract the targeted segment: no-frills approaches for the no-frills traveler, elegance and impeccable service for the extroverted-affluent traveler, and cleanliness and security for the female business traveler. Ads can be placed in local newspapers, regional newspapers of targeted cities, business and trade magazines, and travel and in-flight magazines. Two widely read magazines that target the business traveler are *Business Travel News* and *Corporate and Incentive Travel.* Another advertising option is the *OAG Business Travel Planner* (see Exhibit 5), a hotel directory targeted to frequent business travelers. This guide offers both directory listing and display advertising options and is used extensively by both individual travelers and travel planners.

You can use billboards to attract business travelers on the road and direct mail promotions to promote to specific market segments. One direct-mail strategy that has proven effective is to send periodic newsletters to individual business travelers and corporate planners. La Quinta expanded on that concept by sending quarterly audiotapes titled *Travel Companion* to frequent business travelers; the 40-minute tapes offer property information as well as travel tips, financial advice, and interviews with business celebrities. You can also use radio and television spots to reach business travelers. Television is used primarily by the larger chains. Radio is most effective at reaching businesspeople during the early morning and late-afternoon drive times and on all-news stations.

Exhibit 4 Sample Print Ad Targeting Business Travelers

It isn't just a face lift. It's a whole new kind of Holiday Inn® hotel.

We've designed it to cater specifically to business travelers. With large, comfortable work areas. Two phones with voice mail and dataport. In-room coffee makers, irons and ironing boards. Daily newspaper delivery. Fitness centers. Support services. Executive Edition® rooms with extras like complimentary continental breakfasts and in-room fax machines. Everything your executive travelers need to take care of business, or to forget about it for a while.

So look for Holiday Inn Select℠ hotels in more than 50 U.S., Canadian and Latin American business markets.

It's the new hotel for business travelers who need a better place to do business. And for travel planners who know a good thing when they see one.

Inn Keeping With The Times℠

For reservations, contact your travel counselor or call

1-800-HOLIDAY

HTTP://WWW.HOLIDAY-INN.COM

Many Holiday Inn hotels that had a strong corporate base have been converted to Holiday Inn Select hotels, which were created specifically for business travelers. This print ad, detailing the Holiday Inn Select hotels' business amenities and services, is directed to individual business travelers as well as travel planners. (Courtesy of Holiday Inns, Inc.)

Exhibit 5 Reaching Business Travelers through Directories

Hotels can reach business travelers through listings and display advertising in guides such as the *OAG Business Travel Planner*, which are often used by business travelers when making travel decisions. Note that this is the North American edition; separate editions are published to assist business travelers traveling abroad. Travel guides can be excellent advertising vehicles for chains with international locations, especially since domestic travelers are likely to be familiar with the chain name.

Trade shows can be excellent opportunities to promote a hotel's facilities and services to businesspeople. Trade shows are most often used to reach association and corporate meeting planners.

Public relations and publicity are also excellent ways to reach the business community. You can get publicity for expansions, promotions within various departments, and announcements of special business plans or amenities. Crowne Plaza Hotels & Resorts, for example, received extensive publicity when the chain launched its Sleep Advantage program, which was designed in response to a survey that found that more than half of business travelers don't get enough sleep while on the road. The Sleep Advantage program's goal was to help business travelers perform their best while away from home, and the chain's solution—which included new bedding, guaranteed wake-up calls, designated quiet zones, night lights, drape clips, sleep CDs, sleep tips, and amenities such as eye masks, ear plugs, and lavender spray—was widely publicized in industry magazines and online.

Public relations efforts can include sponsoring a business seminar, donating money for business scholarships, or organizing a "Career Day" at which representatives from a variety of businesses meet with students. Working relationships with the business community can also be cultivated with special "Business Appreciation Days," receptions or tours, and special discount rates for food and beverages, health club facilities, or other recreational amenities.

Conclusion

While business travelers spend billions of dollars annually for transportation, accommodations, and meals, studies have shown that business travelers are still faced with confusion—and a good deal of misinformation—due to today's many travel choices. A study conducted by Marriott Business Travel Institute (MBTI) found that many business travelers didn't know what services were offered in a number of hotels, or that airlines offer over one million fare choices (with over 160,000 of them changing daily). To help business travelers make cost-effective travel choices, the MBTI published a 28-page report, *Business Travelers: The Choice Is Yours (A Guide to Travel Options that Benefit the Travel Planner, Business Traveler and Bottom Line).* This publication details travel options in transportation, lodging, and other travel-related fields.

As a result of surveys and studies such as Marriott's, many hospitality properties are developing special programs and services to appeal to business travelers. Executive or business floors, business services, executive check-in/check-out programs, frequent traveler programs, and all-suite properties are just some of the new facilities and services that have changed the nature of the hospitality industry.

Changing hospitality products and services is only part of serving the business traveler market, however. For many years, the group business market was given top priority when it came to sales efforts; transient business travelers were merely considered "add-ons." But hoteliers came to realize that, while group business had to be cultivated over and over, transient business travelers, who returned to hotels repeatedly on both business and leisure trips, constituted a solid customer base. And since the large number of transient business travelers greatly affects a property's profitability, this segment became more important in terms of sales efforts.

Properties that wish to capture a share of the lucrative business traveler market must stay aware of changes in this growing segment. By responding to the preferences and needs of today's business travelers, properties of all sizes can enjoy increased profitability.

Endnotes

1. *Report to the Nation: Trends in Travel & Hospitality* (Washington, D.C.: Public Affairs Group, 1997), p. 33.
2. *Report to the Nation*, p. 15.
3. MasterCard International Frequent Business Traveler Study. Prepared by MasterCard International, New York, NY 10106. Sample size: 344 telephone respondents.
4. MasterCard International Frequent Business Traveler Study.
5. "Hotels Limit Service with Great Success," Business Travel Section, *USA Today*, 15 October 1996, p. 12B.
6. Judy Liberson, "Appealing to Women," *Lodging*, April 1995, p. 11.
7. The statistics in this section are from the *Report to the Nation.*
8. William Lazer and Robert A. Layton, *Contemporary Hospitality Marketing: A Service Management Approach* (Lansing, Mich.: American Hotel & Lodging Educational Institute, 1999), p. 183.
9. Diana M. Rodriquez, "Nine Zero Goes High-Tech for Opening," *Hotel Business*, July 6, 2000, p. 46.
10. "Real Problem, 'Virtual' Solution," *Hotels*, September 2002, p. 26.
11. The statistics in this list are from Residence Inn's sales literature for prospective franchisors.
12. *Corporate Travel Manager Survey: A Study of the Characteristics and Hotel Bookings of Corporate Travel Managers* (London: Reed Travel Group, 1990). This independent survey was prepared by Market Probe International for *Hotel & Travel Index.*
13. "Making Supplier Connections," *Mastering T&E Expense Management*, December 2007, p. 6.

Key Terms

corporate travel manager—Company manager who handles arrangements for employee business travel.

cost-plus traveler—An extremely cost-conscious business traveler who values no-cost amenities and tends to be sociable.

executive floor—A hotel floor that features exceptional service to business and other travelers. Also referred to as a *business floor* or *the tower concept.*

extroverted-affluent traveler—A business traveler who is typically young, affluent, and either self-employed, a top-level executive, or a professional. These travelers are not concerned with saving money and favor fashionable properties with lots of amenities.

in-room refreshment center—A small refrigerator or cabinet in the guestroom that holds beverages and snack items. Also called a *minibar.*

no-frills traveler—Typically a middle- to upper-management businessperson who only wants a clean, comfortable, and quiet room at a fair price and who has little interest in socializing.

Review Questions

1. What are some of the prime considerations of business travelers in choosing a hotel?
2. What are the three distinct groups of frequent business travelers and what are the needs of each?
3. What factors are important to women business travelers and how are properties meeting their needs?
4. What types of amenities are usually included in a stay on an executive or business floor? What other types of amenities are expected by business travelers?
5. Why are all-suite/extended-stay properties increasing in popularity? How do these properties meet the needs of business travelers?
6. What are some ways to locate local and national business travelers?
7. What strategies do properties use to reach business travelers? What kinds of travel intermediaries generate business traveler bookings?
8. What types of advertising are most likely to attract the attention of business travelers?
9. What types of public relations efforts would attract business travelers to a property?

Internet Sites

For more information, visit the following Internet sites. Remember that Internet addresses can change without notice. If the site is no longer there, you can use a search engine to look for additional sites.

American Marketing Association
www.ama.org

Association of Corporate Travel Executives
www.acte.org

Business Travel Net
www.business-travel-net.com

Business Traveller
www.businesstraveller.com

Choice Hotels International
www.hotelchoice.com

Delta Hotels
www.deltahotels.com

Doubletree
www.doubletreehotels.com

Four Seasons Hotels and Resorts
www.fshr.com

Hawthorn Suites
www.hawthorn.com

Hilton Hotels
www.hilton.com

Holiday Inn
www.holiday-inn.com

Hospitality Sales & Marketing Association International
www.hsmai.org

Hyatt
www.hyatt.com

La Quinta Inns & Suites
www.laquinta.com

Marriott
www.marriott.com

Media Central
www.mediacentral.com

Meeting Professionals International
www.mpiweb.org

National Business Travel Association
www.nbta.org

Ramada Worldwide
www.ramada.com

Ritz-Carlton Hotels
www.ritzcarlton.com

Sales & Marketing Management
www.salesandmarketing.com

Sheraton Hotels & Resorts
www.sheraton.com

urhospitality.com
www.urhospitality.com

Web Digest for Marketers
www.wdfm.com

Westin Hotels & Resorts
www.westin.com

Wingate by Wyndham
www.wingateinns.com

Case Study

Reviving Revenue Management

The Hearthstone Suites Hotel is an all-suite property with 250 rooms. A new property, the Fairmont Hotel, opened near Hearthstone Suites three months ago. Several months before the opening of the Fairmont, Laurie, the GM at the Hearthstone Suites, pushed all her front office and reservations staff to sell as many rooms as possible. As she put it, "Whatever it takes, to stay competitive." The director of sales, Pat, supported the plan from day one, but Jodie, the front office manager, had misgivings from the start. Jodie was concerned that the revenue management program managers implemented a year and a half earlier would be totally useless because of the push for occupancy.

The most recent profit and loss statement indicates that Jodie's fears were fulfilled. Though the occupancy is at budget year-to-date, the average daily rate (ADR) is down by $6. Also, the mix of commercial business is lower than planned—40 percent of guest mix instead of 50 percent. Also, the SMERF segment is higher than it should be—15 percent of guest mix instead of 5 percent. SMERF is a catch-all term for group business—Social, Military, Educational, Religious, and Fraternal groups—at substantially low rates.

Jodie, Pat, and Laurie are in a meeting to discuss these latest figures:

Laurie, the general manager, opens the meeting by saying, "Well, we've weathered the storm caused by the opening of the Fairmont. We managed to hold on to our occupancy level. But it looks like we have some regrouping to do. I trust you've each received the profit and loss statement I sent you. I'm concerned about the fact that we've lost so much of our share of the commercial business. And our ADR is much too low."

"I agree," says Jodie, "but I was just following orders when I had my staff focus on selling rooms. Our good occupancy rate has come at the cost of both yield management and revenue. It will take quite awhile to regain our former position."

"We all sat down and agreed months before the Fairmont opened that we should do our best to keep our occupancy numbers, and that's what we've done," says Pat. "You and your staff have worked hard and are to be commended, Jodie."

"Hear, hear," says Laurie. "And now we have some time to reevaluate our position and start targeting that corporate segment again."

"I just hope it's not too late to win it back from Fairmont," sighs Jodie.

Later that day, Jodie gathers her front desk and reservations team to brief them about re-implementing the revenue management program. "I know you've all been putting a lot of extra effort into filling rooms over the past several months. I'm proud of you; the whole management team is. We've met our occupancy goals. The down side is that our guest mix is off. We've lost some of our commercial segment and gained too much of the SMERF segment. And our ADR is down a full $6. It's time we reviewed the revenue management program we use..."

"The revenue what?" blurts Jack, a fairly new front desk agent. "You never told us about that."

"Now hold on a minute," counters Jodie, "some of you are so new that you haven't been fully trained in this program, but I know I've talked about it to some extent with all of you."

"Sure, you told me a little about it," offers Tracey, a reservationist. "I never have been comfortable with it, to tell the truth. One day I quote a guest $85 and he books a suite. A month later he calls back to book another and I quote $105. Then the guest asks why the rate went up—what am I supposed to say?"

"Well, there are things you can tell guests who ask that, but we're not going to get into that right now," says Jodie.

Bill, the most experienced front desk agent, speaks up. "I've been using the yield management program all along, just like you showed me." He turns to his co-workers. "It's really not unreasonable when you look at the big picture of the hotel's revenue. I just tell inquisitive callers that our rates depend on their arrival dates. Some periods are busier for us than others, and that affects rates."

"Bill, it's good to hear that you continued using the yield management program," Jodie says. "We can get into more detail on applying it in formal training. We've had a lot of changes since the push for volume began—changes in personnel and even changes in the yield management program itself. It's clearly time I evaluated training needs in our department in the area of yield management program execution. You can be confident, Tracey—and all of you—when you quote rates that they are competitive for what we offer. That reminds me," Jodie pauses a moment, "how many of you have actually been inside some of our suites?"

Three of the six employees raise their hands. "How many have seen rooms at the Fairmont or at any of our other competitors?" continues Jodie. Only Bill raises his hand. "So almost none of you have seen the difference between our suites and the single rooms other properties are offering?"

"There hasn't been time to look at what we're selling," protests Jack.

"Much less to look at what anyone else is selling," adds Linda, another reservationist.

"That's what I was afraid of," says Jodie. "In the next two weeks or so, as I'm reevaluating training needs, I'm going to have each of you spend time gaining an appreciation of the value we offer—especially in comparison with the value of Fairmont's offerings and those of our other competition."

"Are we still going to be offering the $84 supersaver rate?" asks Tracey. "We've had a lot of repeat business because of that rate."

"I've had callers tell me we're the best deal in town," Linda says.

But Bill cautions, "We won't need to use it next week. The Home Builders convention is in and every room in town will be booked. We can afford to charge more next week."

"That's good thinking, Bill," says Jodie. "I know it's nice to be popular with guests and it's easy to use that discount whenever a potential guest shies away from a quoted rate, but the supersaver rate is intended to be used only as a last resort or in other special cases. We shouldn't be offering it too frequently. We also need to adjust our selling strategies when special events come along like this convention."

"Speaking of selling strategies, when are we going to get to go through that training module on selling skills you were talking about?" inquires Linda. "I've heard about it but I haven't gone through it yet."

Discussion Questions

1. How can the management team address the problem of low ADR?
2. What are some ways Jodie could make employees like Jack and Tracey more familiar and comfortable with a yield management program?
3. What selling skills should training focus on for the Hearthstone Suites Hotel staff?
4. How can the Hearthstone Suites Hotel regain some of the commercial business it has lost?

Case Number: 370CF

This case was developed in cooperation with Lisa Richards of Hospitality Softnet, Inc., a marketing resources and support company (Sixty State Street, Suite 700, Boston, Massachusetts 02109; www.hospitalitysoftnet.com.

This case also appears in *Contemporary Hospitality Marketing: A Service Management Approach* (Lansing, Mich.: American Hotel & Lodging Educational Institute, 1999), ISBN 978-0-86612-158-3.

Chapter 9 Outline

Competencies

1. Describe how hospitality firms market to families, seniors, baby boomers, GenXers, and other individual leisure travelers. (pp. 327–352)
2. Describe how hospitality firms market to group leisure travelers and the intermediaries who aid these travelers. (pp. 353–365)
3. Explain how small hospitality firms can market to leisure travelers, and explain the concept of vacation ownership. (pp. 365–368)

Insider Insights

Chaney Ross
Director of Sales, In Serve Corporation
Meridian, Mississippi

"It requires an all-out, disciplined effort over a long period of time to get a share of the tour market segment. It's important to build lasting relationships with tour and motorcoach operators, and these relationships can only be built slowly and carefully. They like to do business with hotels that provide good service to their clients, and the entire hotel staff must act to establish this atmosphere. In addition to serving guests, the property must be flexible enough to meet the needs of tour operators—they have unusual problems from time to time, and they need and appreciate assistance. One of the ways a property can tap into the tour market is by maintaining memberships in industry associations and local state and tourist commissions."

9

Marketing to Leisure Travelers

ALTHOUGH MANY HOTELIERS derive much of their business from the business traveler market, you can increase revenues by attracting leisure travelers as well. Leisure travelers differ from business travelers in several ways. First, leisure travel is seasonal, not year-round like business travel. Second, the bookings of leisure travelers change less often than those of business travelers. Many leisure travelers plan their vacations well in advance and for specific dates, while business travel is often booked on short notice and can change due to unforeseen circumstances. Third, leisure travelers tend to look for packages and discounts to make the most of their vacation expenditures.

The leisure traveler market can be divided into two segments: *individual* and *group*. In this chapter we will take a look at the needs of each of these segments; discuss how properties are meeting these needs with discounts, unique marketing methods, special packages, all-inclusive pricing, and programs; and discuss how to reach leisure travelers through advertising, direct mail, travel intermediaries, and other strategies.

Individual Leisure Travelers

Individual leisure travelers can be defined as nonbusiness guests who are traveling independently rather than with a group on a prearranged tour. They can be divided into the following general categories:

- Families
- Seniors
- Baby boomers
- Generation X
- Others

Families

Today's hospitality industry targets a diverse base of family travelers: married couples, couples with children, single parents, and grandparents and other family members traveling with children. It is becoming increasingly common for multi-generational families to travel together. This trend, called "inter-generational travel" or "togethering," is expected to grow, as extended families seek to share additional leisure time and experiences. Families take mini-vacations (weekend trips and other stays of less than a week) and extended-stay vacations, and are also excellent sources of function business for such occasions as reunions and birthday and anniversary dinners.

Selling to the Family Market

Because of the growing number of families traveling, many hospitality chains and properties are researching this lucrative market to determine how to attract it. The Holiday Inn Family Holiday Survey and the Hilton Report on Children and Travel revealed a number of family preferences—and ways for hospitality properties to meet the needs of the traveling family.

Special Rates

While many properties have offered a "Kids Stay Free" option for some time, more and more properties are offering special amenities—cribs, baby-sitting services, planned activities, and so on—at special family rates. In some cases, the family rate includes two adjoining rooms—one for the parents and one for the kids.

Supervised Children's Activities

No longer are parents limited to on-call baby-sitters. Many properties offer licensed child-care services, which provide such supervised activities as crafts, swimming, and off-site excursions to mini-hotels for children. Children's clubs (some with frequent visitor discounts and amenities) are also growing in popularity, with many offering club products and services (tee shirts, monthly or quarterly newsletters, and so on).

Special Children's Menus

Many properties offer children's menus with favorite foods such as tacos, pizza, hamburgers, fresh fruit, and healthy snacks in child-sized portions. At many properties, children eat free when accompanied by an adult.

Family-Oriented Services and Products

Many properties have teamed up with local attractions to offer discount rates, special children's excursions, and learning activities. In addition, property gift shops are stocking up on items popular with traveling families—activity books, crayons, comic books, and toys. Properties are adding video arcades to appeal to young guests.

No matter how a property decides to present its product and services to families, it is especially important to be aware of local and state guidelines (especially regarding child care) and to ensure the safety of parents and children alike.

When marketing to families, your property may wish to consider partnering with a "kid-friendly" organization that caters to your targeted market. For example, Beaches Resorts, a group of all-inclusive Caribbean resorts, partnered with the Sesame Street organization to attract more business from families with young children. The program not only received extensive media coverage, it also increased bookings at Beaches Resorts, due to its appeal and demonstration of the hotel chain's interest in its young guests.

GOING GREEN

According to a survey by the U.S. Travel Data Center, 43 million U.S. travelers are "ecologically concerned," whether they are traveling for business or pleasure. Since many of these travelers specifically look for ecologically-conscious hospitality properties, your property's green program can bring increased business while saving money and helping the environment.

Most travelers are willing to participate in recycling and energy-conservation programs, and your property should provide information on your conservation efforts to make it easier for guests to take part. You can explain your water conservation program, for example, by letting guests know at check-in that towels will only be replaced when they are dropped on the floor or placed in a special receptacle. You can tell restaurant guests that water is available only upon request—and give them a choice of glass sizes. Remind guests of your energy conservation program by placing cards or stickers in close proximity to the air conditioning or heating unit and by using energy-saving light bulbs.

You can offer a card or brochure with handy tips for guests, such as: they can distinguish family members' towels by the colorful pins or stickers provided by the property, and they can use the property's online check-out system to help the property save on paper. To save plastic, you can provide guest amenities such as shampoo and lotion in dispensers, rather than in individual plastic containers. You can get guests involved in your recycling efforts by having recycling bins readily available at convenient locations, such as by the ice machine, pool, and near property entrances.

Finally, you should thank your guests for taking part in your conservation efforts, and ask for feedback, including suggestions to improve your program.

Families—especially those with children—are generally cost conscious. Many married couples without children are also cost conscious, but they tend to place more emphasis on quality. They can afford to spend a little more on a vacation, since in many cases both the husband and the wife work. Married couples without children do not always travel alone; they sometimes travel with other couples.

Meeting the Needs of Family Travelers. Families will usually shop around when looking for lodging. They often prefer resorts or properties that are near a number of attractions. Properties seeking to appeal to families can offer weekend packages, special rates (advance purchase and other discounts, no charge for children staying in the same room with their parents, a "second-room" discount for families traveling with older children or teens who want to stay in their own room, and so on), low-cost recreational amenities (swimming pools and arcade games rank highest in popularity), and kitchenettes (to enable the family to save money on meals). Other conveniences attractive to families include ice and soft-drink machines, parking close to the guestroom, and laundry facilities.

Special services. Special services can make a difference in a family's decision to visit or return to a property. Many properties provide families with free cribs, extra towels, and information of interest to parents, such as the names and telephone numbers of local pediatricians. Items for children in the gift shop, children's menus, and discount coupons for meals and attractions are other special services properties may provide.

Some properties provide recreational facilities designed specifically for children. The Westin Hotel in Winnipeg, for example, offers a weekend child-care center equipped with furniture and play equipment for children between the ages of two and 11. The center is staffed by child-care professionals and has proven to be a business-builder for the property.

Other properties offer guestrooms designed especially for kids. At the Holiday Inn Family Suites Resort in Orlando, for example, some 100 two-room "kid suites" are offered in a variety of themes, from a Coca-Cola suite to educational suites featuring space exploration and environmental themes. Other properties make guestrooms more kid-friendly by stocking them with books and video games and by equipping rooms that will be occupied by younger children with such safety features as night lights, outlet covers, portable gates, and bathtub faucet covers.

Still other properties offer special "camps" and "clubs" for young visitors. Hyatt Hotels, for example, offers Camp Hyatt, featuring planned activities for children and a frequent-stay program for kids. The Embassy Suites Resort Hotel in Palm Beach Shores, Florida, provides children's activities in its Fat Cat Beach Club.

Hilton Hotels offers youth programs at the Las Vegas Hilton and the Flamingo Hilton and Tower in Las Vegas, the Anaheim Hilton in California, and the Hilton at Walt Disney World Village. Activities range from breakfast with Mickey, Goofy, and Donald to pool and playground activities, movies, and arts and crafts. The Walt Disney World Swan and Dolphin Hotel offers bedtime stories over the telephone. Omni Hotels has created a travel planning website just for kids (OmniKidsRule.com) that offers opportunities for kids to download games and coloring books before their stay.

In order to ensure that their young guests and older youth enjoy their stays, whether they take part in a program or not, some chains have hired a teen concierge to offer suggestions for activities and attractions that will appeal to children and teens. Four Seasons Hotels and Resorts, for example, staffs a teen concierge at properties in Manhattan, Chicago, Toronto, and London during July and August. Each teen concierge has grown up in the general area and therefore can convey "what's hot and what's not" to young guests. Other chains, such as Hyatt, have special programs and activities geared to teens. "HyaTTeen Suite 16," for example, offers teens the ultimate sleepover party at participating Hyatt Resorts. The package includes such amenities as a two-bedroom suite for up to two adults and six guests under the age of 18, limo transportation, a Cashmere Spa Robe for the birthday teen, dinner for eight, a special birthday dessert, a continental breakfast on the morning of departure, and a choice of spa treatments or action-oriented activities.

Family travelers also look for free breakfasts or kitchen facilities to enable them to save money for recreation and other family activities. Therefore, properties that wish to attract this segment should consider offering one or both of these options.

Family Travel Trends

- There is a resurgence of interest in families in America. Two-thirds of adults state that their primary source of satisfaction in life comes from their home and family. Spending time with the family is described as "essential" by over 75 percent of Americans.
- Most Americans feel that a vacation is a birthright, and virtually all family travelers believe that travel is an experience that all children should have. Demand from leisure travelers now fills more guestrooms on an annual basis than demand from business travelers.
- Approximately one-third of adults take at least one vacation with children. Many of these trips include multi-generational families (three or more generations traveling together). Fifteen percent of all vacations include participants spanning three generations.
- Children play an increasingly important role in deciding where family travelers vacation as well as where they stay once they get there. Children influence one out of every two lodging selection decisions made by family travelers.
- Business travelers are increasingly likely to mix business with pleasure. One out of every four business travelers take their children on a business trip.
- Seventy percent of Americans who take vacations don't want to vacation where they have been before. Families increasingly say, "Been there, done that," and want to try something new.
- Weekend trips represent over half of all leisure trips taken by Americans. The trend toward shorter, more frequent vacations can be attributed to the time crunch experienced by two-income families, the recognition of the need for short breaks to prevent burnout, and the increasing costs of travel to distant locations.
- The Internet is used by a majority of leisure travelers to plan vacations and make reservations online. Online reviews and blogs are increasingly popular sources of travel information.

Source: Peter Yesawich, "Travel Trends to Watch," adapted from the website of *Hotel Marketing*, January 18, 2008.

Yet another way in which hotels can attract families is to welcome their pets, which are often considered members of the family. According to a Travel Industry Association of America study, 29.1 million U.S. adults have traveled with a pet on a trip of more than 50 miles (one way) in the past three years.[1] Since that number is expected to continue to grow, more and more properties are not only welcoming pets, they are providing special services for them. Loews Hotels became one of the first chains to offer pet services through its Loews Loves Pets program. The general manager at participating properties in the United States and Canada provides pet owners with a welcoming note that lists pet services available on-site as well as information about veterinarians, nearby walking paths, grooming locations, and

INTERNET EXERCISE

Log onto the Internet and research the websites of any three of the following chains: Disney World, Four Seasons, Hilton, Holiday Inns, Hyatt, Loews, Marriott, Radisson, Westin, and Wyndham.

1. Create a spreadsheet to help you compare the children's programs offered by each of the three chains that you chose. On the spreadsheet, include the name of each program, the type of welcome given to young guests, the program's meal options for children, special services provided to children and their families, and other pertinent information.
2. Which of the three programs do you feel is most kid-friendly? Why?

so on. Pets are provided with special beds, complimentary pet treats and toys, food and water bowls and accompanying placemats—there is even a room service menu for four-legged guests. The Starwood chain's Starwood LTD (Love That Dog) program offers similar services, including custom-designed pet beds, canine massages, and plush robes and toys. Other chains offer pet services ranging from doggie day-care to enclosed runs.

Weekend packages. While families are a source of business for extended stays, they are also taking more weekend trips, usually within 200 to 300 miles of home. This can be explained by the increasing number of two-income families. In 1985, 49 percent of U.S. households enjoyed two incomes; that number has risen to 75 percent! While this trend does provide more discretionary income for many families, it results in less leisure time. Properties are taking advantage of this by creating special weekend packages that include quality accommodations and access to a wide range of facilities and recreational amenities.

Weekend packages can be action packed or relaxing, budget or luxury. Exhibit 1 features a print ad promoting a wide variety of weekend packages covering sports and cultural activities as well as a relaxing spa getaway. Many properties have taken creative approaches to attract families and other weekend travelers. Weekend packages, for example, are often more successful when promoted as getaways for groups of four to eight friends, rather than as getaways for individual couples.

Theme weekend packages range from food- or event-related festivals to elaborate murder mystery weekends, such as the one promoted in Exhibit 2. Hyatt has had great success with its Hyattfest Weekends, which are designed around such events as wine tastings and ice cream festivals. Hyattfest Weekends include accommodations, participation in festival events, and discounts on meals and recreational amenities. Murder mystery weekends involve guests in a dramatized "murder" and subsequent "investigation." At the end of the weekend, guests gather to determine who has correctly solved the mystery. This type of package includes accommodations, meals, and the fun of playing detective.

Sports weekend packages are popular with guests who want an active weekend. The Woodlands Inn, located 27 miles north of downtown Houston, is a good example of how a suburban property with appropriate recreational facilities can

Exhibit 1 Weekend Packages

THE CIVILIZED WAY TO EXPERIENCE VERMONT'S GREAT OUTDOORS.

Whether you enjoy golf, tennis, fly fishing, hiking, biking, exploring or simply relaxing, The Equinox has a special package designed for you!

Green Mountain Golf Package • Fun & Fitness Package
Explore Historic Vermont • Equinox Spa Package
Honeymoon/Anniversary Package
Vermont Sportsman Package • Theater in the Mountains

These two- and three-night packages include overnight accommodations plus other exciting features with prices starting at $265*.

To reserve your package or receive our free rate and package brochure, call The Equinox today at 1-800-362-4747; in Vermont, (802)-362-4700 or contact your travel agent.

Historic Route 7A, Manchester Village, Vermont

* per person. Taxes and gratuities are additional.

Travelers with limited leisure time find weekend packages attractive. The Equinox offers a variety of packages to attract weekend travelers. (Courtesy of The Equinox)

attract city dwellers. The Inn's "King of Aces" sports package includes breakfast, unlimited golf on the property's renowned golf courses, use of the tennis facilities and health and fitness center, and a seasonal gift.

Shopping packages can be used both on the weekends and during the week to help boost business. According to the International Council of Shopping Centers, tourists in a dozen U.S. states cite shopping among their top five activities. Shopping ranks as the number one activity of 88 percent of the international travelers who visit the United States.[2]

Exhibit 2 Murder Mystery Weekends

Murder Weekends

Date	Location
January 13th/14th	BLOSSOMS, Chester.
February 3rd/4th	BEECH HILL, Windermere
March 2nd/3rd	ROYAL ALBION, Brighton
March 9th/10th	NEW CLIFTON, Blackpool
March 16th/17th	PRINCE OF WALES, Southport
May 25th/26th	PRINCE OF WALES, Southport
June 29th/30th	PRINCE OF WALES, Southport
July 13th/14th	IMPERIAL, Blackpool
August 3rd/4th	IMPERIAL, Blackpool
August 17th/18th	GOLF HOTEL, Woodhall Spa
September 7th/8th	PRINCE OF WALES, Southport
October 5th/6th	PRINCE OF WALES, Southport
October 26th/27th	ROYAL ALBION, Brighton
November 2nd/3rd	ROYAL ALBION, Brighton
November 9th/10th	PRINCE OF WALES, Southport
November 16th/17th	CAIRN, Harrogate
December 7th/8th	NEW CLIFTON, Blackpool

Other Murder Weekends for Private Parties can be arranged. For any further information contact:

Prince of Wales Hotels,
72 King St., Southport,
England. PR8 1LG.
Tel: (0704) 37700

To attract weekend guests, some properties offer murder mystery weekends. For one inclusive price, guests receive accommodations, meals, and the opportunity to play detective after a dramatized "murder." This concept, which is extremely popular in Britain, is also gaining popularity in the United States. (Courtesy of Prince of Wales Hotels, Southport, England)

An increasing number of hotels have joined forces with local shopping hubs to draw leisure travelers. To augment their packages of discounted rooms and restaurant options, many properties offer free shuttle service to area shopping malls, discount coupons for participating retail outlets, and other services such as personalized shopping services. To further attract leisure travelers, especially those with spouses or children who may not want to shop, some properties include discount admissions to other attractions, such as theaters, theme parks, and museums, in their shopping packages.

Weekend Leisure Travel at a Glance

What: Weekend leisure travel usually includes four room nights or less (one or two-night stays are common), including a Saturday. Popular options include beach and lake vacations, weekend ski trips, and visits to tourist destinations such as Disneyland or cities such as New York, Chicago, or Las Vegas that offer a wide variety of activities in close proximity.

Why: Such factors as the inability to leave work or family for longer periods of time, a lack of vacation days, and economics (higher airfare and gas prices or not enough money for a longer vacation) make shorter vacations more attractive. Travelers are not only finding it more economical to take short trips, they also enjoy visiting a number of different locations and having a variety of experiences during the year.

When: Weekend trips are taken year-round, although work and family schedules as well as such considerations as the weather will affect the scheduling of weekend leisure travel. Some weekend trips are "wrapped around" holidays to maximize vacation time.

How: Properties that realize their peak business during the week can capitalize on weekend leisure travelers by offering special rates to encourage business travelers to stay on for the weekend, or by developing special promotions to attract guests from within a nearby radius. If weekend leisure travel occurs during a property's peak time, it will be necessary to build on added value rather than discounting rates.

Escape weekend packages can vary greatly in price and scope. Often, properties simply discount guestrooms and offer the use of their recreational facilities (swimming pool, health club, golf course, and so on) for the cost of the room. Other escape packages may include special amenities such as breakfast in bed, champagne, and gourmet meals. Whether simple or luxurious, an escape weekend package must be perceived as a real value and targeted to audiences that are within a reasonable distance from home. Some properties have pushed back check-out time to 4:00 P.M. to allow a more leisurely departure day.

A property's target markets, facilities, and in-house amenities, as well as local attractions, will greatly shape the nature and success of packages offered. If your property has an 18-hole golf course, for example, a golf package is a logical choice. But if a hotel across town also has a golf course, your golf package should offer something more, in terms of either value or extra amenities.

Advance-purchase discounts. The family or budget traveler's interest in value has led to a new trend in the hospitality industry: discounts based on advance purchase of rooms. Ramada, for example, offers a discount of 30 percent off rack rates when travelers book 30 days in advance, while InterContinental Hotels Group's discount rate program, "Great Rates," offers discounts of 20 to 40 percent at its Holiday Inn and Crowne Plaza properties. These programs are patterned after supersaver airline fares, and certain restrictions may apply (and will vary from chain to chain). For example, Great Rates cannot be used in conjunction with any other discount, must be guaranteed by credit card, and must be made at least one week (but not more than four months) in advance; any cancellation made within 72 hours of the arrival date results in a $25 fee.

Advance-purchase discounts, also offered by Hyatt, Marriott, and Days Inns of America, are aimed at families, leisure travelers on a fixed budget, and value-conscious travelers who often make airline reservations in advance to save money. While most of these programs are available at any time during the week, Hyatt's program is specifically targeted to the weekend market.

Leisure travelers can also take advantage of discounts offered by organizations or travel suppliers. Special travel rates and services are available to members of the American Automobile Association (AAA), for example. Travelers can often get discounts on room rates and vacation attractions through their employers (many firms negotiate lower rates with hospitality properties and attractions such as theme parks, museums, and other vacation options for their employees). Travel suppliers, such as airlines and car rental agencies, also may offer discounts on hotel rooms to their customers who are leisure travelers.

All-inclusive pricing. Yet another way to save—or at least to know exactly what a vacation will cost—is to select properties that feature *all-inclusive pricing*. This type of arrangement—which is especially popular with people who have hectic schedules, and now accounts for about 20 percent of all vacation travel—offers accommodations, meals, the use of recreational facilities, and other options all for a set price. First popularized at such vacation resorts as Club Med and Sandals, all-inclusive pricing is becoming popular at other resort locations because it eliminates vacation "surprises" and the need for travelers to carry excess cash. Exhibit 3 shows how print ads are used to promote all-inclusive packages at Marriott and Renaissance resorts.

Other properties offer variations on all-inclusive pricing, with special package deals that include property "extras" such as meals, special activities, and the use of facilities. Walt Disney World Resort Vacation Plans, for example, promotes a "Food 'n Fun Plan" that adds meals and the use of recreational activities and facilities to its room packages. Guests receive food credits based on the length of their stay and are given Disney Resort identification cards that identify them as participants in the program.

Still other properties partner with airlines and other travel-related firms to offer all-inclusive packages that include air travel, airport transfers and/or shuttle service, and other off-property services (such as tickets to local attractions) to hotel guests. According to a National Leisure Travel Monitor study by Ypartnership, "56 percent of leisure travelers believe that 'an all-inclusive vacation price that includes air transportation, accommodations, food, transfer to a hotel or escort, and some recreation is extremely/very desirable.'"[3]

When offering discounts or other money-saving values, it is important to keep the programs simple; avoiding confusing restrictions can make the programs more attractive for guests and less troublesome for employees.

Finding Family Travelers. It is generally more difficult to obtain the names of individual leisure travel prospects than it is to find group leisure travelers, but families can be contacted through lists of names from mailing list brokers, membership lists of family-oriented organizations such as the YMCA and YWCA, and

Exhibit 3 Marketing All-Inclusive Packages

Introducing All-Inclusive ValueVacations™
from Marriott and Renaissance Offshore Resorts.

Now all the smiles, seashells,
and strawberry shortcake are included.

Your clients can now enjoy the following all-inclusive package featured at eight of our enticing Offshore Resorts:

- All food and beverages at select restaurants
- Unlimited house-brand cocktails
- Wine and beer by the glass
- Room service
- Complimentary use of the tennis courts
- Complimentary use of the health club
- All applicable room taxes and gratuities

For reservations or information, please call your destination of choice listed on the adjacent page and ask for code IXPA or visit us at www.offshoreresorts.com.

Price range is per person per night, based on double occupancy. Prices valid through 12/20/00. Seasonal price variance may apply. Prices subject to change without notice. Subject to availability. Minimum 5-night stay required, maximum four people per room. Children up to age 11 stay and eat free when staying with parents. No refunds or room credits for unused services, meals missed, or nights of stay unused. Excludes water sports and minibar. Participating food outlets vary by destination. Other restrictions may apply.

All-inclusive vacation packages are becoming increasingly popular and offer a variety of options, from property-wide amenities and services to complete packages that include air travel, transfers, and tickets to local attractions. Note that this ad for an all-inclusive package at eight Marriott and Renaissance resorts clearly spells out what is offered in the package, to eliminate any misunderstandings on the part of potential guests. (Courtesy of Marriott and Renaissance Offshore Resorts)

from referrals, direct mail questionnaires, and previous guest registrations. The most effective way to contact this market may be through travel agents.

Reaching Family Travelers. Family travelers can be reached through a number of avenues: the Internet; direct mail; advertising in newspapers, magazines, and travel guides; collateral materials; radio and television advertising; and public relations efforts. Yellow Pages advertising can also be an important tool to reach families.

Many family travelers use the Internet to research their trips. These travelers can be reached online through property websites and via ads placed on travel supplier sites and on destination city websites.

Direct mail can be especially effective if a member of the family has already visited the property on business or vacation. He or she will appreciate the opportunity to return to the property in response to a special promotion at a special rate. Direct mail can appeal to first-time visitors as well, especially if the direct mail effort follows a recent promotion or publicity-generating event at the property.

Advertising in newspapers, magazines, and travel guides can also get the word out to family travelers. When advertising to families, however, it is important to remember two things: First, most families are not just seeking a hotel; they are seeking a "vacation experience," whether the trip is for the weekend or for an extended period of time. Advertising must communicate the type of experience the family desires, whether it be an active leisure experience or a quiet getaway. Second, many families make impulsive vacation decisions. While some families may plan their vacations a year or more in advance, others decide on the spur of the moment to take mini-vacations or weekend trips. This makes advertising in newspapers especially important, because frequent newspaper advertising keeps the public informed of special packages and events that may stimulate impulse getaways.

Magazine advertising can reach a vast audience. Since many family vacation decisions are made by women, advertising should be placed in both general-interest magazines and women's magazines. Ads can also be placed in special-interest publications (such as golf magazines) that relate to your facilities.

Travel guide advertising can also be an effective way to reach family travelers. Many families seek recommendations from sources such as AAA, CAA (the Canadian Automobile Association), and Mobil travel guides. Along with providing locator maps, these guides list a property's accommodations and services and offer the opportunity for display advertising, as shown in Exhibit 4. They cannot, however, be used to advertise special, short-notice promotions.

Collateral materials designed for families may be placed at bus, train, and airline ticket counters; at car rental counters; and at chambers of commerce in key feeder cities. These materials may also be distributed through direct mail packages, travel agents, or organizations that cater to families.

Radio and television advertising is used by many properties to reach family leisure travelers. While television is usually too costly for the average small or midsize property, these properties can use radio ads to announce family promotions.

Hotels can also reach family travelers through public relations efforts. Properties can build relationships with key members of such organizations as AAA,

Exhibit 4 Travel Guide Advertising

Travel directories, such as those offered by AAA, provide both hotel listings and the opportunity for display advertising. Special discounts are usually offered to AAA members booking at participating properties.

whose chapters offer an Auto Travel Department and Travel Agency to their members. A special family-oriented weekend such as a tennis clinic can generate favorable publicity, both in terms of press coverage and word-of-mouth recommendations. In addition, you can offer special rates that might interest the news media. Properties can also gain media attention by creating special events, such as family-oriented fairs or contests, or becoming involved in community affairs that benefit children and families.

Seniors

Demographers estimate that by the year 2050, one in three people in the United States will be 55 years or older. Since this group currently takes more than 163 million trips a year, its impact on hospitality revenues should become even more significant in the coming years.[4] The average household income for U.S. families between the ages of 50 and 65 is nearly 20 percent higher than the national average. Seniors control nearly half of the nation's discretionary income—an estimated

Exhibit 5 The Seniors Market

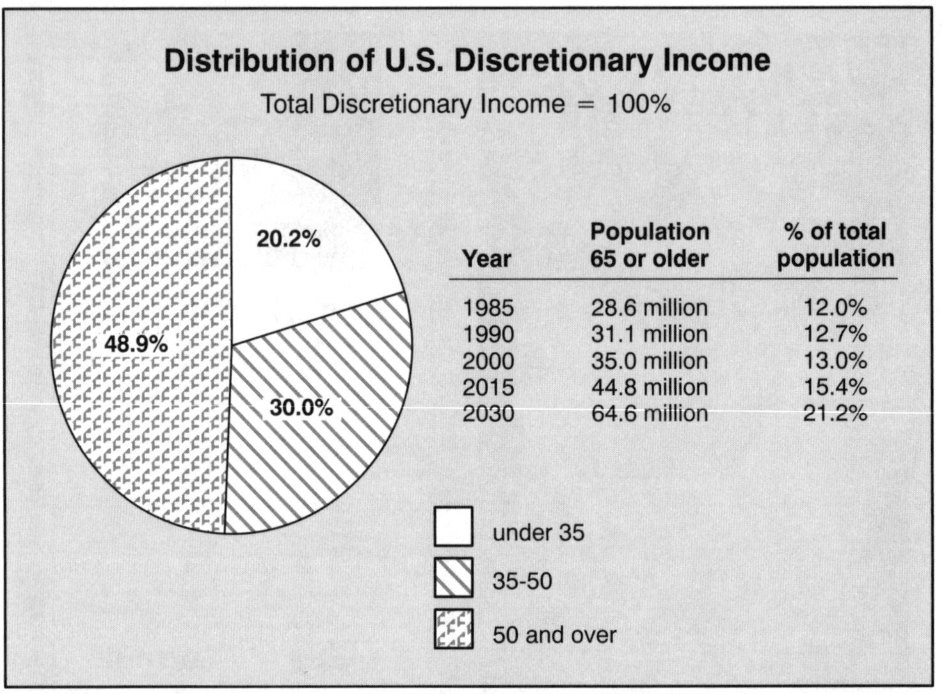

Year	Population 65 or older	% of total population
1985	28.6 million	12.0%
1990	31.1 million	12.7%
2000	35.0 million	13.0%
2015	44.8 million	15.4%
2030	64.6 million	21.2%

In the coming years, the portion of the U.S. population that is 65 or older is expected to dramatically increase. What does this mean to the hospitality industry? Seniors already control nearly half of the discretionary income in the United States, and with the growing number of seniors with more money and leisure time, the hospitality industry is in an excellent position to capture more of this discretionary income in the future. Older travelers can be more flexible about when they travel than families, which makes seniors an excellent potential source of business for the off-season. Source: U.S. Census Bureau projections, and "Midlife and Beyond: The $800 Billion Over-Fifty Market," Consumer Research Center.

$600 billion. The chart in Exhibit 5 shows the impact that seniors and their discretionary income will continue to have on the economy.

The older population in the United States is healthier and more active and diverse than ever before, so it is important not to stereotype mature travelers. For the purposes of marketing, however, seniors can be divided into four segments by age: pre-retirement, young-old, old-old, and 85-plus.

The *preretirement* group consists of working adults between the ages of 50 and 65. They can afford longer vacations and demand excellent service and amenities. The *young-old,* those between 65 and 75 years of age, are generally in good health and like to travel, although some have limited discretionary income and look for value as well as service.

The *old-old* are those between 75 and 85 years of age. A high percentage are single women, and a large number suffer from disabilities, which makes it imperative that properties focus on security and special accommodations to attract this group. Those in the *85-plus* group, a relatively small portion of the population, are likely to suffer from multiple physical ailments and are less likely to travel and dine out. Those who are still active can be served by properties that are willing to meet their needs.

Seniors are especially important to the lodging industry. While some seniors may have less income than other groups, they generally have more disposable income. They can usually travel any day of the week at any time of the year and can stay longer, filling soft spots left by business and seasonal travelers.

Not only can they be an invaluable segment for filling hotel rooms, but restaurants and the tour business can benefit from this group as well. Seniors are frequent users of restaurants, especially those that offer discounts, specials, senior menus, or otherwise provide special services to meet their needs. Bill Watson, vice president of marketing of Steak and Ale Restaurants, states that empty-nesters (couples without children) make up less than 20 percent of the chain's business but generate far more than 20 percent of its sales. A National Restaurant Association study found that empty-nesters spend 65 percent more on dining than couples with children at home.[5] Mature travelers account for 70 percent of the tour industry's business. American Express's tour division focuses much of its marketing attention on the mature market, and the entire museum and historic-sites industry depends heavily on this segment.

As an added bonus, whether they are purchasing hotel rooms, meals, or tours, seniors can be extremely loyal, generating both repeat business and word-of-mouth referrals. Therefore, the mature market can be an attractive segment on which to focus marketing efforts.

Meeting the Needs of Seniors. Like family travelers, many older travelers are value conscious. Many properties now offer clubs or other programs that provide special rates or services to mature travelers. Exhibit 6 illustrates discounts commonly extended to senior hotel guests.

Days Inns of America's September Days Club offers travelers aged 50 or above a ten percent discount on room rates, gift items, pharmaceuticals, and dining at nearly 300 properties across the country. In addition to these discounts, the ten-dollar annual membership fee entitles older travelers to discounts on rental cars and on travel by bus, airplane, and cruise ship.

Membership in the Hilton Senior Honors program, which costs a couple just $50 per year, is a top travel buy for people 60 and over. Membership brings discounts of 50 percent at Hilton hotels worldwide.

Omni Hotels offers a special program for AARP members that includes 50 percent off room rates any night of the week (based on space availability) in 23 luxury hotels nationwide. A complimentary continental breakfast is provided to the guest and the guest's registered companion, and a 15 percent discount is offered on food and nonalcoholic beverages at Omni Hotel restaurants. To qualify for these benefits, guests have only to show their AARP membership cards at check-in.

Other properties offering discounts or special services to seniors include Hampton Inns (Lifestyle 50 program), Sheraton (Retired Persons Plan), Marriott (Leisure Life Program), Travelodge (Golden Guest Program), Choice Hotels (Prime Time), and Ramada (Best Years). Age limitations and membership fees, if any, vary somewhat among these programs.

Exhibit 6 Marketing to Seniors

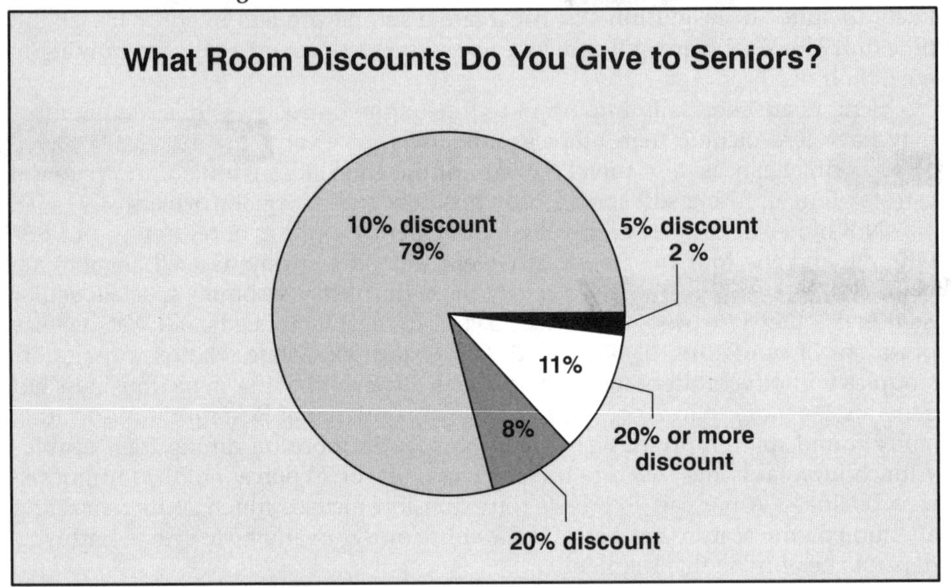

***Lodging Hospitality* asked hotels about their discounts for seniors and got these responses. Because of the emphasis placed on value by older travelers, more hospitality firms are offering discounted rates on both accommodations and food to attract seniors.** Source: *Lodging Hospitality* research.

Many older travelers are value conscious, but they also insist on quality and service. Clean, comfortable rooms and public areas are important to them. Many of these travelers prefer rooms with two beds and look for well-lit public rooms for conversation and card playing. Seniors are interested in safety and security, and they prefer that their assigned guestrooms be located on the ground floor or near elevators.

Some chains are now creating rooms specifically for mature travelers. Choice Hotels International started the trend with its Rodeway Choice Rooms, which are designed especially for those 50 years of age or older. The large, well-lit rooms feature levered doorknobs; shower grab bars; telephones and television remote controls that have large buttons; lighted, easy-to-read alarm clocks; enclosed bed bases and fitted bedspreads; and color-coded handles for hot and cold water. Other amenities preferred by mature travelers include magnifying mirrors, hand-held shower heads, large-print brochures, signs that are easy to read, and no-smoking rooms.

A study of senior Australians found several additional factors to be important in meeting the needs of mature travelers. Lodging attributes identified as being significantly important included a non-slip bathroom floor, anti-slip mats or strips in the bathtub, shower entries without raised edges for easy access, and illuminated light switches. The study also showed that seniors preferred smaller meal portions and menus that addressed specific dietary needs.[6]

Older travelers are also influenced by personal attention. Beverly Garland, the former movie and television star turned hotelier, personally greets senior guests at her North Hollywood Holiday Inn, telling them about the hotel and how it got started. She also distributes tickets to TV game shows and provides a number of amenities appreciated by seniors, including free parking and a complimentary shuttle to Universal City and nearby Burbank.

Many senior travelers prefer to dine and vacation at a leisurely pace; they may feel rushed or distracted by the quick, efficient service that other travelers, such as businesspeople, have come to expect. A property's staff, therefore, should be trained to take a slower approach to serving mature travelers and should take the time to listen to and respond to their special needs. Since many older guests prefer to dine early (so they can avoid driving at night), it is often easy for restaurant staff to provide this extra personal attention. But other personnel who come in contact with older travelers should also be sensitive to them. The front desk staff, for example, can extend special attention to mature travelers. They should be trained to offer general information about hotel services and the local area and to take time to answer questions and assist with special needs. This personalized attention will build guest loyalty and lead to referral business.

Days Inns of America builds rapport through its work force; it staffs senior citizens in a number of front-of-the-house jobs, including front desk clerk, van driver, service person, and housekeeper. In addition, a number of chain properties have mature general managers, and a large number of senior citizens work in reservations centers.

Information is so important to older travelers that Choice Hotels has produced a 40-page booklet, *Tips for Travelers Over 60,* as part of its Prime Time program. This publication lists brief descriptions of hotel types (luxury, all-suite, etc.), their price ranges, and addresses and telephone numbers for major travel associations and senior citizens' organizations. It also gives tips on how to select and work with a travel agent; how to travel by car, airplane, boat, bus, and train; and how to find a property that can meet the needs of older travelers. Such a publication can prove invaluable to seniors when they are making travel decisions.

Restaurants, both hotel and freestanding, can attract seniors by offering healthy and natural foods, special seatings or discounts, and menus that are easily readable. Many seniors have health or dietary concerns, such as heart disease, gastrointestinal difficulties, and diabetes, which can greatly affect their meal selections. Menus should clearly spell out ingredients and offer nutritional information.

Seniors are also influenced by the physical aspects of a restaurant. Restaurants that offer reduced noise levels, adequate lighting, a well-lit parking lot, and easy access to public transportation are popular with seniors. Prompt seating is appreciated by seniors with physical limitations.

Finding Seniors. As with family travelers, it is difficult to solicit individual seniors. You can reach seniors through mailing list brokers, membership lists of senior citizens' organizations, referrals, direct mail questionnaires, and previous guest registrations.

It may be more cost-effective to target older travelers through in-house promotion of your property's senior citizen program. Older travelers are not always aware of these programs, and a point-of-purchase display at the front desk, restaurant, or gift shop may lead seniors to sign up immediately to take advantage of discounts. Their pleasurable stay at substantial savings may lead them to recommend the property to others.

Reaching Seniors. Besides in-house promotions, you might consider promoting to seniors through religious groups and private associations such as local community centers where seniors gather for recreation and friendship. Many of these organizations are delighted to work with hotels to help arrange low-cost vacations for their members.

Print advertising (rather than radio or television) tends to be more effective in reaching seniors. (An example of a typical print ad directed at seniors is shown in Exhibit 7.) Print ads to reach this market may be placed in local and feeder city newspapers and in various magazines. While such organizations as AARP will not release the names of their members, they do offer publications that accept travel advertising. You can also advertise to older travelers in travel guides. In addition to the AAA and Mobil guides, seniors turn to publications available at most local libraries such as *OAG TRAVEL PLANNER/Hotel & Motel RedBook* and *Hotel & Travel Index*.

To effectively sell to seniors, you should customize advertising or other promotional efforts. Value is often of utmost importance, for example, but this doesn't mean that rates have to be slashed; offering an upgrade or a free amenity (such as a complimentary breakfast or tickets to a local cultural event) often results in increased sales. Present your message with a simple, rational approach, rather than an emotional appeal, and spell out costs in full—seniors do not like surprises. Promotional material should reflect seniors as they perceive themselves—active and healthy—and should stress service, convenience, and reliability as well as savings.

Collateral materials that promote special packages for older travelers can be distributed through direct mail campaigns, travel agents, senior citizens' clubs, chambers of commerce, and so on.

Baby Boomers

The baby boomer market consists of the 77 million people born in the United States between 1946 and 1964 and covers a wide spectrum. Baby boomers include single adults, two-income couples without children, couples with children, and blended families. Don Landry, former president of Choice Hotels International, views the aging baby boomers as the growth market for the next decade:

> Ten thousand people a day will turn 50 years old in the U.S. every day for the next 18 years. This is a phenomenal number of people hitting their prime travel years, which bodes well for the limited-service, mid-priced, and economy markets.[7]

The baby boomer generation is wealthier, healthier, and expected to enjoy more years of retirement than any generation before it—and travel is their most desired retirement activity. One study reported that boomers will take an average of four trips per year and spend about $7,700 during them.[8] They are also more likely than any other age group to stay in a hotel or motel.

Exhibit 7 Advertising to Seniors

This ad addresses two issues important to seniors: services and value. The ad promotes the chain's Choice Rooms, which were designed with special features and amenities older travelers desire, and offers a 30 percent discount to travelers over 50. (Courtesy of Rodeway Inn)

Baby boomers are interested in value and quality. Special package prices appeal to all segments of this group, while parents tend to look for facilities and programs that will give them opportunities to spend quality time with their children.

Many baby boomers are especially interested in "adventure travel"—experiences as diverse as house boating, white-water rafting, and vacationing at archaeological digs. They look for unusual activities or sites where few other tourists go. Their combined interests in adventure and family bonding has led to an upsurge in this type of travel that is only expected to grow. Properties that can offer unique experiences (or that are in proximity to such spots) can benefit.

Boomers are also interested in eating healthier. Darden Restaurants, the parent company of Olive Garden, Red Lobster, and Bahama Breeze, has debuted Seasons 52, an upscale-casual grill and wine-bar concept with a focus on low-calorie fare and frequent menu changes to attract baby boomers. As the name implies, the menu will change weekly, featuring fresh, seasonal products to meet boomers' desires for fresher and more healthful food offerings.

Baby boomers generally have little time for television and rarely read the entire newspaper, which makes advertising in these vehicles less cost-effective for reaching them. A combination of radio spots and outdoor advertising is usually the best approach to reach this group. Ads should stress value, quality, and the unique experience your property offers.

Generation X

The baby boom was followed by the "birth dearth" of only 45 million people born between 1965 and 1976. These people were dubbed "Generation X" by author Douglas Coupland, as they fell in the shadow of the boomers and lacked obvious distinguishing characteristics.

The youngest GenXers are now in their early 30s, and this segment has become a viable economic force. Travel spending by GenXers has increased 66 percent over the last five years (compared to a 25 percent increase for baby boomers), and by 2010 they will overtake baby boomers as the primary market for almost every product category, including hotels and restaurants.[9]

GenXers generally care about the environment and respond favorably to socially responsible companies. This segment is also extremely family-oriented, and, in terms of their careers, they work to live instead of live to work, as the boomers did. They look for new, exciting experiences that are meaningful or enrich their lives, especially if they have families. GenXers are as likely as boomers to use travel agents, and they like trendy properties, such as boutique hotels and the latest entertainment "hot spots." They have also proven to be a lucrative market for vacation ownership properties (discussed later in the chapter).

Since GenXers are serious about their leisure, they have specific needs when it comes to hospitality properties. That includes the latest in technology, including WiFi access, flat-screen TVs, on-demand cable television, and CD and DVD players. While these amenities are common in upscale accommodations, GenXers expect them as standard service everywhere when they travel. And, in response to their preference for a more urban environment with a trendy decor, chains are responding with such new brands as Aloft from Starwood, Cambria Suites from Choice Hotel International, and Hyatt Place, a brand converted from the chain's AmeriSuites brand.[10]

Like hotels, restaurants are developing new products and trendy settings to appeal to GenXers. The Kimpton Group in San Francisco, for example, developed

Industry Innovators

Ian Schrager
Chairman and CEO of Ian Schrager Company

Since the 1970s, entrepreneur Ian Schrager has achieved international recognition for concepts that have revolutionized both the entertainment and hospitality industries. His passionate commitment to the modern lifestyle has been expressed through a series of pioneering concepts: The hotel as home away from home, the hotel as theater, "cheap chic," "lobby socializing," the indoor/outdoor lobby, the urban resort, and the urban spa.

His keen instincts for the mood and feel of popular culture were honed during the '70s and '80s, when he and his late business partner, Steve Rubell, created Studio 54 and Palladium. Rubell and Schrager soon turned their attention to the hotel business, opening Morgans Hotel in 1984, which introduced the concept of the "boutique hotel" to the world.

Following this were the equally well-received and highly successful Royalton Hotel and Paramount Hotel, in which Schrager again broke with industry convention by creating "lobby socializing," where the hotel lobby became a new kind of gathering place for guests and New York City residents alike, and "cheap chic," where affordable luxury was offered in a stylish and sophisticated environment. Schrager also received international recognition and acclaim for his one-of-a-kind "urban resorts"—the Delano Hotel in Miami and Mondrian Hotel in West Hollywood. This was followed by the Hudson Hotel in New York, where Schrager realized his "hotel as lifestyle," and continued to refine his concept of "cheap chic," as well as expanding to cities such as San Francisco with the Clift Hotel and London with St. Martins Lane Hotel and the Sanderson Hotel.

Schrager's groundbreaking hotel concepts have changed the business and set industry standards that continue to be imitated throughout the world. He recently completed the new Gramercy Park Hotel in an extraordinary collaboration with artist Julian Schnabel, which presents a completely new and unexpected model for a Schrager hotel.

Mr. Schrager's first residential project, 50 Gramercy Park North, provides unique luxury residences adjacent to the only private park in New York City with world-class service from the Gramercy Park Hotel. 50 Gramercy Park North introduces the concept of "effortless living" and lifestyle management, where owners benefit from a fully staffed household 24 hours a day, 7 days a week, without the bother of managing it, the full expense of maintaining it, or any loss of privacy. The project was designed by world-famous architect John Pawson, known for numerous residential projects that include the Saatchi home in London, the Novy Dvur Monastery in the Czech Republic, and the flagship Calvin Klein store in New York City.

(continued)

Industry Innovators *(continued)*

Mr. Schrager recently completed his second residential project, 40 Bond. The building, designed by eminent Swiss architects Herzog & de Meuron, is an architectural masterpiece. 40 Bond residences will also benefit from 24-hour, 7-day-a-week world-class service from Gramercy Park Hotel.

Mr. Schrager's latest venture, a partnership with Marriott International, intends to create a new brand of as many as 100 hotels that will combine the personal, intimate, individualized, and unique lodging experience that he created with the operational expertise that Marriott is known for on a global scale.

According to J. W. Marriott, Jr., Chairman and CEO of Marriott International, the marriage of the ultimate corporate lodging company and the pioneer of the boutique/lifestyle hotel is an attempt by both to push the boundaries, break new ground, and take the hotel industry to a new level.

The hotels will be located in gateway cities throughout North and South America, Europe, and Asia. With an average size of 150–200 rooms, each of the hotels will reflect the best of the cultural and social milieu of its location and of the time. A diverse set of world-renowned architects and designers will be recruited to create one-of-a-kind buildings spanning the complete range of project types, from new construction, to conversions, to gut renovations. The partners expect these hotels to be not just aesthetically pleasing in their markets but to be environmentally responsible as well.

Sources: *Lodging*, the *Hotel & Resort Insider* online newsletter, and the Ian Schrager website.

a restaurant named Ponzu that features a lounge-like atmosphere and offers a feng shui hour, a popular attraction for this age group that wants something different. Chart House Restaurants have added bright and airy spaces, lots of music, and more seafood and vegetarian specialties to attract GenXers.

Because GenXers are knowledgeable, cautious, and resistant to hype, they must be sold on a product's value. Once won over by a brand, however, they tend to be loyal and may increase business for your hotel or restaurant through word-of-mouth referrals.

GenXers are more likely to reach for a computer mouse than a telephone when it comes to booking travel. They are usually computer savvy and do a lot of online research and comparison before finalizing travel plans. Therefore, you can reach them through your property or restaurant website and by advertising on the sites of travel suppliers or destination city websites. Since GenXers are very likely to provide their e-mail addresses, this group can also be targeted with e-mail advertising. Print advertising can be effective as well, especially in publications targeting the interests of this group, such as magazines about computers, travel, and the environment. To be most effective in reaching GenXers, your ad copy should be casual and hip in tone and offer a benefit (mentioning Internet access is essential, and frequent-guest programs also rank high in appeal). In addition, your property or restaurant can develop packages or offers that can be sold through travel agents.

Others

Other individual leisure travelers include business travelers who are taking a leisure trip either before or after doing business, affluent leisure travelers, active leisure travelers, and single leisure travelers who may be traveling alone or with a group of other singles.

Business/Leisure Travelers. Business travelers are not eligible for low airfares when they don't stay at their destination for a Saturday night. Therefore, business travelers who finish their work during the week may wish to extend their stays over the weekend to take advantage of lower airline rates.

Many businesspeople who extend their stays are interested in some form of self-improvement. A property that offers special programs—from tennis clinics and fitness weekends to language classes and financial seminars—may attract this type of traveler. In addition, there is a growing trend for working women, single parents, and dual-career baby boomer couples to bring their children along on business trips. Therefore, properties that can offer family activities and amenities can also attract business from this segment. InterContinental Hotels, for example, offers "Kid in Tow," a program that offers a free stay in the parents' guestroom, special meals, complimentary family films, and amenities such as baby-sitting services, pager rentals, and take-home backpacks for the kids. Similar programs are being offered at other chains, especially those in family-friendly destinations such as Orlando.

There are a number of ways to reach business/leisure travelers. You can invite convention attendees, for example, to stay after the convention, either indirectly by providing the meeting planner with information about local attractions and special hotel packages, or directly by talking to the delegates as they arrive or at appropriate times during the convention. Delegates, especially association delegates who are attending on a voluntary basis, will often respond to a personal invitation.

You can also reach business/leisure travelers by direct mail. If a businessperson makes a Thursday reservation, for example, don't just send a confirmation notice; include a brochure or flier that invites the traveler to extend the stay through the weekend. You may decide to place ads in the business pages of local and feeder-city newspapers. Radio spots on all-news stations are excellent ways to advertise weekend promotions to business travelers who are looking for mini-vacations.

Affluent Leisure Travelers. The affluent leisure traveler segment is comprised of those who have wealth and those who have a mindset of affluence. While each group has money to spend on hotels and restaurants, each has different needs and interests and must be targeted separately.

People who have wealth may live opulently or modestly, and their values will be reflected in the types of hotels and restaurants they choose. While many affluent travelers will stay at such chain properties as Mandarin Oriental and Four Seasons, others seek unique independent lodging properties and may look to referral services such as the Leading Hotels of the World or Relais & Châteaux when choosing hotels. The very wealthy, of course, can stay and dine anywhere they choose. But people who have accumulated their wealth gradually may live more modestly and still look for value when choosing hotel and dining options.

MARKETING IN ACTION

Starwood's W Hotels—A Popular Choice of Sophisticated Leisure Travelers

Starwood Hotels developed its W brand to attract hip, upscale leisure travelers as well as business travelers looking for an oasis during hectic business trips. Billed as "lifestyle" hotels, W hotels make up the first boutique-hotel chain in the United States and are a variation of the trendy, small European hotels that offer a unique atmosphere and personalized service.

Barry Sternlicht, chairman/CEO of Starwood Hotels, first conceived the W brand as a marriage of substance and style. He wanted to offer the amenities expected by today's business travelers, such as high-speed Internet access, but wanted to create a property with features that he desired in a hotel: a room with a large, state-of-the art television, a comfortable bed, and hip public places. He chose W as the name of the brand to signify "witty, warm, wonderful, worldly, and welcoming."

To ensure that his hotels lived up to his vision, Sternlicht enlisted the aid of Hilary Billings, formerly a member of Pottery Barn's product design team, to create stylish properties that offered more than what guests were getting at other hotels. The resulting guestrooms gave the image of a "private garden." The beds, placed in the center of the room, had woven headboards with flowers and leaves stenciled in browns, greens, and golds, which added to the atmosphere of being away from the bustle of the city. The decor, which also featured upholstered furniture and beds fitted with down bedspreads and pillows, also made use of natural light to make the rooms feel larger.

While the chain's business mix was originally envisioned at 60 percent business, 30 percent groups, and only 10 percent leisure, and its original target market was corporate travelers between the ages of 25 and 35, the chain recognized its opportunity to increase its leisure business. Since properties are located in gateway cities such as Atlanta, San Francisco, Seattle, Chicago, and Los Angeles, they are attractive for both weekend getaways and for travelers who wish to vacation either before or after their business trips. The W properties have also proven popular with older people, especially baby boomers, who are interested in style.

Sources: Kathleen Cassedy, "The Making of a Boutique Brand," *HSMAI Marketing Review*, Spring/Summer 1999, p. 10; and Shannon McMullen, "Starwood's Flagship W Hotel Saturates Road Warriors in Style," *HotelBusiness*, November 7–20, 1998.

Many of today's millionaires live in modest homes and drive older cars, making it difficult to target them through such common marketing efforts as purchasing a mailing list of high-income zip codes or purchasers of luxury cars.

Some of today's wealthy, especially those who made their money quickly, are likely to have an affluent mindset. Their purchases are largely based on image—

they live in upscale neighborhoods, drive luxury cars, wear designer clothes, and, when it comes to hospitality industry purchases, look for the best and the trendy—places to see and be seen. These travelers generally spend money more lavishly—they vacation in style, staying at posh spas, trendy boutique hotels, or upscale resorts, and eat in gourmet restaurants. They want to be pampered and are willing to pay extra for VIP treatment. Whether traveling alone or with their families, it is common for them to spend money on special services, such as VIP tours or reserved seating.

The "new wealthy" often join prestigious clubs, such as country clubs, and you can sometimes reach them through club membership mailing lists. Your efforts will be more successful if others in the group have also experienced your hotel or restaurant, so you may wish to promote special packages to current upscale guests and offer an incentive for them to extend an invitation to their friends.

Affluent travelers can also be reached by advertising in business publications (the *Wall Street Journal, Fortune, Forbes*, and so on), and travel and lifestyle magazines such as *Condé Nast Traveler, Travel & Leisure, Town & Country, Food & Wine*, and *Gourmet*. The wealthy are also more likely than most groups to use travel agents, so you may wish to create and market upscale packages through these travel intermediaries.

Despite their use of travel agents, many affluent travelers also look to the Internet to explore travel destinations and services, so creating a website designed specifically for them or advertising on sites that appeal to high-end travelers may be cost-effective. No matter what advertising media you choose, remember that affluent leisure travelers disdain mediocrity. Your advertising messages should stress quality above all else; appeal to affluent leisure travelers by promoting your excellent level of service and plush facilities and amenities. Once you land affluent leisure customers, you should work hard to retain their loyalty.

Active Leisure Travelers. The active leisure traveler segment includes over 98 million Americans, and continues to be a large and growing market. According to some studies, nearly half of all Americans took an adventure travel trip in the past five years; 46 percent of Americans polled said they planned to camp, hike, or climb on vacation.[11]

Active leisure travel falls into two broad categories: active travel and adventure travel. *Active travel* involves some level of physical activity, from golfing to hiking to horseback riding. Locations can vary—from plush spas to dude ranches—as can activities. Hotels with a number of recreational amenities are attractive to this segment, as are hotels in proximity to other recreational, cultural, and entertainment options. Many hotels are developing packages to attract active travelers and their families and friends. Kapalua Bay Hotel & Ocean Villas in Maui offers the "Maui Experience" package featuring such activities as jet skiing, parasailing, scuba diving, snorkeling, kayaking, whale-watching, horseback riding, pineapple plantation tours, group surfing lessons, and golf or tennis. Loews Ventana, near the Catalina Mountains of Tucson, Arizona, now offers guided hikes and birding in nearby canyons as well as other outdoor activities.

Adventure travel usually involves more strenuous physical activity, such as white-water rafting or mountain climbing, and can vary from a weekend to several weeks (a bicycle tour of Europe would take weeks, for example). Some adventure travel focuses on unusual activities in exotic locations, such as a trip down the Amazon or a safari in Africa. Hotels and restaurants in proximity to remote locations have the opportunity to provide lodging and meals either before or after an "adventure," while hotels adjacent to adventure locations, such as national parks, may develop their own packages for adventure travelers.

There are a number of publications and websites available to travelers interested in active and adventure travel, and you may also advertise in newspapers in key feeder cities to reach this segment. Keep in mind that this is a diverse group—ranging from young people to active senior citizens, for example—so you should target your advertising to those travelers most suited to your property.

Single Leisure Travelers. A growing number of U.S. households have only one member, and "vacations for one" are becoming increasingly common. Many single leisure travelers look for personal enrichment while on vacation, and properties that can offer unique food events, personal enrichment seminars, or recreation activities that enable single travelers to meet other singles are popular.

Women make up a large segment of the single leisure traveler market—unmarried professional women, women who have outlived their spouses, and previously married younger women. The vast majority of these women are well educated and have traveled extensively. Favorite activities include shopping, outdoor activities, and visiting historical sites and museums. However, many single female travelers have begun to venture into traditionally male-dominated travel areas, such as active or adventure travel. This growing interest has fueled the development of books, periodicals, and websites that provide "women wanderers" with information on destinations and vacation values. There also is a growing trend for single women to vacation with other single female friends. Several chains, including Fairmont Hotels & Resorts and Omni Hotels, are responding to this trend with "Girlfriend Getaway" packages.[12] Cruises are also popular options for women traveling alone or in small groups, resulting in increased business for hotels and restaurants in gateway cities.

The singles market, however, is not made up solely of unmarried adults. The increasing number of two-income households has made it more difficult for married couples to take time off together. Married individuals are increasingly traveling without their spouses to vacation.

You can reach single leisure travelers with print ads. A getaway package, for example, can be offered in the entertainment or business section of a key feeder city's newspaper. Many single travelers are attracted to sophisticated consumer magazines, which make excellent vehicles for promoting packages or programs for the single traveler. Broadcast media advertising can also be effective. To reach single women travelers, your hotel or restaurant can contact local women's organizations, including political, business, social, and religious groups, or advertise in publications of interest to women.

A number of single travelers join travel groups. The formation of a singles program within a chain or at an individual property could attract this market segment, as could offering singles' packages through travel agents or direct mailings.

Group Leisure Travelers

Group leisure travel business can greatly benefit a property. First and foremost, groups can be scheduled during soft business periods, generating much-needed room occupancies and revenues. Groups are easier to plan for than individual guests, since you know exactly when the group will arrive, how many people are in it, what services it will require (meal functions, baggage handling, and so on), and the duration of the stay.

Although group leisure travelers are sometimes thought of as simply groups of people taking prearranged vacations, they are actually part of a complex travel and tour system. Services in group **tour** packages range from transportation, accommodations, and baggage handling to more extensive arrangements such as meals, sight-seeing, entertainment, and admission to attractions. Since group tour packages are usually arranged by a travel intermediary, it is important to understand the various types of travel professionals involved.

Tour Intermediaries

Travel professionals who arrange tours are known as **tour intermediaries** or *travel intermediaries*. They include tour brokers, tour wholesalers, and retail travel agents.

U.S. **tour brokers,** also known as *motorcoach brokers* or *tour operators*, are licensed by the Federal Interstate Commerce Commission to put together package motorcoach tours in the United States and, in some cases, Canada. While tour brokers do not actually provide the transportation, they contract with certified carriers such as Greyhound or Continental Trailways for the buses required and with hospitality properties for accommodations or meals. Many tour brokers operate travel agencies through which tours are sold. Motorcoach tours can also be sold by motorcoach companies or travel companies. Tours include motorcoach transportation, room and tax, baggage handling, and tickets to attractions (when applicable). Tour brokers may issue documents called **tour vouchers** or *coupons* to their customers. Travelers exchange their vouchers for accommodations, meals, sight-seeing, and other services.

The tour broker assumes responsibility for the success of the tour. He or she does not work on a commission basis. If seats are not sold, the tour broker must take a loss on the deposits paid out to properties, attractions, and so on.

Tour wholesalers, like tour brokers, put tour packages together, but typically work with airlines rather than ground transportation. Most tour wholesalers contract with hotels, airlines, and other travel and lodging suppliers months in advance, and put packages together that are sold through retail travel agents, incentive travel companies, or their own travel agencies. These packages include air transportation, hotel or motel accommodations, and such extras as meals, sight-seeing, and entertainment, all at prices lower than those a traveler would pay on an itemized or individual basis.

Retail travel agents sell tours offered by tour brokers and wholesalers, as well as tour packages developed by properties.

Exhibit 8 Pricing Rooms for Tour Groups

While many lodging operators believe that tour business is undesirable due to high discounts, selling rooms to this market segment can be profitable. Look at the following example of a hotel charging a $74 rack rate for a commercial single and a $90 rack rate for a motorcoach tour double:

Typical Revenue from a Commercial Traveler (with 10% corporate discount)		$ 74.00 (Single)
Less 10% travel agent commission:		– 7.40
Less 4% credit card cost:		– 2.96
	NET:	$ 63.64
Typical Motorcoach Tour Revenue		$ 90.00 (Double)
Less 20% discount:		– 18.00
	NET:	$ 72.00

In this example, it is more profitable to sell motorcoach doubles at a $72 profit than to sell commercial singles at a $63.64 profit. As in this case, most group tour rates will be equal to or greater than the average daily rate.

Negotiating with Tour Intermediaries. Companies that package tours buy "in bulk" from hotels, sight-seeing businesses, and transportation companies, and then add a markup to all the tour's elements in order to reach an all-inclusive price. Because they block a number of rooms, these tour intermediaries often try to negotiate a significant reduction off the hotel's room rates. Hotel salespeople, therefore, must be well versed in negotiating skills to effectively represent the hotel's interests, while continuing to maintain a good working relationship with tour intermediaries.

The first rule in negotiating is to be prepared. You must have a clear view of your own situation and an understanding of the other party's needs. This type of a foundation results in a climate conducive to negotiating a "win-win" for both parties.

Most properties strive to build a base of both transient and group business. The number of rooms set aside for group and tour business is commonly called the **group sales allotment.** Although these rooms are often sold at discounted rates, called **net wholesale rates,** they can be an important source of revenue. While it may not seem cost-effective to discount rooms at the typical discount of 20 percent off rack rates, guestroom sales to tour groups can actually result in higher revenue than sales to individuals (see Exhibit 8).

Once you clearly understand your property's position, it is easy to go into a negotiating session with a commitment to your product. With a clear understanding of what your property has to offer, it is far easier to overcome the tour intermediary's price objections. However, it is equally important for the negotiator to understand the travel intermediary's point of view. By listening carefully and understanding the other party's needs in terms of services, rates, space, and policies and procedures, you can more easily offer compromise solutions that will be mutually beneficial.

Types of Tours

There are three types of tours commonly taken by group leisure travelers: motorcoach tours, airline tours, and property package tours.

Motorcoach Tours. Motorcoach tours or bus tours fall into two general categories: the overnight or nondestination tour and the destination tour.

Overnight tours are stops en route to another destination. These tours are an opportunity for your property to increase food and beverage revenues as well as guestroom revenues, provided you can give the quick service motorcoach tour groups require for baggage handling and meals.

Overnight tour guests have usually been traveling for many hours and appreciate special services upon arrival. Many properties offer refreshments and an information session while guestroom keys are being distributed to the tour escort and baggage is being unloaded. Depending on departure time, brief local tours may be arranged for overnight guests; in any case, group travelers should be familiarized with your attractions and facilities.

Overnight tour guests appreciate having a wide variety of food choices available. Buffets and cafeteria-style service are popular. Many motorcoach tours cater to older travelers who appreciate light fare or room service. Breakfast service on the morning of departure should be handled quickly. As a precaution, schedule extra restaurant staff to handle the demands of the group on a timely basis.

Destination tour guests are those who will be staying a minimum of two nights either to take advantage of a property promotion or to use the property as a base of operations to tour local attractions. The latter option, called a **hub-and-spoke itinerary,** is especially common in areas where there are sight-seeing attractions and activities in a concentrated area, allowing for day excursions within a reasonable driving distance. Often, destination tour guests have been traveling for a long time and may appreciate a tour of your facilities upon arrival, both to get acquainted with your property and to stretch their legs.

Motorcoach charters are not technically motorcoach tours, since travel intermediaries and special packages are usually not involved. They are another potential source of group business for properties, however. Motorcoach charters are groups of people traveling together who select a destination and then contact a motorcoach company to charter or rent a bus to take them to their destination. Clubs, companies, and schools frequently charter motorcoaches. Overnight stops and the destination property may be decided on by the group; in other cases, the group will ask for the motorcoach company's recommendations.

To attract groups that are traveling on a charter arrangement, you should approach groups or organizations that typically arrange charters. (Charters are not limited to motorcoach companies; airplanes and trains can also be chartered.) Contacts for this type of business are found in both the corporate and the association meeting-planner categories.

Meeting the needs of motorcoach tour travelers. Most motorcoach tour groups enjoy being welcomed. If possible, greet group members on board the bus when they first arrive. Have a greeting on your sign's reader board and hold a reception or happy hour either before or after the group's orientation tour. A welcoming party hosted by your property's manager or another hotel representative

Key Trade Shows to Reach the Group Leisure Market

Travel Industry Association of America (TIA) Pow Wow

This is the largest U.S.A. inbound trade show. U.S. suppliers meet with buyers from around the world.

National Tour Association (NTA) Annual Convention and Marketplace

This is one of the largest North American tour operator shows. North American suppliers meet with buyers from U.S. and Canadian tour companies.

American Bus Association (ABA) Annual Convention & Marketplace

This is the primary convention for U.S. companies owning motorcoaches. Most of these companies package tours as well, so the show is similar to that of the NTA. North American suppliers meet with buyers from North American tour companies.

Rendezvous Canada

This is the largest Canadian inbound trade show. Canadian suppliers meet with buyers from around the world.

Ontario Motorcoach Association (OMCA) Annual Conference & Marketplace

This is the largest Canadian domestic tour operators show. North American suppliers meet with Canadian tour companies.

Dates and locations for the above shows can be found on the website of each organization.

can make a favorable impression on guests and increase your chances for repeat business. Guests may also be impressed by such special features and services as a game room for cards, checkers, and chess; free coffee in guestrooms; free maps of the local area; discount coupons for local attractions; and excursions to nearby points of interest, escorted by a property staff member.

Days Inns' Motor Coach Plus program offers service designed specifically for seniors. Groups are pre-registered and pre-keyed so they don't have to wait in check-in lines. They are met with a red carpet and a welcome reception of light snacks and beverages, and their baggage is carried to their rooms within 20 minutes. Arrangements for group meals are also included in the plan, and a gift is given upon departure.[13]

Both overnight and destination tour travelers look for clean, comfortable rooms and friendly service. Plenty of guestrooms with two double beds should be available, along with a few singles for the group's tour escort, bus driver, and tour guests desiring to room alone. All rooms should be blocked together for group security and the supervision of children, if any. When blocking rooms, consider the nature of the group. For example, older travelers, as previously mentioned, usually prefer ground floors.

Make attention to safety a prime factor when booking groups. Hallways should be well-lit, elevators should have emergency telephones, and simple directional signs should be posted throughout the property. An attractive exterior and interior appearance is also important to both tour operators and guests.

In addition to meeting the needs of motorcoach tour guests, you must provide for the needs of the tour operator or escort, the bus driver, and other staff who may accompany a group, such as an interpreter or a physician. You should provide ample parking for motorcoaches and have all guests preregistered for rapid check-in and distribution of room keys. It is also helpful to assign one staff member to assist the tour escort in dealing with any last-minute changes or problems that might arise during the group's visit. Offering property-sponsored activities (theme weekends, movies, or other entertainment) will also ease the responsibilities of the tour escort. Making the escort's job easier can help generate repeat business, since your initial customer is the tour broker, not the individual guests.

Finding motorcoach tour brokers. Hotels can find the names of motorcoach tour brokers in a number of ways:

- Lists from industry and professional associations. Exhibit 9 provides the most commonly used sources for leads.
- Bus associations such as the Ontario Motor Coach Association and the American Bus Association.
- Sources from the U.S. Travel Service and domestic airlines.
- Travel trade journals such as *Travel Weekly, Travel Trade,* and *ASTA News.*
- Incentive tour operators such as E. F. MacDonald and Maritz.
- Recommendations from personal contacts and independent hotel representatives.

Before attempting to sell to motorcoach tour brokers, however, you should determine exactly what your property has to offer—a location near an airport or major highway, proximity to a number of popular attractions, facilities for large groups, and so on—and contact those brokers who handle the types of tours best suited to your property.

Reaching motorcoach tour brokers. You can reach motorcoach tour brokers directly by sending representatives to motorcoach trade association meetings to promote your group packages and rates, and by participating in motorcoach trade shows. Some chains provide manuals to assist individual properties in reaching this market. Holiday Inns, for example, offers a manual that provides an overview of the market, gives suggestions on what to include in sales letters, and details exactly how individual properties can deliver their messages—from direct selling and telemarketing to direct mail, e-mail, and print media.

Direct mail is one of the most popular avenues of selling to motorcoach tour brokers because it is a way to get answers to a number of questions efficiently and inexpensively. Correspondence with tour brokers should discuss a number of issues, including rates, comps and discounts, services, facilities, and location (see Exhibit 10). Some properties have developed group rate directories that detail group rates at various seasons of the year (see Exhibit 11).

Direct mail letters can be accompanied by brochures detailing what your property has to offer. These brochures should feature photographs of groups being

Exhibit 9 Sources for Group Tour Business

American Bus Association (ABA)
1100 New York Avenue, N.W., Suite 1050 tel: (800) 283-2877
Washington, DC 20005 fax: (202) 842-0850

Hotels and motels can become travel industry members of ABA. Resources and services of this association include the *ABA Directory,* which lists nearly 600 major bus operators and key sales contacts, and an annual convention that matches bus operators with lodging properties in their touring areas.

National Tour Association (NTA)
P.O. Box 3071
Lexington, KY 40596 (800) 682-8886

Hotels and motels can become allied members of NTA. Resources and services include the *NTA Directory,* which lists tour brokers and the areas they service, and an annual convention which features computerized matching of allied members with tour brokers.

Ontario Motor Coach Association (OMCA)
4141 Youge Street, Suite 306
Toronto, Ontario M2P 2A8 (416) 488-8855

Hotels and motels can become allied members of this organization, which, like ABA and NTA, publishes a directory and holds an annual trade show.

United States Tour Operators Association (USTOA)
342 Madison Avenue, Suite 1522
New York, NY 10173 (212) 559-6599

Members of the United States Tour Operators Association are the largest tour companies. The organization's membership includes both motorcoach and air transportation tour companies.

United Motorcoach Association (UMA)
113 S. West Street, 4th Floor
Alexandria, VA 22314 (800) 424-8262

The UMA (formerly the United Bus Owners of America) has a membership of about 850 bus owners and about 2,000 suppliers. While there is a significant membership overlap with the ABA, UMA has quite a few members who don't belong to any other major association, and they are likely to be involved in charter tours, at least on a local or regional basis.

Group Leaders of America (GLAMER)
P.O. Box 129
Salem, OR 44460 (800) 628-0993

GLAMER, which publishes a monthly newspaper, *The Group Travel Leader,* is an organization of about 20,000 group tour leaders. Rather than holding an annual convention, GLAMER stages frequent shows throughout the country that allow suppliers to set up exhibits and talk directly with group leaders from the area. For the most part, the members who attend these shows are very active travel planners.

Exhibit 9 *(continued)*

Student and Youth Travel Association (SYTA)
3048 Clarkston Road
Lake Orion, MI 48362 (800) 509-7982

SYTA is the non-profit professional trade association that promotes student and youth travel. Its members are tour operators, travel agencies, hotels, and destination marketing organizations.

American Society of Travel Agents (ASTA)
1101 King Street
Alexandria, VA 22314 (703) 739-2782

ASTA works with tour brokers and publishes *Motorcoach Touring,* a manual that provides an excellent overview of the motorcoach industry to hotel/motel operators. This manual includes a state-by-state listing of ABA and NTA companies.

Travel Industry Association of America (TIA)
1100 New York Avenue, N.W., Suite 450 tel: (202) 408-8422
Washington, D.C. 20005 fax: (202) 408-1255

TIA publishes the *Discover America Package Handbook.* TIA's annual Pow Wow, usually held in May, is the country's largest tour and travel show (more than 500 international tour buyers from 30 or more countries participate).

served at your property. A brochure should be developed for each group package offered and should speak directly to the needs of motorcoach tour brokers. A brochure that features a locator map of your property and a toll-free number will often get more attention than one that simply describes your property.

You can also acquaint motorcoach tour brokers with your property by offering familiarization tours. These complimentary tours, which can be scheduled for slow business times, allow brokers to experience the property firsthand. The Radisson Hotel High Point in High Point, North Carolina, offered motorcoach tour brokers a Motorcoach Month promotion that featured two room nights, a complimentary breakfast, and a packet of informational materials. The program generated a favorable response from the participants and increased the hotel's tour business.

Motorcoach tour brokers can also be reached through print advertising in travel guides and trade publications. Tour brokers often use *OAG Travel Planner/Hotel & Motel Redbook* and *Hotel & Travel Index* to obtain information about properties in a specific area, although the information within these publications is not usually geared to motorcoach tour brokers. To provide the information most important to motorcoach tour brokers, you may wish to advertise in trade publications such as *Bus Tours Magazine, Leisure Group Travel, Group Travel Leader, Group Tour Magazine,* and *Packaged Travel Insider,* using ads that provide pertinent tour information, your contact person for bus tours, deposit requirements, cancellation policies, and other information. Exhibit 12 shows a sample print ad soliciting tours for a North Carolina resort.

Exhibit 10 Sample Hotel Sales Letter Targeting Tour Groups

Dear [name]:

If you've just returned from the National Tour Association convention in Nashville, chances are that this letter is competing with many others for your attention. So I'll get right to the point:

We want your New England Tours!

Before you finalize your itineraries for the spring, summer, and fall, here are three good reasons why you should consider the [name of property]:

1. LOCATION: We're directly off I-495, just 12 minutes from the Mass Turnpike (I-90), 20 minutes from I-95, and 38 miles from downtown Boston. If you're planning a hub-and-spoke tour, we're the ideal hub. From our location, your tours can easily travel not only to Boston, but also to Plymouth, Cape Cod, Sturbridge Village, and Newport. We're also less than two hours from Mystic Seaport and Franconia Notch, New Hampshire. A shopping center, cinema, and several food outlets are within easy walking distance for the convenience of your passengers.
2. VALUE: Our net tour rates are competitive with rates at any comparable hotel in greater Boston. In addition, we offer special incentive bonuses based on seasonality, volume, and/or arrival-departure patterns. We can also custom-tailor a package to meet the specific needs and interests of your passengers. Our inclusive "Champagne Tour" package is but one popular example.
3. BEYOND THE BASICS: In addition to the excellent facilities and service that you would expect from a hotel, we treat your passengers and staff like guests in our own home. From the moment our general manager, John Smith, and I roll out the Red Carpet (literally!) for your passengers, until we personally distribute departure gifts, your tour will be treated to genuine, first-class hospitality.

To take advantage of all our property has to offer, please take a few moments to jot a short note to me on the back of this letter. I'd be happy to answer your request for more information about [name of property] and the area and answer any questions. I've enclosed a prepaid envelope for your convenience, or, for even faster service, please feel free to contact me at the phone numbers or e-mail address listed on this letterhead.

Thank you for taking the time to respond to this invitation to book your groups at [name of property]. I'm looking forward to hearing from you ... and helping you to create a memorable experience for your groups.

Sincerely,

This letter, designed for tour brokers, focuses on the factors most important to developers of group tours: location, comps and discounts, and services. This letter also promotes services offered to groups—the red carpet treatment and departing gift—and implies that the property is experienced in handling groups.

Exhibit 11 Sample Group Rate Manual

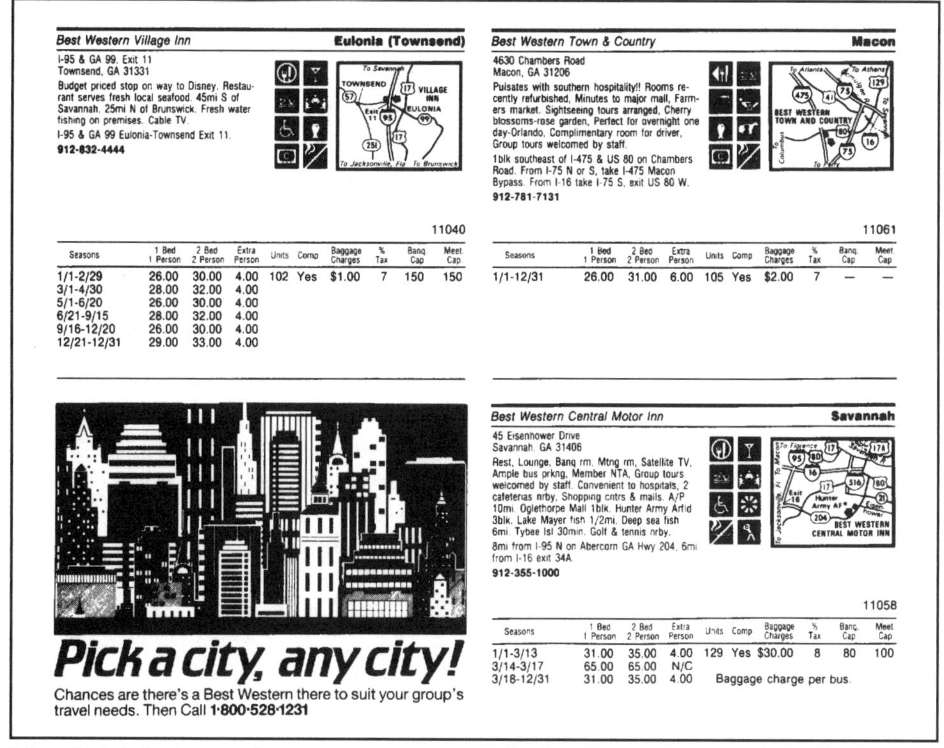

Best Western Village Inn — **Eulonia (Townsend)**

I-95 & GA 99, Exit 11
Townsend, GA 31331

Budget priced stop on way to Disney. Restaurant serves fresh local seafood. 45mi S of Savannah. 25mi N of Brunswick. Fresh water fishing on premises. Cable TV.

I-95 & GA 99 Eulonia-Townsend Exit 11.

912-832-4444

11040

Seasons	1 Bed 1 Person	2 Bed 2 Person	Extra Person	Units	Comp	Baggage Charges	% Tax	Banq. Cap	Meet. Cap.
1/1-2/29	26.00	30.00	4.00	102	Yes	$1.00	7	150	150
3/1-4/30	28.00	32.00	4.00						
5/1-6/20	26.00	30.00	4.00						
6/21-9/15	28.00	32.00	4.00						
9/16-12/20	26.00	30.00	4.00						
12/21-12/31	29.00	33.00	4.00						

Best Western Town & Country — **Macon**

4630 Chambers Road
Macon, GA 31206

Pulsates with southern hospitality!! Rooms recently refurbished, Minutes to major mall, Farmers market. Sightseeing tours arranged, Cherry blossoms-rose garden, Perfect for overnight one day-Orlando, Complimentary room for driver, Group tours welcomed by staff.

1blk southeast of I-475 & US 80 on Chambers Road. From I-75 N or S, take I-475 Macon Bypass. From I-16 take I-75 S, exit US 80 W.

912-781-7131

11061

Seasons	1 Bed 1 Person	2 Bed 2 Person	Extra Person	Units	Comp	Baggage Charges	% Tax	Banq. Cap	Meet. Cap
1/1-12/31	26.00	31.00	6.00	105	Yes	$2.00	7	—	—

Best Western Central Motor Inn — **Savannah**

45 Eisenhower Drive
Savannah, GA 31406

Rest, Lounge, Banq rm, Mtng rm, Satellite TV, Ample bus prkng, Member NTA, Group tours welcomed by staff. Convenient to hospitals, 2 cafeterias nrby, Shopping cntrs & malls. A/P 10mi. Oglethorpe Mall 1blk. Hunter Army Arfld 3blk. Lake Mayer fish 1/2mi. Deep sea fish 6mi. Tybee Isl 30min. Golf & tennis nrby.

8mi from I-95 N on Abercorn GA Hwy 204. 6mi from I-16 exit 34A.

912-355-1000

11058

Seasons	1 Bed 1 Person	2 Bed 2 Person	Extra Person	Units	Comp	Baggage Charges	% Tax	Banq. Cap	Meet Cap
1/1-3/13	31.00	35.00	4.00	129	Yes	$30.00	8	80	100
3/14-3/17	65.00	65.00	N/C						
3/18-12/31	31.00	35.00	4.00						

Baggage charge per bus.

Pick a city, any city!

Chances are there's a Best Western there to suit your group's travel needs. Then Call 1·800·528·1231

Most hotel chains produce group tour manuals that list group rates (usually 10 to 30 percent off) and special weekend rates for tour groups. Group rate manuals are distributed annually to bus companies, tour brokers, and tour wholesalers through direct mail efforts or at travel trade shows. (Courtesy of Best Western International, Inc.)

You can also generate repeat business and word-of-mouth referrals by providing special services. Some properties clean the interior and windows of the bus, while others offer welcome gifts such as fruit baskets or a local product to the tour escort and bus driver. These gestures demonstrate that you care enough about the tour operators and guests to warrant repeat business.

Airline Tours. Airline tours are another excellent source of group business. Airline tours are usually arranged by airline tour wholesalers, who not only contract with properties and attractions, but also promote the tours they develop. This takes a good deal of responsibility for advertising away from the property.

Like motorcoach tour brokers, airline tour wholesalers seek to provide a complete vacation experience for their clients. Properties located in or near popular destination cities or in close proximity to a number of attractions (Disneyland, Knott's Berry Farm, and Universal Studios in southern California, for example) are attractive to airline tour wholesalers, but a property that can offer an extensive recreational package may also be able to sell to this market.

Exhibit 12 Advertising to Tour Brokers

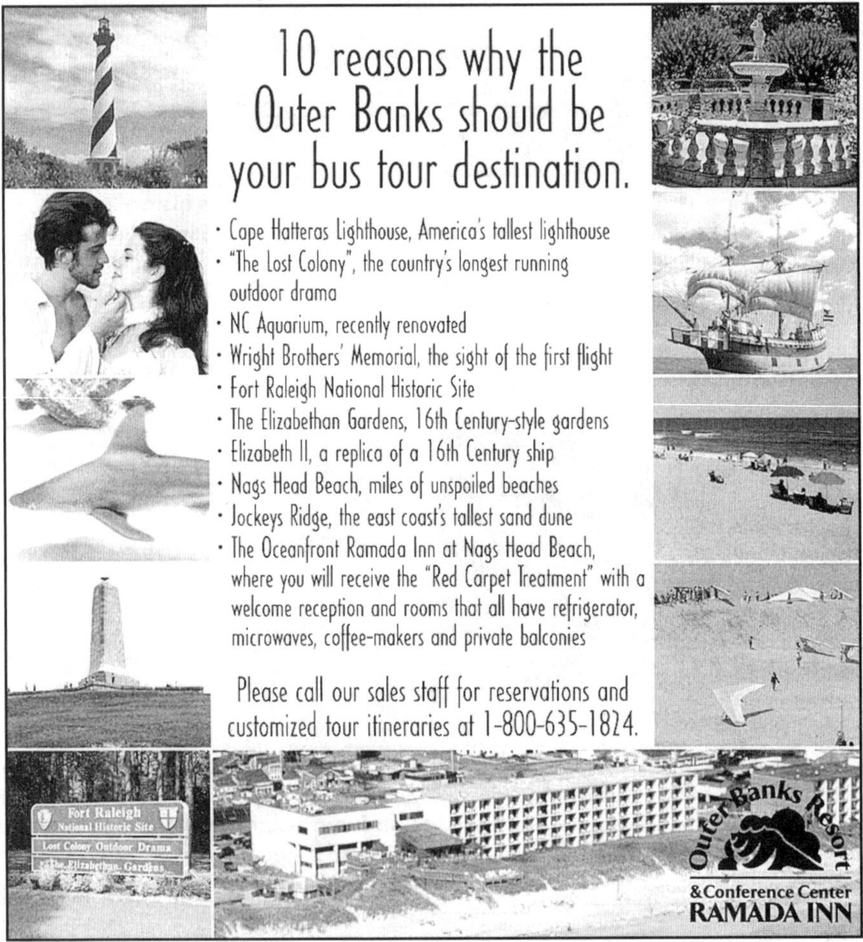

Ads such as this one are used to promote group leisure travel. While this ad primarily stresses the area attractions and offers only a brief mention of services the group will receive, other print ads targeting group leisure travel may include such booking information as group discount rates, property tour policies, and special amenities such as complimentary rooms for the tour guide and driver, discounts to nearby attractions, and so on. (Courtesy of Ramada)

If a property is not located close to an airport, an **intermodal tour** can often be arranged by an airline tour wholesaler. An intermodal tour makes use of more than one form of transportation (air-motorcoach, air-sea, air-car, and so on) and is often used to promote golf vacations, honeymoon trips, and extended group trips such as fall foliage tours. Intermodal tours may include air transportation to the tour's departure city, motorcoach transportation to several points of interest, and even a ferry or boat trip.

Airline tour wholesalers also package group tours that may include cruise ship travel. Air transportation to the port of departure, hotel accommodations and meals while in port, and the cruise itself can all be included in one package price. Properties located in popular ports or near international air terminals have an excellent opportunity to take advantage of this year-round business, especially if they can handle the demands of group travelers.

Property Package Tours. In addition to selling special group rates and services to tour brokers and tour wholesalers who develop tour packages, you can develop your own tour package (see Exhibit 13). Property packages can range from the simple (accommodations and selected meals only) to the elaborate, but should take advantage of the best of what the property has to offer, whether it is a signature dish, its proximity to downtown culture, or its diversity of winter sports. Bretton Woods in New Hampshire, for example, offers a "Midweek Winter Escape" package that includes daily rentals of snowshoes, ice skates, and snow tubes (and facilities to use them), a sleigh ride, and unlimited access to the Bretton Woods Sports Club.

Before you develop your own package, however, you must first familiarize yourself with the tour industry and determine what type of tour (either an independent package or a package in conjunction with other travel suppliers) would work best for your property. An aid in learning about the tour market is the *Discover America Package Tour Handbook,* published by the Travel Industry Association of America. This handbook gives an overall view of the extensive package tour market and provides the names of contacts for assistance or sales leads.

There are several reasons why you should consider developing your own package tour. Property packages can:

- Increase sales by offering consumers convenience and value
- Bring in business when you need it most, such as during the off-season
- Encourage property recognition, especially if the package is innovative or a real bargain

Packages can be simple or complicated. One property may opt for a simple package of one or two room nights with a complimentary continental breakfast, while another may put together a package that includes recreational amenities (golf, tennis, swimming), meals, discounts in the gift shop or discount coupons to nearby attractions, and turndown and valet service. Properties that wish to provide complete vacation packages or weekend getaways can include other travel suppliers (airlines, rental cars, local bus operators, or limousine services) and attractions (amusement parks, historic sites, etc.) in their tour packages.

While developing a tour package can be profitable, it also requires knowledge. You must first determine which markets you will target. Tour packages developed for older travelers may differ greatly from those designed for downhill skiers, for example. Since the needs of each market segment will be different, you have to determine which segments you can best serve.

When promoting tours, it is important to determine the type of group to whom the advertising is being directed. Tour groups can be categorized as active or passive. Your description of your facilities, amenities, and services should appeal to

Exhibit 13 Property Package Tours at a Glance

What:	Property package tours are group tour packages put together by an individual property or a chain. Property package tours offer several travel elements for one price, and may include lodging, meals, baggage transfers, recreational facilities, local guided tours, attractions, and entertainment. Properties that opt to include other travel suppliers—airlines, rental car companies, bus lines, and so on—can also offer transportation as part of the package.
Why:	Property package tours are popular with travel agents and consumers because they can be purchased for one inclusive price. For consumers, this makes it easier to budget. For travel agents, property package tours mean guaranteed availability and lower booking costs—the agent does not have to book the individual components separately.
When:	Property package tours can be developed for those times when business is most needed. They can also be developed to coincide with local events such as rodeos, food festivals, and county fairs.
How:	Property package tours can be developed in a number of ways. The property can package its own services (rooms, meals, entertainment, recreational facilities, etc.) and promote the package through advertising to travel agents and directly to consumers. Many properties, however, have found that developing a package in conjunction with another attraction or travel supplier offers the benefit of the experience of the other package participant(s) and generates a wider customer base. Selling the package to tour brokers after it has been developed is also an excellent way for the property's package to reach a wide base of potential guests.

the type of group visiting the property. An active group, for example, responds to copy promoting the exotic, sensual, and adventurous, while a passive group would be more comfortable with copy that stresses the traditional, well-known, and charming. Having a group profile beforehand will help you better attract and serve each group.

Once a package is developed, the next step is to promote it. You can sell the package to tour wholesalers, travel agents, or the public. If you sell the package through tour wholesalers or travel agents, make it a **commissionable tour** and give it an *IT (inclusive tour) number.* IT numbers are codes used on the hotel's tour folders to assist travel intermediaries in identifying and booking packages.

Property packages can be promoted to tour wholesalers and travel agents through direct contact or through direct mail and print advertising. Advertisements in trade journals will reach many of these travel professionals. Ads should be designed to promote the benefits of the property's tour package to the wholesaler or agent as well as to guests. You can also advertise in the *Consolidated Tour Manual,* a publication sponsored and published by participating U.S. airlines. The manual, which is distributed free to member airline sales offices and certain travel agents, offers hotels a full-page listing in the manual for a fee.

Properties that choose to include other travel suppliers in a tour package may enjoy the benefits of cooperative advertising and the consumer bases of these suppliers. Packages can be promoted through print advertising and by direct sales efforts on the part of not only the property, but also the other travel suppliers involved. Air-ground rooms packages, for example, may be promoted through colorful brochures at airline ticket terminals, at the offices of participating bus lines, and at the property's front desk. Or, the participants in the package could sell the entire package through tour wholesalers, saving on advertising costs.

Whatever option you choose, it often takes time for your tour package to reach consumers. It may take more than one season for a package to consistently fill rooms. You must make sure that a sparsely used package has been properly promoted before deciding it is unsuccessful. Group leisure travelers often book their reservations on a long lead time (up to two years in some cases) and may not be able to take advantage of a particular package when it is first offered. Before dropping a package, you should measure the effectiveness of the promotional campaign and talk to tour wholesalers about their response to the package.

Leisure Travelers and Small Properties

While many of the strategies discussed in this chapter are most applicable to large properties, small properties can also tap into the leisure market—both individual and group—in a number of creative ways. While their promotional budgets may be far smaller than those of large properties and chains, small properties may still take advantage of low-cost advertising in local and regional directories and can reach potential leisure travelers through radio spots and a combination of public relations and promotional activities.

Combining public relations and promotion is an extremely cost-effective way to promote a small property. For example, Bud Schramm, who owned the 31-room Buffalo Trail Motel in Winner, South Dakota, employed several creative and inexpensive ways to keep his property in the public's eye. One of Schramm's promotions was to place jars of red and white mints in gas stations and restaurants in the community. The jars were located by the cash registers and featured signs that said, "You're worth a mint to us," and "Compliments of Buffalo Trail Motel." Not only did the jars provide promotional benefits, but they helped establish contacts with people in the community who could help sell rooms for the property. Another idea that involved community support was the printing of "appreciation cards" that offered a discount at the motel. These cards were given to public-contact people—store clerks, food servers, mechanics, and so on—who handed them out to people passing through town. When enough of the cards were redeemed, the public-contact people were eligible to win a free weekend stay for two at the motel, giving them an added incentive to hand out as many cards as possible.

Small properties can also target the group leisure traveler; in many cases, motorcoach tours stay at small, unique properties close to attractions. This type of stay costs less than one at a larger property at which tour travelers might not have a chance to use all the amenities. Also, the staff at smaller properties can give each group undivided attention. While most motorcoach tour stays are for one night,

INTERNET EXERCISE

Log onto the Internet and research the website of the United States Tour Operators Association at www.ustoa.com.

1. What is the USTOA?
2. What is the difference between a tour and a vacation package?
3. Why would travelers want to purchase a package instead of planning a trip on their own?
4. Test your vacation savvy by taking the true/false quiz on the site.
5. Take the vacation personality quiz to determine the kind of vacation package that bests suits your personality and preferences.

you can encourage longer stays by offering economy packages for two nights or by partnering in the area to provide discounts at local businesses and attractions. Small properties can also add to revenues from groups by offering box lunches, catered picnics at local attractions, and group meals at property restaurants. Even if a group is not staying in the area, hotels and restaurants can take advantage of opportunities to provide meals at bus layover points if they can accommodate groups.

Small properties can sell the uniqueness of their local areas in promotional pieces. They can also join groups or networks that help small properties boost business. The American Hotel & Lodging Association (AH&LA) has a committee on small properties that runs seminars throughout the country. Small properties that belong to AH&LA can also take advantage of AH&LA's Information Center, which provides members with research assistance and help with marketing and promotion.

The Vacation Ownership Option

Yet another way in which the hospitality industry has responded to the leisure traveler market is with vacation ownership properties. **Vacation ownership,** also known as *interval ownership* or *timesharing,* can be defined as purchasing the title to a specific period of time at a particular property's unit (although these units can be traded with other vacation owners). At one time, the vacation ownership industry was a dubious industry at best, with unscrupulous operators selling inferior products at inflated prices. Today, however, the entry of large hotel chains into the field has resulted in an upsurge in sales. Hotel chains have created a greater credibility for the concept, raised the quality of the product, and offer consumers a variety of price points and ownership options. As a result, vacation ownership has evolved into a $3 billion-per-year industry.

The average vacation-ownership package includes a two-bedroom unit and costs about $10,000 for two weeks. Units are usually sold for 50 weeks per year (the other two weeks are commonly set aside for maintenance), generating annual revenue of $250,000 for each unit. Units are sold largely to baby boomers and, increasingly, GenXers.

The vacation ownership market includes such industry giants as Disney, Four Seasons, Hyatt, Hilton, Marriott, Sheraton, and Westin. Some chains, such as Marriott and Hilton, have built timeshare condominiums on the grounds of existing hotel complexes, while some properties have converted a certain number of existing rooms into "urban timeshares." Still other properties are part of international management operations: Interval International serves 600,000 member families in 300 member resorts in 55 countries, while Resort Condominium International boasts 1.9 million members in 2,800 resorts in 81 countries. These firms have centralized reservations services and ensure that quality is maintained in member properties.

Vacation ownership allows travelers the luxury of having a vacation home without the hassle of full-time ownership, and monthly payments are kept affordable. Properties are finding new ways to enhance the condominium vacation experience. Many are now offering increased flexibility through options for members to "split" their purchased weeks into weekend or even daily increments.

Marketing Vacation Ownership

Marketing vacation ownership is often done through direct mail or in-person sales; Marriott sends out 30 million pieces of direct mail annually, targeting people who have stayed at a Marriott hotel and inviting them to visit a Marriott vacation ownership property to hear a sales presentation. Offering a free stay to a potential buyer allows him or her to actually experience the property firsthand.

Face-to-face selling to passersby is common in cities where vacation ownership properties are located. Potential owners are usually promised a free gift—from tickets to dinners or shows to free vacation getaways—for agreeing to take a tour and listen to a sales presentation. This type of "cold calling" is more effective if some form of qualification is conducted beforehand. Many sales representatives ask prospects about basic qualifications (such as minimum level of income) almost immediately after approaching them.

Vacation ownership can also be marketed through property seminars, print ads in travel publications, websites, and e-mail solicitations. New or unique vacation ownership properties can also take advantage of publicity to get their names before the vacationing public.

Conclusion

The leisure traveler market is a large, complex, and valuable source of business for lodging properties. Growth in this market is expected to continue in coming years due to extended holidays, four-day workweeks for a growing number of employees, the increase in the number of dual-career families, longer life expectancies, and increased discretionary income.

Since the leisure traveler market is so large and diverse, many hospitality firms use **focus groups** to determine what leisure travelers look for in a lodging property or restaurant. For maximum effectiveness, focus groups should be comprised of consumers to whom your product is targeted and should be moderated by an experienced marketing person who can accurately determine factors that are most important to group members. Some hospitality firms also use test markets to see if there is an interest in a new product or service. Introducing a change on a small scale can prove extremely cost-effective, especially if the product or service "bombs" with test consumers.

Leisure travelers look for ease and convenience in travel and find special packages like the ones discussed in this chapter particularly attractive. Many packages designed for leisure travelers are sold through travel intermediaries. You should be aware of opportunities to build good working relationships with such travel intermediaries as tour brokers, tour wholesalers, and travel agents.

Endnotes

1. John Boroshok, "It Pays to Welcome Travelers with Pets," *HSMAI Marketing Review,* Fall 2006.
2. Rohit Verma, "What Today's Travelers Want When They Select a Hotel," *HSMAI Marketing Review,* Fall 2002, p. 22.
3. *HSMAI Marketing Review,* Spring 2000, p. 51.
4. Edward Watkins, "The Summit Looks at 97," *Lodging Hospitality,* January 1997, p. 18.
5. John Raymond, "The Joy of Empty Nesting," *American Demographics,* May 2000.
6. Hein Ruyes and Sherrie Wei, "Accommodation Needs of Mature Australian Travelers," *Australian Journal of Hospitality Management,* Autumn 1998, pp. 51–59.
7. *Report to the Nation: Trends in Travel & Hospitality* (Washington, D.C.: Public Affairs Group, 1997), p. 16.
8. Allstate Financial Cost of Leisure Study, *ASTA Travel Agency Management,* May 2002, p. 10.
9. Marilyn Green, "Generation X," *Travel Professional,* October/November, 2007.
10. Dan Philips and Ray Lewis, "Technology in the Crystal Ball," *Hospitality Upgrade,* Summer 2007, p. 168.
11. Cathleen McCarthy, "Tapping Into the Active Travel Market," *HSMAI Marketing Review,* Summer 2002, p. 35.
12. "AAA Survey Finds Girlfriend Getaways Increasing," *TravelAgent,* July 23, 2007, p. 14.
13. Judy Colbert, "Older, Wiser, and Richer Than Ever," *Lodging,* January 2000, p. 59.

Key Terms

airline tour—A tour whose primary mode of transportation is by airplane.

boutique hotel—Generally a small hotel that is trendy, stylish, and unique. Also called "lifestyle" properties, boutique hotels are known for their ambiance, personalized service, and posh amenities.

commissionable tour—Any packaged tour made available to individuals or groups through a travel agency that entitles a travel agent to receive a commission for its sale.

focus group—A group of past or prospective customers assembled to discuss a hospitality product or brand, guided by a trained moderator.

group sales allotment—The number of rooms a lodging property sets aside for group and tour business.

hub-and-spoke itinerary—A group tour that uses a central destination (hub) and supplements the tour itinerary with day excursions (spokes) to other area sites, attractions, restaurants, shopping areas, or entertainment venues.

intermodal tour—A tour that involves more than one form of transportation (air-motorcoach, for example).

motorcoach charter—A group of people traveling together who select a destination and then contact a motorcoach company to charter or rent a bus to take them to their destination.

motorcoach tour—A tour for which the primary mode of transportation is motorcoach or bus.

net wholesale rates—A discounted tour rate offered to a wholesaler or tour operator, who will mark it up before selling tour space to consumers.

tour—Any prearranged (but not necessarily prepaid) journey to one or more places and back to the point of origin.

tour broker—In the United States, a travel professional licensed by the Federal Interstate Commerce Commission to put together package motorcoach tours in the United States and, in some cases, Canada. Also called a *motorcoach broker* or *tour operator.*

tour intermediary—A travel professional, such as a tour broker, tour wholesaler, or retail travel agent, who arranges group tours.

tour voucher—A document issued by tour brokers to be exchanged for accommodations, meals, sight-seeing, and other services. Sometimes called a *coupon.*

tour wholesaler—A travel professional who puts tour packages together that usually involve air transportation.

vacation ownership—Also known as *interval ownership* or *timesharing*; typically involves purchasing the title to a specific period of time at a lodging unit at a particular property.

Review Questions

1. How does leisure travel differ from business travel? What are its benefits to hospitality properties?
2. What are some types of individual leisure travelers?
3. How are properties meeting the needs of family leisure travelers?

4. What are some of the ways to reach the family traveler market?
5. Why is the senior traveler market important to hotels, and how are properties meeting the needs of mature travelers?
6. What is a tour broker? a tour wholesaler? How do properties reach these travel intermediaries?
7. What are three types of tours commonly taken by group leisure travelers?
8. How are properties meeting the needs of motorcoach tour travelers?
9. Why should a property consider developing its own package tour?
10. What is vacation ownership, and how is it different from other aspects of the leisure market?

Internet Sites

For more information, visit the following Internet sites. Remember that Internet addresses can change without notice. If the site is no longer there, you can use a search engine to look for additional sites.

1st Choice Vacation Properties
www.choice1.com

Accommodation Search Engine
www.ase.net

American Association of Retired Persons
www.aarp.org

American Hotel & Lodging Association
www.ahla.com

American Society of Travel Agents
www.astanet.com

Automobile Association of America
www.aaa.com

Bus World
www.busconversions.com

Choice Hotels International
www.hotelchoice.com

Days Inn
www.daysinn.com

Destination Marketing Association International
www.iacvb.org

Doubletree Hotels
www.doubletreehotels.com

Fairmont Hotels & Resorts
www.fairmont.com

Four Seasons Hotels and Resorts
www.fshr.com

Greyhound Lines, Inc.
www.greyhound.com

Hampton Inn
www.hampton-inn.com

Hilton Hotels
www.hilton.com

Hospitality Sales & Marketing Association International
www.hsmai.org

Hyatt Hotels
www.hyatt.com

Marriott International
www.marriott.com

Media Central
www.mediacentral.com/

Meeting Professionals International
www.mpiweb.org

National Tour Association
www.ntaonline.com

Omni Hotels
www.omnihotels.com

Radisson Hotels & Resorts
www.radisson.com

Ramada Worldwide
www.ramada.com

Ritz-Carlton Hotels
www.ritzcarlton.com

Sales & Marketing Management
www.salesandmarketing.com

Sheraton Hotels & Resorts
www.sheraton.com

Travel Industry Association
www.tia.org

urhospitality.com
www.urhospitality.com

Web Digest for Marketers
www.wdfm.com

Westin Hotels & Resorts
www.westin.com

YMCA International
www.ymca.int

YWCA of the USA
www.ywca.org

Case Study

Sales Slump in Sun City

Sun City—how could anyone be unhappy in this vacation paradise where tanned natives and sunburned tourists basked on white sand beaches all year round? But Gregory Earle, general manager of the 122-room Sun & Surf Inn, was unhappy as he gazed out of his office window. Why aren't those tourists at my hotel, he wondered as a sleek, silver tour bus cruised past his property. "Headed for the Beachcomber, I'll bet," thought Greg, picking up the latest sales report from his desk. Tour groups made up only five percent of the Sun & Surf's business, and occupancy was down eight points from budget. Greg couldn't help but think the two were somehow related.

Greg had been general manager of the Sun & Surf Inn for only three months. This was his first position at a travel destination property; the other hotels he'd managed in this national chain drew most of their business from commercial travelers, not tourists. His predecessor left for a new opportunity, followed closely by the resignation of the hotel's sales director, who took with her a couple of profitable accounts with tour operators and wholesalers. Now, Greg's sales staff consisted of his new director of sales, Kendra Wilson, who was promoted from the sales position she held with the hotel for the past two years. Greg called Kendra to his office, hoping she could help him get a handle on their sales picture.

"Kendra, why aren't we pulling in tour groups the way the Beachcomber does?" Greg asked. "Our rates are comparable, we've got the same amenities, and we're actually closer to the beach than they are. So why are we only doing five percent in tour group business?"

Kendra looked uncomfortable. "Well, we lost a couple of key tour accounts when the director of sales left, and she had to work hard to keep them before then. The last general manager wasn't always real good about paying commissions to the tour companies on time. That, and we haven't sent anyone to the Pow Wow or Florida Huddle for a while. We were always arguing over whether trade shows were worth the expense," she said.

Seeing Greg's confusion, Kendra explained that trade shows like the Pow Wow and Florida Huddle, as well as the National Tour Association trade show, were good places to consider for soliciting business from tour companies and wholesalers, which contract with a hotel for a certain number of room nights which they build into tour packages.

"It sounds like we need to get back on the trade show circuit if we're going to boost our occupancy rate," said Greg. "Kendra, I'd like to have you look into those shows and spend some time meeting with tour operators and wholesalers as part of your marketing plan. That should get us back on track."

Kendra shook her head. "It's not that easy, Greg. It takes time to build strong relationships with tour operators and wholesalers. Besides, these folks book their business a year in advance. Even if I start now, we won't see the results on our books until sometime next year. I'm willing to take on the challenge, but we'll need to look at some other marketing strategies that will show results sooner than that."

Greg rolled up his sleeves. "All right, where do we start?"

Kendra showed him her marketing plan. She met regularly with the local convention and visitors bureau to keep on top of events that were bringing groups into town. She read the business pages of the daily newspaper to find new businesses that were coming into the area, and called on them to make them aware of the hotel and to ask for their business. The hotel was listed with two local colleges that recommended the property to students' families during orientation and commencement, as well as to visiting athletic teams. Kendra had also recently updated the hotel's two billboards, which were located in prominent positions along the two major highways leading into Sun City. "We're listed in the AAA book, too," Kendra said.

"That's great," said Greg. "How big is our ad?"

"I didn't say we had an ad; I said we were listed," Kendra replied.

"Oh. Well, how about any of the coupon books for our low-demand dates? At my last property, we were in a couple of travel club programs, like Entertainment Card. No? Maybe you should look into that," said Greg.

"Okay. I've tried to put together some attractive packages to bring in people during our low demand times, but they don't seem to work very well," said Kendra.

Greg asked if the reservation agents were actively selling those packages, and if their chain's central reservations office had an updated listing of the hotel's special rates.

"I don't know," said Kendra. "I gave the information to Luis. I figured it's his job as front office manager to take it from there. I never thought to check out what happened after that."

"Thanks, Kendra," said Greg. "Why don't you meet with Luis about those packages, and we'll all get together to discuss this further."

Discussion Questions

1. What are some of the problems Greg has inherited from the previous general manager, and what steps will he have to take to remedy them?
2. What issues will Kendra need to consider as she begins to solicit business from tour group operators and wholesalers?
3. What are some additional marketing activities the Sun & Surf Inn can implement to increase occupancy in the short term, while the director of sales is building the hotel's wholesaler and tour group business?
4. What are some of the issues that should be discussed with Luis, the front office manager?

Case Number: 370CE

This case was developed in cooperation with Lisa Richards of Hospitality Softnet, Inc., a marketing resources and support company (Sixty State Street, Suite 700, Boston, Massachusetts 02109; www.hospitalitysoftnet.com).

This case also appears in *Contemporary Hospitality Marketing: A Service Management Approach* (Lansing, Mich.: American Hotel & Lodging Educational Institute, 1999), ISBN 978-0-86612-158-3.

Chapter 10 Outline

Competencies

1. Describe travel agencies and the kinds of travelers they serve. (pp. 375–379)
2. Explain how travel agents get information about properties and book reservations, and explain how hospitality firms serve travel agents and their clients. (pp. 379–400)
3. Describe ways in which hospitality salespeople find and reach travel agents and agencies, and summarize issues facing travel agents in the future. (pp. 400–408)

Insider Insights

James P. Tierney, CHSE
Director of Sales and Marketing
World Golf Village Renaissance Resort
St. Augustine, Florida

"Being a travel agent has to be a unique and sometimes frustrating experience. Travel agents are required to work hard to make less money! Clients look for the least expensive airfare, the most economical tour package, and the best possible room rate. In finding these deals, the agent makes less commission. And the agent is held personally responsible if anything goes wrong with the client's vacation or travel arrangements."

10

Marketing to Travel Agents

TEN YEARS AGO, THE U.S. TRAVEL AGENCY INDUSTRY boasted some 400,000 travel agents based in 35,000 full-service travel agencies. A small percentage of these agents were involved in meeting planning, while the majority concentrated on making airline, cruise, and hotel reservations for business and leisure travelers. Since many travel agents served niche markets and focused on special interests and activities for their clients, they became an important source of leisure sales for hotels.

Although travel has become increasingly complex, with a myriad of hotel choices and the airline industry in a constant state of flux, there has been a dramatic decline in the number of travel agents. This is largely the result of smaller agencies closing their doors after the airlines decided they did not need travel agents to sell their seats. With the advent of e-ticketing and direct airline booking sites on the Internet, airlines decided they could cut costs even further by eliminating travel agent commissions. U.S. airlines estimate they will save more than $4 billion annually by eliminating the seven to ten percent commissions that they used to pay to travel agents.

Despite the downturn in the travel agency industry, it still makes good business sense for properties to develop and maintain mutually beneficial partnerships with these travel professionals. There are still large numbers of business and leisure travelers who prefer to rely on the expertise of travel agents (see Exhibit 1), and, industry-wide, travel agents book about 25 percent of hotel room nights (resort hotels receive 50 to 60 percent of their bookings through travel agents). In a 2005 study conducted by H&MM research, travel agents accounted for 30 percent of the resort bookings at Hyatt, and travel agent commissions reached $177 million at Marriott International, where Fred Miller, vice president of global sales for Marriott, says that "agency bookings are always the highest-rated third-party distribution channel; they are the lowest cost distribution channel outside our own sites."[1] Travel agents, therefore, can serve as invaluable extensions of a property's sales force, reaching clients that a hotel might otherwise not be able to specifically target. It costs a hotel just a 10-percent commission on room rates to use the services of travel agents, who now rely more heavily on hotel commissions for their livelihood. Travel agents can be excellent sources of additional bookings and repeat business for hotels that provide good service to them and their clients.

In this chapter, we will take a look at today's travel agents and the diverse types of travelers they serve. We will see how properties are reaching out to these travel professionals and learn what steps hotels can take to meet their needs. We

Exhibit 1 Travel Agents' Influence Growing

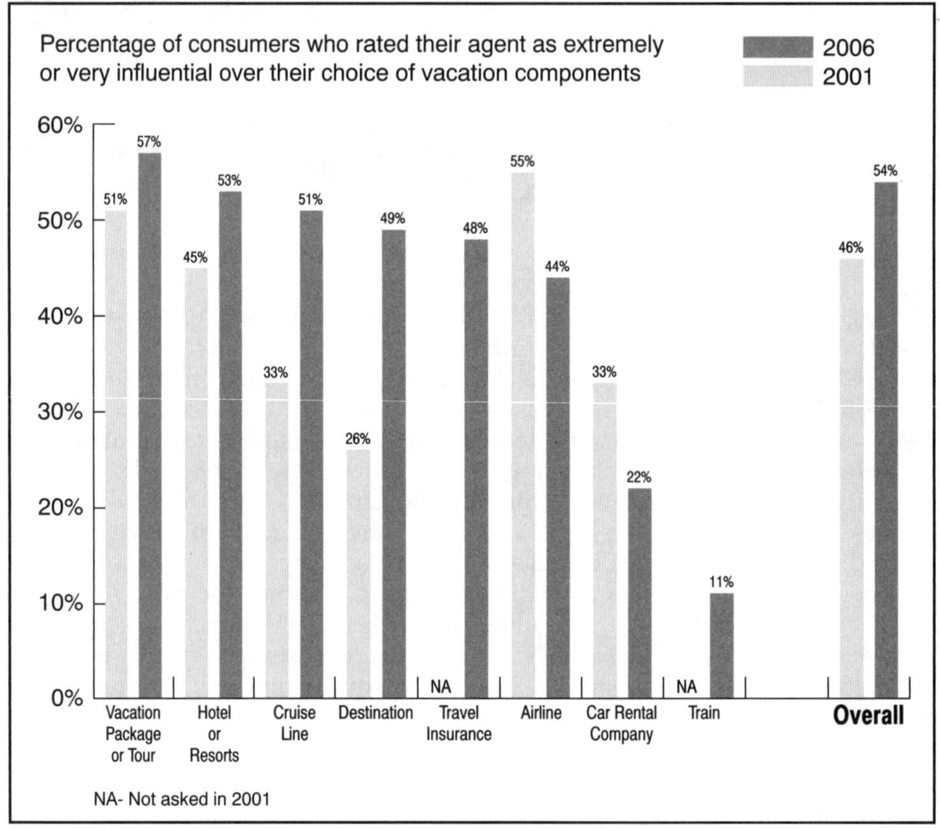

Source: YPB&R May 2001 and 2007 Leisure Travel Monitor.

will conclude the chapter with a discussion of how the travel agency industry is changing, what the future holds for travel agents, and how these changes will impact the hospitality industry.

Travel Agencies

The concept of an individual assisting other individuals with travel plans can be traced to 1841, when a British Baptist minister named Thomas Cook signed up 570 people to accompany him to a temperance meeting. Cook got the group a rate of a shilling per person for the 22-mile round trip from Leicester to Loughborough, and included a picnic lunch and entertainment as part of the "package." His tour proved so popular that by 1856 the enterprising Cook was advertising a "Grand Circular Tour of the Continent." In 1869, Cook introduced his "middle-class-conducted crusades" to the Holy Land.

Most **travel agencies** in the United States began as mom-and-pop establishments that operated on the same principles as Thomas Cook's original tours.

Tours were often "guided" by the owners of the travel agencies, based on personal experiences at the destinations. These early operations are a far cry from the travel agencies and travel agents of today. Today's travel agencies fall into three major categories: travel management companies, consortiums, and independent agencies.

Travel management companies, also called *mega-travel agencies* because of their size and scope, are giant chains that own and control all aspects of their operations. Their extensive buying power enables them to negotiate special rates for their clients, and they provide complete travel services, including arranging and booking transportation, accommodations, and trips and tours. American Express is the largest of these mega-agencies, with 8,000 full-time employees. Other top agencies include Carlson Wagonlit Travel (sister company of Radisson Hotels), Rosenbluth International, World Travel BTI, Sato Travel, Maritz Travel, World Travel Partners, Omega World Travel, Travel and Transport, and Travel One.

Consortiums are groups of travel agents that have partnered to maximize their buying power and share the high cost of today's computer technology. Members of consortiums range from small, independent firms to larger travel companies that may have satellite offices around the country and may focus on travel segments such as business, leisure, or luxury travel. Cahners Travel Group, Hickory Travel System, Travel Savers, Virtuoso, and ABC Corporate Services are examples of travel consortiums.

Independent travel agencies and agents are still viable sources of business, although, as in the hotel industry, there is a trend in the travel agency industry toward consolidation to reduce costs and provide complete services. Independent agencies may serve areas not covered by major agencies or may specialize in corporate travel services or in meeting specialized travel needs.

Today's travel agents use sophisticated technology to research and book some 50 percent of the total reservations made nationwide for air travel, cruises, and rental cars, and are influential in booking corporate and international hotel business as well. The importance of travel agents has not escaped the notice of the lodging industry. Hotels depend on travel agents to serve as a part of their sales force—as salespeople who work at no overhead costs to a property. Michael A. Levin, retired CEO of U.S. Franchise, says that "the travel agent has become a major counselor of the traveler. So, essentially you've added to your sales staff thousands of agents."[2] Other leading hoteliers support Levin's view. Don Landry, past president of Choice Hotels International, states that "travel agents are a very viable source of business. Travel agent business is growing about 30 percent a year in our system."[3] According to leading hotelier Juergen Bartels, travel agents "currently represent a large source of business for the hotel industry, but an even greater potential source of business."[4] Wendy Cole, director of wholesale sales for Hyatt Resorts Caribbean, says that "when the Internet first emerged, everyone said it would be the end of the travel agent, but we never felt that way. The web is very important to us and we work with our wholesalers to develop their own websites that will encourage guests to book online through a retail agent. We are very protective of our relationships with travel agents. We'll always need professionals to help us."[5]

Virtuoso: A Luxury Leisure Travel Consortium

The leading travel agency network for leisure travel, Virtuoso, comprises more than 6,000 elite travel specialists associated with over 300 agencies in 22 countries. Independent travel agents, who join by invitation only, receive sales, marketing, and technology support, specialized training programs, and access to the most exclusive services and products in the luxury market.

Virtuoso, which began in the 1950s as Allied Travel, merged with Percival Tours in 1986 to form Allied Percival International (API), which brought together the best luxury travel agents in the United States. The company was renamed Virtuoso in 2000. Virtuoso's member agencies generate more than $4.2 billion annually in travel sales, and the company is the exclusive travel provider for World Elite MasterCard.

Virtuoso provides a number of specialized services to its travel agents, including marketing services (direct mail, e-mail, and so on), website hosting, and publications (including *Virtuoso Life,* a glossy magazine similar to *Vanity Fair).* Virtuoso's website provides links to upscale hospitality properties, restaurants, and travel providers, making it an attractive advertising option to lodging properties and other high-end hospitality businesses that wish to reach the growing luxury leisure travel market.

Travelers Served

Generally speaking, travel agents serve three types of travelers:

- Business travelers
- Leisure travelers
- International travelers

Business travelers represent about one-third of all business generated by travel agents. Each month, over four million business travelers book rooms through travel agents or through corporate travel planners who use travel agents.[6] Wingate Inns, designed specifically for business travelers, has found great success in filling its 100-plus properties by using the services of travel agents.

In addition to individual business travelers, more travel agencies are serving business groups. This trend has led to the development of agents or separate departments within travel agencies that specialize in business meetings and groups. The fastest growing segment of the business group market is the small meetings segment (meetings for 25 or fewer people). Over 43 percent of travel agents surveyed felt that small meetings would eventually become the backbone of business travel revenue for most travel agencies, especially since many large corporations are consolidating travel purchasing. IBM, for example, consolidated the number of travel agencies it does business with from 1,200 travel agencies to three! And IBM is not an isolated case. The needs of the Fortune 500 companies were once handled by 8,800 travel agencies; today, fewer than 500 agencies assist those companies. Many companies are now setting up their own in-house corporate travel agency or contracting with an established agency to set up and run an in-house agency for them. These agencies are termed **in-plant agencies.**

Leisure travelers often need more assistance in planning their travel than business travelers. Business travelers usually have a predetermined destination and are often restricted by their companies in their choice of hotels, but less than half of all leisure clients know precisely where they want to go. Eighty percent of all individual visitors to resort destinations such as Hawaii, Las Vegas, the Bahamas, and Bermuda use a travel agent to help plan or book their vacations. All-inclusive resorts, such as Sandals and Couples, receive the vast majority of their reservations through travel agents.

To increase their leisure traveler business, many hotels are teaming up with travel agents by creating commissionable weekend packages. Travel agents are big sellers of weekend packages, especially in such markets as New York, Boston, New Orleans, and Washington, D.C. They are attracted to the inclusive prices and easy booking features inherent in many packages.

International travelers can be business or leisure travelers. The number of foreigners traveling to the United States is increasing substantially. To promote a property to international travelers, travel agents must have adequate information. Special services, such as the availability of on-property translators, can help attract international travelers to a property.

Meeting the Needs of Travel Agents

Travel agents deal with a wide range of clients. You must understand what a travel agent needs in order to help him or her successfully promote your property. (Many hotel chains have established advisory boards composed of travel agents to build channels of communication.) The needs of travel agents can be broken down into two general areas: information about the property, and good service to both travel agents and their clients.

Property Information

Hotels can provide property information to travel agents in a number of ways; some of the most common are through global distribution systems, Internet distribution systems, websites, faxes and e-mails, hotel directories, information packages, familiarization tours, and specialized training and education programs. We'll take a look at each of these ways in the following sections.

Global Distribution Systems (GDSs). Hotels can provide basic reservation and rate information to travel agents through the computerized reservations systems developed by the airlines. Several years ago, there were almost a dozen of these systems, developed by both domestic and international airlines. Like hotel systems, these systems initially were called central reservations systems, but they are now known as **global distribution systems (GDSs).** Today, following the consolidation of several systems, there are four major GDSs: Amadeus, Galileo, SABRE, and WORLDSPAN. While travel agents once had exclusive access to these systems, many GDSs now allow access by individual business travelers and corporate travel departments.

Major Global Distribution Systems

amadeus
Your technology partner

Amadeus: A GDS providing online distribution, marketing, and sales tools to travel professionals around the globe. Owned by Air France, Continental Airlines, Iberia, and Lufthansa, its holding company is Amadeus Global Travel Distribution, based in Madrid, Spain.

Galileo
by Travelport

Galileo: One of the world's leading providers of electronic global distribution services, this GDS connects more than 38,400 travel agencies to more than 500 airlines, 45 car rental companies, and major hotel chains and cruise lines worldwide. It is owned by Wyndham, one of the world's largest franchisers of lodging properties.

Sabre Travel Network.

SABRE (The SABRE Group): A world leader in the electronic distribution of travel and a leading provider of information technology solutions for the travel and transportation industry.

worldspan.

WORLDSPAN: Provides global communications and electronic distribution of information for more than 500 of the world's leading travel service providers. Primarily owned by Delta Airlines and Northwest Airlines.

When first introduced, these systems simply offered flight information and availability. Later, basic hotel and car rental information was made available to travel agents via their computer terminals. But a number of other factors, including location, hotel features, guestroom size, amenities, restaurants, special rates, and credit card policies, figure into hotel bookings, and the global reservations systems did not supply this information and were not programmed to answer questions or make alternative suggestions. In addition, travel agents could not book rooms directly on the early systems; they had to check computer listings and then call the hotel or chain to book the reservation or obtain additional information.

Deregulation of the airlines allowed for the computer networks to be developed as separate businesses, and most took advantage of new technologies, including enhanced graphics and displays and video capabilities, to dramatically expand their scope. These systems expanded around the world, creating global automated booking systems for both airline and hospitality travel products.

Although hotels lagged behind the airlines in the area of computerized reservations and global distribution systems, worldwide networks have been developed to improve hotel reservations capabilities. Several hotel chains, including Best Western, Days Inns, Hilton, Holiday Inns, Hyatt, InterContinental, Marriott, Ramada, Sheraton, Forte Hotels, and Westin, are now using electronic distribution systems that link hotel reservation systems with GDSs. The two major developers of these systems were Pegasus and Wizcom, **switch companies** that serve as interpreters to switch the programming language of the GDSs and hotels' reservation

Exhibit 2 Global Distribution Systems

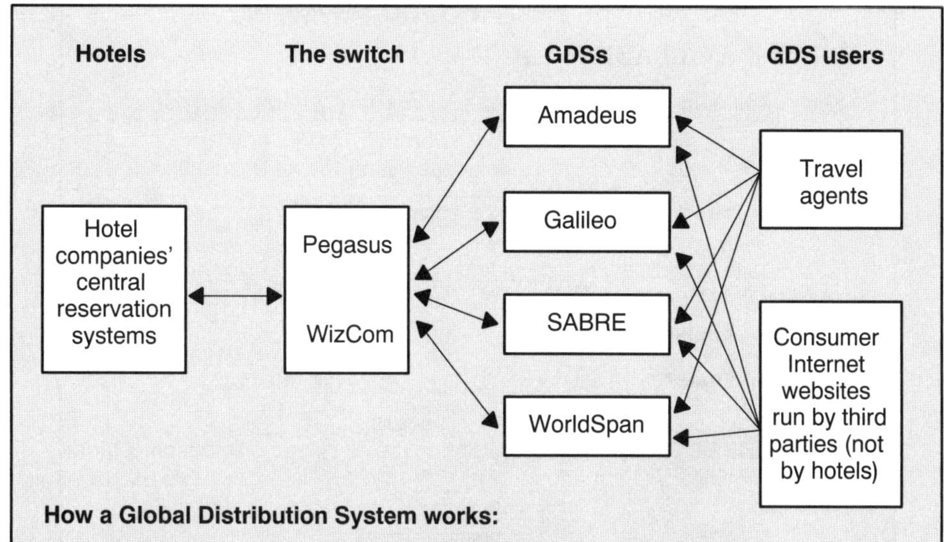

How a Global Distribution System works:

- Hotels deliver rate and room availability to one of the switches.
- The switches deliver rate and room availability to all four GDSs.
- Travel agents and consumer Internet websites use GDSs to access hotel rates and room availability.
- GDSs deliver reservations to hotels' CRSs through the switches.

Global distribution systems (GDSs) allow travel agents to compare the rates of a myriad of hotels and coordinate room reservations with other travel providers, such as airlines and car rental agencies. Switch companies act as an intermediary between the GDSs and hotel chains' central reservation systems. By linking GDSs to lodging properties, switch companies facilitate the relay of information on room availability, rates, and confirmation numbers. Most travel agencies have online access to one or more GDSs and pay a monthly fee for the service. Source: Adapted from Cindy Estis Green, "De-mystifying Distribution: Building a Distribution Strategy One Channel at a Time," from the 2005 booklet *A TIG Global Special Report* published by the HSMAI Foundation, pp. 50–52.

systems to make them compatible. Exhibit 2 illustrates how switch technology allows hotels to connect their reservations systems and room inventory directly to GDSs, allowing viewers to see "real time" hotel inventory and pricing.

Hotels would prefer that travel agents made their reservations through their distribution systems rather than through a GDS (see Exhibit 3). For each reservation received through a GDS, hotels must pay a fee to the GDS and to the switch company (in addition to a membership fee that GDSs charge all properties on their database). These fees total about $6 per reservation. Coupled with the travel agent's commission, these costs cut into profits on rooms, so many hotels encourage travel agents to book directly through property or chain websites; some offer specials to encourage travel agents to do so.

Exhibit 3 Sample Hotel Booking Engine

CHECK AVAILABILITY AND RATES *Step 1 of 4*

1 CHECK AVAILABILITY | 2 SELECT A ROOM | 3 COMPLETE DETAILS | 4 CONFIRM RESERVATION

* Mandatory

Hotel or Resort* Select a Destination

Arrival Date* 31 Mar 2008 Mon

Number of Nights* 1

Departure Date* 01 Apr 2008 Tues

Adults* 1 Children 0

Room* Non-Smoking Smoking

Bed Type King Or Queen

Rate Type Best Available Rate
ID Required at Check-In

Promotional Code

FAmous#

IATA Code

NOTE : For multiple room bookings you will need to Reserve Another Room when you reach the Step 4 of your reservation process.

Check Availability & Rates

Terms & Conditions Currency Converter Privacy Policy

This sample hotel booking engine enables travel agents and others to check availability and rates for selected dates before booking guestrooms in the hotel or resort chosen in the "Select a Destination" box. Hotels prefer that travel agents book directly through hotel booking engines such as this one rather than booking through a global distribution system.

Many chains have also established their own central reservations systems or partnered with GDS providers to provide direct distribution of their products. Sheraton, for example, has linked 17 of its reservations centers around the world and provides toll-free numbers in 44 countries. Radisson Hotels, in cooperation with Galileo, developed a seamless reservation capability, giving agents the ability to enter the chain's reservations system, view the entire inventory, and make a reservation electronically. These types of networks not only provide an additional avenue for booking hotel reservations, but are also used to enhance property management and revenue management as well.

Both of these options save time for travel agents, and, in the highly competitive travel industry, time is money. Booking a $100 room yields a ten percent commission of ten dollars to the travel agent. If the agent has to book the room through a computerized system that does not offer direct booking access or if the agent has to look up a listing in a directory, he or she will have to dial a toll-free number, possibly be put on hold, and then speak to a reservations agent—a process that could take up to ten minutes. If he or she can access a GDS to book the room, however, that ten percent commission could be earned in less than ten seconds!

Therefore, hotels that can offer direct global booking systems have a much greater chance to obtain business from travel agents than those that do not. To assist individual properties, many chains, such as Best Western, offer training and assistance for effectively utilizing global distribution systems. Seminars and other training programs are also offered to both hotels and travel agents by the developers of the GDSs. This growing familiarity with the systems is expected to result in increased direct bookings from travel agents in the future.

Internet Distribution Systems. As use of the Internet to purchase travel products increases, a number of consumer-oriented systems have become available. Sometimes referred to as **online travel agencies,** sites such as Expedia, Orbitz, Priceline, and Travelocity, which are targeted to consumers, are widely used by Internet-savvy individuals to research travel options and book reservations.

The growth of Internet booking sites has made managing hotel rates and inventory online more complex than ever. These sites pose a threat to travel agencies, because they provide consumers with 24-hour access and often offer more affordable rooms. **Internet distribution systems (IDSs)** are a two-edged sword for hotels. On the one hand, they offer great exposure, but, as shown in Exhibit 4, these third-party providers sometimes offer better deals than the hotel's own website. This is possible because the online sites work either directly with hotels and purchase rooms at a discount, or work with **hotel consolidators**—firms that buy rooms in bulk from hotels and hotel chains. Hotel consolidators and online travel agencies get a discount—sometimes called the "merchant rate"—for rooms that hotels don't expect to sell at full price.

The idea of discounting rooms and allowing a third-party Internet distributor to add a markup (this strategy is referred to as the **merchant model**) sounds much like marketing to tour wholesalers. There is a difference, however, between tour wholesalers and IDSs. Tour wholesalers add value and often reach new customers for the hotel. They bundle the rooms with air or ground transportation, sightseeing, and other attractions, and justify selling the rooms at lower rates because they create new demand. IDSs, in contrast, simply offer and resell rooms over the Internet, sometimes competing directly with the hotel. Having such a wide variety of prices can confuse customers and discredit the hotel. Rate integrity is important, and many hotels and hotel chains are moving to **rate parity plans** to maintain consistent rates.

Overall, the GDSs are still a far greater distribution channel than the IDSs, but online distribution sites are growing. According to industry reports, GDSs account for about 50 million hotel bookings, compared with about four million bookings made on the Internet. While online agencies such as Travelocity and Expedia pose

Exhibit 4 Varying Online Rates

Hotel	Orbitz	Travelocity	Expedia	Hotel Site
Sheraton Universal City, Calif.	$175	$120	$149	$165
Marriott Camelback Inn, Phoenix	$149	$149	$135	$149
Quality Inn, Tampa (Fla.) Bears Ave.	$53	$49.95	$53	$62
W Hotel Seattle	$299	$299	$299	$299
New York Hilton (Midtown Manhattan)	$199	$199	$199	$199
Rio Hotel & Casino, Las Vegas	$109	$79.95	$79	$94
Days Inn-Salem, Danvers, Mass.	$139.95	$99.95	$74.95	$74.95
Drury Inn & Suites Overland Park (Kan.)	$101.99	$79.99	$101.99	$107.99
Best Western-Midway Airport-Chicago	$79	$79	$65	$79
Hyatt Regency Atlanta Peachtree	$210	$210	$210	$210
La Quinta Inn Fort Worth (Texas) West	$47.99	$55.95	$47.99	$47.99

These rates, quoted for one person for two nights in July, were taken from the Internet and show how rates can vary from site to site online. In this example, there are only three instances in which the rate offered by the three Internet travel sites and the hotels are the same. Source: Bruce Adams, "Booking Sites Create Challenges, Opportunities," *Hotel & Motel Management,* July 1, 2002, p. 1.

a threat to travel agents who book through GDSs, those who categorize GDSs and travel agents as dinosaurs in the new world of technology should "keep in mind that dinosaurs lasted for a long, long time."[7]

Websites. Another way to use computers is to create a chain or property website, either as part of a travel-related network or as an independent site. Websites offer graphic capabilities for displaying property information and can be easily updated as needed, and travel agents can book rooms online at many sites. Choice Hotels International's Travel Agent City (see Exhibit 5) is fully accessible only to travel agents and provides booking capability at any of the chain's properties. In addition, Travel Agent City calculates commissions, automatically deducting the ten percent discount to agents who reserve rooms online, and offers current "hot agent deals" and travel information.

Hotels can use the services of professional website design agencies or create their own web pages, using a wide variety of graphics and text designs. Use of individual property websites is increasing in popularity as more travel agents and consumers turn to the "information superhighway" to research travel options.

In addition to creating your own website for travel agents, you may want to consider electronic advertising on other travel-related sites. Each GDS offers messages when travel agents sign on as well as on-screen advertising tied to specific sites. Choices include banner ads, advertising space for promotions, and links to your property. TravelClick, a company that sells advertising on GDSs, is used by many lodging properties.

Exhibit 5 Hotel Websites

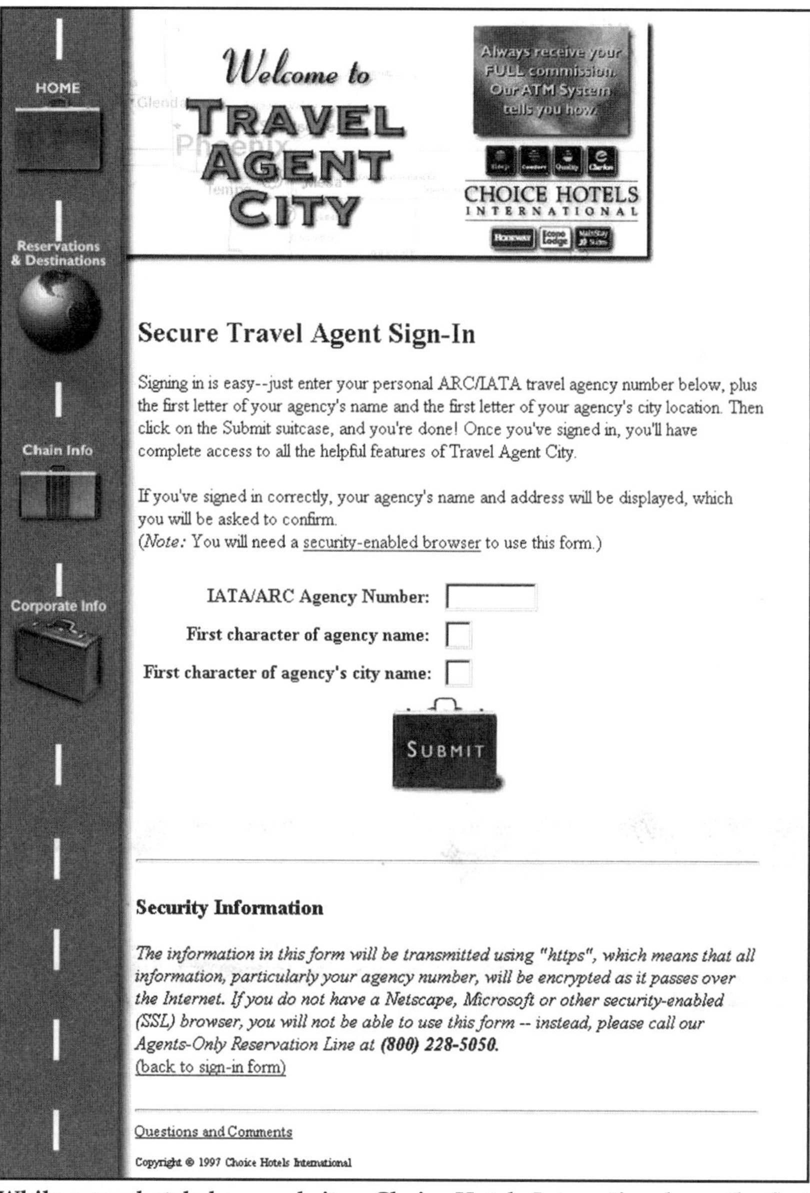

While many hotels have websites, Choice Hotels International was the first chain to offer an interactive website designed exclusively for travel agent use. Although the "Travel Agent City" tab appears on the chain's home page (www.hotelchoice.com), it can only be accessed by special codes issued to travel agents. Travel Agent City enables travel agents to make bookings and also calculates commission payments and alerts travel professionals to special offers. (Courtesy of Choice Hotels International)

Internet Distribution Systems

- Expedia, Hotels.com, and Travelocity represent roughly 75 percent of online agency hotel sales. These agencies receive a 15–30 percent "margin" on the net rate offered by the hotel, as opposed to the customary ten percent commission offered to travel agents.
- Hoteliers are seeking ways to attract customers to their property websites. Reservations booked online, especially those booked directly to the websites of individual properties, cost much less to process than any other distribution method, including 800 numbers, GDSs, travel agents and other intermediaries, and even phone calls made directly to the hotel.
- The balance of power is shifting from online travel agencies to hotels. As more hotels and chains make use of the Internet to make bookings (often offering the lowest available rates), the key clients of travel agents will be smaller hotel operations.
- The Internet is especially attractive to leisure travelers, as they can devote more time to compare prices and take full advantage of lower hotel room rates. Some 85 percent of online consumer bookings are made by leisure travelers looking for weekend stays or promotions.
- Companies are now discovering the advantages of booking travel via the Internet. Charles Schwab, for example, now makes 45 percent of its travel bookings online.

Source: "The Internet Transforms the Traditional Hotel Distribution System," *PricewaterhouseCoopers L.L.P. Industry Study on Hotel Directions,* pp. 19–29.

Faxes and E-mails. Updates on property promotions and special rates can be sent via fax as well as over the Internet. Kathy Grassini, tour and travel account executive for the Resort at Squaw Creek in Lake Tahoe, California, sends a fax newsletter every three weeks to travel agents who have booked at the property. These newsletters feature information on trips, Travel Partner rates and discounts, and packages and events that may be of interest to the travel agents' clients. She also sends property information faxes to travel agents in targeted area codes.

In addition to sending faxes to the agents currently sending clients to your property, you can turn to outside sources to create new business. Hospitality Resources Worldwide sponsors "Deals Digest," a program targeting a travel agency database with direct mailings and fax publications. Participating properties can have updated "broadcasts" loaded onto a private fax wire that distributes the information to carefully screened travel agents who specialize in specific market segments (business, leisure, luxury, etc.). This type of service eliminates the need for hotel salespeople to personally contact and screen agents and ensures that the property's information reaches the agents who will likely produce the most business.

Hotel Directories. Hotel directories provide the detailed information travel agents need to properly serve clients. An agent can compare one property's costs,

Exhibit 6 Hotel Directories

Travel agents make extensive use of hotel directories to research information about properties for their clients. The *Hotel & Travel Index* (left) has been around for over 50 years and is published quarterly; the directory and its supplementary *Hotel & Travel Index ABC International Edition* feature 45,000 worldwide hotel listings, over 300 city locator maps, and global and local reservations information. The *Official Hotel Guide International* (shown open) is published annually and reaches more than 150,000 travel agents. The property information in both directories is classified by location, and both feature listings and offer the opportunity for hotels to place display ads targeted to travel professionals.

location, amenities, facilities, and activities with another's, and make recommendations to clients based on more extensive information than that found in airline reservations systems.

Three of the most widely used guides are the *Hotel & Travel Index*, the *Official Hotel Guide International*, and the *OAG TRAVEL PLANNER/Hotel & Motel Redbook* (see Exhibit 6). Each directory, which is also available online, lists over 30,000 properties worldwide and provides information on hotel locations, accommodations, number of rooms, size of property, rates (including special packages), amenities, and number of restaurants. All three directories include property ads as well as a listing of properties.

A survey of travel agents found that four percent use the listings in hotel directories to select a property, six percent use a hotel's ad, and 90 percent use both to select a hotel.[8] It would be wise, then, for you to purchase a directory ad if possible. To attract attention and get your message across, choose the largest ad you can afford. Some chain properties are eligible for a special discount rate.

There are a number of hotel directories. It is important for you to choose a directory that will reach a large number of readers. The cost of a directory may be an indication of its popularity. In addition to print directories, hotels have the option of taking advantage of today's technology to promote their properties through online directories such as TravelToday.net and WorldTravelGuide.net.

INTERNET EXERCISE

Log onto the Internet and find the website of a large hotel in a city of your choice. Find the booking engine on the site and plug in some arrival and departure dates, select a room type, and record the rates quoted by the hotel. Then search online travel sites such as Expedia, Orbitz, Priceline, and Travelocity. How many prices were you able to find for the same type of room for the same night(s) in the same hotel? Detail your findings on a chart (use Exhibit 4 as an example).

Information Packages. In addition to providing information through computers and hotel directories, many properties offer information packages to travel agents. These packages may include a property information sheet, photographs of the property, a description of property amenities, and information about booking procedures, commission payments, and special travel agent programs. While some properties include rate sheets in their information packages, as a rule travel agents do not use them. Most agents get online or call a property directly to obtain current rate information.

Collateral materials. A property can also include a large quantity of brochures for agency clients in its information package. These brochures should be consumer-oriented and have a blank space for the travel agent's stamp. Other collateral materials, such as colorful posters, can also be sent to travel agents. Agents should be provided with order forms, especially for brochures. Order forms can be included in the information package or mailed with the agent's commission check.

Video/CD brochures and eTools. Your property can also take advantage of today's video technology to get information out to travel agents. Video or CD brochures are an excellent way to give travel agents and their clients a "tour" of your property. Detailed information for the travel agent, such as booking policies and codes and the property's commission plan, can be included with the video/CD or even imprinted on its dust cover.

The Marriott hotel chain makes use of technology by providing several eTools, including a virtual trip kit, eZines, and ePostcards for travel agents. The virtual trip kits enable a travel agent to take a complete tour of a Marriott property and its facilities without leaving his or her computer. Monthly eZines keep travel agents up-to-date with highly customized, interactive content; these publications are also available for specific regions, such as the Caribbean and Mexico. Marriott also sends periodic ePostcards that enable travel agents to personalize their services to their clients.

Familiarization Tours. Many properties offer **familiarization (fam) tours** to travel agents. These tours can be conducted during slack periods and are an effective way to promote the property.

For fam tours to be successful, you must first look at your objectives. What percentage of travel agents are expected to send business to your property following a fam tour? How many room nights do you expect to pick up? If measurable objectives are not set, there will be no way to determine what type of fam tour should be offered and no way to determine a tour's success.

GOING GREEN

Since travel agents deal directly with their clients, they are usually familiar with each client's preferences and will know clients who are interested in staying at properties and eating at restaurants that are environmentally friendly. It is important, therefore, to keep travel agents familiar with your property's environmental programs on a regular basis. You can detail your efforts in brochures or on flyers for travel agents to keep on hand to share with their clients, and provide up-to-the-minute information with e-mail bulletins or e-newsletters. Be sure to include specifics on such topics as your recycling program, your commitment to saving energy, your use of biodegradable materials, your membership in a "green" hotel or restaurant association, and so on.

If your property is located in an area of interest to the environmentally minded, include updates on special programs in the area, such as nature hikes, reforesting efforts, and other activities that will appeal to these travelers—and might result in more bookings for your property. Be sure that travel agents know if your property is involved in such activities as a partnership with an environment-oriented park or your participation in an Earth Day event. And don't forget to mention such other property amenities as environmentally friendly transportation and recreational offerings.

Planning a fam tour includes determining the ideal size of the tour group. Hosting too large a group will not allow the property to show itself off to best advantage. You must also determine exactly what you have to sell and the best way to showcase your property's products and facilities. If your property is noted for its recreational facilities, for example, you should allow the travel agents plenty of opportunity to use them.

Once you've planned a fam tour, you must invite the right travel agents to participate. Travel agents serve different types of clients. If your property caters primarily to leisure travelers, you will not benefit from inviting travel agents who specialize in business travel. The best prospects for fam tours are agents who have recommended clients to the property in the past, and those who serve clients in key feeder cities. Travel agents can be solicited by direct mail or by telephone and should be given a reasonable amount of advance notice (usually four to six weeks). Let agents know exactly what the tour involves: the duration of the tour, what is included (meals, transportation, and so on), whether the event is open to spouses or guests, and other pertinent information.

When the travel agents arrive for the fam tour, each should be greeted personally and given a schedule of events. Most properties assign staff members to handle the on-site details of the tour. A well-planned, well-executed tour will usually result in increased business from the travel agents involved.

While the travel agents' initial reactions to the tour may serve as a general barometer of the tour's success, it is also helpful to obtain an evaluation of your efforts a week or two after the tour. Questionnaires can be sent to participants to determine their perceptions of the strengths and weaknesses of the tour and the property. Of course, the real success of the tour will be measured in the number of bookings it generates.

INTERNET EXERCISE

Log onto the Internet and visit the site of the Interactive Travel Services Association (www.interactivetravel.org), the industry representative for travel distribution companies throughout the world. Review the following links on the ITSA site:

1. An Instructional Guide to Online Travel
2. How the Merchant Business Model Works
3. Fact Sheet about Global Distribution Systems (GDSs)

How did these short articles supplement the material covered in the chapter?

Hyatt does a variation on the fam tour, hosting an annual Travel Agent Exchange Day. About 450 travel agents nationwide participate, visiting a Hyatt property in their area for an overnight stay and in-depth tour. These tours give travel agents a behind-the-scenes look at hotel operations. By watching front desk personnel in action, for example, the agents become familiar with the Hyatt reservations system and learn how reservations are handled. The Travel Agent Exchange Day also includes meetings with hotel executives, such as the general manager, director of sales, executive chef, and executive housekeeper. Hotel managers, in turn, visit travel agencies to see how they operate. While additional bookings are likely to result, the primary objective is to create goodwill by showing the travel agent community that it is important to Hyatt.

In addition to having travel agents come to them, Hyatt has another program, Travel Agency Awareness Days, that is implemented at local levels to build relationships with travel agents by visiting them at their agencies. Ty Helms, senior vice president of sales for Hyatt Hotels, says, "Going into agencies helps us understand what customers are looking for, how we're displayed, and how agents see us, which becomes a great learning experience on our end."[9]

The Philadelphia Convention & Visitors Bureau keeps the fam tour experience fresh in the minds of more than 300 travel retailers who have taken fam trips to the city by sending each of them Phil E. Love, a teddy bear who wears sunglasses and a necktie. Four days after Phil is sent out, agents receive a follow-up letter from his "mom," reminding him to return home for a visit. Five days later, Phil's "dad" sends another letter—usually with information about a hotel promotion. Both of the letters are accompanied by clothing for Phil (a hooded sweatshirt, a leather jacket, and so on). The mailings, which many travel agents look forward to, build client loyalty and keep the agents excited about recommending trips to Philadelphia to their clients.

Specialized Training and Education Programs. Many hotels provide property information and selling tools to travel agents through sales training manuals, educational seminars, and certification programs. For maximum effectiveness, sales training manuals should be informative and interesting, not just a list of dry facts about your property. Educational seminars should be developed with the needs of travel agents in mind. They should be scheduled at convenient times of the day, such as early in the morning or during lunch hour, and they should showcase your services. Travel agents are more likely to become involved if your presentation includes a signature property item, such as a spa treatment or entertainment by the property's lounge act, or if some type of food function is offered during your presentation. These techniques make a far more lasting impression than a two-hour lecture or a notebook of facts.

In order to help travel agents effectively sell hotel properties to their clients, many hotel chains are offering certification programs that combine property facts with selling skills. Fairmont Hotels & Resorts, for example, offers the "Fairmont FAmous" educational program, which teaches key selling points for chain properties, including its Willow Stream spas and its Fairmont Gold hotels. Agents who successfully complete the program receive two continuing education units, which can be used toward their Certified Travel Associate (CTA), Certified Travel Counselor (CTC), or Certified Travel Industry Executive (CTIE) designations from The Travel Institute. They also receive monthly e-mails regarding new hotels in the chain and special offers and programs.

Wingate Inns has implemented a Wingate Inns Specialist program, which also awards continuing education units to participants. Participants receive a certificate from the chain as well, along with a complimentary stay at a Wingate property. Marriott's Hotel Excellence! program, which consists of a ten-chapter self-study workbook, gives a broad overview of the hotel industry and covers such topics as types of travelers, the GDSs, hotel sales, and working with groups, in addition to sections on Marriott products and services. Agents successfully completing the course receive a Hotel Sales Specialist certification from Marriott, "Fam-Tastic" certificates, and a boost in their commissions.

The Internet has made it increasingly easy for travel agents to participate in certification programs offered by these and other hotels. Even destination cities are seeing the value of providing information to travel agents. The Las Vegas Convention and Visitors Authority, for example, offers the Vegas Certified program, which helps travel agents become "go-to experts" on this popular destination city.

Service

The kind of service agents receive from a property is an important factor in whether they will recommend that property again. Service to travel agents also includes service to their clients. Travel agents are often blamed for bungled reservations, specific requests that are not met, and any number of details not handled to the guest's satisfaction at the property. It stands to reason that agents will be far more likely to recommend a property that has treated them and their clients well than a property that hasn't. The Sonesta Beach Resort in Bermuda welcomes guests who have booked through a travel agent with a special gift with the travel agent's name on it; this builds goodwill between the guests and their travel agents and between the travel agents and the hotel. Toll-free numbers, travel agent clubs, commission payment plans, and good service to clients are just some of the other ways properties can provide good service to travel agents. Exhibit 7 shows a print ad that promotes service to both agents and their clients, while Exhibit 8 shows the many different ways Hilton meets the needs of travel agents.

Exhibit 7 Providing Service to Travel Agents

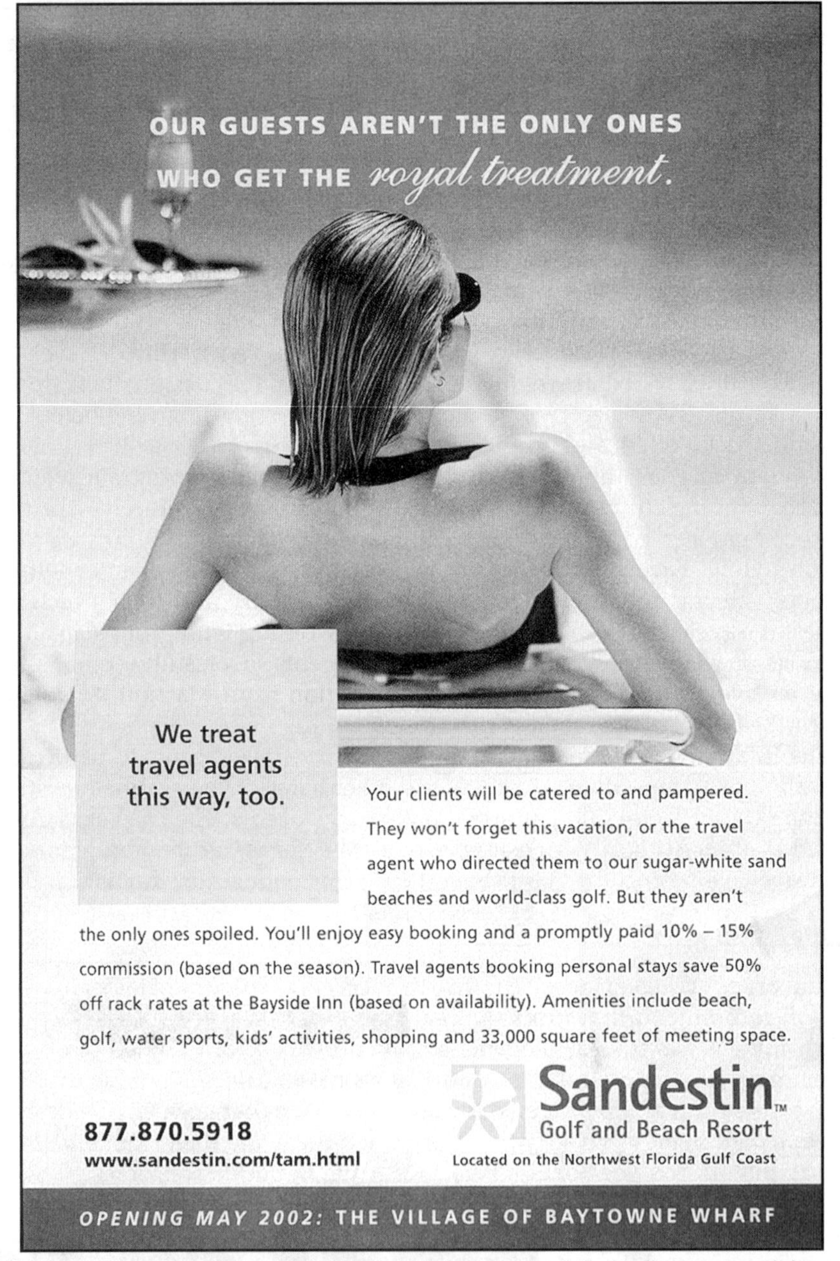

This ad addresses the needs of both travel agents and their clients, promising pampering for the agents' clients, easy booking, a commission plan that pays promptly, and discounts on personal stays for travel agents. Note that the ad provides both a website address and toll-free number for travel agents for easy booking. (Courtesy of Sandestin Golf and Beach Resort)

Exhibit 8 The Hilton Model

Hilton Hotels has initiated a number of comprehensive programs designed to serve agents while bolstering agent recognition and appreciation. Their initiatives include the following:

- **Centralized reservations systems.** Hilton's toll-free Private Travel Agent Reservation Line assists agents with inquiries and reservations for Hilton Hotels nationwide. Staffed by 40 reservationists trained exclusively for work with travel agents, the line offers around-the-clock information every day. Hilton's other central reservation services include automated services such as Apollo, System One, Datas II, and Covia's Inside Availability; expanded rate categories; automatic rate updates; contests; and other marketing messages.
- **Centralized commission payment.** Hilton gives agents consolidated payments for bookings at Hilton Hotels nationwide. Commission checks are issued biweekly for hotels enrolled in Hilton's central commission program, and all other commissions are paid within 48 hours of guest check-out. Check statements include commission amount, folio number, hotel name, number of nights, and guest name. Hilton identifies which rates are commissionable at the time of reservation.
- **Hilton Fam Club.** Recognizing the importance of agent familiarization trips, Hilton introduced its chainwide "fam" policy, which extends to agents a 50 percent savings off the minimum rack rate at each Hilton Hotel.
- **Hilton Direct.** The Hilton Direct toll-free customer-service and meeting arrangement system offers agents information on availability and rates of hotel conference facilities within 24 hours of any inquiry.
- **Travel agent help desk.** The toll-free help line provides agents with research on commission payments, assistance with CRS bookings and format questions, and comprehensive assistance with Hilton's travel agent marketing and sales programs.
- **Travel agent advisory board.** Comprising nine travel-industry professionals and five Hilton executives, the agent advisory board provides feedback for the company's travel agent programs and ensures that relations between travel agents and hotels continue to improve.

Hilton has been cited as the most progressive company in terms of responding to the needs of travel agents. Bruce Rosenberg, director of travel agency marketing for the chain, believes that while 25 to 30 percent of Hilton's bookings are now generated by travel agencies, a realistic goal would be to increase this number to 50 percent. To do so, Hilton has created a number of services for travel agents.

Toll-Free Numbers. While travel agents are increasingly using computers to make hotel reservations, many still book rooms and services over the telephone, and providing a toll-free number is essential. A toll-free number also encourages travel agents to call if they have questions. Agents can explore various options and rates, find out about special events that may interest clients, ask about special services, and receive immediate confirmation of reservations. In some cases, information on a GDS can be different from the information provided by the hotel, and better availability and better rates can still sometimes be found at the hotel level. Special

INTERNET EXERCISE

Hotel Travel Check is one of the many firms that assists hospitality businesses in the design of websites. Log onto the Internet, go to www.hoteltravelcheck.com, and click on the "Web Design" link to view Hotel Travel Check's hotel website design samples.

1. Based on what you have learned in this chapter, critique two of the website samples.
2. What fees does this firm charge for its services?

requests, such as a request that flowers be delivered to a guestroom, are still not managed well in the electronic booking mechanism of the GDSs. Therefore, many travel agents telephone properties when booking VIPs.

A toll-free number serves the property as well as the agent. Property representatives are given the opportunity to sell extra services. In addition, these calls are an excellent way to bring travel agents up to date on property information. The property also can better control its room inventories; rooms may be promoted during slow periods and alternate dates can be suggested for business that cannot be booked due to a full house.

Since travel agents generate so many bookings, some hotels go a step further; they dedicate a special toll-free number for the exclusive use of travel agents. This number is not available to the public and is promoted only through press releases to travel agents or through direct mail and other advertising directed to the travel trade.

Other ways to make it easier for properties and travel professionals to communicate include the use of special fax numbers and e-mail addresses reserved exclusively for travel agents. These technologies can be used to respond quickly to requests for information and to update travel agents on changes or special promotions.

Travel Agent Clubs. Another effective way you can provide service and build rapport with travel agents is through travel agent clubs. Club members are informed of property events and special programs and discounts through direct mail or a club newsletter. Some clubs give prizes to travel agents who book a certain number of room nights at the property; an agent with 100 room nights or "room credits" may earn a watch, for example. Other properties offer even more lavish prizes. In 2004, for example, Hyatt introduced its annual Travel Agent Awards program, which rewards top-producing agents with a free two-day appreciation trip as well as other travel-related prizes, including the grand prize, a Vacation for Life (a one-week ownership at the Hyatt Pinon Pointe, a Hyatt Vacation Club Resort in Sedona, Arizona).

Many clubs offer travel agents such travel-oriented promotional items as tote bags, travel alarm clocks, and baggage tags imprinted with the property's logo and the travel agent's telephone number. Travel agents can use these items to stimulate business for themselves and your property. One of the most successful travel agent clubs is Radisson's "Look to Book," which claims more than half of the world's online agents as members. The club builds travel agent loyalty by rewarding agents with points that can be redeemed for hotel stays, travel, or gifts, based on the number of reservations they book online.

Commission Payment Plans. A very important way that properties are serving travel agents is through commission payment plans. Travel agents earn money in two ways: from the commissions earned by booking clients with travel suppliers, and from fees charged to corporations for travel services. It used to be that travel agents earned the bulk of their commissions from booking airline reservations, but this changed when the airlines stopped paying commissions. When this happened, agents were forced to look for alternatives. Many agents who had previously rebated a part of their commissions to corporations that generated a large volume of business curtailed this practice. Most agents and agencies began charging a service fee to clients booking airline reservations. Others looked to booking more hotel rooms as a way to increase their incomes.

In the past, travel agents were reluctant to rely on booking hotel rooms to generate commissions. First, they generally had to find the best deal for their clients, which translated into smaller commissions. Second, commissions weren't always paid on rooms that were already discounted, such as those for senior citizens or groups. Third, getting paid was often a problem for travel agents; in many cases, the check that was "in the mail" would never arrive. But properties have recognized the need to address these concerns. An increasing number of hotels have developed written commission policies and the hospitality industry has taken giant strides to ensure that travel agents receive commission checks on a more regular basis.

One of the reasons for the sporadic payment of commission checks was that individual properties were responsible for generating the checks. In many cases, a property did not have the technical capabilities to track bookings, and chains that did have these capabilities charged travel agents a fee.

The Holiday Corporation changed all that with the introduction of a centralized commission payment plan. Instead of receiving checks from each property in the chain, travel agents received one monthly check issued automatically through a computer in the chain's corporate office. Travel agents were no longer charged a fee. The program was subsidized through fees charged to individual hotels, but the hotels still saved money since they no longer incurred the administrative, stationery, and postage costs involved in paying travel agents.

Many chains have followed this lead with similar systems. Hyatt, for example, guarantees commission payments within 72 hours of the client's departure. (Exhibit 9 shows a print ad that the chain uses to promote its payment program.) Hilton's policy also is to pay commissions within 72 hours of check-out. Along with the commission check, many hotel chains mail a statement of guest histories for the month, any changes made in a reservation after it was booked by the travel agent, and information relating to new hotel facilities or policies.

To further alleviate commission payment problems, a private company, Pegasus Systems Inc., serves hotels and travel agents worldwide, ensuring that

Exhibit 9 Travel Agent Commission Payment Plans

Our travel agent recognition program will make your job so easy you'll think you're on vacation yourself.

Hyatt's commitment to making travel agents' jobs as easy as possible is the driving force behind our new Special Agent Recognition Program, which includes our Golden Rules for Travel Agents. Key commitments include:

- Commission checks mailed within 72 hours of guest departures
- Guaranteed 10-day response on any late commission notices
- Commissions paid on any additional nights a guest stays
- Commissions paid for any guests relocated with previously confirmed reservations
- 10% commission on all published rates
- Non-commissionable rate information at time of booking
- Written notification if there is a guest no-show or a reservation change
- Commissions deducted in advance from deposits or prepayments sent to Hyatt®
- Special HYschool educational programs
- Preferred treatment while staying at Hyatt
- A toll free Travel Agent Hotline at 1-800-423-2400 to answer any questions concerning commissions, travel and Hyatt programs

The Hyatt CRT code is HY. For more information and reservations call Hyatt Hotels and Resorts worldwide at 1-800-233-1234.

Feel The Hyatt Touch.®

Prompt payment of commissions is an important consideration for travel agents. This ad outlines the Hyatt Hotels & Resorts commission policy and is designed to attract bookings from travel agents. Note also that the ad features a toll-free number and other services for travel agents only.

MARKETING IN ACTION

Hotels Develop Programs to Increase Travel Agent Business

The South Seas Island Resort, Captiva Island, Florida

When the South Seas Island Resort in Captiva Island, Florida, determined that 70 percent of its guest mix was individual leisure travelers—and that 35–50 percent of this business came from travel agents—the property launched a major travel agency marketing program to increase leisure traveler business and make the travel agents' jobs easier. The program included travel trade advertising, a public relations program, attending travel trade shows, a direct mail program, a toll-free number for travel agents, agency familiarization trips, and the creation of the King's Crown Club.

The King's Crown Club, which rewarded top-producing travel agents and agencies, was an important factor in the property's success. In order to get into the club, travel agents initially were required to produce a minimum of $10,000 in room revenue from individual leisure travelers; if the agent or agency also produced group business, the membership minimum was $20,000 (these minimums have now been increased to $12,500 for individual leisure travelers and $25,000 for group business). Once an agent qualified for the club, commissions were increased from 10 percent to 13 percent for the rest of the year.

In addition to higher commissions, qualifying travel agents were also rewarded at the Annual Celebration weekend. The weekend, held from a Thursday through Sunday each spring, included an awards breakfast, receptions and dinner functions, and recreational opportunities. New property information was also distributed to the attending agents. The resort's efforts paid off in happier travel agents—and increased bookings.

Starwood Hotels & Resorts

In order to build stronger relationships with travel agents and agencies, Starwood Hotels & Resorts launched StarwoodPro, a global program that offers travel professionals an enhanced experience when conducting business with the Starwood chain. The program was founded on five pillars—Access, Knowledge, Rewards, Compensation, and Communication. The first pillar, Access, included the launch of a travel agent–dedicated website, StarwoodPro.com, to enable travel agents to easily search for hotels and book properties in any of the chain's nine brands.

The Knowledge pillar of StarwoodPro focused on the development of an educational program, a concept that is being increasingly used by hotel chains. The program includes instruction on sales skills such as upselling as well as information about the chain's various brands. The Rewards program, which was launched in the summer of 2008, focused on providing tangible benefits to top-selling agents. The chain has provided a travel agent educational rate and a travel agency discount program for many years, but the new Rewards program offers special incentives to travel agents, including cash rewards and free stays at Starwood properties.

Communication will be provided through the StarwoodPro website, as well as through continuing face-to-face meetings and interviews with travel professionals to ensure that the chain is meeting the needs of travel agents and their clients.

commissions are tracked and paid promptly (and in the currency of the travel agent's country; previously, agents booking international accommodations were often paid in foreign currency, resulting in the loss of a large part—or all—of the commission). Pegasus' electronic distribution and commission processing greatly simplifies the task of tracking and issuing commissions, providing greater financial motivation for agents to book through member hotels. Travel agents are charged an initial fee for three years of service and pay an additional five to ten percent of their annual hotel commissions; in return, they receive one monthly commission payment from all business booked through participating chains rather than having to worry about sporadic individual commission checks. Pegasus completes the room reservations transaction for more than 100,000 participating travel agencies in 206 countries by collecting and consolidating hotel commissions from more than 25,000 properties.

Many properties give increased commissions to agents who book clients during off-season periods or during certain special package promotions. In recent years, hotels have cultivated relationships with **preferred travel agents**, offering extra commissions or other incentives to selected agents or agencies that book certain volumes of business or take part in chain training programs. Marriott has two commission tiers: a ten percent commission and other benefits for travel agents who have taken part in Hotel Excellence!, a specialized training program offered by Marriott, and an eight percent commission to travel agents who have not been through the program, which is designed to teach agents how to sell hotels (Marriott brands specifically). Some independent hotels, which rely heavily on travel agents for business, have developed programs that offer travel agents higher commissions to attract travel agent business year-round. The Scottsdale Plaza, for example, offers a 20 percent commission on bookings at rack rate in addition to a standard ten percent commission on discounted rates and all-inclusive leisure packages. Sue Perovich, vice president of marketing at the property, says:

> You can't forget the hands that feed you. The thing that has provided us with the greatest amount of success has been our relationship with travel agents and our attitude that views them as travel partners. We independents who don't have a lot of advertising dollars really have to rely on travel agents to do that for us.[10]

Properties can also award special bonuses or free accommodations or trips when an agency exceeds a quota of room nights in a given period. Other properties have found that offering incentives, such as contests and sweepstakes, generates additional bookings. Exhibit 10 shows a shopping spree contest offered by the La Quinta chain, for example.

Serving Travel Agents' Clients. Providing good service to travel agents means providing good service to their clients as well. It is very important to travel agents that their clients be well treated, since a client's experience at a property will likely affect the client/agent relationship. If the client has an enjoyable stay, he or she will be more likely to use the services of the travel agent again. If, on the other hand, the stay does not meet the client's expectations, the agent will lose credibility—and possibly a client.

Exhibit 10 Contest for Travel Agents

Some hotels and chains offer contests and sweepstakes as incentives to build travel agent business. This contest offers chances for a $5,000 shopping spree to travel agents booking at La Quinta Inn and La Quinta Inn & Suites over a specified time period.

Guests booked into the property by a travel agent should be greeted by a friendly staff, and their stay should be made as pleasant as possible. Some properties pamper their travel-agent-booked guests with complimentary wine, fruit baskets, or local specialties delivered to the guestroom with a welcoming note and a card that gives the travel agent credit for the gift. Others may offer special promotional items to guests booked by travel agents, such as the Super Hero Summer items shown in Exhibit 11.

You can easily give special treatment to guests booked by travel agents if these guests can be readily identified. Check guest registrations to determine which guests are commissionable to travel agents. The first time an agent sends a client to your property, you should call and thank the agent. Such actions deliver a powerful message that agents' clients will be well cared for and may encourage agents to recommend the property to other clients.

Checking guest registrations can also lead to identification of travel agents who come to the property unannounced to see what the guest experience is really like. These agents are usually the owners or managers of top-producing agencies. When you identify these travel agent guests, a welcoming phone call can let them know that you care about travel agents' bookings and are receptive to the needs of the travel agency market.

Finding Travel Agents

There are four resources that can help a property identify travel agents and agencies it may want to do business with:

1. The *Official Airline Guide (OAG)*
2. In-house records
3. Outside/industry mailing lists
4. Travel industry trade shows

The *OAG* lists all airline activity between domestic and international cities, and provides valuable information on the flow of airline traffic into a property's locale. While this guide does not specifically list travel agents or agencies, it does target the key cities from which air traffic originates. You can then find out the names of travel agencies in those cities and contact them.

In-house records provide a history of commission payments to travel agents and can help you target agents who have recommended the property in the past. In-house records can also help identify an agent's specific needs. For example, has the agent most often booked individual business or leisure travelers, or does the agent primarily serve the small-meetings market?

You can also use in-house records to develop a travel agent mailing list. The in-house mailing list can be expanded through the purchase of outside mailing lists from other travel industry sources. American Society of Travel Agents (ASTA) mailing lists are some of the most useful. ASTA provides national, regional, and state lists on a cost-per-thousand basis. Other sources of outside mailing lists include the Airline Reporting Corporation (ARC), the government agency that

Exhibit 11 Gifts for Guests Booked by Travel Agents

Many properties offer special amenities to the guests of travel agents. Best Western hotels, for example, promoted a SUPER HERO SUMMER, offering a free Batman Camera and activity book to guests who booked through travel agents.

licenses travel agents to sell airline tickets; Cahner's Travel Agents' mailing list; and lists of travel agency chain and consortium members.

Some properties use industry trade shows as opportunities to meet travel agents. These shows (which will be discussed later in the chapter) allow you to communicate with individual agents and determine specific travel agent needs. Information on these shows can be obtained from ASTA or from trade publications.

Reaching Travel Agents

You can reach travel agents through hotel directories, trade magazines, travel trade websites, direct mail, trade shows, membership in travel agent associations, personal sales, and public relations efforts.

Hotel Directories. As mentioned earlier in the chapter, one effective way to reach travel agents is through advertising in hotel directories. Hotel directories are used by travel agents to book eight out of ten leisure traveler bookings and six out of ten business traveler bookings. The two leading directories used by travel agents are the *Hotel & Travel Index* and the *Official Hotel Guide International,* both of which are also available on CD-ROM. Both print and electronic versions of hotel directories are used extensively even when a computerized system is available: 67 percent of all travel agents say they consult a hotel directory as well as a computerized system.[11]

Since travel agents receive an average of 80 to 100 directories each year, a property's directory ad must attract attention. The headline should include the property's chief benefit, and the ad itself must clearly convey the hotel's name and image. Ads should appeal to a travel agent, not a potential guest.

In a poll taken by Louis Harris and Associates for *Hotel & Travel Index,* travel agents rated the most important elements in directory advertising. A toll-free number ranked highest (96 percent), information on the hotel's location was rated second (92 percent), and a map of the property's location was deemed third most important (88 percent). These elements make it easier for an agent to select and book a property, and a property's ad should feature all three.

In addition to the standard print directories, many of today's properties are taking advantage of computerized hotel directories that provide a full-color look at thousands of participating properties. Some, such as Apollo's Spectrum, offer a number of screens, providing virtual tours and mapping capabilities to provide concise information to travel agents. Others, such as Apollo's Headlines, provide up-to-the-minute information on new products, services, and rates.

Trade Magazines. In addition to directory advertising, many properties advertise in travel trade magazines such as *Travel Weekly, Travel Trade,* and *Home-Based Travel Agent.* These magazines often offer regional circulations or special sections that periodically feature popular destinations. You should request an editorial calendar from these publications and plan advertising accordingly to maximize your property's exposure. Unlike consumer ads, trade ads are often lengthy, since information is so important to travel professionals. Copy should include:

1. *Pertinent location information.* Indicate proximity to major highways and airports or other transportation terminals, distances to popular attractions, mileage to nearby industrial complexes or downtown business areas, and availability of complimentary transportation (airport limousine, hotel courtesy van for trips to shopping malls or attractions, and so on).
2. *Rate information.* List regular rates, group rates, and special rates such as "children free," along with special packages (rates, availability, what is included) and special discounts available for off-season bookings.

3. *Booking information.* Provide toll-free reservation numbers, credit card policies, and other pertinent booking information (such as travel agent guarantees).
4. *Commission information.* Provide information about payment policies and special incentives.

You can use photographs in addition to copy to grab attention and introduce your property to travel agents. Appropriate photos include exterior shots and photos of function areas, guestrooms, and the lobby.

Travel Trade Websites. Many travel agents are turning to travel trade websites to keep up to date on the latest information and promotions. ModernAgent.com is the largest of these travel agent–directed sites, boasting 60,000 travel agent subscribers (75 percent of all U.S.-based travel agents). The site features links to hotels and resorts, travel packages, tours, travel suppliers, special travel offers, and destinations. Advertising on the site works two ways: your property's website can be accessed through the typical links, and your site can also be matched to editorial content. For example, if your property is in New Orleans and ModernAgent.com publishes a story on Mardi Gras, a link to your property (and those of other properties in New Orleans who take advantage of this service) will accompany the article. When travel agents click on your link, they receive an overview of your site, videos on your property and/or local area, your current advertising and promotions, related articles from *Agent@Home* and *Vacation Agent* magazines, current news from ModernAgent's Travel Pulse, and marketing tools to help the agents promote your offers to their clients (travel agents can print out your latest promotions to present to clients, for example). A daily travel show, which presents such programming as destination reports, executive insights, travel technology, and sales and marketing tips, also offers an opportunity for promotion and publicity. In addition, ModernAgent.com tracks your advertising, providing real time statistics on the number of agents who have accessed your page.

While it is not specifically geared to travel agents, a site such as TripAdvisor.com can help agents, especially home-based agents, to keep abreast of consumer preferences. TripAdvisor, a subsidiary of Expedia, Inc., provides unbiased, online reviews that can be invaluable in researching hotels and destinations. Since the site has over five million subscribers and receives over 25 million non-member visits monthly, it is an excellent vehicle for hospitality properties to reach not only the traveling public but those travel agents who also check out the reviews. Advertising options for the TripAdvisor website include traditional listings in the hotel and restaurant pages, advertising on either the home page or other related pages, and sponsorship of editorial content.

Direct Mail. Another way to reach travel agents is through direct mail. Direct mail includes sales letters, collateral materials, promotional giveaways, and newsletters. Collateral materials can be used to introduce new facilities or packages, and can be as simple as printed fliers or as elaborate as full-color folders and special advertising gimmicks. Newsletters are an excellent way to keep in touch with travel agents and inform them of price fluctuations, new promotions, and efforts to better serve travel professionals. Days Inn developed a newsletter called *Travel Days* for travel agents that is mailed to more than 12,000 travel agencies monthly, containing articles and interviews about Days Inn and the travel industry.

Since travel agents receive so much mail, direct mail pieces must be attractive to avoid being thrown away unread. To reinforce the property's message, a series of direct mail pieces is often effective. Series mailings keep the property fresh in the travel agent's mind, especially if they are developed along a theme or are otherwise attention-getting.

Trade Shows. Another, more personal, way to reach travel agents is through attendance at industry trade shows. Trade shows give you the opportunity to talk directly to travel agents and learn their individual needs. Trade shows fall into two categories: major international shows, which are organized and coordinated corporately; and traveling "marketplace" shows, which run for several days in selected cities. The best-known trade shows are the International Tourism Bourse (ITB) in Germany, ASTA conventions, the Travel Industry Association of America's semiannual conference, Travel Age West, the World Travel Market (staged annually in London), and the Luxury Travel Expo, held in Las Vegas.

Travel agents visiting trade shows can be reached through sales presentations and the use of visual aids, including video brochures. Video brochures can be almost as effective as a personal tour of the property. When a video brochure is not available, presenters can use printed brochures and attractive posters—both travel-agent-oriented and consumer-oriented—to help the sales presentation.

Membership in Travel Agent Associations. Allied memberships are available in many associations serving travel professionals, including ASTA, ACTA (the Alliance of Canadian Travel Agents), PATA (Pacific Asia Travel Association), and SGTP (the Society of Government Travel Professionals). Membership benefits often include preferred rates for advertising in association publications, invitations to trade shows, and networking opportunities. In addition, joining forces with travel management companies and consortiums can prove beneficial; most offer current mailing lists, exposure to a large number of travel professionals, and preferred rates for advertising in their directories of member hotels. In most cases, chains are given special membership rates, which are passed on to properties in the chain, and many chains offer marketing programs to help individual properties target travel management companies, consortiums, and trade associations.

Personal Sales. A property may wish to contact local travel agencies that have high business potential through personal sales calls. Many travel agencies are staffed by agents who have specialized areas or client followings, so it may be necessary to call on a number of agents at each agency. Since travel agents are usually busy, it is best to call ahead for an appointment. Avoid calls on Mondays and Fridays, when business volume is heaviest.

Presentations should be brief. Travel agents offer a complex array of properties to clients; therefore, the presentation should clearly differentiate the property from competing properties. A familiarization tour or invitation to view the property's video can be offered. Getting to know travel agents and getting them to learn about the property and its management is one of the keys to success.

A few years ago, Best Western targeted travel agents with what it called "The World's Largest Sales Blitz." Over a one-week period, over 5,000 sales calls were made on travel agencies to spread the word about "Best Request," 16 amenities and services that had become standard at all Best Western properties. The chain followed up the successful blitz the following year with "The World's Largest Thank-You," making 8,000 visits to agents and travel counselors to thank them for their business.

Public Relations. Good public relations may do more to reach travel agents than all the advertising in the world. For example, you might invite travel agents to learn about the inner workings of your property's reservations system. Inviting travel writers to visit the property may lead to travel trade articles that are read by travel agents. Properties can also provide news releases to trade publications that appeal to travel agents. Another public relations idea is to host a "travel agent day" honoring exceptional travel agency partners. Howard Johnson properties, which realize approximately 500,000 room nights and $35 million annually from travel agents, identify their top revenue-producing agents and send thank-you notes to them.

Yet another effective way to build good relationships with travel agents is to establish a travel agency advisory board or offer forums or other ways to open the channels of communication between travel agents and hotels. Or a property could offer a travel agent "help desk" to answer questions and suggest ways to enhance guest satisfaction.

The Future of Travel Agents

We have already seen how today's technology and trends in travel bookings have influenced the travel agent industry. The wealth of travel information to which travel agents had virtually exclusive access via GDSs is now available to travelers on both consumer GDSs and Internet travel sites. In addition, the number of hotels with websites of their own continues to grow, cutting further into travel agent business.

The travel agents of the future will not only have to cope with the widespread use of technology by consumers, but also with other threats to their livelihood, including changes in the way hotels look at rooms distribution. They will have to revamp their business to ensure that clients and suppliers see the value of using travel agents.

A study by PKF Consulting determined that hotels pay about two percent of rooms revenue in travel agent commissions (limited service properties pay about one percent, compared to 2.3 percent for luxury hotels).[12] But although hotels may find other distribution methods (such as their own websites) more cost effective for processing reservations, hotels will continue to need and support travel agents. Small hotels, especially, look to travel agents to fill rooms. Many small hotels do not have large sales forces or marketing budgets, so travel agents serve as their national and international sales force. Large hotels, too, rely on travel agents to fill rooms, even though chains such as Hilton offer incentives for consumers to book over the Internet (Hilton HHonor members earn 1,000 extra bonus points every time they make a reservation online). Although direct Internet reservations cut the cost of distribution and hotels are often willing to pass along a portion of these savings to customers in the form of reduced room rates, chains such as Marriott continue to work with travel agents—especially those that drive business to them.

Both large and small properties find paying a ten percent commission a viable alternative to discounting rooms at 30 percent to hotel consolidators or having vacant rooms. And there are still large numbers of people, especially leisure and international travelers, who prefer travel agents over a faceless transaction over the Internet. Repeat travelers want to be able to call a travel agent who already knows them and their needs; travelers unfamiliar with an area want to speak to someone who can give them advice, reassure them, and be there for them if anything goes wrong.

One of the ways that travel agents can provide additional, personalized service is by attending "destination specialists" programs. These programs are sponsored by countries, regions, and cities, and cover areas as diverse as Austria, the Cayman Islands, Fiji, Great Britain, Pennsylvania, and Switzerland. In these programs, travel agents attend courses and take tests to enable them to better sell an area's facilities and services to clients. Having detailed knowledge helps travel agents to suggest travel options to clients, options that may not be readily available on commonly accessed sources such as city or hotel websites.

The American Society of Travel Agents has reinforced the concept that travel agents are an integral part of a successful vacation or business trip through a series of print ads that promote the expertise of travel professionals (an example is shown in Exhibit 12). Note that the ad promotes travel agents as "the world's most powerful travel search engine"—promising that travel agents "can tell you secrets about your destination that you won't find on any website"—to attract consumers who might be thinking about making their own bookings online.

One thing that seems clear is that more and more travel agents will be working from home in the future, as opposed to storefronts or "brick and mortar" locations. This is another impact of the Internet on the business; it is only because of modern computer and Internet technology that it is now feasible for travel agents to work from home.

Will the distribution systems available on the Internet, so convenient for consumers and travel agents alike, replace travel agents? Not likely. Just as radio survived the advent of television, travel agents will survive and continue to be an important distribution channel for the hospitality industry.

Conclusion

The growing variety of transportation and lodging choices makes travel decisions more complicated than ever before, so meeting the needs of travel agents and maintaining a positive attitude toward travel agencies can mean increased bookings and revenues for your property. Despite the travel information and products available to consumers on the Internet, there will probably always be a need for the personal services of professional travel agents; many consumers do not have the time to research the varied travel options available, or do not trust themselves to find the best value, especially when it comes to multidestination or multicomponent bookings.

Almost all of the major chains have instituted programs to improve relations with travel agents by opening channels of communication and meeting specific needs. Most offer toll-free numbers to answer questions and keep agents advised

Exhibit 12 ASTA Promotes Professional Travel Agents

Connect
with the
world's most
powerful
travel
search engine...

Your travel agent.

Give us your itinerary and we'll hunt through every conceivable option to find you the best value. Give us your vacation budget and we'll meet it. Give us your honeymoon dreams and we'll make them a reality. We can provide options you've never even thought of. We can tell you secrets about your destination that you won't find on any Web site. We know you, your family, your likes and dislikes. Our sole function is to serve your best interests.

And we'll handle all the details. So relax. Your vacation dreams are in the hands of a trusted expert.

Without a travel agent, you're on your own.

These ads were developed by the American Society of Travel Agents for use by individual agents and agencies. The ad's slogan, "Without a travel agent, you're on your own," promotes the expertise of travel agents.

of current product information. Consulting with travel agency organizations, such as ASTA, on how to meet industry concerns and establishing travel agency boards, research panels, and focus groups is also important. The formation of Pegasus

Commission Processing, which provides a centralized commission check and reporting system, and the development of other automation that increases agency productivity have led to a sharp rise in the loyalty of travel agents. Lodging property managers should think of travel agents as professional sales counselors who do not ask for payment until they have booked rooms or packages and who produce a reliable and steady source of business at a fraction of the cost of in-house sales efforts.

Endnotes

1. Harvey Chipkin, "Book It: Travel Agents Still Vital to Hotels," *Hotel & Motel Management,* March 6, 2006, p. 4.
2. *Report to the Nation: Trends in Travel & Hospitality,* (Washington, D.C.: Public Affairs Group, 1997), p. 24.
3. "The Summit Looks at '97," *Lodging Hospitality,* January 1997, p. 67.
4. Harvey Chipkin, "An Interview with Juergen Bartels," *HSMAI Marketing Review,* Summer 2002, p. 29.
5. *World Hospitality,* October 1999, p. 4.
6. Information in this section is based on several studies: "Travel Weekly U.S. Travel Agency Survey," conducted by Louis Harris and Associates (NY, NY); the "North American Travel Agent Usage Study," conducted by Market Probe International; and "Business Travelers' Use of Hotels," "U.S. Meetings Market," and "Corporate Travel Manager Survey," underwritten by *Hotel & Travel Index.*
7. David Jones, "Hotels Ponder Role of Mega–Web Sites," *Travel Agent,* June 12, 2002, p. 8.
8. "An Analysis of the Hotel Selection Process for Business Travelers," an article based on personal interviews of travel agents by the Harvey Research Organization, Inc., for *Hotel & Travel Index.*
9. Erin F. Sternthal, "The Hyatt Touch," from the online newsletter *Travel, The Newsweekly of the Travel Industry* (www.travelagentcentral.com), February 16, 2004.
10. Julie Miller, "Booking Is Believing," *Hotel & Motel Management,* April 3, 1996, p. 18.
11. "Louis Harris Hotel Market Survey of U.S. Travel Agents," a study conducted by Louis Harris and Associates for *Hotel & Travel Index,* 1991.
12. Robert Mandelbaum, "Re-Examine Commission Payment Structure," *Lodging,* July 2002, p. 24.

Key Terms

consortium—A group of travel agencies that have combined their buying power to obtain more favorable rates. A consortium provides its member agencies with all the services required for complete travel. Examples include ABC Corporate Services, Hickory Travel Systems, and TravelSavers.

familiarization (fam) tour—A complimentary or reduced-rate travel program. A familiarization tour is designed to acquaint travel agents, meeting planners, travel writers, and others with a property or destination in order to stimulate sales.

global distribution systems (GDSs)—The electronic networks used by travel agents and some Internet-based distribution channels to make airline, hotel, car rental, and cruise ship reservations.

hotel consolidators—Firms that buy guestrooms in bulk at discounted rates and typically market them via the Internet.

in-plant agency—A retail travel agency that establishes an office on the premises of a corporate client.

Internet distribution system—Internet-based services providing consumers with the ability to book hotel, airline, car rental, and cruise ship reservations.

merchant model—A business model used by online travel agencies. Online travel agencies solicit hotels for deeply discounted room rates (non-commissionable and discounted 20–35 percent below retail levels), and then mark up the rooms a certain percentage for sale on their sites.

online travel agencies—Websites offering travel agent services and a wide range of hotel offerings online. Also referred to as third-party agencies.

preferred travel agents—Agents (or agencies) who are offered above-average commissions or other incentives, usually for booking certain volumes of business.

rate parity plans—The hotels' strategy to maintain consistency of rates among sales channels. Usually enforced through contractual agreements between hotel companies and online agencies, rate parity plans prevent third-party agencies from offering better prices than customers could get if they contacted the hotel directly.

switch company—A firm that serves as an interpreter to make the programming language of GDSs and hotel central reservations systems compatible. Switch companies provide a seamless flow of room and price information between reservation systems.

travel agency—A business that helps consumers with travel planning, serving as a link between consumers and travel suppliers. On the travel supplier side, travel agencies act as agents for airlines, cruise lines, railroads, bus lines, and rental car firms as well as hotels and other lodging properties.

travel management company—A giant chain of travel agencies that has extensive buying power, enabling it to negotiate special rates and provide complete travel services. Examples of such companies include American Express Travel Services, Maritz Travel Company, and Carlson Wagonlit Travel.

Review Questions

1. What factors have contributed to the decrease in the number of travel agents?
2. What are some of the ways properties are meeting travel agents' need for property information?
3. Why are travel agents reluctant to use airline reservations systems for booking hotel rooms?

4. Who are the best prospects for a property's fam tour for travel agents?
5. What are some of the ways in which properties can provide good service to travel agents?
6. From a travel agent's point of view, are there advantages to a centralized commission payment plan? If so, what are they?
7. What are four resources that can help a property identify travel agents and agencies?
8. What is perhaps the most effective way to reach travel agents?
9. What public relations efforts might be used to develop travel agent business?
10. What are some of the challenges and opportunities travel agents will face in the future?

Internet Sites

For more information, visit the following Internet sites. Remember that Internet addresses can change without notice. If the site is no longer there, you can use a search engine to look for additional sites.

Airlines Reporting Corporation
www.arccorp.com

Association of Corporate Travel Executives
www.acte.org

American Express
www.americanexpress.com

American Society of Travel Agents
www.asta.org

Association of Retail Travel Agents
www.artaonline.com

Business Travel News
www.btnonline.com

Expedia (Microsoft)
www.expedia.com

Hospitality Sales & Marketing Association International
www.hsmai.org

Hotels.com
www.hotels.com

Hotwire
www.hotwire.com

JAX FAX Travel Marketing Magazine
www.jaxfax.com

Last Minute Travel
www.lastminutetravel.com

Lowest Fare
www.lowestfare.com

Media Central
www.mediacentral.com

Meeting Professionals International
www.mpiweb.org

ModernAgent Online
www.modernagent.com

OAG Pocket Flight Guide
www.oag.com

OAG Flight Guide North America
www.oag.com

Official Meeting Facilities Guide
www.omfg.com

Orbitz
www.orbitz.com

Pacific Asia Travel Association
www.pata.org

Priceline
www.priceline.com

Sales & Marketing Management
www.salesandmarketing.com

TravelAgent Central
www.travelagentcentral.com

Travel Daily News
www.traveldailynews.com

Travel Industry Association
www.tia.org

The Travel Institute
www.thetravelinstitute.com

Travel Management Daily
www.tmdaily.com

Travelocity (SABRE)
www.travelocity.com

Travel Trade
www.traveltrade.com

Travel Weekly
www.twcrossroads.com

TripAdvisor (Expedia)
www.tripadvisor.com

urhospitality.com
www.urhospitality.com

Virtuoso (U.S. site)
www.virtuoso.com/us

Web Digest for Marketers
wdfm.com

World Travel Guide
www.wtgonline.com

Chapter 11 Outline

Competencies

1. Describe types of association meetings, list possible decision-makers for association meetings, and outline factors association meeting planners consider when planning meetings. (pp. 413–423)
2. Describe types of corporation meetings, list possible decision-makers for corporate meetings, and outline factors corporate meeting planners consider when planning meetings. (pp. 424–432)
3. Identify ways hospitality salespeople can find meetings business and reach meeting planners. (pp. 432–442)

Insider Insights

Michael K. Hausman, CHSE
Director of National Accounts
Renaissance Hotels International
New York City

"The association market is exciting because of its vast size and the dollar value it represents to a hotel. The association market covers myriad associations, from large to small; this means that virtually any hotel can solicit some part of this important market segment. Nothing is more effective than meeting with association executives, either by making trips to association cities, attending various trade shows, or offering fam tours of your property."

11

Marketing to Meeting Planners

PERHAPS THE MOST STABLE and growth-oriented part of a hotel's total guest mix is the group meetings market. Group meetings business can benefit a property in a number of ways:

1. *Additional revenue.* Because group meeting guests are more or less a captive audience, they tend to spend more in the hotel's other revenue centers than do other guests. Spouses and children are accompanying meeting and convention attendees more than ever before, which typically increases business in gift shops, health clubs, and other revenue centers.
2. *Ease in filling slow periods.* Group meetings are an excellent way to generate business during your property's slow periods.
3. *Ease in employee scheduling.* With groups, the length of each guest's stay is usually predetermined. You can schedule employees more efficiently and reduce labor costs.
4. *Repeat business.* Group meetings can result in repeat business from the group organizing the meeting and from individual attendees who are introduced to the property during the meeting. Individuals may later visit the property as business or leisure travelers, and may recommend the property to friends and business associates.

There is yet another benefit to targeting the group meetings market. Group meetings business frequently increases during periods when leisure travel is on the decline due to a struggling economy. A poor economy actually stimulates group meetings business by creating the need for more direct contact among business associates.

The group meetings market can be a consistent revenue-producer for both large and small properties. In this chapter we will explore each segment of the group meetings market in terms of the types of meetings held and the specific requirements of each, including the cycle, pattern, and duration of meetings, and learn how to meet the needs of the people who plan group meetings for associations and corporations. We will also learn how to obtain leads, how to work with decision-makers to generate business, and how to use sales and advertising techniques to build your property's group business.

The Group Meetings Market

According to recent industry-wide studies, nearly 25 percent of U.S. hotel guests are meeting attendees. Of course, for major convention hotels, this figure is significantly higher. According to a Convention Industry Council study, associations spend more than $72 billion a year on meetings; corporations spend over $37 billion. It comes as no surprise, then, that hotel chains such as Hilton, Marriott, Radisson, and Starwood have convention properties in major cities. Complexes such as the Opryland Hotel in Nashville, the New York Marriott Marquis, and the Las Vegas Hilton attribute as much as 80 percent of their total sales volume to convention business.[1]

A common misconception is that all group meetings and conventions are large gatherings of thousands of people. In reality, there are many more small meetings than large ones. Research conducted by industry trade publications shows that 75 percent of all corporate meetings have fewer than 100 people in attendance.[2] This means that group meetings are a potential source of business for lodging properties of all sizes.

The group meetings market can be divided into two segments: associations and corporations. While the needs of these two segments may be the same in some areas, they are quite different in others, and the many organizations within each segment have needs that vary greatly. In fact, it is rare that a single organization's requirements are the same from one meeting or convention to the next! For this reason, each segment—and the organizations within each segment—must be examined separately.

Associations

An *association* is an organization of persons having a common interest or purpose. There are many associations throughout the country and the world, and their sizes, natures, and purposes vary greatly. There are associations for doctors, bankers, and lawyers. There are also associations for magicians, beekeepers, hospital purchasing agents, horseshoe pitchers, fruit growers, and urethane foam contractors. The American Hotel & Lodging Association and the National Restaurant Association are examples of associations in the hospitality industry.

Types of Associations. Associations can be divided into the following general categories:

1. Trade associations
2. Professional and scientific associations
3. Nonprofit organizations

Trade associations are made up of individuals, companies, or corporations that have similar business needs or concerns. Trade associations are usually considered the most lucrative source of group meetings business because their memberships consist largely of successful executives. Most trade associations hold conventions in conjunction with trade shows, such as the trade show staged by the National Restaurant Association. Restaurant and kitchen equipment suppliers exhibit at this annual convention, which draws more than 100,000 delegates to Chicago.

GOING GREEN

The "green" movement is having a significant impact on the hospitality industry. Many corporations and associations place great importance on social responsibility, so "green" hotels and meeting facilities will be increasingly poplar choices for meeting sites in the future.

One of the leaders in the green meeting space movement is the Las Vegas Springs Preserve, which boasts 50,000 square feet of meeting space in 16 separate, flexible meeting areas. Designed to eco-friendly specifications, the site has attracted a number of businesses—including representatives from nearby Las Vegas Strip properties—and nonprofit companies that wish to learn more about environmentally sound meeting practices.

"Green" features at the Las Vegas Springs Preserve include:

- Day-lighting or natural light instead of electric bulbs wherever possible
- Solar panels to generate enough energy for the small amount of electric lighting used
- Carpets made from recycled plastic bottles and corn husks
- Insulation composed of straw and compacted dirt instead of synthetic materials
- The use of regionally grown, organic food whenever possible; if food must be brought in from other areas, careful consideration is given to the distance required

Hospitality firms that cannot make such drastic changes as replacing insulation or adding solar panels can take small steps toward becoming known as being environmentally responsible. These include paperless check-in and check-out options for guests, encouraging guests to use their laptops rather than paper to take notes at meetings, recycling paper or other disposables (such as water bottles and ink cartridges), conserving energy by ensuring that lights and equipment are turned off when not in use, and monitoring the use of heating and cooling systems.

Source: Jennifer Robison, "Meetings Go Green," *Las Vegas Business Press,* reprinted in the *Las Vegas Review-Journal,* December 16, 2007.

Professional and scientific associations are closely related to trade associations, but differ in regard to meeting frequency. Most professional and scientific associations have regular meeting schedules, but it is not unusual for special meetings to be called if a major discovery affects a particular association. Many of these associations are affiliated with national and international associations, and these groups are typically very large. Examples of professional and scientific associations include the American Bar Association, the International Association of Dental Students, and the American Statistical Association.

The medical meetings market may be of particular interest to properties that wish to market to professional and scientific associations. Modern technology is constantly changing the way medicine is practiced, and medical professionals must stay current on the latest equipment, treatments, and techniques. In addition, Continuing Medical Education (CME) credits are required to maintain certifications, providing opportunities for properties to host training sessions and forums.

Industry Innovators

Steve Wynn
Chairman of the Board and CEO, Wynn Resorts

Casino developer Stephen A. "Steve" Wynn is widely credited with Las Vegas' transformation into a world-renowned resort and convention destination. During his tenure as Chairman of the Board, President, and Chief Executive Officer of Mirage Resorts, Incorporated, Wynn totally refurbished the Golden Nugget in downtown Las Vegas, attracting a new, upscale clientele to the former "gambling joint." He later opened the Mirage, Treasure Island (now called TI), and the Bellagio on the Las Vegas Strip, setting progressively higher standards for quality, luxury, and entertainment.

After selling Mirage Resorts, Inc., to MGM Grand in 2000, Wynn bought the historic Desert Inn, which is now the site of the luxurious Wynn Las Vegas. The hotel, which boasts 2,700 rooms, also offers 200,000 square feet of convention and meeting space, and its sister property, Encore, slated to open in late 2008, will offer another 80,000 square feet of convention space.

Wynn's commitment to convention business was evident when he was faced with a dilemma. Wynn, who bought the North American rights (outside Broadway) to the hit Broadway puppet show *Avenue Q* for $5 million, had originally planned to build a separate theater at the Wynn for another hit Broadway production show, *Spamalot*. In addition to the costs for a new theater (about $85 million) for *Spamalot*, the planned new convention space would not be contiguous to the existing space at Wynn Las Vegas with the addition of another venue. Wynn made the decision to close *Avenue Q*, remodeling its theater for *Spamalot*, rather than compromising on the convention space.

His decision, although costly, was understandable, as the city realized $8.2 billion in business from its 6.3 million convention visitors in 2007. Much of their spending was on hotels, restaurants, spas, and entertainment, which began outstripping gaming revenue after Wynn began offering luxurious rooms, upscale restaurants and shopping, spectacular entertainment, and unique attractions at his Strip properties.

In the past, convention business wasn't a prime target for many Las Vegas hotels, primarily because many groups looked for discounted rates and were notorious for light gambling. Wynn's insight that conventioneers were looking for a unique experience and would be willing to pay for added "spectacle" was a major factor in shaping today's focus on convention business as a viable source of revenue.

Sources: Biography on the website of the International Speakers Bureau (www.internationalspeakers.com/speakers); Steven Mihailovich, "'Wynn'-ing Ways," *Las Vegas Business Press*, April 25, 2005; and Steve Friess, "It Didn't Have Spectacle," *Newsweek* magazine's exclusive online archive, February 16, 2006.

Nonprofit organizations are another important source of group business. Because of its makeup of social, military, educational, religious, and fraternal groups, this nonprofit segment has been given the acronym **SMERF.** SMERF groups are now a major market segment for many properties and share a number of characteristics: most meetings are arranged by nonprofessional planners who may change from year to year; most are booked during the property's off-season; and attendees are usually price-sensitive. Since most SMERF meetings are family affairs, print advertising, such as the print ad in Exhibit 1, is often directed toward meeting the needs of families.

Social and military associations include groups reflecting a variety of interests, from garden clubs and bowling leagues to ethnic and military groups. In recent years, military reunions have paved the way for an entire new industry that assists in planning these nostalgic events. Social and military associations may be local, or they may be part of a regional or national organization. While these groups are cost-conscious and meeting frequency may vary widely, they are important sources of both rooms and function business.

Educational associations are groups of teachers or other education professionals and supporters. Although expenses are generally paid by the educational institutions involved, these groups tend to be very cost-conscious. Examples of educational associations include the National Education Association, the Modern Language Association, and the Council of Hotel Restaurant and Institutional Educators.

Religious associations can be divided into two groups: vocational and avocational. Vocational groups include associations of ministers or other clergy; avocational groups include educational and charitable religious groups. Religious associations as a whole are very budget-conscious. Examples of religious associations include Gideons International and the National Conference for Community and Justice. The religious market can boost business on weekdays as well as weekends, since several types of meetings are held: state, regional, and national conferences for various associations and denominations; conferences and retreats for pastors, men, women, couples, singles, and youth; revivals and rallies; and national speakers' symposia.

Fraternal and service groups are made up of individuals who have a similar area of interest, whether it be of a scholastic, philanthropic, or social nature. Members who take part in fraternal or service group meetings typically pay their own expenses. Meetings usually include family participation. Examples of fraternal and service groups include the Benevolent Protective Order of Elks, the Fraternal Order of Eagles, and Soroptimist International.

Types of Association Meetings. With this wide diversity of associations, it is evident that association meetings will vary. Associations generate several types of group meetings business:

- Annual conventions
- State and regional conventions
- Conferences
- Seminars and workshops
- Board and committee meetings

Exhibit 1 Marketing to SMERF Group Meeting Planners

Most SMERF group meetings are family affairs, so properties that provide facilities, services, and special rates for children are especially attractive to this market. This ad promotes both Marriott's Orlando World Center's activities for children and its proximity to Walt Disney World and Universal Studios, popular family attractions. (Courtesy of Marriott's Orlando World Center)

Annual conventions are held by associations of all types. Some conventions are huge affairs attracting tens of thousands of people, while others may have an attendance of fewer than 100. Most annual conventions have a main session for all delegates, supplemented by a number of smaller meetings sometimes called "breakout" meetings. Two-thirds of all annual conventions are held in conjunction with a trade show or with exhibits.[3] In some cases, trade shows may be held without a convention program; these functions are called "exhibitions" or "expositions" and may be sponsored by an association or by individual entrepreneurs or companies for the benefit of the association.

Since annual conventions vary widely, it is necessary to look at the convention needs of the different categories of associations.

Trade associations usually have complex convention programs that include many meetings and social activities. These associations usually make extensive use of sophisticated audiovisual equipment.

Professional and scientific associations also make use of sophisticated audiovisual equipment. Scientific and medical associations typically hold several breakout meetings, and the availability of a number of meeting rooms is more important to these associations than provision for social events.

Social and military groups are ideal customers for properties of every size. Awards banquets, fund-raising events, and installation dinners can adequately be handled by small properties as well as large hotels or restaurants. Some groups also hold shows or reunions, which not only result in sales of meeting space, but also generate additional rooms revenues from out-of-town guests.

Educational associations maximize meetings and minimize social functions at their annual conventions. Meetings are usually scheduled at night as well as during the day. Most educational association conventions are organized around a large general session (often featuring a political speaker), but a number of breakout rooms are usually needed as well.

Religious associations require varied facilities, depending on the nature of the religion. Conservative denominations tend to look for fewer but larger meeting halls, while liberal denominations are more interested in a sufficient number of breakout rooms.

Fraternal and service groups usually have annual conventions built around large general sessions. Attendees often combine vacations with convention attendance, so properties should offer recreational activities. There should also be sightseeing areas and entertainment facilities nearby.

State and regional conventions are smaller in scope than annual conventions and are further limited by geographic restrictions. Although some members elect to fly, most members attending regional conventions drive to the convention site. Therefore, airport properties do not necessarily have an advantage when soliciting state and regional conventions.

Conferences are usually staged to supplement a convention program. A conference supplies information related to new developments of interest to the association's members. Conferences are more common in professional, scientific, and educational associations, although other associations may book conferences following breakthroughs in their fields, changes in tax or corporate law, and other events that would affect the association's members.

Seminars and workshops are similar to conferences but are smaller in scope. They are generally used to train and educate association members. Many seminars are developed by independent seminar consultants who travel around the country, presenting special programs to association members, while other seminars may be developed by the association's paid staff.

Board and committee meetings are the smallest association group meetings in terms of attendance. They are often set in beautiful locales to attract outstanding people to serve on the board or committee, or to reward unpaid association officials. Board or committee meetings may range in size from fewer than ten to more than 100 persons and are ideal for almost any size property. Even a very small property can usually handle a meeting of ten or fewer. A large property may use the success it has with board and committee meetings to generate support for its selection as a convention site.

Planning Factors for Association Meetings. Obviously, there is a wide variety of associations and association meetings. You must identify the individual association's needs and determine ways to meet them if you want your property to be selected as that association's meeting or convention site. However, you should be aware of some factors that all associations must consider when planning a convention or group meeting. These include the timing of meetings, lead time, geographic patterns, geographic restrictions, attendance, and site selection.

Timing. Most association conventions—whether international, national, state, or regional—are held during the same month each year. Some associations, in fact, hold their annual convention during the same week of the same month each year.

Lead time. Most associations plan conventions well in advance. The average lead time is two years, although this varies from as little as one to as many as 15 or more years, depending on the convention's size. This lead time, though frustrating to hoteliers, is necessary for associations to select a site and plan their convention.

Geographic pattern. Many association conventions follow a definite geographic pattern. Often a convention is rotated among three or four cities. Some associations alternate between the East and the West in site selection; a popular variation of this pattern is to select a Midwestern city every third year.

The time of year for which a convention is scheduled may influence which area of the country is chosen. If a Midwestern location is chosen for a winter convention, for example, attendance could suffer in the event of inclement weather. Most **meeting planners** try to avoid weather problems with prudent scheduling, which makes October, May, April, June, and September, in that order, the most popular months for conventions.

Geographic restrictions. Some associations are limited to a site selection in their own states or within a specified distance from headquarters. This is especially true of small or regional associations. However, there is a growing trend to bend these restrictions and choose a site that appeals to the majority of association members no matter where it is located.

Attendance. Since attendance is optional, an association meeting planner must *attract* members to the meeting—and may try to do so with an appealing price, an interesting location, or special programs or events. Exhibit 2 shows a print ad that is used to promote Fairmont Hotels & Resorts in attractive destination cities.

Site selection requirements. While the primary needs for conventions and group meetings are adequate meeting space, a sufficient number of guestrooms, and the services of experienced hospitality employees, associations do consider other factors when selecting a specific site for a convention or group meeting. Transportation is an important factor in selecting a site, for example. If members must fly to the convention or meeting site, an airport property is most convenient;

Exhibit 2 Boosting Association Meeting Attendance

IT'S WONDERFUL
WHEN YOUR GROUP
CAN VISIT THE GREAT
SITES OF NEW YORK.

IT'S EVEN MORE
WONDERFUL WHEN THEY
CAN STAY AT ONE.

A hotel that is, in and of itself, a destination.
The Plaza in New York City. The Fairmont San Francisco. The Fairmont New Orleans.
When you plan a meeting at any one of Fairmont's legendary hotels throughout North
America, you'll be giving your delegates more than something to look forward to.
You'll also be giving them something to look back upon.

For information, please contact 1 866 662 6060.

Places in the heart.

www.fairmont.com

City Hotels: U.S.: Boston • Chicago • Dallas • Kansas City • New Orleans • New York City • San Francisco • San Jose • Santa Monica. Canada: Calgary • Edmonton • Montréal
Ottawa • Québec City • St. John's • Toronto • Vancouver • Victoria • Winnipeg. Bermuda: Hamilton. United Arab Emirates: Dubai. Resorts: U.S.: Scottsdale • Sonoma • Wailea.
Canada: Banff • Charlevoix • Jasper • Lake Louise • Montebello • Kenauk • Mont-Tremblant • St. Andrews • Whistler. Barbados: St. James. Mexico: Acapulco. Bermuda: Southampton

Since meeting attendance is voluntary for a number of groups, especially nonprofit associations, it is often necessary to offer an incentive for members to attend. This ad, targeted toward meeting planners, promotes Fairmont properties in key destination cities that would be attractive to meeting attendees. (Courtesy of Fairmont)

if they usually drive to the convention, a location near an interstate highway is a good choice.

Another factor in site selection is price. Most association conventions average two to four days, and since many delegates pay their own expenses, guestroom

Factors Association Meeting Planners Consider Important in Selecting a Facility/Hotel

Factors Considered Very Important	Major Conventions	Association Meetings
Number, size, and quality of meeting rooms	88%	81%
Number, size, and quality of sleeping rooms	86	68
Cost of facility/hotel	84	86
Negotiable food, beverage, and room rates	83	73
Quality of food service	71	65
Meeting support services and equipment	64	53
Efficiency of billing procedures	61	53
Assignment of one staff person to handle all aspects of meeting	61	48
Availability of exhibit space	57	34
Efficiency of check-in and check-out procedures	53	46
Previous experience in dealing with facility and its staff	49	39
Number, size, and quality of suites	39	15
Proximity to shopping, restaurants, and off-site entertainment	35	22
Meeting rooms with multiple high-speed phone lines and computer outlets	33	24

Although the purpose of a meeting ultimately determines the facility selection criteria, this table gives insight into general factors of importance to association meeting planners. Source: The "2006 Meetings Market Study," conducted by *Meetings & Conventions* magazine.

rates must be within the reach of association members. In some cases, an association meeting planner will select a property that offers the least expensive accommodations; in other cases, the finest accommodations are necessary, and resort or upscale properties will be the meeting planner's first choice. In other words, there is no one right price level. The price an association is willing to pay for guestrooms will depend on the nature of the association and its members' ability to pay.

Whom to Contact. Because of the many factors involved in planning a convention or group meeting and selecting a site for it, the planning and selection process an association goes through is a lengthy and often complex one. It is important for you to become involved in this process as soon as possible. That means getting to know the decision-maker. Who is the decision-maker for an association? Depending on the type of association or the type of meeting, he or she may be one of the following:

- Professional meeting planner
- Association executive

INTERNET EXERCISE

Log onto the Internet and visit AMC Institute's website at www.amcinstitute.org.

1. What is an association management company? Who do these companies serve?
2. What specific services do the AMC Institute's members offer?
3. Association management companies have an average of _____ associations as clients.
4. Can hotels join as associate members?

- Site committee chairperson
- Board of directors chairperson or member
- Local association member

Some associations employ a *professional meeting planner* who is responsible for recommending meeting sites. Others employ an *association executive* who may be given a title such as president, executive vice president, or executive director. No matter what the title, the association executive is usually the key to your sales efforts. He or she is ordinarily involved in the initial screening and final selection of a convention or meeting site. The association executive may either visit prospective sites in person or delegate this responsibility to others. He or she may have an administrative staff that assists with convention planning.

Small associations often cannot afford a full-time association executive and may use a **multiple-association management firm.** These firms serve an association as needed, selecting a site and planning a convention at costs the association can afford.

A *site committee chairperson* may be involved in screening convention sites or deciding on the final site, depending on the size and structure of the association. Chairpersons of other association committees may also be involved with the selection of sites for seminars, especially if the seminar will deal with matters important to their particular committees.

A *board of directors* is not usually involved in the decision-making process until the time for the final site selection. Many boards immediately accept the recommendation of the association executive. Others may take more time, but in the end, most boards of directors agree with the association executive's recommendation.

In many associations, especially professional and scientific ones, local chapters bid for the honor of hosting the national group. In these cases, you can approach a *local association member* and offer assistance in planning a convention or meeting if it will be held at your property. When taking this approach, however, you must demonstrate your property's convention and meetings expertise.

Once the key decision-maker has been identified, the job of selling begins. Techniques for selling to association meeting planners will be discussed in detail later in the chapter.

Corporations

Corporations can be a highly lucrative source of group meetings business. Most corporate meeting planners average 17 meetings or conventions in a single year.[4] The short lead time required for most corporate meetings makes it easier for you to book corporate meetings during slack periods. Corporate groups can be an important source of revenue to small properties as well as large, since, as mentioned previously, 75 percent of corporate meetings average an attendance of fewer than 100 persons.

Types of Corporations. Corporations vary greatly in size and purpose. There are local, state, national, and international corporations that sell products, services, or both. Whatever their size and type, at one time or another most corporations hold group meetings that require lodging facilities.

Types of Corporate Meetings. Corporations hold many types of meetings:

1. National sales meetings
2. Regional or district sales meetings
3. Training seminars
4. New-product introductions
5. Management meetings
6. Stockholder meetings
7. Incentive trips

National sales meetings are the oldest type of corporate meeting. Attendance is usually restricted to senior salespeople and supervisory executives; spouses are not usually invited. Average attendance is 112 persons, and these meetings last an average of 2.8 days.[5] Meeting requirements and site selections are varied. If a national sales meeting is scheduled to introduce new products, for example, it is important that the meeting be held at a site that provides easy access for product delivery. If a sales meeting has been called to develop a new advertising campaign, usually the site is chosen based on ease of access by the participants. The average per-person expenditure is generally above the usual meeting average. Participants tend to stay close to the property and dine in the property's restaurants or make extensive use of room service.

Regional or district sales meetings are usually smaller than national meetings, averaging 65 persons. Ordinarily these meetings are shorter than national sales meetings, although programs are often of the same type. Because regional or district sales meetings have lower budgets and smaller attendance than national meetings, and because they have geographic restrictions, per-person expenditures drop to the medium level.

Training seminars average an attendance of 64 persons and may last from one to five days. This is a no-nonsense type of meeting—there is a high level of double occupancy of rooms, and meeting rooms are often set up like schoolrooms. Since the budget is a prime consideration for this type of meeting, especially when training entry-level employees, the per-person expenditure drops to the low-to-medium level. Training and development meetings are well-suited to small properties regardless of location, especially when a "conference center atmosphere" can be provided.

Comparison of Association and Corporate Meeting Groups

FACTOR	ASSOCIATION	CORPORATION
Attendance Policy	Voluntary	Mandatory
Number of Meetings	Few, but larger attendance	More, but fewer attendees per meeting
Potential for Repeat Business	Some, but must rotate sites	High
Spouse Attendance	Common	Seldom
Exhibits	Frequent; heavy demand for hospitality suites	Less frequent
Geographic Pattern	Rotate geographically	No set pattern
Lead Time	Long (usually two to five years)	Short (often less than one year)
Billing Format	Individual folios	Master account
Price	More price conscious; generally good negotiators	Less price sensitive

New-product introductions are conducted to showcase new products and provide dealer training and motivation. Averaging two to five days, they may be public or private functions and they require a large ballroom or exhibit area and elaborate staging or setup. Most are open to spouses, and top executives often attend; meeting attendees are given the best in accommodations, cuisine, and entertainment, and elaborate food and beverage functions and entertainment events make these meetings some of the most profitable in the corporate meetings market.

Management meetings can also yield high per-person expenditures, since this type of meeting requires the finest accommodations available. These meetings are usually arranged on a short lead time, attendance may vary, and spouses are often invited. Additional revenue can be generated through programs for spouses and the sale of top-quality food and beverages.

Stockholder meetings are the lowest income-producers of all corporate meetings, since the purpose of the meeting is to conduct business as quickly as possible. Stockholders' meetings almost always last one day, and there are no planned food or beverage functions. A property's revenues will come strictly from the rental of a large ballroom or meeting room, room accommodations for a few executives, and meals for some of those coming from out of town.

Incentive trips generally run from five to eight days in length. Spouses are usually invited. Since incentive meetings are rewards for jobs well done, the destination is an important consideration. Almost all trips are to exotic locations, and, as shown in Exhibit 3, these locales are prominently featured in print advertising. Incentive meetings are best suited to resorts or properties in popular getaway spots, although for other properties there is the potential for overnight stays at the point of departure and the point of return if the incentive travel program includes cruise ship or overseas travel.

Exhibit 3 Sample Incentive Trip Ad

You could give them a watch...or send them to a place where they won't want to wear one.

Presenting Individual Incentives by Hyatt.

To reward your top performers, incent your customers and suppliers, or develop motivating sweepstakes and promotions, Hyatt offers two exceptionally appealing and flexible individual incentive options.

- ***Hyatt Nights***™ *certificates let you award rejuvenating stays at Hyatt Hotels and Resorts throughout the U.S., Hawaii and the Caribbean. Each certificate is redeemable any night of the week, and covers the entire cost of a single night's lodging. Best of all, recipients can make their own travel arrangements by calling a special Hyatt toll-free number.*
- ***Hyatt Check***™ *certificates are issued in $25 increments and are redeemable toward sumptuous Hyatt dining, beverages and select services. Use them with Hyatt Nights certificates or separately.*

*So treat people to the ultimate in pampering and personalized service. They're the incentives with the Hyatt touch...and a reward you'll be proud to give. For more information, call Individual Incentives by Hyatt at **1-312-750-8093** or **1-800-872-3600**.*

Feel the Hyatt Touch

Incentive trips reward top producers with getaways at top resort destinations. While incentive trips commonly include a number of qualifiers (over 100 people in some cases), a new trend is to offer "individual incentives"—letting a qualifier choose his or her own destination and/or travel alone rather than as part of a group. (Courtesy of Hyatt)

There are many details to attend to before an incentive meeting gets off the ground. Many large corporations that sponsor incentive travel have their own travel managers who make all travel and hotel arrangements for the group. Smaller companies that do not employ a travel specialist often call on outside **incentive travel companies,** sometimes referred to as "motivational houses," to coordinate their incentive meetings. Incentive travel companies include Maritz Inc., Incentive Travel Solutions, and The Light Group. These companies assist corporate meeting planners with all stages of the travel incentive program, including negotiating with hotels; packaging transportation, lodging, and meeting accommodations; and arranging for meals, tours, and entertainment.

Planning Factors for Corporate Meetings. As with associations, you should be aware of several planning factors common to all corporate group meetings.

Timing. Unlike many association conventions or meetings, there is no particular time cycle for business meetings. Most meetings are scheduled as needed and may occur at any time throughout the year.

Lead time. Lead time is far more flexible for corporate meetings than for association meetings. While annual conventions or sales meetings are usually planned a year or more in advance, training meetings and seminars may be set three to six months in advance, or with even less lead time if the meeting is called to deal with a crisis. Executive conferences and board meetings also may be called on short notice.

Geographic pattern. Corporate meetings are held where they are most needed—close to corporate headquarters, near the field office, or—in the case of an incentive trip—at an attractive location. Training seminars, management meetings, and other corporate meetings are not rotated among a few locations, as are some association conventions. This lack of a geographic pattern opens the door for almost any property, no matter what its location or size, to land corporate meetings business.

Geographic restrictions. Geographic restrictions usually affect only incentive trips. As mentioned earlier, an incentive trip must offer a desirable destination—Hawaii is a popular choice, as are resort destinations such as San Diego, Las Vegas, Miami, and the Caribbean. Some companies may offer trips to exciting cities such as New York or San Francisco.

Attendance. Although there are some exceptions, attendance at business meetings is usually mandatory. Therefore, corporate meeting planners do not have to work as hard as association meeting planners to attract meeting attendees.

Site selection requirements. Companies select the specific site or property for a business meeting because of its meeting facilities and services. Recreational amenities are a secondary consideration.

A resort is an obvious choice for incentive trips, but may also be chosen for a training seminar by a corporate meeting planner who wants meeting attendees to be free of city distractions. An airport location is ideal when convenience and speed are important. A suburban hotel may be best for attendees arriving by automobile or may be chosen because of its proximity to the home or field office. Budget or mid-priced downtown hotels may be the choice of a meeting planner who

Factors Corporate Meeting Planners Consider Important in Selecting a Facility/Hotel

Factors Considered "Very Important"	Corporate Planners
Number, size, and quality of meeting rooms	84%
Cost of hotel or meeting facility	82
Negotiable food, beverage, and room rates	79
Quality of food service	76
Number, size, and quality of sleeping rooms	74
Availability of meeting support services and equipment, such as audiovisual equipment	59
Efficiency of billing procedures	58
Assignment of one staff person to handle all aspects of meeting	54
Previous experience in dealing with facility and its staff	53
Efficiency of check-in and check-out procedures	49
High-speed Internet access	42
Meeting rooms with multiple high-speed phone lines and computer outlets	40
Number, size, and quality of suites	30
Proximity to airport	28

Corporate austerity programs, coupled with a greater awareness of the size of meeting expenditures, have caused corporate meeting planners to rank "cost of a hotel or meeting facility" and "negotiable food, beverage, and room rates" high on their list of factors in booking hotels. "Quality of food service," which was formerly their first priority, dropped to fourth place on the list. Source: The "2006 Meetings Market Study," conducted by *Meetings & Conventions* magazine.

wishes to save money; another meeting planner might choose a luxury downtown hotel to house visiting executives in a posh first-class environment.

Transportation is also an important factor in site selection, especially for annual conventions. For this reason, cities that are transportation hubs are often selected for annual conventions. Many companies return to such locations as Chicago and Dallas year after year because of the convenience factor.

If you want your property to be selected for a convention or group business meeting, you must provide adequate meeting space, guestrooms, security, and service—including convention or meeting planning services if necessary. In many cases, exhibit space will be needed, especially for meetings that launch new product lines. In other cases, a combination of exhibit or large meeting space and breakout rooms will be needed. Many companies prefer to have breakout rooms conveniently located near the large hall or ballroom used for the general session or group meeting.

Whom to Contact. No sales effort succeeds unless it is directed at the person or persons with the authority to make the final site decision, and the corporate sales picture is no different. Your sales pitch is useless unless it is presented to the right person. It can be difficult to reach the right decision-maker, since most of the company meetings planned each year are planned by nonprofessionals.

To find the right person, a hotel salesperson has to ask the right questions. "Who coordinates your meetings?" is not a good question; the person who coordinates the details of a meeting may not be the decision-maker. It is far better to ask, "Who is responsible for deciding which hotels your company uses for meetings?" With this approach, you will be able to save valuable time and effort by making immediate contact with the decision-maker.

Another approach may require slightly more time and effort but may also prove profitable: start at the top of a company and work downward. Speaking with the president of a company may not result in an immediate booking, but the contact can prove valuable in two ways: you won't be referred to someone below the decision-making level, and a referral "from above" may give you opportunities to sell to people who otherwise would not have been interested. A salesperson who can say, "Your president, Mr. Sanchez, suggested that I contact you" has an advantage over someone making a cold call.

Once the key contact is determined, you should also pay attention to tomorrow's decision-makers. As the account is worked and information is obtained on the organizational structure, "peak performers" should be identified and relationships with them cultivated. Knowing the people who are likely to succeed decision-makers when they are promoted or retire can pay big dividends in the future.

As with associations, decision-makers for corporate group meetings vary and can include:

- A full-time meeting planner
- Key executives, such as a president or vice president
- A corporate travel manager
- Division or department heads
- A secretary or associate
- Third-party meeting management firms

Often, large corporations employ *full-time meeting planners* to oversee the organization and implementation of company meetings and conventions. This is ideal for a property, because full-time meeting planners are experienced, usually know what they want, and know how to go about getting exactly what they need for each type of meeting.

Many companies, however, rely on *key executives* (a president or vice president, the chairperson of the board, etc.) to plan meetings and conventions. These executives will never be listed in meeting planner directories, and they do not think of themselves as meeting planners. But since they call meetings, decide where they will take place, and sometimes plan them, these executives are important to the hotel sales staff. Key executives may or may not have meeting planning experience.

According to American Express's most recent Survey of Business Travel Management, corporate business travel and entertainment expenses have escalated

Exhibit 4 The Importance of Corporate Travel Managers to Booking Group Meetings

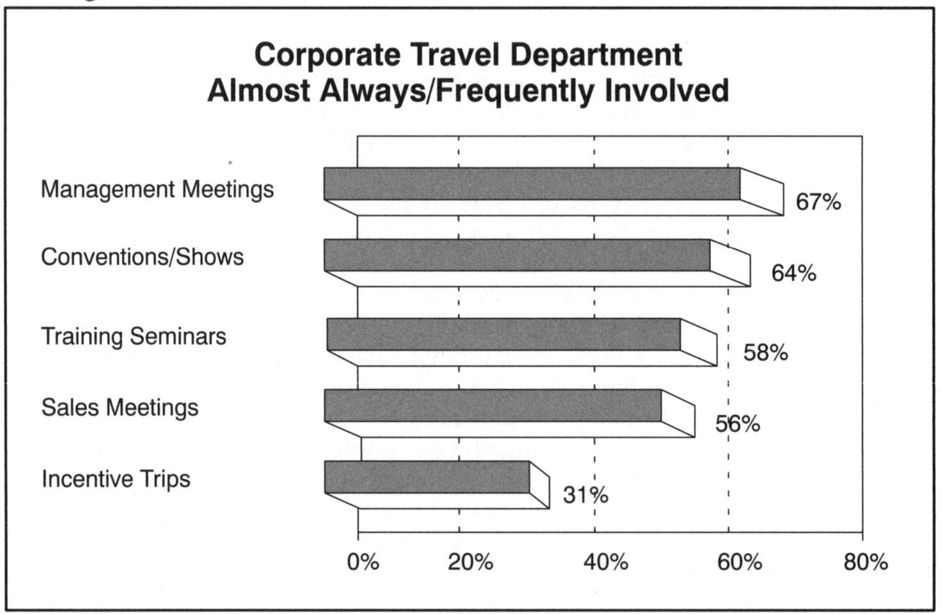

Due to escalating travel costs, a number of corporations have hired corporate travel managers to handle a variety of travel-related activities, from management meetings to incentive trips. Corporate travel managers often are involved in planning these group meetings, making them important contacts for properties wishing to book this business.
Source: *Hotel & Travel Index* Corporate Travel Manager Survey.

to $125 billion annually. In an attempt to manage escalating travel costs more effectively, many corporations have appointed or hired *corporate travel managers.* Corporate travel managers may arrange for a number of trips, from management meetings to incentive trips, and are important contacts for booking a large variety of group meetings (see Exhibit 4).

Division or department heads such as training directors, personnel directors, and advertising managers may also make decisions regarding meetings, seminars, or conferences. Like higher-level company executives, these staff members may or may not have much experience at planning meetings, but are important contacts for the property's sales staff.

Other companies may have *secretaries* or *associates* plan meetings. Although meeting planning may be part of their job descriptions, many secretaries or associates do not know what is required for a successful meeting. They tend to worry about small details while sometimes missing the big picture. In these situations, a property's meeting planning experience can be a deciding factor. A property that will help the secretary or associate plan a successful meeting is more likely to book the meeting than a property that just sells meeting space. Exhibit 5 shows a print ad that illustrates how properties attract business by promoting their expertise.

Exhibit 5 Solving Problems for Meeting Planners

"YOU SAID EXCELLENT SERVICE AT YOUR MEETING MEANS FINDING HELP EASILY. WE AGREE. WITH RED COAT SERVICE, HELP IS ALWAYS NEARBY."

Bill Marriott

You told us what you needed to make your meetings run more smoothly. And we listened.

So now, wherever you hold your meeting across our network of 36 convention hotels and resorts, you'll find "Red Coats." During your meeting, you can turn to them with any request, large or small. Whether you need a last-minute schedule change or extra meals, you'll always find a Red Coat ready to help you.

For more information, or to arrange your next meeting, call **1-800-831-4004.**

WE MAKE IT HAPPEN FOR YOU.

Many meeting planners worry about small details. This ad promotes Marriott's "Red Coat" service, which provides a qualified meeting professional to assist planners with handling their meetings. The chain has at least two Certified Meeting Professionals (a Convention Liaison Council designation) at each of the 41 hotels in its Meetings Network. (Courtesy of Marriott)

Not too many years ago, nearly all corporate meetings were planned by in-house departments and staff. Due to downsizing, many companies, like associations, are looking outside their own organizations for meeting planning services. ***Third-party meeting management firms,*** such as Experient, HelmsBriscoe, and Maritz McGettigan, are frequently hired by corporations to conduct site searches and negotiate rates on behalf of the companies they represent and to assist in conducting the meetings. These third-party planners make their money by charging a flat fee to the meeting organization or by seeking commissions from the hotels at which they book corporate meetings. To demonstrate the importance of these third-party meeting management firms, it should be noted that Experient (because of the number and types of clients it represented) was the single largest customer of Starwood, Hyatt, and Marriott hotels in 2007.

Finding Association and Corporate Group Business

Group meetings business for associations and corporations may be pursued locally and nationally. To reach national and international associations and corporations, the sales staff can consult trade periodicals and directories for leads and the names of key decision-makers.

A local effort can start at the property. Account files of previous group meetings business can be checked for opportunities to rebook associations or corporations. At the front desk, agents can search local newspapers for news of associations and corporate groups. In addition, property salespeople can check the yellow pages of the local phone book and the phone book of the state's capital city (many associations have headquarters in state capitals). Salespeople can also obtain leads from the reader boards of competitors or through word-of-mouth referrals.

Other opportunities can be found at the property level. Suppliers of products or services such as the local dairy operator or insurance agent are potential sources of group meetings business. Even if your property's suppliers do not require meeting space for themselves, many belong to trade, professional, civic, social, or religious organizations. Your suppliers could recommend your property as a meeting site for these organizations.

Your property's employees may also be good sources of meetings business. Many employees belong to organizations that meet regularly or need meeting space for special occasions. Property employees could influence an organization to choose "their" property.

Another effective way to find meeting planners is on the Internet. Many associations are listed on the Internet, and many of their websites offer tools to locate key decision-makers. MPIWeb, the site of Dallas-based Meeting Professionals International, for example, offers a free search service to visitors of the site (who do not have to be members to use it). By entering specific cities and states, you can access updated lists of names and contact information. Hotel salespeople can also search for decision-makers on other sites, including financially oriented sites and the sites of vendors who serve the conventions and meetings industry.

Local and state chambers of commerce, convention and visitors bureaus (CVBs), and industrial commissions can also provide leads for local group meetings

INTERNET EXERCISE

Log onto the Internet and visit the websites of the following third-party meeting management companies:

- ConferenceDirect (www.conferencedirect.com)
- HelmsBriscoe (www.helmsbriscoe.com)
- Experient (www.experient-inc.com)

1. What services do each of these companies offer?
2. What are the benefits for hotels that partner with these companies?

business. There are several ways in which membership or affiliation with these groups can benefit a property. First, CVBs and chambers of commerce are often the first entities that meeting planners contact when considering sites; if your property is listed in the collateral material that these organizations provide in response to these inquiries, you have a head start in attracting business. Second, many CVBs provide leads from groups looking for specific types of properties or facilities for their functions; these groups may want special meeting space, overflow rooms, or services your property can provide. Third, many CVBs promote your area as a destination in advertising and at trade shows; partnering with them in these efforts is a cost-effective way to get your property noticed by interested buyers. Last, but certainly very important, the contacts you make at functions held by these groups can provide leads for both local and national meetings business.

Another good way to develop leads is to visit and exhibit at trade shows, make contacts at annual conventions, and join professional associations—especially those that are users of hospitality industry products. If the property is part of a chain, the regional or corporate office may be able to provide leads.

Reaching Association and Corporate Meeting Planners

Many properties try to reach association and corporate meeting planners haphazardly. They buy a mailing list of meeting planners and send direct mail pieces to everyone on the list, for example. While this technique may produce some results, it is far better to do thorough research and aim selling efforts at a small group of 30 to 40 "hot prospects."

This is not to say that you cannot make use of a mailing list or place ads in trade periodicals, but most properties find it more effective to know something about the person to whom they are trying to sell. If you opt to use a mailing list, you should send out questionnaires to research the needs of those listed before sending an expensive, full-color convention brochure to meeting planners whose requirements you may not meet.

Hotels can also do research locally. The property's staff can gather marketing information by speaking to guests about their businesses or professions. Current guests have the potential to generate group business, and it is far less costly for a hotel to pursue leads right under its roof than to spend considerable time and money on mailing lists, out-of-town trips, advertisements, and sales blitzes.

To target the most cost-effective groups, many hotels use **pace reports** that cover every month for the next five years to track bookings and assist in pricing. Pace reports reveal what definite and tentative revenue is already on the books compared to what should be there based on historical analysis. Warren Breaux, vice president of marketing at the Gaylord Opryland Hotel, says that "we are constantly checking whether we are even, behind, or ahead of pace, so that the rate strategy is adjusted accordingly. If we are below pace in a given month, we are more willing to discount rates or offer other incentives to close business. If we are above pace, we are less willing to discount. The pace reports keep changing every month. A meeting planner can get one set of quotes one month and a different quote a month later for the same time period."[6]

When selling to meeting planners, you also have to understand the **lifetime value of the account.** It may pay to offer concessions for a minor function for the client today if that might result in additional, long-term lucrative business in the future.

Additionally, you must evaluate the total revenue potential of a group, not just guestroom revenue. At meeting-oriented hotels, 44 percent of revenue earned per available guestroom is generated through non-room sources, such as audiovisual rental, greens fees, food and beverage revenue, and meeting room revenue, and each of these has a different profit margin. Warren Breaux explains: "In the association market, we also look for ICWs, short for 'In Conjunction With,' to describe all events that are held in connection with a meeting but are sponsored by individual corporations. These are excellent sources of additional revenue for the hotel, and can serve as bargaining chips. An association might, for example, get a corporation to sponsor a hospitality suite, meal, golf tournament, coffee break, speaker, or event newsletter. When the association controls these events and steers the business to us, we benefit."[7] Before deciding which groups to target, then, you will want to find the right mix that optimizes the profit margin for all your property's departments, not forgetting about **"in conjunction with" business.**

The most effective way to sell to association or corporate meeting planners is face-to-face. A face-to-face presentation provides the opportunity for you to answer any questions and to reassure the meeting planner that your property is experienced at staging successful meetings.

Face-to-face selling can be accomplished in three ways: personal sales calls, sales blitzes, and attendance at trade shows. Personal sales calls focus on selling to individuals, while sales blitzes and attendance at trade shows involve prospecting and selling to a larger number of people over a short period of time.

Personal Sales Calls

Personal sales calls are the best way to sell to meeting planners. You can schedule an appointment call to meet the meeting planner and learn his or her needs. After determining these needs, you can develop a tailored presentation for your sales call.

Sales Blitzes

A sales blitz is essentially an intensive survey of a given geographic area over a specified time period. This time period is usually very short—one to three days is typical. Although the purpose of a sales blitz is largely to gather information, immediate business may be generated.

Planning is the key to a successful sales blitz. Most properties begin planning at least 30 days before the effort. If the blitz concept is new to you, you might plan a one-day blitz as a learning experience before undertaking a more extensive one.

A city directory is essential for planning a sales blitz, since sales routes should be carefully planned for the most effective use of time. Once sales routes have been mapped out, you can write on index cards the names and addresses of individuals or companies to contact, and give the cards and a street map to blitz participants. In most cases, each person is assigned around 30 calls per day and makes approximately 90 to 100 calls over a three-day period.

It is essential that participants have an adequate supply of survey sheets, such as the one shown in Exhibit 6, and collateral materials such as convention brochures and key chains or other low-cost specialty items. All specialty items should be imprinted with the property's name and telephone number.

Property salespeople, other staff members, or outsiders can take part in a sales blitz. A recently rediscovered and increasingly popular approach is to use hotel or marketing students to blitz an area. Nervous students can often get through doors that are closed to experienced salespeople. You should give students a training session and incentives for making calls. Incentives can range from reimbursement for out-of-pocket expenses (gas, parking, meals, etc.) to prizes or cash awards. Hiring students to blitz an area frees the property's sales staff to pursue other business or follow up on leads generated during the blitz.

Trade Shows

Just as a sales blitz may be an effective prospecting and selling tool for properties large and small, attendance at trade shows can help build a client base for all types of properties. The 891-room Peabody Orlando, for example, whose meetings mix is about 60 percent association and 40 percent corporate bookings, is active in meeting planner trade shows and industry meetings, such as those put on by Meeting Planners International and the American Society of Association Executives. Barry Anderson, vice president of marketing for the Peabody Orlando, says that "attending industry meetings allows us to further develop our relationships with our current customer base and develop new relationships through the personal networking available at these high-profile meetings."[8]

There are two types of trade shows. An *exhibit show* features booths that enable exhibitors to distribute materials and talk to buyers. A *marketplace show* offers a structured environment of scheduled appointments between buyers and sellers. Exhibit 7 lists a number of trade shows that can be used to reach the meetings market. Some of these shows are sponsored or attended by local convention and visitors bureaus, and it may be possible for you to share booth space and expenses with your local bureau.

Exhibit 6 Sample Sales Blitz Survey Sheet

Sales Blitz Survey Sheet

Organization____

Address____

_______________**Zip**_______________ **Phone #**_______________

Contact_______________________ **Title**_______________________

Contact_______________________ **Title**_______________________

1. How many meetings do you have a year?__________ When?__________
   Size?____________________ Who plans them?

Contact_______________________ **Title**_______________________

When is your next meeting?___________________________________

Where are meetings usually held?______________________________

2. Do you have incoming visitors that require sleeping accommodations?
   Yes_________ No_________ How many per month? ________________

   If yes, where are they housed?______________________________

   Do you reserve the room? Yes_________ No_________ (If not, who does?)

Contact_______________________ **Title**_______________________

3. Does your organization plan such things as:
   —Christmas Parties? —Retirement Dinners?
   —Award Dinners? —Other Social Events?

   Are you the organizer, or is there a social chairman?
   Yes____ **No**____ **Contact**______________________________

4. Are you, or any of your associates, affiliated with any other organizations or associations that might have need for meeting or banquet space?Yes____ No____

Name_______________________ **Contact**_______________________

Comments:

Taken by:___________________________ Date Taken_______________

Survey sheets are used to obtain information that will be used for personal sales calls if the prospect warrants a follow-up. An experienced sales blitz participant can complete approximately 30 of these forms a day, generating information that may produce future business for the property. Source: Howard Feiertag, "Blitzes and Sales Calls: Indispensable Selling Tools," *HSMAI Marketing Review,* Winter 1987, p. 24.

Exhibit 7 Trade Shows for Reaching the Meetings Market

Exhibit Shows	Number of years	Number of exhibitors	Usual attendance
1. American Society of Association Executives Annual Meeting & Expo	45	800	5,000
2. Incentive Travel & Meetings Exec Show	31	963	14,319
3. Religious Conference Management Association Annual Conference	27	688	1,250
4. Meeting Professionals International Annual Meeting	17	350	1,700
5. Health Care Convention & Exhibitors Association Annual Meeting	42	130	600
6. International Association for Exposition Management	6	125	1,000

Twenty years ago, the only major industry trade show was the American Society of Association Executives Expo. Today, there are a number of shows aimed at different segments of the meetings industry. This is a brief listing of national and regional exhibit shows, the number of years each show has been held, and recent attendance figures. When selecting a show at which to exhibit, keep in mind your primary target markets and plan your trade show strategy specifically for these markets.

Trade show selling should begin long before the show actually starts. You should set goals such as a specific sales volume or number of prearranged appointments. You should target specific prospects, and at least a week to ten days before the show you should send a direct mailing to them. Address this mailing to a key contact, and include a personal invitation to visit the property's booth, a preview of what the booth will be offering, and a response mechanism. Many trade show attendees prefer to plan their itinerary beforehand to visit "must-see" booths, and allowing them to make a preshow appointment may result in sales. Qualified prospects may also be attracted by preshow publicity and advertising.

At trade shows, a property's booth and personnel must accurately reflect the property's image and professionalism. The people who staff the booth should always be courteous, friendly, and informative, and the display should be arranged to involve prospects. Many exhibitors make the mistake of setting tables across the front of their booths; it is usually more effective to place tables at the sides and back of the booth to draw people into the display. In addition, many exhibitors give too many items away. Since most buyers want to travel light, it may be better to show a video brochure or other audiovisual presentation and give prospects just a business card or small brochure.

A property's trade show representatives should make the best use of the time and money spent on the property's exhibit. In other words, you should greet all

INTERNET EXERCISE

The Convention Industry Council (CIC) was formed in 1949 by four organizations: the American Society of Association Executives, the American Hotel & Lodging Association, the Hospitality Sales & Marketing Association International, and the Destination Management Association International (DMAI). The website of the CIC offers a number of resources to help in your understanding of the meetings market. Visit the CIC website at www.conventionindustry.org and answer the following questions:

1. How does one obtain the CMP designation?
2. What is APEX?
3. Click on "Special Projects." What is the CIC's stance on "green meetings"?

prospects who walk into the property's booth, but quickly *qualify* them. Qualifying prospects ensures that you won't spend too much time on browsers.

You can begin the qualifying process by asking questions: "What types of meetings do you hold throughout the year?" or "Has your company ever booked a meeting at our hotel?" These inquiries can lead to other questions that will help you determine the prospect's needs and influence over a meeting-site decision. Additional questions may include: "How many people usually attend your meetings?" "What types of facilities do you need for your meetings?" "How do you decide where to hold meetings?" and "Who determines the location of your meetings?"

Your sales efforts should not end when the trade show closes. For maximum effectiveness, leads must be followed up quickly or business may be lost to competitors. To prevent lost business, deadlines for follow-up should be established before the trade show. Personnel should be designated to handle follow-up to ensure immediate responses to inquiries.

Print Advertising

Many properties use print advertising, such as the ad shown in Exhibit 8, to reach meeting planners. You can place ads in trade journals or magazines, or in the business or social sections of newspapers in key feeder cities. In some instances, you may be able to participate in advertising planned by your local convention and visitors bureau. An entire destination area is usually featured in this type of advertising. You may increase your property's exposure by placing your own ads near the bureau's.

Other Sales Tools

The information theme should be carried through in direct mail and collateral materials, such as the newsletter and brochure shown in Exhibit 9. Meeting planners are not usually looking for romantic photographs; convention brochures and other direct mail pieces should feature room layouts and capacities, special services, and reservations information. In an attempt to provide necessary information, many properties and chains publish full-service meeting guides.

Exhibit 8 Sample Print Ad for Meeting Planners

98 OUT OF 100 PLANNERS WOULD BOOK A WYNDHAM AGAIN.

WE'RE WORKING ON THE OTHER TWO.

According to comment cards, 98% of the planners who have booked meetings at a Wyndham know exactly how dedicated we are to making each and every meeting a success. That's good.

And at The Wyndham Palm Springs Hotel, in particular, our resort-like atmosphere, state-of-the-art facilities, excellent restaurants, nearby championship golf courses, 26,000 square feet of meeting space (also connected to the Palm Springs Convention Center), and expert Wyndham service are enough to bring anyone back. That's also good.

But at Wyndham, we're always striving to be better. That's The Right Way. The Wyndham Way. And why we'd like you to call our sales manager at 619-322-6000 and see how we're coming along.

THE RIGHT WAY. THE WYNDHAM WAY.

888 Tahquitz Canyon Way, Palm Springs, CA 92262

For reservations, call 800-WYNDHAM.
Or for groups, call 800-327-8321.

Print ads directed to meeting planners typically promote a property's meeting and function space, guestrooms, and expertise in handling meetings. Print ads may also promote specific property features and services and other details important to meeting planners, such as the property's proximity to local attractions. This ad further appeals to meeting planners by saying that a large percentage of meeting planners have been satisfied with the hotel's performance. (Courtesy of Wyndham Palm Springs Hotel)

Exhibit 9 Sample Direct Mail Pieces

CENTERLINES

JUNE 1991 INTERNATIONAL ASSOCIATION OF CONFERENCE CENTERS VOL. 8 • NO.2

Conference Scores A Perfect Ten

IACC's Annual Get-Together Is Solid Gold

IACC celebrated its 10th Anniversary at the Annual Conference on April 7-10 at the newly-opened Resort at Squaw Creek in Squaw Valley, California. Themed "Swifter Higher Stronger," the conference carried its Olympic theme throughout the whole schedule of events, from site selection to special events to educational programming.

Upon registration, attendees were assigned to teams in "Olympic Villages," and then members were led by IACC's past presidents through the lobby, marching to the Olympic theme song. Once inside the ballroom, conferees had the chance to see an exciting gymnastics demonstration by Olympic Champion Tim Daggett, and listen to his inspirational account of success and achievement. The Olympic theme continued as villages were split into groups and given pins which had to be exchanged with other team members, until everyone had collected one pin from each of the 10 IACC conferences. This innovative icebreaker, coordinated by Kathleen Zurcher and Jerry Schmidt of the University of Minnesota, generated fun, enthusiasm and the chance to make many new acquaintances.

The "Up Close and Personal" assignment was then outlined for each group, a task involving the creation of a three-minute video which introduced each team member, highlighted some aspect of the Resort at Squaw Creek and wished IACC a happy birthday. (Refer to the "Up Close and Personal" article on page four for the outcome of this activity.)

The conference continued on with fa

Continued on page three

IACC's powwow in Squaw Valley began with the opening parade to hear the keynote address by Olympic gold medalist Tim Daggett (right) and wound up with a closing speech by Peter Burwash (below).

To reach meeting planners, the International Association of Conference Centers uses a newsletter promoting the centers within its network. The Sheraton Colony Square Hotel in Atlanta, Georgia, opened a line of communication to meeting planners by sending a direct mail letter explaining a special property promotion and a colorful brochure outlining meeting facilities and services.

The need for information on the part of meeting planners has led to their increasing use of the Internet. The most recent "Meetings Market Report" determined that over 75 percent of corporate and association meeting planners use the Internet to research possible hotels for their upcoming meetings.[9]

Meeting planners cite a number of benefits to using the Internet, including 24-hour availability, a wealth of up-to-date information on potential meeting sites around the world, and the ability to "interact" on most sites. Using the Internet can save time and money and make the planner's job easier.

There are basically three ways in which properties can use the Internet to reach prospects. The first is to set up your own website, allowing meeting planners and other clients to directly access it for information. The second is to link your website to other meetings-related sites, such as a convention and visitors bureau site, a city site, or the sites of other firms to which meeting planners turn for information. The third is to purchase advertising on sites likely to be visited by meeting planners.

If you opt to develop your own website, you should include features that will provide information required by meeting planners. This includes lists of meeting facilities; floor plan diagrams; the name, telephone number, and e-mail address of a contact person; a form for additional information that can be e-mailed or printed out and mailed or faxed; and a reservations system that allows the planner to guarantee rooms and space with a credit card. Most hotels also offer some form of a "virtual tour" of facilities most important to meeting planners—showing meeting rooms, banquet setups, guestrooms, recreational amenities, and so on. This option, whether it is simply a slide show with color photographs or a graphic presentation with images and sound, is the next best thing to a personal visit to the property.

Since personal experience is a major factor in site selection, familiarization tours and public relations activities can also be effective sales tools. Many meeting planners will not book a meeting before seeing the site. You can maximize site visits in a number of ways. First, schedule tours when the property is busy; full hotels, restaurants, and banquet rooms legitimize claims of quality. There should also be ample time for personal attention to the planner; he or she should be able to sample menus, meet the staff who will be assisting with the meeting, and experience the property on a "guest" level.

The tour itself should include only those items of interest to the planner. The prospect should be questioned before going on a property tour to determine what factors are of interest to him or her; this allows you to plan the tour to show property features and benefits that relate to those factors. State-of-the-art audiovisual equipment may be impressive, but a demonstration of it can be a waste of time for a planner who is arranging a largely social function. Meeting and banquet rooms are most effectively sold when they are shown in use (this helps the planner visualize his or her own function); if this is not possible, they should be shown in four-color photos accompanied by third-party endorsements. Rooms should be shown from the "bottom up"—standard, then luxurious, then suites. Sell the benefits of facilities and amenities as well as their features: "The ballroom is adjacent to the breakout rooms" (feature) "so that attendees can move quickly from the general session to the workshops, which saves time and keeps the meeting on schedule" (benefit).

Public relations activities may include meeting-planning seminars and social functions staged for various types of associations. "Ethnic days" or food festivals may draw local association members and meeting planners.

Conclusion

Although meeting planners can bring much-needed group meetings business to a property, dealing with them can sometimes be challenging. There are many professional meeting planners who are relatively easy to work with because they know the requirements of a business group and what it takes to put on a successful meeting. Other meeting planners are inexperienced, and some individuals—ranging from key executives to secretaries or associates—are called on to plan a meeting with no experience at all.

Almost all meeting planners, experienced or not, tend to be anxious about their meetings or conventions. With their professional reputations at stake, it is understandable that most meeting planners are very concerned about a property's ability to stage a meeting and to respond successfully to the problems that may come up (many veteran meeting planners would change this to "the problems that *will* come up"). That is why properties that sell their meeting planning experience and expertise, rather than just their meeting space, will be the most successful at selling to meeting planners.

Endnotes

1. Milton T. Astroff and James R. Abbey, *Convention Management and Service*, 7th ed. (Lansing, Mich.: American Hotel & Lodging Educational Institute, 2006).
2. "The Meetings Market Report 2006," *Meetings and Conventions*.
3. "The Meetings Market Report 2006."
4. "The Meetings Market Report 2006."
5. This statement and many of the facts cited in this section are from "The Meetings Market Report 2006."
6. "Balancing Yield Management and Meeting Planner Satisfaction," *World Hospitality*, October 2000, p. 5.
7. "Balancing Yield Management and Meeting Planner Satisfaction," p. 5.
8. "Capitalizing on the Steady Meeting Market," *World Hospitality*, May 2000, p. 1.
9. Tyler Davidson, "2006 Meetings Market Report," *Meetings West*.

Key Terms

"in conjunction with" business—Affiliates and subgroups, such as exhibitors, that contribute to the overall value of the meeting. This type of business, which is brought to a facility because of a convention, is also called "auxiliary business."

incentive travel company—Full-time professional travel houses that make arrangements for companies wishing to offer incentive trips. Most represent several different companies.

incentive trip—A trip financed by a business as an employee incentive.

lifetime value of the account—The value or profits expected from a customer's total future purchases. An association or corporation meeting planner who is a satisfied customer and therefore books several meetings with a property over his or her buying lifetime is more valuable than a one-time purchaser.

meeting planner—An employee who makes travel and other arrangements for group meetings.

multiple-association management firm—A company that functions as the executive and office staff for a number of associations.

pace reports—Monthly booking and revenue reports used to assist hotels in pricing and negotiating with group buyers.

SMERF—An acronym for the nonprofit-organization market segment, which is made up of social, military, educational, religious, and fraternal groups.

third-party meeting management firms—Outside individuals or companies that handle meeting planning for associations and corporations that hire them to help with their meetings. Services might include site selection, negotiations with hotels and other suppliers of meeting products and services, and assisting in all phases of staging the meeting itself.

Review Questions

1. What two segments compose the group meetings market?
2. In what ways can each group meetings market benefit a property?
3. What are the categories into which associations are divided and the characteristics of each?
4. What types of meetings business do associations generate?
5. What are some planning factors for an association's annual convention?
6. Who are the possible decision-makers for an association?
7. What are the types of corporate meetings and the characteristics of each?
8. Who are the possible decision-makers for corporate group meetings?
9. What are the three types of face-to-face selling techniques used to reach meeting planners and how can each be used most effectively?
10. What other approaches are used to pursue group meetings business?

Internet Sites

For more information, visit the following Internet sites. Remember that Internet addresses can change without notice. If the site is no longer there, you can use a search engine to look for additional sites.

American Hotel & Lodging Association
www.ahla.com

American Hotel & Lodging Educational Institute
www.ei-ahla.org

American Society of Association Executives
www.asaenet.org

Council on Hotel, Restaurant and Institutional Education
www.chrie.org

Destination Marketing Association International
www.iacvb.org

Gideons International
www.gideons.org

Hospitality Sales & Marketing Association International
www.hsmai.org

International Association of Exhibitions and Events
www.iaee.com

Media Central
www.mediacentral.com

Meeting Professionals International
www.mpiweb.org

National Conference for Community and Justice
www.nccj.org

National Restaurant Association
www.restaurant.org

Professional Convention Management Association (PCMA)
www.pcma.org

Tradeshow Week
www.tradeshowweek.com

Sales & Marketing Management
www.salesandmarketing.com

Soroptimist International of the Americas
www.soroptimist.org

urhospitality.com
www.urhospitality.com

Web Digest for Marketers
www.wdfm.com

Case Study

No Vacancy

Jon Stonewall is a regional manager for IntelTech, a Seattle-based company that produces computer software. He is responsible for planning the annual meeting of his account representatives in District 12, which encompasses the entire Pacific Northwest. The meeting, normally just an opportunity for education and socializing, will be especially important this year because the company is introducing several new products. After reviewing several locations, Jon decided to have the meeting in Sacramento and asked his secretary, Chris, to gather information and solicit bids from at least five Sacramento hotels. Jon is a hard-nosed businessperson who likes to get what he wants. To waste as little time as possible, he systematically examined his choices and narrowed the selection down to two. Now it was time to make a deal.

Jon was in his office when he received a call from Julia Chavez, the sales manager of the Monte Sereno Hotel in Sacramento. She began the conversation by introducing herself and her property, a mid-range hotel with 248 rooms, 8,000 square feet of meeting space, and a 5,200-square-foot ballroom that could be divided into four equal sections.

"We're so pleased you've selected the Monte Sereno as a possible site for your next meeting," Julia continued. "I've spoken at length with your secretary and wanted to speak with you personally to be sure we understand your needs. Do you have a moment to talk?"

Jon was at the start of a busy day and was a little annoyed at the interruption, but brusquely told her to go on. Concerned by his tone, Julia thanked him for his time and proceeded cautiously.

"I understand your group will arrive Sunday afternoon and leave Thursday. You'd like 48 rooms, single occupancy, and an opening-night reception with heavy hors d'oeuvres. Is that correct?"

"Yes," Jon grunted.

"Chris told me that you'll begin each morning with a continental breakfast at 8:00 A.M., followed by a general session at 8:30. The general session meeting room is to be arranged classroom-style, with a luncheon in a separate room beginning at noon. From 1:00 to 5:00 P.M., your account reps will break into groups of 10 to 15 and require separate meeting spaces."

"That's right," Jon replied, "except that everyone will be on their own at lunch time."

Julia had carefully considered this sales opportunity, weighed the options, and decided on an appropriate rate before making the call to Jon. She had taken into account the property's sales history, which showed a 92 percent occupancy rate on the particular days IntelTech had in mind. She was concerned because this meeting would use only 20 percent of the hotel's rooms while using 65 percent of the hotel's meeting space. From her standpoint, it wasn't a great piece of business. Julia Chavez wanted the business, but she wanted it on her own terms. She took a deep breath and continued.

"Well, we do have those dates available for your meeting. We can offer the guestrooms at $99, a reduction from our standard $110 rate, and offer the meeting space you need at $1,000 per day. However, I know that getting high value for your dollar is a consideration for everyone these days, so, if you can be flexible and change your dates to a Wednesday arrival and a Sunday departure, I can offer the rooms to you at $85 and waive the $1,000 charge for the meeting space—if you will hold your farewell banquet with us."

"I can't believe this!" Jon said, his voice rising. "The Salton Hotel down the street has the dates I want *and* they can give them to me at the rate you quoted! Granted, I prefer your hotel overall, but I have to consider my company. This meeting has been set for a long time; some of my people have already made travel plans. We've even scheduled the speakers. I can't go back and change things now! Why are the rates so different later in the week?"

Julia was prepared for this response and answered him as tactfully and honestly as she could. "I'm aware of your concerns and I know it would be difficult to move the meeting, but I wanted to give you the option. Since we're both businesspeople, I know you'll understand that I have to consider my property's financial position in all of this. Our sales history shows that we have our highest occupancy during the first part of the week—between 90 and 100 percent—but later in the week that number declines to around 60 percent; that's why I can give you a lower rate at that time. Because we're sold out or almost sold out from Sunday through Thursday, it doesn't make sense financially for us to offer you the lower rate early in the week."

"Look," Jon said, "I can appreciate where you're coming from, but I don't see how I can change this meeting—even if I can save a lot of money."

"I understand your situation and want to work with you in the future," Julia replied, "but I'm not sure we can meet your needs this time. Down the road, if you bring me your next meeting, I'll throw in a free cocktail party. I think you'd be very pleased with our hotel. We have outstanding food and a very friendly, courteous staff. I hope you'll come and visit us when you're in town."

Jon hesitated. Since he really wanted to stay at the Monte Sereno rather than the other hotel, he didn't want to let the matter drop. "What about this, Julia: if I agree to the higher rates and choose you over a competitor, will you do a few things for me? I'll pay the $99 room rate if you'll throw in the meeting space for nothing. I also want that free cocktail party you just mentioned. In addition, I'd like you to give us turndown service throughout our stay, a free *USA Today* in every room, and, waiting for my account reps when they arrive on Sunday, a mint and a welcome note from me in every guestroom."

Discussion Questions

1. Do you think Julia should agree to host the meeting on Jon's terms? Why or why not?
2. How could Julia further negotiate each of Jon's demands and end with a win-win conclusion?

Case Number: 370CB

This case was developed in cooperation with Bill Flor and Randy Kinder, authors of *No Vacancy: A Tried & True Guide to Get More Rooms Business!*; The No Vacancy Company; Jacksonville, Florida.

This case also appears in *Contemporary Hospitality Marketing: A Service Management Approach* (Lansing, Mich.: American Hotel & Lodging Educational Institute, 1999), ISBN 978-0-86612-158-3.

Chapter 12 Outline

Competencies

1. Outline considerations for marketing hospitality products and services to international travelers. (pp. 449–462)
2. Summarize considerations for marketing hospitality products and services to honeymooners and sports teams. (pp. 462–473)
3. Outline considerations for marketing hospitality products and services to government travelers, travelers with disabilities, and travelers from other special segments. (pp. 473–485)

Insider Insights

John B. Richards
Former Senior Vice President—Marketing
Four Seasons Hotels and Resorts
Toronto, Ontario, Canada

"Hoteliers located in international business centers find it imperative that they not only provide excellent service, but also address the special needs of international guests. One of the ways Four Seasons acknowledges its international guests is by having on staff a number of multilingual concierges who speak a range of languages, including French, Spanish, German, Italian, and Japanese. The smallest gestures can sometimes mean the most—whether it's greeting a guest in his or her native language or having a guest's hometown newspaper available with the morning coffee."

12

Marketing to Special Segments

WHILE BUSINESS AND LEISURE TRAVEL is still the backbone of the hospitality industry, many properties are targeting specialized market segments to ensure consistent occupancy. Reunion groups, juries, out-of-town wedding or funeral guests, truckers, sports teams, and movie crews are just a few examples of the small or special market segments that many properties are now targeting.

Your property's ability to appeal to these segments will vary depending on its products, services, and location. In this chapter, we will take a look at some special market segments that can prove financially lucrative if you are willing to spend the time and money to research them and modify your property's products and services to meet their needs.

International Travelers

One of the fastest growing and most profitable special segments is the international traveler market. International travelers are travelers originating from points outside the United States and are usually divided into three categories: North American travelers, European travelers, and other international travelers (Asian, Australian, African, etc.). Travel and tourism is the United States' top export, ranking ahead of agricultural goods, chemicals, and motor vehicles, and the international market is expected to continue to grow.

It is difficult to give a general profile of the international traveler, but Exhibit 1 provides an overview of this market segment. Visitors from different countries are interested in different attractions and have varying needs. But it is possible to define several patterns in this market:

1. *Point of origin*. While more than half of the international travelers currently visiting the United States comes from Canada or Mexico, the number of North American travelers is on the decline. The market may soon be dominated by Asian, South American, and European travelers, with the biggest increases coming from Japan, Brazil, Argentina, and Korea, although China is also expected to send significantly more travelers to the United States in the future.
2. *Reasons for travel to the United States*. International travelers cite the quality of nightlife, shopping, and accommodations as reasons for visiting the United States. The devalued dollar also played a part in bringing European and Asian travelers (mostly Japanese) to the United States, although the United States is considered a travel bargain regardless of the dollar's strength. Most

Exhibit 1 The International Traveler Market at a Glance

Location: Preferred property locations include gateway cities and locations near hub airports (air tours), main highways (motorcoach tours), cultural and recreational attractions, and natural wonders—the Grand Canyon, Niagara Falls, etc. A large majority are repeat travelers looking for new experiences. Trips to dude ranches and other attractions in the Rocky Mountain region; "adventure trips," such as white-water rafting; tours of the Mississippi River and other destinations in the Midwest; and visits to the "Real America" are increasing in popularity.

Facilities: Preferred facilities include swimming pools, health clubs, and Jacuzzis. Other desirable amenities include multilingual direction signs, gift shops that stock foreign cigarettes and other items, multilingual menus, and security features—safe-deposit boxes or safes, well-lit grounds, and electronic door locks.

Price: Price tolerance depends on the source of business. Tour operators look for low or discounted prices; properties typically offer 20 to 25 percent discounts off rack rates to help absorb their promotional expenses. Travel agents want value but not necessarily the lowest price; their requirements will vary depending on client preferences. Individuals and groups also have varying requirements; some look for budget accommodations, while others opt for luxury vacations.

Services: Preferred services include multilingual staff, bus parking, transportation from airport, group meals (for tour groups), currency exchange, "survival kits" printed in native languages, ethnic selections on restaurant menus, electrical adapters, concierge services, and worldwide reservation services.

Decision-Makers: Individual guests, local or foreign companies, tour operators, or travel agents may make travel decisions.

Best Ways to Reach Market: Goodwill trips and participation in international travel trade shows, personal contacts, direct mail (with an emphasis on group intermediaries), travel writer participation, and placing ads in travel directories, in-flight magazines, and major international magazines and newspapers will reach international travelers. Many properties make use of visual aids, such as slide and video presentations, with audio in the target country's native tongue to overcome language barriers.

international travelers cite the lower costs of U.S. goods and services as an important factor in choosing to travel in this country.

3. *Destinations.* The Japanese usually prefer large cities and tend to stay in just one per trip. The French also prefer cities, including New York and New Orleans, that offer cultural events and nightlife, while the British opt for such destinations as the Grand Canyon or Rocky Mountains. Germans often tour extensively or select beach vacations in Florida or Hawaii.

4. *Length of stay.* Europeans typically receive four to six weeks of leave annually and average 20.6 nights overseas, while the Japanese stay an average of 9.1 nights in the United States on leisure trips. Individual business travelers typically stay one to seven days and often travel on expense accounts (which translates into high expenditures per person). They sometimes take vacation time at the conclusion of the business portion of their trips.

Group leisure travelers account for both short trips and long stays. First-time international visitors often travel in groups and usually prefer three-day to one-week stays. Seasoned international group travelers typically stay longer—sometimes two weeks or more.

Group business travelers generally stay five to seven days and may bring spouses along if the purpose of the trip is to attend a trade show or convention. Group business travelers may also include delegations touring factories or farms, groups traveling to international seminars, and groups stopping over on the way home.[1]

The Decision-Maker

Since the international traveler market is so diverse, properties must market to a number of kinds of decision-makers:

- Individual guests
- Local- or foreign-company managers
- Tour operators and wholesalers
- Travel agents
- Receptive agents

Individual guests usually make travel decisions based on the purpose of the trip. If the trip is for business, the destination is predetermined, and only a property must be chosen. International business travelers tend to choose the familiar. They are likely to choose a chain property that operates in their home country over an independent resort or hotel. Individual leisure travelers, on the other hand, are more likely to choose a property close to interesting attractions. Price is often less important to individual leisure travelers. These travelers are willing to pay higher rates for special amenities or services or for a location close to attractions.

An important trend within the individual travel segment is **foreign independent travel (FIT).** FIT travelers want the convenience and price of an arranged tour (without traveling in groups), usually buy packages at home, and travel unescorted to prearranged destinations. Most FIT travelers have visited the United States in a group, and return on their own. They usually travel individually or in twos; they may be either business or leisure travelers, and they look for a travel "experience"—shopping, sight-seeing, and so on—in addition to competitive hotel rates. Properties in popular destination cities attract the most FIT travelers.

Local- or foreign-company managers are often the decision-makers for individual or group business travelers. Local-company managers frequently make their decisions on the basis of credit arrangements; they will house foreign visitors in properties at which they have charge accounts. Foreign-company managers prefer to do business with familiar properties. They book into chain properties that operate in their home country, or seek a recommendation from the U.S. company with which they are doing business.

Tour operators and **tour wholesalers** usually make the lodging decisions for group leisure travelers and look for a convenient location and good service. Locations easily accessible from main highways (for motorcoach tours) or airports

Trends Among International Travelers

Trends Among Japanese Travelers

- Destination is usually chosen in consultation with a travel agent
- Most popular seasons: winter and summer
- Trip purpose: vacation, 60 percent; business or convention, 22 percent; visit friends or relatives, 11 percent; other, 10 percent
- Top activities (in order of preference): shopping, sight-seeing, dining, water sports
- Children under 18 are rarely included

Trends Among British Travelers

- Most popular months: July, August, September
- Trip purpose: vacation, 54 percent; business or convention, 35 percent; visit friends or relatives, 30 percent; other, 4 percent
- Favorite activities: dining, shopping, and sight-seeing

Trends Among Canadian and Mexican Travelers

- Both groups visit more frequently, stay for shorter periods of time, and spend less money than other international travelers
- Favorite destinations: New York, Florida
- Trip purpose (Canadians): vacation, 62 percent; visit friends or relatives, 20 percent; business or convention, 9 percent; other, 10 percent
- Trip purpose (Mexicans): vacation, 53 percent; business or convention, 30 percent; visit friends or relatives, 27 percent; other, 9 percent (data includes air arrivals only)

The international traveler segment can be an important source of revenue to hotels and restaurants located in key gateway cities or locations in close proximity to natural wonders, recreational sites such as Disney World, and other tourist attractions. By understanding the makeup of this market, you will be able to effectively develop a strategy to reach those international travelers best suited for your property.

(for air/ground packages) and areas that offer a number of attractions within a day's driving distance are favorite choices. Tour operators also want good service, and usually will return to a property that serves group meals promptly, blocks off rooms for the group, and offers discounts or all-inclusive rates.

Tour operators and wholesalers typically receive discounts of 20 to 30 percent off rack rates. In return for these discounts, they will feature your property in annual catalogs and brochures, actively sell your property in their countries, and even develop their own public relations pieces about your destination.

Travel agents are influential in making lodging decisions for individual and group business and leisure travelers. Travel agents also look for a good location, but price plays a lesser part in selection. Since most travel agents work on a commission basis, they won't necessarily seek out the lowest price, but their clients must feel they are getting value for their money. Travel agents insist on good service, and can serve as excellent sources of repeat business if previous clients have been treated well.

Tour operators and travel agents look for U.S. properties with amenities such as swimming pools and saunas (features not common in European hotels). Security may also play a part in their decisions to book with a property. Operators and agents who cater to the Japanese market, especially, look for security. The Japanese are very concerned about their personal safety, and look for hotels that offer safe-deposit boxes or safes, well-lit grounds, and other security measures.

Receptive agents make dealing with visitors from abroad even easier for hotels. A receptive agent is an intermediary who relieves the hotel or other supplier of countless details. Receptive agents work somewhat like tour wholesalers—hotels or attractions negotiate to sell their space at discounts of 30 to 35 percent from rack rates to the receptive operator. The receptive, in turn, works with a series of wholesalers in the region they serve.

A receptive agent can also serve as a domestic wholesaler to foreign wholesalers, collecting the money from abroad and then paying suppliers, facilitating payment transactions for groups. Some large receptive companies provide some or all of the components of a tour package for resale by a motorcoach/air tour wholesaler.

Hotels can reach receptive agents through the Receptive Services Association (RSA). RSA members account for a significant share of bookings into domestic hotels, and the association is also committed to improve the quality of travel-related services for foreign visitors and address economic and policy issues affecting tourism. Hotels and other travel suppliers that become associate members of RSA are listed on the organization's website under the "Associate Members" tab and can establish links to their property or services that can be accessed by both receptive agents and international travelers.

Meeting the Needs of International Travelers

The needs of international travelers vary widely, but there are several areas of common concern:

- *Making reservations*. Whether reservations are made by an individual traveler or by a tour operator or travel agent, easy booking is important. You can meet this need in a variety of ways: establish field offices in key feeder cities (Tokyo, London, Paris, Mexico City, etc.) that offer worldwide reservations services, use Telex machines and toll-free numbers, and create tie-ins with foreign air services.

  The importance of handling international bookings has led Radisson Hotels International to establish a toll-free reservations system in over a dozen

INTERNET EXERCISE

Log onto the Internet and research the website of the Receptive Services Association of America (www.rsana.com):

1. What is the history of this association?
2. What is the purpose and mission of this association?
3. What are the advantages of working with a receptive tour operator?

foreign countries. All of the toll-free calls from these systems ring directly into Radisson's reservation center in Omaha, Nebraska, but they are answered by reservations agents who speak the native language of the caller (a call on the German line, for example, will be answered in German). This system makes it easier for international guests to book reservations and will be expanded into other markets as the need arises.

- *Language barriers.* Many international travelers have difficulty communicating in English. While some international guests speak English quite well, others have trouble with the language, especially with slang and idioms. Hotels that cater to international guests can ease this problem by hiring a multilingual staff and providing multilingual menus and in-house signs. Other useful and appreciated solutions are "survival guides" with text in several languages. These booklets or brochures can serve as a directory of hotel services; give instructions on the operation of the phone system, television set, and air-conditioning unit; and provide additional information to make the visitor feel welcome.

  Today's technology is being used to eliminate language barriers. Two major translation networks are now available to hotels that cater to international guests—the AT&T **Language Line Services** and the **Japanese Assistance Network (JAN).** AT&T's Language Line Services are used at the New York Hilton and Towers, where international travelers account for almost 50 percent of the property's business; the service is accessible from every guestroom and links guests to assistance in 140 different languages. JAN provides Japanese translation for business and leisure travelers. Both services are available 24 hours a day, and can be directly accessed from the concierge desk or from guestrooms.

- *Transportation to the hotel.* First-time international guests traveling by air often have difficulty getting from the airport to the hotel. Many properties offer complimentary limousine service or arrange to have taxis pick up international guests.

- *Methods of payment.* Many international visitors are unfamiliar with the policy of U.S. hotels of prepayment for rooms. Therefore, many chains participate in prepaid **voucher** programs, which are promoted as a service to the international visitor. Days Inn, for example, offers Freedom/Liberty, while Best Western International promotes the North American Guestcheque. Both programs allow international visitors to prepay their accommodations with voucher coupons, eliminating the need for travelers to carry excessive cash.

Of course, many international travelers prefer to use currency or traveler's checks, and you should willingly accept these forms of payment. Properties that accept foreign currency or provide currency exchange services, either in-house or through an agreement with a local bank, can realize a six to ten percent profit as well as offer a much-needed service to their guests. Hotels can either employ an exchange specialist who daily determines the value of foreign currency, or arrange for this service through local banks. Foreign currency usually is sent to a bank daily and a check is returned to the property the following day.

- *Special appliances*. International travelers often bring electric shavers, hair dryers, and travel irons on their trips and have trouble with U.S. voltage. Hotels can provide adapters in guestrooms or offer adapters and small appliances for sale or rent.

Above all, hotels should make international guests feel at home. While some international travelers want a taste of adventure, others feel more comfortable with the familiar.

The Hilton Hotels Corporation, for example, is a leader in catering to Japanese travelers, offering a program called "Yokoso Hilton E" (*Welcome to Hilton* in Japanese) in 20 gateway cities across the United States. Services include complete Japanese breakfasts served in a traditional *binto* box, a Japanese breakfast buffet, a Japanese-speaking staff on duty at all times, and Japanese translations of in-room materials and telephone and safe-deposit-box instructions. The chain also sends periodic cards or letters to Japanese visitors to build guest loyalty.

The Sheraton Carlton Hotel, located just two blocks from the White House in Washington, D.C., hosts a wide variety of international travelers. Its appeal is enhanced by prominently displayed international-time clocks and the availability of foreign-language newspapers and multilingual information brochures and menus. The hotel also offers concierge service (a service prevalent in Europe) and provides on-call multilingual limousine drivers for its international guests.

Another property that caters to international visitors is the Registry Hotel in Minneapolis, Minnesota. Minneapolis is home to several large international companies (3M, Pillsbury, Control Data, etc.) and attracts a number of individual and group business guests from abroad. Registry employees must be fluent in at least one foreign language. The Registry's international guests are further served by multilingual signs, the availability of electrical adapters, and a staff that is sympathetic to their needs.

The Airport Hotels program offered to international travelers at ten Sheraton gateway city hotels includes a number of amenities and services to make travel easier for these guests. Services include overnight and four-hour express laundry and clothes-pressing, Body Clock Cuisine (a selection of menus designed to help guests overcome jet lag), and Day Break Service (three- and seven-hour room rates for at least 50 percent off regular rates, for guests staying only a short time between connecting flights). In addition, guests are offered a "Transit Survival Kit," which includes a toothbrush, tee-shirt, face cream, razor, deodorant, mouthwash, slippers, comb/brush, and other useful stopover items.

A property's efforts do not have to be elaborate to be successful. Doubletree Hotels, for example, shows its appreciation of foreign visitors by flying their national flags, while the Flamingo Hilton in Las Vegas makes international guests feel more welcome with multilingual announcements over the public address system.

Finding International Travelers

Familiarity is important to many international travelers, so sometimes these travelers do not need to be solicited—they contact a U.S. hotel chain property after exposure to the chain's product overseas. Chains such as Hilton, Best Western International, and Sheraton are well-known abroad, and their worldwide reservations systems make it easy for international travelers to book into U.S. properties. Other properties have joined hotel representation organizations such as Leading Hotels of the World, Preferred Hotels Worldwide, Relais & Chateaux, and Small Luxury Hotels of the World to reap the benefits of international recognition.

Independent or small properties cannot boast this advantage, however, and must seek out international travelers. Sources of international business can sometimes be found in a property's own community. Many schools, colleges, and universities bring foreign exchange students or special study groups into the country. These institutions can also assist a property by providing translators and information about foreign customs.

Other local sources of prospects include service and fraternal clubs that may bring in international guests. The local chamber of commerce can provide information on local companies that do business with foreign firms. Many communities have "Sister City" programs that involve international visitors. Other cities may invite international guests for information exchanges, political symposia, and so on. Properties can contact local ethnic groups to request the names of potential visitors, such as students on scholarships or guest speakers from abroad. A property can also obtain information and potential contacts from convention and visitors bureaus (CVBs) or from state tourist agencies.

On the national level, there are a number of resources, including the Travel Industry Association of America (TIA), which publishes international marketing manuals; the American Hotel & Lodging Association's International Travel Committee; and a number of industry associations. The names of other organizations that are involved in international travel are available online or in the public library in such references as the *Encyclopedia of Associations* and *National Trade & Professional Associations.*

Reaching International Travelers

Since the international traveler market is so far-flung, an individual effort may be far too costly for a small to midsize property. Even larger properties may want to consider a cooperative effort when targeting international travelers, such as joining with a travel supplier (airline, tour group, etc.) or an entire destination area's effort to reach overseas visitors.

INTERNET EXERCISE

The Travel Industry Association (TIA) is the authoritative source for travel and tourism information. Log onto the Internet and research the association's website at www.tia.org:

1. What does the TIA do to promote international travel?
2. What types of travel research is done by this organization?
3. What is TIA's "International Pow Wow" trade show and how does it differ from traditional trade shows?
4. What publications are available through the TIA?

Affiliation with a travel supplier such as an airline may involve a number of options—from joint advertising to cooperatively offering complete package vacations or business trips. Some properties can offset the price of this type of promotion by supplying space or services to the travel supplier (convention rooms for a company convention, discounted rooms to airline crews, and so on).

Destination area efforts may be local in scope or part of a state or national campaign to attract international visitors. State tourist agencies may have programs to attract foreign visitors to a state or area; you can advise these organizations of your interest in reaching the international market. The Hawaii Visitors & Convention Bureau, for example, issues meeting planning guides in Japanese, Korean, and Chinese, and plans are underway for additional promotional materials, including business travel videos, press kits, and electronic postcards, to market the area to Asian travelers. Destination area efforts to reach international travelers may also include goodwill tours to "Sister Cities" overseas by municipal governments, CVBs, or chambers of commerce.

Individual property efforts to reach international travelers typically involve many of the methods used to reach other markets: personal selling, participation in trade shows, advertising, the Internet, direct mail, and public relations.

Personal selling often involves an independent hotel representative or rep who specializes in international sales. This rep may maintain a field office overseas, or may make goodwill tours to foreign travel agencies, corporations, and trade shows to promote your property. You must be well-versed in national customs before choosing a rep to send to certain countries. A property should only send male representatives to certain parts of the Middle East, for example.

Face-to-face contacts with potential international guests differ greatly from the face-to-face presentations common in our country. Whenever possible, presentations and written materials should be in the language of the country in which the presentation is taking place; business cards should show titles and other pertinent information in the prospect's native tongue (this is particularly important to the Japanese). Appointments are a must in many countries, especially with tour wholesalers and travel agents. In France, for example, practically the entire country goes on vacation in August, so drop-in calls at that time would be a waste of time and money.

Exhibit 2 Reaching the International Market

Travel Industry Trade and Consumer Shows

Show Name	Location	Audience	Month Held
POW WOW USA	U.S. (city varies)	Trade	May
POW WOW Europe	Europe (city varies)	Trade	September
World Travel Market	London	Trade	November
I.T.B.	Berlin	Trade/consumer	March
VUSAMart	U.S. (city varies)	Trade	September
JATA Travel Trade Show	Tokyo	Trade/consumer	November (every other year)

International travel trade shows can be a cornerstone of any successful marketing plan, providing the opportunity to meet face-to-face with international travel packagers and consumers, interact with media from your target markets, and make valuable contacts with domestic and international suppliers who can later serve as marketing partners.

There are other factors to consider when selling in person to international travelers. Spaniards and Italians often linger over negotiations, so it is unwise to schedule short appointments with them. The Japanese are masters at negotiation and have the patience to wait long periods of time in order to have their demands met. It is often wise to contact potential international guests indirectly, through referral services or professional travel agents.

Another way to reach international travelers is through *participation in trade shows* such as the Discover America International Pow Wow (sponsored by TIA) and the National Tour Association Marketplace. The Pow Wow, which brings together U.S. travel suppliers (hotels, attractions, car rental companies, and so on) and foreign buyers from more than 30 nations, is the major trade show for reaching international business. It is staged in a different U.S. city each year, attracts top international tour wholesalers, and results in $200 to $300 million in travel business from overseas. The National Tour Association Marketplace offers opportunities to reach tour brokers who arrange trips for international travelers. Exhibit 2 lists additional trade shows that will enable you to target the international segment. The names and locations of other shows can be obtained from trade publications such as *Meetings & Conventions* and *Travel Weekly*. Travel agents can be reached through world congresses of the American Society of Travel Agents or through the International Tourism Exchange held annually in West Berlin.

Advertising in international markets can be extremely expensive, so large properties do most of the consumer advertising overseas. Some properties find it more cost-effective to partner with other noncompetitive travel providers, such as airlines and car rental agencies, or to participate in destination advertising with other hotels or local attractions.[2] This type of advertising makes it easier for smaller properties to compete, as does advertising to the travel trade, as shown in Exhibit 3. Specialized "Visit USA" publications are targeted toward travel agents and tour brokers in a number of areas: *El Travel Agent Internacional* is distributed in Mexico

Exhibit 3 Advertising to Travel Intermediaries

NOT ONLY CAN
OUR STAFF ANSWER
THE NEEDS OF YOUR GROUP,
THEY DO SO IN SIX
DIFFERENT LANGUAGES.

A staff should be as versatile as the accommodations. Hence the reasoning behind our multi-lingual, multi-talented staff. They fax memos, arrange meetings, prepare the 20,000 square-foot meeting space. They'll even shine shoes. You can find this dedicated group within the eclectic walls of the ANA Hotel, located opposite the San Francisco Museum of Modern Art and the Moscone Center.

For more details, call 415-974-6400 or 800-ANA-HOTELS.
Till then, ciao. Au revoir. Sayonara. Adios. Auf Wiedersehen.

ANA HOTEL
SAN FRANCISCO

Since most FIT visitors and many international travelers utilize travel agents or tour operators, advertising to travel professionals who specialize in the international market is a wise investment. This ad, directed toward international meeting planners, promotes the hotel's multilingual staff and its services designed to accommodate international guests.

and Central and South America, while *Visit USA* guides are published for Western Europe, Japan, Australia, South America, Mexico, and Canada.

Hotels can also reach overseas travel professionals through directory advertising in such publications as the *OAG TRAVEL PLANNER/Hotel & Motel RedBook* and the *Hotel & Travel Index*. European travel agents seeking information about lodging facilities use hotel directories more than any other information source. Your listing or ad should include specific information such as the proximity of your property to an international airport or **gateway city.** Such information makes it easier for the agent to make a recommendation.

If you have an advertising budget that is large enough to target individual international travelers, there is the option of advertising in foreign newspapers. The names of many of these newspapers can be found on the Internet or in the local library. It is often best to have advertising for international travelers developed by an advertising agency in the targeted country.

Even if your hotel doesn't have the money to advertise in print overseas, you can still reach international travelers by promoting your product and services on the *Internet.* One option is to participate in www.SeeAmerica.org, a site created by the Travel Industry Association of America, a national, non-profit organization that represents the entire U.S. travel industry. This website provides a portal to all the major U.S. travel websites and is a great way for U.S. properties and travel-oriented services to reach the international traveler market. International travelers can search participating travel websites by name, location, activity, and price, and the site helps them find online travel services, travel agents, and tour operators. Any TIA member can have a listing and a link on this site.

Today's technology offers the capability for individual properties as well as hotel and restaurant chains to create a Web presence that can be translated into a variety of languages with the click of a mouse. Howard Johnson International's website, for example, provides the option to change the language to Spanish, while Fairmont Hotels & Resorts now provides hotel information in a multitude of languages and dialects, including Japanese, Spanish, German, and French, as well as newly added translations in simplified Chinese and Arabic. There are also translation services, such as Babelfish, that enable international travelers to translate entire websites into their native language. Some properties, however, opt to create new sites specifically designed for their international markets.

Doris Lundin of the Fairbanks Hotel in Alaska found advertising in foreign countries cost prohibitive, so she hired the Japanese Internet Communications Service to translate her website into Japanese and place it in the top 100 Japanese search engines. She felt it was important to have the translation done by a native speaker who understood subtleties meaningful to her target market (the number four, for example, is considered unlucky in Japan).

No matter what option you choose in creating a website, remember the old adage that "a picture is worth a thousand words." Use photographs to promote your features, and make your site easy for international travelers to navigate.

As with advertising, *direct mail* efforts are more cost-effective when directed toward groups or travel professionals. Direct mail material should always be in the language of the recipients, preferably translated by a native of the country to which it will be sent. In addition to letters, consider developing printed guides or

Exhibit 4 Rack Brochures for International Travelers

AL DESEARLO
SE HACE REALIDAD...

Venga y visite el Walt Disney World Swan y disfrute de la vacación con la cual siempre soñó. Administrado por los Hoteles y Centros Vacacionales Westin, todo lo que usted se imaginó, y aún más, lo encontrará aquí.

LAMPARAS CON
LOROS, Y, PIÑAS

Diseñado por el arquitecto Michael Graves, este centro vacacional es tanto una aventura por dentro como lo es por fuera. Pero no se deje engañar por el aspecto juguetón del sitio. Todas las facilidades y el confort de Westin lo encontrará cuando lo necesite. Servicio especial todas las noches al prepararle su habitación para que se retire a descansar, cajas fuertes dentro de su habitación, mini-bares, entrega del periódico a diario. Todo esto es común en el Walt Disney World Swan.

Español

SOL, ARENA,
Y SURFING

Hay muchas actividades para escoger en el Walt Disney World Swan las cuales incluyen la natación, navegación en velero, el tenis, la practica del golf en cualquiera de los cinco campos profesionales de golf de WALT DISNEY WORLD. ¡ Hasta un gimnasio ! Además, visitar los parques del Centro Vacacional WALT DISNEY WORLD, le queda a un brinco al montarse en un tranvía que lo conduce al EPCOT Center (hasta puede llegar a pie a este lugar), o llegue en la lancha Friendship, al Disney-MGM Studios Theme Park, o, en autobús especial, al Magic Kingdom® Park. Todos los viajes son gratuitos.

DE PIZZAS
A PASTELES

En el Walt Disney World Swan, el desayuno, el almuerzo, y la cena, le ofrece algo especial para todos los gustos. El Garden Grove Cafe para madrugadores así como para trasnochadores. El Palio–nuestro Bistro Italiano. El Splash Grill para comidas rápidas, o comidas para llevar. Y, para cócteles, tenemos el Lobby Court Lounge, o, el Kimonos Oriental Sushi Bar y lounge ofreciéndole el bocadillo especial Japonés–Sushi.

This rack brochure for Westin's Swan Resort at Walt Disney World has been printed in three languages—Spanish (shown here), Portuguese, and German—to promote the property to international travelers. It can be used at both the property level and in direct mail advertising and is extremely cost-effective; photographs and other graphic elements are designed first, and separate printings in specific languages are ordered as needed.

rack brochures in several languages; these can also be used for on-site property promotion (see Exhibit 4).

Public relations can be an effective way to acquaint overseas travel professionals and individual travelers with your property. You may send press releases to trade and consumer publications or offer familiarization trips to international

Exhibit 5 The Destination Wedding and Honeymoon Market at a Glance

Location: Preferred locations include getaway locations, gateway cities (for overseas or cruise ship travel), and adventure locations.

Facilities: Preferred honeymoon facilities include upgraded guestrooms or suites, special in-room amenities (Jacuzzis, round or heart-shaped beds, and so on), meaningful giveaways such as complimentary champagne in souvenir glasses, and recreational amenities.

Price: Newlyweds may prefer anything from economy to upscale accommodations, although most couples will spend in the medium or high ranges. Inclusive-price packages are popular with this market.

Services: Preferred services include limousine service and free continental breakfasts in bed.

Decision-Makers: Traditionally, the bride and bridegroom and their immediate families plan the wedding and honeymoon. Today, couples are more apt to seek advice from friends who have traveled or from travel agents for destination wedding and/or honeymoon location ideas.

Best Ways to Reach Market: Tie-ins with department stores or bridal boutiques, bridal fairs at the property, personal contacts, or ads in consumer magazines will reach this market.

The destination wedding and honeymoon market can be a lucrative one for properties of all sizes if they understand the needs of this market and offer facilities and services to meet those needs.

travel writers. Another way to get publicity is to promote the specialized services you provide for international travelers. One hotel chain received extensive press coverage when it introduced an international traveler program. A property might also hold educational seminars or "international days" to promote its facilities and services and build foreign-guest goodwill.

Creating goodwill seems to be the key to ensuring repeat business from international travelers. If a property can make international visitors feel at home, it may receive one of the most valuable forms of marketing available: word-of-mouth recommendations from satisfied guests.

The Destination Wedding and Honeymoon Market

Since almost all newlyweds plan a honeymoon, this market can be extremely profitable for the hospitality industry. Even if your property is not suited to destination weddings, newlyweds can still prove to be an extremely lucrative segment. Honeymooners are usually loyal guests; many return to their honeymoon property for anniversary visits or recommend it to friends. Favorite honeymoon destinations include Florida, Hawaii, California, Pennsylvania, and New York. Properties in other areas can appeal to this lucrative market if they offer facilities that will help create shared memories—the chief purpose of a honeymoon. Exhibit 5 provides additional information on what is important to this market.

Today's honeymooners are looking for more than just privacy on their honeymoon; while their interests are varied, they look for special activities at their destination location. Since both the bride and the groom are usually employed, today's honeymoons tend to be short; many couples are now looking for honeymoon weekend packages.

Brides and grooms planning their weddings today have typically worked to establish professional careers since their high school or college days, so the majority tend to be in their late twenties or early thirties and are sophisticated and affluent. Many of these couples are opting to travel to an attractive locale for both the wedding and the honeymoon. This trend, which is called the **destination wedding**, can be profitable to properties in a wide variety of locations. Walt Disney World in Lake Buena Vista, Florida, has a complete Fairy Tale Weddings department that offers theme weddings, such as Cinderella and Prince Charming. Other properties, such as the Westin Maui and Marriott Frenchman's Reef Resort in St. Thomas, U.S. Virgin Islands, offer romantic weddings.

To capture their share of the lucrative destination wedding market, many properties have hired **on-site wedding coordinators** to help couples plan hassle-free weddings. Some hotel chains, such as Marriott, offer specialized training for their wedding staff (the chain has over 1,700 certified wedding event planners), while other properties take advantage of training offered by outside sources, including the Travel Institute, which has developed a "Honeymoons and Destination Weddings Lifestyle Specialist" course (a similar course for travel agents is offered through TravelAgent Custom Solutions). In addition to providing on-site professionals to personally assist couples with wedding or honeymoon planning, some chains, such as Marriott and Wyndham, offer specialized wedding websites to provide information—and a dedicated toll-free 800 number—to couples. The Wyndham website includes planning guides, ceremony and reception options, special wedding and honeymoon packages, a wedding album section, and special offers that include discounts on all types of destination weddings. Hotels that do a small destination weddings business can also set up websites featuring wedding information and services. Such properties can hire local wedding planners and contract with suppliers to provide flowers, music, and other products and services of interest to this market.

The Decision-Maker

The bride and groom play the most significant role in making decisions about their wedding and honeymoon, but they often listen to suggestions from their families and other members of the wedding party. Honeymooners may also follow the advice of friends who have previously used a resort, or they may turn to travel agents for recommendations of properties that will meet their needs.

Meeting the Needs of the Destination Wedding and Honeymoon Market

Couples planning destination weddings look for a location that will be attractive to them and their guests, one that offers a number of recreational activities (swimming, golf, tennis, spas, shopping centers, and so on). Obviously, facilities for such wedding functions as the rehearsal dinner, the ceremony, the reception, and perhaps a post-wedding brunch must also be available. While the bride and groom want

Wedding Trends

- Number of U.S. marriages annually: 2.3 million
- Percent of couples who had a destination wedding: 16 (an increase of 400 percent over the last ten years)
- Cost of average destination wedding: $25,806
- Number of wedding guests: almost 380 million, including an average of 63 guests at destination weddings
- Estimated household income: $74,000 (couples who opt for traditional weddings); $93,000 (couples who have destination weddings)

Source: The Condé Nast Bridal Group, "American Wedding Study 2006," February 21, 2007.

to have the opportunity to interact with their guests, privacy in the days after the ceremony is also important. Some hotels offer special honeymoon suites to meet this need. Some newlyweds who have invited family and friends to a destination wedding site opt to honeymoon away from the site—such as on a separate island in Hawaii, for example.

Since destination weddings typically include fewer guests, many hotels, such as Marriott's Frenchman's Reef Resort, offer "Virtual Wedding" services. A custom website is created for each couple, and family and friends back home can view videotaped wedding events and sign an online guestbook via the Internet. Other properties provide live broadcasts of the ceremony and other wedding events to those at home via satellite.

No matter which type of ceremony couples choose—a destination wedding or a wedding nearer home—the large majority of couples plan a honeymoon either immediately following the wedding or within a few months of the ceremony. The average honeymoon trip lasts one to two weeks. Some honeymoons last more than two weeks; some are as short as a weekend. No matter what the length of stay, however, the typical honeymoon couple is looking for a romantic atmosphere, privacy, and a lot of activities at an affordable price.

All-inclusive resorts, which offer packages to couples that cover meals, accommodations, entertainment, sporting equipment, tips, and all other honeymoon expenses, are growing in popularity with newlyweds, especially those on budgets and those who don't want to bother with details. Honeymoon packages offered by hotels usually include accommodations, several meals, and other amenities. The Fairmont Kea Lani on Maui, for example, includes a welcome amenity, one breakfast in bed, a gourmet picnic basket, a couples' massage, and a sunset cruise in its five-night honeymoon package. You should keep in mind that couples usually book honeymoon reservations months in advance; therefore, plan honeymoon packages on a yearly schedule so that they may be promoted in plenty of time for honeymooners to consider them.

Adventure honeymoons have gained popularity. Many couples take art tours of Europe, archeological trips to Mexico, or safaris in Africa. You might still receive business from these couples if your property is located in a gateway city or in the

INTERNET EXERCISE

Log onto the Internet and research Wyndham's and Marriott's websites for weddings:

- www.destinationweddingsbywyndham.com
- www.joyweddingbymarriott.com

1. What services do these two hotel chains offer to wedding groups?
2. As you compare these two websites, which does the most effective job of marketing to the destination wedding and honeymoon markets?
3. What other hotels market to these segments? How do their websites compare with the two listed for this exercise?

city or town in which the wedding takes place. An overnight package with breakfast, complimentary champagne, and transportation to the airport or cruise ship can attract couples who will be honeymooning abroad.

The honeymoon market has long been a mainstay in such places as the Pocono Mountains and Niagara Falls. In the lavish, four-season resorts of the Poconos, couples are treated to breathtaking scenery and rooms that feature plush carpeting, round or heart-shaped beds and bathtubs, and even in-room Jacuzzis shaped like champagne glasses. Most of the honeymoon products and services offered in the Poconos are available for a package price.

Finding the Destination Wedding and Honeymoon Market

Watching for engagement announcements in local newspapers is an excellent way to develop destination wedding and honeymoon market leads. You can also target this market by participating in bridal promotions hosted by local department stores or specialty boutiques. These sources can provide names of prospective brides and may also accept advertising. You may also want to consider participating in a **bridal fair.** If bridal fairs are not held in the local area, you can stage your own event.

Since travel agents now make honeymoon arrangements for so many couples, it is essential that you do not overlook these important travel intermediaries. It is especially effective to invite travel agents to tour the property during a bridal fair. This gives agents an opportunity to experience the facilities and dining offered as part of a honeymoon package.

Reaching the Destination Wedding and Honeymoon Market

The two most effective means of reaching the destination wedding and honeymoon market are direct mail and advertising. Direct mail includes letters of congratulation to couples whose engagement announcements have appeared in newspapers, and invitations to special events at the property. You can also send direct mail pieces to travel agents. These pieces are more effective if they include all-inclusive honeymoon packages.

Exhibit 6 Sample Ad for the Destination Wedding and Honeymoon Market

Sweet. Secluded. Seductive. Your romance continues on the waterfront at The Lodge of Four Seasons on beautiful Lake of the Ozarks, Missouri. (Featured on Lifestyles of the Rich and Famous.)

We make your escape heavenly with a honeymoon package which includes a four-star dinner, a free monogrammed bath robe for each person, and complimentary champagne on arrival. Plus, you'll be served a special breakfast each morning before you spend the day enjoying our many sports activities and guest amenities.

Call 1-800-THE-LAKE now.

All you need is your honey.
We'll provide the moon.

Couples planning a honeymoon as a separate event or as part of their destination wedding can be reached through both print ads such as this one and promotions on the web. Advertising to this market should stress the services and amenities that make a honeymoon special, such as romantic locations, extra services (a champagne toast, breakfast in bed, and so on), and activities that will create special memories.

Advertising in newspapers and magazines can build a property's destination wedding and honeymoon business (see Exhibit 6). If the property is located in a popular destination spot, ads can be placed in newspapers in key feeder cities. Special-interest magazines such as *Modern Bride* are excellent for attracting this market. Your property can also advertise on its own website or on Internet sites that target wedding planners and honeymooners. If your property offers honeymoon packages, for example, an ad or listing on sites such as honeymoonersreviewguide.com or Askabouthoneymoons.com can be extremely effective.

Other ways to reach the lucrative honeymoon market include letting the couple experience the property for themselves during a champagne brunch or giving them a personal tour of the property. Inviting the society writers of local newspapers to property functions encourages good coverage of the property and may lead to personal recommendations. Creating a unique honeymoon package or offering a special honeymoon package as a prize in local or national contests or on game shows may also generate publicity for the property.

The Sports Market

America's passion for sports can provide an excellent opportunity to fill guestrooms and increase food and beverage revenue. Professional and college sports, prep teams, professional and amateur tournaments, special sporting events, and other sports-related activities can generate business. Players, coaches and support staff, and loyal fans can provide year-round business for rooms, meals, and other property services. As with other market segments, the sports market has specific characteristics and needs, as shown in Exhibit 7. Properties that can meet the needs of this market could realize increased business by soliciting one or more segments of it.

Janna Mugnola, national sales manager for the Westin Galleria and Westin Oaks in Houston, says that targeting baseball teams was the property's biggest coup, resulting in 5,000 room nights per season. Bill Bohde, director of marketing for the Marriott in Greenbelt, Maryland (the official hotel of the Washington Bullets basketball team and the Washington Capitals hockey team), says other sports teams also prove lucrative by providing winter business, filling rooms on weekends, spending heavily on food and beverages, and boosting revenue by drawing fans.

Professional Teams

While attracting professional teams can be profitable—and often results in publicity for a property—their impact on business can vary greatly. Professional football teams, for example, play approximately 20 games a year and are in town for one game; American and National League baseball teams play 162 regular-season games annually. These games are played in series, generating additional room nights and food business—and some visiting teams return several times during the season.

Location is the prime factor for professional sports teams in selecting a property; they prefer properties that are no more than a 30-minute drive from the stadium or playing field. After that, service, food, and rates, in that order, are most important. Professional teams expect the best in service and are usually hosted by such chains as Marriott, Starwood, and Holiday Inn. These properties serve the professional market in a number of ways:

1. *Personal greeting.* Most properties assign someone to meet the team and attend to any special needs. This service makes the team feel welcome and makes a good impression on the head coach.

Exhibit 7 The Sports Market at a Glance

Location: Professional teams prefer locations within a 20- to 30-minute drive of the sports arena and in close proximity to the airport or a major highway.

Facilities: Preferred facilities provide guestroom blocks; group function rooms; small meeting rooms; 24-hour room service or late-night restaurants; extra amenities such as a game room, sauna, or swimming pool; and secure storage facilities for equipment.

Price: Amateur teams usually look for low rates; professional teams will pay higher rates. Professional and amateur sports teams look for group rates and complimentary rooms for the head coach and business manager.

Services: Preferred services include discount clubs; preregistration; late check-out; maps of the shortest routes to playing sites; complimentary newspapers; the ability to meet dietary requirements and serve group meals on time; the availability of box lunches for teams traveling by road; a team welcome, including signs or banners (with permission of head coach); bus parking if needed; wake-up service; having the bill ready at the time of departure; and after-stay follow-up.

Decision-Makers: Coaches, athletic directors, or athletic business managers plan sports team travel.

Best Ways to Reach Market: Personal contacts, direct mail, advertisements in college magazines, promotions on the Internet, and newspaper advertising to attract fans will reach this market.

The sports market provides a wide range of business for properties of all sizes. This market can be especially lucrative for properties near sports arenas or in close proximity to an airport or major highway. Properties willing to cater to youth sports teams will also benefit.

2. *Efficient registration.* Most properties receive a rooming list within five days of the team's arrival, and the team is usually housed in one wing or in a quiet area away from other groups. Guestroom keys/cards are made available to the head coach or someone else on the coaching staff for distribution to players.

3. *Food functions.* Food service needs vary by the type of team; in any case, it is important to be aware of any dietary requirements or restrictions in advance of the team's arrival. Football players, who need ample portions and extra table space, are usually served at group functions (arrival dinner, pregame meal, postgame meal, breakfasts, etc.). Baseball and basketball players, however, are usually on their own when it comes to meals; therefore, these players appreciate 24-hour room service, a variety of property restaurants, and the proximity of other food outlets.

4. *Meeting rooms.* Most football teams require at least three meeting rooms and perhaps a room for taping up the players before the game. There is usually a meeting of the entire team at which a film of the competition is shown, and this may be followed by two smaller meetings (usually groups of 35 to 50 people) of the offensive and defensive squads.

If a room is needed to tape up players, it can be set up the morning of the game and should be equipped with two eight-foot tables approximately 12 inches off the floor (this can be accomplished by placing wooden blocks under tables that have their legs folded up). This arrangement eases the strain on the trainers and is a gesture that will be appreciated and remembered.

5. *Other services.* Many properties welcome teams with an outside sign or a sign on the lobby function board, but these must be approved by the head coach. It is also wise to check with the head coach to determine if players may have phone calls or visitors, or if there are any food restrictions (no food after 10 P.M., no alcohol, etc.). Many properties also offer a complimentary room to the head coach, provide daily newspapers to coaches and players, and offer box lunches to teams.

It is important to remember that different teams have different needs and that professional teams are solicited in different ways:

Football teams can be a good source of revenue, but it is important to contact the decision-makers well in advance of the season. Professional teams can be contacted by phone or direct mail or through inquiries to the respective leagues.

Baseball teams can be booked by soliciting major- and minor-league offices. The professional leagues are actively involved in hotel negotiations and recommend certain hotels after a bidding process has been completed. Although individual teams make their own lodging decisions, most follow the recommendations of their league.

Basketball teams typically use fewer rooms than football or baseball teams, but they still offer the potential for increased room occupancies, especially when tournament play is involved. Basketball teams can be solicited through league offices (schedules are available in June).

Other professional teams, such as hockey and soccer teams, can also be solicited through league offices.

Other Teams

The college team sports segment can be a gold mine for your property if you can meet the needs of the various football, baseball, basketball, and other teams of colleges and universities. The needs of college teams vary slightly from those of professional teams; while college teams have similar requirements when it comes to location and services, these travelers do not expect the VIP treatment extended to professional teams. Rates are more important to college teams than to professional teams, since many college teams operate on limited budgets. The Wyndham Hotel Group has found that college teams prefer to stay at hotels that do not charge extra for a third or fourth person in a room, and its quoted rates reflect up to a four-person occupancy per room to ensure customer loyalty.

College teams usually request group meal functions, the timing of which will depend on the time of arrival and the game schedule. As with professional teams, it is necessary to be aware of any dietary restrictions and to have prearranged menus when serving college teams.

College teams can be reached through school athletic offices. Properties can contact coaches, athletic directors, or athletic business managers by obtaining

Contacts for Sports Organizations

College Sports:

National Directory of College Athletics
Collegiate Directories, Inc.
P.O. Box 450640
Cleveland, OH 44145
www.collegiatedirectories.com
800-426-2232 ph
440-835-8835 fx

National Collegiate Athletic Association
6201 College Boulevard
Overland Park, KS 66211-2422
www.ncaa.org
913-339-1906 ph

Professional Baseball:

Major League Baseball Office
350 Park Avenue
New York, NY 10022
www.majorleaguebaseball.com
212-339-7900 ph
212-339-7628 fx

Professional Basketball:

National Basketball Association
645 5th Avenue FL 10
New York, NY 10022
www.nba.com
212-826-7000 ph
212-826-0579 fx

Professional Football:

National Football League, Inc.
280 Park Avenue # 12W
New York, NY 10017
www.nfl.com
212-450-2000 ph
212-758-1742 fx

Professional Hockey:

National Hockey League
1251 Avenue of The Americas
New York, NY 10020
www.nhl.com
212-789-2003 ph
212-789-2020 fx

names from the *National Directory of College Athletics* (which comes in men's and women's editions) or by making contacts at the annual College Athletic Business Manager's Association convention in January (you must be a member of the association to exhibit at this meeting).

High school and other youth sports teams can also be sources of room nights. Youth sports teams include Pop Warner teams, Little League teams, and other teams sponsored by parks and recreation departments, the YMCA, and other groups. Youth sports tournaments have become national in scope, and many take place over weekends and during the weeks of major holidays, such as Thanksgiving and Christmas, when business is typically slow for many properties. For example, one La Quinta Inn and Suites sales manager booked a youth hockey tournament that filled 50 rooms for the week between Christmas and New Year's Eve, traditionally a slow period for the hotel. The same property booked a girls' soccer tournament that filled 100 rooms for three nights a month later. This market can be reached by contacting local high schools, your city's parks and recreation department, and other venues likely to host youth events (soccer complexes, swimming clubs, boxing centers, karate schools, etc.). In addition, many chambers of commerce and CVBs have listings of upcoming youth-sports events.

Many properties find the sports teams market so lucrative that they are developing packages and clubs that offer special rates to teams and fans alike (see Exhibit 8). Days Inns' Sports Plus Club, for example, features team discounts, rental car discounts, free local phone calls, late check-out, and room blocks, and invites athletic administrators and coaches to join its sports advisory board. Winegardner & Hammons, Inc., a hotel management company, promotes a "We Promise" sports program available at such properties as Holiday Hospitality Corporation, Quality Suites, Radisson Hotels, and Comfort Inns.

Another avenue to reach sports teams is the annual "Teams" trade show, which is hosted every fall by Premiere Sports Travel (www.SportsTravel.com). In addition to offering educational sessions on how to market to sports teams, the show also provides an opportunity for exhibitors (which include hotels, airlines, and other travel providers) to have pre-scheduled appointments with members of the sports industry—and to advertise in the show's directory. The 2007 show directory included hotel chains such as Best Western International, Carlson Hotels Worldwide, Choice Hotels International, Crowne Plaza Hotels & Resorts, Hilton, and Marriott, as well as several state and city convention and visitors bureaus.

In addition to the team sports market, properties have the opportunity to host the individual sports market—sports and tournaments in which athletes compete as individuals or in pairs. On the professional level, there are golf and tennis tournaments, professional boxing or wrestling matches, auto races, rodeos, bowling tournaments, and swimming or track-and-field competitions and exhibitions. Many of the organizations that sponsor these events, such as the United States Tennis Association, NASCAR, and U.S. Swimming, Inc., can be contacted directly for information on schedules and how to solicit business.

At the amateur level, tournaments, competitions, and other special events can boost revenues. This business can be solicited by contacting local golf and tennis clubs, bowling alleys, and other organizations, including fraternal organizations that are likely to host sporting events and tournaments. You can also reach this market by keeping abreast of special events in your area: read the local newspaper for news of upcoming events such as competitive runs, gymnastics competitions, cheerleading clinics, and so on; check chamber of commerce and CVB schedules of events; ask current participants for leads on future events; and get to know the people who decide where to house participants.

The Internet can be an invaluable tool for reaching the sports market. Most sports organizations have websites that list the names and telephone numbers of key contacts, publish calendars of events, and provide other useful information. Properties can develop a web page that specifically addresses the needs of athletic groups and create e-mail campaigns targeting key decision-makers.

Last, but certainly not least, don't forget the fans and support personnel! Most sports team business is boosted by the cheerleaders, bands, officials, booster clubs, and avid fans who follow "their" team. Many times, this ancillary business brings in more revenue than the team itself, so you will want to create special programs and services for this market. The support personnel and fan base for the "individual sports" are important markets as well. The Super 8 hotel chain has affiliated itself with NASCAR, which numbers over 75 million fans—many of whom follow their favorite racing drivers and teams around the country. Super 8 sponsors the

Exhibit 8 Discount Rates for Sports Teams

–SPORTS RATES INDIVIDUAL APPLICATION–

Name ____________________ Sports Affiliation (e.g., University, Association, etc.) ____________________

Title ____________________ Phone (____)-____________________

Address ____________________ City ________ State ________ Zip ________

Some hotel chains offer discount rates for sports teams, coaches, recruiters, and fans. This flier for Holiday Inns' Sports Rate program details the benefits of the program and provides an application form. (Courtesy of Holiday Hospitality Corporation)

Exhibit 9 The Government Market at a Glance

Location: The property must be easily accessible; cities to which airlines offer direct flights and discounted fares are given priority.

Facilities: Government groups prefer facilities that offer double-double guestrooms, reasonably priced restaurants, quality facilities, and audiovisual support for meetings.

Price: The government market is price-sensitive. Hotels must meet government per diem guidelines; rates quoted must include taxes when applicable.

Services: This market looks for low-cost or no-cost services, such as airport shuttles, daily newspapers, and so on; meeting planners look for complimentary coffee breaks or waived meeting room rental. IMPORTANT NOTE: Most government employees and agencies are not permitted to accept free goods or services; properties can, however, offer extra services and amenities, such as breakfast included in the room rate quoted, in order to attract guests who are on strict per diems.

Decision-Makers: Agency directors, training officers, contract specialists, and procurement officers at local, state, and federal levels plan travel.

Best Ways to Reach Market: List your property in the *OAG Government Edition;* advertise in trade publications, such as *The Government Executive* magazine; join the Society of Government Meeting Professionals (SGMP), which offers monthly chapter meetings, a national newsletter and directory, and an annual conference for making contacts; or contact governmental offices directly.

Source: Adapted from Milton T. Astroff and James R. Abbey, *Convention Management and Service,* 7th ed. (Lansing, Mich.: American Hotel & Lodging Educational Institute, 2006), p. 187.

Petty Enterprises race team, runs print ads in such publications as *NASCAR Scene* and *NASCAR Illustrated,* and hosts a website aimed at auto racing fans. Holiday Inn, which is billed as the "Official Hotel of Major League Baseball," has also affiliated itself with NASCAR, sponsoring Richard Childress Racing's No. 29 Holiday Inn Chevrolet racecar.

Most supporters want to stay in the same hotel as the team or individual sports stars that they are following. If this is not possible, you may want to stage at least one function at which the team or the stars and their fans can mingle. Other strategies for attracting fans include arranging and advertising package deals for fans through travel agents or in the visiting team's local newspapers, and extending sports club discounts to them. Don't neglect local business: host pregame or postgame parties for locals as well as out-of-town guests, develop special packages for local sports fans, and show your interest in sports by becoming a booster or sponsoring or assisting a local sports team.

Government Travelers

Federal, state, and local governments provide numerous opportunities for properties to increase room occupancies throughout the year (see Exhibit 9). Thousands of government agencies require out-of-town travel to conduct business.

INTERNET EXERCISE

Log onto the Internet and research the following website:

- www.fedtravel.com

This is a commercial website designed to help government officials and employees plan their government-related travel. It includes flight schedules, hotel information, and per diem rates. Click on the FEMA Certified Hotel Listings link to review lodging options listed by state and city. What are the per diem rates for the cities in your local area?

One of the factors that has held many properties back in the government traveler market is the complexity of soliciting government business. Another is the assumption that every piece of government business automatically goes to the lowest bidder. By law the federal government must give every potential supplier a hearing, but the final decision is not made solely on the basis of cost. The final decision is also based on the property's ability to contribute to the efficiency and effectiveness of government operations by providing quality accommodations and service.

Before bidding for government business, you should be aware of the requirements involved in establishing a business relationship with the government. You should also be aware of how expense money is allocated to government travelers.

Straight per diem is a dollar figure allocated to cover lodging, meals, local transportation, and gratuities when government employees travel on official business. This is the most common type of per diem. The amount of money allocated is based on the Consumer Price Index for the government employee's destination and may vary from year to year.

Actual and necessary per diem is the maximum amount an employee may spend regardless of location and is usually equal to or higher than the straight per diem rate. This rate is usually given to upper-level government employees.

The **contract per diem** is the most complex of the pricing arrangements, and incorporates the total cost of accommodations, meals, gratuities, travel expenses, and so on. For example, if a government agency wanted to stage a training program in a hotel, it would put the program requirements out for bid. Private companies or consultants would act as intermediaries between the government agency and travel suppliers, similar to the way tour wholesalers operate. These companies or consultants would contact several hotels for bids and submit a final bid for the entire estimated costs.

Per diems offered to state and local government employees are often less than those offered to federal government employees. State and local employees often incur more unreimbursable expenses, and will be more likely to choose a property that offers low rates.

If you are interested in selling to this market, you have several options. Direct sales can be effective, especially if you assign a dedicated salesperson to the government market. Victoria Dunn, of It Shall Be Dunn in Alexandria, Virginia, suggests that this salesperson be educated on the types of government travelers and the policies and regulations that pertain to government travelers and your hotel.

Dunn also suggests focusing on specific sectors of the government market. If you find that government meetings are best suited for your hotel, for example, you can join the Society of Government Meeting Professionals (SGMP); if your hotel targets transient government guests, consider membership in the Society of Government Travel Professionals (SGTP). The society's website—www.governmenttravel.org—is a good source of information about government travel.

Direct mail is another popular way to reach the government market. The names of various government agencies and officials can be found in government directories available in libraries or on government websites. A direct mail package should contain a government rate sheet or brochure and offer an opportunity for a member of the agency to visit the property.

Advertising can also be used to reach government agencies and officials (see Exhibit 10). The Sheraton chain, for example, launched a successful ad campaign in *The Government Executive* magazine, but only after more than three years of research.

Another important starting point for advertising is the *OAG Official Traveler Travel Guide.* This directory lists government contract airports and airlines and recommended ground transportation and car rental agencies, and includes a directory of domestic hotels and motels, extended-stay apartments, and international lodging facilities. Listings in the directory must fall within government per diem requirements. Properties are listed free of charge in both the printed directory and on the company's new computerized HotelDisk version; advertising space is also available for purchase. Exhibit 11 provides information on the *OAG Official Traveler Travel Guide* and *Innovata's Federal Travel Directory,* the other officially sanctioned government travel directory.

Travelers with Disabilities

The **Americans with Disabilities Act (ADA),** a civil rights statute, makes it easier for people with disabilities, including travelers, to access public facilities. The ADA requires that all public facilities, including hotels and restaurants, offer people with disabilities an "equal opportunity to participate in and benefit from the goods and services" provided by a property. Title III of the statute calls for the removal of architectural barriers that may limit access to those with disabilities, but this is only a small part of serving this growing market segment. Exhibit 12 lists the special features mandated by the ADA that hotels must provide for hotel guests with disabilities.

Individuals with disabilities are divided into three categories: those with mobility impairments (defined as people who use wheelchairs), those with hearing impairments, and those with visual impairments. While adding ramps, widening doors, and providing special parking spaces helps people with mobility impairments, this is not of much benefit to the other two groups.

Guests with visual impairments should have access to directories and menus printed in braille, raised room numbers, and braille labels in elevators. In addition, most guests with visual impairments appreciate being given instruction on the location and use of in-room features, such as temperature controls (at some properties, instructional cassettes are available; at others, hotel personnel provide this

Exhibit 10 Sample Ad for the Government Market

FROM PARIS TO PEORIA...
FOR GOVERNMENT RATES, WORLDWIDE,

CALL 1-800-HOLIDAY.

One easy toll-free number, 1-800-HOLIDAY, is all it takes for Government Rates information and reservations. We have over 1200 participating Holiday Inn® hotels in 32 countries. And you can guarantee your reservations and Government Rates with the same call!

Worldwide Government Rates, 1-800-HOLIDAY, and convenient locations are just some of the reasons why more Government travelers choose Holiday Inn hotels than any other hotel chain in the world!

Government Rates rooms are limited and subject to availability, so make your travel plans early!

Advertising to the government market is most effective when it stresses value, as most government employees are traveling on per diems.

service). And the housekeeping staff should be instructed to clean around items left in these guests' rooms.

Restaurants are also responding to visually impaired guests. The Olive Garden chain, for example, not only offers braille menus, but also provides a "Menu on Cassette," which allows visually impaired guests to hear the menu on tape—especially helpful to those who have not learned braille.

Exhibit 11 Sources for Reaching the Government Market

OAG Official Traveler Travel Guide

Provides free basic listing for all hotels meeting government requirements. Offers printed and CD-ROM versions. Contact:

OAG Worldwide, Government Business Unit
2000 Clearwater Drive,
Oak Brook, IL 60253
fax: 630-574-6750

Innovata's Federal Travel Directory

Offers printed and CD-ROM versions. Contact:

Innovata, LLC
3985 Old Mundy Mill Rd.
Oakwood, GA 30566
fax: 770-534-8688

Guests with hearing impairments should be offered amplified phones, special telecommunications services such as Telephone Typewriters (TTY) or a Telecommunications Device for the Deaf (TDD) system (text telephones should have caption decoders), and Visual Alert Systems (VAS). VASs include sound-sensitive lights that let hearing-impaired guests know when someone is at the door, that the telephone is ringing, or that there is an emergency such as a fire. Most properties find it beneficial to offer the first two options in all public areas and have specialized equipment available on an as-needed basis.

When this equipment is portable and easy to set up, more flexibility in room assignments can be offered, which is an important consideration; the ADA specifies that individuals with disabilities may not be segregated from other guests (they must be allowed to make the same room requests as other guests).

In addition to removing barriers and meeting other specific needs of guests with disabilities, staff awareness and sensitivity play a large part in attracting and serving these travelers. Employees should be sensitive but not overly solicitous when serving guests with disabilities. InterContinental, Sheraton, Hilton, Best Western, Ramada, Hyatt, and other hotel chains have implemented employee training programs that focus on the needs of this market. Microtel Inns & Suites, for example, has implemented a training program called "Opening Doors." The program, which was developed by W. C. Duke Associates, trains staff in disability etiquette skills as well as in basic safety and emergency procedures. During the training, employees make use of wheelchairs, blindfolds, earplugs, and other

Exhibit 12 Accommodations for Travelers with Special Needs

- The hotel entrance must be level or have a ramp.
- ADA rooms must be available on the ground floor or, if this is impractical, elevators must be large enough to accommodate a wheelchair.
- All public areas must be accessible to wheelchairs.
- In-room switches, locks and climate controls must be low enough to be accessible to someone in a wheelchair.
- There must be a telephone by the bedside.
- Beds must be low enough to allow easy transfer from a wheelchair to the bed.
- The bathroom must be able to accommodate a wheelchair when the bathroom door is either open or closed.
- The bathtub must have safety bars and the wash counter must be at an accessible height.
- Special equipment should be available to the hearing impaired.

The Americans with Disabilities Act mandated that all people with disabilities be offered an equal opportunity to participate in and benefit from the goods and services provided by a hotel or restaurant. This required hotels to make changes to their guestrooms and other areas.

devices that put them in touch with the limitations faced by guests with special needs. This enables the staff to provide relevant as well as courteous service.

A property does not have to be a member of a chain to train employees in the proper way to serve guests who have disabilities. Information is available from organizations such as the Society for Accessible Travel & Hospitality (SATH), or from local organizations of people with disabilities. In addition, hospitality professionals can take advantage of seminars and special events that focus on travelers with disabilities. For example, SATH holds an annual World Congress that addresses issues ranging from interacting with guests who must use oxygen to providing adventure travel experiences for guests with physical limitations.

There are several ways a property can reach travelers who have disabilities. The employees of many properties find it personally rewarding to affiliate themselves with such organizations as Easter Seals, United Cerebral Palsy, and the United Way. These employees can make important contacts while serving the community. In your consumer ads to business and leisure travelers and your trade ads to tour operators and travel agents, you can indicate your property's ability to accommodate travelers with disabilities. Other options include direct mail (obtain names from referral sources or from directories of key feeder cities' associations for people with disabilities) and public relations and publicity. For example, properties that sponsor fund-raising events with the United Way and other organizations may receive favorable publicity. A property can also contribute a lump sum to organizations that help people who have disabilities, or donate an amount that is based on a special sales promotion.

Other Special Segments

There are a number of other (and often overlooked) market segments that can increase occupancies and revenues: reunion attendees, travel crews and distressed passengers, truckers, construction crews, movie crews, military personnel, sequestered juries, and overflow/local business.

Reunion Attendees. The fast-growing reunions market consists of family, class, and military reunions. Recent interest in nostalgia has led to an upsurge in family and class reunions. Most are hosted by nonprofessionals, but there is also an association for reunion planners—the National Association of Reunion Planners, based in Rockville, Maryland.

This market segment is usually very cost-conscious (most attendees pay their own way) and often requires extensive help with planning. If you want to attract the reunions market, you should focus your sales presentations on value and professional expertise. Exhibit 13 gives an example of an advertisement that appeals to this need to be reassured of professional assistance. Selling points should include your property's accessibility, affordability, and facilities (recreational amenities, activities for all age groups, shuttle service, etc.) as well as your proven ability to handle group needs.

Military reunions typically draw 100 to 300 people and are much more frequent (meeting annually or biannually) than most class or family reunions. Since there are more than 13,500 different military groups that meet for reunions (generating some seven million room nights), military reunions can be an important segment for properties of all sizes. Military reunions usually don't require a lot of meeting space, they generally book off-season, and their dates are flexible. Attendees spend about $80 per person per day in addition to their room rates.[3] Like class and family reunion attendees, military reunion attendees are very cost-conscious. Many military reunions in the past were planned by nonprofessionals, but this is changing. Because of the rising interest in military reunions, publications focusing on them (*Reunion* and *Military Reunion News*) have appeared, and The Reunion Network, an organization offering reunion-planning assistance, has been established.

The Reunion Network publishes *TRN News*, a newsletter for military reunion planners. *TRN News* is an excellent vehicle for advertising to this market segment (the organization provides a list of "reunion-friendly" hotels to its members). Other avenues for reaching military reunion planners include direct mail (mailing labels can be obtained from the Service Reunions National Registry) or advertising in military magazines.

Travel Crews and Distressed Passengers. Travel crews include airline personnel, train crews, and bus drivers. Travel crews often have layovers or waiting time between trips, with stays usually ranging from 12 hours to three days. In most cases, airport properties have the advantage in attracting this market segment, but, especially in the case of layover crews or "commuting employees," downtown properties may also be considered by these travelers, due to the proximity of these properties to shopping and cultural activities.

Some properties, such as the Congress Hotel in Chicago, have taken extra steps to attract airline travel crews—the property offers a "crew lounge" that

Exhibit 13 Attracting the Reunions Market

While some reunions are handled by professional reunion planners, many reunions are still planned by nonprofessionals who need help to stage a successful event. Some properties and chains, such as Holiday Inn hotels, offer free reunion-planning guides to attract business from this growing market segment.

includes a washer and dryer and an iron and ironing board for crews on a short layover. There are a number of other needs that must be considered before marketing your property to travel crews. First, these guests need their rest; providing blackout shades, scheduling housekeeping around their sleeping schedules, and providing 24-hour wake-up-call service can sway business in your direction, as can providing rooms in areas away from the street and heavy-traffic areas (such as lobbies and areas near elevators or ice machines) and reducing the time needed for check-in (rooms should be available and assigned before crew members arrive). Free and timely shuttle service to and from the airport is also important to travel crews, as is 24-hour room service. Most airlines also look for short-term contracts and value; room rates can be up to 40 percent off regular rack rates, and most crew members are on per diems, which makes it necessary to offer discounts on food and beverages as well as rooms.

The extra business generated by travel crews provides another benefit—travelers who see crews at a property tend to perceive it as a quality hotel. Travel crews can be reached by contacting local airport station managers (each airline at an airport has its own station manager).

Properties may also wish to contract with major travel suppliers to service "distressed passengers" (those whose transportation has been delayed by inclement weather or mechanical problems). Be sure to establish a direct bill and voucher program with the airlines and other travel suppliers for payment for the distressed passenger rooms they book for their passengers. Bill Baxter, general manager of the Four Point Sheraton at Los Angeles International Airport, builds distressed-passenger business through public relations efforts targeted to airline employees. He regularly sends Sheraton staff members to the airport with "goodies" for airline employees, and hosts an annual party for airline personnel. As a result, his hotel often is the first to come to mind when airline personnel must find accommodations for distressed passengers.

Truckers. The trucking industry employs more than 9.5 million Americans, including over three million heavy-duty truck drivers. Truckers, who often drive in husband-and-wife teams, realize annual incomes ranging from $25,000 to over $65,000 annually and account for from two to nine room nights per month. This segment can be extremely lucrative, especially to budget and mid-price properties located on well-traveled highways. Exhibit 14 will help you determine if your property should target this segment.

Truckers fall into two general categories: *fleet drivers* and *independent drivers*. Fleet drivers are employed by a single company and do not always have discretion on their choice of lodging; an effective selling effort, therefore, should be directed to negotiating contracts or being placed on the preferred hotel lists of trucking companies. Independent drivers, who account for 50 percent of those making overnight trips, make their own hotel choices. Since they are paying for lodging out of their own pockets, these drivers look for value.

There are a number of ways to reach truck drivers: (1) direct sales, by making contacts at local, regional, and national trucking firms, at local businesses serving the trucking industry, and at trade shows); (2) advertising in print and on the web; and (3) direct mail. Knights Inn, for example, attends the Mid-America Trucking Show, maintains a Trucker On-Line Resource Center on the web, and offers a King of the Road Club. The club offers free local calls, prepaid calling cards, and a free fill-up of coffee upon departure. Full tractor-trailer parking is available at most Knights Inns.

Construction Crews. Construction crews are also an excellent source of business for budget and mid-scale properties. Out-of-town contractors—and local contractors using out-of-town subcontractors—frequently need rooms during the week

Exhibit 14 The Trucker Market at a Glance

Location: As a rule, truckers do not stop in big cities. They usually look for locations no more than three miles from an interstate.

Price: Fifty percent of truckers making overnight stops are independent contractors or "owner-operators" who look for value. Corporate headquarters of trucking firms can be contacted with a written proposal.

Services: Ample and secure parking; clean, comfortable guestrooms; 24-hour food service on site or within walking distance; modem accessible phones; 24-hour check-in and wake-up services; and courtesy transportation from the hotel to the nearby trucking company terminal.

Decision-Makers: Owner-operators; independent contractors; officials in local, regional, and national trucking company offices.

Best Ways to Reach Market: Direct sales, direct mail, and advertising are the methods most commonly used to sell to truckers. This market can be reached by attending trade shows, including the Mid-America Trucking Show and the International Trucking Show; obtaining membership lists of trade associations, such as the American Trucking Association (ATA) and the National Association of Truck Stop Operators (NATSO); advertising in publications such as *Professional Truckers Guide* and *The Professional Truckers Truckstops;* developing a web page directed to truckers; and making contacts at truck stops and repair stations in the area.

and look for properties that can offer nightly or four- to seven-night rates, free coffee, and early-morning wake-up calls.

To reach construction crews, subscribe to your area's *Construction Bulletin* and the *F. W. Dodge Reports;* both publications detail current and upcoming projects. Visit sites in person, but dress casually, be sensitive to busy times (early in the morning and just before lunch and quitting times), and limit your visit with the project superintendent to five minutes. This market does not respond well to "sales pitches"; simply express your desire to serve the crew and leave a flier printed on colorful paper. You may also wish to place ads in the *Construction Bulletin, F. W. Dodge Reports,* and other trade publications to establish your presence in this market.

Movie Crews. Movie crews typically stay on location from six to ten weeks, generating rooms and food and beverage business—and publicity for the property if a movie star is involved in the production. Movie crews usually require 40 to 70 guestrooms and four to six rooms for office facilities. Rooms for the crew should be similar (usually with one double bed), while special accommodations must be provided for the stars, producer, director, and executive secretary. Room rates are usually discounted somewhat and office space offered free of charge in consideration for the amount of business the crew generates. In addition, such amenities as flowers for the cast and free newspapers are often included.

To meet the needs of this specialized segment, Hilton International has launched "Master Shot," a service package for media companies and crews, at 160 of its hotels worldwide. The program's manual outlines how hotel personnel can best meet the specific needs of production companies on location, and a Master Shot manager is on call throughout the group's stay to ensure that personal needs are met, in addition to helping arrange for such details as local office space, parking, storage facilities, security, and transportation.

To reach movie crews, you can contact your state's movie commission or CVB as well as make personal contact with movie production offices. Producers usually are the decision-makers regarding hotel accommodations, so you may want to offer familiarization tours to them to showcase your property.

Military Personnel. If your property is near a military base, there are a number of possibilities for business, including hosting military reunions, leisure and social functions, and meetings, and providing rooms for out-of-town visitors and personnel relocating from other bases. Much of this business can help boost your weekend occupancies, especially if you offer special rates or packages for military personnel and their out-of-town guests.

Ways to reach the potentially profitable military market include contacting the base's Scheduled Airline Travel Office (SATO), which handles most vacations and leaves for military personnel, and developing relationships with officers of the base's various military clubs (NCO club, etc.) and the base's athletics director and contracting officer. The latter two contacts can advise you of upcoming events, such as tournaments involving visiting teams, and of the needs of outside construction contractors performing work at the base. You may also wish to place ads in base newspapers or in publications serving the military, develop fliers that can be displayed on base, or promote your property with a direct mail campaign.

Sequestered Juries. Properties located near courthouses can take advantage of their location and serve sequestered juries. The needs of this market will be determined in part by the county sheriff's office or by an appointed court official. In most cases, the jurors, the officer of the court, and other court personnel must be housed on one floor for security reasons, and telephones, television sets, and newspapers must be removed from rooms. Sequestered juries must have no contact with hotel employees. All arrangements for meals and transportation are made through the officer of the court.

Overflow/Local Business. In addition to the markets mentioned previously, you don't want to overlook potential business right in your own backyard. Overflow business from other properties in your area may be an excellent way to fill rooms during slow periods. Although you may be in competition with these other properties, they may not always be able to provide the rooms necessary for a group or even transient business during peak times and would welcome the opportunity to refer overflow guests to a nearby property. Make it a point to visit other properties in your area to let them know that you would be willing to accommodate overflow business; conversely, when your rooms are full, send your overflow business to the properties that can benefit you the most.

Finally, become involved in your community (see Exhibit 15). Network with other business professionals, join community groups, participate in charitable activities, and keep abreast of current events and trends. Having a presence in

Exhibit 15 Targeting Local Sales Prospects

Office Buildings and Industrial Parks

Call on every business. Try a creative approach, such as offering to host a free morning or afternoon break in the office building in order to reach prospects.

City Department of Parks and Recreation

Contact the person who handles events. Obtain a list of contacts for teams visiting for softball tournaments, swim meets, soccer tournaments, basketball games, and other park-related events.

Shopping Malls

Contact the general manager and leave brochures that will introduce your property to visiting regional managers, auditors, buyers, and so on. Ask for a calendar of mall events (if a mall hosts a craft show or similar activity, ask if you can become the host hotel). Ask about placing an ad in newsletters distributed to mall merchants. Free-standing retail outlets and chain restaurants should also be contacted.

Arenas, Auditoriums, and Fairgrounds

Obtain a calendar of events and a mailing list of contact persons for upcoming events.

High Schools, Colleges, and Trade Schools

Contact the school district office, head of the athletic department, head of the music department, principals and deans, and so on. The following departments are also good sources for lodging possibilities: alumni, housing, student affairs, admissions, dean's office, president's office, conference services, and purchasing office. Obtain a calendar of events, taking note of visiting teams, reunions, and so on.

Nursing Homes, Rehabilitation Centers, and Hospitals

Contact the administrator and the social services, human resources, and continuing education directors regarding the need for guestrooms for visiting family members, doctors, training seminar attendees, and so on. You can also approach these groups regarding group functions, such as volunteer recognition banquets or installation banquets. If possible, distribute fliers to personnel who may have need of your facilities and services.

Real Estate Agents

Real estate agents can provide leads for the relocation market. They will be eager to cooperate with you if you offer an incentive to encourage referrals, such as free meals or the use of your facilities.

Attorneys

Attorneys can be sources of leads for witnesses coming from out of town and professional functions such as banquets or seminars.

(continued)

Exhibit 15 *(continued)*

Funeral Homes
Contact funeral directors for leads on out-of-town guests attending funerals.

Insurance Companies
Contact local insurance companies to prospect opportunities for training workshops, the relocation market, and auditors and other traveling employees. Building relationships with local agents can open doors with company offices in feeder markets and provide opportunities for booking regional and national meetings.

Bowling Alleys
Call the manager to ask if the facility holds competitions. Your hotel or restaurant can participate in a number of ways: providing accommodations, catering an awards banquet, building community goodwill with a sponsorship, and so on.

Most properties can find a large amount of business within a five-mile radius of their location. These ideas identify a number of sources for potential business.

your community will lead to a number of sources of potential business—as well as enhance your reputation as a hotelier who cares.

Conclusion

While the primary focus of hospitality sales and service should be on meeting the needs of a property's principal markets, demand from principal markets does not always keep occupancies at acceptable levels year-round. Therefore, make an effort to seek out new markets to fill rooms and to increase food and beverage sales.

International travelers, honeymooners, sports teams and their fans, government travelers, travelers with disabilities, and other special markets offer an excellent opportunity for increased room occupancies—and profits—to properties with the time and budgets to research these markets and sell to them. As today's hospitality industry becomes increasingly competitive, special markets will become even more important. Properties that take the initiative to target these markets will be in a position to capture their share of the billions of dollars in revenues that special markets generate.

Endnotes

1. Some of the facts and figures in this section were taken from two publications by the American Hotel & Lodging Association: *The Care and Feeding of Guests from Abroad* and *The World Is Your Market*.
2. Kathleen Cassedy, "The World Market: How Small Properties Can Score Big with International Visitors," *Lodging*, April 1996, p. 118.
3. Howard Feiertag, "Call to Action: Get Your Share of the Military Reunion Market," *Hotel & Motel Management*, August 2006, p. 7.

Key Terms

actual and necessary per diem—The maximum amount a government employee may spend regardless of location; usually equal to or greater than the straight per diem rate.

all-inclusive resort—A resort that includes accommodations, meals, entertainment, and activities for a single price. The resort may also offer free wedding ceremonies, or ceremonies at reduced rates, for couples that bring a certain number of guests.

Americans with Disabilities Act (ADA)—U.S. legislation requiring commercial operations to remove barriers to people with disabilities in the workplace and provide facilities for customers with disabilities.

bridal fair—An event showcasing a wide variety of wedding-related products and services for brides and grooms.

contract per diem—A dollar figure that is allocated to government employees traveling on official business that incorporates the total cost of accommodations, meals, gratuities, travel expenses, and so on.

destination wedding—A wedding held at the honeymoon site.

foreign independent travel (FIT)—A custom-designed prepaid tour arranged by a travel agent for individual travelers traveling in foreign countries.

gateway city—A city with an airport that handles direct flights from other countries.

Japanese Assistance Network (JAN)—A service that provides Japanese translation via telephone for business and leisure travelers.

Language Line Services—A service provided by AT&T that links guests via telephone to interpreters; the service is available for more than 140 languages.

on-site wedding coordinator—The person at the hotel or wedding venue who is in charge of all wedding-related details.

receptive agent—A person or company that serves as an intermediary between a hotel and the global tourism industry. These agents may act as a domestic wholesaler or provide some or all of the components of a tour. Other services provided by receptive agents may include meet-and-greet services, sight-seeing tours, access to ground transportation, and vendor selection.

straight per diem—A dollar figure allocated to government employees who are traveling on official business; the amount covers lodging, meals, local transportation, and gratuities.

tour operator—A tour wholesaler or other tour company or an individual who operates packages or tours—that is, provides the necessary ground transportation and guide services.

tour wholesaler—A company or individual who plans, prepares, markets, and administers travel packages, usually combining the services of several travel and tourism suppliers and carriers.

travel agent—A person or organization that reserves and sells the services of travel and tourism suppliers to individual and group customers, and receives commissions for these efforts.

vouchers—Documents having a predetermined cash value issued by travel suppliers such as hotels, motorcoach tour operators, and so on. Vouchers can be exchanged for accommodations, meals, sight-seeing, and other services with contracted vendors.

Review Questions

1. Why is the United States a popular destination for international travelers?
2. What are some typical lodging needs of international travelers? How are lodging properties meeting these needs?
3. How can properties market to international travelers?
4. What avenues can be used to target the destination wedding and honeymoon market?
5. How do the different types of sports teams differ in their lodging requirements?
6. Why is targeting government business sometimes a challenge? What are the differences between a straight per diem, an actual and necessary per diem, and a contract per diem?
7. What are the three major categories of travelers with disabilities, and what are properties doing to accommodate the special needs of each?
8. What are the different types of reunion groups, and how can a property reach each group?
9. What are the advantages of attracting travel crews to a property? What types of properties best meet the needs of this market segment?
10. How do other specialty markets, such as truckers, construction crews, movie crews, and so on, impact a property's profitability? What are the special needs of these segments, and how can properties target them?

Internet Sites

For more information, visit the following Internet sites. Remember that Internet addresses can change without notice. If the site is no longer there, you can use a search engine to look for additional sites.

American Association of People with Disabilities
www.aapd.com

American Hotel & Lodging Association
www.ahla.com

Best Western International
www.bestwestern.com

Days Inn
www.daysinn.com

Destination Marketing Association International
www.iacvb.org

Doubletree Hotels
www.doubletreehotels.com

Hilton Hotels
www.hilton.com

Hospitality Sales & Marketing Association International
www.hsmai.org

Meeting Professionals International
www.mpiweb.org

Meetings & Conventions
www.meetings-conventions.com

Modern Bride
www.modernbride.com

National Association of Reunion Managers
www.reunions.com

National Directory of College Athletics
www.collegiatedirectories.com

Radisson Hotels International
www.radisson.com

Receptive Services Association of America
www.rsana.com

Reunions Magazine
www.reunionsmag.com

Sales & Marketing Management
www.salesandmarketing.com

Sheraton Hotels
www.sheraton.com

Society for Accessible Travel & Hospitality
www.sath.org

Society of Government Meeting Professionals
www.sgmp.org

Travel Industry Association of America
www.tia.org

Web Digest for Marketers
www.wdfm.com

Westin Hotels & Resorts
www.westin.com

Chapter 13 Outline

Competencies

1. Summarize trends affecting the food and beverage industry, and describe positioning strategies and techniques for restaurants and lounges. (pp. 491–503)
2. Explain how managers can merchandise food and beverages. (pp. 503–519)
3. Describe basic types of restaurant and lounge promotions. (pp. 519–527)
4. Explain how managers can build repeat business in restaurants and lounges, and describe these other hotel food service operations: room service and limited-service operations. (pp. 527–534)

Insider Insights

Bruce MacKenzie
Former Director—Food and Beverage
Town & Country Hotel
San Diego, California

"We began to see a trend in our guests: they were going off-property more often to eat. So we began placing "mini menu" handouts in display racks and handing out brochures featuring food and beverage outlet descriptions. The in-house TV channel advertised our restaurants and lounges, and bellpersons described them as they escorted guests to their rooms. Once inside the restaurants and lounges, our guests are exposed to visual promotions—bakery cases, refrigerated dessert carts, and so on. Suggestive selling is also used. If we can entice one of every two hotel guests to use one of our outlets, we will realize an increase of approximately $950,000 in food sales each year!"

13

Marketing Restaurants and Lounges

A CAREER IN FOOD AND BEVERAGE SERVICE puts you into one of the most exciting—and challenging—areas in the hospitality industry. Today's business climate offers a myriad of food service career choices—from fast food to specialty items to gourmet eateries. Yet studies conducted by Cornell and Michigan State universities show that one in four restaurants closes its doors before its first anniversary, and 60 percent fail within five years of opening.[1]

To be successful in this fast-paced, consumer-driven business, you must keep abreast of developments in the industry, recognize the differences between food fads and trends, and offer products and services that meet the ever-changing preferences of the public. Some of the trends that are affecting the food and beverage industry today include the following:

1. *Celebrity involvement.* The profitability of the restaurant business has not escaped the notice of celebrities, and many have invested in food and beverage establishments. In most cases, the celebrities have little to do with the restaurant's actual operation, although they may participate in grand openings and other promotions. Other celebrities are actively involved in the development of products and the promotion of their outlets.

   Many hotels are building business by introducing celebrity chain brands or partnering with celebrity chef consultants. The MGM Grand in Las Vegas, for example, offers the Louisiana cooking of Chef Emeril Lagasse. The Hôtel Plaza Athénée in Paris hired famed chef Alain Ducasse as a consultant to add his expertise at their Plaza Athénée Restaurant. He revamped the restaurant and brought in a team of chefs that he had trained at his other restaurants. Sofitel Hotels and Resorts, Paris, recently created their Café du Chef program, in which celebrity chefs consult with each hotel. Wyndham International formed a partnership with Shula's Steak House, an upscale dining establishment named after former football coach Don Shula. Shula's celebrity status helps draw more guests from outside the hotels—business has tripled since the chain purchased part ownership in Shula's company.

2. *Theme restaurants.* When the first Hard Rock Café opened in London in 1971, it set off a boom in theme restaurants. Planet Hollywood features movie memorabilia. The Harley-Davidson Cafés feature motorcycles. The Jekyll & Hyde Club serves up food and beverages in a "haunted house." The food is considered secondary at most theme restaurants; the main draw is the experience.

Operators further romanticize the experience by selling clothing and other merchandise as souvenirs of guests' visits. These sales can result in more profit than the food; they can contribute 30 to 50 percent of the outlet's revenue.

Most theme restaurants are located in such major tourist centers as New York, Orlando, Las Vegas, and London, because theme restaurants depend on tourists for the majority of their business. Dick Clark's American Bandstand Grills are an exception; they have attracted local followings in such cities as Indianapolis, Indiana; Columbus, Ohio; and Kansas City, Missouri.

3. *Dining entertainment options.* Since many diners today are looking for an experience rather than just a meal, tableside cooking, action stations, buffets with theme decorations, and interactive dining options have increased in popularity. The entertainment experiences that were previously available only at dinner theaters are now supplemented by interactive dining options. In Las Vegas, for example, dinner—and magic—is served up in Caesar's Magical Empire, and at the Excalibur Hotel's "King Arthur's Tournament," guests can eat Cornish hens with their hands while cheering on jousting knights. But restaurants don't have to offer expensive entertainment to attract guests; thanks to virtual-reality effects and a few props, restaurant guests in Chicago can enjoy a meal in a "tropical" setting on a blustery winter day.

4. *Increased competition.* In addition to competing with other restaurants and catering services, dining establishments must compete with nontraditional outlets. Convenience stores, for example, now offer popular fast foods (hot dogs, hamburgers, nachos, etc.), microwavable meals, and full-service delis. Many grocery stores feature deli departments and offer a growing array of "heat-and-eat" entrées.

   Today's busy lifestyle has led many consumers to look for "meal solutions," and supermarket "home-meal replacements" are perceived to be healthier and more nutritious than fast food. Choices range from pre-cooked meat and vegetable dishes that can be taken home for reheating, to exotic menu items such as sushi. As these easy-to-prepare items are gaining in popularity, supermarkets are moving them closer to the check-out lines, enabling customers to dash in to pick up quick meals for themselves and their families. In supermarkets where take-out food is prepared on-site, dining areas are sometimes added, adding yet another source of competition for traditional restaurants.

   Supermarkets that do not have the facilities or expertise to prepare take-out meals have begun teaming up with established food companies to enable them to cash in on this trend. For example, The Wolfgang Puck Food Company has established Wolfgang Puck Express units in upscale supermarkets, while the Vons chain has partnered with Panda Express to offer Chinese take-out at some of its locations.

5. *Takeout and delivery.* Many consumers with hectic schedules rely on takeout and delivery food to save time. In response, takeout has expanded beyond the traditional pizza, burgers, and chicken. A growing number of restaurants are packaging meals (including gourmet meals) "to go" and are offering delivery

service. Applebee's, for example, offers a popular To Go menu featuring appetizers, salads, grilled specialties, platters, burgers and sandwiches, desserts, beverages, and a kid's menu. Customers call in their order, pull into designated "To Go" parking spaces at participating restaurants, and their food is brought out to their cars. Other restaurants, such as Romano's Macaroni Grill, Chili's, Ruby Tuesday, and Outback Steakhouse, also offer curbside service. Some restaurants offer delivery as well as customer pickup. These outlets may hire their own drivers or contract with delivery services.

6. *Hotel and restaurant branding partnerships.* Since food service can be a losing proposition for some hotels, especially those with limited services, a number of properties are joining forces with outside food vendors and operators to provide a wide range of food choices, from in-room pizza delivery to food courts to gourmet restaurants.

   Ned Barker, vice president of food and beverages for InterContinental, says there are three types of branding solutions for hotels:

   - Taking a full-service branded restaurant concept (Red Lobster, T.G.I. Friday's, Denny's, Steak & Ale, Shula's Steak House, and so on) and placing one in a hotel. This is often successful because it matches a well-known restaurant brand with a well-known hotel brand.
   - Using the products of branded, leading food service companies and placing them on the menu.
   - Taking several quick-service brands and bundling them into a food court or offering a quick-service alternative, such as a Pizza Hut Kitchen, as the main restaurant.[2]

   The first concept can be illustrated by the pairing of the Palace Hotel in New York City with Le Cirque, an upscale restaurant that was looking for a new location. The restaurant works independently of the hotel, although the two share a common clientele. Other restaurants also look for properties that would be a good match for their product—Texas-based Metromedia Restaurant Group, for example, looks to four- and five-star hotels for its Steak and Ale brand, which has a high-check average.

   Several hotel chains offer branded products, such as ice cream, baked goods, or pizza, on their menus or as part of their room service offerings (pizza, for example, may be prepared on-premises or ordered directly from the pizza outlet). Other hotels have teamed up with other food service operators, from fast-food chains to upscale restaurants, to diversify their food offerings or eliminate the need to operate hotel kitchens. At the Embassy Suites, Center City Philadelphia, for example, T.G.I. Friday's operates the lunch and dinner menu for the hotel and provides the complimentary breakfast buffet that is part of the Embassy Suite package.

   Hotel chains such as Choice Hotels and Holiday Inns have partnered with a number of food service providers to offer food courts or kiosks featuring well-known brands. This concept, which is known as dual- or multiple-branding,

Hotel and Restaurant Branding Partnerships

Sheraton
- Starbucks Coffee
- Ruth's Chris Steak house
- Pizza Hut

Holiday Inn
- Denny's
- Pizzeria Uno
- Red Lobster

Hilton
- Benihana Japanese Restaurants

Choice Hotels (six different hotel brands)
- Bennigan's
- Steak and Ale
- Bonanza
- Ponderosa

Marriott
- Pizza Hut
- Nathan's
- TCBY
- Popeye's Chicken
- Burger King

offers a win-win situation for all concerned—customers readily accept branded dining options, the restaurant operators realize additional business, and the hotel cuts costs. Depending on the arrangement, hotels may realize additional revenue from these food service providers through space rental deals.

7. *Multiple-branding among restaurants.* A number of restaurants are teaming up to offer customers "two-for-one" (or more) choices at the same outlet. For example, Taco Bell and Pizza Hut have teamed up within the same building at many locations to offer diners a choice. Taco Bell has also opened dual units with its sister company, KFC.

   These "within brand" arrangements can prove profitable as target markets may be diverse. In the case of Taco Bell–KFC, for example, Taco Bell enjoyed a larger lunch business than KFC, which outpaced Taco Bell at dinner. This arrangement also saves on real estate costs—the partners can share rental and other costs associated with operating a restaurant.

   While multiple branding is generally practiced by quick-service restaurant chains, middle-market restaurants are also considering sharing space under one roof, whether in a freestanding facility or as part of a hotel food court. Darden Restaurants, owner of Olive Garden, Red Lobster, and Bahama Breeze, does not see cannibalization of its brands at shared space, citing that each brand offers a different type of dining experience and the proximity may increase visits to outlets that diners had previously not tried.

To succeed in the competitive food and beverage business, you need to know how to merchandise your product, create promotions that will help you stand out from the crowd, and generate staff involvement to provide a "diner-friendly" experience. While these basics apply to all restaurants and lounges, they are especially important when promoting hotel food and beverage outlets.

MARKETING IN ACTION

Taco Bell and Pizza Hut Team Up to Offer a Diverse Dining Experience

Taco Bell and Pizza Hut, two of the five brands under the Yum! Brands Inc. umbrella (the others are KFC, A&W Restaurants, and Long John Silvers), are just two of the fast-food outlets that share space in order to diversify their menus, serve different groups of diners, and save on real estate costs. Jonathan Blum, a senior vice president at Yum!, says that "multi-branding is our key growth strategy. It offers more choice and convenience and it overcomes the veto vote."

According to research by Yum!, customers preferred visiting a multi-branded location six-to-one. Therefore, Yum!, which has 32,000 units across its five brands, now operates about 1,800 domestic multi-branded outlets and projects an additional 375 annually in the future. By late this decade, it will have more than 5,000 dual- or multi-branded outlets.

One of the principal challenges faced by the dual Taco Bell–Pizza Hut outlet was at the back of the house. Prep areas had to be reconfigured (they were essentially split into two dedicated areas) and each brand required different prep skills, resulting in the need for cross-training of both staff and management.

The dual-branding of Taco Bell and Pizza Hut has proved popular, however, giving diners additional menu choices at one convenient location, and the chain has added other dual-branding concepts, combining Taco Bell (usually an impulse dining choice) and KFC (a "destination" purchase).

Sources: Milford Prewitt, "Brand Bundling Booms as Fast Feeders Exploit Variety," *Nation's Restaurant News,* October 21, 2002; Tim Hillard, "Co-Branding," *Foodservice and Hospitality,* March 1998, p. 34; and Cathy Enz, "Multi-branding Strategy—the Case of Yum! Brands," *Cornell Hotel and Restaurant Administration Quarterly,* February 2005, p. 85.

Positioning Restaurants and Lounges

In this section, we will discuss the positioning of hotel restaurants, the positioning of freestanding restaurants, and positioning research.

Positioning Hotel Restaurants

There was a time in the not-too-distant past when U.S. hotel managers considered in-house restaurants a necessary evil. Hotel restaurants are very popular in other parts of the world. In Europe and Asia, hotel dining rooms are commonly the best dining facilities in the city and are heavily patronized by both hotel guests and local clientele. The Movenpick Hotel in Zurich, Switzerland, for example, which offers several theme restaurants, often has to turn away local business in order to accommodate hotel guests. In Asia, revenue from hotel restaurants can account for up to 75 percent of the hotel's revenue, as compared to an industry average of 35 percent in the United States.

Today's U.S. hotel operators are increasingly beginning to see in-house dining facilities as more than just a convenience for their guests, although the **capture rate**—the percentage of hotel guests who eat meals at the hotel—is still considered important and is measured regularly. Hotel restaurant operators in the United States have become more aware of the importance of non-hotel customers and the need to offer food and ambiance reflecting the tastes of their surrounding area. Therefore, hotel restaurants are becoming more relaxed and less formal and many have become "in" places that attract patrons from the surrounding community as well as hotel guests.

Today's hotel restaurants range from the bright and cheery to the intimate and elegant, from coffee shops to lavishly decorated gourmet rooms. The Ritz-Carlton hotel chain, for example, has updated its formal restaurants, redesigning them for today's more casual atmosphere. Now they feature exhibition kitchens, windows that look out onto the street, and décor reflecting the history and ambiance of the local area (such as the colors and tastes of Cuba at its Miami property).

It is becoming increasingly common for hotels to open unique, new dining options that range from trendy fusion restaurants, such as Asia de Cuba, to hip Japanese restaurants, such as Sushi Roku. It is important that hoteliers weigh the pros and cons of such trends. Will a typically older resort guest base embrace high-energy and somewhat louder dining venues? Will increased business from younger diners offset potential losses from diners who prefer more traditional hotel restaurants? Are there "happy mediums" that will please the majority of diners? Sometimes, the solution to the trendy restaurant dilemma can be as simple as offering restaurants opened by high-profile or celebrity chefs who enjoy large and loyal followings in other cities.

Despite improvements in hotel restaurants, some surveys continue to show that many hotel guests prefer to eat in an outside establishment. With dramatic changes taking place, why aren't more guests discovering and frequenting hotel restaurants? The answer is *positioning*. Many guests don't feel that a hotel restaurant or lounge is as good as a freestanding restaurant or night spot. This view presents a challenge to hoteliers. Their food and beverage outlets must be positioned (in terms of physical location, atmosphere, and prices) to compete with freestanding eateries and lounges despite this negative view. Exhibit 1 shows how one hotel used a clever promotion to convince its guests that its restaurant offered better food and service than what a guest might expect to find at a hotel restaurant.

Several hotels have remodeled their restaurants to resemble freestanding establishments. Curtis Nelson, president and CEO of Country Hospitality Worldwide, believes that "you need an exterior entrance, definitive curb appeal with awnings, a facade, and signage." Don Cronk, vice president of development for T.G.I. Friday's, agrees: "Access through hotels is not sufficient."[3] Giving a hotel restaurant a separate identity is a good way to enlarge your guest base; hotel

Exhibit 1 Building the Image of Hotel Restaurants

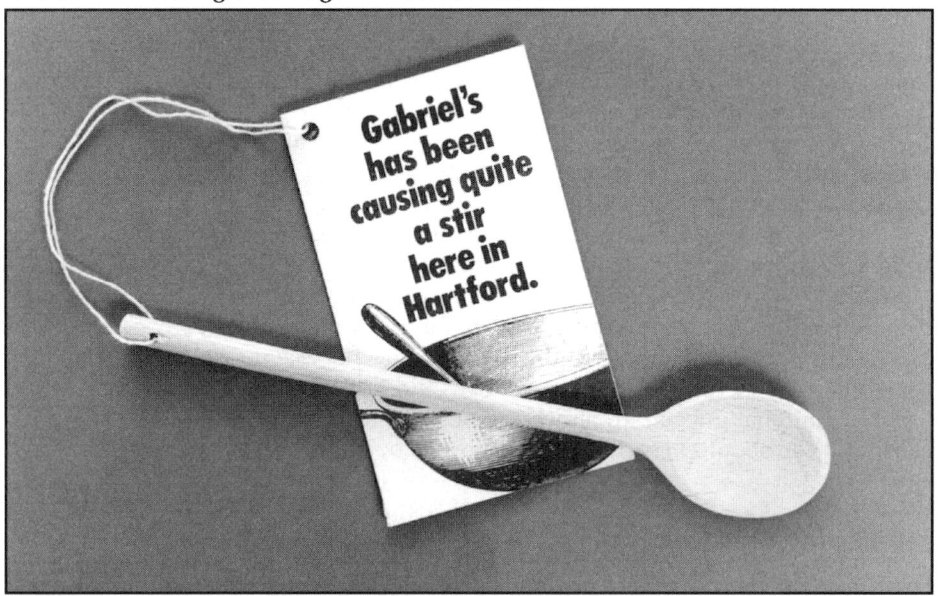

This eye-catching promotion, featuring a wooden spoon attached to a brochure, was placed in guestrooms at The Summit Hotel in Hartford, Connecticut, to promote the property's restaurant, Gabriel's. This campaign is typical of those that try to upgrade the image of hotel restaurants in the minds of guests. The brochure was designed to convince guests that Gabriel's offered better food and service than what a guest would expect to find at a hotel restaurant. It also stressed the convenience factor. There was no need to drive or take a cab to find superior food; the restaurant was just an elevator ride away. (Courtesy of The Summit Hotel, Hartford, Connecticut)

restaurants with outside entrances, a canopy, and valet parking have seen their guest counts go up.

Positioning Freestanding Restaurants

Positioning is equally important for freestanding restaurants, especially those located in an area where there are multiple dining opportunities. If that is the case, the restaurant may position its products against those of a competitor. Such was the case during the "Burger Wars" of a few decades ago, when Wendy's ran its "Where's the Beef?" campaign against McDonald's and Burger King, and Burger King used its flame-broiled campaign against McDonald's.

Service differentiation can also be used to position a restaurant. A restaurant, for example, may offer such amenities and services as advance reservations, "white glove" service, or gifts of roses or corsages to women diners on Mother's Day, as a way of setting themselves apart from competitors.

A restaurant can also use its location or ambiance to distinguish itself from competitors. The Hard Rock Café restaurant chain, for example, has created an environment that is hard to duplicate with its displays of memorabilia, while other restaurants can offer a unique dining experience in a tropical setting or "fun" environment.

Whatever type of positioning your restaurant uses, it is important that customers have a consistent image of your establishment. Many restaurateurs make the mistake of experimenting with different slogans or products, which leads to customer confusion—and loss of business. If you are unsure of how to position your restaurant, it is perhaps better to call in a professional to ensure that your positioning adequately reflects what you have to offer.

Even successful restaurants can benefit from repositioning. McDonald's dispelled its image as an impersonal, "cookie-cutter" chain with "My McDonald's" positioning, which promoted each outlet as owned by someone in the local community who cared about his or her outlet. This positioning strategy was developed after McDonald's managers sought to discover who was in the guest base, why these guests were dining out, and what would appeal to them (and what would attract additional guests). In short, the new positioning resulted from using the same tool you should use to determine how to position your restaurant—*thorough research.*

Positioning Research

Positioning research should become an ongoing part of the operation of any restaurant. Positioning research falls into five basic areas: trading-area research, guest-profile research, situation (current business) research, competition analysis, and trend research.

Trading-Area Research. Research into who guests are and where they come from is critical in restaurant positioning. An important factor often overlooked is the **trading area** (also known as the "catchment area") from which business is derived. The catchment area for a restaurant is typically a three- to five-mile radius (usually a travel time of ten minutes or less). Therefore, it is generally much smaller than that of a lodging facility, which attracts guests from far-flung locations.

Your trading areas may vary greatly, depending on a number of factors. You may have an entirely different group of guests on the weekends than you serve on weekdays, for example. Your guest mix may even vary by meal period. Your lunch crowd, for instance, might consist largely of businesspeople within a ten- to 15-minute drive or a five-minute walk, while dinner guests may be residents within a ten- to 15-mile (16- to 24-kilometer) radius. Knowing exactly where guests are coming from and how they are getting to the restaurant can provide valuable insights that will help you in directing mailings, choosing media for advertising, and creating menus that will appeal to each trading-area group.

Many restaurants, in fact, attribute their success to **neighborhood marketing,** since probably 70 percent of their revenue comes from people who live, work, shop, or visit within a ten-minute drive. Develop a database of your potential local clientele, separating them by categories such as employers, churches, schools, residential customers, and so on, and mail offers of interest to each group. Your mailing to a church, for example, may include a fund-raising proposal, while your mailing to senior citizens in a nearby complex might offer early-bird specials available only to them.

INTERNET EXERCISE

Log onto the Internet and find the website of the Quantified Marketing Group (www.quantifiedmarketing.com). Click on "Learning Center" and choose "Articles." Read two articles and write a brief report on what you have learned.

Even large, established chains do not neglect neighborhood marketing. McDonald's is known for catering to the local markets it serves, such as when 300 restaurants added bratwurst sandwiches to their menus to cater to the unique tastes of the Midwesterners they served, or when McDonald's outlets in India replaced its hamburgers with veggie burgers and other choices, since the majority of customers there considered cows sacred and would not eat beef.

Guest-Profile Research. Once the trading area has been determined, research into a guest's age, gender, type (new or repeat), and employment can enhance restaurant positioning. If you find that you are catering primarily to businesspeople at lunch and hotel guests in the evening, for example, it makes it easier to design menus that appeal to each group.

Information for guest profiles can be more difficult to obtain in restaurants than at the front desk. If a hotel restaurant patron is a hotel guest and charges his or her meal to the room, the patron's room number can be noted and information can be obtained at the front desk from the patron's registration form. In cases where a great deal of business consists of walk-in guests (whether local or traveling), there are a number of ways in which guest profile information can be obtained:

Personal conversation or observation. The host or food server can get information by conversing with guests, or by observing details such as an out-of-town driver's license used as identification when cashing a check, or a briefcase or business conversation that identifies a guest as a businessperson, and so on. When a patron has been identified as a local, make a special effort to obtain his or her zip code.

Special promotions. If the restaurant caters to a business trade, it can run a free-meal promotion and request the business cards of patrons as entry forms. One or more of the cards can be drawn on specified dates, and the winner(s) given a complimentary meal. This type of promotion yields names, occupations, addresses, and telephone numbers, and is extremely cost-effective.

Guest surveys. Questionnaires or evaluation forms are excellent sources of information that can assist in menu planning and the planning of promotions for certain target markets. Charlie Trotter's restaurants continually ask guests for their opinions. All diners are given satisfaction surveys asking them to rate food, service, ambiance, price, efficiency, aesthetics, attention to detail, and execution. Trotter says that "guest satisfaction surveys help us to make decisions—from lighting, to the price of meals, to the number of courses, to attitude of service staff, to pricing the wine list."[4] Applebee's uses customer-focused menu development, testing its new products (40 to 50 annually) at selected restaurants and in consumer focus groups that provide feedback on the products being tested. Other chains, such as Olive Garden, offer seasonal and "test" menu items to solicit customer feedback.

Questionnaires vary in content. A restaurant targeting business lunch guests, for example, may use a questionnaire that asks questions relating to favorite food selections, speed of service, and other factors that would make the restaurant more attractive to the business community. A questionnaire could also focus on food preparation (such as the trend from fried foods to broiled and steamed items), type of service (whether guests prefer buffets or table service), or general demographics (to get an accurate breakdown of market segments currently using the restaurant).

Completed guest surveys can assist the restaurant staff in serving present markets and can give clues as to markets being missed. They can also aid management in making pricing decisions.

To encourage guests to fill out questionnaires or other survey forms, a server can draw attention to the form and tell guests that they will receive a gift or discount coupon if the form is filled out and presented when making payment. The restaurant can also provide a complimentary pen to make filling out the form easier, or an envelope for the completed survey. A guest who has received less-than-perfect food or service may feel intimidated when turning in an unflattering survey to his or her food server; an envelope ensures anonymity and may encourage more guests to respond. Still other food and beverage outlets provide stamped, self-addressed survey cards or questionnaires that may be filled out and returned at the diner's convenience.

Increasingly, guest surveys are going high-tech. For example, Smokey Bones restaurants invite selected diners to visit the Smokey Bones website within 48 hours of their dining experience. Once at the website, they type in a code identifying the outlet at which they dined, then fill out a short survey online. At the end of the survey, they are given a "special code" that they can write on their restaurant receipt. At their next visit to a Smokey Bones outlet, they can turn in the receipt with the special code and receive $4 off their next meal.

Situation (Current Business) Research. Situation (or current business) research can be used to identify market segments. If situation research shows that most of the property's lunch guests are businesswomen, for example, the property can appeal to that market segment with an eye-catching salad bar and specially priced small lunch portions for light eaters. T.G.I. Friday's, which always had an all-day menu, now has different lunch and dinner menus to enable it to better segment the daytime market.

The singles market is a rapidly growing segment for many restaurants. Restaurants with a large singles clientele have developed a number of innovative ideas to profit from this lucrative market. One idea is the "Friendship Table." Friendship tables are designed to provide single diners with company and conversation if they don't want to eat by themselves. Exhibit 2 shows creative ways that Friendship Tables are being used to attract lone diners. While this idea has long been used on cruise ships, it is relatively new to the hospitality industry and has become a popular addition in many restaurants.

The Wyndham Hotel in Chicago has done a variation on the Friendship Table with its "Networking Table," which gives women traveling alone the opportunity to dine with other women travelers. The Peninsula in Hong Kong offers yet another dining option for single diners, The Chef's Table. Guests are

Exhibit 2 The Friendship Table

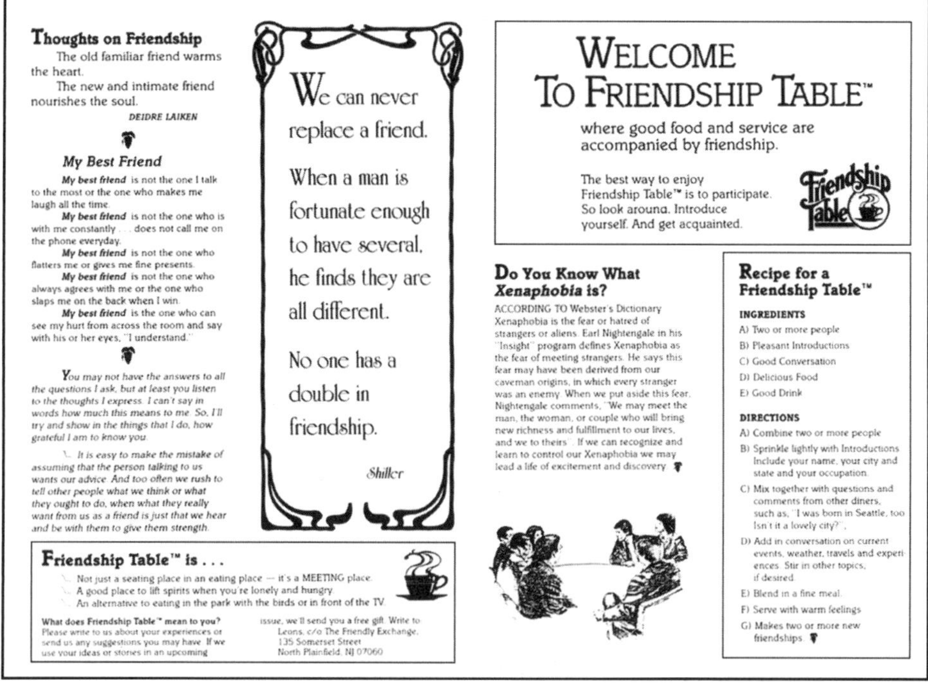

Thoughts on Friendship

The old familiar friend warms the heart.

The new and intimate friend nourishes the soul.

DEIDRE LAIKEN

My Best Friend

My best friend is not the one I talk to the most or the one who makes me laugh all the time.

My best friend is not the one who is with me constantly . . . does not call me on the phone everyday.

My best friend is not the one who flatters me or gives me fine presents.

My best friend is not the one who always agrees with me or the one who slaps me on the back when I win.

My best friend is the one who can see my hurt from across the room and say with his or her eyes, "I understand."

You may not have the answers to all the questions I ask, but at least you listen to the thoughts I express. I can't say in words how much this means to me. So, I'll try and show in the things that I do, how grateful I am to know you.

It is easy to make the mistake of assuming that the person talking to us wants our advice. And too often we rush to tell other people what we think or what they ought to do, when what they really want from us as a friend is just that we hear and be with them to give them strength.

We can never replace a friend.

When a man is fortunate enough to have several, he finds they are all different.

No one has a double in friendship.

Shiller

WELCOME TO FRIENDSHIP TABLE™

where good food and service are accompanied by friendship.

The best way to enjoy Friendship Table™ is to participate. So look arouna. Introduce yourself. And get acquainted.

Friendship Table

Do You Know What *Xenaphobia* is?

ACCORDING TO Webster's Dictionary Xenaphobia is the fear or hatred of strangers or aliens. Earl Nightengale in his "Insight" program defines Xenaphobia as the fear of meeting strangers. He says this fear may have been derived from our caveman origins, in which every stranger was an enemy. When we put aside this fear, Nightengale comments, "We may meet the man, the woman, or couple who will bring new richness and fulfillment to our lives, and we to theirs". If we can recognize and learn to control our Xenaphobia we may lead a life of excitement and discovery.

Recipe for a Friendship Table™

INGREDIENTS

A) Two or more people
B) Pleasant Introductions
C) Good Conversation
D) Delicious Food
E) Good Drink

DIRECTIONS

A) Combine two or more people
B) Sprinkle lightly with Introductions. Include your name, your city and state and your occupation.
C) Mix together with questions and comments from other diners, such as, "I was born in Seattle, too. Isn't it a lovely city?".
D) Add in conversation on current events, weather, travels and experiences. Stir in other topics, if desired.
E) Blend in a fine meal.
F) Serve with warm feelings.
G) Makes two or more new friendships.

Friendship Table™ is . . .

- Not just a seating place in an eating place — it's a MEETING place.
- A good place to lift spirits when you're lonely and hungry.
- An alternative to eating in the park with the birds or in front of the TV.

What does Friendship Table™ mean to you? Please write to us about your experiences or send us any suggestions you may have. If we use your ideas or stories in an upcoming issue, we'll send you a free gift. Write to:
Leons, c/o The Friendly Exchange,
135 Somerset Street
North Plainfield, NJ 07060

Friendship tables are relatively new to hotel restaurants but are rapidly gaining in popularity with singles, senior citizens, and business travelers who prefer not to dine alone. Friendship tables provide the opportunity to just socialize or to network with fellow diners, and even those who are initially shy about joining a group often warm up once they become more familiar with the "social dining" concept. A newsletter such as this one published by Leon's Restaurant Services, North Plainfield, New Jersey, can provide conversation starters.

shown around the kitchen and a special menu is devised for them, to show off the chef's talents. The concept, which was originally started to get publicity for the new chef, has proven so popular that there is now a three-month waiting list for the table for four.

The senior citizens market may be important in a restaurant's positioning, especially if the restaurant is located in a hotel or another area that is popular with seniors. Many restaurants offer special menus, portions, and discounts for senior citizens.

Situation research also entails a look at statistics. Nearly all hotels make use of room occupancy statistics, but fewer have access to restaurant occupancy data such as total **covers** and **table turnover** ratios per meal. Tracking covers, for example, helps to identify slow, medium, and busy periods, and also helps to determine patterns of spending and menu choices. For best results, covers should be broken down into the six weekly meal periods or dining segments:

Creating an Enjoyable Dining Experience for Single Diners

Restaurateurs who wish to attract the large number of solo diners among business travelers, leisure travelers, and local customers must work to create a climate in which solo diners are welcomed and shared seating is comfortable and acceptable. Here are a few ideas:

- Develop a truly welcoming greeting for solo diners. Avoid "body count" greetings, such as, "Only one?"; instead, say warmly, "Thank you for joining us for dinner this evening."
- Offer a variety of seating options—from a single table, to cluster seating, to variations on community tables. A diner who is shy about eating with a large group may be open to sharing a table with just one other solo diner.
- Place explanatory messages on tables. This demonstrates your restaurant's support of "social dining" options and casts a mantle of acceptability on the concept. These messages announce the dining option to all guests; some couples may welcome the opportunity to become acquainted with others.
- Make solo dining a special experience whether the diner chooses to dine alone or join another diner or group. Provide special attention to solo diners and offer an amenity, such as a complimentary appetizer, beverage, or dessert, to show your appreciation for their patronage.

Give "social dining" options time to work. Ask for feedback and work out any problems guests might have with the options you offer. Publicize your single-dining options, detailing their benefits, such as the opportunity to network over a meal or simply enjoy the company of fellow women business travelers, for example.

- Weekday breakfast (Monday–Friday)
- Weekday lunch (Monday–Friday)
- Weekday dinner (Monday–Thursday)
- Weekend breakfast (Saturday–Sunday)
- Weekend lunch (Saturday–Sunday)
- Weekend dinner (Friday–Sunday)

Using these meal periods makes it easier to track such statistics as customer check average (dollars); entrée average (dollars); and number of beverages, desserts, and side items sold during each period. These statistics help managers to analyze strengths and weaknesses and to take steps to increase sales, such as asking food servers to make a special effort to sell desserts during a meal period that is typically slow for dessert sales. In addition, a breakdown by meal period provides invaluable information for staff scheduling and for tailoring service to the specific needs of guests.

Determining what is important to each meal period's customers can help you more cost-effectively develop promotions for each category of diner. For example, it would be helpful to know that the weekday breakfast and lunch crowds are interested in speed and value, while customers during the same periods on the weekend are looking for relaxation and ambiance.

Competition Analysis. While in-house research is extremely necessary, it is equally important to be aware of what the competition is doing. Study the competition's:

- Menu items and prices
- Facilities and services
- Mix (source and volume) of business
- Extra amenities—parking facilities, special menus or discount clubs for seniors, and so on
- Promotional efforts

Analysis of the competition for a hotel restaurant should be used as it is by the rooms division—to determine property strengths and weaknesses and develop ways to differentiate the property's facilities from those of the competition. While questioning competitors and filling out forms is useful, it is far more effective to actually experience what the competition has to offer. Restaurant staff should visit competitors at various times (breakfast, lunch, and dinner; traditionally slow periods; and peak times) to get a complete picture of service and atmosphere.

Trend Research. In addition to the trends mentioned in the opening of the chapter, you should keep abreast of changing demographics and dining trends. For example, the population in the United States is getting older and there has been a growth in the number of single diners; these trends can impact the type of foods desired, the ambiance of a restaurant, and even the size of portions. In addition, children are becoming increasingly important to restaurateurs, as they often influence decisions on where the family will eat out. Therefore, if you are located in an area where there is a large population of families, you may want to consider developing a children's menu or take steps to make your restaurant more "family-friendly."

You should also examine food trends and eating habits. Over the past several years, the trend has been away from heavy meals to lighter, healthier fare such as salads, fresh fruits and vegetables, and lean meats and fish. While some restaurants have been left behind by changing trends and have suffered financially, your restaurant can avoid this problem by supplementing traditional menu selections with trendy specialties. Menus can be changed each night to alleviate "menu boredom"; dining "adventures" (a sushi bar, a "select-your-own-lobster" seafood buffet, meals prepared tableside, etc.) can be introduced, and special menus can be created for dieters and the health-conscious.

Merchandising Food and Beverages

Food and beverages can be merchandised by special packaging and pricing, promotional materials such as posters and table tent cards, and suggestive selling by food servers. But perhaps the most important merchandising tool is the restaurant's menu. A good menu, through the types of items offered and the presentation of those items, can enhance the image and increase the profits of any food and beverage operation.

Industry Innovators

Steve Ells
Founder and CEO, Chipotle Mexican Grill

Steve Ells learned classic French cooking skills at the Culinary Institute of America and had hopes of opening his own large-scale "fancy" restaurant before he made a decision that changed his career—and American perception of fast food. Ells' previous experience with Mexican food had been burritos smothered with green chile salsa, presented on a plate, but then, while visiting *taquerias* in San Francisco, he discovered giant flour tortillas filled with such ingredients as rice, beans, meat, and salsa, rolled up and wrapped in foil. Thinking that he could make the food lighter and more upscale, Ells opened his first Chipotle Mexican Grill in Denver, Colorado, in July 1993. Customers flocked to his restaurant to enjoy gourmet burritos and tacos in a trademark setting of such basic construction materials as plywood, corrugated metal, stainless steel, and exposed ductwork. Ells subsequently opened a number of equally successful restaurants.

Ells' first investor was his father, who not only loaned his son over $1.5 million, but also helped him put a business plan and a board of directors together. Ells then sought a partner who could continue to fund the business. He sent the business plan to McDonald's, and the company not only liked his plan, it invested about $360 million into Ells' business over a seven-year period. It was a unique arrangement, in that McDonald's did not impose its style, brands, values, or mode of operation on Ells' chain—the fast-food giant allowed Ells to be himself, which meant foregoing the usual highly processed food used by McDonalds in favor of quality raw ingredients and prep work that rivaled what was done in the finest restaurants.

Always concerned with serving the finest-quality food in a hip, friendly atmosphere, Ells took Chipotle's philosophy of "Food with Integrity" a step further in October 2000 when he began purchasing only naturally raised pork. Today, 80 percent of the chain's chicken and 50 percent of its beef also comes from naturally raised sources.

Ells' restaurants appeal to diners seeking fresher, healthier meals. His restaurants are also known for serving up respect for their employees, their suppliers, and the environment.

Creating Menus That Sell

A menu must reflect the restaurant's positioning or image, provide information, and serve as a suggestive-selling tool. While this may seem like a monumental

Exhibit 3 Sample Restaurant Menu

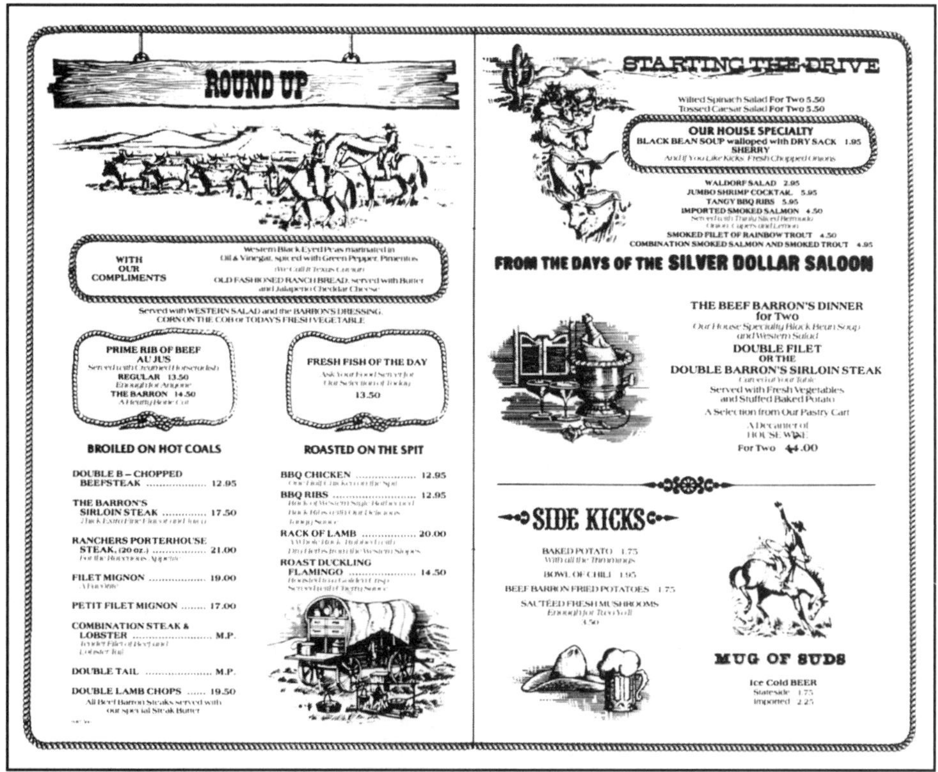

Menus should be designed to reflect the character or image of the restaurant. The headings in this menu from the Beef Barron are reminiscent of the Old West. Important dishes are encircled by lariats, and line drawings reinforce the Western theme. (Courtesy of Hilton Hotels Corporation)

challenge, it is actually quite easy when you follow a menu development cycle that includes image, price, message, and design.

Image. The menu development cycle begins with your restaurant's positioning or image (see Exhibit 3). Your restaurant's image refers to how your restaurant is perceived by your patrons. What image does your restaurant create? What type of ambiance or atmosphere do you offer? When people visit, do they expect a romantic atmosphere or a casual dining experience? While there are a myriad of menu options, your menu must live up to your guests' expectations.

Since a restaurant's image is determined in part by the type of clientele the restaurant attracts (or hopes to attract), it is important to determine whether patrons are coming from inside or outside the property (or a mixture of both) and what market segments your restaurant serves. Does the restaurant cater primarily to the health-conscious? Do business travelers, who usually prefer rapid service during their lunch hours, make up the largest number of patrons? Or does the restaurant serve a great number of families and therefore need a more varied menu?

GOING GREEN

Restaurants Rally to Save the Environment

Just as many hotels are doing, many restaurants are increasing their commitment to protecting the environment. Since restaurants account for about one-third of all retail electrical use, many of their efforts focus on the reduction of energy consumption through the use of energy-efficient lighting and appliances as well as other energy-saving strategies. Many restaurants also are installing water-saving devices such as low-flow spray nozzles, flow-restricted faucets, and ultra-low-flow toilets in order to use less water.

Recycling has also become an important part of restaurant environmental efforts. Programs that recycle paper products such as hand towels, napkins, and carry-out bags are popular, and many restaurants are recycling food products and grease as well. These programs also help to reduce pollution, as does the use of organic food products that are free from harmful pesticides.

The demand for organic food has increased 25 percent over the past few years, and eco-friendly restaurants are committed to meeting this demand by offering organic produce, hormone-free meats, and sustainable seafood. Celebrity chef Wolfgang Puck has developed a program, "Wolfgang's Eating, Loving, and Living" (WELL), for his Puck Gourmet Express restaurants. The program, which reflects his philosophy that healthy eating and gourmet dining can go hand-in-hand, provides for existing recipes to be adapted to all-natural USDA organic ingredients. Under the WELL program, Puck's eateries and catering ventures serve organically grown fruits and vegetables. All meat and seafood come from humanely raised animals and certified sustainable seafood sources. The focus is on using produce and meat with minimal pesticides, hormones, and antibiotics. Puck's first eatery to go eco-friendly was the Springs Cafe, located in Las Vegas at the Springs Preserve, an eight-acre botanical garden dedicated to conservation and promoting green living.

Several organizations have been established to assist restaurants in implementing "green" strategies. A national association, the Green Restaurant Association (www.dinegreen.com), offers environmental guidelines as well as an endorsed-products list. The association also offers a listing of restaurants that meet the guidelines established to help properties qualify as a "green restaurant."

Area associations, such as Green My Cuisine (www.greenmycuisine.com), which serves the San Francisco Bay area; and Going Greener (www.greenrestaurants.org), which is based in Chicago, also provide tips for conservation and using eco-friendly foods and products. Certification requirements vary, as do inspection programs that ensure compliance with area guidelines.

Restaurants can encourage patrons to participate in their environmental efforts by providing tips to reduce waste, such as suggesting that patrons carry bottled water (rather than using restaurant glasses that need to be washed), use travel mugs or reusable cups to minimize the use of Styrofoam, and (if patrons expect to have leftovers) bring plastic bags, aluminum foil, or a reusable plastic container for take-home food. Restaurant customers can also help the environment by taking only the number of condiment packets that they will actually use.

Source: Erica Vital, "Even the Food Is Green at Springs Cafe," *Spring Valley View,* February 12, 2008.

INTERNET EXERCISE

Log onto the Internet and research the website of Lettuce Entertain You Enterprises (www.leye.com). This company offers over 30 restaurant brands. Click on the "Restaurants" link, choose three of the brands, and do a menu analysis of the three menus:

1. Do the menus reflect each restaurant's image? Why or why not?
2. Does the menu copy describe the food in a complete and appetizing manner?
3. How do the menus help differentiate each brand from the other restaurants operated by the company?

Price. Price information is a critical menu consideration. Your pricing strategy should be determined long before your menu is designed, and should correspond with your positioning. What prices do your guests expect to pay for menu items? Will items be priced individually (à la carte) or as full meals? Will prices appear at all?

According to a study detailed in the *Cornell Hotel and Restaurant Administration Quarterly,* restaurants can charge different prices for the same menu items during lunch and dinner without risking customers' perceptions of fairness. In addition, the study found that variable pricing on weekends versus weekdays is also likely to be acceptable with customers.[5] These factors, then, should also be taken into consideration when planning your pricing strategy.

Determining prices. Food service operators generally base menu pricing on four critical factors: cost, the type of operation, guest perception and demand, and competition. Unlike freestanding restaurants, which operate with established overheads, hotel restaurants often share facilities (kitchens, storerooms, etc.) with other arms of the food and beverage department, making it difficult to determine operating costs or to properly price menu items. For this reason, hotel restaurants price menu selections primarily on a cost-of-merchandise basis. Since the cost of merchandise can vary significantly, it is impractical to use a general percentage for all items. Common cost-of-merchandise targets are 30 to 40 percent on food, 17 to 22 percent on bar drinks, and 33 to 50 percent on wines. Therefore, to determine the selling price of a menu item, you must divide the cost of the item by the desired cost percentage. Labor costs for certain items (oysters must be shucked, for example) should also be considered.

It is important to remember that you "can't bank percentages" and that a lower cost-of-merchandise percentage does not always mean higher profits. Exhibit 4, which lists Tuesday and Wednesday covers, foods costs, and revenue, shows how average gross profit per guest can differ substantially from day to day. Even though Tuesday shows the lower food cost percentage, it was the less profitable of the two days.

Menu pricing is also difficult because restaurants face the problem of changing market conditions, including fluctuating wholesale prices for merchandise and alterations in what the competition is offering and charging. Menu prices in

Exhibit 4 Menu Price Analysis

	Tuesday			Wednesday		
Menu Item	Covers	Food Cost	Revenue	Covers	Food Cost	Revenue
Chicken	550	$1,650	$4,950	150	$450	$1,350
Prime Rib	200	$1,200	$2,800	400	$2,400	$5,600
Crab Legs	150	$1,350	$2,700	350	$3,150	$6,300
TOTAL	900	$4,200	$10,450	900	$6,000	$13,250
Food Cost %	$4,200 ÷ $10,450 = 40.2%			$6,000 ÷ $13,250 = 45.3%		
Total Gross Profit	$10,450 – $4,200 = $6,250			$13,250 – $6,000 = $7,250		
Average Profit/Guest	$6,250 ÷ 900 = $6.94			$7,250 ÷ 900 = $8.05		

Basing a menu's pricing upon food cost alone will not ensure the greatest profitability. A 40.2 percent food cost figure on Tuesday is not necessarily more profitable than a 45.3 percent figure on Wednesday. This chart for two separate days illustrates how the average profit per guest can differ substantially. While Tuesday has the lowest food cost percentage, it is also the least profitable.

most establishments must be monitored constantly and adjusted for seasonal and competitive changes.

In addition to cost, the following factors should be considered in order to properly price menu items for hotel restaurants:

1. *Type of operation.* Is the restaurant a coffee shop, a multipurpose dining room, or an elegant supper club? Does the restaurant offer a varied menu or are selections fairly consistent? Offering a consistent menu may keep costs down. If the restaurant caters primarily to guests who stay at the property for an extended period of time, however, a varied menu that could keep extended-stay guests interested in on-property food facilities may be more cost-effective.
2. *Guest perception and demand.* How do guests perceive the restaurant? Do they expect to pay high prices for superior service and menu selections, or do they see the restaurant as a casual dining room and expect to pay low prices?
3. *Competition.* How many restaurants are nearby, and how do their prices, food, service, and atmospheres compare with your own? When a patron has a special occasion for dining out, does he or she have only a few acceptable restaurants to choose from or are there many high-quality restaurants in the vicinity?

Message. Think of your menu as your restaurant's brochure—but remember that customers spend an average of three minutes with a menu, so make the most of that time. Make sure your menu is organized, readable, and conveys the tone of your restaurant. It's message—the written information it contains—is an important part of the menu's appeal. Will your menu simply list the foods and beverages offered, or will it also include the size of the items, the cooking methods, the main ingredients, and methods of service? In addition to describing menu selections, will the menu provide information such as restaurant hours, payment options, special dietary information, and cross-selling messages for other property facilities? A restaurant with historic significance may opt for menus featuring background stories; a "fun" restaurant (a restaurant that features zany decor or that involves guests in sing-alongs, for example) may feature offbeat information.

Menu copy should describe food in an honest and attractive manner. It is important that guests know exactly what they are getting ("served with your choice of soup or salad, vegetable of the day, and dinner roll or garlic toast"). The menu should feature the actual name of the item. "Steak and eggs," for example, is too vague; is it a sirloin steak, a T-bone steak, or a minute steak? Menu descriptions should also include:

- The cooking method ("deep-fried in vegetable oil," "broiled to your specification")
- Other main ingredients (descriptions can be kept brief, but should focus on the freshness and quality of additional ingredients)
- Descriptions of any sauces used ("brown butter sauce," "white clam sauce," etc.)
- Information about unusual presentations ("wrapped in parchment," "stir-fried at your table")
- Health-related information (information about fat, cholesterol, sodium, and calories is especially important to today's health-conscious consumers)

When writing menu copy or checking menu copy written by a menu specialist or advertising agency, it is important that your restaurant's image not be tarnished by the use of sexist language, negative restrictions ("Your credit card welcomed here" is far more diplomatic than "Positively no personal checks"), or poorly designed promotions. One of the most common errors—and a striking example of poor taste—is the lumping together of a senior citizens' menu and a menu for children: "For those under 12 and over 65."

Design. The menu's message is only part of the presentation. An attractive design will enhance the copy and draw guests to featured items and specials. As shown in Exhibit 5, there are many layouts for menus. There are also many styles of menus, from a simple blackboard on the wall to parchment paper tied with a gold cord. The factors previously mentioned (image, price, and message) will play an important role in determining the menu's design. A restaurant with contemporary positioning and an emphasis on fresh foods, for example, may select a menu enhanced by color photography. A family restaurant or a coffee shop that caters to a variety of tastes may prefer using a menu divided into categories: a breakfast section, a light-lunch section, a "hearty-fare" section, a dessert section, a "for-the-youngsters" section, and so on.

Good menus, no matter what the format, share the following design characteristics:

Exhibit 5 Basic Menu Layouts

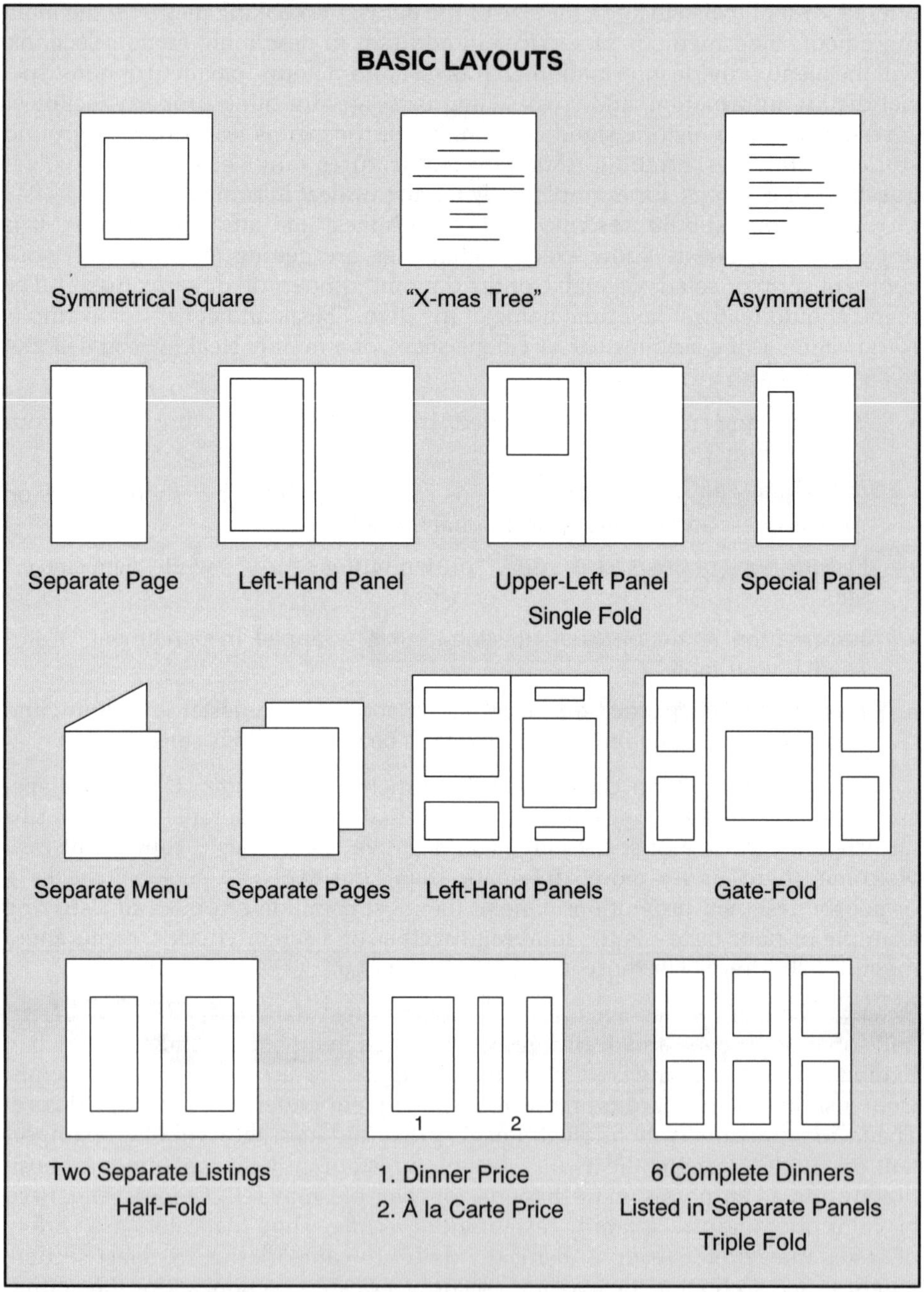

BASIC LAYOUTS

Symmetrical Square

"X-mas Tree"

Asymmetrical

Separate Page

Left-Hand Panel

Upper-Left Panel
Single Fold

Special Panel

Separate Menu

Separate Pages

Left-Hand Panels

Gate-Fold

1

2

Two Separate Listings
Half-Fold

1. Dinner Price
2. À la Carte Price

6 Complete Dinners
Listed in Separate Panels
Triple Fold

Menus can be designed in a variety of styles and layouts. Whatever style or layout is chosen, it should reflect the restaurant's positioning and provide enough room for menu items to be uncluttered and readable.

Exhibit 6 Menus and Eye Movement

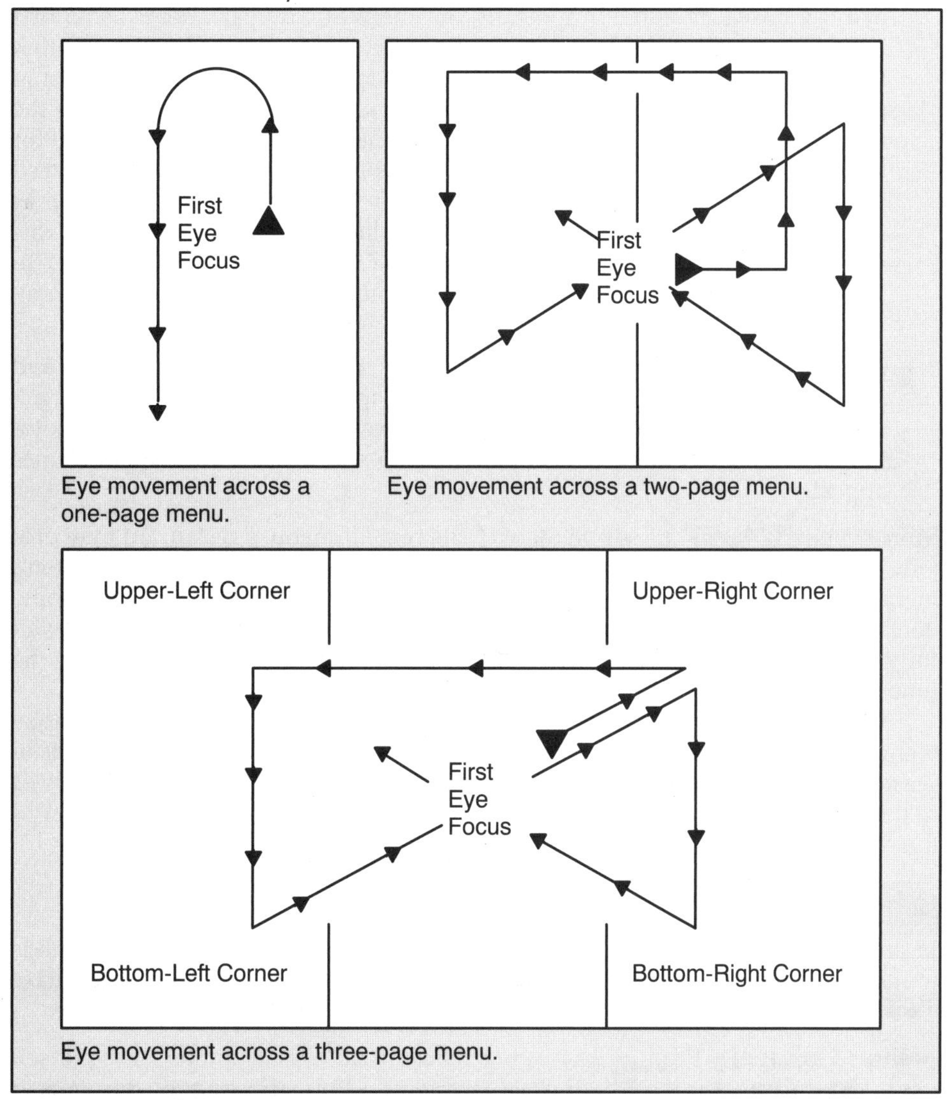

This chart details typical eye movement over various styles of menus. To make the most effective use of menu space, high-profit items should be placed in the locations where they will receive the most notice.

1. *Effective use of space.* The menu must be clean and uncluttered. Wide borders, space between selections, and large type are effective ways to increase the menu's readability.
2. *Effective layout.* As shown in Exhibit 6, your guests' eyes will be attracted to particular areas of the menu, depending on its style. The most popular items,

or those that the restaurant wants to promote, should be placed at the head of a list, boxed, featured graphically, or otherwise set apart. Items listed first in each category sell best (we are psychologically conditioned to assume that the first item on a list is the best), so place items you wish to sell the most in this first position.[6] If a two-page menu is used, the right-hand page gets the most attention; with three-panel menus, the middle panel should be used for special promotions. And last but certainly not least, prices should be placed at the end of each item (this can increase the check average by as much as six percent).[7] Many restaurants mistakenly line up prices on the right; this approach leads many customers to base their menu selections on price. To play down price, use boldface type for the names of entrées, center them on the page, and place prices at the end of the descriptions of items offered.

3. *Eye appeal.* Good menus are attractive. The choice of paper, type style, and artwork is important. The color of ink and paper affects readability. Dark ink on light-colored paper is best, especially if restaurant lighting is dim. Photographs or illustrations can also be added to add interest and enhance sales appeal.

Supplemental Menus. As supplements to its regular menu, a restaurant may provide drink menus and wine lists, children's menus, and dessert menus. Children's menus, such as the one shown in Exhibit 7, are often designed as colorful take-home items, and may feature games or stories to keep children occupied while they wait for the meal. Dessert menus are an effective addition to the regular menu; by the time the meal is over, guests may have forgotten which desserts are available.

Clip-ons are used to avoid expensive reprinting when restaurants supplement the regular menu with daily specials, theme meals, or special menu items in season. If a restaurant plans to use clip-ons, appropriate space should be allotted in the menu's design. Perhaps a blank inside flap or a blank space in the center of the menu can be set aside so the clip-on does not obscure other entrées.

Other F&B Merchandising Methods

In addition to menus, restaurants can use the following merchandising methods to increase sales: product packaging, added-value alternatives, point-of-purchase merchandising, suggestive selling, and special promotional items.

Product Packaging. Product packaging relies on an appeal to the senses to sell items. Product packaging—both table setting and the garnishing of the food or beverage—usually involves producing a special visual impact that can turn something ordinary into a special delight.

Product packaging can begin at the restaurant's entrance—a display of wines, a tempting dessert cart, or an attractive display of fresh produce are all effective sales tools. A display of fresh produce not only whets the appetite but also conveys the message that the restaurant uses only the freshest ingredients. This message can be carried throughout the restaurant through salad bars and table decor.

Product packaging can inspire promotions that generate additional business. Cracker Barrel restaurants, for example, have featured an apple promotion that includes theme posters, recipe brochures, bushel-basket displays of apples, special

Exhibit 7 Sample Children's Menu

The Red Robin chain provides a special children's menu to guests 10 and under (just the cover is shown here). Games and other activities keep kids occupied while waiting for the meal. Children's menus position restaurants as family-friendly. (Courtesy of Red Robin)

menu items such as baked apples and apple bread, and a free apple with each deli soup and sandwich lunch.

Many food and drink items can be made special through product packaging. Colorful garnishes of fresh fruits or vegetables create a feeling of quality and abundance and can make even simple food and beverage items more appetizing and salable. A bowl of dry cereal, for example, becomes a more memorable breakfast when served with a choice of colorful fruits (bowls of bananas, strawberries, raisins, and so on). A simple salad can become a work of art when enhanced with skewers of fresh fruits or vegetables.

Unusual presentations can also be used for eye appeal. A hollowed-out avocado can serve as a unique bowl for homemade guacamole; chicken curry or a special salad can be showcased in a pineapple half; and a fresh, crispy tortilla bowl can hold a taco salad. Drinks, too, whether alcoholic or nonalcoholic, can generate impulse sales when presented in unique ways. An unusual glass; the addition of attractive garnishes, whether as simple as a few grapes placed in a glass of wine or as elaborate as artistically arranged skewered fruit in frosted glasses; and the use of specialty items (tiny umbrellas, unusual stirrers, or even a clay parrot or sombrero attached to a wooden skewer) can generate interest and sales.

Novelty serviceware might also increase food sales. Eggs served in cast-iron skillets, bread warm from the oven and offered on miniature breadboards, and soups brought to the table in small covered kettles are all examples of creative merchandising that sells.

Creativity is equally important in how the food is offered to guests. When every restaurant in town is serving prime rib, for example, why should a guest choose yours? One answer might be your restaurant's unique way of serving the meal. At Lawry's Prime Rib restaurants, ribs are brought to each table on a serving cart; guests choose their cuts and watch them being sliced to order. A food server could prepare a salad at the guest's table instead of the kitchen, spinning the salad while sprinkling dressing over it. In either case, the difference is *entertainment value*. Dining becomes more than satisfying hunger—it becomes an experience to be enjoyed.

Sales can be increased by presenting a spectacular dessert early in the evening. A complimentary dish such as bananas flambé can be presented to one table of guests (the guests can be told they have been chosen to receive the dessert for any number of reasons), and sales of that item are almost guaranteed to increase as other guests are impressed by the flaming presentations. The ways that creative product packaging can be used to boost sales are almost endless.

Added-Value Alternatives. Not all guests are influenced by showmanship, however; there will always be guests who are most interested in getting value for their money. The principle behind added-value alternatives is simple—the guest is given an opportunity to purchase the greatest value among several alternatives. The ways in which to offer greater value are limited only by the imagination of the restaurant manager.

One way to provide value alternatives is to offer various sizes of items, whether the item is a cup of coffee or a steak. Salad items can be sold on different-sized plates; steak can be sold by the ounce to appeal to those with small

Exhibit 8 Sample Point-of-Purchase Display

Some point-of-purchase displays are as elaborate as this six-panel, full-color tent card promoting exotic drinks. Point-of-purchase materials are used to encourage impulse sales. (Courtesy of Flamingo Hilton and Tower, Las Vegas, Nevada)

appetites. When large sizes are offered, it is important to note that although the cost-of-merchandise percentage rises, the contribution margin or profit per guest also rises.

Another option that will appeal to value-conscious guests is offering price alternatives—the choice of full meals or à la carte entrées, for example. Other examples of price alternatives are salad bars priced both with and without a dinner entrée, pie offered with or without ice cream, and drinks offered with or without appetizers. For this method to be effective, guests must see real value—an alternative that appeals to their lifestyle.

Package pricing is another way to provide added-value alternatives. This technique is often used in restaurants, and involves including a number of items in one selection; the price of the items, of course, would be higher if purchased separately. Examples of this type of alternative include offering a glass of wine with dinner; a sandwich served with a choice of soup or salad and beverage; a dinner that includes a choice of salad, vegetables, breads, and dessert; and so on.

Point-of-Purchase Merchandising. Sometimes guests are not influenced by either product packaging or value factors, and must be coaxed into making selections. **Point-of-purchase merchandising** can be used to promote specialty or high-profit items to best advantage. Merchandising at the point of purchase makes extensive use of display advertising such as posters, tent cards on tables (see Exhibit 8), and additional graphic reinforcement such as strategically placed salad bars, displays of wines, and dessert carts.

Some restaurants also use tabletop selling—for example, a bottle of wine labeled with a tag identifying it as the "wine of the month," or complimentary samples of appetizers or entrées that the restaurant is promoting. When using tabletop selling, the restaurant must make it clear whether the item is complimentary or for sale. If a bottle of wine is for purchase only, it must be clearly identified as such and guests must not feel obligated to buy. If a fruit basket contains complimentary fruit and is not on the table strictly for decoration or for sale, a simple banner ("With our compliments") can clear up any confusion and make guests feel more at home.

In order to make the most of point-of-purchase merchandising, one strategy is to divide your restaurant into five zones and use different promotional items in each: *lobby zone* (danglers, easel posters, decals, suggestion boxes); *front counter zone* (register toppers, matches, and brochures); *bar zone* (posters of dramatic drinks, and point-of-purchase opportunities); *dining room zone* (specials boards, danglers, tabletop displays/tent cards, menus, napkins, wine lists, and after-dinner mints); *bathroom zone* (point-of-persuasion opportunities such as music and displayed newspaper ads).[8]

Point-of-purchase merchandising can lead undecided guests into making impulse decisions, but, like a menu, it has a limitation: it is a one-way communications medium. There is still a missing ingredient: people.

Suggestive Selling. Food servers and other restaurant personnel play an important part in merchandising food and beverages. One of their most effective merchandising tools is **suggestive selling.** Suggestive selling can begin from the moment a guest is seated. The food server can suggest a cocktail from the bar or a special appetizer to begin the meal. A group can be offered an appetizer sampler plate, and the food server can suggest several appetizers that can be ordered by various members of the group and shared. Entrées may be suggested or upgraded with a few suggestive-selling phrases. After the meal, the food server can suggest a choice of desserts rather than just asking if anyone would like dessert (the chances of sales success are enhanced with the use of an attractive dessert cart).

Suggestive selling can also be used in a lounge. The bartender or cocktail server can suggest appetizers or specialty drinks: "We have a terrific new tropical drink that I know you'd enjoy. It's made with a blend of fresh pineapple juice and orange juice with our quality rum, and is served in a tall, frosted glass."[9]

Suggestive-selling responsibilities should be part of a food or cocktail server's job description, and wait staff should be trained in the proper use of suggestive selling techniques. Suggestive selling should never be perceived as an attempt to railroad guests into buying items they really don't want, or as an effort to "bump up" a check. Instead, suggestive selling should be viewed as a part of good service, a way to serve the best interests of guests and make their visits more enjoyable.

Since some servers feel uncomfortable with the idea of suggestive selling, Bill Marvin, a noted restaurant consultant and trainer, suggests that they simply make personal recommendations. He advises servers to tell guests what they like, what they think are the best things on the menu. Not only is sharing a personal favorite a lot more personal, but servers are expressing their own ideas and will have a natural enthusiasm and sincerity.

Food servers often use dessert trays to enhance their suggestive-selling presentation.

Management should make sure that food and beverage servers understand the principles behind suggestive selling and which audiences are most receptive to this sales technique. Leisure travelers, for example, may be more receptive to taking their time and trying new dishes than guests having a business lunch.

Special Promotional Items. Some restaurants use special promotional items (see Exhibit 9) such as recipe cards, postcards depicting drinks, and souvenir menus. (If a menu is expensive to produce, a smaller, souvenir version can be designed to take home.) If the restaurant is part of a chain, special promotional items may be available through corporate headquarters. They can also be specially designed by an advertising agency, a free-lance artist, or a menu specialist. If outside sources are used, however, the food and beverage manager should approve the final design and ensure that the copy and design accurately reflect the positioning of the property.

Promotional items, especially tee shirts, have become so popular that a number of restaurants—especially theme restaurants—realize a large percentage of revenue from the sale of souvenirs. Logo items have become so popular that Planet Hollywood, Hooters, and other restaurants have established adjoining stores to sell merchandise. The Cracker Barrel has designed its outlets so that customers must go through the gift shop to get to the restaurant.

Logo items boost revenues and serve as an extension of advertising efforts; guests become "walking billboards" for the restaurant. But some restaurants, such as New York's 21, shy away from the souvenir clothing market. Instead, they may offer such items as signature steak sauces and marinades. Marie Callender's has

Exhibit 9 Special Promotional Items

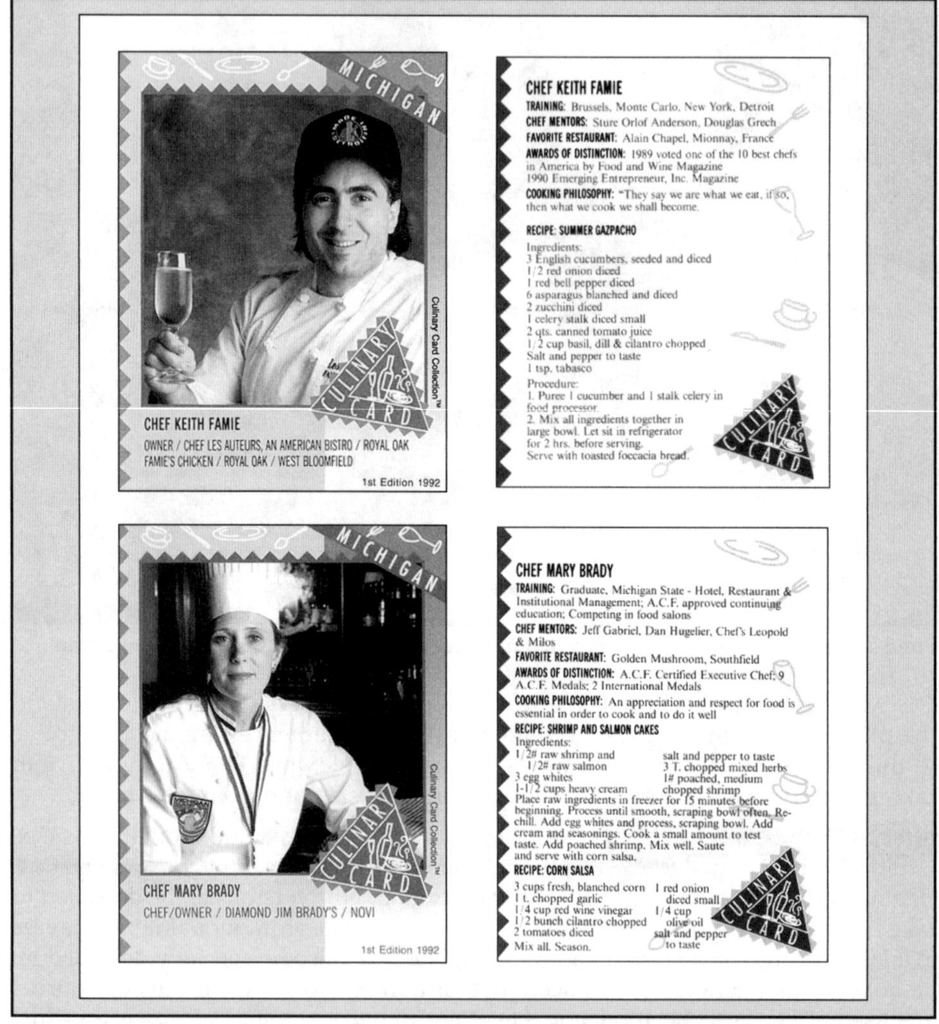

These collectible cards featuring Michigan chefs are the brainchild of Chef Keith Famie and General Manager John Messina of Les Auteurs, a restaurant in Royal Oak, Michigan. The cards generated a lot of publicity for the restaurant, including a mention in *USA Today* and an interview on CNN. "You beat your head against the wall, marketing your restaurant, then do something crazy like this and get all sorts of national attention," says Messina. Plans are in the works to produce a set of cards for chefs in Chicago and New York City as well.

The cards are slightly larger than a baseball card; the front features a color photo of the chef, the back has information about the chef and a favorite recipe. The cards are sold in packs, and ten percent of gross sales go to the nonprofit Rainbow Connection, which fulfills the wishes of terminally ill children. (Courtesy of Chef Keith Famie, Owner, and John Messina, General Manager, of Les Auteurs, Royal Oak, Michigan. CREATORS OF THE CULINARY CARD COLLECTION)

adjoining bakeries that sell thousands of freshly made pies and pastries to dining and nondining customers alike. The chain's bottled salad dressings became so popular that they—and a full line of entrées—are now sold in major grocery stores.

The success of merchandising special promotional items depends on a number of factors. First, the right merchandise must be selected; this means matching merchandise to your clientele. If your restaurant caters to families, for example, you will want to offer low-cost items that appeal to all age groups. If yours is an upscale eatery, you may want to forgo tee shirts and offer specialty gifts, such as engraved logo mugs or golf towels featuring your logo.

Second, you must find a way to differentiate your merchandise from similar merchandise; you must give your guests a reason to spend more for a baseball cap that advertises your establishment than they would pay for one that does not. Some chains, such as Planet Hollywood and the Hard Rock Café, print the locations of their restaurants on logo items, giving guests an opportunity to collect merchandise from around the world. Some restaurants offer dated logo items, making each year's offering a collector's item, while other operations, such as ethnic or specialty restaurants, can capitalize on their uniqueness when designing merchandise.

Third, where the merchandise is displayed can play an important role in sales. Some restaurants choose to use the restaurant's entrance or waiting area, which can be especially effective if there is typically a wait for seating. Others use in-house space, such as countertops, island fixtures, and the cashiering area. Restaurants with extensive merchandise operations often offer two separate entrances; this approach keeps merchandise customers out of the restaurant area.

No matter what approach is used, merchandise should be attractively and creatively displayed. It should be placed at eye level and should be accessible; a display of expensive merchandise in a glass case may draw attention, but customers are more likely to buy merchandise they can touch. Merchandise should be changed periodically, especially if you cater to a base of repeat customers. The change doesn't have to be elaborate or expensive; it can be as simple as changing a color, adding a date, or replacing an item that is not selling well with a potentially more profitable one.

Promoting Restaurants and Lounges

While word-of-mouth referrals lend exceptional credibility to a restaurant, they are usually not enough to properly promote the facility. Even if a restaurant has a popular menu, a good atmosphere, and an excellent staff, it won't be profitable if no one (or only a small group of loyal patrons) knows it's there. The restaurant must be promoted in order to attract guests and make a profit.

Types of Sales Promotions

Sales promotions are useful for generating quick sales increases and can be targeted to times when business is most needed. Promotions can also be used to introduce new products or services, generate excitement and entertainment for both guests and employees, and build repeat business.

There are three basic ways to promote a restaurant: personal promotions, in-house promotions, and outside promotions.

"Four Walls" Sales Promotion

The three major purposes of sales promotions are to increase guest traffic, increase the frequency of guest visits, and increase the average guest check. While there are many ways to accomplish these goals, some of the best opportunities to increase business can be generated within the restaurant's own four walls. Tom Feltenstein, founder of the West Palm Beach, Florida–based Neighborhood Marketing Institute, developed the "four walls" marketing system. His "four pillars" of the four walls marketing system include: (1) your menu, (2) your employees and internal customers, (3) your "zones" (the areas in and around your restaurant), and (4) your data capture (using strategies that build repeat business, including such innovations as an "Insider's E-Mail Club").

Stimulating Lunch Business. Lunch business can be increased by offering "express" lunches (meals guaranteed to be served within 15 minutes or the meal is free) or by offering salad bars (this option not only provides variety, but allows guests to serve themselves).

Stimulating Dinner Business. One of the most effective ways to increase dinner business is by offering "early-bird specials," dinners served at a reduced rate before the regular dinner crowd arrives.

Using Special Promotions. Two other promotions that generate additional traffic are birthday clubs and gift certificates. Birthday clubs usually offer the birthday guest a free item (from a dessert to a complete meal) or a meal at a reduced rate. The honored guest rarely comes alone—he or she will usually bring along at least one other person who will dine at regular prices. Similarly, gift certificates often result in additional sales. In many cases, the recipient will spend more than the gift certificate amount—and will usually not dine alone.

Increasing Guest Visits. Two popular options for increasing guest visits are the use of frequent customer cards and bounce-back coupons. Frequent customer cards usually are printed with a number of boxes that are marked or punched on each visit; when purchase requirements are met, the customer receives a specified item at no charge. Bounce-back coupons, which offer additional discounts at a later time, are a good way to build business during weak periods. If Tuesday dinner business is slow, for example, a weekend guest can be given a coupon good only on Tuesday night. An interesting—and profitable—variation to the bounce-back is the "split meal" offered by hotels in the theater districts of London and New York. Dinner guests are given a dessert coupon to be used following the show, which stimulates additional beverage sales (coffee, tea, liquor, cordials, wines, etc.) later in the evening.

Building Name Recognition. Giving guests something to take home often stimulates repeat sales. Popular items are calendars, pads of paper, pins or buttons, pens, matchbooks, and the business card of the manager.

Source: Tom Feltenstein, "Building from the Inside Out: Tools for Future Growth Already Gathered within Your Four Walls," *Nation's Restaurant News,* July 7, 2003, pp. 34, 61.

Personal Promotions. Personal promotions include sales calls (both telephone and in-person) and sales letters to introduce prospective guests to the restaurant. Restaurant sales calls differ very little from sales calls made for rooms or banquet business. Whether the sales call is made by the restaurant manager or a member of the food service or sales staff, it should follow the basic presentation sales call format: an opening, getting prospect involvement, the presentation, overcoming objections, and closing the sale. Restaurant representatives should thoroughly familiarize themselves with these steps before attempting to make telephone or in-person sales calls.

Sales letters are another important phase of personal promotion, and may be used either as introductory tools or as follow-up tools to supplement telephone or in-person sales calls. Sales letters should be tailored to individual needs—a restaurant manager should not send the same letter to a business group and a bride!

In-House Promotions. In-house promotions range from coupons and contests to drawings and special events. The types of in-house promotions a restaurant engages in depend on the size, type, and staff of the restaurant as well as its typical markets and target markets. Promotions must be consistent with the positioning of the facility and present a good reason for guests to patronize it. Creative promotions not only generate additional business, but also help to build guest goodwill and word-of-mouth referrals. In-house promotions that are cost-effective, build enthusiasm among the staff, and provide a benefit to guests (whether value or excitement) greatly enhance the image of the restaurant as a friendly, comfortable place to eat and be entertained.

Some of the most popular in-house sales promotions include coupons; premiums; sweepstakes, games, and contests; specials or special discounts; special-occasion clubs; gift certificates; sampling; and food festivals and other special events.

Coupons. Coupons are a popular way to offer a discount, introduce new items, or boost sales of a particular item. There are many types of coupons that can be used; Exhibit 10 lists types of coupons commonly used by restaurants. While all of the coupons listed in Exhibit 10 can generate immediate sales, coupons also have disadvantages. Peter Boyle, resident manager of the Feathers Hotel in Woodstock, England, for example, is opposed to coupons that offer two-for-the-price-of-one meals, feeling that these promotions tend to attract people who only take advantage of the offer—they don't buy wine or even coffee with the meal—and don't return until another promotion is offered. Some food outlets have overused coupons, continually discounting the same item and thus leading guests to perceive the coupon price as the true value of the item so that they are reluctant to purchase the item at its regular price. At one time, for example, the major pizza chains distributed coupons nearly every week, leading customers to believe they were not getting a value if they purchased a pizza without a coupon. To avoid this type of perception, Applebee's and some other restaurant chains avoid using coupons altogether; they choose instead to make menu changes to promote value.

To avoid misunderstandings and ill will, coupons should always be specific—the terms of the offer and any restrictions ("not valid on weekends," for example) should be clearly spelled out, and each coupon should include an expiration date. Guest contact employees should always be informed of any coupon offers and redemption procedures.

Exhibit 10 Types of Coupons

Buy-One-Get-One-Free (also known as Two-For-One)
No charge for an item or meal of the same or lesser value with the purchase of the promoted item.

FREE APPETIZER
Value up to $4.75
Choose from a variety of delicious appetizers including:
Clam Chowder
Hot Pops
Fried Cheesesticks
Chicken Wings
Fried Mushrooms
Calamari Rings
Red Lobster.
Authorized Signature

Single- or Multiple-Item Discounts
A discount such as $1 off the purchase of two salad bars or half off one dinner.

Combination Meal at a Discount
A special price for a promoted meal (may include dessert and beverage, appetizers, and so on).

Discounts on Selected Sizes, or a Large Item for the Price of a Smaller Item
Discounts on a medium-size item, a large coffee for the price of a smaller coffee, etc.

Discounts on Specific Purchase Amounts
Can be offered as percentages (20% off all checks over $25) or discounts ($1 off all purchases over $5).

Free Item with Purchase of Another Item
Free cup of coffee with dessert, free salad bar with dinner entrée, and so on.

Time-Fused Coupons
A series of coupons that are good during specific times of a particular promotion; perhaps a different special each week, or a different individual item offered each week during the promotion.

BURGERS
Buy One - Get One FREE
GOOD ALL DAY
THURSDAY, FRIDAY & SATURDAY ONLY!
That's right ! Buy any one of our half pound burgers, and get the second one free. Please present this coupon when ordering.
One Coupon Per Customer.
Sneakers
2250 East Tropicana Ave.
In the Renaissance Center

Bounce-Back Coupons
Coupons that are given for future purchases. These are usually handed to guests when they leave, or they may be included on place mats or affixed to or inserted into "to go" packaging. Like time-fused coupons, bounce-back coupons can be used to stimulate business during otherwise slow periods—bounce backs should be good only on "slow" days or be for specific items that need increased sales. To create a sense of urgency and build sales during otherwise slow periods, bounce-back coupons are often designed to become invalid after a short period of time.

Coupons can be an effective way to introduce new restaurants and products, stimulate sales on slow-moving items, and build repeat business.

Premiums. Premiums are items that are either given away free or sold at cost. The most successful premium promotions involve a series of items given out over multiple purchases—one item at each visit. McDonald's and Burger King have been highly successful with this approach. McDonald's has offered Barbie dolls, Hot Wheels cars, miniature Fisher-Price toys, and toys from a number of Disney movies. Burger King premiums have included popular television characters, CDs by the Backstreet Boys, and characters from the *Lord of the Rings* movie trilogy. One of its most successful premium offerings was 57 different Pokemon figures. These premiums, which were offered at eight per week, led to near riots in some locations when supplies were exhausted. This prompted the chain to set up special family trade nights: on Tuesdays between 5:00–8:00 P.M., kids and their families would get together to trade Pokemon characters to complete their collections.

To be effective over the long term, premiums must reflect the positioning of the restaurant and appeal to the restaurant's target market. An upscale restaurant, for example, would not want to give away cheap toys or novelties; conversely, a budget family restaurant probably would not find it cost-effective to promote a top-of-the-line premium. But the right premium can lead to phenomenal success. Pat O'Brien's in the French Quarter of New Orleans became a major tourist attraction as a result of serving Hurricanes in commemorative glasses; the Raffles Hotel in Singapore, the birthplace of the Singapore Sling, sells thousands of the drinks in souvenir glasses. A number of other restaurants and lounges, such as those in the major Las Vegas hotels, have seen beverage sales skyrocket after offering "signature" glasses and mugs.

Sweepstakes, games, and contests. Sweepstakes, games, and contests are exciting ways to generate interest and build business, and are even more effective if they require multiple visits.

Sweepstakes winners are chosen at random. There are no games to play and no skill is required—guests simply register or fill out an entry form. **Games** are similar to sweepstakes, but utilize game "pieces," such as match-and-win game pieces or scratch cards that reveal the prizes contestants have won. **Contests**, unlike sweepstakes and games, require the entrant to demonstrate some skill in order to win. Exhibit 11, for example, illustrates a promotion in which contestants must correctly guess the exact score of a football game and which team will win.

Specials or special discounts. One of the most popular specials is the "Early-Bird" dinner. Other discount options include offering discounts to seniors, students, and military personnel; offering free meals to children dining with their parents; and featuring discounts on a traditionally slow night (no coupon required).

Special-occasion clubs. Special-occasion clubs require a guest to register information regarding his or her birthday, anniversary, or other special occasion. An invitation, which offers a discounted or free meal or item, is then mailed to the guest in time for his or her special day.

Gift certificates. Gift certificates can be issued in a variety of denominations or for specific meals (free dinner, for example), and they represent prepaid sales. In some cases, certificates are not redeemed, providing pure profit.

Sampling. Sampling—offering samples of new or specialty products—is an excellent way to generate interest and build sales. Free samples give guests

Exhibit 11 Contests as In-House Promotions

Games, contests, and sweepstakes are often used to generate interest and build business. This contest, promoted by Marriott Hotels and Resorts, gives lounge customers the chance to win roundtrip tickets for two on Continental Airlines. (Courtesy of Marriott Hotels and Resorts)

the opportunity to taste new items without having to pay for an entire dish. This type of promotion is especially effective if it includes some form of showmanship. Employees giving out samples of Swiss mocha cheesecake can be costumed in colorful Swiss outfits, for example.

Food festivals and other special events. Theme events, ethnic nights, and other promotions, such as a "Meet-the-Chef" night or a "Chocolate-Fantasy" festival, are excellent ways to generate interest and business. One restaurant staged a "Price Roll-Back" promotion to celebrate its 25th anniversary. Prices were reduced to reflect those on its first menu, and, while the promotion was initially costly, it generated tremendous crowds, and many guests returned after the promotion.

Cost-effective promotional packages can be created by forming partnerships with vendors. During football season, for example, beer vendors that sponsor professional games can supply promotional items such as team flags, banners, and tableware; or a restaurant can arrange a promotion around a particular product—a certain brand of wine, a seafood specialty, and so on. These "piggybacking" efforts not only benefit your customers—and your bottom line—but also help forge stronger relationships with your suppliers.

Restaurants can also create their own special events. For example, The Egg & I, a restaurant in Las Vegas that serves only breakfast and lunch, put together a murder mystery dinner theater for the evenings, when the restaurant would normally be closed. For one price, guests get a three-course meal and participate in the mystery—the "killer" is seated among them. Time is allotted throughout the show and meal for guests to mingle and try to figure out the clues, and the show changes every eight weeks to keep things fresh and patrons coming back.

Planning ahead is the key to successful in-house promotions. Generally, major promotions should not run for more than four to six weeks and should be spaced with minimal intervals of two to three months. Maintaining a promotions calendar can help managers organize their promotions ahead of time, keep major holidays from sneaking up on them, and spark ideas for new promotions. April 29, for example, is celebrated as "Zipper Day" in Dunedin, New Zealand, to commemorate the invention of the zipper in 1913. Prizes are awarded for the most zippers on an outfit, and for telling the most outrageous "my-zipper-was-stuck" stories.

Outside Promotions. Outside promotions fall into two general categories: paid advertising and supplemental promotion. Franchise restaurants usually participate in national advertising campaigns that are supplemented on a local level, while independent operations can plan their own advertising strategies.

Most restaurants, whether they are hotel outlets or freestanding facilities, make extensive use of a number of forms of paid advertising—both print (newspaper, magazine, direct mail, and so on) and broadcast. Paid advertising offers the advantage of controlling the message to the consumer. Exhibit 12 provides examples of the types of creative advertising that can be used to promote a restaurant to both new and repeat guests.

Another creative way to advertise is on the web, where restaurants can be listed in searchable databases. Internet advertising is growing in popularity with restaurant owners because it is relatively inexpensive and offers a variety of advertising options. Restaurants can post testimonials and their menus and hours, offer food and dining tips, promote specials, or even take reservations over the Internet.

In addition to having a presence on the web, restaurants can also take advantage of technology to market to customers via e-mail, which is far less costly than direct mail and is generally well received. E-mail marketing can include newsletters, notification of special offers (sometimes only available to online customers), promotions (such as birthday or other special occasion communications), and surveys that can be completed and returned in a matter of minutes.

Supplemental promotion includes the use of sales materials—discount coupons, fliers, offers of giveaways, and so on—and promotional pieces such as newsletters. A newsletter not only provides information about the restaurant's latest promotions or special offers, it also serves to keep the restaurant's name in front of the public. Since nearly everyone has an interest in food, this type of promotional literature is likely to be kept and referred to a number of times. Newsletters are usually extremely cost-effective in comparison with other print advertising. Having your chef write a weekly column for the food section of your local newspaper or answer food-related questions on a radio talk show increases awareness of your restaurant and enhances your restaurant's image in the eyes of your community.

Although not as common as newsletters (because they are more expensive), magazines are used by some properties as supplemental promotion pieces. Diana Moxon, director of public relations for the London Hilton, created a food magazine

Exhibit 12 Examples of Restaurant Advertising

These ads feature humorous headlines and illustrations to capture the attention of potential guests. Restaurant ads often feature specialty dishes or views of the dining room to offer a preview of the restaurant's fare or ambiance.

as a direct-mail piece for the hotel. She states: "I employ a respected food writer who presents stories informatively, an art director, and a good photographer. The magazine has helped establish the reputation of our Austrian chef in London. He now gets asked to run master classes at exhibitions and gourmet clubs, and I hope this will lead to TV coverage."[10]

Supplemental promotion also includes publicity. Marcia Yudkin, a Boston-based public relations consultant, says that "a lot of people assume you have to do something earthshaking to earn publicity. That's not true. You just have to do something unusual. And it helps to have a human-interest angle."[11] Publicity can play an important part in public awareness of a restaurant, and opportunities to receive free publicity are almost everywhere. Local newspapers may eagerly snap up news of restaurant expansions, special promotions and offers to local patrons, and feature stories about employees or special recipes. One restaurant demonstrated how it baked breads on a local television station; another handed out recipe cards for its signature dish, which generated free press coverage in the food section of the local newspaper.

Building Repeat Business

Repeat business is a significant factor in the success of restaurants. Therefore, it is important to cultivate guest loyalty.

The Importance of Employees

Guests do not buy just a meal or a few drinks; they buy a social experience as well. Social experiences always involve people. Food and beverage employees can help make dining or relaxing over a drink a pleasurable occasion. Well-trained employees dedicated to serving guests can make the difference between a highly successful operation and empty seats. Adrian Stevens, the co-owner of New Jersey Innkeepers, which includes four casual dining restaurants and bars in three New Jersey townships, says, "Our employees are our biggest assets. You can have the best location in the world, the best chef in the world, the best ambiance in the world, but if your server is not courteous, does not respect the guest, then you've ruined it. You can have a great menu, but horrendous service and the guest will walk out unhappy. But if the server is on his game, and knows how to smooth things over, the guest will come back."[12]

One way to build and retain a staff of loyal, conscientious employees is to offer ownership in the operation—either financial or psychological ownership. The option of financial ownership, which is common in other industries, is fairly new in the restaurant business. Starbucks Coffee is a leader in this area; its "Bean Stock" program allows employees to buy company stock at a discount.

At restaurants where financial ownership is not possible (franchise operations, for example), employees can be motivated to provide consistent service when they are treated as integral members of the restaurant's team and made to feel like co-owners of the outlet. In some cases, this means getting to know them and helping them reach their personal and professional potential; in others, it means involving them in planning efforts or empowering them to personally handle specific situations, such as allowing substitutions or adjusting a guest's check when food or service did not meet the guest's expectations.

A good manager will make sure that his or her staff not only serves guests but makes friends of them as well. Managers should start with personable employees who are truly interested in each guest and eager to give guests the three free "gifts" that can make each visit memorable and build guest loyalty: recognition, recommendations, and reassurance.

Recognition. Employee recognition of guests is one of the most effective tools for building guest goodwill and repeat business. Almost everyone likes to hear his or her name and feel valued.

Name recognition should begin as soon as a guest walks into the restaurant. This important part of guest relations can take a number of forms. In some restaurants, guests are greeted personally by the manager. If this is not feasible, a host can make guests feel welcome and introduce them to their food server, or give the food server the names of the guests before he or she waits on them. Food servers should use the guests' names often while greeting and serving them.

Recommendations. Recommendations are another part of the server's job that can help build repeat business. Good recommendations depend on both food and service knowledge. Servers should be fully informed about each item on the menu and should be ready to respond when guests ask for suggestions. Far too many servers are inadequate in this area.

Recommendations can both help the guest and increase the size of the check, so each food server should know the ingredients in each dish, the method of preparation, and the approximate preparation time. In addition, servers should taste-test each menu item so they can knowledgeably answer questions about the dish's flavor, spiciness, consistency, and so on. When a food server can tell a guest what he or she likes best on the menu or what he or she plans to have at the end of a shift, the server projects a natural enthusiasm and sincerity.

For even better results, the restaurant's staff should occasionally eat at the establishments of competitors. If the server has dined at a competitor's restaurant, he or she can honestly tell the patron the difference between the French onion soup offered by the competitor and the French onion soup served in your restaurant.

When food servers have this extensive knowledge, they find it far easier to assist the restaurant's guests in making selections, which helps build guest trust and loyalty.

Reassurance. Reassuring guests means making them feel at home. Food servers can use conversation and personal observation to tailor their service to each guest. A leisure diner, for example, has time to talk to the server and taste-test different foods, linger over a meal that took time to prepare, and enjoy a dessert. A businessperson, on the other hand, may want to place an order immediately and may prefer to order foods that can be prepared quickly. A group of guests engaged in an animated discussion may not want to be disturbed; in this case, the food server should simply take the order and interrupt as seldom as possible.

Food servers should be sensitive to the special needs of certain guests. Diners eating alone, for example, may feel conspicuous, or families dining with small children may feel uncomfortable if the children become restless or cranky. In these cases, the food server can become a public relations ambassador by meeting the unique needs of these guests.

If a lone diner apologetically says, "There's just one today," for example, the host or food server can project a friendly image, be sure that the lone diner is not seated in an out-of-the-way location, and check back to make sure that everything is all right. Some restaurants offer a daily newspaper to guests dining alone, or (as previously mentioned) offer to seat them at a "Friendship Table" or "Networking Table" for company and conversation. Providing these special touches can prove to be enormously profitable for the restaurant. Lone diners who are treated well are more likely to become repeat guests and may bring their friends to the restaurant as well.

In the case of a family dining situation, the food server can be friendly and attentive and can assure the family that the children are welcome. The food server should take the order promptly and, if possible, offer a light complimentary snack to the children to help prevent restlessness. Most children are satisfied when given a cracker, a piece of fresh fruit, or some type of "finger food" to occupy them while they wait for the meal. A little extra personal attention helps keep children (and parents) content.

Food servers can make all guests feel at home by engaging them in conversation, truthfully answering questions, and involving them in the restaurant by sharing "trade secrets" or asking for feedback about the food or service. This usually enhances a guest's restaurant experience and provides an excellent reason for the guest to return to the restaurant.

Guest Follow-Up

One of the easiest and most inexpensive ways to build guest goodwill and loyalty is with a follow-up telephone call. Telephone numbers can be obtained from the reservations book or a guest survey card provided at each table. The call should be brief, but should express the fact that the guest is valued by the restaurant. Asking if everything was satisfactory can give guests an opportunity to express themselves. If the guest has negative feedback, the call can serve as a way for restaurant representatives to handle complaints and obtain information to help serve guests better.

Keeping in touch with past patrons through the mail also helps build repeat business. Personal notes or mailings are an excellent way to provide guest follow-up; notes may be sent after a telephone call or may be used to thank a guest for completing a guest survey. Another way to encourage guests to come back is to print a monthly calendar of events, such as the one shown in Exhibit 13. This type of general mailing can be used to announce special promotions, new menu items, or upcoming events. Some restaurants send out an annual calendar, which often includes discount coupons that can be redeemed each month. This type of thank-you keeps the restaurant's name in front of the patron all year long—and provides an incentive to return.

Customer Loyalty Programs and Other Business-Building Strategies

Like many hotels, many restaurants have established customer loyalty programs to recognize and reward their frequent customers. Some of these restaurant programs, like hotel programs, award points for customer purchases. Participants in T.G.I. Friday's Gold Point Program can redeem their points for gift certificates, stays at Radisson's Country Inns and Suites, and premiums from participating retailers such as Toys "R" Us. Other loyalty programs make use of punch cards, or membership cards that can be swiped at the point of purchase. When a certain number of purchases (or visits) have been punched on the punch card or a certain level has been reached on the computer-supported membership card, the diner typically receives a free product or meal.

Database marketing has made it easier for restaurants to identify and track frequent guests and their preferences. In many cases, guests can even apply for membership in a loyalty program online. Restaurants using punch cards can ask for guest information that can be entered into the database before issuing cards, or

Exhibit 13 Sample Calendar of Events

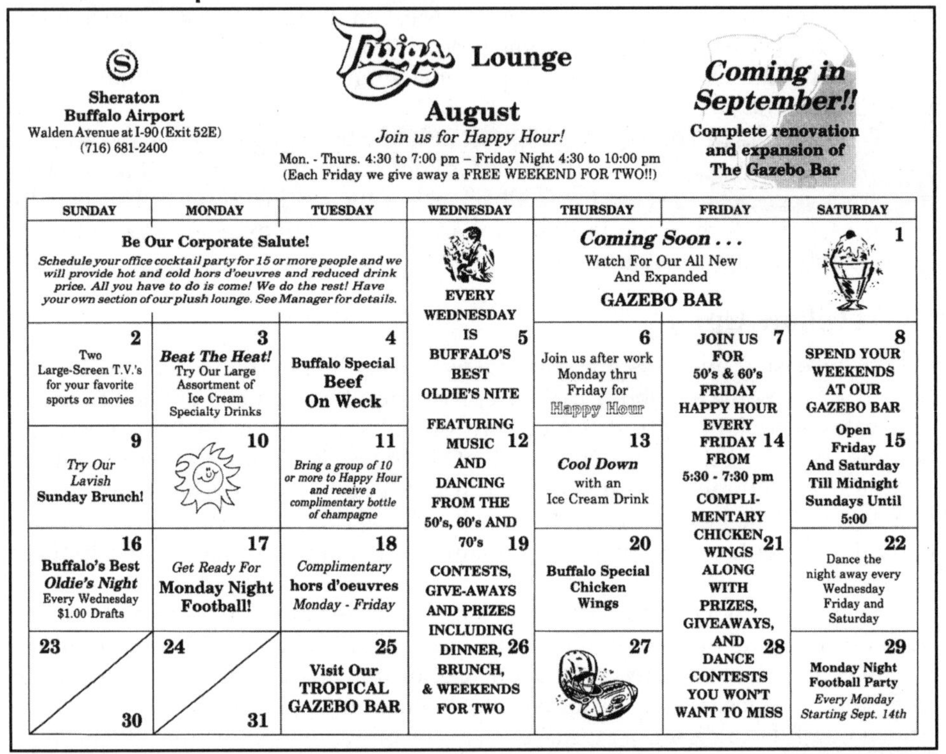

Many restaurants use calendars to promote their special events and menu items. Monthly calendars can be printed in newspapers, distributed to local businesses, or mailed to regular patrons. Yearly calendars are often mailed as a "thank-you" to customers. Annual calendars often include discount coupons good for specific periods of the year. (Courtesy of Sheraton Buffalo Airport Hotel, Buffalo, New York)

have a system in place for monitoring punch card customers. If, for example, it is noted that a punch card customer comes in every Friday evening, the restaurant can be prepared with a special table, service, or amenity.

Most restaurateurs recognize that true customer loyalty goes beyond frequent visits and repeat purchases. The most important type of customer loyalty is an emotional commitment to the restaurant. A patron who has developed strong emotional ties to your establishment is willing not only to return to it but also to recommend it. This type of loyalty must be cultivated through relationship marketing.

Recognition is often the most important aspect for building customer loyalty. Repeat guests should always be greeted by name whenever possible and their needs anticipated. Regulars at Deleece in Chicago, for example, find their favorite cocktail waiting for them when they arrive. Recognizing birthdays and other special occasions is also important, whether the restaurant simply sends a card or rewards the celebrant with a special amenity. The upscale Palm chain, for example, rewards loyal customers with a complimentary three-pound lobster dinner

Exhibit 14 Hotels with Room Service, by Segment Type

Luxury	Upscale	Mid-Priced	Economy	Budget
66%	56%	29%	9%	6%

Source: RealTime Reports and the American Hotel & Lodging Association.

on their birthdays. A number of restaurants also offer free meals on customers' birthdays. Free birthday cakes are also common.

Other ways to create a memorable experience for your loyal guests include hosting special events for them. Lettuce Entertain You, for example, gives loyal patrons dinners with guest winemakers and chefs. At other restaurants, the chef may make a personal visit to the table of frequent guests to thank them for their patronage. Sometimes display items are used to recognize frequent visitors—lounges may display mugs engraved with the names of patrons, while restaurants may name a dish after a patron who has suggested the item or often orders it. Some establishments take photographs of regular customers and display them in prominent places, resulting in additional business as the "honored guests" bring family and friends to view the photos.

Other Food Service Operations

Hotels offer more food and beverage options and outlets than just restaurants, coffee shops, and lounges. While room service has long been a staple at many properties, a growing number of hotels are making changes in room service operations and are looking to a number of limited-service options for providing food and beverage service to guests.

Room Service

Many properties offer room service for the convenience of their guests (see Exhibit 14). Many managers consider room service a costly amenity because of the long and odd hours of operation and the impossibility of predicting the volume of business. Labor shortages and soaring overhead costs have also had a negative impact on room service operations. In terms of labor, for example, additional staff is required, including preparation cooks, stewards, order-takers, and delivery personnel, who must be willing to work the often inconvenient hours associated with room service operations. In addition, room service operations cannot take advantage of quantity cooking; meals must be prepared to order, which means a greater per-meal cost.

Nevertheless, many managers feel that room service is a key to keeping guests over the long term. Luxury hotels that cater to business travelers, convention groups, and the upscale leisure market generally feel it is necessary to offer 24-hour room service, but an increasing number are limiting menu items to food that will retain its quality from the kitchen to the guestroom. If managers consider room service essential to guest service, they should come up with action plans to increase room service profitability and maximize effectiveness.

Some hotels have found it more profitable to offer alternatives to traditional room service. They may opt for specialty kitchens that offer a single item, such as pizza, fried chicken, burgers, or sandwiches. They may also focus on a single meal, such as breakfast. Other properties feature delis where guests can pick up their favorite foods and prepare them in their rooms. There are a number of limited-service operations in hotels today that have dramatically changed the nature of room service.

Limited-Service Operations

Hotels are finding that many guests, especially business travelers, are looking for cheaper alternatives to full-service hotels and choose properties that offer fewer services and amenities. Most of these guests eat lunch outside the hotel (they are usually out calling on customers) and spend evenings either at a freestanding restaurant or in their guestrooms with pizza or other takeout. However, hotel guests usually want to eat breakfast at the property. More properties are catering to this need by including free breakfasts and offering other options, such as coffee carts, in-room minibars, and kitchenettes stocked with microwavable items, instead of offering full-service restaurants and room service.

Many hotels now offer breakfast to their guests at no (or a nominal) cost (see Exhibit 15). Some chains, such as Baymont Inns & Suites, Comfort Inns, Fairfield Inns, Hampton Inns, and Holiday Inn Express, offer free continental breakfasts either delivered to the room or served in a public area. Other properties, including Embassy Suites, Hilton Suites, and Quality Suites, serve complimentary cooked-to-order breakfasts.

Hotels have found that guests, especially business travelers, seniors, and families, are enthusiastic about the free-breakfast concept, both in terms of price and convenience, and many properties are featuring this option. When complimentary breakfasts are offered, the guest saves money and time and receives an added value for the price of the room; the hotel can save money by providing meals or other food service without the overhead of a full-service restaurant; and free breakfasts enable mid-priced and budget properties to better compete with upscale properties that offer more amenities.

Exhibit 15 Hotels with Complimentary Breakfast, by Segment Type

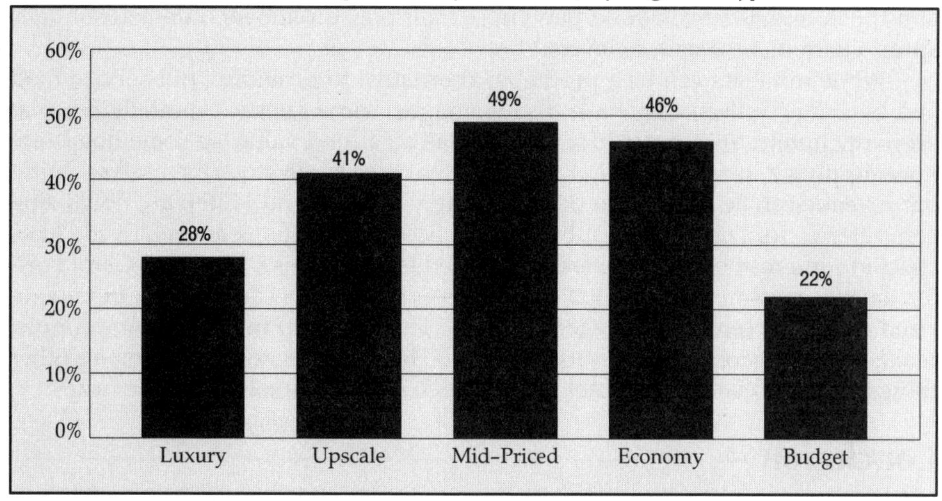

According to a 2007 survey by Ypartnership, 53 percent of business travelers and almost half of leisure travelers expect a free breakfast to be included with their room rate. Hampton Inns was the first major chain to introduce and popularize the free breakfast, which is now offered by hotels in every segment. Sources: RealTime Reports and the American Hotel & Lodging Association, "Survey Shows Travelers' Eating Habits, Preferences," from www.meetingsindustrymegasite.com, posted May 16, 2007; and David Wilkening, "What's for Breakfast?" www.hotelinteractive.com, posted September 24, 2007.

On the downside, the property may have to raise room rates to cover food expenses, additional workers may be needed to run breakfast bars or delivery services, and extra costs may be incurred for cleanup. But overall, properties are finding that the benefits of serving "free" breakfasts far outweigh the disadvantages, especially in terms of generating guest relationships. At Hampton Inns, for example, breakfast is served in a living-room environment that brings guests together as "one big family." Mark Wells, vice president of marketing for Hampton Inns, states that guests at Hampton Inns get a high-quality breakfast and build friendships with the people staying at the chain and the staff members serving the breakfast. This strategy builds a camaraderie that creates the potential for repeat business.[13]

Another option for serving guests who are in a hurry is the *coffee cart.* These carts can offer a wide array of products (coffee, tea, gourmet and specialty coffees, bagels, muffins, juices, etc.) and can be placed in high-traffic locations such as lobbies, pedestrian skywalks, and meeting room areas. In addition to breakfast items, carts (and kiosks) can offer anything from yogurt to pizza. In many cases, properties contract with outside vendors, such as Dunkin' Donuts or Pizza Hut, to provide this type of food service.

Yet another way to bring food and drink to the guest is with in-room *minibars,* which are most often stocked with bottled water, soft drinks, juices, alcoholic beverages, snack foods, and candy. (Some hotels have also begun stocking minibars with sundry items guests might need. The Ritz-Carlton Atlanta, for example, sold thousands of pairs of men's black socks after it began including them in minibars, and the hotel has since added pantyhose, nail polish remover, non-aerosol hairspray, vitamins, and pain relievers.)

While minibars can be a profitable alternative to providing full-service food and beverage outlets, they have disadvantages. Some guests, especially those at economy hotels, do not perceive minibars as an added value, so some hotels are now supplying in-room mini-refrigerators that guests can stock themselves. Minibar revenue can be lost due to theft, although Marriott and Hilton are now using computer-controlled units that bill guests' accounts as items are removed. Also, checking and restocking minibars is an added labor expense. However, Carol Poister, a spokesperson for Swissotel, maintains that minibars can certainly be categorized as a profit center if managed properly. The Swissotel in Boston, for example, realizes a 37-percent profit on its minibars. They are stocked with (among other things) the hotel's own Swissotel water, which accounts for 10 percent of sales.

Conclusion

Today's food and beverage industry is constantly evolving, and food service professionals must stay abreast of trends that affect the way they market their restaurants and lounges. In this chapter, we've looked at a number of these trends. We've also learned the importance of research, and how to best position a restaurant to capture the most desirable marketing mix. We've discussed the factors that must be considered when creating a restaurant menu. We've detailed methods for merchandising food and beverage products, and looked at various types of sales promotions managers use to attract customers and build repeat business. By following these guidelines—and using them as a starting point for your own creative strategies—you can successfully market your restaurant or lounge to attract and keep patrons in today's competitive marketplace.

Endnotes

1. Barry Cohen, "The 'WOW' Effect," *Cornell Hotel and Restaurant Administration Quarterly,* April 1997, p. 75.
2. Mike Feldott, "Trends," *Lodging,* April 1998, p. 109.
3. Judy Liberson, "A Working Marriage," *Lodging,* February 1996, p. 64.
4. Paul Clarke, *Lessons in Excellence from Charlie Trotter* (Berkeley, Calif.: Ten Speed Press, 1999), pp. 214–215.
5. Sheryl E. Kimes and Jochen Wirtz, "Perceived Fairness of Demand-Based Pricing for Restaurants," *Cornell Hotel and Restaurant Administration Quarterly,* February 2002, p. 31.
6. Tom Feltenstein, *Foodservice Marketing for the 90s* (New York: John Wiley & Sons, Inc., 1992), p. 63.
7. Herme Shore, "Money-Making Menus," *Restaurant Business,* 1 May 1990.
8. Tom Feltenstein, "Profit from In-House Marketing," *Restaurant Hospitality,* September 2000, p. 48.

9. Serving alcoholic beverages properly is the subject of the videotape and workshop *CARE for Servers* (Lansing, Mich.: American Hotel & Lodging Educational Institute).
10. *World Hospitality,* April 2000, p. 8.
11. Phillip Perry, "Put Your Restaurant's Name in Headlines," *Restaurants USA,* November 1998, p. 12.
12. Dina Berta, "Promoting Inside Your Own 4 Walls: Image Is Everything," *Nation's Restaurant News,* May 19, 2003, p. 166.
13. Edward C. Achorn, "Food Fight: The Free Breakfast War," *Lodging,* December 1990.

Key Terms

capture rate—The percentage of hotel guests who eat meals at the hotel.

contests—Marketing promotions that require entrants to demonstrate knowledge or some skill.

coupons—Vouchers that entitle users to a discounted or free product/service; frequently used to attract first-time buyers or to introduce a product.

covers—Food service term denoting the number of meals sold. For example, 150 dinners sold equals 150 covers.

games—Marketing promotions that involve the use of game cards; chances of winning are often associated with additional purchases.

neighborhood marketing—Marketing aimed at a geographic area in close proximity to a restaurant—within a three- to five-mile radius, or a ten-minute drive, for example. This area, sometimes called the "trading" or "catchment" area, represents the most fertile ground for attracting loyal guests, as research has shown that 70 percent of a typical restaurant's clientele originates within a ten-minute drive time.

point-of-purchase marketing—Promotion that is done at the point of customer purchase, such as at the cash register or the front desk. The display of promotional materials at these points can stimulate impulse buying.

premiums—Marketing items, such as toys or apparel, given away free or sold at cost; usually given away with the purchase of a product.

sales promotion—Short-term incentives (other than advertising or public relations) aimed directly at stimulating sales of specific products at a specific time.

sampling—Free samples of a product given away to encourage customers to purchase the product.

suggestive selling—A sales technique in which employees suggest or recommend additional or higher-priced items or services. Also known as upselling.

sweepstakes—Marketing promotions based on chance that require entrants to submit their names and addresses.

table turnover—The number of times a table at a restaurant is used to serve new customers during a meal period or some other time period.

trading area—The neighborhood from which all, or at least the majority, of a restaurant's customers come. Also known as the catchment area.

Review Questions

1. What are some of the trends affecting the restaurant industry today?
2. What problems are unique to hotel restaurants and how can these be addressed to ensure greater success?
3. What areas must be researched before positioning a restaurant?
4. What factors must be considered when creating a restaurant menu? How does the design of a menu influence food sales?
5. What methods are used to merchandise food and beverage products?
6. How can restaurants and lounges be promoted? Under what circumstances is each method most effective?
7. What strategies can be used by restaurant and lounge employees to build sales and repeat business?
8. What are some of the methods of guest follow-up commonly used to build repeat business?
9. How have room service operations changed? What new options are hotels using to make room service more cost-effective?
10. What types of limited-service operations are being used by hotels as alternatives to traditional dining and room service?

Internet Sites

For more information, visit the following Internet sites. Remember that Internet addresses can change without notice. If the site is no longer there, you can use a search engine to look for additional sites.

American Culinary Federation
www.acfchefs.org

American Hotel & Lodging Educational Institute
www.ei-ahla.org

American Institute of Wine and Food
www.aiwf.org

Applebee's Neighborhood Grill & Bar
www.applebees.com

Benihana
www.benihana.com

Burger King
www.burgerking.com

Chili's Grill & Bar
www.chilis.com

Cracker Barrel Old Country Store
www.crackerbarrel.com

Cuisine.com
www.cuisine.com

DineSite.com
www.dinesite.com

Food Institute
www.foodinstitute.com

Going Greener
www.greenrestaurants.org

Green My Cuisine
www.greenmycuisine.com

Green Restaurant Association
www.dinegreen.com

Hard Rock Café
www.hardrock.com

International Hotel & Restaurant Association
www.ih-ra.com

KFC
www.kfc.com

McDonald's
www.mcdonalds.com

National Restaurant Association
www.restaurant.org

Nation's Restaurant News Online
www.nrn.com

Olive Garden
www.olivegarden.com

Outback Steakhouse
www.outbacksteakhouse.com

Pizza Hut
www.pizzahut.com

Rainforest Café
www.rainforestcafe.com

Red Lobster Restaurants
www.redlobster.com

Restaurant Hospitality
www.restaurant-hospitality.com

Restaurants & Institutions
www.rimag.com

Romano's Macaroni Grill
www.macaronigrill.com

Ruth's Chris Steak House
www.ruthschris.com

Society for Foodservice Management
www.sfm-online.org

Spaghetti Warehouse
www.meatballs.com

Steak and Ale
www.steakale.com

Taco Bell
www.tacobell.com

T.G.I. Friday's
www.tgifridays.com

Walt Disney Company
www.disney.com

Wendy's
www.wendys.com

Chapter 14 Outline

Competencies

1. Identify the duties and responsibilities of positions typically found in a hotel catering department, and describe the department's marketing plan development. (pp. 539–549)
2. Describe catering promotions and summarize how salespeople develop leads and follow up inquiries in building business for the catering department. (pp. 549–554)
3. Describe sales strategies and procedures for selling to catering clients, explain how catering functions are planned and managed, and identify ways the catering department can follow up accounts. (pp. 555–567)
4. Explain how food and beverage functions other than banquets can increase catering department revenues. (pp. 567–575)
5. Summarize issues involved in meeting room sales, including types of meeting rooms, meeting room setups, how meeting rooms are booked, and how meetings are managed. (pp. 575–580)

Insider Insights

Gus Moser, Director of Catering
Las Vegas Hilton
Las Vegas, Nevada

"A catering career is diverse, with clients booking everything from early-morning breakfasts and sales meetings to late-evening receptions. And there's the ever-increasing market for special events, which range from boxing matches to concerts. A catering director must be able to adjust to different clients from appointment to appointment—switch from the hard-driving sell required for a meeting planner or a training director, for example, to the gentler approach necessary for a nervous bride-to-be. The client that genuinely trusts the catering director and his or her staff will generate much-needed repeat business."

14

Marketing Catered Events and Meeting Rooms

AT LARGE PROPERTIES, the primary profit center is guestrooms, with the catering department the second-most-profitable operation. The catering department of a hotel can produce additional, often high, revenues and generate positive guest relations through well-run banquets and other functions.

A hotel with a strong catering program can generate positive word-of-mouth referrals throughout the community, and a properly catered event is a marketing opportunity that can lead to a significant amount of new business. A wedding reception for 200 guests, for example, represents 200 future customers; if just ten percent of them booked a similar function, the effect on food and beverage revenues would be substantial.

Successful banquets can contribute greatly to the overall profitability of the hotel. Banquets are the most profitable area of a hotel's food and beverage operation, accounting for as much as 60 percent of a hotel's annual food and beverage revenue. The profit margin on sales for banquets often reaches 35 percent, as opposed to 15 percent for hotel restaurants. There are several reasons for this difference:

1. Banquet sales volume often exceeds restaurant volume at a large hotel—in some cases by a margin of two to one.
2. Banquets allow flexibility in pricing. Prime rib priced at $28 on the restaurant menu may bring $42 at a banquet. (Part of this increase is due to the cost of erecting and tearing down the banquet setup.)
3. Food costs are lower due to volume preparation. Since you know how many people you will serve and what they will eat, you can predetermine a price to avoid losing money on a catered event. Also, no large inventory is needed for a banquet kitchen to function, since ordering can be done as needed.
4. Beverage costs can be controlled through pricing flexibility and volume purchasing.
5. Labor costs are lower. Since banquet servers can be supplemented by part-time employees on an as-needed basis, the regular banquet serving staff can be kept small. The cost of restaurant employees, in contrast, is largely fixed; restaurants must maintain a regular staff even during slow periods.
6. Additional income can be generated through ancillary sources, such as photographers, entertainers, florists, and printers. Many hotels work with preferred suppliers who pay a commission to the hotel for business generated from functions.

In this chapter, we will take a look at the dynamics of a successful catering operation—its staffing, responsibilities, and role in relation to overall hotel sales—and learn how catering and meeting-room business contributes to a property's overall image and profitability. The chapter is divided into two parts. The first part will focus on the catering department. This department provides services for banquets, parties, and other business or social functions involving food and beverages. The second part will discuss the sale of meeting rooms, which, unlike banquet business, is most often handled directly by the hotel's marketing and sales office.

The Catering Department

Most catering departments have two basic responsibilities: (1) to sell food and beverage functions to businesses and individuals in the local community, and (2) to service in-house convention and group functions sold by the property's marketing and sales office.

To plan and manage functions, catering department personnel must possess extensive knowledge of sales, service, the use of facilities and function space, food production, menu planning, and cost control. Selling food and beverages involves different strategies than selling rooms.

The size and organizational structure of the catering department depend on the size of the property and amount of function space available, the types of catering to be handled, the property's business mix, local and regional competition, and departmental budgets. Exhibit 1 details the structure of typical catering departments at both a small hotel (200 rooms or less) and a large convention hotel.

At most large properties, the catering department and catering sales are arms of the food and beverage department, while at smaller properties catering sales are often handled by a salesperson in the marketing and sales office. For example, Deanna Davis, director of sales for The Inns of Iowa, is in charge of both booking and planning catering events at the hotel. Davis' day includes such activities as answering the phone and responding to voice and e-mail messages, booking event information, negotiating contracts, and problem-solving for clients, which entails such diverse responsibilities as making changes to room layouts or contracts and being present at the start of a scheduled event (and being available throughout the event, should a problem arise). Although her clients know her as the "go-to" person at the property, Davis works with five other departments to ensure that catering events are properly planned and executed.[1]

Catering Department Personnel

At large properties, catering is usually headed by a director of catering who supervises a banquet or catering manager, catering salespeople, clerical staff, and service personnel (food servers, buspersons, and so on).

As seen in Exhibit 2, the *catering director's* primary responsibilities are the sales and administrative aspects of the catering operation. As the hospitality industry becomes increasingly competitive, the catering director's sales responsibilities become more crucial; today's catering director may give a great deal of attention to soliciting or servicing accounts. The catering director is also responsible for the

Exhibit 1 Sample Organization Charts for Catering Departments

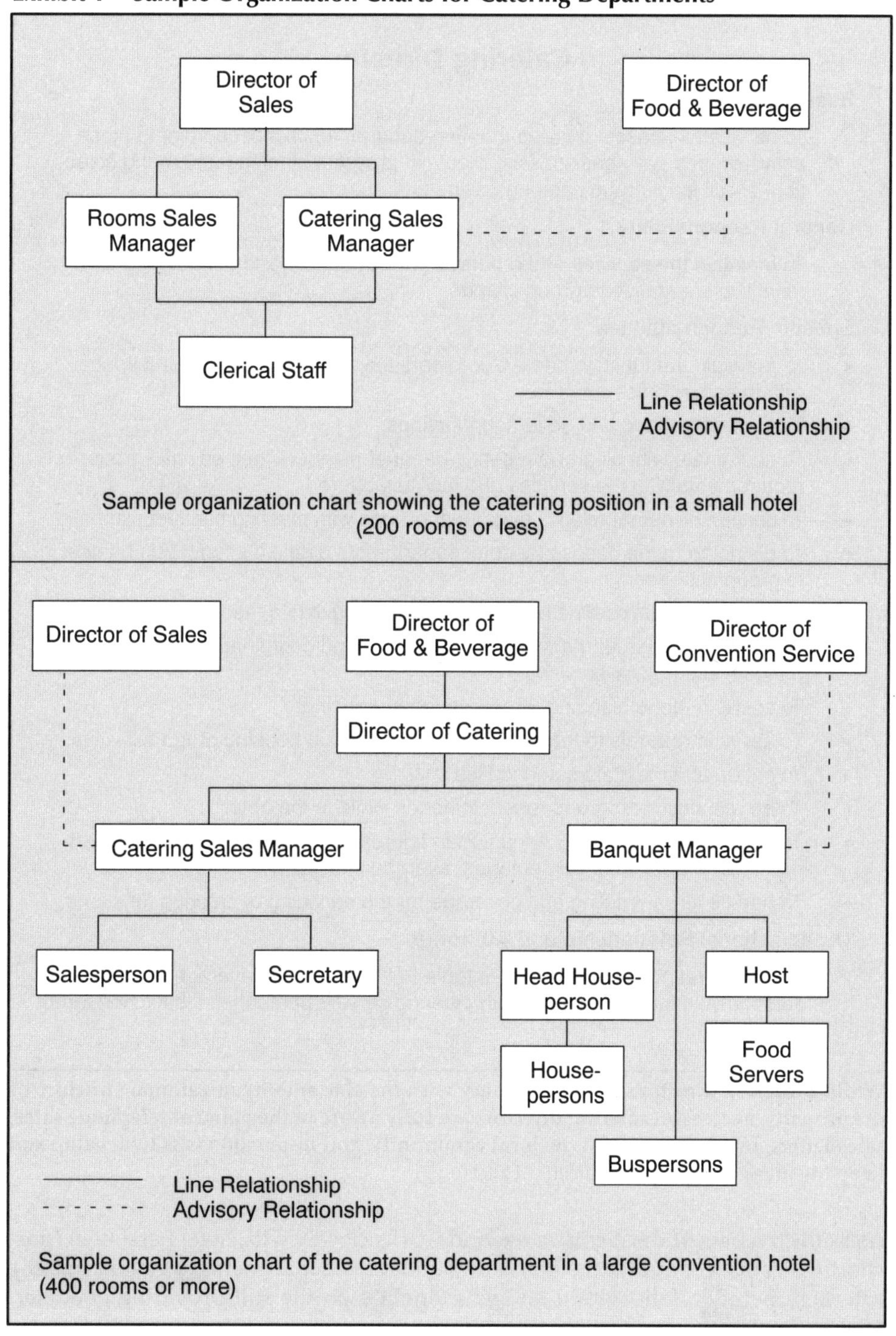

Exhibit 2 Sample Job Description for a Catering Director

Catering Director

Basic Function

To service all phases of group meeting/banquet functions; coordinate these activities on a daily basis; assist clients in program planning and menu selection; solicit local group catering business.

General Responsibility

To maintain the services and reputation of Doubletree and act as a management representative to group clients.

Specific Responsibilities

- To maintain the function book. Coordinate the booking of all meeting space with the sales office.
- To solicit local food and beverage functions.
- To coordinate with all group meeting/banquet planners their specific group requirements with the services and facilities offered.
- To confirm all details relative to group functions with meeting/banquet planners.
- To distribute to the necessary hotel departments detailed information relative to group activities.
- To supervise and coordinate all phases of catering, hiring, and training programs.
- To assist the banquet manager in supervising and coordinating meeting/banquet setups and service.
- To assist in menu planning, preparation, and pricing.
- To assist in referrals to the sales department and in booking group activities.
- To set up and maintain catering files.
- To be responsive to group requests/needs while in the hotel.
- To work toward achieving Annual Plan figures relating to the catering department (revenues, labor percentages, average checks, covers, etc.).
- To handle all scheduling and coverage for the servicing of catering functions.

Organizational Relationship and Authority

Is directly responsible and accountable to the food and beverage manager. Responsible for coordination with catering service personnel, the kitchen, and accounting.

While a catering director's duties may vary with the size and organizational structure of the property, successful catering directors are fully aware of the value of telephone sales, sales letters, involvement with the local community, and in-person visits to develop and keep business. (Courtesy of Doubletree Hotels)

cost-effectiveness of the department, and works closely with hotel personnel (purchasing agents, chefs, and the marketing and sales department) to ensure that the catering operation falls within budget guidelines while still providing good service to clients.

The *banquet* or *catering manager* is responsible for overseeing food and beverage functions and supervising service personnel, and may be directly involved in setting up function rooms. At large convention hotels, however, setup duties are often handled by a convention service manager, whose job is to manage the logistics of functions: the room preparation, setup, maintenance, and so on. Banquet managers also schedule personnel, prepare payrolls, and work with the catering director on special functions.

Catering salespeople are often employed by large properties to actively solicit business not brought in as part of conventions or meetings, such as weddings, Rotary luncheons, and similar food functions. These salespeople should also be available to follow up on written, telephone, and walk-in inquiries. Catering salespeople must know the proper procedures to follow to develop leads, process paperwork for an account, and follow up the account after a function. Knowledge of what type of business to book and when is also important. For example, catering salespeople should avoid booking a social function such as a bridge tournament luncheon in the ballroom on a weekday. Such a booking could prevent booking a four-day corporate meeting with rooms business and breakfast, lunch, and dinner business each of the four days.

The catering department may employ a *clerical staff* to maintain the paperwork generated by business solicitation, handle routine inquiries, and follow up on accounts. In large properties, a catering secretary may assist the catering director with administrative duties or manage the catering office.

Service personnel serve food and beverages, set up function rooms, and maintain banquet areas and equipment. Service personnel include hosts, food servers, buspersons, and maintenance or setup crews.

All of the employees just mentioned are involved in sales, whether they are actually selling banquets, servicing existing accounts, or simply projecting a friendly and hospitable image as they serve guests. Members of the catering department should see themselves and the department as important parts of the property's overall marketing and sales effort. This sales orientation is extremely important, since banquet sales at some properties represent 50 to 60 percent of the total revenue generated by the food and beverage department. Starwood Hotels, for example, realizes more than 50 percent of its food and beverage revenue from banquets and catering operations.

Deborah Libster, marketing director of the Holiday Inn Crowne Plaza in Tampa, Florida, said the catering potential at her hotel was not being exploited to its full potential when she first joined the property's staff: "People would go 15 miles away to downtown [Tampa] instead of here in their own backyard....We knew we had all the components, but we had to change [potential customers'] habits. We just ask them for one chance." After the staff was trained to go after business, food and beverage revenues increased 40 percent over the previous year![2]

The Marketing Plan

The catering department's marketing plan development should closely follow the five steps of the development of the property's overall marketing plan:

- Analyze your property and the competition—conduct a marketing audit

INTERNET EXERCISE

Log onto the Internet and, using the search engine of your choice, search for "catering sales positions." Review three sites that have posted job openings for catering personnel. Review job qualifications, responsibilities, and salary offered. What level of education is required for these positions?

- Identify key catering markets—select target markets
- Position your department—emphasize the differences between you and your competition
- Set goals—set objectives for your operation, and develop action plans to enable you to meet your objectives (your action plans should include defining the roles of staff members)
- Evaluate results—monitor and evaluate the results of your marketing efforts

Analyze Your Property and the Competition. An analysis of the competition is needed to determine the catering department's strengths and weaknesses in relation to competitors. Factors to consider include the location of each competitor, the size of the function space available, the aesthetic quality of function rooms, the availability of equipment such as audiovisual equipment and portable dance floors, and the competitor's reputation. In addition, you should compare menus, specialties, prices, and types of service available. The use of a banquet competition and pricing comparison sheet (such as the one shown in Exhibit 3) can make comparison easier and provide invaluable information for positioning the property's facilities.

While hotels, which can offer many services and have sufficient space to service events, generally have an advantage in the catering field, it is important for hotel catering managers to remember that there is nonhotel competition as well. Independent banquet and conference facilities, restaurant and banquet facilities, and mobile caterers should also be considered when analyzing the competition.

Identify Key Catering Markets and Position the Department. Once the department's strengths have been determined and weaknesses corrected, key catering markets must be identified. There are three types of local business that can prove profitable: business from local corporate sources, business from civic and academic sources, and social business. Local corporate business might include sales meetings, conventions, breakfasts or dinners with lectures, and other meetings requiring the use of food and beverage service. Civic and academic business can include fundraising banquets, conventions, annual parties, and special-project events such as a hotel-based telethon or beauty pageant for such groups as the Jaycees. Social business includes weddings, parties, family reunions, and similar events. Exhibit 4 lists sources, contacts, and types of events for each of these types of local business.

Exhibit 3 Sample Banquet Competition and Pricing Comparison Sheet

Prepared by ______________ Date______________

BANQUET COMPETITION AND PRICING COMPARISON

HOTEL NAME	YOUR HOTEL HERE	HOTEL A	HOTEL B	HOTEL C	HOTEL D
LOCATION Address & Phone Number	(xxx) xxx-xxxx	(xxx) xxx-xxxx	(xxx) xxx-xxxx	(xxx) xxx-xxxx	(xxx) xxx-xxxx
BANQUET SPACE	**# of Rooms/sq ft**	**# of Rooms/sq ft**	**# of Rooms/sq ft**	**# of Rooms/sq ft**	**# of Rooms/sq ft**
Ballroom	1-7,050	1-5,500	1-4,000	1-15,000 1-4,578	1-2,178 1-3,608
Board Rooms	3-608		11-350 each	5	1-276
Meeting Rooms	2-304		2-1,200 each	6	10-5,779
Prefunction	1-1,218			1-3,044	
Other			a lot of pre-function space!	Theater	
MEAL PRICING	**B L D**	**B L D**	**B L D**	**B L D**	**B L D**
Lowest pkg	7.50 7.95 13.50	5.59 6.95 11.75	5.50 7.50 13.50	7.25 8.25 12.75	5.95 7.25 9.95
Highest pkg	11.50 12.75 22.00	8.95 9.95 16.00	8.50 12.95 25.00	13.50 14.25 23.75	8.95 10.95 18.95
Est Avg Ck	9.50 10.35 17.75	7.45 8.45 13.88	7.00 10.23 19.25	10.25 11.25 18.25	7.45 9.10 14.45
BEVERAGE	**HOST CASH**	**HOST CASH**	**HOST CASH**	**HOST CASH**	**HOST CASH**
House Brands	2.25 2.50	2.00	2.25 2.00	2.25 2.50	Bottle only 2.00
Call Brands	2.50 2.75	2.25	2.50 2.25		$48-$60 2.50
Premium Brands	2.75 3.00	Bottle avail.		2.50 2.75	per bottle
Beer/Wine	1.75 2.00	1.50/1.75	1.75 1.75	1.75 beer 2.25 beer 13.50 bottle 2.75 wine	1.75
PERCEIVED POSITIONING	Highly social, Corporate rooms	Corporate 16% gratuity	Corporate 16% gratuity	group/convention some social	corporate/airport
PERSON CONTACTED AND TITLE		Linda Smith DOS	Don Marcos DOS	Mary Giesling SALES MANAGER	Ed Fisher SALES MANAGER

B = Breakfast L = Lunch D = Dinner

A sheet like this one can be used to compare the property's positioning to that of competitors and to record information that may be used to differentiate the property's catering services. (This is only one of several sheets that would be used.) You might also consider how your competitors serve clients—how they respond to inquiries, their sales policies, and their brochures and other promotional materials and strategies.

Exhibit 4 Sources of Local Business for the Catering Department

LOCAL CORPORATE BUSINESS

Sources:	Chambers of commerce, yellow pages, business section of the newspaper, trade journals, property staff members, competition's reader boards, referrals, past accounts.
Contacts:	Sales managers, personnel directors, department or division officers or heads, key secretaries.
Types of events:	Sales meetings (refreshment breaks, lunches, receptions); conventions (refreshment breaks, breakfasts, lunches, dinners, receptions); trade displays and exhibits (refreshment breaks); seminars and demonstrations (meals and refreshment breaks); retirement dinners; office and holiday parties; incentive vacations (meals included).

CIVIC AND ACADEMIC BUSINESS

Sources:	Chamber of commerce listings; club directories; yellow pages; society, local news, and sports sections of local newspapers; competition's reader boards; referrals; past accounts.
Contacts:	Organization officers, committee chairpersons, officers of alumni associations, social chairpersons of sororities or fraternities, coaches, key secretaries.
Types of events:	Banquets; conventions (meals and refreshment breaks); annual parties; special project events (refreshments, beverage sales); class reunions (meals and refreshments); dances (refreshments, beverage sales); receptions.

SOCIAL BUSINESS

Sources:	Society section of local newspaper; bridal fairs; mailing lists; personal contacts (jewelers, photographers, and so on); competition's reader boards; referrals; past accounts.
Contacts:	Church secretaries, direct contact with the prospective client.
Types of events:	Weddings (luncheons and teas, bridal showers, bachelor and bachelorette parties, rehearsal dinners, receptions); parties (holiday, anniversary, birthday, cocktail); family reunions (banquets, receptions); bar and bat mitzvahs; church-related functions (lunches, receptions).

These sources can be used to build catering sales. Since most competitors have access to the same sources, however, it pays to be creative. One successful catering manager, for example, visits local funeral directors twice a year, bringing wine, cigars, or other appropriate gifts along with information cards offering special rates for group dinners. His approach is rewarded by business from out-of-town families who are unfamiliar with the area's eating places.

To solicit this business, you must position your food operations to effectively showcase your major selling points. Your positioning should highlight such factors as location (your convenience, view, etc.), decor, pricing, food (specialties, attractiveness of presentation, etc.), service, and your willingness to negotiate customer-friendly contracts.

For maximum effectiveness, leads should be qualified before a great deal of time is spent soliciting business. A potential client's creditworthiness can be checked through such organizations as TRW or Credit Bureau/Equifax, or may be checked in business financial listings such as Dun & Bradstreet. In some cases, a credit application, such as the one shown in Exhibit 5, may be given to a potential client. If the client's credit is approved by a hotel credit manager, a master account may be set up. If credit is denied, the client will be required to pay in advance. (One of the major reasons hotels are reluctant to extend credit except to large, established firms is that the services provided are completely consumed; they cannot be repossessed as can tangible goods.)

Set Goals and Develop Action Plans. After identifying potential sources of local business, the sales goals of the department can be set. When setting these goals, it is important to focus sales efforts on valley and shoulder periods. This is only possible when accurate information on function room usage is available. Useful function-room statistics to monitor include:

- Function room occupancy by meal period
- Types of functions
- Pattern of unused times and days
- Use of guestrooms by function groups
- Popularity of individual banquet-menu items
- Sales revenue per square foot of function space
- Average banquet check by type of function
- Average number of persons by type of function

After sales goals have been set, action plans to reach those goals can be implemented. If a property has set a goal to increase wedding business by 65 percent over a specific three-month period, strategies might include the development of wedding brochures and planners; promotion of special wedding packages; attendance at local bridal fairs; and soliciting leads from local jewelers, photographers, and bridal boutique owners.

Action plans will vary with the goals set, target markets, budget available for promotion, and so on. Action plans may range from the simple to the elaborate. An action plan at one property might be to make 15 sales calls per week on local businesses to increase public awareness, while another property in the same city may stage a spectacular event for the same purpose.

Evaluate Results. Evaluating the results of sales and promotional efforts can reveal successful strategies as well as areas that need improvement or new action plans. Action plans should be monitored on a monthly or quarterly basis. An "action calendar" is an effective way to keep track of activities and results. This calendar maps out sales, advertising, and public relations activities for each month. It allows the marketing and sales team to identify the time of year to approach each market.

Exhibit 5 Sample Credit Application Form

CREDIT INFORMATION FORM

RETURN TO: RADISSON HOTEL ST. PAUL
CREDIT MANAGER
11 EAST KELLOGG BLVD.
ST. PAUL, MN 55101
(612) 292-1900

NOTE: TO BE CONSIDERED FOR DIRECT BILL PRIVILEGES, APPLICATION MUST BE FILLED OUT COMPLETELY!

NAME OF COMPANY ______

COMPANY ADDRESS ______

CITY ______ STATE ______ ZIP CODE ______ PHONE ______

NAME OF PERSON RESPONSIBLE FOR PAYMENT ______ POSITION ______

NAME OF BANK AND ADDRESS ______

ACCOUNT IN THE NAME OF ______ A/C # ______

REP. ______ PHONE ______

REFERENCE #1 (hotel or vendor) ______

CITY ______ STATE ______ PHONE ______

DATE OF FUNCTION ______

REFERENCE #2 (hotel or vendor) ______

CITY ______ STATE ______ PHONE ______

DATE OF FUNCTION ______

I HEREBY GIVE MY PERMISSION TO RADISSON TO VERIFY ANY OR ALL FACTS DISCLOSED AND UNDERSTAND THAT IF CREDIT IS ACCEPTED RADISSON'S PAYMENT POLICY REQUIRES ALL ACCOUNTS BE PAID IN FULL WITHIN (30) DAYS FROM THE CLOSE OF OUR FUNCTION. IN CASE OF A QUESTION OR ERROR IN BILLING, IT WILL BE THE ORGANIZATIONS RESPONSIBILITY TO CONTACT THE HOTEL ACCOUNTING OFFICE IMMEDIATELY TO CLEAR UP ANY PROBLEM.

ACCEPTANCE

IT IS AGREED BY THE PARTIES THAT THE FOREGOING WITH SUPPLEMENTS AS PRESCRIBED (if any) SETS FORTH THE ENTIRE AGREEMENT BETWEEN RADISSON HOTEL ST. PAUL

AND THE ______

TO PERFORM ALL POINTS CONTAINED HEREIN AND THAT THERE SHALL BE NO RIGHT OF TERMINATION FOR THE SOLE PURPOSE OF HOLDING THE SAME FUNCTION IN SOME OTHER FACILITY OR CITY.

THE PERFORMANCE OF THIS AGREEMENT BY EITHER PARTY IS SUBJECT TO ACTS OF GOD, WAR, GOVERNMENT REGULATIONS, DISASTER, STRIKES, CIVIL DISORDER, CURTAILMENT OF TRANSPORTATION FACILITIES OR OTHER EMERGENCY MAKING IT INADVISABLE, ILLEGAL OR IMPOSSIBLE TO PROVIDE THE FACILITIES OR TO HOLD THE FUNCTIONS. IT IS PROVIDED THAT THIS AGREEMENT MAY BE TERMINATED WITHOUT LIABILITY FOR ANY ONE OR MORE OF SUCH REASONS BY WRITTEN NOTICE FROM ONE PARTY TO THE OTHER.

ORGANIZATIONS CANCELLING FUNCTIONS OTHER THAN SPECIFIED WILL BE ASSESSED CHARGES AS PRESCRIBED HEREIN.

ACCEPTED AND AGREED TO:	ACCEPTED AND AGREED TO:
(ORGANIZATION)	(RADISSON HOTEL ST. PAUL)
(ACCEPTED BY)	(ACCEPTED BY)
(TITLE)	(TITLE)
(DATE)	(DATE)

In some cases, hotel catering operations offer credit to qualified buyers. To determine a client's creditworthiness, a salesperson must fill out an application on the client and submit it for the approval of the hotel's credit manager. (Courtesy of Radisson Hotels International)

It also enables the sales manager to spread the workload and assign salespeople to specific solicitation dates. Periodic meetings of the catering sales staff will help ensure that goals and objectives are met for each market segment targeted.

Catering Sales

Catering salespeople use a number of different strategies to sell food and beverages. While most catering sales result from conventions and meetings sold by the property's marketing and sales office, catering department salespeople in midsize to large properties are responsible for selling to local meeting planners and other local clients (in conjunction with marketing and sales office staff). In this section we will look at the strategies used by catering department salespeople to increase food and beverage sales.

Catering Promotions

Advertising and promotion play a key role in the success of a catering department. All advertising and promotional strategies used should be targeted to specific audiences and reflect the professionalism and creativity of the catering services being offered. Each should give potential customers a way to respond (a reply coupon, a toll-free number, a fax number, an e-mail address, etc.).

Print ads can be effective in local newspapers (especially in the society and business pages), ethnic publications, and specialty newspapers and newsletters, such as those directed to reunion planners. Catering departments with large advertising budgets might also advertise in magazines that target meeting planners, wedding planners, or other users of banquet services. Direct mail, including sales letters, postcards, and mailings that include brochures, fliers, or menus, can be sent to specifically targeted customers such as meeting planners, reunion planners, and others. Exhibit 6 shows a print ad and a direct mail postcard targeting the weddings market.

Brochures and *fliers* can be used both in-house and outside the establishment to attract customers. A property or club located near a business district, for example, may distribute fliers to businesses in the area. In-house promotions include the use of table tent cards, posters in high-traffic areas (entrances, guest elevators, etc.), fliers (as part of in-room information packages), and advertising on the property's marquee or on the closed-circuit televisions in guestrooms to promote the catering department. A property can also advertise to both in-house guests and potential clients on its website—which can be particularly effective if the catering section includes menus. A property may also offer samples of catering specialties at its restaurant's Sunday brunch or during the lounge's happy hour.

Developing Leads

A major factor in the success of catering department sales efforts is the development of leads. Salespeople can develop leads through in-person soliciting, telephone soliciting, sales letters, or responses to inquiries.

Exhibit 6 Advertising for the Weddings Market

Hotels who wish to reach the lucrative weddings market can advertise in bridal magazines and special publications targeting brides-to-be. For example, this ad (top) was placed in a wedding planner published by Bridal Spectacular Events, Inc. The postcard offers a free wedding planner to respondents. It was developed by Holiday Inn to be used for sales blitzes, direct mailings, and distribution at bridal fairs. The back of the postcard provides room for properties to print or stamp their contact information.

In-Person Soliciting. Personal selling involves contacting the owners of businesses frequented by members of a targeted market segment. The catering director may call on public relations firms to attract business from cultural organizations, for example. Or, as mentioned previously, the catering director or a catering department salesperson may call on the owners of jewelry stores, bridal boutiques, or photography studios for wedding business referrals. Photographers are an excellent source of information regarding family reunions, wedding anniversaries, and other family social activities.

Property tours can be used in conjunction with an outside solicitation program to promote the property to local corporate sources and civic organizations whose members can provide future business (Rotary Club, Kiwanis, Chamber of Commerce, and so on).

Telephone Soliciting. Telephone soliciting is another excellent way to develop leads. Selling over the phone involves far less time than in-person visits. If the catering director has hired a sales-oriented staff, the staff can make most of these calls, freeing the catering director for other duties.

Successful telephone solicitation begins with a plan that includes your targeted prospects, the information you wish to convey, and the results you expect to achieve. Since you have a limited time to present your services, preparing a script that contains your key points is essential. But callers should rehearse the material until it sounds natural and conveys interest in the prospect. In this example, the goal is to obtain an appointment:

> Good morning, Mrs. Alvarez. This is Carl Benson from the Midtown Hotel's catering department. I read the announcement of your daughter's wedding in the *Times* and would like to extend our best wishes to your family. I would also like to offer our catering services for the reception. As you may know, our goal is to make every event a memorable one, and we specialize in wedding receptions. It would be our pleasure to cater your daughter's reception, and I'd be delighted to meet with you to discuss how we can make your daughter's reception special.

Ideally, a telephone solicitation will result in a tentative reservation or an appointment to discuss the event. At the very least, try to get permission to send a copy of the catering department's brochure; this will both supply the prospect with additional information and provide you with an opportunity to follow up with the prospect.

Sales Letters. Sales letters are another effective way to build business. Sales letters can be categorized as form letters or personalized letters. Form letters are most commonly used by the sales office to solicit out-of-town convention and meetings business, while the catering department usually writes personalized letters to solicit local business. Writing a personalized letter does not mean the property cannot use a format that is easily modified. Today's word-processing capabilities make it easy to personalize a letter by changing names, adding a date, or mentioning facts gained through stories in the press or other sources.

A sales letter should be written with the prospective client's needs in mind. The requirements of a meeting planner will be far different from those of a wedding party, and letters should be prepared accordingly. No matter what target market is selected, the letter should attract the prospect's *attention,* create an *interest* in and then a *desire* for the product, and give the prospect a means to take *action* (a telephone number, an invitation to stop by for a visit, and so on). This is known as the *AIDA formula.* Sales letters should be kept to one page, and be simple and to the point. They should open with a benefit to the reader and close with a call to action. They should be personally signed, preferably with blue ink, to distinguish the signature from the black type. A sample sales letter is shown in Exhibit 7.

Don't overlook the sales potential of follow-up letters. A written thank-you after an interview or event conveys your commitment to service and can result in additional business. Like sales letters, thank-you letters, confirmations of bookings, and annual follow-up letters can be developed and stored on a computer to be personalized later for individual clients.

Responses to Inquiries. No matter what type of inquiry you receive, you should obtain pertinent information about the client, the client's organization (if applicable), and function needs *before* trying to make a sale. Inquiries are made in writing, by fax or e-mail, by telephone, or in person.

Written inquiries. A letter from a prospective client should not be answered in writing! A telephone call will reach the client (who has probably written to a number of properties) much faster.

Another reason for replying by phone is that letters from prospective clients are rarely specific. Few letters include the client's exact specifications. Will the function be formal or informal? What is the budget limit for the function? Does the potential client expect special services or setups? By talking with the client over the phone, the catering director or salesperson can determine exact needs, give details about function rooms and banquet menus, and negotiate terms. If a written communication is needed (a letter or proposal to be submitted to a board, for example), it can then be tailored to address specific needs.

In today's fast-paced world, fax transmissions and e-mail are also used to make inquiries. Replying to a fax inquiry with a fax gives you the advantage of responding immediately without interrupting a potential client. Likewise, e-mail inquiries should be answered by e-mail. E-mail provides an immediate reply—and messages can be printed out to help ensure the preservation of the correspondence. E-mail messages can also be forwarded to other people in the department who will be involved in the event, and information can be stored for use at a later date. When using either of these media, responses should be prompt and professional. Fax replies should be typed, not handwritten, and both fax and e-mail responses should be checked for errors and followed up with a mailing of any requested information (catering brochures, banquet menus, etc.).

Telephone inquiries. Telephone inquiries from prospects must be handled quickly and efficiently to ensure that business is not lost. All personnel should try to answer the phone within three rings, project a pleasant and courteous image, and avoid placing callers on hold if possible. If the employee must put the caller on hold, he or she should ask if the caller minds holding and should periodically advise the caller of how much longer the wait will be. A prospect who is put on

Exhibit 7 Sample Sales Letter

[Date]

[Name of Prospect]
[Address]

Dear Mr./Ms.:

I've learned that the international sales force of the ABC Corporation is scheduled to come to our city during the month of July 20XX. I'd like you to consider the XYZ Hotel as the site of your 20XX sales convention. Our convenient location, only five minutes from the city's center, is favored by numerous firms and organizations who have found that meetings held at the XYZ Hotel are highly successful.

We have meeting rooms that will accommodate from 20 to 2,000 persons. They are well-located and equipped with the finest audiovisual aids. In addition, they are ideal for exhibits and displays of merchandise and equipment. We can offer you a variety of setups to meet your needs. Our staff is at your disposal to assure efficient, smooth-running service for your convention programs.

XYZ Hotel offers comfortably furnished and attractively decorated guestrooms, each with a private bath and balcony. All rooms are equipped with air conditioning and color TVs. The members of your sales force can relax in these pleasant surroundings and will feel refreshed and attentive for each day's meetings.

We know that the success of any meeting is strongly related to the quality of the food served. We are proud of our reputation with the many companies who have discovered that we serve the finest foods for the functions required on a convention program like yours. We think that the consistent excellence and pleasing variety of our menus are ways of instilling a positive attitude in your convention participants. We'll be happy to submit suggested menus for your selection.

We're eager to serve you and the associates of ABC Corporation. I would appreciate an opportunity to show you our facilities personally if you find it convenient to be in our vicinity in the near future. In the meantime, please call me at 1–800–555–5555 if you have any questions.

Sincerely,

[Name and title of writer]
XYZ Hotel

An effective sales letter is short and to the point. This sample sales letter details property benefits and asks for an opportunity to provide additional information. A sales letter should make it easy for potential clients to contact the catering department; direct telephone numbers, a fax number, and an e-mail address usually are included on the finished version of a letter such as this one.

hold for too long—or is transferred from one department to the next—will usually try another property.

The catering director or catering salespeople should handle banquet inquiries. If they are not available, the clerical staff can be trained to take routine information (name of caller, type of function desired, preferred date, etc.) and can assure the caller that the catering director will return the call as soon as possible.

For inquiry calls to be handled efficiently, the function book and other information (sample menus, room capacities, price lists, and so on) should be readily available. In addition, catering department salespeople must have the ability to obtain enough pertinent information over the phone from a prospective client to accurately quote prices, suggest serving styles, and book the request.

In-person inquiries. In-person inquiries should also be handled efficiently and hospitably. When someone drops in unexpectedly and inquires about function space, the following steps should be taken:

1. A member of the staff (the front desk staff if the person is asked to wait in the lobby, the catering staff if the person is shown to the catering department) should welcome the prospective client and offer him or her a seat.
2. The client's name should be taken and given to the catering director or a catering salesperson immediately. If there is going to be a wait (which many clients will expect due to the nature of walk-in calls), the client should be advised of the approximate time he or she will be seen.
3. The client should be offered coffee or tea and some reading material. The reading material should relate to the catering department—a photo album of previous functions, scrapbooks containing publicity features and photographs, brochures or information sheets, sample menus, and so on. This type of material may answer some of the client's questions or give him or her a better idea of what is available.

Since many catering sales are made in the catering office itself, your catering office must make a positive first impression; it should serve as a marketing tool. It should indicate that your operation is well-organized and professional. Your catering office should be easy to find and tastefully decorated—both with fresh flowers or plants and with potential sales aids, such as posters of room configurations, color photographs of room setups or past events, and framed news releases, professional affiliations, and awards. In addition, a book of testimonials can be placed in the waiting area to help presell the client.

In addition to the waiting area, the catering office should have a quiet, private area with seating for four to six people. In such an area, you can meet with your client and provide frequently requested information, such as menus, brochures, price lists, lists of staging and audiovisual equipment, recommended suppliers, and costs and sources of all rental equipment. Like the waiting area, this space should be comfortable and inviting, and decorated with visual aids to enhance your sales presentation. At some properties, a sample place setting or empty bottles of quality champagnes and wines are displayed on a credenza to assist in upselling the event.

Selling to Clients

The key to successful selling is putting yourself in the client's place. When a client books a catered event, he or she often perceives a certain element of risk; the client may be inexperienced and concerned about the impression he or she will make on business contacts or guests. Therefore, he or she may be concerned about the quality of food and service, the cost involved (including any "hidden" costs), and what will happen if something goes wrong. The client wants to be assured of a worry-free event, and it is your job to become a consultant and problem-solver.

You first need to establish a personal relationship with each client in order to be able to turn his or her negative concerns into positive expectations. Once you have established this relationship, determine the client's needs and objectives before you begin selling food, beverages, and services. By determining what is most important to the client, you can focus your sales presentation on that area. For example, a client who is staging a regional dinner and wants to impress company officials may be more concerned with the menu and the type of service than with the cost. The catering director could meet the needs of the client—and increase banquet revenues—by suggesting three different levels of service:

> Mr. Rodriguez, our property offers three different types of functions—each featuring a superb sit-down meal. The difference is in the level of service. Our standard service is one server for every 20 persons, our first-class service provides one server for every 15 persons, and our regency or premiere service offers the ultimate in personal attention by providing one server for every ten persons.

Given alternatives, the client will often "trade up," especially if alternatives are presented as answers to specific needs. In the previous example, the client will likely choose the regency service, as he has already expressed an interest in impressing company officials. This technique of forced-choice suggestive selling or *upselling* can be used in all situations, whether the client's concern is for upgraded or budget service. In addition to offering upgraded service, you can boost the bottom line and client satisfaction by suggesting special china, glassware, linens, props, and the use of action stations (chef service for omelets, crepes, meat carving, etc.). Even prospects who are looking for bargains can be offered extras, such as centerpieces, candles, fancier desserts, and so on, in place of discounts on established prices. In other words, maintain the perception of value not by dropping prices but by offering something special.

Another way to sell function space is to offer a tour of the facilities, preferably when the ballroom or an appropriate function room is set up. It is far easier for the client to picture a successful event if he or she has seen the facilities, decorations, and table service that will be used.

Experienced hoteliers report that less than five percent of catering sales are made on the first contact. Catering department salespeople will need to follow through with additional contacts to book business. Since new business is so difficult to come by, catering departments rely heavily on past business—clients who know the product and are satisfied. In many catering departments, sales efforts are focused more on these repeat clients than on developing new business, but whatever the business mix, develop an efficient filing and trace system to service catering accounts.

Catering Sales Procedures. Like the guestroom sales department, the catering sales department should have clearly defined standard operating procedures. A banquet sales manual should include instructions explaining how recurring catering activities should be handled, including catering filing and tracing procedures, solicitation and booking procedures, methods used to prepare banquet event orders and other planning sheets, dates and space reservations policies, confirmation procedures and cancellation procedures, function room rental rates and setup charges, deposits and refund policies, credit procedures, and guarantee policies.

If a property is to stay competitive today, computers are a necessity for keeping track of sales records, and having a computerized catering office will ensure that your catering operation runs smoothly. In addition to the usual accounting and word-processing programs, there is specialized software available to assist catering operations, including CaterMate, Scheduler Plus, and Breeze, the catering program by Newmarket Software Systems. Any of these software packages can help a catering operation be more responsive to changing market needs. They store standardized menus, food costing and pricing data, and banquet event orders. Computerized catering systems also can be used to schedule rooms and functions, to create customized floor plans for each event, to update arrangements and menus, and to assemble nutritional analyses of menus. Exhibit 8 shows an example of how this software is used to generate a function sheet and develop a room setup.

Although computers have greatly reduced the amount of time needed to track the components of a function, it is still necessary to have a "paper trail" for the event. All catering inquiries should be recorded on a catering inquiry form (such as the one shown in Exhibit 9), whether the inquiry is from a new client or a previous one. The top part of the form lists the name of the organization, the address, the telephone number, and the name of the contact person. Spaces are usually provided for recording the type of function, the date and time of the proposed function, and the number of people expected to attend. The middle portion of the form is used to determine the action to be taken: Does the client want additional information? Is he or she asking for a definite date? At the bottom of the form is a section that specifies the materials to be sent to the client (menus, additional information sheets, a confirmation letter, and so on).

Before taking action on a request or inquiry, check the function book to determine if space is available (a page from a sample function book is shown in Exhibit 10). Since the function book is generally kept in the sales office, properties without a computerized function book should have the catering department and marketing and sales office in close proximity. If the date of the function is tentative, the booking can be entered in pencil and an alternate date may also be penciled in.

In an automated sales office with a computerized function book, these time-consuming administrative tasks are easier to do. Automated systems provide up-to-the-minute information on the availability of function space, enabling salespeople to be more effective in selling space and providing customer service.

Exhibit 8 Sample Computerized Function Sheet and Banquet Floor Plan

Crown Jewel - North

12 8 1 5 13 14

1

NEWMARKET
HOTEL AND TOWERS
at Commerce Way
135 Commerce Way • Portsmouth, NH 03801 • Phone (603)436-7500 • Fax (603) 436-1826

EVENT ORDER #110

Grp #: 15456 **Rep: Dan Hira** **Date Booked: 10/18/X3**
Event Date: 10/11/X4 **DAY: Saturday** **Distribution Date: 6/14/X3**

ACCOUNT: **Bose Speakers - Tweeter Division**
POST AS: **Bose Speakers - Board Meeting**
CONTACT: **Mr. Henry Bose** TITLE: **President**
ON-SITE CONTACT: Ms. Tanya Tweeter
ADDRESS: 45 Bose Way
CITY: Framingham STATE: MA ZIP: 01701
TELEPHONE: **617-555-7520** FAX: 617-555-3443

ALL SERVICES, EQUIPMENT, AND ROOM RENTAL ARE SUBJECT TO AN 18% SERVICE CHARGE AND 6% SALES TAX.

Date	Time	Room	Function	AGR	EXP	GTD	Rental
10/11/XX	12:00PM - 1:30PM	Crown Jewel - North	Awards Banquet	170	165	168	$500.00

SET UP	MENU
Two (2) 6ft. registration tables with chairs in foyer. Fourteen (14) rounds of Eight (8). Head table in front of room on risers. Number cards in center of tables. White tablecloths with red colored napkins.	**FAJITA BAR** Sizzling beef and chicken sautéed with onions and peppers, served with soft flour tortillas, sour cream, pico de gallo, guacamole, and jalapeño peppers @ $6.95++/person.

SPECIAL ARRANGEMENTS

Dance floor, 30'x40'.
Piano along North wall.
Six (6) potted plants around curve of room.

BEVERAGE REQUIREMENTS

One bar located in NW corner, with a second bar located in the SE corner of the room.
Bars to be stocked with house brands, domestic beers and wines, with an assortment of micro-brewed beers.
CASH BAR.

The Hotel will consider the above 'expected' number of persons as the final 'guaranteed' attendance. Should the client fail to communicate a final 'guaranteed' number of guests **72 HOURS** prior to the above function(s), the above expected number of guests will be the basis for the billing charges. To confirm these arrangements on a definite basis, please carefully review each **Banquet Event Order**, sign below and return to your Catering Representative. Additionally, please review the enclosed **Banquet General Information Sheet**, initial, and return with your signed Banquet Event Order.

Organization's Authorized Signature Title Date

This software program displays function sheet information in a standardized format and can be used with a room layout program to quickly generate room plans for the setup crew. Source: Delphi 7/Newmarket Software Systems, Inc., Durham, New Hampshire.

After the inquiry has been noted and the function entered as tentative or definite in the function book, an account file is created for the client. This file includes all information pertinent to the account: details of telephone calls, written inquiries and return correspondence, contracts, and so on. After functions have taken

Exhibit 9 Sample Catering Inquiry/Lead Form

RMI

EXAMPLE

TIME: 2:35 P.M. SALES MANAGER: SS

DATE: 3/9/XX

CATERING INQUIRY

ORGANIZATION: Carter/Hale Wedding

ADDRESS: 1414 E. 14th St., Anywhere STATE: AZ ZIP: 81414

NAME: Mrs. Andrew Hale PHONE: 262-2626

TITLE: Mother of the Bride

BUSINESS POTENTIAL

TYPE OF FUNCTION: Wedding Reception TIME: 7 P.M.–12:30 A.M.

NO. OF PERSONS: 175 DATE: 8/22/XX

ALTERNATIVE DATE: None

GUEST ROOMS: 5 ROOM RATE: (current rack)

Have you ever used the Ramada Anywhere?
Where are/were functions held? No, but neighbor had her reception here last year

---

ACTION: X TENTATIVE BOOKING
____ DEFINITE BOOKING
____ FUTURE BOOKING

MENU ACTION:

TO BE MAILED: YES X NO ____ MENU: Wedding package

OTHER: ____

FOLLOW-UP BY: 3/18 HOLD SPACE UNTIL: 4/9

REPORT ON FOLLOW-UP—LOST DUE TO (check one)

SPACE RELEASE POLICY ____

PRICE ____ NO SPACE ____ SPACE NOT SATISFACTORY (reason below)

OTHER ____

NO EXPLANATION GIVEN ____

CHECK LIST

ENCLOSURES REQUIRED FOR LETTER(S) CHECKED-OFF:

BUSINESS CARD	X
CATERING MENU BROCHURE	X
MENU PRICE LIST ONLY	
LETTER	X
CREDIT APPLICATION	
RACK BROCHURE	
AIRPORT TRANSPORTATION BROCHURE	
A/V SHEET	
WEDDING INFORMATION	X

Catering Administration Manual

This form can be used for all kinds of inquiries—written, telephone, or in-person—and serves as an information base for the client's file. Note that the form makes provision for potential business (tentative booking, definite booking, and future business) and provides a space for recording follow-up results.

Exhibit 10 Sample Function Book

ROOM	A.M.		P.M.	
IMPERIAL ROOM	Organization		Organization	
	Function		Function	
	Time	Number	Time	Number
	Tentative	Confirmed	Tentative	Confirmed
	Engager		Engager	
	Booked By	Type Setup	Booked By	Type Setup
SALON ROOM	Organization		Organization	
	Function		Function	
	Time	Number	Time	Number
	Tentative	Confirmed	Tentative	Confirmed
	Engager		Engager	
	Booked By	Type Setup	Booked By	Type Setup
BOARDROOM	Organization		Organization	
	Function		Function	
	Time	Number	Time	Number
	Tentative	Confirmed	Tentative	Confirmed
	Engager		Engager	
	Booked By	Type Setup	Booked By	Type Setup
CONVENTION REGISTRATION OFFICE	Organization		Organization	
	Function		Function	
	Time	Number	Time	Number
	Tentative	Confirmed	Tentative	Confirmed
	Engager		Engager	
	Booked By	Type Setup	Booked By	Type Setup
THEATER OF PERFORMING ARTS	Organization		Organization	
	Function		Function	
	Time	Number	Time	Number
	Tentative	Confirmed	Tentative	Confirmed
	Engager		Engager	
	Booked By	Type Setup	Booked By	Type Setup
TOWER-CAMELOT POOL	Organization		Organization	
	Function		Function	
	Time	Number	Time	Number
	Tentative	Confirmed	Tentative	Confirmed
	Engager		Engager	
	Booked By	Type Setup	Booked By	Type Setup

The function book must be kept up-to-date to ensure that function rooms are used to best advantage. When a date is requested, a member of the catering department checks the function book for the day and time requested. If the inquiry date is open, an entry (either a tentative, a hold, or a definite commitment) is made in the function book for the date and time requested. In addition to the time the room will be in use, each entry includes the name of the organization requesting the room, the name of the contact person, the type of function, and the salesperson's name. When confirming or denying that function space is available, it is important to check the times that the space is booked. A small function can often be booked between other functions.

place, account files should be separated into "repeat" and "nonrepeat" categories; the nonrepeat files (weddings, companies that have gone out of business, etc.) should be placed in a "dead" file, but the repeat files should be organized into a trace file for periodic action. A trace file is especially useful in catering sales, since it may take four or five contacts with a new account to close a sale, and because past accounts are the backbone of catering sales.

Most past clients should be contacted several months prior to their previously scheduled function date. Many companies, associations, and clubs stage banquet functions at the same time each year, making it easier to set up a trace file for these accounts. You can call the past account's contact person, tell the client that the catering department is preparing a schedule of events, and ask if the client would like to rebook.

If the client responds negatively, it is important to find out why the account has been lost. If a specific reason is given, you should look into the problem. After a week or so you can send a letter thanking the client for his or her suggestions and informing him or her of steps taken to remedy the situation. The following week, a personal call should be made. At that time, you can again thank the client for his or her suggestions and invite the client to take a firsthand look at the improvements that have been made. If the client is still adamant about using another property, the account can be filed and followed up in another year or two.

Whatever the type of account—new or repeat business—no inquiry should be dropped without final resolution. If business is lost or cancelled, a lost business report should be filed; if business is booked, a definite status should be entered in the function book, a confirmation letter sent to the client, and further arrangements made.

Planning the Function

After a date has been confirmed, you must work with the client to plan the function. Your emphasis here shifts from sales to service, and you will want to demonstrate your ability to provide dependable, timely service of food that is well presented in a setting that meets the client's expectations. You will also want to stress your department's attention to detail and your ability to handle last-minute requests and crises efficiently. Your client should be able to relax so much that he or she feels like a guest and not like the host of the function. This will both increase customer satisfaction and help generate repeat business and positive referrals.

Most properties use a banquet/catering checklist to ensure that all requirements are met for both meeting and food and beverage functions (see Exhibit 11). This checklist can be used for telephone and in-person contacts and will help build client confidence in the department's thoroughness as well as provide instructions for the proper management of the function.

The client should know just what is available: a dinner, for example, may be a sit-down meal or a buffet, formal or informal, set with round banquet tables (called *rounds*) or rectangular tables. The number of people expected, the theme or atmosphere desired, and the client's budget will all play a part in the final decision.

If you put yourself in the client's place, you can make use of suggestive selling to both increase revenues and ensure a successful function. A meeting planner, for

Exhibit 11 Sample Banquet/Catering Checklist

RMI

BANQUET/CATERING CHECKLIST

I. MEETING

1. Time: ______
2. Location: ______
3. Expected Attendance: ______
4. Setup:
   - ______ Classroom
   - ______ Theater
   - ______ U-Shape
   - ______ Hollow Square
   - ______ Other ______
5. Speaker Requirements:
   - ______ Headtable
     - ______ Size
     - ______ # People
     - ______ Draping
     - ______ Other ______
   - ______ Tabletop Podium
   - ______ Standing Podium
   - ______ Risers
   - ______ Other ______
6. Audiovisual Requirements:
   - ______ Hotel Provide
   - ______ Client Provide
   - ______ Delivery Time
   - ______ Setup Time
   - ______ Screen(s)
     - Size ______
     - Price ______
   - ______ Projector(s)
     - ______ 16mm—Price
     - ______ 35mm—Price
     - ______ Lens Size—Price
     - ______ Overhead Projector—Price
     - ______ Acetate Roll—Price
     - ______ Grease Pencils—Price
     - ______ Other
   - ______ Other
   - ______ Microphones— ______ Stands
     - ______ Table
     - ______ Floor
     - ______ Lavalier—Price
     - ______ Handheld—Price
     - ______ Other
     - ______ Mixer—Price
   - ______ Flip Chart—Price (includes 2 markers and 1 pad)
   - ______ PA System (other than existing hotel system)
     - ______ Type ______
     - ______ Size ______
   - ______ Video Recorder/Player
     - ______ Type/Player-Recorder (circle one or both)
     - ______ 3/4" VTR—Price
     - ______ 1/2" BETA—Price
     - ______ 1/2" VHS—Price
     - ______ Other
   - ______ Monitor(s)
     - ______ Size
     - ______ Color ______
     - ______ Price ______
   - ______ Advent Screen ______
     - ______ Size ______
     - ______ Price ______
   - ______ Other ______
7. Registration Requirements:
   - ______ Time ______
   - ______ Setup ______
     - ______ Draped Table(s)
     - ______ Chair(s)
     - ______ Telephone
     - ______ Message Board
     - ______ Wastebasket
     - ______ Signage
     - ______ Other
8. Coffee Break Requirements:
   - ______ Times ______
   - ______ # People ______
   - ______ Location ______
9. Breakout(s):
   - ______ Time
   - ______ # People
   - ______ Location
   - ______ Setup
   - ______ Audiovisual Requirements ______
10. Meeting Room Charge: ______
11. Shipments: ______
12. Security: ______
13. Reader Board Posting Policy: ______

Catering Administration Manual

This form is designed to aid the catering director or salesperson in determining specific client needs. It can be used when dealing with the client face-to-face or over the telephone, and can be customized to include pertinent details for individual properties.

INTERNET EXERCISE

Experient (www.experient-inc.com) is a leading meeting planning company. With the aid of Hilton Hotels, it has published a *Guide to the Food & Beverage Experience,* a booklet that provides a wealth of information on catering and meeting room sales. Log onto the Internet, go to Experient's website, then drop down to the "Knowledge Center" sub-menu. Once there, click on "Experient Publications." After you register (enter the name of your school in the "Company" box, and "hospitality student" under "Other"), you can access the online version of *Guide to the Food & Beverage Experience.*

1. What are the three basic choices for breakfast meetings?
2. What are the two general choices for planning breaks?
3. What factors should be considered when ordering food for receptions?
4. What is meant by a "banquet ticket exchange"?

example, may be worried that a luncheon won't finish on time; you can suggest a buffet or a simple menu so that the meal can be eaten quickly. Refreshment breaks a couple of hours before the luncheon or serving dessert at an afternoon break are other time-saving suggestions that can (1) help build the meeting planner's confidence that the meeting will be successful, and (2) increase sales of profitable food items as well.

Menus. A well-designed menu that features tempting dishes can be an important sales tool (see Exhibit 12). A menu should be printed on durable, high-quality paper and should be easily readable. The menu should be user-friendly, which means listing the prices of each item or choice whenever possible. "Bingo" menus, which list items by letters or numbers that are cross-referenced on a separate price sheet, are inconvenient to customers. If you must use a separate price sheet, however, be sure to date it in order to avoid misunderstandings with clients who may have an out-of-date copy.

Innovative items should be offered, but descriptions should be kept clear and simple; keep your menu free of pretentious foreign words or culinary jargon. Also, preparation and presentation techniques should be detailed (photos or drawings will help you better describe your offerings), nutritional information should be provided, and any substitutions that are available (lowfat gravy, nonfat milk, etc.) should be listed. Enhance the role of your menu as a selling tool by suggesting complementary wines in various price ranges after each entrée's description; identify wines by color and sweetness or dryness.

When it comes to the food offered, providing banquet menus that are cost-effective yet appropriate for the function is an important responsibility of the catering director. At some properties this is handled by the food and beverage director, although the catering director, working with the client, has the option of creating custom menus.

The catering director should try to sell banquet menus that can be prepared at different stations throughout the kitchen. A menu featuring cold hors d'oeuvres,

Exhibit 12 Sample Creative Banquet Menu

THE FRENCH BANQUET GUIDE

INTRODUCTION

Fine food, superior service, cordiality and hospitality: this is what Sofitel is all about. In all things and in all ways it's l'amour toujours. Because at Sofitel we love what we do and we believe that we do it well. "It" is the business of serving you, your friends, your company, and your guests.

As the first French hotel company to enter the United States, Sofitel has created its own niche in the industry, built upon 20 years of fine service. "Classic Comfort with a French Accent" is our philosophy. At each Hotel in the U.S. you will find a consistent level of quality in service, accommodations, and cuisine... all with a distinctive French touch.

Meeting planners will be especially pleased to learn about creative accents that add sparkle to ordinary events. Having won a Gold Platter Award for superiority in food and beverage service, we think we can help. All food and beverage outlets are managed by master chefs from France. Sofitel's commitment to fine French cuisine is so distinct that in 1981 L'Hotel Sofitel School of French Culinary Skills was opened in Minneapolis. It is the only private Cooking School in the world certified by the French Ministry of Education.

Long ago, the French discovered that hospitality and gastronomy are both serious arts and serious business. The chef even becomes part of the team to help customize your event.

Regardless of where you hold your next meeting, we would like to make your job a little easier. We created this guide after many planners told us that their principal concern is the planning and selection of their food and beverage activities.

Use this guide with our compliments.

John F. Lehodey
Executive Vice President

Seeking to take away the mystery—but keep the mystique—of superb French food and beverage service, Sofitel Hotels has developed a banquet menu/beverage guide for meeting planners. This elegantly designed reference booklet, featuring a French Impressionist painting on the cover, not only suggests memorable theme events focusing on French foods and wines, but also contains such sections as "How Food Makes Your Meeting a Success," "Planning the Courses," and "Special Touches." A glossary translates French food and beverage terms into English to help meeting planners with menu planning. (Courtesy of Sofitel Hotels, a division of ACCOR)

cold salads, and deli plates puts the burden of preparation on one station; a combination of hot and cold hors d'oeuvres, a cold salad, and a conventional meal would spread the preparation around. For this reason as well as others, the catering director should try to sell banquet menus that have already been developed whenever possible. With ready-made menus, costs are already known, while custom meals may require extra staff and costly ingredients. If a custom menu is requested, however, the catering director should consult with the chef for suggestions to keep costs as low as possible. A food cost chart may also be helpful when customizing menus.

A variety of tempting menus can be created. When developing menus, strive for a balance of colors, textures, shapes, and temperatures in addition to nutritional content. Today's clients tend to eat lighter and healthier, so items that are broiled, baked, or poached should be offered in addition to sautéed or fried dishes. Appetizers and desserts that are low in fat, cholesterol, and salt are also popular, but watch out for the "food fads" trap; mesquite grilling, for example, died quickly in most areas of the country.

Instead, if you wish to update a menu, go with trends, such as healthy foods, ethnic foods, and popular local or regional dishes. Sheraton boosted its catering sales with the introduction of its "Cuisine of the Americas," a menu of 365 dishes prepared to regional tastes. Catering departments can capitalize on local specialties, such as mahi mahi, avocados, and so on, when creating restaurant or banquet menus.

Types of Service. An important planning decision is the type of service to be used at food functions. The kind of banquet service selected influences pricing, staffing, and the overall effect of the function.

The most common form of banquet service is **plate service** (also called American service). Plate service requires a large kitchen and serving staff for a short service time. The food is plated in the kitchen. Cold food may be plated ahead of time and stored in large roll-in refrigerators or carts. Hot food must be plated at the time of service, and is sometimes served from a number of stations set up in the kitchen.

With **Russian service**, food is served from platters or other large dishes by servers, and sufficient food for one table is placed on each platter. One food server serves the meat and sauce while another serves the potato and vegetables, so a large labor force is needed.

With **English service,** food on platters or in bowls is placed on the table, and guests help themselves. The main meat item is presented to the host, who either cuts the main course him- or herself or chooses to have the cutting done by the server.

In **French service** (also called cart or tableside service), items are prepared tableside from a cart or guéridon. This requires food servers with specialized skills and experience. Sufficient space is needed between tables to enable food servers to move about freely.

Buffet service is suitable for all types of meals and all types of functions—from informal breakfasts to formal dinners served in silver chafing dishes. Hot and cold foods are attractively displayed, and guests walk up and help themselves. Service personnel may be required to assist—carvers at dinner meals, omelet-makers at breakfast buffets, and so on—but labor costs are reasonably low.

Preset service is sometimes used for lunch meetings or for other occasions when time is short. The first course (a cold soup, salad, or appetizer) is set on the table before guests sit down; in some cases, the dessert may also be preset. While this type of service may be necessary at times, preset food is rarely as attractive as food that is set in courses during the meal.

Receptions or cocktail parties typically feature **butler-style service.** Hors d'oeuvres are placed on platters and circulated among the guests by servers. When food is served at receptions, it is common to staff one server per 50 people.

À la carte catering is a new trend in food functions. With this option, two or three items are offered instead of a set menu, and guests can choose their own entrées. Marriott makes extensive use of à la carte catering and even provides menus to the seated guests to impart a sense of fine dining. Service requirements for this type of catering are similar to those for plate service.

A combination of service styles is often used for wedding receptions or corporate dinners. Many wedding receptions feature a buffet of appetizers and then a sit-down dinner. Another common combination is having the first course and dessert served by servers, with a main-dish buffet.

Seating arrangements may affect service style and prices and should be determined before plans are finalized. Hotels generally staff more servers per guest as the price per cover increases. While the minimum ratio for standard plated dinners is one server per 20 guests (at tables seating ten, one server per two tables; at tables seating eight, two servers per five tables), when price and service warrant it, the ratio may go as low as one to 12. If the menu calls for wine service poured by wait staff, the minimum is one server per 16 guests. For large parties, there should be one captain for every 150 guests.[3] Other factors that will influence the choice of service style include the size of the room, the size of the tables, the type of function, and the number of people attending.

Beverage Plans. Alcoholic beverages are a part of many functions. Properties may use one or a combination of the following popular beverage plans to provide alcoholic beverages.

Cash bar. At a **cash bar,** also called a *no-host bar,* each guest pays the bartender for his or her own drinks. Sometimes a ticket system is used at a cash bar for control purposes. With this system, guests pay a cashier for their drinks and are given tickets to present to the bartender. The food and beverage manager generally sets drink prices, which can be the same as or different from normal selling prices. Frequently, management will reduce drink prices from the normal lounge rates in order to attract beverage business.

Host bar. With a **host bar,** guests do not pay for drinks; rather, the host pays for the drinks consumed. These charges may be figured *by the hour, by the bottle,* or *by the individual drink.* When groups are charged by the hour, a fixed rate is charged for each person present during a specified time period. Therefore, hotels that use this system need an accurate way to determine attendance, such as collecting tickets or invitations at the door.

The host can also pay by the bottle, paying for all bottles opened, including partially full bottles. Hosts who use this method often request that staff close banquet bars in a staggered order (called *marrying the bars*), moving the partial bottles to open bars to minimize the number of partial bottles.

The last method, paying by the individual drink, is often the most economical method of payment if the group is smaller than 100 or if it has many nondrinkers. To ensure proper payment, there should be an agreement between the host and the catering department on drink sizes (a double would be charged as two drinks, for example) and on a way to determine how many drinks are served. Tickets may be used, or drinks may be recorded on a tally sheet or rung up on a register.

Additional labor charges are usually incurred for functions that involve liquor. As a general rule, one bartender is staffed for each 75 to 100 people. Cashiers or ticket-takers may also be required when liquor is priced by the drink or by the hour.

Finalizing Arrangements. Once the menu, beverage plan, and other arrangements have been set, the catering director or salesperson must complete a **banquet event order** (BEO), also called a *function sheet* or *banquet prospectus* (a sample computerized function sheet was shown in Exhibit 8). This sheet acts as a final contract for the client and serves as a work order for the catering department. The form includes the time and place of the function, physical arrangements of the function room, menu (foods are listed in the sequence in which they will be served), prices quoted for the menu items, beverage requirements, special requests, service notes (number of staff, special costumes, and so on), personnel required (servers, cashiers, checkroom personnel, and so on), tax and gratuity, payment arrangements, and guarantee clause.

A **guarantee clause** requires groups booking food functions to give the hotel a count of the expected attendance prior to the function—usually 72 hours in advance. This count is the minimum expected or guaranteed attendance; the group is charged for its guaranteed number even if actual attendance falls below the guarantee. Most hotels will agree to set tables for a percentage above the number guaranteed in order to accommodate additional guests. Many properties set for an additional ten percent; others hold to five percent. The guarantee clause is important because it helps catering managers control labor and food costs.

Managing the Function

As noted earlier in the chapter, the banquet manager is primarily responsible for the management of the actual function, and supervises room arrangement, service personnel, and service procedures. It is his or her job to see that the instructions on the function sheet are followed and that food is prepared and served at the designated time.

The banquet manager should make sure that the function room is set up as far in advance as possible and that the appropriate number of extra settings over the guaranteed attendance are set up (if the number of guests exceeds the guarantee, time will be saved if tables are preset). A bulletin board in the service area outside the function room also helps to facilitate function preparations. The bulletin board should list the name of the group, the time the function room doors should be opened, the names of food servers and other service personnel needed, the menu that will be served, which items can be preset (if any), service assignments, and special notations (when to serve courses or bus tables).

Just prior to the function, the banquet manager should check to be sure that the appetizers and desserts are ready to serve and that tables are properly set. He or she should also check with the chef to ensure that food preparation is proceeding on schedule and should advise the chef of any last-minute changes in the number of guests.

During the function, the banquet manager should be present to see that everything is going smoothly and the order of service is followed (see Exhibit 13). In some cases, the banquet manager presents the bill to the client. The banquet manager should be sure to thank the client for the opportunity to serve the group—this is the first step in following up on the account.

Following Up Accounts

Follow-up service is an important step in building a base of repeat clients. Immediately following the function, a thank-you letter and an evaluation form should

Exhibit 13 Sample Order of Service

This is a typical order of service followed in serving a banquet. This order may vary in certain circumstances—the dessert may be served following a speaker's presentation, and so on—but service should always be handled as efficiently and quietly as possible.

1. The head table is always served first, no matter what type of service is ordered.
2. The appetizer should be placed on the table just before or as guests are seated. Appetizer dishes should be cleared away before salads are served if the party is small; for larger parties, service is faster if the salad is placed on the left side of the plate immediately after placing the appetizer.
3. All appetizer dishes, bar glasses, empty salad bowls, and salad dressings should be removed before serving the entrée. If cracker baskets were placed with the salad course, they should now be replaced with bread baskets.
4. The entrée should be served, more water poured, and the beverage served.
5. Coffee can be served throughout the entire course of the meal.
6. Entrée dishes should be cleared from the table and water glasses filled.
7. Before serving dessert, all items not needed should be removed from the table. A dessert utensil, coffee spoon, glass of water, and beverage cup or glass should be the only items on the table when dessert is served.
8. The dessert should be served.
9. Dessert dishes should be removed, and additional coffee and water poured.

be sent to the client. A notation should be made in the trace file and a follow-up note sent if the evaluation is not received within a specified length of time. While it is not a replacement for checking on the success of the function in person, an evaluation form is an important source of feedback, both on the positive and negative aspects of service (see Exhibit 14). Any negative information can be used to correct flaws in service or avoid similar problems with other clients, while positive comments can be a source of encouragement for employees.

If problems occurred, adjustments in charges may have to be made; at the very least, a letter of apology is in order. The client should be given a reason to try the property again and recommend the property to others.

Other Food and Beverage Sales

While banquets are important sales, other food and beverage functions can increase catering department revenues as well. The following list suggests a few of the opportunities a creative catering director has to serve guests, create repeat business, and increase sales.

Creative Refreshment Breaks

Refreshment breaks are usually scheduled at mid-morning and mid-afternoon, normally last 15 to 30 minutes, and are intended to alleviate boredom and sharpen the attention and enthusiasm of meeting attendees. Typical refreshment break fare

Exhibit 14 Sample Evaluation Form

RAMADA®

— SERVICE CRITIQUE —

Group Name: ______________________ Date of Function: ______________

Type of Function: ______________________

	Excellent	Good	Fair	Poor	Comments
REGISTRATION					
EMPLOYEES' ATTITUDES					
Banquet Staff					
Sales & Catering Staff					
Restaurant Staff					
Front Desk Staff					
Telephone Operators					
Bell Staff					
Housekeeping Staff					
RESTAURANT					
Food & Beverage Quality					
Food & Beverage Service					
LOUNGE					
Beverage Quality					
Beverage Service					
BANQUET FUNCTION					
Room Appearance					
Food & Beverage Quality					
Food & Beverage Service					
MEETING ROOM FUNCTION					
Room Appearance					
Equipment					
Lighting					
Temperature					
Reaction of your guests					

ADDITIONAL COMMENTS: ______________________

A thank-you letter and an evaluation form should be mailed to the client as soon as possible after the function. (Courtesy of Ramada, Inc.)

includes a variety of hot and cold beverages, muffins and other types of bread and pastries, fruits (both fresh and dried), cut vegetables, and peanuts. Whatever the choice, speed is often a major consideration for refreshment breaks; menu items should include only those foods that attendees can pick up quickly.

An alternative to the typical refreshment break is a theme refreshment break. Examples include a New York Deli refreshment break featuring vegetable juice, lox and bagels, cream cheese, jellies, and cream sodas; and a Mexican refreshment break with exotic fruits and juices, Mexican pastries, and so on. Refreshment breaks can also feature unusual house specialties—hot spiced cider, a variety of breads, dried fruit and assorted nuts, and so on.

When setting up for refreshment breaks, you should usually plan to have one beverage station per 75 to 100 attendees, and you should space the stations so that bottlenecks are minimized. One server should be staffed per 100 people, and stations should be laid out for quick service. Coffee cups should be next to caffeinated and decaffeinated coffee, tea bags, and hot water. Cream, sugar, sweetener, and spoons should be available on a separate table a short distance from the beverage station. Coffee and soda stations should be separated, and hot beverages should be identified with signs. Open the stations farthest from the main entrance first to draw people into the room; toward the end of the break, coffee stations can be "married" to speed cleanup.[4]

Hospitality Suites

Hospitality suites are often sold to sponsors of an event or to vendors or attendees as a place to do business and socialize. In many cases, a hospitality suite is set up in two or more guestrooms with connecting doors, or the hospitality suite may be located near the meeting area.

Most hospitality suites are open only in the evenings, but some may be set up as around-the-clock "open houses" that offer refreshment break snacks during the day and another menu (that often includes liquor) in the evenings. Hospitality suite charges must reflect not only the cost of the food and beverages, but also any labor costs for servicing the function. Hospitality suites are not usually serviced by the catering staff; in many cases, they are handled by room service personnel.

Receptions

Receptions are an excellent way to generate revenues at a low cost. Most receptions involve a host or cash bar and simple hot or cold hors d'oeuvres. Such parties require little in the way of setup time (many receptions require only a few chairs around the room). When taking orders for receptions, the catering director should determine the purpose of the party, budget limits, and method of pouring drinks (measured or as requested).

Special Functions

Staging special functions, such as theme parties, family reunions, and wedding receptions, can be the most challenging—and rewarding—aspect of the catering business. Making these special events truly memorable to both your clients and their guests shows your willingness to get involved with your clients and pay attention to even the smallest details. Success with special functions can lead to repeat business and word-of-mouth referrals.

Food and Beverage Allowances for Hospitality Suites

(All quantities are per person)

Hors d'oeuvres	3 oz.
Nuts	3 oz.
Dry Snacks	4 oz.
Cheese	3 oz.

Average Liquor Consumption

All Male Attendees	2.5 first hour, 2 each additional hour
All Female Attendees	1.5 first hour, 1–1.5 each additional hour
Mixed Group	2 first hour, 1.75 each additional hour

Source: Excerpted from Best Western International's *Meeting Resource Guide*, p. 44.

Perhaps the most personal of these special events are wedding receptions and ceremonies. These occasions are so special to the wedding party and their families and guests that quality and perfection are expected—and cost often becomes a secondary concern. Therefore, a catering department should offer a number of options to enable the couple to "trade up" for all aspects of the event.

The five elements of a wedding reception sold by the catering department are the *menu and beverages, disposables, equipment, decor,* and *service.* While the program can range from a simple hors d'oeuvres reception to an elegant sit-down dinner, the tastes of the bride and groom should be of paramount concern. The catering department should be capable of tailoring menus to the desires of the bride and groom while still keeping the menus within budget guidelines. Disposable items, such as personalized matches, napkins, and favors, should also be offered. Catering departments should keep abreast of trends in this area, but should also be ready to provide traditional items, as many couples prefer "old-fashioned" weddings.

Promote your silver service, champagne fountains, or other equipment that can add ambiance to the special day. Decor, too, can be simple or elaborate. In some cases, catering departments have gazebos, trellises, centerpieces, and other decorating items in stock; other departments rent the needed equipment from outside vendors and charge the couple as part of a package.

The scope of services that catering departments provide varies greatly, but service plays an important part in special events. Catering departments may offer table-waiting, food presentation (French service, action stations, etc.), and cleanup services. Flowers, entertainment, photography, and transportation are usually

Tips for Making Your Property Wedding-Friendly

- Cross-train your entire team to be wedding-savvy.
- Have a quiet, private sitting area where you can talk to the bride without distractions.
- Convey enthusiasm by asking the bride-to-be about her dream wedding.
- Have bridal magazines available for perusal.
- Provide examples of successful weddings you have staged, using framed photographs, wedding photo albums, and recommendation letters or thank-you notes from previous brides.
- Prominently display certificates of advanced training you and your staff members have earned in the hospitality and wedding industries.

Source: Adapted from Nelson Clark, "How to Expand Your Wedding Business by Finding Your Unique Selling Proposition," *HSMAI Marketing Review*, Fall 2002, p. 41.

provided by contractors, but some hotel catering departments provide these services as well.

Since there is so much involved in planning a wedding and reception, it is becoming more common for couples to have their ceremony as well as their reception at a hotel in either their home city or their honeymoon destination city. That way, the wedding party and guests do not have to travel to the wedding site and then to the reception; all details are handled by a single person ("one-stop shopping"); and the couple can save money. Independent wedding consultants typically charge 15 percent of the gross wedding costs; by servicing all the events, you provide added value to the wedding party.

In an effort to better serve the weddings market, the Marriott chain developed a program to train and certify wedding planners. While the chain has always been in the weddings business, averaging about 100,000 weddings a year worldwide, Bruno Lunghi, director of food and beverage development, said the chain felt the need to further educate sales and event managers on wedding traditions and current trends. Maria Synder, director of marketing and public relations, says Marriott is "courting a long-term relationship" via the program, explaining, "We want them [the couples holding their weddings at Marriott] to come back for anniversaries, birthdays, etc."[5]

Hotels and clubs that offer complete wedding and reception services have found this a profitable business. Besides the revenues generated from the event, income is earned from the commissions paid by the outside vendors. Therefore, a number of hotels have added wedding chapels or set up outside wedding areas, complete with gazebos and elaborate staging, to attract couples. At the Orlando Peabody, for example, about 80 percent of the weddings business it books includes a ceremony. Social Catering Manager Bonnie Garfield steers couples away from wedding packages, preferring to design events that offer "more individuality, rather than the feeling of a staged, planned event." She says, "We are very flexible and are sensitive to the couple's preferences."[6]

Attracting the Bridal Market

Today's wedding industry generates $80 billion a year in revenue and continues to grow, proving itself to be virtually recession-proof through economic downturns. There are many ways to attract bridal market business to your property. Here are just a few:

Stage a Bridal Show

Join forces with local wedding-related businesses and hold a bridal show or fair. When the Super 8 Motel in Saukville, Wisconsin, held its bridal show, invited businesses included local jewelry stores, bridal boutiques, florists, printers, bakeries, travel agents, and hair stylists. The property booked 15 weddings and over 300 room nights as a result of this promotion—as well as generated additional business from rehearsal dinners, receptions, bridal showers, bachelor parties, luncheons, and teas.

The Ritz-Carlton Osaka (Japan) partnered with a local wedding agency and invited the area's most eligible couples to a mock wedding to show them exactly what their "special day" would be like at the hotel. The hotel picked up the food and beverage tab, but individual vendors sponsored everything else—from flowers and dresses to laundry and lighting. Of the roughly 100 couples that attended, 13 were married at the hotel (in Japan, it is very prestigious for couples to get married in hotels), generating some $30,500 per ceremony (or roughly $396,500 in all) on a total investment of $10,000 for the property.

Offer a Wedding Booklet

While the menu may seem the most important consideration to a person booking a wedding or reception, following traditional etiquette is a prime factor in wedding or reception planning. Offering a booklet on wedding etiquette—especially one covering everything from initial planning to the final toast—is usually greatly appreciated. The booklet should include fill-in charts, such as timetables, decorations needed, and spaces for the names of printers and florists, and should also promote the services offered by the property.

Larger properties or properties that do a large volume of wedding business might also consider either hiring a full- or part-time wedding consultant or contracting with an outside consultant and offering his or her services in the package price.

Create Deluxe Wedding Packages

Most people want to go first-class when it comes to a wedding, reception, or honeymoon, so hotels should not be afraid to prepare a deluxe package. Rather than offering the deluxe package first, it is best to present three options (deluxe, mid-priced, and budget). In many cases, purchasers will opt for the deluxe package for this "once-in-a-lifetime" occasion.

To capture your share of this market, build trust and confidence with your potential clients. This means listening, taking notes, and sharing your enthusiasm. Using visual aids, such as photos of decor, table settings, and cake-decorating options, will enhance your sales presentation, but the most important aspect of selling to this market is your expertise—being able to deliver a memorable, worry-free event.

Exhibit 15 Ad Promoting Kosher Service

Many hotels offer kosher service when it is requested for weddings, bar and bat mitzvahs, and other special occasions. This brochure, printed by the Hilton International in Sydney, Australia, promotes kosher services available at the property. (Courtesy of the Hilton International Sydney, Sydney, Australia)

Other special functions may include requests for kosher service (see Exhibit 15) or requests for menus to meet dietary restrictions. When preparing for these types of functions, the catering director and kitchen staff must pay close attention to special requirements for purchasing and preparing foods.

MARKETING IN ACTION

Wyndham's Creative Marketing Captures Weddings Business

The weddings market can be a lucrative market for properties that can offer the products, services, and expertise required by today's busy couples. Wyndham Hotels & Resorts put together a wedding-specific sales program, adding wedding consultants to the staffs of some hotels and resorts, and at other properties training existing sales managers in how to handle the details involved in landing local weddings business. While the program was successful in building business, research done by Wyndham indicated that as many as 300,000 destination weddings (weddings where a couple married away from home with or without family and friends) took place annually, and the chain decided to target this segment of the weddings market.

Demographics of the Wedding Market

The following information is based on information from the U.S. Census Bureau and other U.S. government agencies unless otherwise indicated.

2.4 Million Weddings Annually

1.6 million engaged women (or 63% of all marriages) are marrying for the first time.

88% use the Internet to plan, according to Bride's magazine.

28 is the average age of an engaged woman.

29 is the average age of her fiancé.

Brides today have their own money to spend and annually, weddings generate **$80 billion a year** in consumer spending.

Weddings Take Place Year-Round. The year-round wedding industry is called recession-proof by financial analysts, and brides and grooms are among the most desirable consumer groups today.

Household Income of Today's Bride	
$40,000+	53.5%
$50,000+	43.0%
$60,000+	33.0%
$100,000+	10.8%
Median HHI: $43,052	

Employment	
Employed	53.5%
Employed full-time	43.0%
Professional/Managerial	33.0%

David Riley, vice president of catering, and Michael Curran, the chain's director of e-commerce, worked together to develop a comprehensive website designed specifically for today's computer-savvy brides and grooms. The site, www.destinationweddingsbywyndham.com, offers a number of options to cover all phases of destination weddings. The "Destinations" tab, for example, showcases Wyndham's resort folio. Divided into several geographic categories, "Destinations" includes virtual tours of Wyndham properties, and, once a possible destination has been selected, all future information provided will relate to that destination. The site also includes such tabs as "Ceremony" (ideas for ceremonies at a variety of locations at each resort), "Celebration" (sample menus, price quotes, and special touches for a reception), "Wedding Album" (photos, reviews, and suggestions from previous users of Destinations Weddings by Wyndham), "Special Offers," and the all-important "Planning" tab. Clicking on the "Planning" tab provides access to a wedding planner ("Planning Your Wedding The Wyndham Way") full of checklists, charts, worksheets, and helpful planning tips; and a "Contact a Wedding Coordinator" link that directs the couple to a wedding consultant who serves the selected property.

Initial results from the website have been impressive. Wyndham plans to make the site even more interactive, offering the opportunity for couples to communicate with their guests and potential guests via the site, and enabling guests who are unable to attend the wedding to enjoy photos and the wedding story online. To make planning via the site even more convenient for couples, the chain will be partnering with airlines and other travel and hospitality providers to ensure that couples can take care of just about every wedding detail using the Wyndham site.

Source: Nelson Clark, "The Wedding Market: A Growing Resource," *HSMAI Marketing Review,* Spring 2002, p. 31.

Off-Premises Catering

Off-premises catering can be divided into two categories.[7] The first, which is offered by many hotels, involves a function that is not held in the banquet room but is still on the property, such as a poolside party or barbecue, a garden wedding, or a function held under tents pitched on the property's grounds. This type of catering is popular with many guests, and has the added advantage of being in close proximity to the hotel's kitchen and any equipment that is needed to service the function.

The second category of off-premises catering involves servicing functions away from the property, and is offered by far fewer hotels. One of the primary reasons for the reluctance to enter this area is the high initial startup cost for transportation and equipment to keep foods at appropriate temperatures, and high inventory costs for items such as tables, chairs, and tents. In addition, there are costs for labor (drivers and setup personnel), insurance (both for the vehicles and for liability), and health permits.

Despite these factors, many hotels and restaurants—especially those in areas in which there is no strong independent catering competition—have found off-premises catering an extremely lucrative addition to their food and beverage bottom line. David Beecham, general manager of the Hyatt Regency Tech Center near Denver, says, "If you're going to grow revenue in today's market, with flat outlet sales, with flat to lowering beverage sales, and, in some cases, flat banquet sales, off-premises may be the key to start that revenue growth in food and beverage. It certainly has been for us."

Beecham's hotel teamed up with the Hyatt Regency in downtown Denver to win the catering contract for the gala that opened Denver's international airport. His hotel has participated in several other high-profile events, including the opening of *Miss Saigon*. The Dallas Sheraton has also profited from off-premises catering; it catered a society gala at the Dallas Museum of Art. With its new contacts there, it wasn't difficult to contract with the city to cater all events held at the symphony center.

Even small properties can benefit from offering off-premises catering. The 92-room Little Nell hotel in Aspen, Colorado, capitalizes on its location by catering functions at the top of Aspen Mountain as well as at off-site weddings and functions in the town's symphony hall. Jaime Pavey, director of catering at the property, says that her hotel has an advantage over the other caterers in the area. Since it is open year-round, the hotel employs a full-time staff; other caterers in the area are seasonal and have to rehire every year. And since the hotel is perceived as a luxury hotel, its ambiance and quality are strong selling points.

Meeting Room Sales

Meeting rooms are usually sold by salespeople in the hotel's marketing and sales office who sell group guestroom business to corporations and associations. At some large properties, a separate convention department may solicit meetings and convention business. However meeting room sales are handled, it is important to understand the dollar value of meeting room space and to keep these points in mind:

1. The amount of revenue that can be generated relates directly to the amount of space available. By arranging for the most effective use of meeting room space—for example, meetings following meetings in the same room rather than a banquet following a meeting—costs can be kept down and more space can be sold.
2. Selling the least desirable space first increases maximum space usage. If the least desirable space is sold, it is far easier to sell the desirable space at a later date. If the desirable space doesn't sell, the previously booked meetings can be moved into the prime space.
3. "Holds" that reserve space for all day or all evening should be questioned; few meeting planners need rooms for an entire day or evening, and a few hours of "dead" time can be used for another meeting.
4. Salespeople should concentrate on selling space during times when business is usually slow. Meeting rooms will practically sell themselves during peak periods, so sales activity should be aimed at valley and shoulder periods.

At large properties, a convention service manager may set policies on selling meeting rooms, while at a smaller property the sales director or manager may deal with this aspect. Meeting rooms were often provided free of charge in the past if a banquet was involved; today, however, there is a trend to charge for meeting rooms even if the group uses banquet facilities. This makes it even more important to provide clients with the services they require.

Types of Meeting Rooms

Meeting rooms fall into three basic categories: exhibit halls, ballrooms for large meetings or banquets, and conference meeting rooms. The type of room used will depend on a variety of factors: the type of meeting, the number of people expected to attend, the size and layout of the room, and special requirements (audiovisual equipment, access to freight elevators, and so on). A meeting planner may also be interested in such room features as ceiling height, the location of electrical outlets, proximity to elevators, the locations of exits, the number of doors and windows, and the presence of pillars or other potential obstructions.

Meeting Room Setups

As shown in Exhibit 16, there are various meeting room setups that can make the best use of space while still meeting the client's needs:

1. *Theater setup* (also known as a *cinema setup* or an *auditorium setup*)—Chairs are set up in straight rows (with aisles) parallel to the head table, stage, or speaker's podium.
2. *Senate setup*—Same as a theater setup, except chairs are placed in a semicircle rather than in rows.
3. *V-shaped setup*—Same as a theater setup, except that chairs are placed in a *V* (the base of the *V* begins at the center aisle).

Exhibit 16 Sample Meeting Room Setups

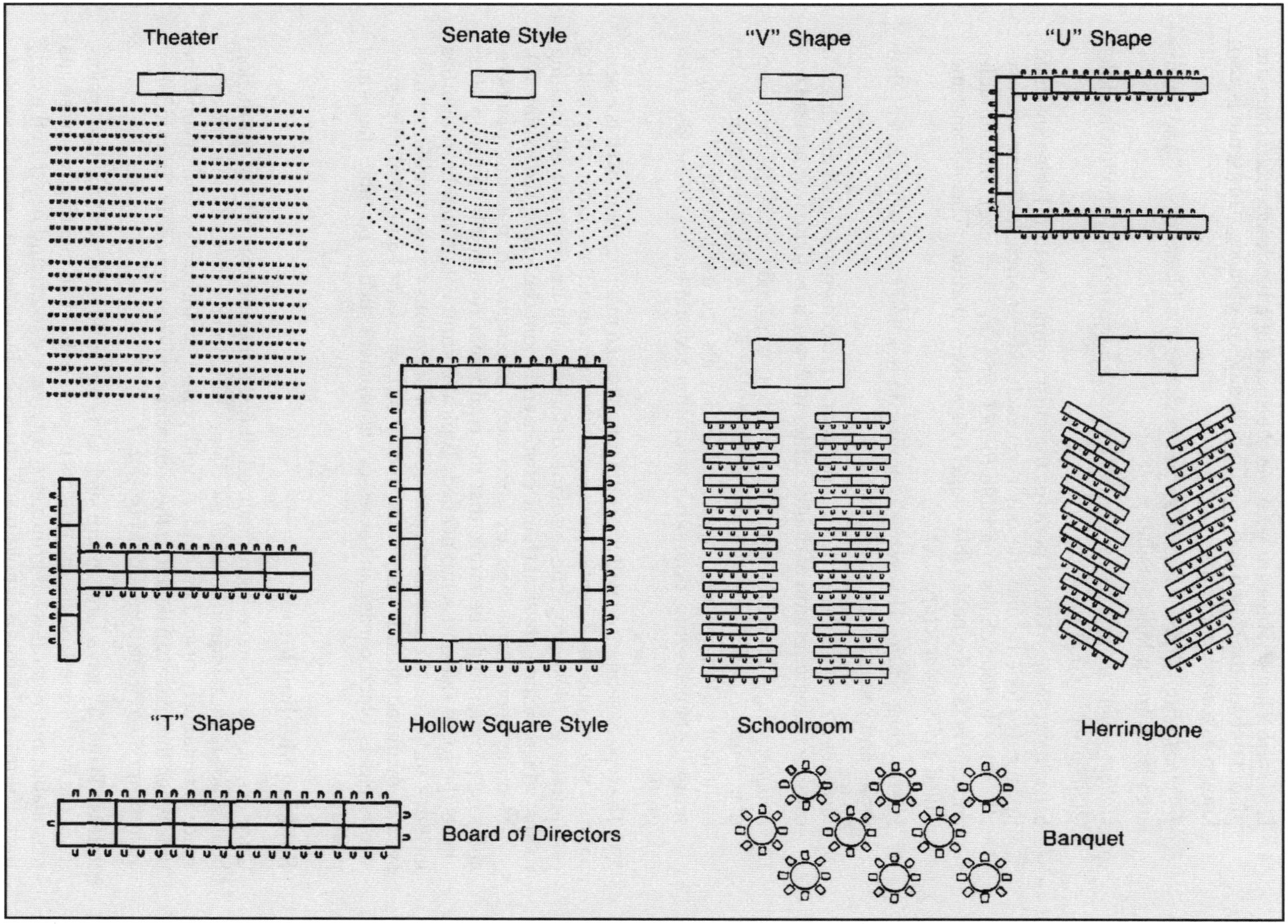

Theater

Senate Style

"V" Shape

"U" Shape

"T" Shape

Hollow Square Style

Schoolroom

Herringbone

Board of Directors

Banquet

Source: Adapted from Convention Liaison Council, *The Convention Liaison Council Manual,* 7th ed. (Washington, D.C., 2000).

4. *U-shaped setup*—Tables are set up in the shape of a block-letter *U*; chairs are placed outside the closed end and on both sides of each leg. This setup is also known as a *horseshoe setup*.
5. *T-shaped setup*—Tables are set up in the shape of a block-letter *T* and chairs are placed around the outside.
6. *Hollow-square setup*—A series of tables forms a square with a hollow middle; chairs are placed around the outside.
7. *Schoolroom setup*—This is perhaps the most common setup. Tables are lined up in rows (one behind the other) on each side of an aisle. There are usually three to four chairs to a table (depending on table size), and all tables and chairs face the head table, stage, or speaker's podium. This is sometimes called a *classroom setup*.
8. *Herringbone setup*—This setup is similar to a schoolroom setup except that tables and chairs are arranged in a *V*.
9. *Board-of-directors setup*—This is a popular arrangement for small meetings. It calls for a single column of double tables with seating all the way around.
10. *Banquet setup*—A meal setup that generally uses round tables. The most popular round is a five-foot (1.5-meter) table that seats eight to ten people. An eight-foot (2.4-meter) rectangular table may also be used, set in a U-shaped setup, T-shaped setup, or another setup that accommodates the needs of the group.

The type of setup used will affect the capacity of a meeting room, so it is essential that salespeople be knowledgeable about room capacities under all possible configurations. Most properties provide detailed scale drawings of all meeting rooms, which include physical characteristics and room capacities (see Exhibit 17).

Meeting room capacities are extremely important to meeting planners, and salespeople should be aware that the equipment required by a group often affects the room size and setup needed. Typical equipment offered by properties includes audiovisual equipment (microphones of various types, a public-address system, overhead or slide projectors, and so on), speakers' equipment (flip chart stands, easels, blackboards), and accessory equipment such as portable stages and podiums.

Booking Meeting Rooms

Once arrangements have been finalized, the salesperson can fill out a function book space-request form and detail the client's function room needs. In some cases, space is tentatively placed on hold. A hold period should not extend beyond the time when the space can be sold if the commitment is not firmed up. To avoid this, an appropriate release date should be set.

Release Dates. When a large group such as a convention buys out the vast majority of the hotel's guestrooms, the group's request to hold all meeting rooms seems reasonable. But regardless of group size, a **release date** should be set in the contract. The reason for this is simple: many groups estimate requirements for meeting

Exhibit 17 Sample Meeting Room Plans

CARAVAN EXHIBIT HALL
School Room Style Seating Approx. 450
Theatre Style Seating Approx. 800
Banquet Style Seating Approx. 650

MONACO ROOM
School Room Style Seating Approx. 250
Theatre Style Seating Approx. 500
Banquet Style Seating Approx. 300

Fluorescent Ceiling Lights
220 110 Outlets
Exit Lights
Electric Floor Outlets
Recessed Ceiling Lights
Wall Bracket Light Outlets
Telephone
Air Wall Room Dividers
Ceiling Speakers
Plumbing Outlets
Duplex Recp't. Outlets
Portable Transformers Available
Ample Stage Lighting
Rheostat Lighting
Movable Spotlights in Ceiling for Displays
Closed Circuit T-V Facilities Beside Telephone Jacks
Ceiling Height of Caravan Exhibit Hall — 13 Ft
Ceiling Height of Monaco Room — 12 Ft

Meeting room plans showing such details as exits, electrical outlets, telephone jacks, lighting, door openings, and ceiling heights are often requested by experienced meeting planners, and are an aid in making a sales presentation. Note that this drawing also presents the room's capacities for schoolroom, theater, and banquet seating.

space a year or more prior to the actual event, based on a rough outline of the convention program. As the convention draws nearer, meeting planners may make extensive program changes. With a release date (usually 60 or 90 days prior to the event), meeting rooms that are not needed can be released, and the hotel can then sell this space to other groups.

In many instances, another group can be given a tentative booking if, as in the example above, a group seems to have reserved more space than it will need. If the tentative booking cannot be filled because it turns out that the first group does indeed need all the space it reserved, the second group must be notified immediately and a lost business report filled out.

Managing Meetings

While policies for managing meetings will vary from property to property, there are certain requirements that are followed almost universally. First, rooms are set up well in advance if possible. This allows for any last-minute changes. Setup teams vary with a property's size: small properties may use house attendants, medium-sized properties may rely on crews supervised by the banquet manager, and large convention properties may have special setup crews.

Most properties provide general meeting room accessories. These include draped head tables and pitchers of ice water with glasses. If the meeting is scheduled to run more than two hours, setup personnel or food servers usually freshen up the room by removing dirty or wet linens, straightening chairs, refilling water pitchers, and replacing glasses with clean ones.

Setup crews may also be involved in setting up exhibit booths or display areas. Many properties offer partitions that can be used to divide a room into smaller rooms or be opened to provide display or ballroom space. This option offers flexibility, and is popular with training directors who wish to divide meeting attendees into small groups after a general training session. Partitions also benefit the property by enabling better space control. Putting a meeting of 20 persons in a room built for 100, for example, wastes space and cuts into profits; with partitions, the room can be divided to accommodate several small groups at a time.

After a meeting, follow-up should be taken care of promptly—a thank-you letter and an evaluation form should be sent and traced. Providing hassle-free meeting space and personalized service can help ensure repeat and referral business and keep the meetings business profitable.

Conclusion

In this chapter, we have taken a detailed look at the scope and function of the catering department, which can be one of a property's most lucrative profit centers. We have seen how the catering function is sold and managed, and explored ideas for creative functions that can add to a hotel's profit margin. We have also discussed types of meeting rooms and detailed how to reach meeting planners to sell these meeting rooms to groups that can provide the best profit mix.

No matter what facilities your property has to offer, with a little creativity and a focus on customer service, even the smallest hotel can handle food and beverage functions and host meetings—and enjoy repeat business and word-of-mouth referrals. Using the techniques presented in this chapter, you can take advantage of opportunities to sell functions to a wide variety of groups that will boost revenues and fill guestrooms during periods when business is needed most.

Endnotes

1. April Thorn, "Behind-the-Scenes Work Is Necessary to Make Hotels Run without a Hitch," adapted from the online edition of the *Times-Republican,* a Central Iowa daily newspaper, posted Tuesday, October 23, 2007.
2. Jill Jusko, "Proper Preparation Can Lure Non-Guests into Eateries," *Hotel and Motel Management,* 15 August 1994, p. 23.
3. Milton T. Astroff and James R. Abbey, *Convention Management and Service,* 7th ed. (Cranbury, N.J.: Waterbury Press; and Lansing, Mich.: American Hotel & Lodging Educational Institute, 2006), p. 448.
4. Astroff and Abbey, p. 434.
5. Barbara Capella Loehr, "Marriott Bolsters Wedding Business with a New Certification Program," *HotelBusiness,* April 7–20, 2002, pp. 7, 15.

6. Shannon McMullen, "Hotels Diversify Services to Capture Lucrative Wedding Market Business," *Hotel Business,* 21 April–6 May 1995, p. 28.
7. Quotes and examples in this section are from Ron Ruggless, "Catering to the Off-Premises Request," *Nation's Restaurant News,* 29 November 1993, pp. 28–29.

Key Terms

à la carte catering—Catered events in which guests may choose from a number of entrées.

banquet event order (BEO)—Also called a *function sheet* or *banquet prospectus,* a form that serves as a final contract for the client and serves as a work order for the catering department.

buffet service—A food service style in which hot and cold foods are attractively displayed, and guests help themselves.

butler-style service—With this type of food service, food—usually a variety of hors d'oeuvres—is placed on platters and circulated among guests by service staff. Butler-style service is typically used at receptions.

cash bar—A beverage plan for a banquet or other function in which guests pay cash to the bartender who prepares their drinks. Sometimes called a *COD bar* or an *à la carte bar.*

English service—With this type of food service, food on platters or in bowls is placed on the table and guests serve themselves. In some cases, the host cuts the main meat item(s); the host may also elect to have the server perform this task.

French service—Food service in which items are prepared tableside from a cart or guéridon.

guarantee clause—A clause in a banquet event order or contract in which the client gives the hotel (usually 72 hours in advance of the banquet) a count of the number of persons to be served. Payment is made on the basis of the guaranteed number or the total number actually served, whichever is greater.

hospitality suite—Guestroom or suite used for receptions and entertainment, usually stocked with beverages and light food. Often used by exhibitors at trade shows to entertain and sell delegates on their firms' products.

host bar—A beverage plan for a banquet or other function in which guests do not pay for drinks; rather, the host is charged by the drink, by the hour, or by the bottle. Sometimes called a *sponsored bar.*

plate service—A food service style in which food is plated in the kitchen, then served to guests.

preset service—A food service style in which the first course is set on the table before guests sit down; in some cases, the dessert may also be preset.

release date—A date agreed upon by the event organizer and the hotel; by this date, the organizer will either confirm his or her reservation for the space or release the space so the hotel can sell it to someone else. Release dates are usually 60 or 90 days prior to the event.

Russian service—A food service style in which food is served to guests from platters or other large dishes by the food servers, and sufficient food for one table is placed on each platter.

Review Questions

1. Why is the profit margin for banquets often greater than the profit margin for a hotel's restaurant?
2. What are two basic responsibilities of most catering departments?
3. What are the catering director's primary responsibilities?
4. What steps should be included in a catering department's marketing plan?
5. What are the basic ways to generate sales leads for functions?
6. What components are most important for creating a successful catering office?
7. How are each of the following used by the catering department: catering inquiry form, function book, banquet or catering checklist, banquet event order (BEO), and lost business report?
8. What are some of the different types of service used for functions? What factors determine the type of service needed?
9. What types of food and beverage sales contribute to the profitability of a catering operation besides banquets?
10. What are some of the different kinds of meeting room setups? When is each most commonly used?

Internet Sites

For more information, visit the following Internet sites. Remember that Internet addresses can change without notice. If the site is no longer there, you can use a search engine to look for additional sites.

American Marketing Association
www.ama.org

CaterWare Inc.
www.caterware.com

CuisineNet
www.cuisinenet.com

Experient
www.experient-inc.com

Food Network
www.foodtv.com

Hospitality Sales & Marketing Association International
www.hsmai.org

Hyatt Hotels
www.hyatt.com

Marriott International
www.marriott.com

Meeting Professionals International
www.mpiweb.org

Newmarket International
www.newsoft.com

Professional Convention Management Association
www.pcma.org

Sales & Marketing Management
www.salesandmarketing.com

Sheraton Hotels
www.sheraton.com

Case Study

Distributing Sales Functions between a Hotel's Sales and Catering Departments

Carla Mills is the general manager of the Woodfield Plaza, a 400-room first-class/suburban hotel. It's early July, and Carla has just reviewed the forecasted year-end profit and loss statement. A couple of areas concern her. First, assuming the hotel will hit budget the rest of the year, banquet food sales will be down $60,000 to budget. Also, the audiovisual revenues and room rental revenues will miss budget by $30,000. Carla calls a meeting with her director of catering, Alan Jenkins, to discuss ways to remedy the situation.

Carla opens the meeting by contrasting the forecasted statement with the budget and asks Alan what he plans to do about the decrease in banquet food sales.

"You've been here sixty days now, Alan. You should have a good feel for the property and the community. Tell me, why are sales down in your area?"

Alan shifts in his seat. He thinks about the question for a moment, then responds. "Well, I think ultimately it comes down to a problem with selling," he says. "The sales staff knows how to sell guestrooms, but they don't seem to sell function rooms. They don't seem to be aware of opportunities to sell catering, or how to take advantage of those opportunities. I can't remember one event since I've been here that was generated by sales. And from what I've seen in past reports, this has been an ongoing problem."

"OK. That's a legitimate point," Carla replies. "Salespeople certainly could take advantage of those kinds of opportunities. Sales and catering aren't often as united as they could be when it comes to selling our services—"

"It's just that no one in sales will take ownership for selling catering," Alan interrupts.

"Then you take ownership of it," replies Carla. "Look, in fairness to sales, it's not their job to sell function rooms and banquet events, primarily. Their job *is* to sell guestrooms. In some situations they could probably work a little harder on selling function rooms. But the responsibility for selling catering events ultimately belongs to catering, not sales. And since you're so concerned about *sales* selling *functions,* how many *guestrooms* has *catering* sold? The street goes both ways."

Alan sits back in his chair, thinking about what Carla has said. "Not many, actually," he finally says. "As far as catering taking responsibility for its own sales, you're right. We need to. But we're so busy taking the calls coming in, trying to process them as fast as we can, we haven't had time to focus on increasing our sales skills."

"You can't continue to be just order-takers and expect your sales to do fine," Carla says. "You need to take responsibility for your sales. You need to take an active role in this. In your own words, you need to take ownership of it. Let me ask you: Do you know where you're losing business, and why?"

"Not offhand, no."

"Do you know how you're going to solve the problem?"

"Well, I think I can come up with a solution," Alan replies.

"I know you can. And I know your staff is capable. What I'd like you to do is come up with a plan as to how you'll sell catering, and how you'll work with the sales staff to sell catering. Could you get that to me ... let's see," Carla looks at her calendar. "Two weeks from today?"

"I think I can do that."

"Great. Now on to my next concern." Carla holds up the forecasted statement. "As you can see from this forecast, by the end of the year audiovisual revenues and room rental revenues will miss budget by $30,000—that's if all goes well the next six months. Now, what do you suggest we do about *that?*"

Alan thinks about the problem. "With the room rentals, I think the problem is that we're giving function space away to book more room nights. I understand we have to do this, to some degree, but we're losing money doing it."

"But don't you think that's a worthy trade-off, to get more room nights?"

"It would be if it were necessary. But I don't think it is."

"What do you mean?" Carla asks.

"I think we can keep the room nights without losing the room rental completely, if we institute a sliding-scale function fee."

"Yes," Carla nods.

"For example, if the customer picks up 80 to 100 percent of a room block, there's no rental. If they pick up 50 percent of the room block, they'll get 50 percent off the rate, and so on."

"Excellent idea. That should increase room rental revenues. You may want to consider putting a similar scale in place for catering revenues."

"Hmmm. Come to think of it, my staff does seem a little too eager to lower rentals. Maybe scales will help them deal more effectively with that issue."

"Good. Now, what about audiovisual rentals?"

Alan pauses. "I need to look into that. I know there are several ways to increase the A.V. revenues, as well as additional ways to increase room rental revenues. How about if I think about the problem in the next couple of weeks, and include my proposals in my plan?"

"I trust your judgment. Let's get together again in two weeks and see what you've come up with."

"Great. I'll see you then."

Alan leaves the room. Both he and Carla feel that they made some progress in solving their budget problems. And they're confident that in two weeks they'll have a plan in place to help prevent similar problems in the future.

Discussion Questions

1. In an ideal situation, what should the distribution of sales functions between a hotel's catering and sales departments look like?
2. Given the responsibilities of a hotel's catering department, what challenges will the director of catering face as the department shifts from simply being production-focused to being sales-focused?
3. How could the catering department at the Woodfield Plaza recover more audiovisual and room rental revenues?
4. What steps should the director of catering at the Woodfield Plaza take to identify the specific causes of his budget problem? Once the specifics of the budget problem have been identified, how should he address the problem?

Case Number: 370CG

This case was developed in cooperation with Lisa Richards of Hospitality Softnet, Inc., a marketing resources and support company (Sixty State Street, Suite 700, Boston, Massachusetts 02109; www.hospitalitysoftnet.com).

This case also appears in *Contemporary Hospitality Marketing: A Service Management Approach* (Lansing, Mich.: American Hotel & Lodging Educational Institute, 1999), ISBN 978-0-86612-158-3.

Discussion Questions

Index

A

B

D

E

F

G

H

Q–R

T

U–V

W

Y–Z